KT-449-733

# Children and Young People's Workforce

## EARLY LEARNING AND CHILD CARE

Carolyn Meggitt
Teena Kamen
Tina Bruce
Julian Grenier

DYNAMIC
LEARNING

HODDER
EDUCATION
AN HACHETTE UK COMPANY

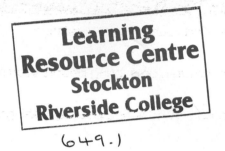
Orders: please contact Bookpoint Ltd, 130 Milton Park, Abingdon, Oxon OX14 4SB. Telephone: (44) 01235 827720. Fax: (44) 01235 400454.
Lines are open from 9.00 to 5.00, Monday to Saturday, with a 24-hour message answering service. You can also order through our website
www.hoddereducation.co.uk

If you have any comments to make about this, or any of our other titles, please send them to
educationenquiries@hodder.co.uk

*British Library Cataloguing in Publication Data*
A catalogue record for this title is available from the British Library

ISBN: 978 1444 11799 8

This edition published   2011
Impression number      10 9 8 7 6 5 4 3 2 1
Year                   2015, 2014, 2013, 2012, 2011

Hachette UK's policy is to use papers that are natural, renewable and
recyclable products and made from wood grown in sustainable forests.
The logging and manufacturing processes are expected to conform to the
environmental regulations of the country of origin.

Cover photo © mitgirl – Fotolia.com.
Typeset by Servis Filmsetting Ltd, Stockport, Cheshire.
Printed in Italy for Hodder Education, an Hachette UK Company, 338 Euston Road, London NW1 3BH by Printer Trento

# Contents

**Additional free material** on the web at
www.hoddereducation.co.uk/cache covering Unit CYPOP 7: Promote creativity and creative learning in
young children.

# Acknowledgements

I would like to thank the following people for their contributions: Laura Meggitt (Community Play Specialist) for her valuable insights and for providing many of the early years case studies; Gill Hutt (Youth Worker) for help with information on young people's services.

I would also like to thank the editorial team at Hodder Education – in particular Colin Goodlad, Publisher, Deborah Edwards Noble, Managing Editor, and Llinos Edwards, copy editor, for all their hard work and support.

– Carolyn Meggitt

Many thanks to the children, families, students and colleagues who I have worked with over the years including: the Marr family and the Pinder family; The Badger's Sett Play Scheme; St. Thomas's Rainbow Guides; Rood End Primary School; Withymoor Primary School; Birmingham College of Food, Tourism and Creative Studies; Sandwell College of FE and HE. Special thanks to Rebecca Brown, Derek Gannon, Terry James and Pauline White for their support and invaluable contributions during the writing of this book. To my son, Tom Jennings, with love and affection.

– Teena Kamen

Since 1996 when we wrote our first textbook together, I have valued and enjoyed working with Carolyn Meggitt, and a friendship between our families has developed. It has been a pleasure to add Julian Grenier to our team, and we have memories to be treasured of our three families joining together to celebrate our work together, Carolyn, Julian and myself. Colin Goodlad at Hodder has been a tower of strength throughout.

– Tina Bruce

I would like to thank Tina, Carolyn and all the writers and editors who have worked to create this book, everyone on the staff team at Kate Greenaway and our colleagues in Islington, and of course Caroline and Maisie.

– Julian Grenier

Thanks to Michele Barrett and the children, families and staff at Kate Greenaway for their help with many of the photographs, taken by Andrew Callaghan and Justin O'Hanlon.

Andrew Callaghan took the photos on the first page of each section and the following figures: 1.3, 3.1, 3.3, 5.8, 5.10, 5.11, 8.3, 12.2, 12.3, 15.3, 17.1, 19.1, 20.1 and 21.2.

Justin O'Hanlon took figures 2.1, 2.2, 3.2, 6.2, 7.1, 7.2, 7.4, 11.3, 12.6, 12.7, 13.2, 13.4, 13.7, 13.8, 13.10, 13.11–14, 14.2, 14.4, 16.1, 16.2, 16.4–6, 18.3 and 20.3.

Every effort has been made to trace the copyright holders of material reproduced here. The authors and publishers would like to thank the following for permission to reproduce copyright illustrations:

Figure 1.1 Stephanie Matthews/Hodder Education; figure 1.2 © Dmitry Naumov – Fotolia; figure 5.3 © Mariusz Blach – Fotolia; figure 5.4 © Ken Welsh/Alamy; figure 5.5 © Renata Osinska – Fotolia; figure 5.6 © Jose Manuel Gelpi – Fotolia; figure 5.7 © ping han – Fotolia; figure 5.9 © Jose Manuel Gelpi – Fotolia; figure 5.12 © pressmaster – Fotolia; figure 5.13 © Monkey Business – Fotolia; figure 8.1 © sciencephotos/Alamy; figure 8.4 © GUSTOIMAGES/SCIENCE PHOTO LIBRARY; figure 9.1 (centre) © Adam Borkowski – Fotolia; figure 11.1 Council for Disabled Children; figure 12.4 © Pavel Losevsky – Fotolia; figure 14.4 David Meggitt; figure 16.7 © Jamie Pham Photography/Alamy; figure 17.2 courtesy of the Scottish Government (Getting it Right for Every Child team); figure 17.3 David Meggitt; figure 18.1 © DR P. MARAZZI/SCIENCE PHOTO LIBRARY; figure 18.2 courtesy of Community Hygiene Concern; figure 20.2 © Freeze Frame Photography – Fotolia; figure 21.3 © Paula Solloway/Photofusion.

Figure 11.1: **The Council for Disabled Children (CDC)** is the umbrella body for the disabled children's sector in England, with links to the other UK nations. CDC has a wide range of information and resources developed for a variety of audiences including parents, young people, voluntary sector and public sector professionals. www.ncb.org.uk/cdc

**Participation Works** is a partnership of six national children and young people's agencies that enables organisations to effectively involve children and young people in the development, delivery and evaluation of services that affect their lives. www.participationworks.org.uk

# SECTION 1

# Mandatory shared core units

1. Promote communication in health, social care or children and young people's settings (SHC 31)

2. Engage in personal development in health, social care or children and young people's settings (SHC 32)

3. Promote equality and inclusion in health, social care or children and young people's settings (SHC 33)

4. Principles for implementing duty of care in health, social care or children and young people's settings (SHC 34)

# 1 Promote communication in health, social care or children and young people's settings: Unit SHC31

Effective communication is the cornerstone of work in all care settings with children and young people. Being able to communicate well helps in forming effective relationships, with colleagues, children, young people and their families.

## The importance of communication in the work setting

When working in care settings, you need to be able to communicate effectively with a wide range of other people, such as:

- children and young people
- their parents, families and carers
- colleagues and managers
- different **professionals**, such as teachers, doctors, nurses and social workers.

Communication may take the form of **one-to-one** interactions, with a child or a parent, or **group** interactions, such as activities with children or young people, case conferences, and staff meetings.

## Reasons why people communicate in work settings

The main reasons why people communicate in care settings are given below, with examples:

1 **To promote relationships and to offer support**: a social worker arranges regular contact with a family 'in need' and builds up a mutual system of support.
2 **To maintain relationships**: a child's key person will ensure that he or she gets to know the child and his or her family, so that a trusting relationship is built and maintained.
3 **To exchange information**: for example, a patient visiting their GP will supply the doctor with information about their symptoms. They will in turn receive information that will enable them to understand more about their medical problem.
4 **To negotiate and liaise with others**: an Early Years setting manager will liaise with other professionals, parent groups and committees to discuss policies and procedures.
5 **To express needs and feelings**: children and young people should be given opportunities to express themselves freely, confident that adults will acknowledge them and meet their needs.

## How communication affects relationships in the work setting

Establishing effective relationships in the work setting enables you to support other people and also to expect support from them in times of stress or difficulty. If you work alongside practitioners whom you like and respect – and whom you know will be there to support you – then you will help to create a **positive working environment** in which:

- both you and your colleagues experience job satisfaction
- children and young people's holistic development is supported
- practitioners work together in a team – with the common aim of providing the best possible service for children and young people
- transitions (such as settling in to a new setting) are managed sensitively
- parents and carers know that they can trust practitioners, because information is regularly shared and any concerns addressed within an environment that encourages open communication.

# Meeting the communication and language needs, wishes and preferences of individuals

The way in which we communicate with other people should always take account of each individual's needs, wishes and preferences. For example, parents and carers may express a preference to be addressed by their full title, or they may ask to be addressed by their first name. There may be a required way in which the work setting requires parents to be addressed.

## Empathetic listening

Empathy means being able to 'project' yourself into the other person's situation and experience, in order to understand them as fully as possible. Practitioners need to be able to listen with sympathy and understanding, and give support at the appropriate time. They also need to be able to encourage people who lack confidence that other people will value what they say.

(For more information on how to communicate well with children and young people, see Chapter 9, Unit CYP Core 3.5.)

## Communicating with parents

You will find that there are many occasions when you are responsible for passing information clearly to parents. However, parents will also want to talk to you, as well as listen. You will therefore need to develop effective listening skills. Try to set a particular time for parents so that they do not take your attention when you are involved with the children or young people. For some parents this can be very difficult to arrange, especially if they are working.

## Factors to consider when promoting effective communication

The key to effective communication is the consideration of **individual needs**. Practitioners need to be flexible in their choice of communication method and to be aware of the need to ask for help if they perceive any barriers to communication. There are many factors to consider when promoting effective face-to-face communication.

## Environment

Various environmental factors influence communication, such as:

- the design or layout of the space
- decoration
- lighting
- colour
- furniture
- smells
- noise.

A busy, noisy environment will inhibit effective communication, and practitioners often need to find a quiet place in order for children and young people to feel relaxed and for the practitioner to convey genuine warmth when responding to their needs.

## Personal space

The concept of personal space means the distance you are in relation to another person. It is sometimes called **proxemics** or physical proximity. Psychologists now believe that air rage and other violent outbursts are often caused by 'invasions' of personal body space. In care relationships, those

## Guidelines: How to communicate well with parents, carers, young people and colleagues

1 Maintaining eye contact helps you to give your full attention to someone. It is important to be aware that, in certain cultures, mutual eye contact is considered disrespectful.

2 Remember that your **body language** shows how you really feel.

3 Try not to interrupt when someone is talking to you. Nod and smile instead.

4 Every so often, summarise the main points of a discussion, so that you are both clear about what has been said.

5 If you do not know the answer to a question, say so, and that you will find out. Then, do not forget to do this!

6 Remember that different cultures have different traditions. Touching and certain gestures might be seen as insulting by some people, so be careful.

7 If the other person speaks a different language from you, use photographs and visual aids. Talk slowly and clearly.

8 If the other person has a hearing impairment, use sign language or visual aids.

### Reflective practice: Being aware of personal space

- Think about an occasion when you have felt uncomfortable, or have felt that your personal space has been invaded.
- How do you protect your own personal space in the library, in a queue or on a crowded train?
- How could care settings such as hospitals or residential homes, take account of people's need for personal space?

giving care should be conscious of the power they may have over the physical and personal space of the person receiving care.

## Communication methods and styles

Effective communication involves **listening**, **questioning**, **understanding** and **responding**. It is important to remember that communication does not only happen through the spoken word, but also involves:

- facial expressions and eye contact
- body language: posture and actions or gestures which help to convey meaning
- tone of voice: this can alter the meaning of what has been said. For example, a sharp tone of voice could express disapproval
- pauses
- turn taking.

It is thought that more than 70 per cent of messages are conveyed through **non-verbal** ways.

When communicating with other people, it is also important to:

- take account of culture and context, such as where English is an additional language
- build a rapport by showing understanding, respect and honesty.

In order to meet individual needs, you will need to know how to choose the most effective method of face-to-face communication. This will include both non-verbal and verbal communication methods.

# Non-verbal communication

The ways in which we express ourselves and communicate without using words is a very important part of effective communication. It is also called **body language**.

## Eye contact

People's eyes can express a wide range of emotions. Before beginning a conversation, people will usually make eye contact as a signal that they are ready to speak or listen. Once a conversation is underway, regular glances lasting several seconds show interest and friendliness. The more eye contact someone has with another person, the closer they tend to feel to him or her. People who do not like each other tend to avoid eye contact.

Eye contact has five important functions in communication:

1 **It regulates the flow of conversation**: gazing during social interaction can signify whose turn it is to talk; for example, when person A finishes speaking, he looks at Person B to signal that it is B's turn to speak. Person B, in turn, will tend to look away after he begins his response, especially if he intends to speak for a long time, or the material he is dealing with is difficult to understand. In general, people look more as they **listen** than as they **speak**.
2 **It controls intimacy in a relationship**: in an experiment, researchers discovered that when there was a status difference between participants communicating, the person having the higher status (whether male or female) had a longer gazing pattern. Women tend to gaze more than do men. This could be because women display a greater need for a connection, or regard eye contact as less threatening; as a result, they are less likely to break eye contact than men in similar situations.
3 **It gives feedback** to the speaker on what has just been communicated, and gathers information in turn.
4 **It expresses emotion**: we appear to make more

and longer eye contact with people we like, but this varies between males and females.
5 **It informs both speaker and listener** of the nature of their relationship.

People who have strong emotional needs for approval tend to make more eye contact than others. Speakers also feel that if people are not looking at them, they may be either bored or showing dislike. A practitioner who is listening to a child, young person, parent or carer will therefore use eye contact to express sincerity and **empathy** – and to show that he or she is attending carefully. However, it is important to be aware that, in certain cultures, mutual eye contact is considered disrespectful. Practitioners should adapt their use of eye contact accordingly.

> ## Key term
>
> **Empathy** – the ability to understand and share the feelings of another.

## Facial expressions

Some facial expressions have the same meaning all over the world. One example is the 'eyebrow flash': when people greet each other, they rapidly raise and lower their eyebrows. Some cultures inhibit the expression of certain emotions, such as anger or disgust. Those working in care settings often have to hide their feelings by controlling their facial expressions, for example to spare a patient embarrassment when attending to intimate bodily functions.

## Posture: open and closed postures

Posture, or how people stand or sit, is an important aspect of body language. People may want to appear to others in a certain way, but body posture or small unconscious gestures (which demonstrate, for example, nervousness or anxiety) often give away how they *really* feel. An open posture when seated will encourage communication, whereas a closed position may be a barrier to communication (see Figure 1.1).

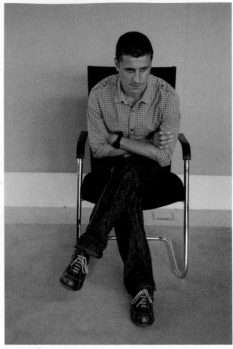

**Figure 1.1** (a) An open posture encourages communication (b) A closed posture inhibits communication

## Gesture

People who are communicating with each other often show 'postural echo'. This means that they copy or mirror the gestures and posture of the person to whom they are talking. This demonstrates attentive listening and **empathy**. Many gestures (such as head nodding, bowing or giving a 'thumbs-up' sign) are culture-specific; that is, they mean something to people from one culture, but may mean nothing (or something completely different) to those from another culture. British Prime Minister Winston Churchill insisted on using the victory salute during the Second World War, although the way in which he raised two fingers (palm inwards) was even then considered a very rude gesture. In Italy, people communicate using many more gestures than in the UK.

Some of these gestures may be used as part of a *signed* language – such as **Makaton** - or as an aid to verbal communication in a noisy environment, such as the floor of a busy factory.

## The importance of physical contact or touch

Touch is one of our most basic forms of communication. Our first contact with the outside world comes through tactile experiences, such as the midwife's hands as the baby is delivered, and the parent's or carer's hands which feed, bathe, caress and comfort the baby throughout his or her waking hours. Early tactile explorations seem to be crucially important to children's subsequent healthy emotional and social development. Studies in orphanages and hospitals have shown that infants deprived of human skin contact lose weight, become ill and even die. Premature babies given periods of touch therapy gain weight faster, cry less, and show more signs of relaxed pulse, respiration rate and muscle tension.

Touch is something we naturally associate with comfort. If we are hurt, upset, happy or sad, we will typically seek some form of physical contact. Even when we do not know someone particularly well, we will often reach out and touch their arm or hand as a

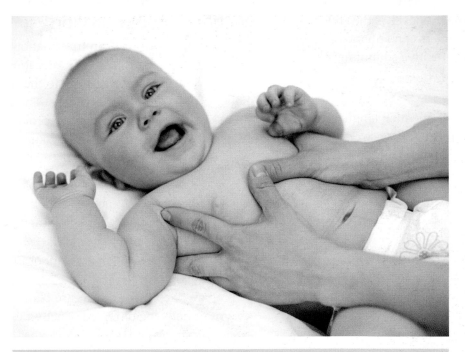

**Figure 1.2** Touch is very important for a baby

means of comfort. Similarly, it is also comforting to be the one doing the touching; many people find that stroking a cat or petting a dog is very relaxing and therapeutic.

## Cultural variations in touch

The amount of everyday touch which we will allow people to have with us is also culturally determined. There are certain groups within the community who very rarely touch each other; elderly people with no close relatives and widowed people receive little or no bodily contact specifically planned to fulfil their emotional needs. In care settings, touch can be used as a means of conveying warmth and understanding.

A number of professionals touch people in the normal course of their work: for example, nurses, doctors, physical education teachers, health visitors, hairdressers, masseurs and physiotherapists. Those who work with distressed people who are in shock, pain or bereavement, know that there are times when touch – for example, holding hands – is comforting and quieting when no suitable words exist. However, it should be remembered that not all

people would welcome such contact. Some might view it as intrusive or even patronising.

See Chapter 9 (Unit CYP Core 3.5) for guidelines on physical contact with children and young people.

## Dress and personal grooming

Personality characteristics can be reflected in the style of clothes worn. Paediatric (children's) nurses usually wear practical tabard aprons decorated with nursery rhyme or cartoon characters. Early years practitioners and children or young people's social care workers often wear a customised sweatshirt and trousers, if any uniform is worn.

People working in care settings are aware that both dress and personal appearance convey important messages. Personal grooming is also important. Hair should be clean, and clothes well cared for and also appropriate to the setting.

## Verbal communication

It is important to adapt the way in which we speak – and the vocabulary we use - so that the person we are speaking to can understand. By actively listening, and being on the same eye level as the child or young person, practitioners can enhance their verbal skills and so promote effective communication.

## Paralanguage

Paralanguage is the *way* in which language is spoken. By altering our **tone** of voice or changing its **pitch**, we can convey different emotions. An example of paralanguage is whispered speech, which in many languages adds an aura of secrecy or conspiracy to the words being spoken. Paralanguage features include the tone of voice (such as flat or bright), the tempo (fast or slow) and the way in which we emphasise certain words.

- When someone is in a highly emotional state, for example angry or anxious, they tend to stutter, repeat themselves and make more slips of the tongue than usual.
- When someone is unsure of what they are saying, or uncertain of how it will be received, they tend to say 'er' and 'um' more often than usual.
- Very slow speech may indicate that a person is uncertain of what they are saying. Rapid speech can indicate that a person is excited or anxious.
- The way in which language is spoken varies greatly between cultures. For instance, a 'breathy' or husky voice conveys deep feeling in many languages, but in Japanese, it is routinely used as a way of conveying respect or submission.
- **Motherese** is spoken in many, but not all, cultures. In motherese, adults speak differently to babies and very young children from the way they speak to adults: they use a higher-pitched voice, talk more slowly and with emphasis on key words.

### Key term

**Body language** – Body language is also known as **non-verbal communication**. It includes facial expressions, eye contact, tone of voice, body posture and motions, and positioning within groups. It may also include the clothes we wear.

## Written communication

Most care settings have an Information Board where notices are displayed to give information about a wide variety of matters relating to the setting's policies, procedures and activities. There are many occasions when you may need to provide written information about children and young people in your care. For example, depending on where you are working, you may need to:

- complete a chart in the Baby Room of a nursery to detail an individual child's feeding and sleeping patterns and bowel movements
- record the details of an accident or injury in the Accident Report Book
- prepare or contribute to a care plan
- write a daily log or record of activities and significant events
- contribute written evidence to a document for assessment purposes.

(See Chapter 10, Working together for the benefit of children and young people; Unit CYP3.6, for information on how to prepare written reports.)

## Appropriate responses

Effective communication involves knowing how to respond to others – to pick up on the cues or signals they are giving us. The key to this is **active listening.** On the whole we tend to be poor listeners. Sometimes we only hear items in which we are interested, and do not attend to others. If we are bored or dislike the speaker's personality, mannerisms, accent or appearance, we may 'switch off' and follow more interesting thoughts of our own.

Active listening, the listening required in any care relationship, calls for concentration; it is hard work and tiring. The following skills are important for active listening:

1 **Maintain eye contact**: face the speaker and maintain eye contact to show that you are interested. Remember that, in certain cultures, mutual eye contact is considered disrespectful.
2 **Maintain an open posture**: keep your body and hands neat and relaxed. An occasional nod acts as positive reinforcement; it can encourage the other

person when he or she is saying something useful or helpful.

3 Show that **you are listening**: for example, by prompting the speaker to continue, saying 'Yes' or 'go on'.

4 **Listen with undivided attention**, without interrupting: let the speaker finish.

5 **Listen also to what is not openly said**: the speaker's body language will help you to 'listen' to what may not be said openly but may be felt (the hidden feelings).

## The use of open-ended questions

Closed questions such as 'How old are you?' or 'What is your date of birth?' are only appropriate when brief factual material is needed. They do not encourage conversation or expression of thoughts and feelings.

In contrast, open-ended questions give the person responding an opportunity to give a fuller and deeper answer. The '5WH Test' is a useful standby formula to obtain information in a fact-finding interview. This acronym stands for questions which start with 'Wh':

- Why? (use this sparingly)
- Who?
- What?
- When?
- Where?
- How? (a sixth useful question).

Sensitive use of these key words can draw much basic information. For example, a parent tells you that they are worried because their child refuses to eat properly at home. You could try asking: **What** is the problem? **When** did it start? **Who** could help? **Where** should we begin to sort it out? **How** have you managed so far?

### Key term

**Active listening** – Active listening is about focusing not only on what is being said, but the accompanying emotions and feelings that are also being expressed. It provides a safe structure for a child voice his or her concerns, and to receive feedback from the adult.

### Reflective practice: Communicating with children and young people

As practitioners we need to think carefully about what we say and how we say it, and we should also be fully aware of what our **body language** is communicating.

- Do we look interested when a child is talking to us?
- How do we make sure that the child knows we are listening?
- How do we convey the feeling that what the child is saying and feeling is important to us?
- How could you improve the ways in which you communicate with children or young people?

# Barriers to effective communication

When communications are difficult it is often because of 'barriers' of one kind or another. The first step in overcoming such barriers is to identify them.

## Identifying barriers to communication

### The physical environment

Communication may be blocked by the environment. The design of a building, lack of access for people who use wheelchairs, noise and lack of privacy are all factors which can inhibit effective communication. For example, too much background noise can prevent a message being fully understood; there may be too many people talking at the same time, or there may be a lack of privacy.

### Disability and impairment

Practitioners need to be trained to recognise the influence of hearing impairment, limited mobility, visual and verbal impairments and conditions such as autism on a child's ability to communicate. For example, a child may have a physical impairment such as cleft palate and harelip, or speak with a stammer or stutter.

## An additional language

Children and young people's home language must be valued. Adults should recognise that these children and young people are probably very competent communicators at home, and need support to develop an additional vocabulary which, for the very young child, may only apply in the early years setting.

## Attitudes

If practitioners are unaware of the stereotypes and prejudices they hold in their own minds, these will unconsciously act as a barrier to communication. The word **stereotype** refers to forming an instant or fixed picture *of a group of people*, usually based on false or incomplete information. Stereotypes are often negative. For example, stereotyped thinking can deflect you from seeing someone as an individual with particular life experiences and interests, and so prevent effective communication.

## Distractions

A continuous noise outside an interview room is a distraction, but interaction between two people will be inhibited far more by interruptions. Suppose a young person is telling their personal story to a practitioner when the phone rings or there is a knock at the door. The practitioner takes their attention from the young person and talks for some minutes to the person on the telephone or the person at the door, about another matter entirely. The young person will feel devalued, that their key communication is unimportant, and therefore that *they* are also unimportant. The young person may feel angry, and when the practitioner at last turns back, might have decided not to reveal any more about themselves. Practitioner/young person communication will have broken down.

Any interruption should therefore be dealt with briefly, with the practitioner making it clear to the young person that their problems are the current priority.

## Dominating the conversation

Practitioners are there to listen and should put their own concerns to one side. However, it is possible to dominate the conversation in any of three ways, even unintentionally:

1 Making the young person's story his or her *own* story: 'Oh, I'm sorry to hear that happened to you. My own sister had a similar experience . . .'
2 By assuming responsibility for working out the problem and giving the young person only a minor role. An extreme example would be to set out a treatment or care plan, and then impose it on the young person.
3 By trying to scrutinise every area of the young person's life, regardless of the actual support he or she may need.

## Blocking the other's contribution

During one-to-one, face-to-face interaction, one participant may block communication in a number of ways, both verbally and non-verbally. The practitioner may block the communication of the other person in these **non-verbal** ways:

- a look of boredom
- a yawn
- the slightest expression of disgust
- a smile at the wrong time
- withdrawal of eye contact, turning away
- drumming the fingers or fidgeting.

The practitioner may block the communication of the client **verbally** by:

- changing the subject
- being critical
- misunderstanding
- joking at the client's expense.

# Effects of different backgrounds and factors on communication

## Respect for other people's beliefs and views

We all have different ideas about how we conduct our lives. It is inevitable that every practitioner will encounter people with vastly different backgrounds, beliefs and outlooks on life. Only if people feel that their individual values and beliefs are respected, will they develop the confidence to express themselves freely and make choices.

## Confidence and self-esteem

Some children and young people lack confidence in expressing themselves, both verbally and in writing. If they are not encouraged to practise their communication skills, they may seek to avoid communication for fear of making mistakes.

## Family background

Every child's family background is unique to him or her. A child with many siblings will probably have a very different home life from that of an only child. Children and young people may hear more than one language being spoken, or may frequently hear swearing at home. This experience will affect the ways in which the child or young person communicates with others.

## Language and literacy skills

Some children and young people have poorly developed language and literacy skills. This may be because of a specific learning difficulty, or because they are not yet fluent in the language used in the setting.

> ### Reflective practice: Recognising barriers to communication
>
> Think about a situation in which you have found communication unsatisfactory. Why do you think this occurred? Try to identify any possible barriers, and think about how you could improve your own communication skills.

## Overcoming barriers to communication

Barriers to communication can occur for a variety of reasons. If you can identify the particular barrier, then you will be better equipped to overcome it.

## Clarifying misunderstandings

It is important to be able to identify when misunderstandings have occurred, and to find ways of clarifying them. Misunderstandings can cause resentment and lack of trust, both of which will affect relationships. Often it will become apparent that there is a misunderstanding during the conversation, and then careful, sensitive questioning will help to resolve the problem.

There are two useful techniques for checking understanding: paraphrasing and reflection.

 **In Practice**

### Overcoming barriers to communication

❑ **Allow sufficient time for communication**: if you appear to be in a rush to get to your next task, the other person will sense this and feel that their contribution is unimportant.

❑ **Avoid making assumptions or judgements**: do not assume that you already know what the person is trying to say. Some people find it difficult to express themselves – either verbally or in writing – and you should always check that you have understood what they are communicating.

❑ **Put the other person at ease**: this may mean adapting the environment, such as finding a quiet place to talk where you will not be interrupted, and using effective body language.

❑ **Speak clearly and maintain eye contact**: try to empathise with the other person. People with language needs or a hearing impairment may find it difficult to understand you if you speak too quickly, or if they are unable to see your face clearly. Remember that, in certain cultures, mutual eye contact is considered disrespectful. Practitioners should adapt their use of eye contact accordingly.

## Paraphrasing

Paraphrasing means using your own words plus the important main words of the other person, to check accurate understanding of what he or she has said. In this way, the practitioner can check that he or she really has understood what the other person has said; the other person will also be helped by having his or her story presented concisely and clearly back to them.

An example of paraphrasing:

*Learner*: The problem is getting from my technology class, which doesn't end until 3 p.m., in time to catch the bus to the sports centre with the other students.

*Tutor*: So there's a real timetabling problem for you here.

## Reflecting

Reflecting is similar to paraphrasing, but rather than restating the content, it reflects back the feeling being communicated in the message. In this way, the emotional content of the message is clarified. This helps the other person to understand and appreciate the effect which the problem is having on his or her life. The practitioner also reflects feelings of empathy.

An example of reflecting:

*Learner*: I've been to six interviews and still haven't got a job. I always prepare myself. I don't know what's happening.

*Tutor*: You have obviously tried very hard and are upset and frustrated by what has happened.

# Extra support or services to enable individuals to communicate effectively

In order to promote effective communication, practitioners need to know when to call in help from outside, and whom to approach when more specialist expertise and help is needed. Support services include:

- **specialist teachers** for children and young people who are learning English as an additional language
- **translation and interpretation services**
- **advocacy services**: an advocate's role is to represent the wishes and feelings of children and young people to the courts, and to provide a view of the child's best interests
- **speech and language therapists** assess and treat children and adults who have difficulties with speech and language
- **specific 'sign' languages** – such as Makaton, Signalong and Picture Exchange Communication system (PECS).

## Makaton

The Makaton Vocabulary is a list of over 400 items with corresponding signs and symbols, with an additional resource vocabulary for the UK National Curriculum. The signs are based on British Sign Language (BSL), but are used to support spoken English.

The Makaton Project publishes a book of illustrations of the Makaton vocabulary. Most signs rely on movement as well as position, so you cannot properly learn the signs from the illustrations. Facial expression is also important for many signs. If a child at a school or in an early years setting is learning Makaton, the parents should be invited to learn too. The Makaton Project will support schools and parents in this, as they know that everyone involved with the child must use the same signs.

**Figure 1.3** Using Makaton can help to promote communication

## Signalong

Signalong is a sign-supporting system that is also based on British Sign Language. It is designed to help children, young people and adults with communication difficulties (mostly associated with learning disabilities) and is user-friendly for easy access. The Signalong Group has researched and published the widest range of signs in Britain.

## Picture Exchange Communication system (PECS)

PECS begins with teaching children to exchange a picture of an object that they want with a teacher, who immediately gives it to them. For example, if they want a drink, they will give a picture of 'drink' to an adult, who directly hands them a drink. Verbal prompts are not used; this encourages spontaneity and avoids children being dependent on the prompts.

The system then teaches recognition of symbols and how to construct simple 'sentences'. Ideas for teaching language structures such as asking and answering questions are also incorporated. It has been reported that both pre-school and older children have begun to develop speech when using PECS. The system is often used as a communication aid for children and adults who have an autistic spectrum disorder.

### Research Activity

#### Different ways of communicating with children and young people

Find out more about methods of communicating with children and young people such as Makaton, Signalong and PECS. (See the list of useful websites on page 16.)

### Assessment practice

#### Research into communication in the work setting

1. Identify the main reasons why people communicate in your work setting. For each reason identified, provide an example of the methods in which communication is carried out.

   (For example, in an early years setting, one reason people communicate may be: 'To share information with parents or carers about the key person approach.' One method of communication could be a leaflet or brochure produced by the setting and given directly to the parents. For information about the key person system, see Chapter 12, Unit EYMP1.)

2. Explain how communication affects relationships in your work setting.

   (For example, you could look at:

   (a) the ways in which colleagues communicate with each other

   (b) how information is shared with other practitioners

   (c) the nature of the relationship between children or young person and their key person.)

# The principles and practices relating to confidentiality

Confidentiality is very important when working in settings with children and young people. Any practitioner working with children will need to practise confidentiality, whether in an early years setting, a care environment, a school or in the family home.

## What is meant by confidentiality?

Confidentiality means respect for the privacy of any information about a child and his or her family. You will be entrusted with personal information about children, young people and their families, and it is important that you do not abuse this trust. The giving or receiving of sensitive information should be subject to a careful consideration of the needs of the children, young people and their families; for example, if a child is in need of protection, all relevant information must be given to all the appropriate agencies, such as social workers or doctors.

### Key term

**Confidentiality** – The preservation of secret (or privileged) information concerning children, young people and their families which is disclosed in the professional relationship.

## Maintaining confidentiality in day-to-day communication

Some information *does* have to be shared, but only with your line manager. For example, if you suspect there may be a child protection issue, this should be shared with your line manager in the strictest confidence. Parents need to be aware of this policy from the outset of your partnership. They need to understand that although they may tell you things in confidence, you may have to share the information with your line manager. It is not fair to encourage parents to talk about confidential things with you unless they understand this principle.

Some information has to be shared with the whole staff team, such as information about diet, allergy, and if the child is being collected by someone else. Make sure that parents are clear about the sort of information that *cannot* be confidential.

In many instances, you will be working under the supervision of others and it is likely that parents will pass confidential information directly to a more senior staff member. However, there may be occasions on which *you* are given information and asked to pass it on, or that you may hear or be told confidential information in the course of the daily routine. You may be entrusted with personal information about children, young people, parents and staff, either directly (being told or being given written information) or indirectly (hearing staffroom

### Progress check

**Your role in maintaining confidentiality**

Children, young people, their parents and carers need to feel confident of the following points:

- You will not interfere in their private lives; any information you are privileged to hold will not become a source of gossip. Breaches of confidentiality can occur when you are travelling on public transport for example, and discussing the events of your day. Always remember that using the names of children or young people in your care can cause a serious breach of confidentiality if overheard by a friend or relative of the family.
- You will ensure that personal information related to any child or family is restricted to those who have a real **need to know**, such as when a child's family or health circumstances is affecting their development.
- You understand when the safety or health needs of the child override the need for confidentiality. Parents need to be reassured that you will always put the safety and wellbeing of each child before any other considerations.

discussions, parental comments or children's or young people's conversations), and it is important that you do not repeat any of it at home or to friends. The incidents may be discussed in your teaching sessions among your learner group, with permission to do so from your placement, but you should not identify the children or young people concerned, and it must be agreed that they are not talked about beyond the group.

## The Data Protection Act 1998

Under the Data Protection Act 1998, all schools processing personal data must comply with the eight principles of effective practice. Data must be:

- fairly and lawfully processed
- processed for limited purposes
- adequate, relevant and not excessive
- accurate
- not kept longer than necessary

## Case Study    Marsha

Marsha is a student on the CACHE Level 3 course and her first placement is in a private nursery. She enjoys most of the work at the nursery, but is unsure of how to react when children show behaviour which is not acceptable in the setting, such as name-calling, biting and pulling the hair of other children. Her supervisor has arranged to hold a special evening session on 'unacceptable behaviour' and has encouraged Marsha to attend if she can.

Marsha usually catches the same bus as a fellow student, Sadie, who is working at a nearby primary school. One day, she pours out all her pent-up feelings of frustration to her on their journey home. She is particularly anxious about Isobel, a three-year-old child who has started biting the other children in her group, and tells Sadie that Isobel has a young, inexperienced mother whose partner has recently left her for another woman. She says that she feels sorry for the mother, but that there

is no excuse in her mind for any child to bite another child, and she thinks the mother is to blame.

Also on the bus that afternoon, sitting directly behind Marsha and Sadie, is Isobel's auntie. She realises it is her niece being talked about and is very upset. She does not say anything to Marsha, but decides to phone the nursery manager to complain when she gets home. When Marsha arrives at the nursery the following day, she is called in to see her supervisor about the incident, and soon realises that she has made a dreadful mistake.

1 Which fundamental principle has Marsha ignored by her behaviour on the bus?

2 Give three examples of information that Marsha spoke about to Sadie.

3 Would the situation be any different if Marsha and Sadie were the only people on the bus, and if so, how?

- processed in accordance with the data subject's rights
- secure
- not transferred to other countries without adequate protection.

## What does personal data cover?

Personal data covers information (both facts and opinions) about a living individual. It covers:

- **ordinary** personal data – name, address and telephone number
- **sensitive** personal data – relating to racial or ethnic origin, political opinions, religious beliefs, trades union membership, health, sex life and criminal convictions.

Personal data can be held in the following format:

- computer files, including word processor, database and spreadsheet files
- paper files
- microfiche, CCTV pictures, audio.

 **In Practice**

### Confidentiality

Find out about your setting's confidentiality policy. What sort of personal information does your setting hold with the permission of parents and guardians? What sort of records are *you* expected to keep, and how are they kept accurate and secure?

## A breach of confidentiality

This week a dinner lady at a village primary school was sacked for telling a child's parents that she was sorry their daughter had been attacked in the playground at school. The dinner lady had found a seven-year-old girl tied up by her wrists and ankles, surrounded by four boys, having been whipped with a skipping rope across her legs. The dinner lady had rescued the child and taken the boys to the headteacher. That night she bumped into the parents, who were friends of hers, and offered her sympathy. It instantly became clear that the parents had not been told the story by the school. Their daughter had arrived home traumatised and refusing to talk about what happened, with a note saying only that she had been 'hurt in a skipping-rope incident'. As soon as the school discovered that the dinner lady had told the parents the truth, she was first suspended for several months, and then sacked by the governors for 'breaching pupil confidentiality'.

(Story adapted from *The Guardian*, 24 September 2009)

This news report caused a fresh debate over the complex issue of confidentiality. The dinner lady had not revealed to the parents the names of the children involved in the incident, but was deemed to have breached confidentiality as she had not followed the correct procedure for reporting what she had witnessed.

1. Do you agree with the school governors that the dinner lady had breached confidentiality?
2. What should you do if you witness an incident of bullying in the playground?

## Potential tensions between maintaining confidentiality and disclosing concerns

Confidential information received by you should *not* be disclosed unless required by law or to protect the interests or welfare of the child. If sharing information or disclosing concerns will help to ensure a child's safety, you must do this. In nearly every case, you would start by explaining to the parent why you wish to share the information and how this would help the child. If a parent refuses, ask for advice from the named person for safeguarding or the manager/head of the setting.

 Useful resources

**Organisations and websites**
**Makaton** was developed to help people with learning disability to communicate. It is now widely used with a variety of children with communication difficulties: **www.makaton.org**

**The National Youth Advocacy Service (NYAS)** is a UK charity providing children and young people's rights and socio-legal services. It offers information, advice, advocacy and legal representation to children and young people up to the age of 25, through a network of advocates throughout England and Wales: **www.nyas.net**

**Picture Exchange Communication** (**PECS**) uses functional and practical interventions to teach individuals how to communicate, function independently, and be successful in their schools, homes, places of employment and the community: **www.pecs.org.uk**

**Signalong** empowers children, young people and adults with impaired communication to understand and express their needs, choices and desires by providing vocabulary for life and learning: **www.signalong.org.uk**

# 2 Engage in personal development in health, social care or children's and young people's settings: Unit SHC 32

Personal development and reflective practice are both fundamental to those who work with children in a wide range of settings. Engaging in personal development has a positive influence on improving the status of early years practitioners, as well as enabling them to share examples of effective practice with others. Early years settings benefit from employing early years practitioners who are able to reflect on and improve their professional expertise.

## Learning outcomes

By the end of this chapter you will:

1. Understand what is required for competence in your own work role.
2. Be able to reflect on practice.
3. Be able to evaluate your own performance.
4. Be able to agree a personal development plan.
5. Be able to use learning opportunities and reflective practice to contribute to personal development.

## Competence in your own work role

Having satisfactorily completed the Level 3 Diploma for the Children and Young People's Workforce, a professional early years practitioner will be qualified to work in a variety of settings: nursery, infant or primary schools or classes, Sure Start Children's Centres, family centres, hospitals and the private and voluntary sectors.

## Values and principles

All early years practitioners should work within a framework that embodies sound values and principles. The **CACHE Statement of Values** is a useful tool for checking that you are upholding important child care values.

## CACHE statement of values

You must ensure that you:

1 Put the child first by:
   - ensuring the child's welfare and safety
   - showing compassion and sensitivity
   - respecting the child as an individual
   - upholding the child's rights and dignity
   - enabling the child to achieve his or her full learning potential.
2 Never use physical punishment.
3 Respect the parent as the primary carer and educator of the child.
4 Respect the contribution and expertise of staff in the child care and education field, and other professionals with whom they may be involved.
5 Respect the customs, values and spiritual beliefs of the child and his or her family.
6 Uphold the Council's Equality of Opportunity Policy.
7 Honour the confidentiality of information relating to the child and his or her family, unless its disclosure is required by law or is in the best interests of the child.

**Figure 2.1** It is important to be patient and helpful to children as they play; sometimes a little bit of help at just the right time will mean that next time a child can do something by him or herself

# Duties and responsibilities of the practitioner

There are lots of different settings for children and young people, and each one will offer its own mix of benefits and drawbacks. This section makes some general comments about working in children and young people's settings, but you should judge each setting on its own terms. Spend time there and watch how the children play, and how they seem when they arrive and leave. Talk to staff, and read the information provided (such as leaflets and booklets for parents and carers, and Ofsted reports – Ofsted is the Office for Standards in Education, Children's Services and Skills).

Effective practice as a team member will depend on liaising with others, and reporting on and reviewing your activities. Conflicts between team members often arise from poor communication; for example, an early years practitioner who fails to report (verbally and in writing) that a parent will be late collecting his or her child on a particular day, may cause conflict if a colleague challenges the parent's conduct.

Your duties and responsibilities as a professional practitioner are explored below under the following headings:

- Respect the principles of confidentiality.
- Commitment to meeting the needs of the children and young people.
- Responsibility and accountability in the workplace.
- Respect for parents, carers and other adults.
- Communicate effectively with team members.
- Work effectively with professionals from other agencies.

## Respect the principles of confidentiality

Confidentiality is the preservation of secret (or privileged) information concerning children and their families which is disclosed in the professional relationship. It is a complex issue, which has at its core the principle of trust. Chapter 1 (Unit SHC 31) covers this area extensively.

## Commitment to meeting the needs of children and young people

The needs and rights of all children and young people should be paramount, and the practitioner must seek to meet these needs within the boundaries of the work role. Any personal preferences and prejudices must be put aside; all children and young people should be treated with respect and dignity, irrespective of their ethnic origin, socio-economic group, religion or disability.

## Responsibility and accountability in the workplace

The supervisor, line manager, teacher or parent will have certain expectations about your role, and your responsibilities should be detailed in the job contract. As a professional, you need to carry out all your duties willingly and be answerable to others for your work. It is vital that you know who your manager is, and how you would raise any concerns or seek guidance or support.

All staff need to know how to obtain clarification of their own role and responsibilities, and to know how well they are carrying out that role. If you do not feel confident in carrying out a particular task, either because you do not fully understand it or because you have not been adequately trained, you have a responsibility to state your concerns and ask for guidance. If you have a difficulty or disagreement with another member of staff, you must handle this in a professional manner. This means raising your concern directly with that person, or with an appropriate manager. You should not complain about colleagues in the staffroom, in front of parents, carers or outside work with friends or family.

## Respect for parents, carers and other adults

The training you have received will have emphasised the richness and variety of child-rearing practices in the UK. It is an important part of your professional role that you respect the wishes and views of parents and other carers, even when you may disagree with them. You should also recognise that parents and

...who know their
...ealings with parents,
...you must show that you
...values and religious beliefs.

The ...aining you have received will have emphasised the importance of effective communication in the workplace. You will also be aware of the need to plan in advance for your work with children and/or young people. Knowledge and understanding of the developmental needs of children and young people will enable you to fulfil these responsibilities within your own work role.

## Work effectively with professionals from other agencies

Working with children and young people is increasingly about coordinating services for the benefit of children, young people and their families. This places new demands on practitioners. It is very important that you are confident about your own training and expertise. For example, if you are a child's **key person** in an early years setting, you will know a great deal about the child's development, learning and emotional wellbeing. You will need to communicate what you know in a concise and clear way. If an assessment of the child's development is needed, you could offer records in the form of observations and assessments for your setting or school. (For more information on the key person system, see Chapter 12, unit EYMP1.)

It will also be important that you are able to listen carefully and take note of what other professionals have to say; for example, a paediatric dietician may need you to keep an accurate record of what a child is eating in an early years setting, and may ask you to follow a particular approach to encourage a child to eat more healthily. It is important that families do not receive conflicting advice from different professionals, so you will need to follow the dietician's advice and avoid putting across your own personal views. If you feel that there is a conflict between what you are being asked to do and what you see as effective early

years practice, it is important to discuss this with your manager, headteacher or special educational needs coordinator (SENCO).

## Expectations for your own work role

You also need to understand the expectations about your own work role as expressed in relevant **standards**, including codes of practice, regulations, minimum standards or national occupational standards. For example the government document published in 2005 by the DfES, *Key Elements of Effective Practice* (KEEP), provides a framework for early years practitioners to do the following:

- reflect on their work
- understand what effective practice looks like
- record their qualifications
- formulate their self-development plan
- allow managers to understand staff experience/ qualifications and training needs to support the development of the setting.

KEEP supports self-appraisal, appraisal, quality assurance, self-evaluation and performance management as it links the needs of children, young people, parents, carers, the setting *and* practitioners.

KEEP has been developed alongside and is consistent with the *Common Core of Skills and Knowledge for the Children's Workforce*, which sets out the six areas of expertise that everyone working with children, young people and families should be able to demonstrate:

- effective communication and engagement with children, young people and families
- child and young person development
- safeguarding and promoting the welfare of the child or young person
- supporting transitions
- multi-agency and integrated working
- information sharing.

# Reflecting on practice

Effective practice requires committed, enthusiastic and reflective practitioners with a breadth and depth of knowledge, skills and understanding. To be an

**Progress check**

- Working as a team, show your commitment to the CACHE statement of values in your daily practice.
- Outline the standards of professional practice expected from you and your colleagues. (This information may be included in a code of practice for staff in the staff handbook and/or set out in best practice benchmarks, such as KEEP.)

effective, reflective practitioner, you should use your own learning to improve your work with children and their families in ways which are sensitive, positive and non-judgemental. Through initial and ongoing training and development, the KEEP framework requires you to develop, demonstrate and continuously improve your:

- relationships with both children and adults
- understanding of the individual and diverse ways that children develop and learn
- knowledge and understanding in order to actively support and extend children's learning in and across all areas and aspects of learning
- practice in meeting all children's needs, learning styles and interests
- work with parents, carers and the wider community
- work with other professionals.

## Techniques of reflective analysis

As a professional practitioner you need to know and understand the techniques of reflective analysis:

- questioning what, why and how
- seeking alternatives
- keeping an open mind and viewing from different perspectives
- thinking about consequences
- testing ideas through comparing and contrasting; asking 'what if?'
- synthesising ideas; seeking, identifying and resolving problems (National Day Nurseries Association (NDNA), 2004).

# Evaluating your own performance

You need to know and understand clearly the exact role and responsibilities of your work as a professional practitioner. Review your professional practice by making regular and realistic assessments of how well your working practices match your role and responsibilities. Share your self-assessments with those responsible for managing and reviewing your work performance; for example, during your regular discussions/meetings with your colleagues or with your line manager. You should also ask other people for feedback about how well you fulfil the requirements and expectations of your role.

You can reflect on your own professional practice by making comparisons with appropriate models of effective practice, such as the work of more experienced practitioners within the setting.

## Self-evaluation

Self-evaluation is necessary to improve your own professional practice, develop your ability to reflect upon routines/activities, and modify plans to meet the individual needs of the children and/or young people with whom you work. When evaluating your own practice, you should consider the following questions:

- Was your own particular contribution appropriate?
- Did you choose the right time, place and resources?
- Did you intervene enough or too much?
- Did you achieve your goals (such as objectives/outcomes for the child or children and yourself)? If not, why not? Were the goals too ambitious or unrealistic?
- What other strategies/methods could have been used? Suggest possible modifications.
- Who should you ask for further advice: perhaps a senior practitioner, setting manager, other professional?

## Performance management and appraisal

An employer looks for a range of personal and professional qualities in any employee. A system of performance management or appraisal helps you and your manager or employer to assess how you are performing in your job and whether you are happy. Usually, goals will be set and your performance will be measured in relation to these targets.

## Guidelines for performance management or appraisal meetings

- Prepare for the meeting. Spend some time thinking about what you think is going well and what you are finding difficult. If you need help or support with something in particular, think ahead about how you will raise this topic. Look back at your targets from the previous year: did you meet them, or even exceed them? Did anything arise that prevented you from achieving them?
- The meeting provides an opportunity for both you and your employer or manager to identify any aspects of the job that you are doing very well, and any that need to be improved. It is on these occasions that you can raise any problems you have, such as dealing with particular situations, children, young people, parents, carers or staff.
- The meeting is also an opportunity to ensure that you understand the current priorities and aims of the setting and how your work contributes to these.
- If you can show that you are carrying out your entire duties well, you may be given more responsibility, or moved to work in a different area to develop your experience with other age ranges or activities.
- Appraisals should be viewed by staff as a positive action which helps to promote effective practice within the setting. This holds true even when there are criticisms of your performance. If you are starting to feel upset or nervous during the meeting, or if you feel that unfair criticisms are being made, ask for the meeting to pause for a few minutes so that you can collect your thoughts. If appropriate, ask whether a colleague could accompany you for the rest of the meeting.

- Usually, there is an annual cycle of performance management, including observation of your work and review meetings.
- Appraisals are also useful in identifying staff development needs; for example, an early years practitioner who is unassertive may be sent on an assertiveness training course. All early years settings and schools are required to identify the training needs of staff and how they plan to meet them.

### Key term

**Appraisal** – also called performance management, this is a formal system that your manager uses to evaluate how well you are doing in your job, and to set targets for further improvement over the year ahead.

###  Progress check

- How do you monitor the processes, practices and outcomes from your work?
- Give examples of how you evaluate your own practice, including the following: self-evaluation; reflections on your interactions with others; sharing your reflections with others; using feedback from others to improve your own evaluation.
- Describe how you have used reflection to solve problems and improve practice.

## Agreeing a personal development plan

You can take part in continuing professional development by identifying areas in your knowledge, understanding and skills where you could benefit from further development, and creating a plan to achieve this. You should seek out and access opportunities for continuing professional development as part of this plan, to improve your professional practice (NDNA, 2004).

## Identifying your personal development objectives

To develop your effectiveness as a professional practitioner, you should be able to identify your own SMART personal development objectives:

- **S**pecific: identify exactly what you want to develop, such as the particular skills you need to update or new skills you need to acquire (such as first aid or ICT skills).
- **M**easurable: define criteria that can be used to measure whether or not your objectives have been achieved (for example, best practice benchmarks, course certificate of attendance or qualification).
- **A**chievable: avoid being too ambitious; set objectives which you know are attainable.
- **R**ealistic: be realistic about what you want to develop.
- **T**ime-bound: plan a realistic timeframe within which to achieve your objectives.

> What are your own SMART personal development objectives?

## Your own personal development plan

You should discuss and agree your objectives with those people responsible for supporting your professional development, with the aim of drawing up a **personal development plan**. For example, you may consider that some of your work tasks require modification or improvement, and therefore wish to discuss possible changes with your line manager; you may feel that you lack sufficient knowledge and skills to implement particular activities, and need to discuss opportunities for you to undertake the relevant training.

To achieve your personal development objectives you should make effective use of the people, resources (such as the internet, libraries, journals) and other professional development or training opportunities available to you (see below). When assessing your

personal development and training needs, you need to consider the following:

- your existing experience and skills
- the needs of the children with whom you work
- any problems with how you currently work
- any new or changing expectations for your role
- information and/or learning needed to meet best practice, quality schemes or regulatory requirements.

### ✓ Progress check

- Describe how you have identified and developed areas in your knowledge, skills and understanding. Include information on the following: your existing strengths and skills; skills and knowledge you need to improve; plans for improving your work; preparing for future responsibilities.
- Give examples of how you access opportunities for continuing professional development.

## Learning opportunities and personal development

Training courses and qualifications can have a positive influence on improving the status of early years practitioners, as well as enabling them to share examples of effective practice with others working with children. Children's settings also benefit from having professional practitioners who are able to improve their expertise and increase their job satisfaction. Specific training and recognised qualifications for the children and young people's workforce are available; for example, Level 2, 3 and 4 qualifications, as well as a wide range of training courses for professional practitioners.

### Qualifications for early years practitioners

Working in the field of early years care and education can be physically and emotionally exhausting, and professionals will need to consolidate their skills and

**Figure 2.2** Liz Dolan conducted research into children's sleep in her nursery for her BA (Hons) in Early Childhood Studies at London Metropolitan University; her research highlighted the importance of children getting ready for sleep in an unhurried way, and having special bedding and objects around them to help them feel relaxed

develop the ability to be reflective in their practice. It is important to keep abreast of all the changes in child care and education practices by reading the relevant magazines, such as *Nursery World* and *Early Years Educator,* and by being willing to attend training courses when available.

There are greater opportunities than ever before for practitioners to enhance their qualifications up to and beyond degree level. It is clear that the future in the children and young people's workforce will favour the best qualified people.

## The Qualifications and Credit Framework

The introduction of the Qualifications and Credit Framework (QCF) has simplified the structure of qualifications for early years practitioners by reducing the number of qualifications available. For example, the Level 2 Certificate for the Children and Young People's Workforce and the Level 3 Diploma for the Children and Young People's Workforce are now the two essential qualifications for working with children and/or young people. The QCF also offers qualifications in a modular format, enabling learners

to develop knowledge and understanding which is not only tailored to their existing training needs but also allows for greater flexibility as their work roles and responsibilities change over time. For example, a practitioner with a Level 3 qualification who has taken the Early Years Mandatory Pathway would only need to take some additional units to be qualified to work with older children or young people in an extended school. It would not be necessary to start a whole new course.

## Degree level

Degrees for early years practitioners include foundation and full honours degrees in Early Years Education and Child Care (Level 5).

- **Foundation degrees** are intended to be vocational in their emphasis; they are studied part-time and build on the learner's practical, workplace experience. These courses are offered by colleges of higher education and universities.
- **Honour degrees** can be studied full-time or part-time, usually at university. Many early years practitioners study part-time for degrees with a modular design, which enables the learner to fit studying around work.

## Postgraduate training

The **Early Years Professional (EYP) status** is a specialist postgraduate qualification for practitioners working with children in the Early Years Foundation Stage (EYFS). The status sits alongside Qualified Teacher Status (QTS). It is currently recommended that staff with QTS working with children from birth to 5 years should also undertake EYP status. Staff with EYP status are not, however, qualified to lead nursery or reception classes in schools.

Depending on their previous experience, practitioners (including childminders) can gain EYP status through the following routes:

- four-month part-time validation programme
- six-month part-time, short extended professional development (EPD) pathway
- twelve-month full-time training pathway.

Practitioners with an early years foundation degree (Level 5) or an equivalent qualification are eligible for the long EPD pathway, which lasts 15 months and tops up a foundation degree to a full honours degree.

## Short courses for early years practitioners

Professional development and training opportunities for early years practitioners include short courses in the following areas:

- play and child development
- supporting children's literacy and numeracy activities
- developing ICT skills
- strategies for dealing with challenging behaviour
- first aid training including paediatric first aid
- child protection
- equal opportunities workshops
- disability and inclusion training
- supporting specific special needs
- conflict resolution
- working with parents or carers
- arts and crafts workshops
- drama and storytelling workshops
- children's sports or games workshops.

Other professional development and training opportunities include: training to be a QCF assessor and quality assurer; staff training manager; work with local authorities or regulatory bodies as an early years advisor or quality assessor; work with children in different sectors.

### Research Activity

Find out about the professional development and training opportunities for early years practitioners in your local area.

## Professional portfolio

A professional portfolio highlighting your existing experience and qualifications can form the basis for assessing your training needs. This portfolio will also be a tangible record of your professional development, and will help to boost your self-esteem. In addition, a well-presented portfolio containing all relevant and required documents for an interview, will demonstrate to potential employers that you are well organised and have a professional attitude towards your work with children and young people.

Your professional portfolio may include the following documents:

- your *curriculum vitae* (see below)
- school examination certificates
- college certificate or diploma
- first aid certificate
- basic food hygiene certificate
- statement of your child care philosophy
- examples of previous work with children, such as activity plans
- relevant college assignments.

### Preparing a *curriculum vitae*

It is always useful to compile a *curriculum vitae* (CV) and to keep it up to date. The purposes of a CV are to provide a brief outline of your life history, set out basic factual information in a concise manner, and assist in filling out application forms. Most software packages contain templates for a CV or resumé (for example, Microsoft® Word and OpenOffice).

The main headings to include in a CV are:

- **First name and family name**
- **Personal details** – full postal address, telephone number, email address
- **Education and qualifications** – include names of schools and colleges attended, with dates and qualifications obtained
- **Employment history** – if you have not already held a full-time post, include babysitting experience, college work experience and Saturday or holiday jobs
- **Other experience** – include any voluntary work, involvement in local organisations or groups, sport and leisure interests
- **Referees** – give the names, positions and addresses of two people who are willing to provide references for you; always ask them first.

CVs should be well presented and free of any mistakes. Use your spellchecker, and also ask a friend to check it through for you. In general, if you are applying for a post in a school or local authority children's centre or day nursery, CVs will not be accepted; you may need to complete an application form instead. Read the guidance on job applications very carefully before you complete the forms to apply for a post.

## Key term

**Curriculum vitae (CV)** – *Curriculum vitae* is Latin for 'course of life'. Your CV is a brief summary of your education, training, qualifications and experience that you provide for a prospective employer. A CV helps an employer to decide whether or not an applicant might be suitable for the job.

 Progress check

- Think ahead about which direction you would like your career to take, and what training and development this will require.
- Prepare a draft version of a CV before you start seeking employment.
- Compile your own professional portfolio if you do not already have one.

 Useful resources

**Organisations and websites**
**Council for Awards in Care, Health and Education (CACHE)** is the specialist awarding organisation for qualifications in children's care and education, such as the CACHE Level 3 Diploma for the Children and Young People's Workforce:
**www.cache.org.uk**

**Daycare Trust** is a national child care charity that provides information for parents, child care providers, employers, trades unions, local authorities and policymakers:
**www.daycaretrust.org.uk**

**Health and Safety Executive (HSE)** is a government-funded organisation which works to protect people against risks to health or safety arising from work activities:
**www.hse.gov.uk**

**MIND** is the UK's leading charity providing advice and support about all aspects of mental health and wellbeing. MIND also campaigns to improve public understanding of mental health issues such as depression and anxiety:
**www.mind.org.uk**

*Nursery World* is the leading magazine for everyone working in early years education and care. It includes job adverts, news and in-depth articles on effective practice:
**www.nursery-world.co.uk**

*The Key Elements of Effective Practice* (KEEP) is a framework for early years practitioners:
**www.standards.dfes.gov.uk/primary/
    publications/foundation_stage/keep/**

*The Common Core of Skills and Knowledge for the Children's Workforce* sets out the six areas of expertise that everyone working with children, young people and families should be able to demonstrate:
**www.cwdcouncil.org.uk/assets/0000/9297/
    CWDC_CommonCore7.pdf**

# 3 Promote equality and inclusion in health, social care or children and young people's settings: Unit SHC 33

Equality and inclusion are moral and legal obligations and rights for people working in and using public services. As a practitioner, you have a role to play in ensuring that in all aspects of your work every person is given real opportunities to thrive, and that any barriers that prevent them from reaching their full potential are removed. The principles of equality and inclusion are at the heart of work with children and young people in every kind of setting.

## Learning outcomes

By the end of this chapter you will:

1. Understand the importance of diversity, equality and inclusion.
2. Be able to work in an inclusive way.
3. Be able to promote diversity, equality and inclusion.

# The importance of diversity, equality and inclusion

## What is meant by diversity, equality and inclusion?

### Diversity

Diversity refers to the differences in values, attitudes, cultures, beliefs, skills and life experience of each individual in any group of people. In the UK, early years curriculum frameworks emphasise the importance of developing each child's sense of identity and promoting a positive sense of pride in each child's family origins. Starting with themselves, young children can develop a sense of belonging to the local community, and begin to understand and respect less familiar cultures.

## Equality

Equality does not mean that everyone has to be treated the same. People have different needs, situations and ambitions. Practitioners have a part to play in supporting children and young people to live in the way that they value and choose, to be 'themselves' and to be different if they wish. Every person should have equality of opportunity. This means opening up access for every child and family to the full participation in all services for children and young people. Lack of access causes:

- poor self-esteem
- misunderstandings
- stereotyping and discrimination
- lack of inclusion
- lack of respect
- lack of confidence.

## Inclusion

Inclusion is a term used within education to describe the process of ensuring the equality of learning opportunities for all children and young people, whatever their disabilities or disadvantages. This means that all children and young people have the right to have their needs met in the best way for them. They are seen as being part of the community, even if they need particular help to live a full life within the community.

# The potential effects of discrimination

## What is discrimination?

Discrimination is the denial of equality based on personal characteristics, such as race and colour. Discrimination is usually based on prejudice and stereotypes.

- **Prejudice** literally means to prejudge people based on assumptions. For example, racial prejudice is the belief that physical or cultural differences (in skin colour, religious beliefs or dress) are directly linked to differences in the development of intelligence, ability, personality or goodness.
- The word **stereotype** comes from the process of making metal plates for printing. When applied to people, stereotyping refers to forming an instant or fixed picture of a group of people, usually based on false or incomplete information. Stereotypes are often negative.

We need to be aware of different forms of discrimination so that we can act to promote equality.

### Case Study    Sade

Sade is a four-year-old, British-born Nigerian girl, but she has never been to Nigeria. Both Sade's parents were born in the UK and grew up there. Sade only eats Nigerian food at family gatherings which happen a few times a year when relatives visit. She finds it rather hot and spicy compared with the European food that she usually eats at home and at nursery. She does not understand her key worker's question about the spices her mother uses to cook at home.

## Racial discrimination

Racism is the belief that some races are superior, based on the false idea that things like skin colour make some people better than others. Examples are refusing a child a nursery place because they are black; failing to address the needs of children and young people from a minority religious or cultural group, such as children and young people from traveller families; and only acknowledging festivals from the mainstream Christian culture, such as Christmas and Easter.

### Institutional racism

Following the Macpherson Inquiry (1999) into the murder in 1993 of Stephen Lawrence, a black teenager, this has been defined as

'the collective failure of an organisation to provide an appropriate and professional service to people because of their colour, culture or ethnic origin. It can be seen or detected in processes, attitudes and behaviour which amount to discrimination through unwitting prejudice, ignorance, thoughtlessness and racist stereotyping which disadvantage minority ethnic people.'

It can be difficult to detect and combat institutional racism as it tends to be integrated into an organisation's culture and practices as a result of its past history. For this reason, it is vital that all early years settings adhere to an up-to-date policy of equal opportunities, and that the policy is implemented and regularly monitored.

## Disability discrimination

Children and young people with disabilities or impairments may be denied equality of opportunity with their non-disabled peers. Examples are failing to provide children with special needs with appropriate facilities and services; or organising activities in a nursery setting in a way that ignores the special physical, intellectual and emotional needs of certain children.

## Sex discrimination

This occurs when people of one gender reinforce the stereotype that they are superior to the other. Examples are routinely offering boys more opportunities for rough-and-tumble play than girls; or encouraging girls to perform traditional 'female' tasks such as cooking and washing.

No law can prevent prejudiced attitudes. However, the law can prohibit discriminatory practices and behaviours that flow from prejudice.

## Case Study
### Childminder escapes jail for racial assault on two-year-old child

A childminder who crayoned the word 'nigger' on the forehead of a two-year-old girl in her care narrowly escaped jail after a judge accepted pleas that she was 'ignorant rather than evil'. The 57-year-old childminder made different excuses during her trial, when a jury found her guilty of aggravated racial assault. She thought up the name crayoning as a way of entertaining a group of children she was minding at her home. She scrawled the first names of the others, who were all white, on their foreheads, but then wrote 'nigger' on the little girl's. At first she claimed that the word was a private joke between her and the girl, but then changed her story to say that she had meant to write 'Tigger', because the child had been playing the character in a game based on AA Milne's book, *Winnie the Pooh*.

The insult was still visible when the child returned home, and police and social workers were called in. The childminder tried to laugh the incident off when first interviewed by officers, claiming that the girl had 'pestered' her to use the word instead of her actual name. The recorder told her: 'You abused this girl by demonstrating the clearest hostility to her mixed race status by writing the word nigger . . . You told the police you only wrote the word because she asked you to and that she often referred to herself as the little black bastard. But where did a young girl get that phrase from? This child was brought up in a climate of neglect, hostility and racial abuse, and it is clear that on this occasion when she was in your care you simply continued the abuse.'

(Adapted from a news story in *The Guardian*, September 2005)

Read the case study above and discuss the following questions:

1 Was the two-year-old girl a victim of **direct** or **indirect** discrimination?
2 What are the likely consequences for the child's self-esteem?

## Types of discrimination

Children and young people can experience the effects of discrimination in a number of ways. Discrimination can be direct or indirect.

### Direct discrimination

This occurs when a child is treated less favourably than another child in the same or similar circumstances; for example, when a child or young person is bullied by being ignored, verbally or physically abused, or teased. (See also pages 132–5 on bullying.)

### Indirect discrimination

This occurs when a condition is applied that will unfairly affect a particular group of children or young people when compared to others. This may be either deliberate or unintended; for example, when children from a minority ethnic or religious group (such as Sikh, Muslim or Plymouth Brethren) are required to wear a specific school uniform that causes difficulties within their cultural code.

Discrimination of any kind prevents children and young people from developing a feeling of self-worth or self-esteem. The effects of being discriminated against can last the whole of a child's life. In particular, they may:

- **be unable to fulfil their potential**, because they are made to feel that their efforts are not valued or recognised by others
- **find it hard to form relationships** with others because of low self-worth or self-esteem
- be so affected by the **stereotypes or labels** applied to them that they start to believe in them and so behave in accordance with others' expectations. This then becomes a self-fulfilling prophecy: for

example, if a child is repeatedly told that he is clumsy, he may act in a clumsy way even when quite capable of acting otherwise (see also information about self-fulfilling prophecy in Chapter 5)

- **feel shame** about their own cultural background
- **feel that they are in some way to blame** for their unfair treatment, and so withdraw into themselves
- **lack confidence in trying new activities** if their attempts are always ridiculed or put down
- **be aggressive towards others**: distress or anger can prevent children and young people from interacting cooperatively with other children and young people.

## Key terms

**Anti-discrimination** – An approach which challenges unfair or unlawful treatment of individuals or groups based on a specific characteristic of that group (such as colour, age, disability, sexual orientation etc.).

**Diversity** – The differences in values, attitudes, cultures, beliefs, skills, knowledge and life experience of each individual in any group of people.

**Discrimination** – Treating a person less favourably than others in the same or similar circumstances.

**Equality** – Ensuring that everyone has a chance to take part in society on an equal basis and to be treated appropriately, regardless of their gender, race, disability, age, sexual orientation, language, social origin, religious beliefs, marital status and other personal attributes.

**Inclusion** – Ensuring that every child, young person, adult or learner is given equality of opportunity to access education and care, by meeting their specific needs.

**Inclusive practice** – Inclusion in education and care is one aspect of inclusion in society, and means taking necessary steps to ensure that every child, young person, adult or learner is given an equal chance of taking advantage of the opportunities offered to them.

## How inclusive practice promotes equality and supports diversity

Inclusive practice (also referred to as inclusive education, inclusive schooling or educational inclusion) is a term used within education to describe the process of ensuring **equality of learning opportunities** for all children and young people,

whatever their disabilities or disadvantages. This means that all children and young people have the right to have their needs met in the best way for them. They are seen as being part of the community, even if they need particular help to live a full life within the community.

# Be able to work in an inclusive way

Laws in the UK deal with the overt discrimination that results from prejudice, especially when combined with power. Practitioners should work in an inclusive way, taking into account both the statutory legal framework in the UK and the policies and procedures in your setting. You need to value, and show respect to, all those you encounter in your setting as individuals. Examples of ways of working inclusively are given below.

## Legislation and codes of practice

The laws and codes of practice relating to equality, diversity and discrimination are listed here:

- The Equality Act (2010): this new Act has simplified the legal structure by bringing together nine different pieces of equality legislation

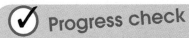 **Progress check**

### Understanding and promoting equality of opportunity

Practitioners should:

1. Know their Equalities Lead Officer or Equalities Coordinator
2. Receive support and ongoing training in this area
3. Work to improve his or her own practice
4. Report all incidents of discrimination (an incident is discriminatory if it is felt to be so by anyone involved, even an onlooker)
5. Take active steps to make sure that everyone knows about the available services and is able to access them.

Think about different ways in which you have encouraged equality of opportunity in your work with children and young people. How can you ensure that your practice is not discriminatory? How can you promote equality of opportunity? Write a short account of ways in which you can ensure that no child, young person or adult is treated unfavourably compared with others.

- The Special Educational Needs and Disability Act 2001
- The Race Relations (Amendment) Act 2000
- Convention on the Rights of the Child (UN, 1989)
- The Human Rights Act 1998
- The Special Needs and Disability Act (SENDA) 2001.

The legislation should have an influence on the way in which organisations provide and organise services, and how practitioners approach their work. You need to be aware of the law as it stands in relation to promoting equality of opportunity, although you do not need to know the details.

## Respecting the beliefs, culture, values and preferences of others

Much can be gained from respecting different ways of bringing up children and young people. For example, the Indian tradition of massaging babies is now widely used in British clinics and family centres, as is the way in which African mothers traditionally carry their babies in a sling on their backs. It is important to understand and respect what the child has been taught to do at home. In some cultures it is seen as disrespectful for a child to look an adult directly in the eye, whereas in other cultures children are considered rude if they do not look at an adult directly.

Adhering to the following guidelines will help children and young people to form positive images of people.

### Storytelling

You could ask storytellers (such as parents) from different ethnic groups to tell stories in their own languages, as well as in English. This helps children and young people to hear different languages, so that

**Figure 3.1** All parents or carers were given the opportunity to attend a massage session with their babies

**Figure 3.2** Reading a picture book in Portuguese

the idea becomes familiar that there are many languages in the world.

## Use arts, crafts and artefacts from different cultures

You could use fabrics, interest tables, books, posters, jigsaws, etc. from different cultures. This helps children to realise for example that not everyone uses a knife, fork or spoon when eating; they might use fingers or chopsticks instead. Children and young people are helped to learn that there are different ways of eating, something which might seem strange to them at first.

## Include music and dances from different cultures

In every culture children love to stand at the edge while people perform. Children often 'echo-dance', which means copying the movements. Look out for this the next time you visit a fair or fête. If there are Morris dancers or folk dancers, you are likely to see children watching them and echo-dancing at the sides.

Being introduced to different cultures in this way helps children not to reject unfamiliar music. For example, Chinese music is based on a pentatonic scale, whereas European music and classical music are usually based on a chromatic scale. A child who has never before seen ballet or Indian dancing might find these beautiful but strange at first.

## Cookery from different cultures

You might have multi-language, picture-based cookery books that families can borrow (or you could make these). For example, there could be a copy of a recipe for rotí in English, Urdu and French, or for bread in English, Greek and Swahili; the choice of languages would depend on which were used in the setting or the local area.

### Plan the menu carefully

Make sure that the menu includes food that children will enjoy and which is in some way familiar. One of the things which young children worry about when they are away from home is whether they will like the food. Food and eating with others is a very emotional experience.

## Help children to feel that they belong

Ensure that children who look different, because they are from different cultures or because they have a disability, feel at ease and part of the group.

# Promoting diversity, equality and inclusion

## Modelling inclusive practice

As practitioners, we are responsible for ensuring equal opportunities within our settings. There are many ways in which we can promote diversity, equality and inclusion; some guidelines follow.

## Promote a sense of belonging

As children grow up, they need to feel that they belong to the group, whether that group is their family, their culture, the community they live in and experience, or their early years setting, school or college.

## Value cultural diversity and respect difference

In the UK we live in a diverse and multicultural society. This means that it is important to appreciate, understand and respect different cultural and religious ideas. The whole environment of every setting needs to reflect a multicultural and multilingual approach. For example, the home area in an early years setting, like every other area of the environment, should include objects which are familiar to children and link with their homes and culture. These are often called **cultural artefacts**.

## Give individual children individual help

There may be children with special educational needs using for example the home area, and they may need to have special arrangements to allow them access. A child in a wheelchair will need a height-appropriate table so that a mixing bowl can be stirred; it might be necessary to make a toy cooker of an appropriate height. Children love to construct their own play props, and allowing them to do so creates a much more culturally diverse selection, because they can say what they need in order to make a play setting like their homes.

## Understand different religions

In order that every child feels accepted beyond their home, those working with children and young people and their families need to learn about belief structures other than their own. It is also important to remember not to judge people or make assumptions about their values or behaviour based on whether they believe in any god, gods or no god. Some children are brought up in families that follow more than one religion. For example, there might be a Roman Catholic Christian father and a Muslim mother, or a Hindu father and a Quaker Christian mother.

## Include children with disabilities

Inclusion is about being able to support, encourage and provide for all with individual needs, whether they are temporary or permanent. Excluding disabled children from everyday experiences, which are the norm for most children, can lead to a lifetime of segregation. In addition, lack of contact with disabled people can lead to fear and ignorance of those who seem 'different'.

## Have an awareness of gender roles

Creating an environment where girls and boys are respected and cared for equally in early childhood is the first step towards breaking cycles of discrimination and disadvantage, and promoting a child's sense of self-worth as it relates to their gender. It is important to remember that some children will have learned narrow gender roles. In the traditional home situation, mothers usually do housework and fathers mend cars. Children need to see adults taking on broader gender roles, and to learn about alternative ways for men and women to behave as themselves.

## Avoid stereotypes

When adults fill in forms they decide whether to be described as Mr, Ms, Mrs or Miss, and whether or not they wish to describe themselves according to different ethnic categories. An adult with a hearing loss can also choose whether to be described as deaf, hearing impaired or aurally challenged.

Children need to be given as much choice as possible about these aspects of their lives. If adults describe a child as 'the one with glasses', or comment 'What a pretty dress,' or talk about 'the Afro-Caribbean child', they are stereotyping these children and seeing them narrowly rather than as whole people. Children and young people need to hear and see positive images of themselves and of other people.

# Supporting others to promote equality and rights

In the UK legislation exists on race, gender and disability discrimination, which helps teams of people working together to have an impact on racism, sexism, and disablist attitudes and work practices, however unconscious these may be.

In addition, it is important that each of us inspects what we do so that we become aware of our attitudes and values. Only then can we act on the unwittingly discriminatory behaviour that we will almost inevitably find. Discriminatory behaviour occurs when we are sexist, racist or disablist, even if this is not our intention; for example, an early years practitioner might ask for a strong boy to lift the chair. We need to explore whether what we *say* we believe, matches what we actually *do*, and then address this issue if we are being discriminatory. Each of us has to work at this all the time, right throughout our lives. It is not useful to feel guilty and dislike yourself if you find you are discriminating against someone, but it *is* useful to do something about it.

The process of inspecting our basic thinking needs to be done on three levels:

1 within the legal framework
2 in the work setting as part of a team
3 as individuals.

## Working as a team

It is important to pause at regular intervals and examine what happens in every work setting. Does what the team members *say* they believe in, match what they *actually* do? Identifying problems in the way in which children and adults relate to each other is essential before positive action can be taken by the whole team. It helps to work as a team when doing this because it is hard for individual team members to inspect their own thinking in isolation from other people. It helps to share and discuss different issues with colleagues. The team should devise a policy and procedure of equality of opportunity, ensure that they are implemented and then, as a team, review them regularly:

- The policy states the values of the team and the aims of its work.
- The procedure sets out how the team will put the policy into practice.
- The review process covers all aspects of the team's work in relation to its policy and procedure.

## Guidelines to help individuals promote diversity, equality of opportunity and inclusion

- Remember that you are part of a multiprofessional team, and that each member has something different to bring to their work. You cannot be an expert in every area, but you *can* be an effective networker. This means linking people together who might be useful to each other. Get in touch with people who know about:
  - welfare rights and social services
  - health services
  - voluntary organisations and self-help groups.
- Be willing to find out about different religions and to respect them. For example, there are Hindus, Sikhs, Jains, Orthodox and Reform Jews, Roman Catholic Christians, Church of England Christians, Methodist Christians, Quaker Christians, Jehovah Witness Christians and Mormon Christians. Every religion has variety within it. Ask religious leaders and parents or carers for information.
- Find out about different disabilities. Ask parents,

**Figure 3.3** It is important to be warm towards children

carers and voluntary organisations (such as SCOPE, RNIB, RNID) to help you. Do not be afraid to say that you do not understand many issues surrounding disability, but that you want to find out and learn more. Remember that minority groups of all kinds are as important as the majority groups, and should be included as part of the whole group.

- Respect and value the child's home language. Think how you can make yourself understood using body language, gestures and facial expression: by pointing, using pictures or using actions with your words. Try asking children if they would like a drink using one of these strategies. You could use objects as props. It is important to be warm towards children: remember to smile and to show that you enjoy interacting with them.
- Set children and young people tasks that will help them to make decisions and exercise choice. It is important to let all children make choices and decisions so that they feel a sense of control in their lives. When people feel they have some control over what they do, their learning improves; it gives them greater equality of opportunity and feelings of self-worth.
- Respect yourself and others alike. Try to think why

people hold different views and customs from yours. Keep thinking about what you do: consider issues of race, gender, sexual orientation, age, economics, background, disability, assertiveness, culture and special educational needs. Be determined to change whatever you dislike about what you do, without feeling guilt or shame.

## Identifying and challenging discrimination in the work setting

The first step in being able to challenge discrimination is to identify when it is taking place. The most obvious and common form of indirect discrimination is when labels are applied to children. You may believe in private, for example, that Mark is a 'spoilt' child who is allowed to behave in a way which you personally think is unacceptable. It would be unnatural not to have an opinion on such matters. However, you should not initiate or join in any discussions which result in Mark being labelled as a 'difficult' or 'spoilt' child. Equally, you will find some children more likeable than others; again this is quite natural. What is important is that you are fair in your treatment of all the children in your care. You should ensure that you value each as an individual and treat them with respect.

## Activity

### Working together to promote equality of opportunity and inclusivity

The following activities can often be done as a group exercise. Each provides useful opportunities for you to develop these important skills:

- observing children or young people
- planning to meet the needs of all individuals
- implementing and evaluating the activities and observations.

1 **Plan a multicultural cooking library.** Make six cookery books with simple recipes from a variety of cultures. Find or draw pictures to illustrate the books. Write the text in English and another language if possible. If you write in Urdu or Chinese, remember that you will need to make two separate books, as Urdu and Chinese text runs from right to left. Use the books with groups of children and run a series of cookery sessions.

- **Observe** the way in which the children use and respond to the cookery books.
- **Evaluate** the aim of your plan, the reason for the activity, how the activities were carried out and what you observed in the children's cooking activities.

2 **Story-telling.** Plan a story that you can tell (rather than read from a book). Choose a story which you enjoy, and make or find suitable props. You could make puppets out of stuffed socks, finger puppets out of gloves, stick puppets or shadow puppets, dolls, dressing-up clothes and various other artefacts.

- **Observe** the children listening as you tell the story.
- **Evaluate** your activity.
- Focus on their understanding and their language, especially children whose first language is not English.

3 **Religious festivals.** Plan how you can make the children you work with more aware of religious festivals in a variety of cultures. For example, how could you introduce the children to Diwali in a way that is not a token effort? Remember to offer children meaningful first-hand experiences.

- **Observe** the children and assess how much they understand.
- **Evaluate** your plans and observations.
- Look particularly at the reactions of children who are familiar with the festival you choose, and compare their behaviour to that of children for whom this is a new experience.

4 **Inclusion.** Plan how you would include a child with a special need or disability in your setting. Remember that your plans will be different according to each child's needs. A child with a hearing impairment will need different help from a child who is a wheelchair user, for example. Also plan how you would include a child who has a temporary disability, such as deafness from the condition 'glue ear'. Also plan for a child with emotional needs – e.g. a child whose daily life has been disrupted through a family bereavement.

- Carry out and **observe** your plan in action.
- **Evaluate** your plan.
- Focus on how you meet each child's individual needs through your plan.

5 **Equality of opportunity.** Read your setting's policy on equality of opportunity, and look at actual practices in the daily routine, such as mealtimes, looking at books. Does what happens match the policy?

## Activity

- **Evaluate** your observations.

6 **Musical development**. Plan a series of activities which introduce children to the music of a variety of cultures. You will need to help children to listen to and make music. Make musical instruments out of cardboard boxes, elastic bands, yoghurt pots, masking tape and other materials.

7 **Booklet**: Plan a booklet which introduces different religious festivals and helps parents and carers to understand different religious perspectives in your early years setting. Make the booklet and use it in your setting.

- **Evaluate** it.

8 **Display**: Plan and make a display using a multicultural theme.

- **Evaluate** it: how did the adults use it? How did the children react?

9 **International book**. Choose one picture, book, story or poem from each of the five continents: Africa, America (North and South), Asia, Australasia and Europe. Make the collection into a book that you can use with children aged between three and seven.

- **Evaluate** the activity.

10 **Multicultural provision**. Plan an area of provision that is multicultural in approach, such as the home area. Perhaps you can add more ideas to those suggested in this section.

- Implement and **evaluate** your plan.

## Challenging discriminatory behaviour

### The role of the individual member of staff

Each individual worker needs to be committed and empowered to carry out the team's policy using the procedure or code of practice. You can have a great impact on the lives of the children and families you work with, and you can have an influence on combating discriminatory behaviour.

It is important to be **assertive** but not aggressive. Being assertive means talking clearly and politely about how you feel, which is very different from being rude and angry. For example, you might say, 'I felt very uncomfortable when you asked me to give a drink to the girl with a hearing aid. I felt I needed to know her name, because I am worried that I might stop seeing her as a person if I just think of her as "the girl with a hearing aid".'

### Challenging situations

If you see a child hurt or insult someone, explain that such behaviour is not acceptable. Never ignore or make excuses for a child's discriminatory behaviour towards another person. Explain to the child why such behaviour is unacceptable, and encourage them to see how hurtful their comments or actions appear to the other child. Criticise the behaviour rather than the child.

### Being aware of discrimination in children's resources

Books which are discriminatory can be discussed with other practitioners, removed and replaced with others (chosen as a team) which contain positive images of people with disabilities, from different cultures and of different genders.

## Learning from experience

From time to time you will make mistakes, and regret things which you have said or done. For example, someone who had lived in Dorset all her life came to London and laughed at the idea of people eating goat meat. She quickly realised how insulting this was to her new friends, and apologised, explaining that it was simply a new idea to her.

## Learning about other cultures and respecting the differences

It is very important to try to pronounce and spell names correctly, and to understand the systems which different cultures use when choosing names for people. It is also very important to learn about the types of clothes which people wear in different cultures, and to try to learn what these garments are called.

# Teaching children and young people to be assertive

We have seen that being assertive is important for staff, but it is also vital for children and young people. Children need to feel protected from aggression and to be able to assert themselves sufficiently to take a full part in the activities provided. Children often pick on weaker children or those who are different; they may tease them or

make racial, gender or disability insults. Both the bully *and* the child being bullied need help to be assertive: one needs help with aggression, and the other with timidity. Visualisation techniques can help children and young people to use positive images (seeing themselves as assertive) rather than negative images (being the bully or victim of bullying).

## Assessment practice

### Understanding equality, diversity and inclusion

Every setting should have a policy and procedure on equal opportunities. Look at the relevant policy in your own settings and then answer the following questions, making brief notes on current practice:

- How do you show that you value differences between children, and ensure effective communication and liaison with parents and carers to ensure that the records for children and young people contain relevant information?

- How do you develop children's sense of identity and raise their self-esteem?

- How does the curriculum planning reflect equal opportunities within every activity and area of learning?

- What do you do to acknowledge the diversity of backgrounds and cater for the individual needs of the children and young people in your setting? (This should include dietary, medical and cultural needs.)

- To what extent do your resources reflect a full range of the diversity within society, avoid stereotypes and promote positive images?

- Who is responsible for planning resources, and how often are the resources reviewed?

- How do you value different spoken and written languages and other forms of communication encountered in your setting?

- To what extent do you take into account the requirements of those with special educational needs and disabilities?

For each question, identify any areas that could be improved, and suggest ways in which this could be achieved.

## ✓ Progress check

### Inspecting your own feelings and attitudes

- Know the legislation on discriminatory behaviour.
- Work within the team to construct a policy on equality of opportunities.
- Use the procedure or code of practice drawn up by the staff in the work setting.
- Make sure that your team reviews the code of practice together regularly.
- Be assertive (not aggressive) and try to work towards greater equality of opportunity in your work setting.

Useful resources

**Organisations and websites**
**Early Education** is the leading national voluntary organisation for early years practitioners and parents, and promotes the right of all children to education of the highest quality:
**www.early-education.org.uk**

**Equality and Human Rights Commission (EHRC)** has a statutory remit to promote and monitor human rights; and to protect, enforce and promote equality across the seven 'protected' grounds – age, disability, gender, race, religion and belief, sexual orientation and gender reassignment:
**www.equalityhumanrights.com**

**National Children's Bureau (NCB)** is a charitable organisation dedicated to advancing the health and wellbeing of all children and young people across every aspect of their lives, and providing them with a powerful and authoritative voice:
**www.ncb.org.uk**

**Organisation Mondiale Education Pre-Scholaire (OMEP)** is an international, non-governmental organisation founded in 1948 to benefit children under the age of eight years throughout the world. OMEP's aim is to promote the optimum conditions for all children, in order to ensure their wellbeing, development and happiness, both within their family unit and the wider communities in which they live:
**www.omep-international.org**

# 4 Principles for implementing duty of care in health, social care or children and young people's settings: Unit SHC 34

This chapter is aimed at people who work with children or young people in a wide range of settings. It considers how duty of care contributes to safe practice, and how to address dilemmas or complaints that may arise where there is a duty of care. It also includes information about responding to complaints relating to duty of care.

### Learning outcomes

By the end of this chapter you will:

1. Understand how duty of care contributes to safe practice.

2. Know how to address conflicts or dilemmas that may arise between an individual's rights and the duty of care.

3. Know how to respond to complaints.

## Understand how duty of care contributes to safe practice

Many professions contain a 'duty of care', including health, social care and education. Duty of care requirements tend to be involved in occupational situations such as working in health or social care settings, or working with children or young people in a wide range of settings. To understand how duty of care contributes to safe practice, you need to understand what duty of care actually means.

## What is a 'duty of care'?

A duty of care involves an obligation that a person in a specific role has to ensure that others are taken care of and not harmed during a particular task. This involves giving appropriate attention, watching out for potential hazards, preventing mistakes or accidents, and making wise choices about steps undertaken in a role. If a duty of care is not met in a role that requires it, then the responsible person can be held accountable for allowing negligence to occur (Lutzenberger, 2010).

A standard of care is the benchmark, minimum amount or quality of care that should be provided under a duty of care. For example, medical staff have a duty of care for a patient with a laceration, which involves a standard of care to provide an appropriate bandage. A large gaping wound treated only with a plaster would not meet an expected standard of care from a doctor or nurse, but a set of butterfly bandages or stitches combined with a protective cover and elastic wrap bandage would be closer to the standard of care expected (Lutzenberger, 2010).

## Duty of care in children and young people's settings

The Early Years Foundation Stage (EYFS) is the framework that provides assurance to parents and carers that the early years providers which they choose will keep their children safe and help them to thrive. The overall aim of the EYFS is to help young children achieve the five *Every Child Matters* outcomes (staying safe, being healthy, enjoying and achieving, making a positive contribution, and achieving economic wellbeing) by improving quality and consistency in the early years sector through a universal set of standards which apply to all settings.

Early years providers include maintained schools, non-maintained schools, independent schools and childcare registered by Ofsted on the Early Years Register, all of which are required to meet the EYFS requirements. From September 2008 it is the legal responsibility of these providers to ensure that their provision meets the learning and development requirements and complies with the welfare regulations, as required by section 40 of the Childcare Act 2006.

The legal requirements relating to welfare (safeguarding and promoting children's welfare; suitable people; suitable premises, environment and equipment; organisation; and documentation) are set out in section 3 of the *Statutory Framework for the Early Years Foundation Stage*. The welfare requirements are given legal force by Regulations made under section 39 (1)(b) of the Childcare Act 2006. Together, the Order, the Regulations and the Statutory Framework document make up the legal basis of the EYFS. The requirements in this document have statutory force by virtue of section 44 (1) of the Childcare Act 2006 (DCSF, 2008).

In addition, the government document *Working Together to Safeguard Children* sets out specific expectations on what must be done to ensure that children and young people are safeguarded and their welfare promoted through assessment, advice, support and intervention.

## How duty of care contributes to safeguarding and protecting individuals

There is one aspect of work with babies, toddlers and young children that must always come first: the requirement to keep them safe, and to protect them from significant harm. The guidance from the *Every Child Matters* framework reminds us that:

'all those who come into contact with children and families in their everyday work, including practitioners who do not have a specific role in relation to safeguarding children, have a duty to safeguard and promote the welfare of children'.

The EYFS sets out the general welfare requirements for safeguarding and promoting children's welfare:

- The provider must take necessary steps to safeguard and promote the welfare of children.
- The provider must promote the good health of the children, take necessary steps to prevent the spread of infection, and take appropriate action when they are ill.
- Children's behaviour must be managed effectively and in a manner appropriate for their stage of development and particular individual needs.
- Providers must ensure that adults looking after children, or having unsupervised access to them, are suitable to do so. (DCSF, 2008)

(For more information, see Chapter 7, Unit CYP Core 3.3.)

### Key term

**Safeguarding** – This term includes all the steps you would take in an early years setting or school to help children feel safe and secure; protecting children from neglect or abuse; and ensuring that children stay safe, healthy and continue to develop well.

### Research Activity

Take a look at the grids on pages 22–40 of the statutory framework for EYFS.

Summarise the key points.

## Addressing conflicts or dilemmas that may arise between an individual's rights and the duty of care

Children and young people are entitled to basic human rights such as food, health care, a safe home and protection from abuse. However, children and young people are a special case because they cannot always stand up for themselves. They need a *special* set of rights that take account of their vulnerability and ensure that adults take responsibility for their protection and development.

The UN Convention on the Rights of the Child applies to all children and young people under the age of 18 years. It spells out the basic human rights of children and young people everywhere. All children have the right to: survive; develop to their fullest potential; be protected from harmful influences, abuse and exploitation; participate fully in family, cultural and social life; express and have their views taken into account on all matters that affect them; play, rest and enjoy leisure. (See Chapter 3, Unit SHC 33.)

A parent or primary carer is responsible for the care and upbringing of their child. The Children and Young Persons Act 1933 imposed criminal liability for abandonment, neglect or ill treatment of a child under 16 years, on any person over the age of 16 years who is responsible for that child. Because parental responsibility cannot be surrendered or transferred, parents and carers are liable for neglecting their child if they choose an inadequate babysitter.

The best approach to working with parents or carers is to develop a culture of mutual trust, respect and sharing of information. Involving parents or carers and upholding their rights fosters a positive relationship between them and the early years practitioner. Accessing their children's records should be a straightforward process for parents or carers, however they are kept. Parents and carers will expect to be offered regular meetings to discuss their children's progress, when achievements can be celebrated and concerns can be raised and discussed.

The EYFS states:

'Parents must be given free access to developmental records about their child (for example, the EYFS Profile). However, a written request must be made for personal files on the children, and providers must take into account

data protection rules when disclosing records that refer to third parties.'

It is important not to make assumptions about any individual, as this can lead to stereotyping (see Chapter 3, Unit SHC 33, page 28). You need to get to know the children and young people in your care (and their parents or carers), so that you consider each child as an individual with his or her own **unique needs**.

## Potential conflicts and dilemmas

Many difficult issues arise when professionals record and share information about children and young people. Information on a child or young person should only be collected and stored with the consent of their parents or carers, who should have free access to this information on request. Information should only be shared between professionals with the express consent of parents and carers, which should be gained formally with a signature. The only exceptions are the very small number of cases where the child might otherwise be at risk of immediate and significant harm if you shared a piece of information with the parent (see Chapter 7, Unit CYP Core 3).

Safeguarding children and young people requires practitioners to make difficult judgements, which must be consistent with the equal opportunities approach outlined in Chapter 3 (Unit SHC 33). As an early years practitioner, your first duty is to promote the welfare, development and learning of each child. Sometimes this means raising difficult or sensitive issues with a parent or carer. A key person might for example need to share a concern with parents that a child may have special educational needs (discussed in more detail in Chapter 18, Unit CYPOP 2), and is not receiving sufficient support and help at home, or that his or her needs are being neglected (discussed in more detail in Chapter 17, Unit CYPOP 1).

All of these are sensitive issues. It is important that they are raised in a way that shows concern for a child or young person, and not criticism of a parent or carer. In general, if a discussion is sensitively arranged in a confidential space and with a clear focus on the child or young person's best interests, the vast majority of parents or carers will be supportive, even if their first reaction is negative. It is always important to involve senior staff in such discussions, such as the headteacher, setting manager or SENCO.

## Balancing individual rights against the duty of care

The physical layout and organisation of the setting must keep children and young people safe and secure. However, it is important that this emphasis on safety is balanced with opportunities for children and young people to explore and take risks. When children and young people are placed in an environment that is too safe, they may lack the stimulation that comes from being challenged, and they may not develop the ability to evaluate risks and make judgements. If there is no challenging climbing equipment for example, children will not learn the skills of judging how high they can go. An appropriately safe and secure environment will include opportunities, inside and outside, for children to challenge themselves and take some risks. It will however exclude aspects that are merely hazardous, like a poorly designed or uneven surface, which is a tripping hazard.

Some children in an early years setting may present with delayed development, or emotional and social difficulties. These may result from adverse early experiences, such as witnessing domestic violence, or growing up with a parent who has mental health difficulties. Extra support could include helping a mother join a 'Stay and Play' group, to make friends and find support, or working with the clinical psychology service to give advice about bedtimes or mealtimes. This work can be coordinated under the **Common Assessment Framework (CAF)**, which is discussed in Chapter 7 (Unit CYP Core 3.3).

Some children and young people are at risk because of the actions of their parents or carers (for example, physical abuse like hitting, or sexual abuse), or because their parents or carers fail to act to keep them safe and well (for example, neglect). In these cases, different agencies still work together to provide support and help to the parents or carers, but there may also be actions that the parent is required to take, which can be checked through unannounced visits and compulsory medical, developmental and psychological assessments.

## Sources of additional support and advice

Colleagues within your own setting may be able to provide additional support and advice about conflicts and dilemmas, such as your line manager or the setting manager. In addition, a wide range of organisations can provide additional support and advice for those working with young children and their families. These include statutory services and voluntary services, such as:

- **local education authority** – special needs advisors, education welfare officers
- **health services** – paediatricians, health visitors, school nurses
- **social services department** – social workers, specialist social workers
- **charities and voluntary organisations** – Barnado's, NSPCC, Save the Children.

Always remember to follow your setting's guidelines regarding confidentiality and the sharing of information when concerned about the welfare of a child or young person. (See Chapter 7, Unit CYP Core 3.3.)

### Key terms

**Statutory service** – Any service provided and managed by the state or government; for example, the NHS or a local authority day nursery.

**Voluntary organisation** – An association or society which has been created by its members rather than having been created by the state; for example, a charity.

**Progress check**

- Working in a team, you should discuss your concerns about children or young people in meetings or with senior staff, as appropriate.
- Understand why you would ask a parent for consent before sharing confidential information with another professional.
- Understand that there are times when you would share information without consent.

# Know how to respond to complaints

Always follow your setting's procedures for responding to complaints from parents and carers. This may mean taking direct action and/or reporting your concerns to someone who has the authority to deal with these difficulties if you cannot resolve them, or they are outside your role/beyond your capabilities (such as the senior practitioner or setting manager).

Difficulties can arise even in the best-run settings. The resolution of difficult situations within the setting requires the senior practitioner to work with colleagues. Whenever possible it is better for colleagues to find their own solutions, with the senior practitioner or manager acting as a **facilitator** or **mediator**. Sometimes a colleague may not make allowances for the parent's or carer's particular problems, or does not show respect for the needs and rights of parents and carers. Difficult situations need to be handled sensitively and resolved as quickly as possible to avoid creating a negative, unpleasant atmosphere for all those in the setting, which can have a detrimental effect on the wellbeing of the children or young people.

## Responding to complaints

Whatever kind of setting you work in, situations may arise in which you need to respond to complaints. There may be times when another person, such as a parent or carer, will be critical of something that either you or your colleagues have done, and will tell you about it. People react differently in such situations depending on the circumstances, who is involved and their own temperament. When responding to a complaint, it is important to take into account the other person's point of view and to find a constructive solution to the problem. The complaint may be delivered with some tact or the other person may be quite hostile. Nobody likes to be criticised, even when a complaint is justified; it may shake your confidence or may leave you feeling upset and angry, especially if the complaint is expressed with hostility and aggression. You should aim to deal with any complaint in a constructive, rather than destructive way, in order to maintain positive working relationships.

These four positive steps may help you to respond to complaints in a constructive manner:

## Keep cool: avoid escalation

The person who is making the complaint may feel angry or anxious; you may also feel your emotions rising. However, it is your responsibility to ensure that your own feelings do not get in the way of professional practice. If you feel yourself becoming angry or agitated, either count to ten or tell yourself to keep calm. If the other person is very angry or upset, it might be better to postpone the discussion for five minutes or longer to take the heat out of the situation.

If you wish to postpone the discussion or to move the conversation to a more suitable location, remember not to appear dismissive of the person or their complaint. Explain that you are taking the complaint seriously, but that you will be able to give it more careful consideration in a quieter place, or at a time when you can give it your full attention. Be specific about arranging a time and a place which will suit you both.

## Listen: show you understand

Listening carefully to the complaint is important – let the other person have their say, without interrupting. Let them know that you understand the basis for their complaint by **reflecting back** what they have said. Reflecting back means repeating the main thing which the person has just said, as though you were a mirror for them; this will demonstrate that you are listening properly and have understood their complaint. If you have misunderstood, the person will certainly be quick to correct you! The person making the complaint needs to know that you understand their point of view and that you are taking their complaint seriously.

## Apologise if necessary, and rectify actions caused by misunderstandings

If you are in the wrong, you should always apologise. Perhaps you have misunderstood or forgotten an instruction, or did not realise how your actions would affect another person. The most reasonable and respectful way forward is to acknowledge that the other person has a justifiable cause for complaint. You should say that you are sorry, and where appropriate, outline the steps you will take to put things right. In some situations, all that is needed to address the complaint is to rectify the situation caused by a misunderstanding.

## Try for a win/win solution

If the complaint cannot be resolved by an apology or a simple explanation, then the most helpful attitude, as in any conflict, is to discuss and negotiate a compromise that suits everyone to bring about a win/win solution to the situation. There are only three possible ways to resolve conflicts:

- to fight or bully: being **aggressive**, 'I win so you lose'
- to submit or retreat: being **submissive or passive**, 'I lose because you win'
- to discuss and negotiate: being **assertive**, 'I win and you win'.

Complaints (and conflicts) need to be discussed in a calm manner so that a mutually agreed compromise can be reached. Remember, compromise equals wise! (Petrie, 1997)

When responding to complaints you should remember these important points:

- Focus on the facts by stating the exact nature of the problem.
- Avoid making personal comments – be tactful!
- Suggest a possible and practical solution.
- Be prepared to compromise if at all possible.

Always follow your setting's procedures for dealing with conflicts with (including responding to complaints from) parents and carers.

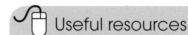

### Activity

List the main points of your setting's procedures for responding to complaints.

### 🖱 Useful resources

**Organisations and websites**
**Early Years Foundation Stage (EYFS)** – the statutory requirements and practical guidance can be found at:
www.nationalstrategies.standards.dcsf.gov.uk/earlyyears

**National Children's Bureau** is a charitable organisation dedicated to advancing the health and wellbeing of all children and young people: www.ncb.org.uk

**National Society for the Prevention of Cruelty to Children (NSPCC)** campaigns against cruelty to children, offers services to support children and families, and can investigate cases where child abuse is suspected:
www.nspcc.org.uk

*Working Together to Safeguard Children* is an inter-agency guide to working to safeguard the welfare of children:
www.education.gov.uk/publications//eOrderingDownload/00305-2010DOM-EN.PDF

# SECTION 2

# CYP core units

# 5 Understand child and young person development: Unit CYP Core 3.1

Child and young person development is an essential subject of study for everyone who works with children and young people. Looking after other people's children gives you different responsibilities from caring for your own children. People who work with other people's children therefore need to be trained properly and carefully, and be informed about how children and young people develop and learn.

## The expected pattern of development from birth to 19 years

The key to understanding child development is 'wholeness'. Studying **holistic** child development means regarding children in all aspects of their lives.

### Aspects of development

The whole child may be looked at under six headings, or aspects. To help you remember these aspects, note that they make up the acronym **PILESS**:

- physical development
- intellectual development
- language development
- emotional development
- social development
- spiritual development.

The various aspects of development are intricately linked: each affects all the others. For example, once children have reached the stage of emotional development when they feel secure being apart from their main carer, they will have access to a much wider range of relationships, experiences and opportunities for learning. Similarly, when children can use language effectively, they have more opportunities for social interaction. If one aspect or area of development is hampered or neglected in some way, children will be challenged in reaching their full potential.

### The contextualised child

Researchers in the field of child development now realise that when for example children quarrel, it is almost impossible to say which aspect of their behaviour is:

- emotional (anger)
- physical (stamping with rage)
- intellectual or language (what they say or do).

In order to understand what is happening in this instance, it is very important to identify who or what made a particular child angry, starting the quarrel. This is the **context** of the behaviour. So, it is important to contextualise the child when studying child development. By looking at child development in context we recognise that the biological part of

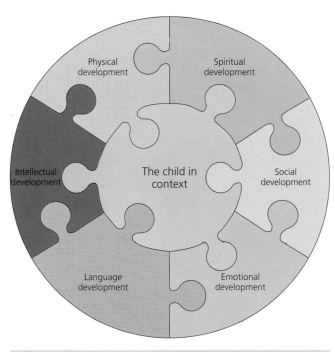

**Figure 5.1** Studying integrated development is like looking at the pieces of a jigsaw

## Key terms

**Holistic** – Seeing a child in the round as a whole person: emotionally, intellectually, socially, physically, morally, culturally and spiritually.

**Development** – The general sequence in the way that the child functions in terms of movement, language, thinking, feelings, etc. Development continues from birth to death and can be likened to a web or network.

**Context** – The context for a child's development is their environment, which is created by the people that surround them. It affects the child's access to learning and the ethos in which the child learns.

**Ethos** – The characteristic spirit and values of a group of people or community; for example, a happy ethos, a caring ethos.

development (physical development and genetic factors) is integrated with the cultural part of development (social, cultural, intellectual and linguistic factors).

# The difference between sequence of development and rate of development

## Sequence of development

Children across the world seem to pass through similar sequences of development, but in different ways and different rates according to their culture. The work of Mary Sheridan on developmental sequences has been invaluable, but she suggests that children move through rigidly prescribed stages that are linked to the child's age: the child sits, then crawls, then stands, then walks. In fact, this is not the case. Not all children crawl: blind children often do not, and other children (such as Mark in the case study) 'bottom-shuffle', moving along in a sitting position.

A traditional approach to child development study has been to emphasise **normative** measurement. This is concerned with 'milestones' or stages in a child's development. These show what *most* children can do at a particular age. In reality, there is a wide range of normal development which is influenced by genetic, social and cultural factors. Children have been labelled as 'backward' or 'advanced' in relation to the so-called 'normal' child, which is not always helpful.

## Rates of development

It is important to be aware that normative measurements can only indicate general *trends* in development in children across the world. They may vary considerably, according to the culture in which a child lives. It is important to understand that while the sequence of development is fairly general to all children, the **rate** – or speed – of development can vary a great deal. When children do things earlier than the milestones suggest is normal, it does not necessarily mean that they will be outstanding or gifted in any way. Parents sometimes think that because their child speaks early, is potty-trained early or walks early, he or she is gifted in some way. You should handle these situations carefully, as the child may not be gifted.

Children with special educational needs often seem to 'dance the development ladder': they move through sequences in unusual and very uneven ways. For example, they might walk at the normal age, but they may not talk at the usual age. As researchers learn more about child development, it is becoming more useful to think of a child's development as a network that becomes increasingly complex as the child matures and becomes more experienced in their culture. So, instead of thinking of child development and learning as a ladder, it is probably more useful to think of it as a web.

## Key term

**Norm** – The usual or standard model or pattern.

## Case Study

1 Mark moved around by bottom-shuffling and did not walk until he was two years old. He began to run, hop and skip at the normal times. Walking late was not a cause for concern, and he did not suffer from any developmental delay.

2 African children living in rural villages estimate volume and capacity earlier than European children who live in towns. This is because they practise measuring out cups of rice into baskets from an early age as part of their daily lives. Learning about volume and capacity early does not mean that children will necessarily go on to become talented mathematicians. Children who learn these concepts later might also become good mathematicians.

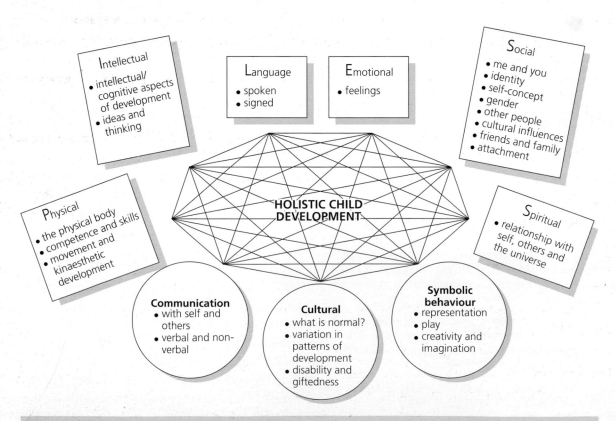

**Figure 5.2** Thinking of child development as a web

## Holistic development: The first month

### Physical development

| Gross motor skills | Fine motor skills |
|---|---|
| • The baby lies **supine** (on his or her back).<br><br>• When placed on his or her front (the **prone** position), the baby lies with head turned to one side, and by one month can lift the head.<br><br>• If pulled to sitting position, the head will lag, the back curves over and the head falls forward. | • The baby turns his or her head towards the light and stares at bright or shiny objects.<br><br>• The baby is fascinated by human faces and gazes attentively at carer's face when fed or held.<br><br>• The baby's hands are usually tightly closed.<br><br>• The baby reacts to loud sounds but by one month may be soothed by particular music. |

### Communication and language development

- Babies need to share language experiences and cooperate with others from birth onwards. From the start babies need other people.

- The baby responds to sounds, especially familiar voices.

- The baby quietens when picked up.

- The baby makes eye contact.

- The baby cries to indicate need, e.g. hunger, dirty nappy etc.

- The baby may move his or her eyes towards the direction of sound.

### Intellectual development

Babies explore through their **senses** and through their own activity and movement.

**Touch**

- From the beginning babies feel pain.

- The baby's face, abdomen, hands and the soles of his or her feet are also very sensitive to touch.

- The baby perceives the movements that he or she makes, and the way that other people move them about through his or her senses.

- For example, the baby gives a 'startle' response if they are moved suddenly. This is called the '**moro**' or startle reflex.

**Sound**

- Even a newborn baby will turn to a sound. The baby might become still and listen to a low sound, or quicken his or her movements when he or she hears a high sound.

- The baby often stops crying and listens to a human voice by two weeks of age.

**Taste**

- The baby likes sweet tastes, e.g. breast milk.

**Smell**

- The baby turns to the smell of the breast.

**Sight**

- The baby can focus on objects 20 cm (a few inches) away.

- The baby is sensitive to light.

- The baby likes to look at human faces – eye contact.

- The baby can track the movements of people and objects.

- The baby will scan the edges of objects.

- The baby will imitate facial expressions (e.g. he or she will put out their tongue if you do). If you know any newborn or very young babies, try it and see!

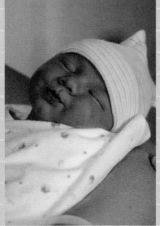

**Figure 5.3**

## Holistic development: The first month (cont.)

### Emotional and social development

- A baby's first smile in definite response to carer is usually around 5–6 weeks.
- The baby often imitates certain facial expressions.
- The baby uses total body movements to express pleasure at bathtime or when being fed.
- The baby enjoys feeding and cuddling.
- In the first month babies are learning where they begin and end, e.g. his or her hand is part of them but mother's hand is not.

**Table 5.1** Holistic development: the first month

## Holistic development from one to four months

### Physical development

| Gross motor skills | Fine motor skills |
|---|---|
| **From four to eight weeks:**<br>- The baby can now turn from side to back.<br>- The baby can lift the head briefly from the prone position.<br>- Arm and leg movements are jerky and uncontrolled.<br>- There is head lag if the baby is pulled to sitting position. | - The baby turns his or her head towards the light and stares at bright or shiny objects.<br>- The baby will show interest and excitement by facial expression and will gaze attentively at carer's face while being fed.<br>- The baby will use his or her hand to grasp the carer's finger. |
| **From eight to twelve weeks:**<br>- When lying supine, the baby's head is in a central position.<br>- The baby can now lift head and chest off bed in prone position, supported on forearms.<br>- There is almost no head lag in sitting position.<br>- The legs can kick vigorously, both separately and together.<br>- The baby can wave his or her arms and bring his or her hands together over the body. | - The baby moves his or her head to follow adult movements.<br>- The baby watches his or her hands and plays with his or her fingers.<br>- The baby holds a rattle for a brief time before dropping it. |

### Communication and language development

**From four to eight weeks:**

- The baby recognises the carer and familiar objects.
- The baby makes non-crying noises such as cooing and gurgling.
- The baby's cries become more expressive.

**From eight to twelve weeks:**

- The baby is still distressed by sudden loud noises.
- The baby often sucks or licks lips when he or she hears sound of food preparation.
- The baby shows excitement at sound of approaching footsteps or voices.

## Holistic development from one to four months (cont.)

### Communication and language development

**During the first three months:**

- The baby listens to people's voices. When adults close to the baby talk in motherese or fatherese (a high-pitched tone referring to what is around and going on) the baby dances, listens, replies in babble and coo.
- The baby cries with anger to show they are tired, hungry, and to say they need to be changed.
- The baby is comforted by the voices of those who are close to them and will turn especially to the voices of close family members.

### Intellectual development

- The baby recognises differing speech sounds.
- By three months the baby can even imitate low- or high-pitched sounds.
- By four months the baby links objects they know with the sound, e.g. mother's voice and her face.
- The baby knows the smell of his or her mother from that of other mothers.

### Emotional and social development

**Four to eight weeks:**

- The baby will smile in response to an adult.
- The baby enjoys sucking.
- The baby turns to regard nearby speaker's face.
- The baby turns to preferred person's voice.
- The baby recognises face and hands of preferred adult.
- The baby may stop crying when he or she hears, sees or feels his or her carer.

**Eight to twelve weeks:**

- The baby shows enjoyment at caring routines such as bath time.
- The baby responds with obvious pleasure to loving attention and cuddles.
- The baby fixes his or her eyes unblinkingly on carer's face when feeding.
- The baby stays awake for longer periods of time.

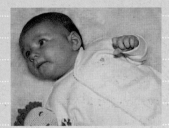

**Figure 5.4**

**Table 5.2** Holistic development from one to four months

## Holistic development from four to six months

### Physical development

| Gross motor skills | Fine motor skills |
|---|---|
| • The baby is beginning to use a **palmar grasp** and can transfer objects from hand to hand. | • The baby now has good head control and is beginning to sit with support. |
| • The baby is very interested in all activity. | • The baby rolls over from back to side and is beginning to reach for objects. |
| • Everything is taken to the mouth. | • When supine the baby plays with his or her own feet. |
| • The baby moves his or her head around to follow people and objects. | • The baby holds his or her head up when pulled to sitting position. |

## Holistic development from four to six months (cont.)

### Communication and language development

- The baby becomes more aware of others so he or she communicates more and more.

- As the baby listens, he or she imitates sounds he or she can hear, and reacts to the tone of someone's voice. For example, the baby might become upset by an angry tone, or cheered by a happy tone.

- The baby begins to use vowels, consonants and syllable sounds, e.g. 'ah', 'ee aw'.

- The baby begins to laugh and squeal with pleasure.

### Intellectual development

- By four months the baby reaches for objects, which suggests they recognise and judge the distance in relation to the size of the object.

- The baby prefers complicated things to look at from five to six months and enjoys bright colours.

- The baby knows that he or she has one mother. The baby is disturbed if he or she is shown several images of his or her mother at the same time. The baby realises that people are permanent before they realise that objects are.

- The baby can coordinate more, e.g. the baby can see a rattle, grasp the rattle, put the rattle in his or her mouth (they coordinate tracking, reaching, grasping and sucking).

- The baby can develop favourite tastes in food and recognise differences by five months.

### Emotional and social development

- The baby shows trust and security.

- The baby has recognisable sleep patterns.

Figure 5.5

**Table 5.3** Holistic development from four to six months

## Holistic development from six to nine months

### Physical development

| Gross motor skills | Fine motor skills |
|---|---|
| • The baby can roll from front to back. | • The baby is very alert to people and objects. |
| • The baby may attempt to crawl but will often end up sliding backwards. | • The baby is beginning to use a **pincer grasp** with thumb and index finger. |
| • The baby may grasp feet and place them in his or her mouth. | • The baby transfers toys from one hand to the other and looks for fallen objects. |
| • The baby can sit without support for longer periods of time. | • Everything is explored by putting it in his or her mouth. |
| • The baby may 'cruise' around furniture and may even stand or walk alone. | |

### Communication and language development

- Babble becomes tuneful, like the lilt of the language the baby can hear (except in hearing-impaired babies).

- Babies begin to understand words like 'up' and 'down', raising their arms to be lifted up, using appropriate gestures.

- The baby repeats sounds.

## Holistic development from six to nine months (cont.)

### Intellectual development

- The baby understands **signs**, e.g. the bib means that food is coming.

- From eight to nine months the baby shows that he or she knows objects exist when they have gone out of sight, even under test conditions. This is called the concept of object constancy, or the **object permanence test (Piaget)**. The baby is also fascinated by the way objects move.

**Figure 5.6**

### Emotional and social development

- The baby can manage to feed him- or herself using his or her fingers.

- The baby is now more wary of strangers, sometimes showing **stranger fear**.

- The baby might offer toys to others.

- The baby might show distress when his or her mother leaves.

- The baby typically begins to crawl and this means he or she can do more for him- or herself, reach for objects and get to places and people.

- The baby is now more aware of other people's feelings. For example, he or she may cry if their brother cries.

**Table 5.4** Holistic development from six to nine months

## Holistic development from nine to twelve months

### Physical development

| Gross motor skills | Fine motor skills |
|---|---|
| <ul><li>The baby will now be mobile – may be crawling, bear-walking, bottom-shuffling or even walking.</li><li>The baby can sit up on his or her own and lean forward to pick up things.</li><li>The baby may crawl upstairs and onto low items of furniture.</li><li>The baby may bounce in rhythm to music.</li></ul> | <ul><li>The baby's pincer grasp is now well developed and he or she can pick things up and pull them towards him or her.</li><li>The baby can poke with one finger and will point to desired objects.</li><li>The baby can clasp hands and imitate adults' actions.</li><li>The baby can throw toys deliberately.</li><li>The baby can manage spoons and finger foods well.</li></ul> |

### Communication and language development

- The baby can follow simple instructions, e.g. kiss teddy.

- Word approximations appear, e.g. 'hee haw' to indicate a donkey, or more typically 'mumma', 'dadda' and 'bye-bye' in English-speaking contexts.

- The tuneful babble develops into 'jargon' and the baby makes his or her voice go up and down just as people do when they talk to each other. 'Really? Do you? No!' The babble is very expressive.

- The baby knows that words stand for people, objects, what they do and what happens.

### Intellectual development

- The baby is beginning to develop images. Memory develops and the baby can remember the past.

- The baby can anticipate the future. This gives the baby some understanding of routine daily sequences, e.g. after a feed, changing, and a sleep with teddy.

- The baby imitates actions, sounds, gestures and moods after an event is finished, e.g. imitate a temper tantrum he or she saw a friend have the previous day, wave bye-bye remembering Grandma has gone to the shops.

T041625

## Holistic development from nine to twelve months (cont.)

### Emotional and social development

- The baby enjoys songs and action rhymes.
- The baby still likes to be near to a familiar adult.
- The baby can drink from a cup with help.
- The baby will play alone for long periods.
- The baby has and shows definite likes and dislikes at mealtimes and bedtimes.
- The baby thoroughly enjoys peek-a-boo games.
- The baby likes to look at him- or herself in a mirror (plastic safety mirror).
- The baby imitates other people – e.g. clapping hands, waving bye-bye – but there is often a time lapse, so that he or she waves after the person has gone.
- The baby cooperates when being dressed.

Figure 5.7

**Table 5.5** Holistic development from nine to twelve months

## Holistic development from one year to two years

### Physical development

| Gross motor skills | Fine motor skills |
|---|---|
| **At 15 months:**<br>- The baby probably walks alone, with feet wide apart and arms raised to maintain balance. He or she is likely to fall over and often sit down suddenly.<br>- The baby can probably manage stairs and steps, but will need supervision.<br>- The baby can get to standing without help from furniture or people, and kneels without support. | - The baby can build with a few bricks and arrange toys on the floor.<br>- The baby holds a crayon in palmar grasp and turns several pages of a book at once.<br>- The baby can point to desired objects.<br>- The baby shows a preference for one hand, but uses either. |
| **At 18 months:**<br>- The child walks confidently and is able to stop without falling.<br>- The child can kneel, squat, climb and carry things around with him or her.<br>- The child can climb onto an adult chair forwards and then turn round to sit.<br>- The child can come downstairs, usually by creeping backwards on his or her tummy. | - The child can thread large beads.<br>- The child uses pincer grasp to pick up small objects.<br>- The child can build a tower of several cubes.<br>- The child can scribble to and fro on paper. |

### Communication and language development

- The child begins to talk with words or sign language.
- **By 18 months**: The child enjoys trying to sing as well as to listen to songs and rhymes. Action songs (e.g. 'Pat-a-cake') are much loved.
- Books with pictures are of great interest. The child points at and often names parts of their body, objects, people and pictures in books.

## Holistic development from one year to two years (cont.)

### Communication and language development

- The child echoes the last part of what others say (**echolalia**).
- The child begins waving his or her arms up and down which might mean 'start again', or 'I like it', or 'more'.
- Gestures develop alongside words. Gesture is used in some cultures more than in others.

### Intellectual development

- The child understands the names of objects and can follow simple instructions.
- The child learns about things through trial and error.
- The child uses toys or objects to represent things in real life (e.g. using a doll as a baby, or a large cardboard box as a car or a garage).
- The child begins to scribble on paper.
- The child often 'talks' to him- or herself while playing.

### Emotional and social development

- The child begins to have a longer memory.
- The child develops a sense of identity (I am me).
- The child expresses his or her needs in words and gestures.
- The child enjoys being able to walk, and is eager to try to get dressed – 'Me do it!'
- The child is aware when others are fearful or anxious for him or her as he or she climbs on and off chairs, and so on.

**Figure 5.8**

**Table 5.6** Holistic development from one year to two years

## Holistic development from two years

### Physical development

| Gross motor skills | Fine motor skills |
|---|---|
| • The child is very mobile and can run safely. | • The child can draw circles, lines and dots, using preferred hand. |
| • The child can climb up onto furniture. | • The child can pick up tiny objects using a **fine pincer grasp**. |
| • The child can walk up and downstairs, usually two feet to a step. | • The child can build a tower of six or more blocks (bricks) with longer concentration span. |
| • The child tries to kick a ball with some success but cannot catch yet. | • The child enjoys picture books and turns pages singly. |

### Communication and language development

- Children are rapidly becoming competent speakers of the languages they experience.
- The child over-extends the use of a word, e.g. all animals are called 'doggie'.
- The child talks about an absent object when reminded of it; e.g. seeing an empty plate, they say 'biscuit'.
- The child uses phrases (**telegraphese**), 'doggie-gone' and the child calls him- or herself by name.
- The child spends a great deal of energy naming things and what they do – e.g. 'chair', and as they go up a step they might say 'up'.
- The child can follow a simple instruction or request, e.g. 'Could you bring me the spoon?'
- The child increasingly wants to share songs, dance, conversations, finger rhymes.

## Holistic development from two years (cont.)

### Intellectual development

- The child has improved memory skills, which helps his or her understanding of **concepts** (e.g. the child can often name and match two or three colours – usually yellow and red).
- The child can hold a crayon and move it up and down.
- The child understands cause and effect (e.g. if something is dropped, he or she understands it might break).
- The child talks about an absent object when reminded of it (e.g. he or she may say 'biscuit' when seeing an empty plate or bowl).

### Emotional and social development

- The child is impulsive and curious about his or her environment.
- **Pretend play** develops rapidly when adults encourage it.
- The child begins to be able to say how he or she is feeling, but often feels frustrated when unable to express him- or herself.
- The child can dress him- or herself and go to the lavatory independently, but needs sensitive support in order to feel success rather than frustration.
- By two and half years the child plays more with other children, but may not share his or her toys with them.

Figure 5.9

**Table 5.7** Holistic development from two years

## Holistic development from three years

### Physical development

| Gross motor skills | Fine motor skills |
| --- | --- |
| The child can jump from a low step. | The child can build tall towers of bricks or blocks. |
| The child can walk backwards and sideways. | The child can control a pencil using thumb and first two fingers – a **dynamic tripod grasp**. |
| The child can stand and walk on tiptoe and stand on one foot. | The child enjoys painting with a large brush. |
| The child has good spatial awareness. | The child can use scissors to cut paper. |
| The child rides a tricycle, using pedals. | The child can copy shapes, such as a circle. |
| The child can climb stairs with one foot on each step – and downwards with two feet per step. | |

### Communication and language development

- The child begins to use plurals, pronouns, adjectives, possessives, time words, tenses and sentences.
- The child might say 'two times' instead of 'twice'. The child might say 'I goed there' instead of 'I went there'. The child loves to chat and ask questions (what, where and who).
- The child enjoys much more complicated stories and asks for his or her favourite ones over and over again.
- It is not unusual for the child to stutter because he or she is trying so hard to tell adults things. The child's thinking goes faster than the pace at which the child can say what he or she wants to. The child can quickly become frustrated.

## Holistic development from three years (cont.)

### Intellectual development

The child develops **symbolic behaviour**. This means that:

- The child talks.
- The child **pretend plays** – often talking to him- or herself while playing.
- The child takes part in simple non-competitive games.
- The child represents events in drawings, models, etc.
- Personal images dominate, rather than conventions used in the culture, e.g. writing is 'pretend' writing.
- The child becomes fascinated by cause and effect; the child is continually trying to explain what goes on in the world.
- The child can identify common colours, such as red, yellow, blue and green – although may sometimes confuse blue with green.

### Emotional and social development

Pretend play helps the child to **decentre** and develop **theory of mind** (the child begins to be able to understand how someone else might feel and/or think).

- The child is beginning to develop a gender role as they become aware of being male or female.
- The child makes friends and is interested in having friends.
- The child learns to negotiate, give and take through experimenting with feeling powerful, having a sense of control, and through quarrels with other children.
- The child is easily afraid, e.g. of the dark, as he or she becomes capable of pretending. The child imagines all sorts of things.

Figure 5.10

**Table 5.8** Holistic development from three years

## Holistic development from four years

### Physical development

| Gross motor skills | Fine motor skills |
|---|---|
| - A sense of balance is developing – the child may be able to walk along a line. | - The child can build a tower of bricks and other constructions too. |
| - The child can catch, kick, throw and bounce a ball. | - The child can draw a recognisable person on request, showing head, legs and trunk. |
| - The child can bend at the waist to pick up objects from the floor. | - The child can thread small beads on a lace. |
| - The child enjoys climbing trees and frames. | |
| - The child can run up and downstairs, one foot per step. | |

### Communication and language development

- During this time the child asks why, when and how questions as he or she becomes more and more fascinated with the reasons for things and how things work (cause and effect).
- Past, present and future tenses are used more often.
- The child can be taught to say his or her name, address and age.
- As the child becomes more accurate in the way he or she pronounces words, and begins to use grammar, the child delights in nonsense words that he or she makes up, and jokes using words.

## Holistic development from four years (cont.)

### Intellectual development

- At about age four, the child usually knows how to count – up to 20.
- The child also understands ideas such as 'more' and 'fewer', and 'big' and 'small'.
- The child will recognise his or her own name when it is written down and can usually write it.
- The child can think back and can think forward much more easily than before.
- The child can also think about things from somebody else's point of view, but only fleetingly.
- The child often enjoys music and playing sturdy instruments, and joins in groups singing and dancing.

### Emotional and social development

- The child likes to be independent and is strongly self-willed.
- The child shows a sense of humour.
- The child can undress and dress him- or herself – except for laces and back buttons.
- The child can wash and dry his or her hands and brush his or her teeth.

Figure 5.11

**Table 5.9** Holistic development from four years

## Holistic development from five to eight years

### Physical development

| Gross motor skills | Fine motor skills |
| --- | --- |
| **From five years:** | |
| • The child can use a variety of play equipment – slides, swings, climbing frames. | • The child may be able to thread a large-eyed needle and sew large stitches. |
| • The child can play ball games. | • The child can draw a person with head, trunk, legs, nose, mouth and eyes. |
| • The child can hop and run lightly on toes and can move rhythmically to music. | • The child has good control over pencils and paintbrushes. He or she copies shapes, such as a square. |
| • The sense of balance is well developed. | |
| • The child can skip. | |
| **Six and seven years:** | |
| • The child has increased agility, muscle coordination and balance. | • The child can build a tall, straight tower with blocks and other constructions too. |
| • The child develops competence in riding a two-wheeled bicycle. | • The child can draw a person with detail, e.g. clothes and eyebrows. |
| • The child hops easily, with good balance. | • The child can write letters of alphabet at school, with similar writing grip to an adult. |
| • The child can jump off apparatus. | • The child can catch a ball thrown from one metre with one hand. |

## Holistic development from five to eight years (cont.)

### Communication and language development

- The child tries to understand the meaning of words and uses adverbs and prepositions. The child talks confidently, and with more and more fluency.
- The child begins to be able to define objects by their function, e.g. 'What is a ball?' 'You bounce it.'
- The child begins to understand book language, and that stories have characters and a plot (the narrative).
- The child begins to realise that different situations require different ways of talking.

### Intellectual development

Communication through body language, facial gestures and language is well established, and opens the way into **literacy** (talking, listening, writing and reading).

- The child includes more detail in their drawings – e.g. a house may have not only windows and a roof, but also curtains and a chimney.
- The child will recognise his or her own name when it is written down and can usually write it him- or herself.
- Thinking becomes increasingly coordinated as the child is able to hold in mind more than one point of view at a time. **Concepts** – of matter, length, measurement, distance, area, time, volume, capacity and weight – develop steadily.
- The child enjoys chanting and counting (beginning to understand number). The child can use his or her voice in different ways to play different characters in pretend play. The child develops play narratives (stories), which he or she returns to over time. The child helps younger children into the play.
- The child is beginning to establish differences between what is real and unreal/fantasy. This is not yet always stable, so the child can easily be frightened by supernatural characters.

### Emotional and social development

- The child has developed a stable **self-concept**.
- The child can hide their feelings once they can begin to control them.
- The child has developed a stable **self-concept**.
- The child can hide their feelings once they can begin to control them.
- The child can think of the feelings of others.
- The child can take responsibility, e.g. in helping younger children.

**Figure 5.12**

**Table 5.10** Holistic development from five to eight years

## Holistic development from eight to eleven years

### Physical development

| Gross motor skills | Fine motor skills |
|---|---|
| **From eight to nine years:** | • The child can control his or her small muscles well and has improved writing and drawing skills. |
| • The child can ride a bicycle easily. | • The child can draw people with details of clothing and facial features. |
| • The child has increased strength and coordination. | • The child is starting to join letters together in handwriting. |
| • The child plays energetic games and sports. | |
| **From ten to eleven years:** | • The child tackles more detailed tasks such as woodwork or needlework. |
| • Children differ in physical maturity. Girls experience puberty earlier than do boys and are often as much as two years ahead of them. | • The child is usually writing with an established style – using joined-up letters. |
| • The child's body proportions are becoming more similar to adults. | |

### Communication and language development

**From eight to nine years:**

• The child uses and understands complex sentences.

• The child is increasingly verbal and enjoys making up stories and telling jokes.

• The child uses reference books with increasing skill.

**From ten to eleven years:**

• The child can write fairly lengthy essays.

• The child writes stories that show imagination, and are increasingly legible and grammatically correct.

### Intellectual development

**From eight to nine years:**

• The child has an increased ability to remember and pay attention, and to speak and express their ideas.

• The child is learning to plan ahead and evaluate what they do.

• The child has an increased ability to think and to reason.

• The child can deal with abstract ideas.

• The child enjoys different types of activities – such as joining clubs, playing games with rules, and collecting things.

• The child enjoys projects that are task-orientated, such as sewing and woodwork.

**From ten to eleven years:**

• The child begins to understand the motives behind the actions of another.

• The child can concentrate on tasks for increasing periods.

• The child begins to devise memory strategies.

• The child may be curious about drugs, alcohol and tobacco.

• The child may develop special talents, showing particular skills in writing, maths, art, music or woodwork.

### Emotional and social development

**At eight or nine years old:**

• The child may become discouraged easily.

• The child takes pride in their competence.

• The child can be argumentative and bossy, but can equally be generous and responsive.

## Holistic development from eight to eleven years (cont.)

### Emotional and social development

- The child is beginning to see things from another child's point of view, but still has trouble understanding the feelings and needs of other people.

**At eleven or twelve years old**:

- The child may be experiencing sudden, dramatic, emotional changes associated with puberty (especially girls, who experience puberty earlier than boys).
- The child tends to be particularly sensitive to criticism.
- The child prefers to spend leisure time with friends and continues to participate in small groups of the same sex, but is acutely aware of the opposite sex.
- The child succumbs to peer pressure more readily and wants to talk, dress and act just like friends.

Figure 5.13

**Table 5.11** Holistic development from eight to eleven years

## Holistic development from 12 to 19 years

### Physical development

**From 12 to 16 years**

Physical development during adolescence is known as **puberty**. The age at which puberty starts varies from person to person but on average it begins between 9 and 13 in girls and 10 and 15 in boys. Many physical changes occur during puberty:

- **Growth** accelerates rapidly – often called a **growth spurt**. This usually happens in a particular order from outer to inner:
  1. the head, feet and hands grow to adult size
  2. the arms and legs grow in length and strength
  3. the trunk (the main part of the body from shoulder to hip) grows to full adult size and shape.

This sequence of growth means that, for a brief period, adolescents may feel gawky and clumsy, as they appear to be 'out of proportion'. The average boy grows fastest between 14 and 15. Girls start earlier, growing fastest when 12 and 13. Girls also finish their growth spurt earlier, at 18, while boys need another two years before they finish growing aged 20.

- **Secondary sex characteristics** develop; these are external traits that distinguish the two sexes, but are not directly part of the **reproductive system**; for example, the growth of pubic hair in both sexes, facial hair and deepened voice for males, and breasts and widened hips for females.
- Primary sex characteristics develop; these are the penis and sperm in males and the vagina and ovaries in females. During puberty, hormonal changes cause a boy's penis and testicles to grow and the body to produce sperm. Girls start to menstruate – to have their monthly period. Both these events signal **sexual maturity** – the ability to reproduce.

| | |
|---|---|
| The first *external* sign of puberty in girls is usually breast development, often accompanied by a growth spurt. The main features of physical development in puberty in girls are as follows. | The first *external* sign of puberty in most boys is an increase in the size of the testicles and then the penis. This is followed by the growth of pubic and underarm hair. At the same time, the voice deepens and muscles develop. Lastly, boys grow facial hair. |

## Holistic development from 12 to 19 years (cont.)

- **Breasts develop**: at first, the nipples start to stick out from the chest (often called 'budding'). Behind the nipple, milk ducts begin to grow. Next, the flat, circular part of the nipple, the areola, rises and starts to expand. Glands that make sweat and scent develop beneath it. The breast begins to fill out as fat is deposited around the nipple. Some girls feel a tingling sensation or have tender breasts. Initially, the breasts stick out or have a conical shape. As growth continues, they gradually round off into an adult shape.

- **Body size and shape** grows taller. Hips widen as the pelvic bones grow. Fat develops on the hips, thighs and buttocks, and the ratio of fat to muscle increases. The waist gets smaller and the body develops a more curved shape.

- **Menstruation** – having periods – is part of the female reproductive cycle that starts when girls become sexually mature during puberty. During a menstrual period, a woman bleeds from her uterus (womb) via the vagina. This lasts anything from three to seven days. Each period begins approximately every 28 days if the woman does not become pregnant during a given cycle. The onset of menstruation is called the menarche; it can occur any time between the ages of 9 and 16, most commonly around the age of 12–13. It means that the body is capable of **reproduction**.

The main features of physical development in puberty in boys are as follows.

- **Voice breaking**: testosterone causes the voice box or larynx to enlarge and the vocal cords to become longer. Sometimes, as the voice changes to become deeper, it may change pitch abruptly or 'break' at times. The voice box tilts and often protrudes at the neck – an 'Adam's apple'. (Many boys start to develop breasts in their teenage years, but this disappears as testosterone levels increase.)

- **Body size and shape** grows taller. The body takes on a new, more muscular shape as the shoulders and chest become broader and the neck becomes more muscular.

- **Chest hair** may appear during puberty, or some years later.

- **Penile erections** – these occur spontaneously, even from infancy, but during puberty they become more frequent. Erections can occur with or without any physical or sexual stimulation and can cause acute embarrassment.

- **Sperm**: once the testicles begin to grow, they also develop their adult function – to produce sperm. Mature sperm is present in the male body towards the end of puberty (most commonly between ages 13–15) and means that the body is capable of **reproduction**.

Some physical developments occur during puberty in both girls and boys:

- **Pubic hair** starts to grow around the genitals, and becomes coarse, dark and curly. In girls, pubic hair forms an upside-down triangle shape; in boys, the hair grows between the legs and extends up from the penis to the abdomen.

- Hair grows in the armpits and on the legs.

- A different kind of **sweat** is now produced in response to stress, emotion and sexual excitement. It is produced by the apocrine glands and occurs only in the armpits, belly button, groin area, ears and nipples. As bacteria break down the sweat it starts to smell strongly – this is known as body odour (BO).

- **Oil-secreting glands** in the skin can become over-active. This can cause skin to become greasier and may cause acne.

## Communication and language development

### From 12 to 19 years

During this period, young people become increasingly independent and spend much of their day outside the home – at school or after-school activities, and with peers.

- The young person has a fast, legible style of handwriting.

- The young person communicates in an adult manner, with increasing maturity.

- The young person understands abstract language, such as idioms, figurative language and metaphors.

- The young person is able to process texts and abstract meaning, relate word meanings and contexts, understand punctuation, and form complex syntactic structures.

## Holistic development from 12 to 19 years (cont.)

### Intellectual development

#### From 12 to 19 years

Around this time, young people experience a major shift in thinking from **concrete to abstract** – an adult way of thinking. Piaget described this as the **formal operational stage** of intellectual development. This involves:

- *thinking about possibilities* – younger children rely heavily on their senses to apply reasoning, whereas adolescents think about possibilities that are not directly observable.

- *thinking ahead* – young people start to plan ahead, often in a systematic way; e.g. younger children may look forward to a holiday, but they are unlikely to focus on the preparation involved.

- *thinking through hypotheses* – this gives them the ability to make and test hypotheses, and to think about situations that are contrary to fact.

- *thinking about their own thought processes* – this is known as **metacognition**; a subcategory of metacognition is **metamemory**, which is having knowledge about your memory processes – being able to explain what strategies you use when trying to remember things (e.g. for an exam).

- *thinking beyond conventional limits* – thinking about issues that generally preoccupy human beings in adulthood, such as morality, religion and politics.

They approach a problem in a systematic fashion and also use their imagination when solving problems.

### Emotional and social development

- The young person may become self-conscious or worried about physical changes (e.g. too short, too tall, too fat, too thin).

- The young person develops a sexual identity; self-labelling as gay or lesbian tends to occur around the age of 15 for boys and 15 and a half for girls, although first disclosure does not normally take place until after the age of 16 and a half years for both sexes.

- The young person often feels misunderstood.

- The young person can experience wide emotional swings (e.g. fluctuate between emotional peaks of excitement and depths of moodiness).

- The young person wants to become accepted and liked.

- The young person tends to identify more with friends and begin to separate from parents; they are less dependent on family for affection and emotional support.

**Table 5.12** Holistic development from 12 to 19 years

| Spiritual aspects of a child's development | |
|---|---|
| **The first year** | Even a tiny baby experiences a sense of self, and of awe and wonder, and values people who are loved by them. Worship is about a sense of worth. People, loved teddy bears, a daisy on the grass grasped and looked at (or put in the mouth!) are all building the child's spiritual experiences. This has nothing to do with worship of a god or gods. Spirituality is about the developing sense of relationship with self, relating to others ethically, morally and humanely and a relationship with the universe. |
| **One to three years** | Judy Dunn's work suggests that during this period children already have a strongly developed moral sense. They know what hurts and upsets their family (adults and children). They know what delights them and brings about pleased responses. Through their pretend play, and the conversations in the family about how people behave, hurt and help each other, they learn how other people feel. They learn to think beyond themselves. |

| Spiritual aspects of a child's development (cont.) | |
|---|---|
| **Three to eight years** | With the help and support of their family, early years practitioners and the wider community, children develop further concepts like being helpful and forgiving, and having a sense of fairness. By the age of seven years, they have a clear sense of right and wrong – e.g. they realise that it is wrong to hurt other people physically. |
| **Eight to eleven years** | By eight or nine years, children continue to think that rules are permanent and unchangeable because they are made up by adults, who must be obeyed and respected. They have a clear idea of the difference between reality and fantasy, and are highly concerned about fairness.<br>By ten and eleven years, children understand that certain rules can be changed by mutual negotiation; often, they do not accept rules that they did not help make. They may begin to experience conflict between parents' values and those of their peers.<br>These concepts become more abstract – such as justice, right, wrong, good versus evil, beauty and nature, the arts and scientific achievements. |
| **Twelve to nineteen years** | Young people are able to think beyond themselves more and to understand the perspective of another. They are developing their own ideas and values, which often challenge those of home; they may deliberately flout rules or keep to them only if there is otherwise a risk of being caught. |

**Table 5.13** Spiritual aspects of a child's development

# Factors that influence development

Many factors affect the healthy growth and development of children and young people. These include personal factors such as genetic influences and health status, and external factors such as poverty and deprivation.

## Personal factors influencing development

### Genetic influences

Scientists believe that both our environment and our genes influence the person we become. Genes are found in our chromosomes, and parents pass these on to their offspring in their sex cells (the egg and the sperm). Different versions of the same gene are called **alleles**, and these can determine features such as eye colour, and the inheritance of disorders such as cystic fibrosis. A baby's development can also be affected during pregnancy, at the time of birth and after the birth. In the very early weeks of pregnancy, a woman may not even know she is pregnant; however, the first twelve weeks of life in the womb

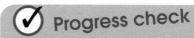

**Progress check**

**Aspects of development**

1. Explain the sequence and rate of each aspect of development from birth to 19 years.
2. What is the difference between the **sequence** and **rate** of development, and why is this difference important?

(or uterus) are the most crucial as this is when all the essential organs are being formed.

- **Antenatal** – the time from conception to birth. Aspects of the mother's lifestyle affect the development of the child, such as her diet, whether she smokes and consumes alcohol, and whether she is fit and healthy.
- **Perinatal** – the actual time of the birth. A baby who is born prematurely (before 37 weeks' gestation) may need intensive care and may have problems which affect development. Difficulties around the birth itself (such as the baby lacking adequate oxygen) can also affect future development.

## Health status

Children and young people's health status is determined by their genetic inheritance as well as other factors, such as diet, environment and the health care that they receive. Some children and young people are born with a condition that could adversely affect their holistic development; for example, cystic fibrosis, Down's syndrome or a heart defect. Children and young people who develop a chronic illness (such as diabetes or asthma) may find that their activities are restricted by their condition, or that their schooling is interrupted by frequent hospital visits.

# External factors influencing development

External factors that influence development include the following:

- poverty and deprivation
- family environment and background
- personal choices
- being a looked-after child
- education.

## Poverty and deprivation

Many of the factors that adversely affect child health and development are closely interrelated, and make up a **cycle of deprivation**. For example, poorer families tend to live in poorer **housing** conditions and may also have an inadequate **diet**; this may not include sufficient minerals and vitamins, leading to an increased susceptibility to **infectious diseases**, and so on. Poverty is the single greatest threat to the healthy development of children and young people in the UK. Growing up in poverty can affect every area of a child's development: physical, intellectual, emotional, social and spiritual.

- **Accident and illness**: Children and young people from the bottom social class are four times more likely to die in an accident and have nearly twice the rate of long-standing illness, than those children living in households with high incomes.
- **Quality of life**: A third of children and young people in poverty are deprived of the meals, toys or the clothes that they need.

- **Poor or unbalanced diet**: Living on a low income means that children and young people's diet and health can suffer. Eating habits developed in early life are likely to be continued in adulthood. This means that children and young people who eat mainly processed, convenience foods will tend to rely on these when they leave home. Conditions that occur in early life are directly related to a poor or unbalanced diet, such as anaemia and an increased susceptibility to infections such as colds and bronchitis.
- **Space to live and play**: Poorer children and young people are more likely to live in sub-standard housing and in areas with few shops or amenities, where children have little or no space to play safely.
- **Growth**: Children are also more likely to be smaller at birth and shorter in height.
- **Education**: Children and young people who grow up in poverty are less likely to do well at school and have poorer school attendance records.
- **Long-term effects**: As adults, they are more likely to suffer ill health, be unemployed or homeless. They are more likely to become involved in offending, drug and alcohol abuse, and abusive relationships.

## Family environment and background

A child or young person who is miserable and unhappy is not developing in a healthy way, although he or she may *appear* physically healthy. All children and young people need the following:

- **love and affection**: to receive unconditional love from their parents or primary carers
- to feel **safe and secure**
- **stimulation**: healthy growth and development can be affected when a child receives too little (or too much) stimulation
- **opportunities to play**: all children need to play, and young people need to have leisure opportunities, such as playing a sport or a musical instrument, or joining a club.

Children and young people's social and emotional development is strongly influenced by family and culture. The majority of parents or carers provide a nurturing environment for their children. However, there are some parents or carers who, for a variety of reasons, do not manage to provide the secure base that every child or young person needs. Common problems within the home occur when one or both parents or carers neglect their children because of:

- mental health problems, such as depression
- drug misuse, particularly alcoholism
- marital conflict and domestic violence.

## Personal choices

The lifestyle choices that young people make can also affect their development. Young people may choose to smoke, drink alcohol or take drugs – all of which can impact on the healthy development of their brain. These lifestyle choices are often difficult to give up, and set an unhealthy pattern for the future.

## Looked-after children

Children and young people who are in the care of **local authorities** are described as 'looked-after children'. They are one of the most vulnerable groups in society. The main reason for children and young people being under the care of their local authority is that they lack a stable, warm and consistent environment, and many of them will not have formed secure attachments. This impacts on their emotional and social development – particularly developing trust in others – and also affects their ability to do well at school. The majority of children and young people who *remain* in care are there because they have suffered some sort of abuse or neglect. Some children and young people are in residential care or living with foster families. Others who also have **care status** may live with their

### Key term

**Care status** – When a child or young person is the subject of a care order that places him or her under the care of a local authority. The local authority then *shares* parental responsibility for the child or young person with the parents or carers, and will make most of the important decisions about the child or young person's upbringing, such as where they live and how they are educated.

parents or carers, but are the responsibility of the local authority.

## Education

The quality of education received in childhood is very important. This is not just the formal education received in schools, but the quality of the learning environment which children experience, within their families and in wider social and cultural networks, such as sports clubs and places of worship.

Some children and young people do not benefit from quality education. They may fail to attend school regularly, and this will affect their future cognitive development as well as their employment opportunities.

 **Progress check**

### Influences on development

How is the development of children and young people influenced by:

- a range of external factors
- a range of personal factors?

## Theories of development and frameworks to support development

A theory of child or young person development is an idea or set of principles about how a child or young person might develop. Theories help people to predict for example that before children talk, they usually babble. Theories about how children or young people develop are products of research and so are influenced by the culture in which they are carried out. Research provides evidence for and against various theories of child or young person development. It is very important to remember this, because people are not always objective: they agree and disagree. There is no such thing as 'the truth' about child or young person development. We always need to stop and ask: who is doing the research? Who is formulating the theory?

Two examples illustrate this point:

- The child psychologist **Vygotsky** (1896–1935) grew up in the Soviet Union, where Marxist and Communist ideas dominated. He came from a large family. Is it coincidence that his theory emphasises social relationships and the community?
- The psychologist **Piaget** (1896–1980) grew up in Europe. He was an only child. Is it coincidence that his theory emphasises the child as an individual and as an active learner trying to experiment and solve problems?

## Using theories in your work

You need to have an open mind and look at different theories, bringing together those ideas that are useful from each so that you can use them in your work. Some theories will help you to make predictions about a child or young person's learning. You need to see where different theories overlap and where they diverge. Sometimes the differences between theories are so considerable that it is not possible to use them together. However they are often similar (as with Piaget's and Vygotsky's work), and can be blended into a useful template for our work with children and young people. The theories of Piaget and Vygotsky both help us to look at how children and young people learn.

Historically, theories of child and young person development have tended to fall into one of two groups:

1 Some theories take the view that learning is closely linked with development. Examples of this type of theory are '**leave it to nature**' theories and **social constructivist** theories.
2 The other group of theories dismisses the importance of a child or young person's development as the basis of learning. These theories follow the **transmission** model: children learn what they are shown by adults.

When describing how children and young people learn, it is important to say which theory is being used. In the following section, we will look first at transmission theories, and then at 'leave it to nature' and social constructivist theories.

## Transmission theories: classical and operant conditioning

In the seventeenth century, the British philosopher John Locke thought that children were like lumps of clay, which adults could mould into the shape they wanted. At the beginning of the twentieth century, an American psychologist John Watson, and the Russian psychologist Ivan Pavlov, were developing similar theories about how people learn. These theories have had a strong influence on thinking about development.

### Key term

**Transmission** – Shaping the child's behaviour so that the child has the knowledge the adults wants to transmit (or send) to him or her.

## Classical conditioning

**Ivan Pavlov** (1849–1936) experimented with conditioned responses in dogs. He liked to be described as a physiologist rather than as a psychologist, because he believed that psychological states (such as conditioning) are identical to physiological states and processes in the brain. He thought this approach was useful and scientific.

Classical conditioning is the way in which responses come under the control of a new stimulus. In his experiments, there was a neutral **conditioned** stimulus: a church bell ringing. This was paired with food, which was an **unconditioned** stimulus. The dogs were fed when the church bells rang. This produced an **unconditioned** response, which was saliva flowing in the dog's mouth when the food appeared. Gradually, the sound of any bell would produce a **conditioned** response in the dogs, which would produce saliva ready for the food that usually accompanied the ringing of the bell.

Food normally produces salivation. Classical conditioning changes the stimulus, so that the sound of a bell produces salivation. Pavlov would have fed the dogs, whether or not they salivated at the sound of the bell.

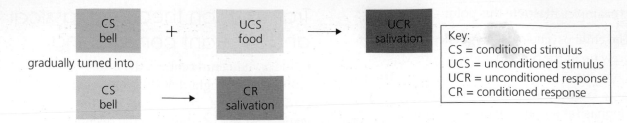

```
CS          +    UCS              →     UCR
bell             food                   salivation
```

gradually turned into

```
CS          →    CR
bell             salivation
```

Key:
CS = conditioned stimulus
UCS = unconditioned stimulus
UCR = unconditioned response
CR = conditioned response

**Figure 5.14** A summary of Pavlov's experiment

**Figure 5.15** Pavlov's dog: an illustrated summary of the experiment

## Operant conditioning

**B. F. Skinner** (1905–90) was a behavioural psychologist who worked in the USA. He did not believe it was useful to theorise about mental states that could not be observed, and thought to be unscientific. Whereas Pavlov fed his dogs when the bell rang whether or not they salivated, in Skinner's experiments he only fed rats or pigeons if they behaved as he required.

- He gave rats a reward of food if they pressed a lever. This was **positive reinforcement**: the desired behaviour was rewarded.
- Conversely, undesired behaviour could be **negatively reinforced**. The rats would receive an electric shock every time they went near one area of a maze, and would begin to avoid that area. The undesired behaviour was extinguished and the desired behaviour was encouraged.

### Links to practice

An example of negative reinforcement would be that while playing in the water tray, a toddler might try to take a jug from another child. Neither child will let go, and both look to the nearest adult with cries of distress to receive attention. If in the past, this has led to a satisfactory conclusion (such as the adult finding a bottle which one child accepts as a substitute), the children will repeat the behaviour in the future.

## Bribery and behaviour shaping

**Bribery** is quite different to **behaviour shaping** or **behaviour modification**. We might want a child to put away the floor puzzle that she has been working on and which is spread all over the floor. If we tell her she can play with a favourite toy if she tidies it up, this *is* bribery. The child understandably feels she is being given a choice and weighs up the behaviour against the reward. Is it worth it? She may decide it is not – and she will be baffled if the adult is displeased with her choice. (Older children may see this as an opportunity to negotiate, asking for two toys!) With bribery, the child learns that the point of the behaviour is to please the adult and gain the reward (in this case playing with a toy), not to ensure that all the pieces of the puzzle are stored safely for another time.

## Case Study    An example of learning through classical conditioning

Year 2 children (aged six and seven years) in a primary school were working in different groups, either painting, writing, playing a maths game or cooking. The school bell rang. Immediately, the children stopped what they were doing and started to tidy up quickly and go out to play. The children were conditioned to expect playtime when the bell sounded, so they tidied up in readiness. They would have tidied up even if they had not been allowed subsequently to go out to play.

bell (CS) + playtime (UCS) = tidy up (UCR)

bell (CS) = tidy up (CR)

(CS: Conditioned Stimulus; UCS: Unconditioned Stimulus; UCR: Unconditioned Response; CR: Conditioned Response.)

| Subject | Behaviour | Reinforcer | Outcome |
|---|---|---|---|
| child | has tantrum in supermarket | GETS sweets | POSITIVE REINFORCEMENT – BEHAVIOUR WILL BE REPEATED |
| salesperson | meets sales target | GETS bonus | |
| teenager | pushes over old woman in street | GETS money from handbag | |
| dog | sits up and begs | GETS food | |
| baby | points to toy | GETS toy handed to her | |
| holidaymaker | puts on suntan oil | AVOIDS sunburn | NEGATIVE REINFORCEMENT – BEHAVIOUR WILL BE REPEATED |
| tutor with headache | takes aspirin | STOPS headache | |
| driver | slows down before speed camera | AVOIDS speeding ticket | |
| student | hands medical certificate in | AVOIDS losing bursary | |
| baby with wet nappy | cries | STOPS discomfort (adult changes nappy) | |
| neighbour | complains about loud music next door | STOPS noise | |

**Table 5.14** Operant conditioning (With permission from Chris Rice, Clydebank College)

## Links to practice

In behaviour shaping or modification, there is no 'if' and no mention of reward. The reinforcer comes only *after* the behaviour has appeared, usually in a way that is linked to the behaviour. For example, the adult might say, 'Well done, you have tidied that up quickly.'

When using behaviour shaping, the only time that there is any mention of future outcome is in terms of what will be happening next; for example, 'When everyone is sitting quietly, then we can start the story.'

Just as positive reinforcement must not be confused with bribery, negative reinforcement must not be confused with **punishment**. Ignoring undesirable behaviour (leading to extinction, or its disappearance), together with clear and consistent reinforcement of desired behaviour, is more effective than punishment.

## Problems with using behaviourist techniques

It is important that adults are very clear about their purpose if they use these techniques:

● What behaviour is to be extinguished?
● What behaviour does the adult want to increase?

The adult must make sure that what they intend is what actually happens, and that the child does not pick up an entirely different message. For example, a child may learn that, if he says sorry within an adult's hearing and quickly enough after hitting another child, he may avoid punishment irrespective of whether or not he has any feelings of remorse.

Often, adults ignore children and young people when they are behaving appropriately, only giving them attention when they are disruptive. However, children and young people need to realise the advantages (enjoyment and satisfaction) of cooperating with others in different situations, so that enjoyment and satisfaction become the reinforcers. Other kinds of reward are not then necessary.

## 'Leave it to nature': a *laissez-faire* model

In the eighteenth century, the French philosopher Jean Jacques Rousseau thought that children learned naturally, and that they were biologically programmed to learn particular things at a particular time. He thought that just as a flower unfolds through the bud, so a child's learning unfolds – for example, babbling leads into language and then into reading and writing, and kicking the arms and legs leads to crawling and walking.

In this approach, adults help children to learn by making sure that the environment supports the child's learning as it unfolds. For example, children learn the language that they hear spoken as they grow up. If children hear Chinese, they learn to speak Chinese; if they hear English, they learn to speak English. If children hear more than one language, they are able to learn more than one language and become bilingual or multilingual. This model of learning suggests that children are naturally programmed to learn languages.

This view of learning suggests that children naturally do what they need to do in order to develop and learn. It sees children as *active* in their own learning. Children may be helped by other people or may learn on their own. Because adults need not act, this is sometimes referred to as a *laissez-faire* view of how children learn.

## Arnold Gesell

In the 1930s, **Arnold Gesell** (1880–1961) mapped out some norms of development (normative measurement was discussed earlier in this chapter). These were used to chart milestones in the child's development as it unfolded. Gesell believed that normal development progressed according to a set sequence. His milestones could be used to check that the pattern of development was 'normal'. Gesell's developmental scales looked at motor, adaptive, language and personal–social areas. If children reached particular milestones such as walking within the 'normal' age range, then their development was said to be making 'normal' progress.

This approach is depressing if used with children with special educational needs as they are constantly labelled 'abnormal'.

## Sigmund Freud, Anna Freud and Melanie Klein: psychoanalytic theorists

**Sigmund Freud** (1856–1939) did not focus on the development of the youngest children. However, his daughter **Anna Freud** did, and so did **Melanie Klein** who was working at the same time as Anna Freud. Anna Freud and Melanie Klein were both nativists, believing that children are born with the capacity to learn a language.

Sigmund Freud and other psychoanalysts (such as Anna Freud, her student Erik Erikson and Klein) argued that development in children unfolds quite naturally. They also thought that when children suffer trauma, they could be helped to heal by being given as normal a childhood as possible and by experiencing loving relationships. They believed in the power of love, security, play and interesting experiences, as well as in being valued. A few children may need additional help through therapy.

Anna Freud worked with children in Nazi Germany but had to escape to England with her father. Based in Hampstead, north London, she later cared for children who had survived concentration camps in Nazi Germany. There is now a museum in

## Case Study    An example of learning through a 'leave it to nature' approach

Because most children of around three to four years of age begin to enjoy drawing and painting, the rooms in a nursery school were set up to support this activity. Great care was taken in the way that a variety of colours were put out in pots, with a choice of thick and thin paintbrushes. Children could choose paper of different sizes. A drying rack was close to the area and children could choose to paint at a table or on an easel.

Adults would be on hand to help if needed, but would be careful not to talk to children while they were painting, in case they cut across the children's thinking. Adults would not 'make' children paint, because not all children would be ready to do so. Readiness is important in this approach to learning.

| Advantages | Disadvantages |
|---|---|
| • Adults can learn about how to offer the right physical resources, activities and equipment for each stage of development. | • Adults may hold back too much because they are nervous of damaging the child's natural development: for example, by not talking to a child while she is drawing or by holding back from playing with children. |
| • Children can actively make choices, select, be responsible, explore, try things out and make errors without incurring reproach or a feeling of failure. | • Adults only support children in their learning, rather than extending the learning children do. |
| • Adults value observing children and act in the light of their observations. This might mean adding more materials, and having conversations with children to help them learn more. | • Children might be understimulated because adults are waiting for signs of readiness in the child. The signs might never come! Adults wait too long before intervening. |
| • Adults are able to follow the child's lead and be sensitive to the child. | • Children might not be shown how to do things in case it is not the right moment developmentally to teach them, which leaves them without skills. |
| | • Children with special educational needs or from different cultures might be labelled 'abnormal' or 'unready'. In fact, they might reach a milestone earlier or later, but still within the normal sequence. They might develop unevenly but in ways which make 'normal' life possible. Milestones in one culture might be different in another culture. |

**Table 5.15** Advantages and disadvantages of the 'leave it to nature' view of development and learning

Hampstead that honours her work with children, and the Anna Freud Centre that works with children and their families.

Sigmund Freud emphasised the **unconscious** mind, unlike Pavlov and Skinner, who both emphasised observable behaviour. Freud believed that:

• our unconscious minds influence the way in which we behave

• our early experiences cause later adult behaviour
• symbolic behaviour is important, and he tried to interpret dreams.

Freud linked thinking, feeling, and sexual and social relationships with early physical behaviour, such as breastfeeding, toilet training and separation from parents.

# The social constructivist approach: Piaget, Vygotsky and Bruner

In the eighteenth century, the German philosopher Immanuel Kant believed that a child's learning was an *interaction* between the developing child and the environment. He said that children constructed their own understanding and knowledge about the world. The approach is called a **social constructivist** view of how children learn. This model:

- is the approach currently most favoured by early years practitioners
- has the best support from research into child development in the western world
- draws on both the transmission model and the *laissez-faire* ('leave it to nature') model of a child's learning, rearranging elements of both into a model which is helpful to those working with children.

## Jean Piaget

Jean Piaget (1896–1980) was a **cognitive** theorist. He developed a theory of how children learn, claiming that they:

- go through **stages** and **sequences** in their learning
- are **active learners**
- use **first-hand experiences** and prior experiences in order to learn
- **imitate** and transform what they learn into **symbolic behaviour**.

Piaget did not explicitly emphasise the importance of social and emotional aspects of learning, and he did not dwell on social relationships as much as other social constructivists. He took social and emotional development for granted, and did not write about it in detail. Instead, his writing emphasises intellectual or cognitive development and learning. Piaget's theory is called **constructivist** (rather than social constructivist) for this reason.

## Lev Vygotsky

Lev Vygotsky (1896–1935) stressed the importance for development of being near someone who knows more than the child, who can help the child to learn something that would be too difficult for the child to do on his or her own. Vygotsky described:

- the **zone of potential development**, sometimes called the zone of **proximal** development. It means that the child can do with help *now* what it will be possible for him to do alone without help *later in life*.
- the **importance of play** for children under seven years. Play allows children to do things beyond what they can manage in actual life (such as pretend to drive a car). It is another way through which children reach their zone of potential development.
- the **zone of actual development**: what the child can manage without help from anyone.

Vygotsky believed that **social relationships** are at the heart of a child's learning, so his theory is called a social constructivist theory. Barbara Rogoff (1950– ) has extended Vygotsky's work and wrote about the way in which adults and toddlers co-construct their learning; they each learn from each other (1997).

## Jerome Bruner

The essence of Bruner's (1915– ) theory is that children learn through:

- **doing** (the **enactive** mode of learning)
- **imaging** things that they have done (the **iconic** mode of learning)
- making what they know into **symbolic codes**, for example talking, writing or drawing (the **symbolic** mode of learning).

Adults can tutor children and help them to learn. They do this by 'scaffolding' what the child is learning in order to make it manageable for the child. This means that children can learn any subject at any age. They simply need to be given the right kind of help.

For example, when a baby drops a biscuit over the side of the high chair, the baby can learn about gravity if the adult **scaffolds** the experience by saying something like, 'It dropped straight down on to the floor, didn't it? Let's both drop a biscuit and see if they get to the floor together.' Bruner's theory

## Case Study

### An example of a social constructivist view of development and learning

Using a team approach to record-keeping in an early years setting, staff had built up observations of children. They noted that Damian (aged five years) kept punching; he punched other children, furniture and other objects. It seemed to be his main way of exploring.

The staff decided to introduce activities that allowed punching:

- They put huge lumps of clay on the table.
- They made bread and encouraged energetic kneading.
- They sang songs like 'Clap your hands and stamp your feet' and 'Hands, knees and bumps-a-daisy'.
- They encouraged vigorous hand printing and finger painting.

- They helped children to choreograph dance fights when acting out a story.
- Damian told the group about 'baddies' from another planet.
- He helped to 'beat' the carpet with a beater as part of spring-cleaning.
- He spent a long time at the woodwork bench hammering nails into his model. He soon stopped hitting other children, and began to talk about what he was doing in the activities with adults and other children.

Observation enabled adults to support Damian's learning in educationally worthwhile ways. Adults were able to extend his learning so that hitting people stopped, and he learned to use physical force in a rich variety of ways that did not hurt anyone.

 Progress check

How is current early years practice influenced by theories of development?

is also called a social constructivist theory, as social relationships are central to scaffolding.

## The nature–nurture debate

The nature–nurture debate is concerned with the extent to which development and learning are primarily to do with the child's natural maturing processes, and the extent to which development and learning progress as a result of experience. The debate has been very fierce, and it is not over yet. Modern psychologists such as Sir Michael Rutter believe that the child's learning is probably about 60 per cent nature and 40 per cent nurture (Rutter 2005). Neuroscientists such as Colin Blakemore stress the importance of relationships (nurture), and how these

actually cause the brain to change and remain physically altered (Blakemore and Frith, 2005). What do you think, having read about different theories of development? We can consider the developmental theories in terms of nature and nurture:

- The transmission approach stresses experience and nurture.
- The 'leave it to nature' approach stresses maturation and nature.
- The social constructivist approach to learning stresses both nature and nurture. A modern way of describing this is to say that both the biological and socio-cultural paths of development are important for learning.

## Adults' learning

Remember, theories about learning are not just about how children learn; they are about how adults learn too. Adults who enjoy learning and being with children are much more likely to provide a high-quality early years setting for children and their families. When a setting is described as

| Advantages | Disadvantages |
|---|---|
| ● This approach is very rewarding and satisfying because adults and children can enjoy working together, struggling at times, concentrating hard, stretching their thinking and ideas, celebrating their learning, and sharing the learning together. | ● It is very hard work compared with the other two approaches to learning that we have looked at in this chapter. This is because there is much more for adults to know about, more to think about, more to organise and do. |
| ● Trusting each other to help when necessary creates a positive relationship between children, parents and staff. It means taking pride in the way that indoor and outdoor areas of the room are set up, organised, maintained and cared for. | ● It is much more difficult for those who are not trained to understand how to work in this way. |
| ● It means teamwork by the adults, which is the way to bring out everyone's strengths in a multiprofessional group of teachers and early years workers. | |
| ● It means sharing with parents and children all the learning that is going on. | |
| ● It means adults need to go on learning about children's development. When adults continue to develop as people professionals, learning alongside children, they have more to offer the children. | |
| ● In Sweden there are now local plazzas where early years workers explain the way they work to parents, those working with older children, governing bodies and politicians. | |
| ● Adults and children respect and value each other's needs and rights, and help each other to learn. | |
| ● Although it takes time, training and experience for adults to build up skills for working in this way, it is very effective in helping children to learn during their early years. | |

**Table 5.16** Advantages and disadvantages of the social constructivist view of learning

demonstrating effective practice, or high-quality practice, it is usually seen that adults and children are *both* active in their learning.

## Activity

### Remembering our own learning

Think about your own experience at school. Were any of the lessons based on a transmission model of learning? Evaluate your learning experience.

## A humanistic approach: Maslow and Pringle

**Abraham Maslow** (1908–70) developed a **humanistic** approach to create a theory of human needs which is relevant to all ages, not just for children. He described five levels of need – physical, safety, social, self-esteem, creativity – and proposed that each level must be met before progressing to the next level. It is difficult to reach one's full potential unless the lower level needs have been met.

Maslow's theory is relevant to child development and care. For example, at the basic level of physiological needs, a child who is cold or hungry will be unable to respond effectively to planned activities.

**Mia Kellmer Pringle** (1920–83) suggested that there are four significant developmental needs that have to be met from birth: love and security, new experiences, praise and recognition, and responsibility.

### The need for love and security

This is probably the most important need as it provides the basis for all later relationships. The

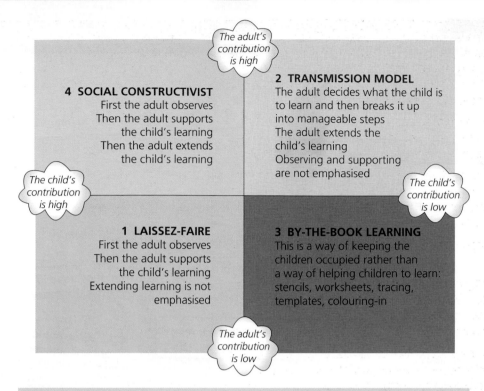

**Figure 5.16** The four approaches to development and learning

## ✓ Progress check

### Guidelines for using the different approaches to development and learning

1. Figure 5.16 shows that in a 'leave it to nature' approach to learning, children make a very high contribution to the learning they do, but adults hold back and take a very small part.
2. This is very different from the transmission model. In this approach the adult has a very high input into the child's learning, taking control over the child's learning. The child's contribution is quite low.
3. The 'by-the-book' approach to learning is not valuable and has not been covered in this chapter. Here, both the adults and the children have a very low level of participation. It is not really an approach to learning; it is just a way of keeping children occupied. Worksheets, colouring in, tracing, templates, filling in gaps and joining the dots all fall under this heading.
4. In the social constructivist (sometimes called 'interactionist') approach to learning, both the adult and the children put an enormous amount of energy into active learning.

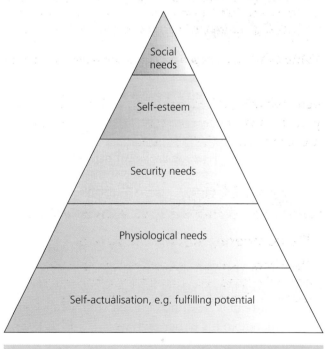

**Figure 5.17** Maslow's hierarchy of needs

## Activity

## Models of learning

Make a chart with these three headings:

1 Transmission model of learning

2 *Laissez-faire* or 'leave it to nature' model of learning

3 Social constructivist or interactionist model of learning.

Which of these sentences should be placed under which heading on your chart?

1 Adults should mould children's learning. After all, adults know more than children.

2 Children know what they need in order to learn.

3 Do you want to have a story first, or tidy up first?

4 We need to tidy up; we will have the story afterwards.

5 Children are full of ideas if they are encouraged to have them.

6 Do it because I say so.

7 That child has been 'off task' all morning.

8 Children are born with everything they need in order to learn.

9 Children enjoy conversations with adults.

10 Children must be free to try things out.

11 Children will learn when they are ready and not before.

12 That child performed the task successfully today.

13 Nature knows best.

14 Adults know best.

15 Children must be free to try things out and to learn from the mistakes they make.

Compare your answers with a partner. Discuss your answers together.

young child instinctively wants to move away and become more independent, but separating from the parent figure may be difficult. Each child deals with this challenge in his or her own way.

- **Security**: In their first year, the child's need for security may be met by having a comfort blanket or a favourite toy; Donald Winnicott (1896–1971) called this a **transitional object**.
- **Routine**: Another aspect of the child's need for love and security is the need for routine and

predictability. This is why having daily routines is so important in childcare. By meeting children's need for routine, carers are helping the child to feel acknowledged and independent, and this increases their self-esteem.

- **Attachment:** Pringle (like Bowlby, see below) recognised the children's need to have a steady, durable and caring relationship with empathetic adults. A continuous, reliable, loving relationship first within the family unit, then with a growing number of others, can meet this need. It can give the child a sense of self-worth and identity. In childcare settings, the **key person** system helps to meet this need.

## The need for new experiences

New experiences are a fundamental requirement for cognitive development. Children learn from their experiences.

- In early life it is largely through play and language that the child explores the world and learns to cope with it. As children pass through each stage of development, they often return and work on a previous level in a new way. For experiences to be meaningful, they must extend what children have already learned; they should present children with social, intellectual and physical challenges.
- In adolescence, another form of play is important – the young person experiments with different kinds of role, such as girlfriend, boyfriend, worker or leader. Language remains a crucial factor in intellectual growth; it helps in learning to reason and think, and in making relationships.

## The need for praise and recognition

Growing up requires an enormous amount of learning, emotional, social and intellectual. Consequently, strong incentives are necessary for children to continue through the difficulties and conflicts that they will inevitably encounter. The most effective incentives are praise and recognition sustained over time.

- **Self-fulfilling prophecy**: The lower the expectation of the parent or carer, the lower the level of effort and achievement of the child. This is sometimes called a self-fulfilling prophecy.
- **Intrinsic motivation**: If you make children feel anxious when they have not succeeded, they will avoid activities likely to lead to failure. It is important to praise children appropriately when they try hard or achieve something new, however small it might seem. This will motivate children to greater effort and lead to the desire to achieve something for its own sake; this is called intrinsic motivation.

## The need for responsibility

Being responsible involves knowing what is to be done and how to do it. Children have different levels of understanding at different ages. Your role is to structure the environment to provide challenging tasks according to their different interests and ability levels. The need for responsibility is met by allowing children to gain personal independence, firstly through learning to look after themselves in matters of everyday care; then through a gradual extension of responsibility over other areas until they have the freedom and ability to decide on their own actions. Cooperation rather than competition allows children more freedom to accept and exercise responsibility. You can help by building group work into your planning activities.

## Social learning theory: Albert Bandura

The theory developed by Albert Bandura (1925– ) emphasises that young children learn about social behaviour by:

- watching other people
- imitating other people.

Albert Bandura found that children tend to imitate people in their lives whom they believe hold status, especially if those people are warm or powerful personalities. This research study did not replicate a natural situation for the children, but it does suggest that adults can be very influential on a child's behaviour. This should lead us to think about our own behaviour and the effect we have on children:

- If children are smacked by adults, they are likely to hit other children.
- If children are shouted at by adults, they are likely to shout at others.
- If children are given explanations, they will try to explain things too.
- If children are comforted when they fall, they will learn to do the same to others.

People who work with young children are very important status figures in the child's social learning.

### Links to practice

Children copy directly what adults do, but they also pretend to be adults by role-playing when they begin to play imaginatively. The indoor role-play area is an important place for this, as is the outdoor area, which

## Case Study — Bandura's work

Bandura showed three groups of children a film in which an adult was hitting a Bobo doll and shouting at it. The film had a different ending for each of the three groups:

1 **First ending**: the adult was given a reward for hitting the doll.

2 **Second ending**: the adult was punished for hitting the doll.

3 **Third ending**: nothing was done to the adult for hitting the doll.

Then the children were given a similar Bobo doll to the one in the film. The children who saw the adult rewarded for hitting the doll tended to do the same.

can become all sorts of places (for example, shops, markets, streets and building sites).

The problem with this approach is that it does not regard role play as children experimenting with different ways of doing things: it suggests that children merely copy what they see. We now know that role play is a more complex activity than the social learning theory would suggest.

## Attachment theory: Bowlby

Babies and the people who care for them usually form close bonds. As the baby is fed, held and enjoyed, these emotional, loving relationships develop and deepen. Babies who find that adults respond quickly to their cries become trusting of life and are securely **attached** in stable, warm relationships. They know that they will be fed,

## Case Study — Joe, four years old

Joe pretended to be an early years practitioner. He told a story to a group of dolls and imitated the way in which the worker talked gently to the children, smiling and holding the book.

changed when soiled, comforted when teething, and so on. Babies and parents who, for one reason or another, do not make close emotional bonds experience general difficulty in forming stable, warm and loving relationships.

**John Bowlby** (1907–90) looked at:

- how babies become attached to the mother figure (**attachment**)
- what happens when babies are separated from the mother figure (**separation**)
- what happens when babies experience loss and grief after being separated from the people to whom they feel close.

**Mary Ainsworth**, who worked with Bowlby, found that if adults responded quickly to a baby's cries, the child was less demanding by three years of age than those babies who had generally been left to cry. The individual temperament of a baby becomes obvious very early on and has an effect on the carers. For instance, some babies become hysterical very quickly when hungry, while others have a calmer nature. Bonding is partly about adults and babies adjusting to and understanding each other; learning how to read each other's signals.

Bowlby thought that early attachment was very important – that the relationship between the mother figure and the baby was the most important. This was because in the 1950s mothers tended to be at home with their babies. He did not believe that the most important attachment figure must be the natural mother, but he did say that babies need *one central person*, or a mother figure. It is now understood that babies can have deep relationships with several people – mother, father, brothers, sisters, carers and grandparents. Indeed, babies develop in an emotionally and socially healthy way only if they bond with several different people. In many parts of the world and in many cultures, this is usual.

Babies might enjoy playing with one person and having meals with another. It is the quality of the time which the child spends with people that determines whether or not the child becomes attached to them. Attachment can be difficult at first, especially in cases where it is hard for the adult and child to communicate; for example:

- the birth has caused mother and baby to be separated, and the mother is depressed
- the child is visually impaired and eye contact is absent
- the child is hearing-impaired and does not turn to the parent's voice; eye contact is also harder to establish here because the child does not turn to the parent's face when he or she speaks
- the child has severe learning difficulties and needs many experiences of a person before bonding can become stable.

## Links to practice

Bowlby's work on attachment was important because it led to the following changes in practice:

- the introduction of the **key person** system in early years settings (for more information on this system, see Chapter 14)
- parents can often stay in hospital with their children; there may be a bed for a parent next to the child's bed
- social workers are more careful about separating children and parents when families experience difficulties
- most early years settings have policies on how to settle children so as to make it a positive experience
- children are fostered in family homes rather than placed in large institutions.

## Separation anxiety

By five or six months, many babies are so closely attached to the people they know and love that they show separation anxiety when they are taken away from these attachment figures. Researchers have found that toddlers will happily explore toys and play with them if an attachment figure (usually their parent) is present. If the parent goes out of the room, however, young children quickly become anxious, and stop exploring and playing. They need the reassurance of someone they know to be able to explore, play and learn. Children who have had many separations from those with whom they have tried to bond find it very difficult to understand social situations and relationships.

### Key term

**Attachment** – An enduring emotional bond that an infant forms with a specific person. Usually the first attachment is to the mother, formed between the ages of six and nine months.

# Monitoring development

The aim of monitoring children and young people's development is to identify those children and young people who are not matching the expected pattern of development, and then to plan and provide more accurate support for each child or young person to make appropriate progress.

## Different methods of monitoring and assessing children and young people

Children and young people are assessed throughout their lives, by a variety of professionals and using a range of different methods. At the time of birth for example, the health of a baby is assessed using the Apgar score. In the months and years following birth, a child will be continuously assessed and monitored by doctors and health visitors to ensure that he or she is progressing according to the recognised developmental norms.

Observations are a valuable method of assessing children's development, and are used to plan activities for groups of children. (This topic is covered in Chapter 6, Unit CYP 3.2.) In education settings, children and young people are monitored and assessed using formative assessment frameworks, such as the Early Years Foundation Stage Profile.

## Involving parents, carers and others in assessing children

Parents and primary carers have a wealth of knowledge about their children. Practitioners should try to build up a fuller picture of the children they are assessing by:

## Case Study — Assessing Jack's needs

Jack is a three-year-old child who lives with his young mother, Samantha, in a small flat in an inner city area. He does not have brothers or sisters. Jack's mother is increasingly unable to cope with Jack's behaviour. Every weekday, Samantha drops Jack off at his childminder's house at 8.15 am and goes to a department store where she works as a catering assistant. She picks him up again at 5.45 pm and rushes home to prepare the evening meal. Jack always watches television while she cooks and then they eat their meal together.

As soon as he has finished, Jack starts demanding attention. First he wants a story, then he wants to play a space adventure game that his grandma gave him; and then he starts throwing his toys around. Samantha usually reacts to his demands by shutting him in his room and telling him that he can only come out again when he has learned how to behave. At other times she threatens to cancel the Sunday outings with his father.

Weekends are usually taken up with household chores. Jack's father takes him to the park or to his grandparents' house on Sundays. Jack loves these visits, but Samantha finds that he demands even more of her attention when he comes home.

1 Look at the four needs described by Pringle on pages 76–8. For each need, list the possible consequences of failure to meet that need, in terms of the effects on the child.

2 Identify any needs that are not being met for Jack's healthy development. Try to think of ways in which all the needs could be met, both for Jack and for his mother, Samantha.

- asking parents and carers to tell you what children do at home
- comparing the way in which children play at home to the way in which they play in the setting
- finding out about the child's family and culture.

Parental views and comments should be included in the child's records whenever possible. Children and young people can contribute to their own assessments by being encouraged to express their preferences for certain activities, and to talk about what they found hard or easy to do.

## The reasons why development may not follow the expected pattern

It is not always possible to determine why a child or young person's development is not following the expected pattern, but some of the more usual reasons are given in Figure 5.18.

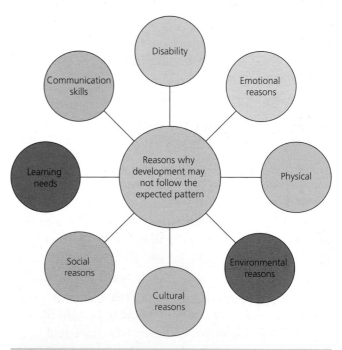

**Figure 5.18** Reasons why development may not follow the expected pattern

## How disability affects development

For more information on disability and development, see Chapter 11 (Unit CYP Core 3.7).

## Different types of intervention

A range of professionals can be called upon to help and support families and children whose development is delayed; see Table 5.17. Some work independently, but the majority work in a multi-agency partnership so that the child receives the best holistic care possible.

All early years settings are expected to have a special educational needs co-ordinator (SENCO).

**Assistive technology** can also be used to support children and young people. This includes specially designed mobility aids, standing chairs, feeding equipment and voice-activated computer programs. (See page 88 for Ability Net's website.)

 **Progress check**

### Assessment checklist: Development and interventions

1. Explain why children and young people's development may not follow the expected pattern.
2. Explain how disability may affect development.
3. Explain how different types of interventions can promote positive outcomes for children and young people where development is not following the expected pattern.

# The importance of early intervention to support speech, language and communication needs

Chapter 16 (Unit EYMP5) looks in more detail at the importance of speech, language and communication to children's holistic development. This chapter looks at the importance of identifying speech, language and communication delays and disorders. It can be very difficult for some children and young people to communicate (to listen and to talk); for example, for those who have a hearing impairment, severe learning difficulties and moderate learning difficulties, or physical challenges such as cerebral palsy.

It is very important that every child is encouraged to find ways of communicating with other people. Many children and young people are now helped to learn sign language or sign systems (Makaton), or to use personal references that help them to communicate. Remember that gestures and touch are effective forms of communication, as well as shared signs, finger spelling and computers and keyboards.

## Early identification of speech, language and communication delays and disorders

Recently there has been an emphasis on encouraging communication and language development in the first five years. **Every Child a Talker (ECaT)** is a developmentally appropriate approach that emphasises the importance of a supportive and stimulating environment in which children are encouraged to develop communication and language. It supports the work of the Early Years Foundation Stage in England, in home learning environments (childminders) and in group settings of all kinds.

| Professional | Role of professional |
|---|---|
| Educational psychologist | An educational psychologist is a qualified teacher who is also trained as a psychologist. They help children and young people who find it difficult to learn or to understand or communicate with others. |
| Health visitor | A registered nurse or a midwife with additional training. They visit families at home to give help, advice and practical assistance about the care of very young children. Some areas have specialist health visitors who have particular experience and expertise supporting families with a young disabled child. |
| Learning support assistant | A learning support assistant or teaching assistant is someone who works alongside teachers. They support individual children or small groups to help them learn and take part in activities in schools or nurseries. |
| Nurse specialist | The special needs school nursing service aims to provide specialist holistic care for all special needs children and their families and carers by placing highly trained paediatric nurses and trained support staff in the school and home environment. |
| Paediatric dietician | A dietician is a health professional who gives advice about nutrition and swallowing or feeding difficulties. |
| Paediatric occupational therapist | A paediatric occupational therapist helps children with difficulties in carrying out the activities of everyday life, such as sitting in a chair, holding a spoon and fork or drinking from a cup. They carry out assessments to see if the child would benefit from using specialist equipment such as adapted cups, buggies or chairs. They can also advise parents and carers on lifting and handling the child safely. |
| Paediatrician | A doctor who specialises in treating babies and children. They are often the first point of contact for families who find out that their child has an impairment or medical condition. |
| Physiotherapist | A health professional who specialises in physical and motor development. They can assess the child and develop a plan that might include helping a child to control head movement, sit, crawl or walk. |
| Portage home visitor | An educational professional who can come to the home of pre-school children with special educational needs and their families. |
| Psychiatrist | A doctor who specialises in psychiatry – the branch of medicine that deals with the study, prevention and treatment of mental illness. |
| Social worker | A professional who provides practical help and advice about counselling, transport, home help and other services. Social workers are normally employed by the local council. |
| Special education needs coordinator (SENCO) | Member of staff of an early years setting or school who has responsibility for coordinating SEN provision within that setting. In a small setting, the manager or headteacher may take on this role. In larger settings there may be an SEN coordinating team. |
| Speech and language therapist | Speech and language therapists assess and treat children and adults who have difficulties with speech and language. |
| Youth Justice Board | The Youth Justice Board oversees the youth justice system in England and Wales, and works to prevent offending and reoffending by children and young people under the age of 18. This organisation also ensures that custody for them is safe and secure, and addresses the causes of their offending behaviour. |

**Table 5.17** Professionals who offer different types of intervention

ECaT helps practitioners to do the following:

- **identify** what helps communication and language to develop
- **review** their language provision and **plan** appropriately
- **work with children** with English as an additional language (EAL)
- **make the most of everyday activities and experiences** that promote communication and language
- make an effective **partnership with parents**.

## Language delay

There are a variety of reasons why language may be delayed:

- The child may be growing up and spending time in environments which do not support the development of communication and language.
- The child may have a learning difficulty that makes it a challenge to process language, such as

aphasia, Asperger's syndrome, autism or Down's syndrome.
- The child may have a hearing or visual impairment.

## How multi-agency teams work together to support speech, language and communication

For children with a language delay or disorder, it may be necessary to support their language development with the help of a speech and language therapist, a specialist language teacher or an educational psychologist, and with other professionals such as a health visitor who works in the home context with families and young children. Teams need to work together in collaboration with the child's parents to ensure that the right support is offered.

### Key terms

**Aphasia** – Aphasia is a language disorder where people have problems speaking and writing, and also understanding both the spoken and written word. Aphasia is not a condition in itself; it is a symptom caused by pre-existing brain damage.

**Asperger's syndrome** – Asperger's syndrome is a form of **autism**, which is a lifelong disability that affects how a person makes sense of the world, processes information and relates to other people.

### Involving parents and carers in supporting children's speech, language and communication

Spend some time thinking about the possible reasons why parents and carers with whom you work may not be fully engaged in supporting their child's communication development. Every setting and every parent or carer is unique, so there may be a variety of reasons that you could discuss with others in your group. For example, both parents or carers may be working full time and cannot visit the setting during the working day, or parents may be unaware of the importance of communication as a basic skill, and how and when children develop certain language skills.

### Case Study — Communication-friendly spaces

At Barnaby's Nursery, staff are using the ECaT (Every Child a Talker) initiative. They made a plan of the room and then over a few sessions monitored the whole room in terms of the amount of communication in each area. They put green stickers where they observed a great deal of talking, and red stickers where they observed little or no talking. Staff then used this information and discussed why certain areas seemed conducive to talking, while others were

not. They rearranged these areas, and observed the children to see what their reaction was to the new arrangement. They then carried out a new survey to see if there was any improvement in talking in the newly arranged areas. Their findings were that there was a marked improvement in communication with the new arrangement. (See page 351 for more information on communication-friendly spaces.)

## Supporting the development of speech, language and communication through play

Play is vital to developing language, and children learn particularly well when they are having fun. There are some simple activities and games that we can play with young children to support their language development, and be entertaining at the same time. These include the following:

- **Song and rhyme box or bag**: Collect objects that match songs that the child knows. Encourage the child to select the object for the song they want to sing, for example, a bus for 'Wheels on the Bus'; a star for 'Twinkle twinkle little star'; a sheep for 'Baa baa black sheep' etc. During the singing, leave gaps at the end of some lines to let the child supply the word. The bag or box can also be used in whole group singing so that the children become very familiar with the songs, and the objects can be left out for the children to explore.
- **Using music to develop language**: Try singing to everyday activities in the setting using the tune, 'Here we go round the mulberry bush'. When you are at the water tray, you might sing, 'This is the way we sail a boat. . .' etc.
- **Books:** Sharing storybooks with an adult is regarded as one of the most important ways of developing young children's spoken and written language, as well as promoting their knowledge and understanding of the world. Books that use

much repetition are particularly effective: Peep-O and The Hungry Caterpillar are appropriate examples.

- **Small-world play:** Using small wooden or plastic animals and figures can help children to progress to creating imagined stories without objects – a skill needed later on for creative writing.
- **Roleplay:** Taking on roles and dressing up promotes imaginative play and provides endless opportunities for conversation.
- **Blowing bubbles**: Recent research suggests that infants who can blow bubbles and lick their lips are more likely to pick up language quickly.
- **Involving parents**: use the Parents' Message Board to keep parents informed about what is happening in the setting. For example, 'Today we have been talking about. . .'. Parents and carers can then talk about this at home with their children.

# The potential effects of transitions on children and young people's development

## What are transitions?

A transition is a change of passage from one stage or state to another. Children and young people naturally pass through a number of stages as they grow and develop. Often, they will also be expected to cope with changes such as movement from nursery education to primary school, and from primary to secondary school.

You may have just made the transition from secondary school to a tertiary college or sixth form. Along with the excitement of a new course and possibly making new friends, you are likely to have felt some apprehension about the change to your life. This is likely to affect you more if you have experienced many changes in your life.

These changes are commonly referred to as **transitions**. You can learn more about how to offer support during transitions in Chapter 6 (Unit CYP3.2).

## Types of transitions

Transitions can affect all areas of the development of children and young people:

- **Emotional**: personal experiences, such as parents separating, bereavement, entering or leaving care
- **Physical**: moving to a new educational setting, a new home or care setting
- **Intellectual**: moving from nursery to primary school, or primary to secondary school
- **Physiological**: puberty or a long-term medical condition.

## Expected transitions

Many transitions are universal; they are experienced by almost everyone, and can usually be anticipated, or expected.

**Babies** experience transitions when they:

- are weaned onto solid food
- are able to be cared for by others, such as at nursery or a childminder's home
- progress from crawling to walking
- move from needing nappies to being toilet trained.

**Children** experience transitions when they:

- start nursery and then primary school
- move up to secondary school.

**Young people** experience transitions when they:

- go through the physical and emotional changes caused by puberty
- attend college or university
- leave home
- start work.

**Adults** experience transitions when they:

- get married
- become separated or divorce
- have children
- change jobs
- experience a death in the family, which changes the family structure.

## Unexpected transitions

Not every transition is experienced by every child, and not all transitions can be anticipated. These unexpected transitions include:

- the birth of a new baby in the family (although this is a very common transition, it is not always expected)
- an unexpected change of school or child care provider
- moving house
- violence or abuse within the family
- parents divorcing; having a new step-parent and perhaps new step-family
- serious illness, accident or death in the family.

## The possible effects of transitions on children and young people

You need to be able to identify transitions and understand what you can do to support children through them.

Many of the problems associated with transitions in childhood are associated with **separation**. As children become older, they start to cope better with being separated from their parents or main carers, but the way in which they cope will still depend on their early experiences of separation and how earlier transitions were managed. Children and young people who have had multiple transitions (perhaps changing schools or homes many times, possibly caused by changes to a parent's job) often find it harder to settle in and make new friends and relationships.

Transitions can affect the development of children and young people in different ways. There can be positive as well as negative effects; they can also be short-term or long-term, depending on the individual child or young person and on how effectively they are supported. Possible effects of transitions are given in Table 5.18.

## The importance of positive relationships during periods of transition

Children and young people need practitioners who are able to recognise the importance of attachment and emotional wellbeing during periods of transition, and who are able to identify the needs of an individual child and his or her family. The **key**

| Experience of the child or young person | Effect of this experience |
|---|---|
| **Withdrawal** | Children may withdraw from new relationships with other children and with carers, because they do not trust the separation not to happen again. |
| **Disorientation** | No sooner have children settled in one place and got to know a carer, they may be uprooted and have to face the same process again. |
| **A sense of loss** | Each time children and young people make a move, they lose the friends they have made and also the attachments they have formed with their carers. |
| **Regression** | Reverting to behaviour usually shown by younger children; for example, a child who was previously dry at night may start to wet the bed, or an older child might start to talk in a more 'babyish' way. |
| **Depression** | This may show in a number of ways: sadness, problems sleeping, crying and lack of appetite. |
| **Separation anxiety** | Children become clingy and need to be near their parent or primary carer to feel reassured. |
| **Changes in behaviour** | Young children may have more frequent outbursts of temper, and young people may become aggressive, often shouting and swearing. |
| **Lack of motivation** | Children and young people may have difficulty in concentrating on schoolwork and become easily distracted. |

**Table 5.18** Effect of transitions on children and young people

**person** approach is vital to supporting young children through transitions, and is also frequently used in health care and social care settings when transitions are necessary.

## Reflective practice: Transitions

- Does your setting have a policy for transition and continuity which is shared with everyone involved, both in and beyond the setting?

- How do you help children and families who are new to the area or your setting to settle in and get to know people? What is the role of the key person in supporting transitions?

- Think about a child or young person you know who has experienced a transition. How was he or she supported, and could the experience have been improved?

 Useful resources

**Organisations and websites**
**Abilitynet** is a national charity helping people with disabilities to use computers and the internet by adapting and adjusting their technology:
**www.abilitynet.org.uk**

**Afasic** is a UK charity representing children and young adults with communication impairments, working for their inclusion in society and supporting their parents and carers:
**www.afasicengland.org.uk**

**The Communication Trust** highlights the importance of speech, language and communication needs across the children's workforce, and aims to enable practitioners to access the best training and expertise to support the communication needs of all children:
**www.thecommunicationtrust.org.uk**

**Books**
Ahlberg, J. and Ahlberg, A. (1997) *Peepo!* Viking Kestrel Picture Books.

Blakemore, S.-J. and Frith, U. (2005) *The Learning Brain: Lessons for Education*. Blackwell.

Carle, E. (1995) *The Very Hungry Caterpillar*. Puffin.

Rutter, M. (2005) *Genes and Behaviour: Nature–Nurture Interplay Explained*. Wiley-Blackwell.

# 6 Promote child and young person development: Unit CYP Core 3.2

As we have seen in Chapter 5 (Unit CYP Core 3.1), every child or young person develops in a unique way. When promoting child and young person development, you need to learn how to meet every child and young person's individual needs. Observing children and young people in a structured way enables you to discover their individual needs and how best you can promote development. Similarly, drawing up an individual plan for each child helps the practitioner to promote development.

## Learning outcomes

By the end of this chapter you will:

1. Be able to assess the development needs of children or young people and prepare a development plan.

2. Be able to promote the development of children or young people.

3. Be able to support the provision of environments and services that promote the development of children or young people.

4. Understand how working practices can impact on the development of children and young people.

5. Be able to support children and young people's positive behaviour.

6. Be able to support children and young people experiencing transitions.

## Assessing the development needs of children or young people and preparing a development plan

Becoming skilled in observation and assessment is one of the most important parts of your training and developing practice. By **observation**, we mean closely watching, listening to and generally attending to what a child is doing, and recording your findings as accurately as you can. While you are observing, you try to avoid drawing any conclusions, and you try to stay as focused on the child or young person as possible.

By **assessment**, we mean making judgements about what your observation says about the child or young person's development, learning, health and wellbeing.

Through careful observation, you can begin the following process:

- Get to know each child or young person as an individual.
- Evaluate each child or young person's health and wellbeing.
- Think about each child or young person's interests, strengths and needs.
- Reflect on each child or young person's development and think about how to support and extend their learning.
- Gather information to share with parents and carers, and show how you value parents' and carers' observations of their own children.
- Gain an impression of how children and young people experience life in the setting, how they interact with others and behave.

- Think about the quality of care routines and interactions.
- Evaluate the quality of the learning environment and the curriculum.

> ## Key terms
>
> **Assessment** – Assessment involves practitioners, parents/carers and children/young people. It is about establishing what children and young people understand, are interested in and what they can do.
>
> **Assessment for learning** – Assessment for learning means using assessment information to help plan for children's next steps of development and learning. This planning could include activities, resources, talking and playing, or trips away from the setting.

# Factors that need to be taken into account when assessing development

## Confidentiality: the importance of appropriately sharing confidential information

Many difficult issues arise when professionals record and share information about children and young people. These include the issues of consent and confidentiality.

### Consent

Information should only be collected and stored on a child or young person with the consent of their parents or carers, who should have free access to this information on request. Information should only be shared between professionals with the express consent of parents or carers, which should be gained formally with a signature. The only exceptions are the very small number of cases where the child or young person might otherwise be at risk of immediate and significant harm if you shared a piece of information with the parent or carer (see Chapter 7, Unit CYP Core 3.3, for specific guidance on safeguarding).

### Confidentiality

It is important that information is securely stored so that it cannot be freely accessed by anyone. Practitioners, including learners, should not discuss or otherwise share this information, for example when chatting in the staffroom or with friends at the weekend. If information is kept on a computer or sent by email, steps must be taken to ensure that it could not fall into the hands of other people (for example, the use of encryption software).

## Children's wishes and feelings

It is very important to remember that everything that happens in the setting must, as far as possible, be in the children's interests. Children cannot give informed consent in the way that adults can, but you can follow the same principles with the children:

- If you think that your observation might be causing distress or discomfort, you should stop. Look out for times where the child:
  - keeps looking at you and seems inhibited from playing
  - seems uncomfortable
  - shrinks or looks away when you get close enough to observe
  - indicates through body language or words that she does not want you to observe her.
- If a child asks you what you are doing, or shows interest:
  - explain that you are watching her play and that you are very interested in what she is doing
  - show the child your notebook or paper and explain that you are writing things down
  - wait patiently for the child to go back to her play or activity, without trying to shoo the child away. You will usually find that children get used to observations and stop noticing you.
- If a child might be about to have an accident, or if you think a child is about to be hurt or bullied, you will need to stop your observation and intervene (or ask for a member of staff to help).

## Ethnic, linguistic and cultural background

It is important to find out from parents and carers about a child's home language development, including if a child is learning English as an additional language (including the children of deaf parents or carers who use British Sign Language at home). If their grasp of English is at a very early stage but they are talking fluently in their home language, this is not a language problem. On the other hand, if a child is hardly talking at home, then it will be important to involve speech and language therapy to enable the child to start using English in nursery. Where appropriate, bilingual support services should be used to help communication between practitioners and parents or carers.

It is also important to understand the child or young person's family and culture. The child or young person who seems 'withdrawn' may come from a family or culture where showing respect to adults is important. This might explain why a child is slow to speak to adults in an early years setting and is easily embarrassed. If the child is showing an interest in others and in early years activities, then it will be important to act with cultural sensitivity and avoid situations where the child has to answer direct questions. Gradually, with support, the child will manage to move between the different cultures of home and the early years setting. However, if a child shrinks away, is afraid of adults, and fearful, then you will need to discuss your concerns with the manager or setting head.

## Disability or specific requirements

A child or young person who has a disability or an additional need may need extra time or structured support when being assessed. For example, a young child with a serious lung disease used oxygen to help his breathing; this meant that his speech was very slow to develop, but in all other areas, his development was sound. Also a child with dyslexia may need extra time to complete assessment tasks or tests.

## Reliability of information

Observations that try to record what children and young people do and say will be less biased and give a clearer picture of what is really happening. You should be as objective as possible: record factual information (what you actually see and hear) rather than information you have already begun to interpret.

## Avoiding bias

When you are observing and assessing children and young people, you will need to be able to work towards putting into practice the anti-discriminatory, anti-bias approaches outlined in Chapter 3 (Unit SHC 33). Child development charts, including the *Development Matters* section in the Early Years Foundation Stage (EYFS), can be criticised for trying to 'normalise' every child. In other words, instead of seeing development as varied and influenced by different cultures and background, charts can present an 'ideal child'. This is a problem if any child who develops differently is seen as abnormal and problematic.

It may not be possible to completely avoid **cultural bias**, or any other kind of bias, when observing children and young people. However, we must minimise bias by:

- focusing on what children and young people actually do and say
- raising our awareness of cultural diversity
- learning from parents and carers about how they play and talk with their children at home, and what they value
- involving children and young people – by asking them to tell us what *they* think about what we have noticed and heard.

It is important not to confuse anti-bias practice, with holding back from making judgements. If you never make judgements about children and young people's development, then you will never notice which children and young people are experiencing difficulties and know who needs extra help. Although you will be trying to uphold equal opportunities, the result will be that children with special needs and other difficulties will miss out on the extra help they need.

When you are observing and assessing children, you need to make robust judgements about:

- the child's approach to play and learning – such as their involvement, enjoyment, and toleration of frustration
- the child's rate of progress – can you see development over time?
- whether the child is making sound progress, or needs extra help.

The important thing is that you try to base your judgements *on the information you have recorded*, not merely on your opinions and impressions. You should also be open to the views of others – parents, and your colleagues for example. Be prepared to explain why you have formed your opinion, but be open to change your mind.

## Key term

**Anti-bias practice** – Anti-bias practice means going beyond equal opportunities and actively opposing forms of discrimination and prejudices in your work; for example, letting all children take part in a woodwork activity upholds equal opportunities. Inviting a woman joiner into the nursery, displaying pictures and books about women doing woodwork, and talking these issues through with children, is an anti-bias approach.

On an outing to a live music event, a class of 28 children was seated in the front rows. They all thoroughly enjoyed the jazz-style pieces and many of them were standing up and swaying or moving in time with the music. Chantelle was the only mixed-race child present, being African-Caribbean and part White English. After the concert, when the children have all gone home, an adult helper (who had watched the children with pleasure) says to you, 'I suppose it's because she's black that Chantelle has such a good sense of rhythm.'

You think that this adult has based her comment on a stereotypical view of black children. What might you say to her? How could her stereotypical view get in the way of her observing Chantelle? Could it also get in the way of her observing the other children?

## Assessing development
### Assessment frameworks

In the EYFS, observation, assessment and planning make up one of the commitments under the heading of *Enabling Environments*. The EYFS requires all practitioners to:

- make systematic observations and assessments of every child's achievements, interests and learning styles
- use these observations and assessments to identify learning priorities and plan relevant and motivating learning experiences for every child
- match their observations to the expectations of the Early Learning Goals.

The frameworks for early years education in Scotland, Wales and Northern Ireland also emphasise the importance of practitioners closely observing children in order to assess their progress.

## Different approaches to observation and assessments

It is generally accepted practice to observe children and young people in a familiar environment, interacting with family and friends. In educational and care settings, the EYFS promotes **observation-based assessment**. Observations are assessed using the *Development Matters* scales, or the EYFS Profile (at the end of the Reception year). There are other scales to help assess particular areas of development, for example in the Every Child a Talker (ECaT) programme.

## Techniques for observation and assessment

Practitioners are increasingly using video, photography and audio recording of children and young people. There are many advantages that have come with new technology, especially as digital cameras and MP3 recorders are cheap and easy to use. For example if you want to study a child's language development and discuss it with parents, an audio or video recording might be a very effective way of doing this. Similarly, nothing records a child's construction or model as well as a carefully taken photograph.

## In Practice

### Observing children

If you are on placement in an early years setting, and you are going to observe a particular child over a period of time, you should do the following:

❏ **First of all, speak to your supervisor or mentor**. Make clear the requirements of your course, and think together about which child or children might be suitable. For example, if a child is subject to a safeguarding plan, then she is already being observed and assessed by many different people. Also, some children are very self-conscious; being observed might stop them from playing. Ask for advice and help.

❏ **Ask the parent or primary carer for consent**. It is helpful if the child's key person or the nursery manager/head meets the parent with you, to provide reassurance. Explain the requirements of your course, and how having opportunities to observe children will help you to become a better practitioner. Answer any questions openly and honestly, and if you are not

sure of something, say so and assure the parent that you will find out and answer the question in due course. Offer parents regular opportunities to look at your observations.

❏ **Ask for a signature to show formal consent**.

❏ **Maintain anonymity** (for example, refer to children only by their initials, not their full names) and confidentiality (do not discuss with friends or family what you find out about children).

❏ **Plan when, where and how often you will observe the child**, and make sure that everyone in the staff team is aware. You do not want to create a situation where colleagues are expecting you to supervise an area and play with children, but you are expecting to be able to hold back and spend time observing.

❏ **Share your observations** with staff in the setting – you can help them with their record-keeping, assessment and planning.

## Evaluating the selection of the assessment methods used

It is only by practising the skills of observing children and young people that we can learn which methods are the most effective to use in each situation. You may feel that time constraints or lack of resources may lead you to select one method over another. Table 6.1 details some of the more common advantages and limitations of different assessment methods.

Each observation and assessment method should have a clear aim, and when evaluating the method chosen, you may find that you have not achieved the stated aim. This is useful information and will help you to select the appropriate method next time.

## Developing a plan to meet development needs

When you compare more than one observation on an individual child, you may not be able to see

## Progress check

### Equal opportunities and assessment

- Practise observation that accurately records what children and young people do and how they set about it.
- Work with the team to involve parents in the observation and assessment of children and young people's development.
- Review any checklists you use, and consider whether these might disadvantage children with English as an additional language, or children from poorer backgrounds.

development; you will need to consider whether the child or young person might need some additional help or support. You should discuss this with your manager or head, and then talk over your concerns with the child or young person's parents or carers.

| Technique | Description and advantages and limitations |
|---|---|
| **Narrative**<br>Methods of narrative observation include:<br>• descriptive/running record<br>• video recording<br>• tape and transcript<br>• diary description<br>• anecdotal record<br>• target child | The most common type of observation used. It attempts to record everything that happens, as it happens, with plenty of detail. Usually recorded over a short period of time.<br>**Target child or young person observation** involves observing individual children and young people over 10 to 20 minutes and includes a coding system to help you to interpret your findings. An **anecdotal record** is a brief note of the key point you observed (e.g. 'Charlie did a painting for the first time today').<br>*Advantages*: Can be used frequently – often without children being aware. Target child observation enables observer to focus clearly on one child.<br>*Limitations*: Difficult to note down everything a child or young person says and does in the descriptive record. With photos, video and tape recordings, children and young people might be aware of being filmed and change their usual behaviour and play. |
| **Time sampling**<br>Usually using a prepared chart | This involves making a series of short observations (usually up to two minutes each) at regular intervals over a fairly long period. The interval between observations and the overall duration is your decision, depending on exactly what you are observing and why. For example, you may choose to record at 20-minute intervals over the course of a whole day, or every 15 minutes during a half-day session.<br>*Advantages*: Can observe different activities and areas of development.<br>*Limitations*: May miss observing things outside the sampling time; can be difficult to interrupt what you are doing regularly. |
| **Event sampling**<br>Usually using a prepared chart | Usually used to observe a particular aspect of a child or young person's behaviour or development whenever it occurs; e.g. how a child or young person communicates with others, or observing when a child or young person behaves aggressively towards others.<br>*Advantages*: Focus is always on one type of behaviour.<br>*Limitations*: Event observed may not explain reasons for behaviour. |
| **Checklist**<br>Using a prepared list of skills | This is carried out with a prepared list of skills or competencies that are being assessed, and is often used for 'can do' or 'is able to' checks in the context of a structured activity.<br>*Advantages*: The same list can be used for several children and results are easily understood.<br>*Limitations*: May not give a true picture if child is less cooperative or unwell on the day. Observer may be tempted to tick against a skill observed previously, showing a lack of objectivity. |
| **Diagrammatic charts**<br>Pie charts, flow diagrams, sociograms, bar charts and growth charts | These provide a visual and accessible display of collected information; e.g. a bar chart could be used to plot the heights of each child; or a sociogram could be used to show an individual's social relationships within a group.<br>*Advantages*: Fairly quick to complete and easy to understand.<br>*Limitations*: Does not always provide useful information about individual children. Relationships within the group (in the case of a sociogram) may change from day to day. |
| **Standardised tests** | The EYFS Profile is a formal assessment carried out on every child at the end of the reception year. During the school years, standardised tests are used to assess children's skills in literacy, mathematics or cognitive development.<br>*Advantages*: These are closed methods of recording information which are not subject to observer bias. |

| Technique | Description and advantages and limitations |
|---|---|
| | *Limitations*: Children are being assessed on a particular occasion and may not perform as well as on another day. Some children may receive private coaching that will result in better performance. |
| **Information from parents, carers and colleagues** | Parents and carers know their child best and can provide information about their child or young person's favourite activities, how they play when at home etc.<br>*Advantages*: Parents and carers may be able to explain certain preferences and behaviour, which will help practitioners to gain a more rounded picture of the child, and assist their planning.<br>*Limitations*: Parents and colleagues may show bias. |

**Table 6.1** Techniques for observing and assessing children

Observation, assessment and planning are in a continuous cycle. Children and young people are regularly observed by practitioners, and those observations are used to assess children's development and learning and to inform planning.

Some practitioners collect a great deal of information about children and young people, through observations, photographs and collecting drawings. But the value of their work is limited if they just collect information and do not put it to any use. Equally, other practitioners plan activities for children and young people without any thought to what they have observed the children and young people doing. They simply pluck ideas from the air – 'Let's do play dough with glitter on Wednesday; we have not done that for a while.' This makes it unlikely that the children or young people will be able to build on their learning over time.

**Planning**
**What next?**
Experiences and opportunities, learning environment, resources, routines, practitioner's role.

**The child**

**Start Here**
**Observation**
Look, listen and note.
**Describing**

**Assessment**
Analysing observations and **deciding** what they tell us about children.

KEEP: Key Elements of Effective Practice

**Figure 6.1** Observation, assessment and planning are a continuous cycle of activity in the early years

**✓ Progress check**

**Assessing children's development across the EYFS**

- Use a single, long observation to tell you about a child's all-round development in the six areas set out in the EYFS.
- Work as a team to find out whether there are some areas of development and learning that you do not observe often, and think about how you will address this problem.
- Spend time talking to parents, children and colleagues about your observations, so that you gain other perspectives.

## Research Activity

This activity will help you to practise using observation and assessment to:

- evaluate the quality of the provision, and consider how well it meets the EYFS commitments

- a child's starting points in an early years setting

- consider what you might plan to do next, in order to support the child and young person's development and wellbeing.

Before you start, have a copy of the EYFS at hand or go to this website: www.nationalstrategies.standards.dcsf.gov.uk/earlyyears

First, carefully read the case study on Tyrone.

## Case Study  Tyrone

Tyrone is six months old, and it is his third day during his settling-in period at nursery. His mother carries him into the nursery and they are both greeted by their key person, Debbie. Tyrone's mother sits down next to Debbie and then places Tyrone on her lap. Debbie starts to sing a song that Tyrone had enjoyed the day before in nursery and he smiles briefly. Tyrone explores the Treasure Basket that is in front of them briefly, putting a few different objects in his mouth, but he is not really involved in the Treasure Basket and keeps looking at his mother.

Tyrone's mother says goodbye to him and agrees with Debbie that she will leave him for ten minutes. She says that Tyrone may be hungry, and that she has left some baby rice in his bag. Tyrone starts to cry as his mother is leaving and he reaches towards her, so Debbie has to hold him on her lap. She starts singing again, and this soothes Tyrone a little bit, but he is not happy. A few minutes later he starts to explore another item in the Treasure Basket, but his main focus is on the door. Debbie continues to sing and Tyrone moves a little in rhythm with the song. Then he starts to cry again. Debbie soothes him and, wondering if he is hungry, gets out some baby rice. Tyrone angrily rejects the baby rice and pushes the spoon away. When his mother comes back a few minutes later, Tyrone is still crying. She cuddles him, and when she offers him some rice he eats it hungrily.

(Grenier and Elfer, 2009)

Under the EYFS *Positive Relationships* heading, the *Key Person* section states that:

- A key person helps the baby or child to become familiar with the setting and to feel confident and safe within it.

- A key person develops a genuine bond with children and offers a settled, close relationship.

- When children feel happy and secure in this way, they are confident to explore and to try out new things.

- Even when children are older and can hold special people in mind for longer, there is still a need for them to have a key person to depend on in the setting, such as their teacher or a teaching assistant.

1. How well do you think that this setting is working towards meeting the EYFS commitment to positive relationships?

2. What next steps would you take, if you were Debbie, to continue to meet this commitment?

We can also use observations to assess children's development, learning and wellbeing. These assessments help us to think about how we might work with parents and our colleagues to provide further support for children in order to meet their needs, and build on children's development and learning.

Look at the *Personal, Social and Emotional Development* section in *Development Matters*, which is part of the EYFS. Carefully read the *Birth to 11 months* sections.

1. What evidence can you find to show that Tyrone's development is securely in this band? For example, do you think the observation shows that he can 'Gain physical, psychological and emotional comfort from "snuggling in"'?

2. Now read the 'Look, listen and note' column. What might you be looking out for next, as you observe Tyrone? For example, one suggestion is to look for 'How young babies respond to attention, such as making eye contact or vocalising'. Do you think this would be an effective focus for future observations of Tyrone?

3. Read the 'Effective practice' column. Does this give you some useful ideas of what you might do next, if you were Tyrone's key person? For example, the guidance suggests that you should 'talk to a young baby when you cannot give them your direct attention, so that they are aware of your interest and your presence nearby'. Do you think that this would help Tyrone?

4. Finally, read the 'Planning and Resourcing' column. What might you plan to do next, in discussion with Tyrone's family and your colleagues? For example, the guidance suggests that you should 'Have special toys for babies to hold while you are preparing their food, or gathering materials for a nappy change'. Is this something you might plan to do?

5. Now turn to other sections of *Development Matters*. What does this observation tell you about different areas of Tyrone's development, such as communication or physical development?

This shows how just a few useful quality observations can inform you about a child's starting points. Quality observations help you to evaluate your practice and think of next steps for the child. Perhaps most importantly, observations like this help you to get to know a child, and give a focus for discussions with the child's parents.

## In Practice

### Develop your skills in observation and assessment

The following points will help you to develop your skills of observation, both as you start out on your work with children, and as you develop into an experienced practitioner.

- **Plan ahead**: think about when the majority of the children are likely to be settled enough in what they are doing, so that you can start your observation.

- **Think about what exactly you need information about**: if you are observing a baby's feeding routine and the baby's responses, you will need to know exactly how much milk the baby has, how the baby likes to be held, what interaction soothes the baby and makes the experience enjoyable, and what happens at the end of the feed. Equally, if you have pages of observations of a child's early writing and lots of examples, then you will need to plan to gather information about an area you know less about.

- **Choose your approach with care**: if you are building up a profile of a child, you might plan to observe the child systematically over a number of days, choosing different times and places. You can gather information about the start of the day, different types of play inside and out, mealtimes, settling to sleep or resting, etc. If your focus is assessment for learning, then you need to find times when the child is involved in something worthwhile, so that you will have plenty of material to think about. An observation of a child drifting from one table to the next and looking bored will tell you little about the child's development and learning; it might be better to help the child there and then.

- **Respond quickly on the spur of the moment**: life with young children is unpredictable, which is what makes it so interesting. You may be busy with a hundred

## In Practice (cont.)

different things but notice out of the corner of your eye that William has gone to the easel and is doing a painting for the first time; or you might be cooking with three children and need to concentrate totally on helping them with the recipe, but also be noticing lots of things about what they can do. These are times to write a quick note on a Post-it when you get a moment, or at the end of the session, to add to children's records. Just state very briefly what you saw which was important, and always include the date.

❑ **Try to observe as accurately as possible**: focus on what you see and hear, and try to note everything down with as much detail as possible.

❑ **Take photos or collect examples where possible**: subject to the policies of your setting, a series of photos of a child painting will really bring an observation to life. Photocopy a child's early attempts at writing his name, as well as observing how he did this.

❑ **Share your thoughts with others**: ask the child or young person to talk to you about what you observed, share the observation with a colleague, and talk to the child or young person's parents. You will deepen your understanding by doing this.

# Promoting the development of children or young people

## Implementing the development plan

Many plans are drawn up in consultation with colleagues, and they can be plans for individual children or focused more broadly on a whole group or class of children or young people. You need to ensure that you prepare for the implementation; for example, by:

- organising a time slot
- providing equipment and resources
- arranging for others to help if necessary.

## Roles and responsibilities

Your role and responsibilities in implementing the plan should be clearly defined. You can still be flexible in making minor changes to the plan as you go along, but if for example your role is defined as promoting physical activity in the outdoor play area for a specific timed session, then you must implement the plan according to your agreed role.

## Development is holistic and interconnected

If we focus solely on children and young people's needs, we are in danger of using a **deficit model** of working with children. A deficit model focuses on 'negative' assessments of children and young people's development and wellbeing, rather than on their abilities, interests and preferences. We need to observe children to find out what they can already do and, most importantly, what they enjoy doing. This should then be incorporated into the plan.

## Evaluating and revising the development plan

The development plan should be evaluated by considering whether the targets or aims were fully met or only partially met. You should also evaluate it in terms of how enjoyable it was for the child/children or young person/people. Having evaluated the plan, you then need to consider if it could be improved; it is important to let children and young people have a role in reviewing the plan and in suggesting possible changes.

### Key term

**Evaluate** – Review evidence from different perspectives and come to a valid conclusion or reasoned judgement.

## Activity

### Developing a plan

Most of this Unit will be assessed in the work environment. One of the assessment tasks is to show that you can develop a plan to meet the developmental needs of a child or young person. The following guidelines will help you to develop a plan. Use the information in this chapter, particularly the section 'In practice: Develop your skills in observation and assessment', to do the following:

1 Having used different observational techniques, make an assessment of a child or young person's developmental needs. Remember to practise confidentiality and anti-bias practice.

2 Encourage the child or young person to take responsibility for his own development plan. Even young children can help in planning activities by suggesting things they enjoy doing. Young people may set their own targets and also suggest how they plan to achieve them.

3 Involve parents or carers in the assessment of their children.

4 Devise a structure for the plan (your setting may use a regular format for plans). Include the following details:

- the date and the child or young person's name
- the aim and purpose
- the period of time involved – or timescale
- the activities suggested to meet the child's needs, including a list of resources
- the targets or goals to use in order to measure the success of the plan
- the name of the person/s responsible for implementing the plan
- the date for review of the plan.

 **Progress check**

### Reviewing the plan

- Are you meeting your aims?
- Is the child or young person's development being supported by the activities?
- Is the child or young person enjoying the activities?
- Are there any difficulties in implementing the plan?
- Are there any changes you could make to improve the plan?

## The importance of a person-centred and inclusive approach

A child-centred organisation focuses its practice on improving outcomes for children and young people. It also works with others to promote and contribute to better outcomes for all children and their families. Child-centred practice involves more than focusing on the rights and responsibilities of the child or young person. To reflect a genuinely child-centred approach, practitioners should:

- place observation, planning and assessment at the heart of their practice
- acknowledge and value the child or young person's voice in the planning process where possible.

Every child and young person needs to be *included* and to have full access to the curriculum, regardless of his or her ethnic background, culture, language, gender or economic background. No child should be held back in their learning because of restricted access to learning opportunities. Some children with complex needs will be assessed using additional tools, but the EYFS aims to be inclusive. Inclusivity means that the welfare, learning and all-round development of children with different backgrounds and levels of ability, including those with special educational needs and disabilities, should be of concern to early years practitioners.

## Key term

**Child-centred practice** – Where the needs, views, interests and concerns of the child or young person influence all decisions about their care, learning and development.

## Listening and communicating in ways that encourage children and young people to feel valued

We need to listen carefully to children or young people and show interest. This will help them to feel valued and appreciated, and to communicate well with you and with others. You can read more about the importance of effective communication in encouraging children to feel valued in Chapter 9 (Unit CYP Core 3.5).

## Encouraging children and young people's active participation in decisions affecting their lives

It is important to recognise that young people have a right to participate in the key decisions that affect their lives. Article 12 of the United Nations Convention on the Rights of the Child states that children and young people should have the opportunity to express their views on matters that concern them, and to have those views taken into account when decisions are made. It is good practice to share your observations with the child, taking account of their age and development. With very young children, you may want to look at photos together and consider the child's responses (smiles, frowns, lack of interest, etc.). Many children from the age of three upwards will be able to talk to you for a time.

Using feedback from young children, you can consider their personal choices and preferences when deciding on the provision of activities. Older children and young people can be encouraged to express their opinions and feelings about their learning activities, the targets set for them and how to achieve these. Recent research into consultation with pupils found that children's learning experiences could be improved if tasks were more closely aligned with the social worlds in which they lived, both inside and outside the setting. Participants said that they found

## Activity

### A child-centred approach

1. Observe a child over a period of a week or longer, and then record:

   a) the child's interests

   b) whether he or she is alone or in a group when following his or her own interests.

2. Consider the adult role and the resources required to support the child's learning and development.

   - What would be your next step in planning to support the child's development?
   - How would you evaluate the effectiveness of your plan?

it helpful when teachers used materials, objects and images with which they were already familiar. See also Chapter 11 (Unit CYP Core 3.7) for more information on involving children and young people in decision-making.

Article 12 of The United Nations Convention on the Rights of the Child says that children have a right to express an opinion. Their opinion should be taken into account, if any matter or procedure affects them.

 **Progress check**

**Active participation**

- Plan the provision of play or leisure so that it meets the child or young person's individual needs.
- Encourage children and young people to make choices and to set their own priorities.
- Observe and take account of individual and group needs and interests when planning the next steps.
- Involve children and young people in selecting, organising and using resources.

 **In Practice**

**Share your observations with children and young people**

- ❏ Show a child or young person some photos you have taken, and talk together about them. Try to discover the child or young person's point of view. What does the child or young person think he or she was learning to do?

- ❏ Tell a child or young person about what you have observed and what you think, and ask for his or her comments. For example: 'I have noticed you spending lots of time with the blocks. What do you like about playing with them?'

- ❏ Ask a child or young person what they would like to do next, or make suggestions. For example: 'I know you really like playing with the trains. Shall we go to the station one day and see some real trains?'

# The provision of environments and services that promote development

Children or young people need adults to provide a safe and predictable environment, and a warm, affectionate atmosphere. Children and young people learn only if adults are sensitive to their needs and interests, provide stimulating things to experience, and encourage them to have a go at things, explore and be independent.

## The features of an environment that promotes the development of children and young people

The environment or service should provide holistic care and education, by addressing the range of children's developmental needs – that is, their physical needs, intellectual and language needs, and emotional and social needs. In order for children and young people to develop holistically, the environment or service should have the following features:

- **Be stimulating and attractive**: children and young people need broad and varied experiences that enable them to explore and investigate.
- **Be well-planned and organised**: the setting should take account of each child and young person's individual needs and provide for them appropriately.
- **Be personalised and inclusive**: learning should be personalised through building on individual children's interests, skills and strengths. For inclusion to be successful, the child, parents/carers and family must be at the centre of the processes, practices and decision-making.
- **Encourage and practise participation**: children and young people should be encouraged to review their own learning strategies, achievements and future learning needs.
- **Meet regulatory requirements and follow high quality policies**: all child care and education

settings are required to comply with government legislation, such as health and safety legislation and the statutory frameworks, such as the EYFS. Each setting establishes policies and procedures to ensure that the requirements are met. These policies have to be regularly reviewed and evaluated.

- **Be varied**: there should be a wide range of activities that encourage experimentation and problem-solving. Activities should be regularly reviewed to maintain children's interest.
- **Meet individual and group needs**: the setting should provide appropriate levels of assistance for individual children and young people, while ensuring that the needs of the whole group are also met.
- **Provide appropriate risk and challenge**: children and young people must be provided with opportunities or challenges for them to be active, to take risks, to make mistakes and to learn from these.
- **Involve parents and carers where appropriate**: practitioners should develop positive relationships with parents and carers in order to work effectively with them and their children.

# Organising your own work environment to promote development

When organising environments to meet children and young people's needs, adults need to focus on the value of talk, play, paying attention, interacting and spending meaningful time with children and young people. For example loose and flexible plans allow adults to choose the moment that is right for the child, either to introduce something new, or to step back and not invade the child's play.

## Personal and external factors

The way in which a work environment is organised will always be affected by the preferences, philosophy and experiences of the adults working within it. Adults who are sensitive and attentive can help to create play environments that encourage and support children, and enhance their play. External

factors such as the location, the building and the services offered, will also affect the working environment. Settings which share premises with other organisations need to develop flexible ways of planning the use of play areas.

## Providing specific activities

Planning flexibly for children and young people also involves understanding the importance of continuity and familiarity to children and the importance of the day-to-day happenings in their setting. Children and young people like to return to and revisit things that were important to them that morning, the day before, or the previous week. Specific activities are important, such as visiting children in their homes as part of a 'settling-in' policy or providing opportunities for parents to meet informally.

## Providing services

All settings provide a service to children or young people. Some (such as Children's Centres) provide further support, for example, outreach services, home visiting and family support services.

## Measuring outcomes

Outcomes relating to children and young people may be child-specific, such as the improved learning attainments of a particular child; or they may be more general, such as reducing rates of teenage pregnancy across a defined population. Outcomes are measured using a range of methods, including parent questionnaires and formal assessment frameworks.

## Communicating effectively, showing empathy and understanding

All settings should provide an environment that promotes effective communication. For more information, see Chapter 1 (Unit SHC 31).

## Supporting participation

Practitioners should find ways to seek children's opinions and to involve them in their learning. For example:

- brainstorm with small groups around topic themes and ask the children to suggest stories and activities
- ask children to suggest resources for a new, imaginative play area
- ask children to think about what they would like and intend to do that day, the following day or week.

## Involving parents and carers

Parents not only benefit from being involved in their child's care and education, they also have a right to feel included. One way of ensuring this is to consistently share important information with parents on a daily basis, where possible.

## Supporting children and young people's rights

Planning needs to be informed by the child or young person's interests, needs, capabilities and preferences. There are many factors which affect children and young people – for example, the local environment, their opportunities for play and social interaction, the impact of traffic and noise pollution on their lives, the quality of the streets and housing for children. On each of these issues, children and young people will have a view and a valid contribution to make.

## Adult-led practice

There will always be aspects of children and young people's care and education that require practitioners to take the lead. This is called adult-led practice. In early years settings, practitioners lead activities which encourage children and young people to use language, practise skills and develop thinking. Adult-led and adult-intensive activities may include the following:

- story and song times
- activities such as cooking with small groups
- trips into the local community
- a new game
- shared reading and writing
- scientific investigations
- new, imaginative play settings.

# How working practices can impact on development

Children and young people need the sort of environment which is most likely to promote effective and confident child development, where they can experience an environment of mutual respect and trust and open communication. Where large numbers of children and young people are being cared for together, it is even more important to be aware of the influence of the environment on children and young people's wellbeing and sense of self.

 **In Practice**

### Involving parents and carers

Practitioners could do the following:

❏ Use informal (verbal) exchanges of information as parents or carers drop off and collect their children.

❏ Use more formal exchanges of information, such as baby care sheets, parent held records, documented observations of the child or young person during the day and children and young people's profiles.

❏ Provide displays of children and young people's work.

❏ Have digital photographs of the day's events on display where parents can choose whether or not to look at them.

❏ Provide video footage, where parents agree, for parents to take home with them of their child that day.

❏ Provide opportunities for parents to spend time in the setting and opportunities for support and discussion with parents within the home.

(This learning outcome is linked to Chapter 10, Unit CYP Core 3.6 and Chapter 11, Unit CYP Core 3.7).

## How your own working practice can affect development

It is important to develop the skills of being a reflective practitioner. By reflecting on your own practice, you can evaluate the contribution you have made to the support of children and young people's development, and you can seek ways to improve your practice.

### Reflective practice: Supporting children and young people's development

Reflect on:

- the ways in which you communicate with children and young people
- the variety of activities you provide for children and young people – both indoors and outdoors.

Think about these aspects of your work in relation to supporting children and young people's developmental needs. For example:

1. Do you vary your method of communication to account for the individual child's needs and stage of development?
2. Do you provide a wide range of activities which are designed to promote particular skills?
3. Do you plan activities to promote development for individual children?

After considering these questions, can you think of ways in which you could improve your practice?

## How institutions, agencies and services can affect development

A multi-agency approach is the best way of ensuring that all the child or young person's developmental needs are met. Multi-agency working is covered in depth in Chapter 10 (Unit CYP Core 3.6).

# Supporting children and young people's positive behaviour

Behaviour refers to the way we act, speak and treat other people and our environment. Children and young people who develop well socially and emotionally at an early age are more likely to make friends, to settle well into school and to understand how to behave appropriately in different situations. They have strong self-esteem and a sense of self-worth, but also have a feeling of empathy for others. They understand what the boundaries are, and why they are necessary. A child with lower social and emotional development may be at risk of poor relationships with peers and unwanted behaviour. In turn, behaviour has a significant impact on current and later success for children and young people, in terms of their social skill development, education and employment.

## Encouraging positive behaviour

### Needs, feelings and behaviour

Children and young people can present difficult behaviour for many reasons, some of which are explored below.

### Feeling insecure

If a child has experienced early neglect at home for example, he or she might not feel confident that anyone is thinking about him or her in particular, or will respond to his or her needs. The child may feel that the only way to get attention, or to get what he or she needs, is to demand it or fight for it.

### Feeling unsure

If there are different rules depending on whether a child is at home, with grandparents or at nursery, the child may genuinely be unsure of what is expected of him or her.

### Lack of appropriate care in the early years setting or school

Examples of this include young school children being sent into the playground for long lunch periods, without any familiar staff being available. While some children will respond by becoming sad or withdrawn, others may become rather wild and defiant.

## Lack of appropriate stimulation and educational experiences

Boredom leads to misbehaviour. This can occur because there is not enough to do, the adults themselves seem rather bored, or when activities are too difficult for some of the children to access or enjoy (presenting fiddly puzzles to toddlers will often result in frustration and tantrums). Additionally, unsuitable expectations are sometimes made of young children, such as to sit quietly through long school assemblies or to line up and wait for long periods of time. Lining up and waiting often lead to pushing and shoving, and it is only to be expected that a young child who cannot see or really understand an assembly or a long story session will start to fidget and talk.

Young children feel things very intensely, and they find it much more difficult to regulate their emotions than adults. When a young child wants something, such as a particular toy, he or she may impulsively reach or grab for it, or even hit or hurt another child. As adults, we all know the feeling of really wanting something and finding it hard to wait, but we have experience of how to manage such feelings, so that we can wait in the expectation that we will get a turn, or do something else instead. Children often act much more impulsively on their feelings than adults.

Similarly, children can feel losses during their day very intensely, like the departure of their mother or father at the start of the day. Some children become sad or withdrawn, but others may feel angry at being left, and may express this through angry behaviour. Psychodynamic theorists (for example, Freud) argue that if a child cannot tolerate a feeling, he or she will try to get rid of it by passing it on to someone else. The child who cannot bear feeling sad might hit another child to make him or her sad, so moving the sad feeling away from him or herself and on to another person.

Finally, children often get tired during the day, and they may also get very hungry. Tiredness and hunger

**Figure 6.2** Sometimes young children want to go quickly or make big, energetic movements, which can be misunderstood as difficult or over-boisterous behaviour; this boy is being given enough space to learn how to ride a bike, so that his energy and speed are positive, not problematic

can lead to difficult behaviour. It is very useful to look for patterns in a child's difficult behaviour. If difficulties largely occur at the same time, in the same area or with the same children, you may be able to plan ahead and avoid those 'triggers' by guiding the child elsewhere, to play with other children, or by ensuring that the child has a rest or something to eat.

## Helping children and young people to recognise their emotions

Child development theory emphasises how children use **social referencing** to make sense of situations. In other words, children look back to see adults' expressions and pay close attention to their tone of voice and what they say. In practice, this can be used to help children understand situations and their emotions – for example, a smile and approval for a child as he or she plays positively with others

**In Practice**

## Factors influencing behaviour

If the behaviour of a particular child or young person in your setting is difficult, consider the following factors:

❏ Does the child or young person have a strong relationship with a key person?

❏ Are there plenty of stimulating things to do which match the child or young person's interests?

❏ Are routines and demands appropriate for the child or young person's development and age?

❏ Might the child feel tired or hungry?

❏ Have there been any recent changes in the child or young person's family life that may have unsettled him or her?

You could share your thoughts with other members of staff in your setting, and discuss how you might improve the situation for the child or young person.

It is important that you do everything you can to establish a positive relationship with the child or young person's parents or carers. If a child or young person has similar difficulties at home, and behaviour remains difficult over time in the early years setting or school, you may decide that this is a special educational need (SEN), and seek help and support from the special educational needs coordinator (SENCO). (For more information on behavioural, emotional and social difficulties (BESD) refer to Chapter 10, Unit CYP Core 3.6.)

## Case Study    Learning to share

An experienced early years practitioner sees a child snatch a toy train from another child, who starts to cry. She goes over to the children calmly and says, 'I can see you really wanted that train, Harry. But Iqbal really wants it too.' After a moment, she asks Harry, 'Can you see that Iqbal is sad?' Harry nods, so she asks, 'What could we do to make him feel better?' Harry is not sure and does not answer. So she asks Iqbal, who points at the train. After a minute or so, Harry hands the train to Iqbal. The practitioner says, 'I wonder what you could do next time when you really want something like the train.' Harry does not reply, so she suggests, 'Maybe you could say, "Can I have a turn next?" Or perhaps you could look for another train?' Then she checks to see if Iqbal is all right, and suggests, 'Next time, if someone

grabs something from you, you could say, "No, it is mine," or "Stop it. I do not like that." Shall we try saying that together?'

Consider the following questions:

1 How has the practitioner helped the children to acknowledge their feelings?

2 How has the practitioner given the children ideas to manage their behaviour in the group?

3 This approach would take a lot longer than just telling Harry off and making him give the train back to Iqbal. Do you think that the extra time and attention is worthwhile?

4 What might be the longer-term benefits of dealing with the incident in this way?

reinforces the child's inner sense of enjoyment. Where children and young people are in conflict, adults might intervene sharply to say 'No,' or to reprimand with terms like 'naughty' and 'nasty'.

These responses can lead children and young people to associate those situations with anger and criticism, and a cycle of difficult behaviour can arise. An alternative approach is to try to help the children to understand what has happened and what they might be feeling. This means approaching an incident of inappropriate behaviour rather like a problem to be solved together.

## Different approaches to supporting positive behaviour

### Containment

From psychodynamic theory comes the notion of **containment**, developed by Wilfred Bion (1897–1979). In Bion's model, a baby has an experience of frustration, such as hunger. If an adult (such as the baby's mother) can receive this unprocessed emotion from the child and think about it, by interpreting the cry as meaning hunger, then the understanding is 'given back' to the baby. Bion conceptualised this by saying that the baby projects the sensation or feeling into the mother. The mother processes this through what Bion calls her **reverie**, and returns the projection in a way that the baby can manage. A parent picking up a distressed infant and helping the infant to cope with the feeling by singing, feeding, repositioning or talking to the baby is an example of containment. A parent becoming angry or distressed with a baby's communication (crying, 'whingeing', seeking attention, and so on) is probably failing to contain the baby.

The regular experience of containment helps the baby to develop the capacity to think, and to turn the raw experience of discomfort into a thought: 'I am hungry'. On the other hand, if the baby's raw experience is rejected (the adult is cross at the constant crying and shouts angrily at the baby), the baby is simply given back the raw emotion and does not develop the structures for thinking. According to

this theory, if the baby experiences enough containment, he or she becomes increasingly able to manage frustration by thinking. Those thoughts might include being confident that he or she will be fed soon, or being able to communicate hunger. If the baby constantly experiences the raw emotion being returned, thinking will not develop and the baby will be terrified by powerful emotion.

The baby's needs can never be fully met. There will always be times when it is not possible for the adult to offer the function of containment. If the frequency or intensity of these times is not overwhelming, the child manages through **symbolisation** – representing things in play or in language, for example. So a toddler who is angry about parting from his or her mother at nursery might direct this angry energy into very focused play in the home corner, and not wish anyone to disturb or interrupt him or her.

The pattern of this development is formed in the baby's early experiences, and remains as a pattern through childhood and into adult life. Bion's theory

### Case Study — Containment

Jaydeen is three years old. It is five o'clock in the afternoon on a hot day. Her key person, Tara, sees out of the corner of her eye that Jaydeen is struggling to put the marble run together. After a few minutes, Jaydeen flings a piece to the floor in frustration and shouts so loudly that the child playing next to her starts to cry. Tara comes over and sits close to Jaydeen, comforting the child who is crying. Then she says to Jaydeen, 'I think you are probably fed up because you are hot and tired. Shall we all sit together and have a cuddle and a story?' Jaydeen puts her thumb into her mouth and snuggles up to Tara.

Consider these questions:

1 How does Tara provide a containing function for Jaydeen's emotions?

2 How might this change things for Jaydeen?

## Key terms

**Containment and reverie** – These terms refer to an adult's state of mind in relation to a baby or young child. Through **containment**, the adult can receive the baby's communications of anxiety, pain, distress or pleasure. This happens on an unconscious level: the adult cannot mean or plan to do this, but he or she can try to be open to the baby's emotional state by being close to the baby and not distracted by other tasks or thoughts.

Through **reverie**, the adult can process the baby's communications and hand them back to the baby, either sharing the pleasure in a loving and intimate interaction, or handing back distressing thoughts in a way that the baby can manage. This model was developed by the psychoanalyst Wilfred Bion.

**Social referencing** – When children check how adults respond to a situation as part of their own emotional response, this is called social referencing. An example would be a baby who sees something on the grass in a park and looks back at her mother before deciding whether to crawl confidently forward to grab it, or to stay away and watch warily.

is not therefore only about very young babies; you can use it when thinking about older children, too. An example of how baby-like feelings around feeding might be understood to affect us in adult life, is that an adult in a difficult meeting might say, 'I'm fed up with all this change. If they carry on like this, we will all crack up.' Here, you can see how baby-like, intense experiences around hunger and the fear of falling apart can remain with us.

## The difference between being caring and being excessively permissive

In the examples provided by the case studies in this chapter so far, practitioners have supported children and young people by being aware of their emotional state and helping them to understand their feelings and manage them. Understanding children's emotional states is not the same as permitting them to act out their emotions however they wish to. Young children have powerful urges. Their loving and forgiving ways can be accompanied by intense feelings of rivalry, aggression and hatred. Children often need adults to help them, by standing up against these intense feelings. Looking back to the case study on containment: if Jaydeen keeps shouting

at children, for example, it will be important for the adults to make very clear that this is not allowed, and that she must find some other way of expressing her anger. Adults should not permit children to be aggressive through a misplaced belief that they are being caring. The adult is required to support the child's sociable urge, the desire to relate to others, to belong and to be liked.

 Progress check

### The importance of feelings

- Understand how children's feelings might influence their behaviour.
- Use some strategies to help children become more aware of how they are feeling.
- Work within the team to create an atmosphere that shows understanding towards children's feelings, but also puts some limits on how they can express those feelings.

## Behaviour modification: positive reinforcement

This theory can be applied to the management of children and young people's behaviour. Behaviour is understood as a response to positive reinforcements – for example, if a child has a tantrum and is given sweets to help him or her to calm down, the sweets become a positive reinforcement, so the child may start to throw tantrums in order to get sweets. Following the approach of learning theory, if the parents stop giving the sweets, the learned behaviour will no longer be reinforced and will wither away. This approach is often called **behaviour modification**, and it is used a great deal in early years settings and schools. It is underpinned by the following theories:

- Most behaviour – appropriate or inappropriate – is learned.
- If behaviour is reinforced when it occurs, it will increase.
- If behaviour is ignored or punished when it occurs, it will decrease.
- Behaviour can therefore be changed, if consequences are always applied *immediately*.

Rewards will increase the desired behaviour, and negative consequences (such as time out, ignoring) will decrease the undesirable behaviour.

- The timing of the reinforcements is crucial, especially for young children: it has to be immediate, otherwise the reward or punishment may not be associated with the behaviour.

(Adapted from Sylva and Lundt (1982), page 198)

## Advantages of this approach

This approach to managing behaviour can work well in certain circumstances. Parents and carers often use it successfully to manage difficult issues such as going to bed or toileting, using star charts linked to rewards ('if you go to bed on time, you get a star; if you get five stars, you will get a reward, like a small toy'). In an early years setting or school, it may be the only effective strategy if a child's behaviour is very difficult to manage; for example, aggressive behaviour could lead consistently to spending time out (sitting out and not being able to play for a short period of time, like one minute), while cooperative behaviour (such as managing to play alongside another child for two minutes) could be consistently rewarded with praise, and special time on a favoured activity.

## Drawbacks of this approach

Children and young people might not be able to generalise. A child might be punished consistently for drawing on books at home until this behaviour dies away, but then goes to his or her grandparents' house and draws on the walls. The child has stopped the *specific* behaviour, but does not understand the *general* requirement to be careful and avoid doing damage. Another drawback is that children and young people might start doing things for rewards, which will affect their curiosity and general motivation. Marion Dowling gives the following example:

'In one study in a nursery school, a group of children were provided with drawing materials and told that they would receive a prize for drawing which, in due course, they did. Another group were given the same materials but with no mention of prizes. Some time after, drawing was provided as one of a range of optional activities . . . significantly, the children who chose to spend the least time on drawing were those who had been previously rewarded.'

Another drawback or limitation to this approach is that it takes no account of the child or young person's inner world. A child or young person's behaviour may be difficult because of previous experiences, such as experiencing the trauma of losing a parent in early childhood. Behaviour modification would only seek to control the child or young person's behaviour, rather than seeking to help the child or young person to grieve and find ways of expressing his or her feelings of sadness and anger.

### Key terms

**Behaviourism** – Behaviourism is an approach to understanding child development which proposes that everything a child does should be observed and thought of as a behaviour. Behaviourists would argue that this is the only objective, scientific way to approach child or young person development, without having to imagine what a child is thinking or feeling inside.

**Behaviour modification** – An approach to working with children and young people who have BESD which draws on the theory of behaviourism. In order to change the child or young person's behaviour, the adult focuses on what is observable and tries to change it. For example, if a child frequently becomes disruptive at group time, the adult would observe the behaviours around this time closely. This might lead to a plan of action around seating the child in a particular place, because it is noticed that the child finds being touched, or feeling squashed, stressful. The adult leading the group would aim to praise the child for positive behaviour at the start of the group, continue to reinforce this positive behaviour with regular praise throughout the group, and would try to end the group while the child is still behaving as expected. In this way, the child would begin to associate group time with the reward of praise, and perhaps other rewards too, such as stickers. Considering the root causes of the child's disruptive behaviour and planning a therapeutic intervention would not be part of this approach.

## Therapeutic help

If a child or young person's behaviour is very difficult, other professionals may be called on to offer therapeutic help to them. Some of these professionals are art, music or play therapists and child psychotherapists. In contrast to the behavioural modification approach outlined above, a **therapeutic approach** will generally involve an attempt to find the underlying causes of the child or young person's difficult behaviour. Through play, art, music or talking in a free way, the child or young person can be helped to express his or her feelings. The therapist can help by giving the child or young person a safe space for expression, and by interpreting the child or young person's communications in a way that makes it more possible for the child or young person to live with feelings of anger, loss or unhappiness. As the child is increasingly able to express and find ways of living with difficult emotions, he or she becomes more able to develop and grow throughout childhood, instead of being 'stuck'.

## Research Activity

1. To find out more about therapeutic help, read *Dibs: In Search of Self* by the American play therapist, Virginia Axline (see page 115 for a full reference).

2. Find out more about how therapeutic ideas can be used in mainstream early years settings and schools, by reading *Wally's Stories* by Vivian Gussin Paley (see page 115 for a full reference).

# Methods of supporting positive behaviour

## Least restrictive principle

The least restrictive principle refers to the ethos of the setting and to the adult's response to challenging

## In Practice

### Guidelines for dealing with inappropriate behaviour

1. **Try to remain calm**: it is easier to control a child or young person behaving inappropriately if you are in control of yourself. Listen to both sides of the story when there is conflict, and apologise if you have made a mistake.

2. **Ignore attention-seeking behaviour**: children or young people who desperately want adults to notice them will call out, interrupt, ask questions and frequently push in front of other children or young people to show something they have made or done. It is important to ignore such behaviour as much as possible and to reward them by giving them attention *only* when they have waited appropriately, so that they are encouraged to do so again.

3. **Use a distraction or diversion**: if two children are arguing over a toy, you could distract them by offering an alternative activity: 'Shall we go and play with the blocks instead?' Or you could use a volunteer task as a distraction, such as helping with handing out resources.

4. **The behaviour, not the child**: when you need to talk to a child or young person about their behaviour, it is important for them to feel that it is not personal – that you do not dislike them, only his or her behaviour.

5. **Give them a choice**: explain that they can choose how to behave. For example, you might say: 'Bailey, you now have a choice. You can stop throwing the toys and play nicely with them, or I'm afraid I will have to take them away.' Allow them a few minutes to decide what to do. If he or she refuses to comply, follow through with the sanction by removing the toys.

6. **Firmly state the rule in your setting if a child or young person uses unacceptable language**: this includes swearing and name-calling that often result from children and young people repeating what they have heard. Sometimes they are unaware that it is unacceptable in one setting but not another. In these cases they need to be told firmly not to say those words 'here' – you cannot legislate for language they may use at home or criticise their families. Some children will deliberately use unacceptable language to shock or seek attention. In these cases you should state the rule calmly and firmly.

behaviour. It aims to allow maximum freedom with minimum rules, so that children and young people learn responsibility for their own behaviour. When faced with **challenging behaviour**, you may have to physically intervene to prevent harm to others. This intervention must be in the **least restrictive** way necessary to prevent them from getting hurt, and used only after all other strategies have been exhausted.

## Modelling

Modelling positive behaviour is a useful way of helping children to resolve conflicts. For example, when talking to a pair of children who have been fighting, an adult might say, 'I wonder how Jason could have said he wanted the train, instead of grabbing it?' or 'Serena, I wonder how you could stop Jason grabbing the train, without hitting him?'

## Positive culture

It is important to encourage a culture where children can say how they are feeling. Sometimes it may feel like children, or a particular child, keep coming to you for help, and this may become wearing. But it is important that on every occasion you listen with sympathy and try to help the child. Adults can encourage children to be *assertive*. For example, they can help children to use phrases like 'I want a turn', 'Can I go next?', and 'Can I have a turn when you're finished?' Encourage children to respond to things they do not like, by saying 'No' or 'I do not like that'.

## Looking for reasons for inappropriate behaviour and adapting responses

It helps to try to find out why a child is behaving inappropriately so that we can adapt our response accordingly. For example, if you see that a child is tired and becoming irritable, you could suggest a drink of water and encourage a quiet activity. Children and young people with communication difficulties often become frustrated when trying to express themselves, and this can result in inappropriate behaviour. By supporting a child's need to communicate effectively (for example, by using gesture or signing systems, such as Makaton), adults can often reduce their frustration and so improve their behaviour.

## Individual behaviour planning

If a child or young person frequently displays challenging or inappropriate behaviour, practitioners should observe and monitor the behaviour; perhaps implement a chart to record the child or young person's behaviour patterns, when it occurs and the circumstances. It is also important to monitor how both adults and children respond to the behaviour. This helps to build up a picture of the child or young person's behaviour patterns.

An **individual behaviour management plan** can then be drawn up. As with the individual plans described earlier, the plan should be drawn up with the child or young person's parents and, where possible, also in consultation with the child or young person. When various aspects of problem behaviour need to be addressed, the individual behaviour plan may be divided into **phased stages**. Clearly defined goals or targets are set to an agreed timescale, and a date for review is arranged to assess progress. It is important that everyone involved with the individual child or young person follows the plan and communicates well with the parents and everyone within the staff team.

## De-escalate and diversion

Young children find it difficult to control their emotions, and are not easily able to understand that what they are doing is unacceptable. Practitioners can help to prevent inappropriate behaviour from escalating by providing a distraction or diversion.

## Boundary setting and negotiation

It is important that adults provide **boundaries**: they clearly tell children when their behaviour is not acceptable. Some young children bump into others, grab for equipment first, give others an aggressive look or generally intimidate other children. Other children say things to make others feel left out or foolish – 'You are not coming to my party' or 'Do not play with stupid Eleanor'. Behaviour like this can quickly escalate to more serious forms of bullying like open aggression, which is either **physical** (hitting, pushing) or **verbal** (name-calling). It is important that adults look out for this sort of behaviour and encourage other children to say confidently how it affects them.

**Be consistent**: It is normal for children to push at the boundaries set by adults. It is often tempting to 'overlook' inappropriate behaviour when we are feeling stressed or overworked, but children will better understand how you want them to behave if you always respond in a consistent manner.

## Supporting children and young people to reflect on and manage their own behaviour

In order to help children or young people to learn positive behaviour in a group, one particularly important area to consider is how children or young people can learn to manage the conflicts that will inevitably arise. If children or young people are taught to depend on adults to sort out every dispute, their development will be held back.

## Anti-bullying strategies

The EYFS requires that 'children's behaviour must be managed effectively and in a manner appropriate for their stage of development and particular individual needs'. Schools are also legally required to have policies and procedures in place to identify and prevent bullying. Every early years setting needs to develop a policy around the support of children or young person's behaviour and the prevention of bullying. In any group, there are likely to be instances of bullying, including early years settings and schools.

Supporting children or young people to become assertive and to resolve conflicts can help to minimise bullying. But remember that, in the end, it is the adults' responsibility to uphold acceptable behaviour. Some children and young people may not be able to stop others from being aggressive and domineering, however much they try to be assertive. When inappropriate or bullying behaviour occurs, take firm action when necessary. You may have to

say to a child, 'Pushing like that is not allowed. Do you remember yesterday when Jason said he felt sad when you pushed him? So I am going to have to take you away from the trains for two minutes.' You can help the child by saying clearly which part of their behaviour is not acceptable, while not being negative towards the child personally. This is why you would *not* say, 'You are being naughty'. It is important that you follow this up by settling the child back into the play – 'We can go back to the trains, but I need you to remember that there is no pushing' – and then spend time in that area, helping the children to play together.

## Key term

**Challenging behaviour** – The term 'challenging behaviour' has been used to refer to the unwanted or unacceptable behaviours that may be shown by children or adults (usually, but not always) with a learning disability. Such behaviours include *aggression* (hitting, kicking, biting), *destruction* (ripping clothes, breaking windows, throwing objects), *self-injury* (head banging, self-biting, skin picking), *tantrums* and many other behaviours. Normally, challenging behaviour puts the safety of the individual or others in some jeopardy, or has a significant impact on their quality of life.

## Progress check

### Helping children and young people to develop self-discipline

- By 'tuning in' to children and young people and responding positively and warmly to them, you can help them to become aware of how they are feeling.
- Work with the team to set and maintain clear and agreed boundaries, so that children and young people know what sort of behaviour is acceptable.
- Spend blocks of time with an individual child or young person who is experiencing difficulties with behaviour, to build a close relationship with him or her.
- Help children and young people to negotiate solutions to conflicts and disputes rather than just telling them off, so that in time they can solve problems themselves.
- Helping children to understand cause and effect relationships is important.

# Supporting children and young people who are experiencing transitions

The different types of transitions children experience are discussed in Chapter 5 (Unit CYP Core 3.1), page 86. This learning outcome requires you to understand *how to support children and young people* who are going through transitions.

For the majority of children and young people, the key transitions from infancy to adulthood will take place in a relatively secure home and educational environment, but change may still present difficulties. Children and young people need sensitive support to cope with transitions such as:

- moving to different surroundings
- adapting to being without a close friend or their key person when they leave a setting
- bereavement or adjusting to a close family member being ill.

Parents also need support to cope with change and new situations. Ensuring smooth transitions needs to involve, on an equal basis, the children, young people, parents and carers and all the staff within the setting.

## Ways of supporting children and young people

- **Ensure that there is continuity of experience**: whenever there is a transitional point for a child and family, it is important to look at *what went before* so that we can learn about and tune in to the child, and support them and make as seamless a transition as possible. There should be continuity, not discontinuity, of experience for the child and family. This means that every practitioner working with children in the birth to 19 years' range should know what comes before and what comes after the time the child will spend with them.
- **Ensure that the child or young person is at the centre of the process**: by placing the child or young person at the centre, practitioners can

ensure that the individual's needs and preferences are respected throughout the process.
- **Explain what is happening**: reassure children, young people and those caring for them by explaining what is happening, and by exploring and examining possible actions to deal with new and challenging situations.
- **Discuss what is happening**: identify opportunities to discuss the effects and results of transition.
- **Share information**: make sure that relevant information transfers *ahead* of the child or young person when appropriate, and respect other professionals when sharing information.
- **Be positive**: where appropriate, illustrate the benefits of transition.
- **Access further support**: make effective links with other practitioners should further support be necessary.

## Loss and grief

Children will often become aware for the first time of death and dying when they are in a setting or school. A child or young person's grandparent may die, for example, or another close family member. People say different things when someone dies. For example, they may tell children that the person has:

- gone to heaven
- gone to sleep
- gone away
- turned into earth.

Children can become very confused, and frightened that they will be taken away to this place called heaven, or that if they go to sleep they might not wake up. Children need honest, straightforward explanations of death that make it clear that the person will not come back, and that it is not their fault that the person has died.

## Structured opportunities to explore the effects of transitions

The activities and opportunities used will depend upon the individual, the type of transition, what has gone before and the specific needs of the child or young person.

## Guidelines on helping children and young people to grieve

1  Explain issues – for example, that someone is terminally ill, that parents are divorcing or that a person is going to prison. Children and young people need to be told of the reality of the situation.

2  Make sure that they do not feel responsible for what has happened.

3  Do not exclude them – let them be part of the family. If someone has died, let them go to the funeral or visit the grave and share the sadness.

4  Be especially warm and loving; hug them, be calm and quietly be there for them.

5  Give them reassurance that they are allowed to feel grief. Help them to know that, although these feelings will last for a long time, they are normal. Tell them that the pain will ease over time.

6  Find photographs and evoke memories.

7  Some children and young people are helped by play therapy.

8  Be prepared for them to regress; do not demand too much of the child or young person. When they begin to show an interest in things once more, gently encourage them.

## Case Study — Dealing with loss

Anna is a four-year-old child in your setting. She has missed a few days of nursery; as you are her key person, you phone home to find out if everything is all right. Anna's mum, Doreen, answers the phone and soon breaks down into tears. 'Her great aunt's died. She was old and not very well, but it has still been a shock,' she says. 'I do not want to upset Anna, so I have not told her; it will make her too sad. But she does not seem to want to go anywhere and I cannot get her to nursery.'

With a partner or in a small group, discuss what you would say to Doreen.

## Routines

Daily routines (for example, around mealtimes and bedtimes) can be very useful in helping young children to adapt both physically and emotionally to a daily pattern, which suits both them *and* those caring for them. This is especially helpful during times of transition and change in their lives, such as starting nursery or moving house. If certain parts of the day remain familiar, they can cope better with new experiences.

## Anchor activities

Children and young people need to be with their key person when they part from their parent or carer. They benefit from a familiar and comforting activity, with the adult close to them, talking with them and helping them to make the transition from home into the early childhood setting. Playing on a rocking horse, or with sand or dough are examples of activities which are often used in this way, in the planning of the day.

## Visits

Planning a series of structured visits to the new setting helps to ease the transition. These could be informal visits at first, such as children from the Foundation Stage taking a piece of work to show a Year 1 teacher. Then plans could be developed to allow a small group of children to spend short periods in the Year 1 class, and so on.

The visits should have a clear aim and involve staff from both settings – and parents and carers where appropriate.

## Role-play and drama

Use situations which promote and stimulate a variety of emotions associated with transitions.

## Circle time activities

These need to be focused on listening skills, turn-taking, and understanding other people's points of view. A group of children joining a new class or school would be able to share their feelings by being directed by the teacher: 'What are you excited about joining Class X? What are you nervous about joining Class X?' Children and young people would soon realise that most people are apprehensive about big changes in their lives.

### Reflective practice: Supporting children and young people through transitions

- What methods do you currently use to ease transitions for children and parents?

- Think about one experience of transition from your recent experience: what would have been ideal from the child or young person's point of view, and how far did you achieve it?

- How do you ensure that children and young people's needs and wishes are taken seriously – and how are their decisions incorporated into your practice?

- How do you plan for individual time with children and young people? How often does this not work out? Try to analyse the weaknesses in your plans and how you might manage to fulfil them better.

- How do you communicate with parents about the way in which you are dealing with transitions in the setting?

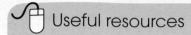

## Useful resources

**Organisations and websites**

**Anna Freud Centre** was established in 1947 by Anna Freud to support the emotional wellbeing of children through direct work with children and their families, research and the development of practice, and training mental health practitioners:
www.annafreud.org

**HighScope** is an American approach to early education and care, with several decades of research into its effectiveness. The website includes books, DVDs and news of training events and conferences in the UK:
www.high-scope.org.uk

**Kate Greenaway Nursery School and Children's Centre** – this website includes news and policies for a centre based in central London:
www.kategreenaway.ik.org

**Kidscape** is a charity established specifically to prevent bullying and child sexual abuse. The website includes resources for parents, children and professionals, and details of campaigns and training events:
www.kidscape.org.uk

**The National Strategies (Early Years)** is the government's programme for developing practice in the early years, including statutory requirements, advice on best practice, and research findings:
www.education.gov.uk, search for early years.

**Books**

Axline, V. (1971) *Dibs, In Search of Self*: *Personality Development in Play Therapy*. Penguin.

Dowling, M. (2010) *Young children's personal, social and emotional development*. 3rd Edition. Sage Publications.

Paley, V.G. (1981) *Wally's Stories*. Harvard University Press.

Sylva, K. and Lunt, I. (1982) *Child Development*: *A First Course*. Blackwell.

# 7 Understand how to safeguard the wellbeing of children and young people: Unit CYP Core 3.3

All settings working with children and young people should establish and maintain a safe environment and deal with circumstances where there are welfare concerns. Through their protection policies and procedures for safeguarding children and young people, settings which work with children and/or young people have an important role in the detection and prevention of abuse and neglect. This includes helping children and young people to protect themselves from abuse, as well as dealing with bullying (both physical and through communication technology) and understanding e-safety.

## Learning outcomes

By the end of this chapter you will:

1. Understand the main legislation, guidelines, policies and procedures for safeguarding children and young people.

2. Understand the importance of working in partnership with other organisations to safeguard children and young people.

3. Understand the importance of ensuring children and young people's safety and protection in the work setting.

4. Understand how to respond to evidence or concerns that a child or young person has been abused or harmed.

5. Understand how to respond to evidence or concerns that a child or young person has been bullied.

6. Understand how to work with children and young people to support their safety and wellbeing.

7. Understand the importance of e-safety for children and young people.

# Legislation, guidelines, policies and procedures for safeguarding children and young people

All practitioners working to safeguard children and young people must understand fully their responsibilities and duties as set out in government legislation, regulations and guidance.

## Current legislation, guidelines and policies

The *United Nations Convention on the Rights of the Child 1989* (UN, 1989) was ratified by the UK on 16 December 1991. It includes children's rights to protection from abuse, the right to express their views and be listened to, and the right to care and services for disabled children or children living away from home. Although different British governments have said that it regards itself bound by the Convention and refers to it in child protection guidance, it has not become part of UK law. There is no single piece of legislation that covers safeguarding children and young people in the UK; different laws and guidelines cover different parts of the UK – England, Wales, Scotland and Northern Ireland (NSPCC, 2010; page 1).

## Safeguarding children in England

*Working Together to Safeguard Children* (2010) applies to those working in education, health and social services as well as the police and the probation service. It is relevant to those working with children and their families in the statutory, independent and voluntary sectors. The document covers the following areas:

- A summary of the nature and impact of child abuse and neglect.
- How to operate best practice in child protection procedures.
- The roles and responsibilities of different agencies and practitioners.
- The role of Local Safeguarding Children Boards (LSCBs).
- The processes to be followed when there are concerns about a child.
- The action to be taken to safeguard and promote the welfare of children experiencing, or at risk of, significant harm.
- The important principles to be followed when working with children and families.
- Training requirements for effective child protection.

It is not necessary for all practitioners to read every part of *Working Together to Safeguard Children* in order to understand the principles and to perform their roles effectively. However, those who work regularly with children and young people and who may be asked to contribute to assessments of children and young people in need should read Chapters 1, 2 (relevant sections, such as schools and further education institutions), 5 and 11; it may also be helpful to read Chapters 6, 8, 9, 10 and 12.

For the full text, see this website: http://publications.dcsf.gov.uk/eOrderingDownload/00305-2010DOM-EN.pdf

*Framework for the Assessment of Children in Need and their Families* (2000) provides a systemic framework to help professionals identify children and young people in need and assess the best approach to help them and their families (see Chapter 14, Promote children's welfare and wellbeing in the early years: Unit EYMP 3 for more information on supporting

early intervention for the benefit of children and families).

*What to do if you're worried a child is being abused* (2003) is a guide for professionals working with children which explains the processes and systems contained in *Working Together to Safeguard Children* and *Framework for Assessment of Children in Need and their Families.*

As a further safeguard to children's welfare, The Protection of Children Act 1999 requires childcare organisations (including any organisation concerned with the supervision of children) not to offer employment involving regular contact with children, either paid or unpaid, to any person listed as unsuitable to work with children on the Department of Health list and the Department for Education and Employment's List 99. The Criminal Records Bureau acts as a central access point for criminal records checks for all those applying to work with children and young people.

The Children Act 2004, sections 1–9, created a Children's Commissioner for England. However, the English Commissioner does not have the remit to promote children's rights, unlike the commissioners for the rest of the UK. As well as creating a Children's Commissioner for England, the Children Act 2004 placed a duty on local authorities to appoint a Director of Children's Services and an elected lead member for Children's Services, who is accountable for the delivery of services. It placed a duty on local authorities and their partners (including the police, health service providers and the youth justice system) to cooperate in promoting the wellbeing of children and young people and to make arrangements to safeguard and promote the welfare of children. It put the new Local Safeguarding Children Boards on a statutory footing (replacing the non-statutory Area Child Protection Committees), and gave them functions of investigation and review (section 14), which they use to review all child deaths in their area as required by the *Working Together to Safeguard Children* statutory guidance.

The Children Act 2004 also revised the legislation on physical punishment by making it an offence to hit a child if it causes mental harm or leaves a lasting mark on the skin (section 58). This repealed the section of the Children and Young Persons Act 1933 which provided parents with the defence of 'reasonable chastisement' (NSPCC, 2010, page 5).

## Safeguarding children in Wales

The Children Act 1989 legislates for England and Wales. The current guidance for Wales is *Safeguarding children: working together under the Children Act 2004* (Welsh Assembly Government, 2006). The Children's Commissioner for Wales Act 2001 created the first Children's Commissioner post in the UK. The principal aim of this position is to safeguard and promote the rights and welfare of children.

In June 2010, the Welsh Assembly Government laid down the Proposed Rights of Children and Young Persons (Wales) Measure, which if passed by the National Assembly for Wales, will embed the principles of the UN Convention on the Rights of the Child into Welsh law (NSPCC, 2010).

## Safeguarding children in Scotland

The Children (Scotland) Act 1995 has similar principles to the law in England and Wales, but has its own guidance: *Protecting children: a shared responsibility: guidance on inter-agency co-operation* (Scottish Office, 1998). Subsequent legislation created a Children's Commissioner for Scotland (Commissioner for Children and Young People (Scotland) Act 2003) to safeguard and promote the rights and welfare of children (NSPCC, 2010).

## Safeguarding children in Northern Ireland

The Children (Northern Ireland) Order 1995 has similar principles and has its own guidance: *Co-operating to safeguard children* (DHSSPS, 2003). In addition, in Northern Ireland it is an offence not to report an arrestable crime to the police, which by definition, includes most crimes against children.

Subsequent legislation created a Children's Commissioner for Northern Ireland (Commissioner

for Children and Young People (NI) Order 2003) to safeguard and promote the rights and welfare of children (NSPCC, 2010).

## Keeping children safe – everyone's responsibility

There is one aspect of work with babies, toddlers and young children that must always come first: the requirement to keep them safe, and to protect them from significant harm. The guidance from the *Every Child Matters* framework reminds us that:

> 'all those who come into contact with children and families in their everyday work, including practitioners who do not have a specific role in relation to safeguarding children, have a duty to safeguard and promote the welfare of children'.

Schools and early years settings are places where children and young people spend a considerable amount of their lives. Early years practitioners are some of the most important adults that young children will come into contact with. As a staff team, they can create an atmosphere and ethos which profoundly affects the child's experience of being cared for, listened to, valued, guided and stimulated. Early years settings and schools therefore play a considerable part in promoting – or, sadly, sometimes neglecting – children's best interests.

- For some children, universal services like early years education and health visiting are not enough to ensure their healthy, safe and happy development. These children might, for periods of time, be vulnerable. They may experience emotional difficulties, fall behind in their development or learning, or suffer the adverse effects of poverty, poor housing or ill health. The Common Assessment Framework (CAF) exists to support children and families with timely help and advice for a brief period.
- There are also **children in need**, who are judged to be unlikely to reach or maintain a satisfactory level of health or development unless they are offered additional services. This group includes children with disabilities.

- Finally, there are children who are subject to an inter-agency **child protection plan**. These children are judged to be at risk of significant harm without the provision of additional services, as well as close and careful monitoring by specialist children's social workers.

All this work with children and families falls under the umbrella term of safeguarding. The Government has defined safeguarding as:

'the process of protecting children from abuse or neglect, preventing impairment of their health and development, and ensuring they are growing up in circumstances consistent with the provision of safe and effective care that enables children to have optimum life chances and enter adulthood successfully.'

You might already be starting to understand how complex this can be. No two people will be able to agree on exactly what is meant by 'optimum life chances' for a child, or having a 'successful adulthood'. Different families, communities, cultures and indeed individuals will disagree about what makes for 'sound development' or 'good health'. In this chapter, we explore some of these complexities, and also explain how judgements might be reached by professionals on the basis of the best possible assessments. Although there is much that is complex and worthy of debate, it is a priority for professionals to take swift action where necessary.

This chapter offers concise, useful and accurate information about safeguarding. If you have any doubts or concerns about a child, however trivial you might think they are, we strongly advise you to speak to the manager or headteacher of the early years setting or school where you are working. Always ask for information and guidance.

### Key term

**Safeguarding** – This term includes all the steps you would take in an early years setting or school to help children and young people to feel safe and secure; protecting children and young people from neglect or abuse; ensuring that children and young people stay safe, healthy and continue to develop well.

## The child's interests are paramount

All the legislation and guidance in recent decades, including the Children Act 2004, make it clear that the child's interests must come first. All professionals must work together to promote the child's welfare before all else. For example, imagine that you found out that a father has slapped his child on the face, leaving a mark. You may have developed a very close relationship with this parent and you may be very sympathetic to the difficulties he is experiencing. You may feel that this incident is a 'one-off', that he genuinely loves and cares for the child, and that he would be devastated if you did not keep this to yourself. All the same, you are required to put the child's interests before your feelings about the family. The actions you might take are discussed later in this chapter (page 130).

All early years settings and schools must nominate a member of staff to oversee safeguarding and child protection. This person must be specifically trained to undertake this role. The whole team (including volunteers and students) must work together to promote children's welfare and keep them safe. The whole team will need regular training and updating, and it is best practice that such training provides staff with time to explore different experiences, attitudes and opinions as steps towards agreeing policy and practice.

## Inquiries and serious case reviews

Regulation 5 of the Local Safeguarding Children Boards Regulations 2006 requires LSCBs to undertake reviews of serious cases. These reviews are known as serious case reviews (SCRs). Chapter 8 of *Working together to safeguard children* (2010) sets out the purposes of and processes for undertaking SCRs.

SCRs are undertaken when a child or young person dies (including death by suspected suicide), and abuse or neglect is known or suspected to be a factor in the death. Additionally, LSCBs may decide to conduct an SCR whenever a child or young person

**Figure 7.1** Helping children to feel safe and secure is the cornerstone of safeguarding

has been seriously harmed in any of the following situations, and the case gives rise to concerns about the way in which local professionals and services worked together to safeguard and promote the welfare of children and young people (including inter-agency and inter-disciplinary working):

- A child or young person sustains a potentially life-threatening injury or serious and permanent impairment of physical and mental health and development through abuse or neglect.
- A child or young person has been seriously harmed as a result of being subjected to sexual abuse.
- A parent or carer has been murdered and a domestic homicide review is being initiated under the Domestic Violence Act 2004.
- A child or young person has been seriously harmed following a violent assault perpetrated by another child, young person or an adult.

The purpose of SCRs is to:

- establish what lessons are to be learned from the case about the way in which local professionals and organisations work individually and together to safeguard and promote the welfare of children and young people

- identify clearly what those lessons are both within and between agencies, how and within what timescales they will be acted on, and what is expected to change as a result
- improve intra- and inter-agency working, and better safeguard and promote the welfare of children and young people.   (DfE, 2010)

## Sharing information to safeguard children and young people

Safeguarding children and young people raises issues of confidentiality that must be clearly understood by everyone within the setting. You must be absolutely clear about the boundaries of your legal and professional role and responsibilities, with regard to the confidentiality of information relating to abuse and neglect. A clear and explicit confidentiality policy that staff, children, young people and parents can all understand should ensure effective practice throughout the setting.

Practitioners have a legal duty of confidence with regard to the personal information they hold about children, young people and their families. Any information you receive about children/young people (and their families) in the course of your work should only be shared within appropriate professional contexts.

All information including child protection records should be kept securely. The law allows the allegation of confidential personal information in order to safeguard a child or children. Usually personal information should only be disclosed to a third party (such as social services) after obtaining the consent of the person to whom the information relates. In some child protection matters, it may not be possible or desirable to obtain such consent. The Data Protection Act 1998 allows an allegation without consent in some circumstances, for example to detect or prevent a crime, to apprehend or prosecute an offender.

The safety and wellbeing of children and young people must always be your first consideration. You cannot offer or guarantee absolute confidentiality, especially if there are concerns that a child or young person is experiencing, or is at risk of, significant harm. You have a responsibility to share relevant information about the protection of children and young people with other professionals, particularly the investigative agencies such as social services and the police. If a child or young person confides in you and requests that the information is kept secret, it is important that you explain to the child in a sensitive manner that you have a responsibility to refer cases of alleged abuse to the appropriate agencies for their sake. Within that context, the child or young person should, however, be assured that the matter will be disclosed only to people who need to know about it.

# Understand the importance of working in partnership with other organisations to safeguard children and young people

It is important to work in partnership with other organisations to safeguard children and young people in order to share relevant information and to take appropriate action to safeguard and protect. A wide range of professionals and organisations share the responsibility to safeguard and protect children and young people.

When working with other organisations to safeguard children and young people, it is important to have a child-centred approach. Any procedures should take the child's feelings and experiences into account and should avoid causing further distress to an already hurt or confused child. However, remember that no matter how concerned you are about a child or young person's welfare, you must always act within the law (Lindon, 2008).

## What is partnership working?

Partnership working is important to ensure that children and young people's welfare is safeguarded regardless of where they are and who is looking after them. For example, where children receive education and care in more than one setting, practitioners must ensure continuity and coherence by sharing relevant

## Activity

- What are your role and responsibilities for reporting information on possible abuse to a senior colleague or external agency?
- How and to whom should you pass on information from a child or young person's personal allegation of abuse? For example, your role and responsibilities for providing information on the allegation to a senior colleague or external agency.
- Find out about your setting's policy and procedures with regard to the confidentiality of information in child protection matters.

information with each other and with parents or carers.

Patterns of attendance should be a key factor in practitioners' planning. Close working between early years practitioners and parents is vital for the identification of children's learning needs and to ensure a quick response to any area of particular difficulty. Parents and families are central to a child's wellbeing, and practitioners should support this important relationship by sharing information and offering support for extending learning in the home. Practitioners will frequently need to work with professionals from other agencies, such as local and community health services, or where children are looked after by the local authority, to identify and meet needs and use their knowledge and advice to provide children's social care with the best learning opportunities and environments for all children (DCSF, 2008; page 10).

Different professionals and agencies should work together to help the child/young person and family early on when there are difficulties. They should not wait until something serious happens before taking action. For example, a health visitor might notice that a mother is getting very stressed by the behaviour of her toddler and is struggling to cope. Early intervention might involve talking to the mother, showing sympathy, and perhaps finding some support for her at the local children's centre or setting up a programme of home visits. This would be much better than waiting to see if the situation becomes worse before doing anything. Although there is still a common view that social workers swoop in to take children away from their families, in reality, the vast majority of social work is about helping different agencies work together to support

the family, so that the child or young person's safety and wellbeing are assured.

## Inter-agency child protection

You may have heard about children being 'on the child protection register', but technically they should be described as having an **inter-agency child protection plan**. To give an idea of the scale of child protection work in England (comparable statistics are not easy to discover for the other countries in the UK):

- There were 547,000 referrals to children's social care departments in the year ending 31 March 2009.
- These referrals led to social workers completing 349,000 **initial assessments**.
- 37,900 children became the subject of an **inter-agency child protection plan** – this is fewer than 0.5 per cent of all children, or fewer than one child in 200.

## Initial assessment

**Initial assessments** are undertaken by specialist children's social workers in response to referrals made by schools, doctors, nurses and early years settings, for example. The initial assessment informs the decision of what to do next. Possible decisions include the following:

- **Offering services** to support the child and family, if it is judged that the child is not at immediate risk of harm but is at risk of poor developmental outcomes.
- **Urgent action** to protect the child from harm – for example, applying for a court order to take the child into care. Social workers cannot take children away from their parents; only the courts can direct this. However, a police officer can take a child into police protection in an emergency.
- **Holding a strategy discussion**. This would happen where the assessment indicates that the child may be suffering significant harm. Other professionals who know the child and family, such as GPs, health visitors, teachers and early years practitioners, may be invited to this discussion. Specialist police officers must always be represented in strategy discussions. Where

### Key term

**Early intervention** – This approach seeks to offer extra help and support to a family before the child starts to lag behind in development or experience neglect or abuse. Early intervention is about working cooperatively with parents and carers, giving them a chance to make choices about which services they need.

appropriate, a **child protection conference** will be arranged (see below).

It is important to remember that staff in early years settings and schools should *not* investigate possible abuse or neglect. The role of the early years practitioner is to refer concerns to children's social care, to contribute to the initial assessment and to attend meetings as requested.

The initial assessment can lead to:

- further work and assessment being undertaken by specialist children's social workers – this is called the **Core Assessment**
- help being offered to the child and family on a voluntary basis, usually coordinated under the **Common Assessment Framework** (CAF)
- a **child protection conference** being convened: key staff working with the family, along with the child's parents, will be invited to this conference. The meeting will be organised by an independent chairperson who has not previously been involved in the case in any way, and who reports to the Director of Children's Services.

## Child protection conference

The child protection conference seeks to establish, on the basis of evidence from the referral and the initial assessment, whether the child has suffered ill-treatment, or whether his or her health or development has been significantly impaired as a result of physical, emotional or sexual abuse, or neglect. A professional judgement must be made about whether further ill-treatment or impairment is likely to occur. It is possible to hold a child protection conference prior to birth if there are significant concerns that the newborn baby will be at risk of immediate harm; for example, in a family where there has been significant previous child abuse, or where a mother has abused drugs or alcohol during pregnancy.

If this is established, the child will be made the subject of an **inter-agency child protection plan**. The child's early years setting or school should be involved in the preparation of the plan. The role of the school or early years setting to safeguard the child, and promote his or her welfare, should be

clearly identified. Examples of this role might include:

- carefully monitoring the child's health or wellbeing in the setting on a daily basis
- making referrals to specialist agencies – for example, educational psychology
- offering support and services to the parents – for example, a parenting class run at the setting
- monitoring the child's progress against the planned outcomes in the agreed plan.

- One of your key children is subject to an inter-agency child protection plan, under the category of neglect. During the day, you notice that the child looks rather grubby. Other children are avoiding him because he smells.
- Discuss how you would talk to the parent at the end of the day, and what information you would pass on to the child's social worker.

## Drawing up an inter-agency child protection plan

The core group of professionals and the child's parents must meet within ten working days of a child being made subject to a child protection plan. The group will be called together by the child's social worker in the role of the **lead professional** (sometimes called the key worker), and will then meet regularly as required. This group should include a member of staff from the child's early years setting or school.

The core group develops the child protection plan into a more detailed working tool, outlining who will do what and by when. Both this working plan and the overall child protection plan should be based on the assessments undertaken by the specialist social worker and others, and should address the issues arising in relation to:

- the child's developmental needs
- parenting capacity
- family and environmental factors.

There should be a **child protection conference review** within three months of the initial conference. Further reviews should be held at least every six months while the child remains subject to a child protection plan. The plan may be ended if it is judged that there have been significant improvements to the wellbeing and safety of the child. These improvements might have taken place as a result of:

- a change in circumstances – for example, the abusing parent has moved out of the family home and no longer has unsupervised contact with the child
- the family is responding positively to the requirements set out in the plan, and following advice given
- the child is being given the medical or other treatment that he or she needs.

At this stage, there might be no further involvement from Children's Services, or the family may continue to be offered further help and support by the different agencies, usually coordinated under the CAF. This only happens once Children's Services are satisfied that their involvement is not required

### Key term

**Inter-agency protection plan** – If a child's health or development has been significantly impaired as a result of physical, emotional or sexual abuse or neglect, an inter-agency protection plan may be drawn up. The plan will identify the steps that the family needs to take to safeguard the child, with the support of Children's Services and other agencies. The child's safety, health, development and wellbeing will be regularly monitored throughout the plan.

### ✓ Progress check

- Working in a team, you should help work towards the plan in a CAF, or offer additional help to a child who has been identified as being vulnerable.
- Know about the definition of a child in need.
- Know who can take children into protective care if they are in immediate danger.
- Understand why a child might be made subject to an inter-agency child protection plan.

because the child is no longer considered to be 'in need'.

# Understand the importance of ensuring children and young people's safety and protection in the work setting

## Why children and young people must be protected from harm in the work setting

Ensuring children and young people's safety and protection in the setting is an essential part of safeguarding and promoting their welfare. Every adult working in the setting must be a suitable person to work with young children, and must have been checked by the Independent Safeguarding Authority. This includes students on placements and regular volunteers.

Practitioners need to actively promote the wellbeing of every child. This includes providing opportunities for children and young people to develop and learn, to play, communicate and socialise with each other in the setting. Children and young people also need healthy, nutritious and enjoyable food, and opportunities to move and exercise their bodies. They need to be able to make decisions and develop a level of independence that is appropriate to their age and development.

Practitioners also have responsibilities for providing extra support to children and young people whose needs are not being met, working with parents and other professionals. Some children in an early years setting may present with delayed development, or emotional and social difficulties. These may result from adverse early experiences, like witnessing domestic violence, or growing up with a parent who has mental health difficulties. Extra support could include helping a mother join a 'Stay and Play' group, to make friends and find support, or working

| Policies and procedures for safeguarding children and young people | |
|---|---|
| Working in an open and transparent way | Physical contact |
| Listening to children and young people | Intimate personal care |
| Duty of care | Off-site visits |
| Whistle-blowing | Photography and video |
| Power and positions of trust | Sharing concerns |
| Propriety and behaviour | Recording/reporting incidents |

**Table 7.1** Policies and procedures for safeguarding children and young people

with the clinical psychology service to give advice about bedtimes or mealtimes. This work can be coordinated under the CAF.

Practitioners also need to protect the small number of children and young people who may be at risk of significant harm as a result of their home and family circumstances. Some children and young people are at risk because of the actions of their parents – for example, physical abuse like hitting, or sexual abuse – or because their parents fail to act to keep them safe and well – for example, neglect. In these cases, the different agencies still work together to provide support and help to the parents, but there may also be actions that the parent is required to take, which can be checked through unannounced visits and compulsory medical, developmental and psychological assessments.

## Policies and procedures for safeguarding children and young people

It is important to have clear policies and procedures to ensure children and young people's safety and protection in the setting. Table 7.1 lists the different policies and procedures which should be in place for safe working.

The setting's policy for safeguarding (or child protection) should state the following:

- The name of the setting and the type of service(s) provided for children, young people and/or families; the name of the setting's designated child protection officer.

- The importance of child protection with an outline of the main legislation and guidance relevant to that part of the UK.
- The responsibility of everyone within the setting to be active in safeguarding and preventing abuse or neglect.
- How the setting will meet this obligation, for example through safer recruitment of staff or active support for children and/or young people.
- The safeguarding commitment works together with other policies such as equal opportunities, behaviour and partnership with parents.

(Lindon, 2008; pages 143–4)

The procedures should set out how the policy will be put into practice on a daily basis. The procedures should make clear the responsibilities of the setting's designated child protection officer, and the responsibilities of practitioners both as individuals and as members of the team. The procedures should be clear about the following points:

- The obligation to respond appropriately, and in a timely way, to any concerns, whomsoever raises them.
- A brief summary of signs that should concern practitioners with a reference to the relevant guidance document.
- The steps that should be taken when there are concerns, and the boundaries to the role of a familiar practitioner or the designated child protection officer.
- Details of the services, including names and telephone numbers of those who should be contacted or consulted locally.
- Specific guidance about how to behave if a child or young person alleges an abusive experience.

**Figure 7.2** Children need to be cared for by suitably qualified staff who enjoy their company

- How a safeguarding procedure is supported by other procedures such as written records or dealing with allegations of abuse or malpractice.
- Effective safeguarding includes helping children and young people to learn skills of personal safety, for example, explaining the rules about internet use and e-safety.

(Lindon, 2010; page 145)

## Whistle-blowing

Sometimes a person inside an organisation knows that something is going wrong and is being covered up. This could affect the safety and wellbeing of children and young people. Examples of this in early years settings and schools include the following:

- A member of staff has reported a number of concerns about a child's welfare. The child's parents are on the management committee of the nursery, and the manager says, 'They are not the sort of people who would harm their child.'
- There are consistently too few staff on duty in the nursery. When the local authority come to visit, supply staff are hired, and during an Ofsted inspection, management and office staff are brought into the room so that legal ratios are met.

In cases like these, it is very important that action is taken before there is a serious incident. If a member of staff has spoken to the manager, headteacher or other appropriate person, made clear that a situation is dangerous and illegal, and no action is taken, it is necessary to 'blow the whistle' and report the concerns directly to an outside body, such as the local Children's Services, Ofsted or the NSPCC.

If you act to protect children and young people and to keep them safe, you are clearly protected by the law. In general, employees who blow the whistle are legally protected against being bullied, sacked or disciplined, if they have acted in good faith.

### Research Activity

- Find out more information about whistle-blowing at this website: www.direct.gov.uk/en/ Employment/ResolvingWorkplaceDisputes/ Whistleblowingintheworkplace
- Search online for 'Protection of whistle-blowers'.

## Allegations made against staff

Schools and settings are usually some of the safest places for children and young people to be. However, sadly there have been incidents when children and young people have been harmed or abused by the adults who work with them and care for them. Cases include the murders in 2002 of Holly Wells and Jessica Chapman by their school caretaker Ian Huntley, and the discovery in 2009 that a nursery nurse, Vanessa George, had taken and distributed indecent pictures of some of the children in her care.

Generally, a setting or school keeps children safe by having effective procedures around safer recruitment, management and its general operating policy; for example, if children and young people are encouraged to speak out when they feel unhappy or uncomfortable, they will be much less vulnerable to abuse. Children's intimate care (nappy-changing, toileting, dressing and undressing) should be coordinated by a key person. This means that children should not expect that anyone can take them aside and undress them; their right to privacy is upheld.

It is effective practice, where developmentally appropriate, to ask children to consent to offers of intimate care and to give them as much control as possible. So you might say to a toddler in the toilet, 'Would you like me to help pull your pants down?' rather than just going ahead and doing it.

However, no system alone can protect children and young people: what matters, beyond effective policies and procedures, is that adults are confident to raise concerns, and that children and young people are encouraged to say if they are unhappy or uncomfortable with anything that happens to them.

All early years settings and schools are required to have a policy to deal with allegations made against staff. This will cover cases where a child makes an allegation, or an adult is seen or overheard behaving in an inappropriate way. But there are other examples that might give rise to a concern, without a specific allegation being made:

- a child who seems fearful of a particular member of staff
- a member of staff trying to develop a very close relationship with a child – for example, offering small presents and special treats, or arranging to meet the child outside of the setting or school
- a parent expressing a general concern about how a member of staff relates to their child, without being able exactly to say what is wrong.

In cases like these, you will need to discuss your concerns with the named person for safeguarding. Discussions like these are awkward, but it is important to share any concerns you have: the child's welfare is paramount.

## Off-site visits

When participating in off-site visits, all practitioners (including volunteers) have a duty to take reasonable care to avoid injury to themselves and others, and to cooperate to ensure that statutory duties and obligations are fulfilled. Adults in charge of children or young people during an off-site visit have a duty of care to make sure that the children/young people are safe and healthy. Practitioners have a common law duty to act as would a reasonably prudent parent. Practitioners should not hesitate to act in an emergency and to take life-saving action in an extreme situation. As a safeguard to children and young people, volunteer helpers on off-site visits must be appropriate people to supervise children/young people, should be trained in their duties, and have had a CRB check. Unqualified staff or volunteers must not be left in sole charge of children/young people except where it has been previously agreed as part of the risk assessment. There should normally be a minimum of two adults with any group involved in an off-site visit or activity; the exact ratio of adults to children/young people depends on their ages and should be appropriate for the needs of the group and in line with the relevant guidelines. Practitioners and volunteers should not be in a situation where they are alone with one child or young person away from the rest of the group.

# Understand how to respond to evidence or concerns that a child or young person has been abused or harmed

Practitioners are good at recognising when all is not well with a child or young person. Historically, the biggest difficulty has not been in recognising problems, but in communicating concerns to others (including parents or carers) and acting on them. Often practitioners worry about the consequences of passing on information, and worry that it might lead to the family being split up. It is important to remember that in the vast majority of cases the different services will work *with* the family to ensure the child or young person's safety. But the decision about what is best for the child or young person should be made by a trained social worker, acting on the best possible information. When practitioners feel worried but do not communicate their concerns to others, a child or young person can be put in danger.

## Definitions of abuse and neglect

'Abuse and neglect are forms of maltreatment of a child. Somebody may abuse or neglect a child by inflicting harm, or by failing to act to prevent harm. Children may be abused in a family or in an institutional or community setting, by those known to them or, more rarely, by a stranger, for example, via the internet. They may be abused by an adult or adults, or another child or children.' (*Working Together to Safeguard Children: A Guide to Inter-agency Working to Safeguard and Promote the Welfare of Children*, DCSF, 2010)

There are four categories of abuse: physical, emotional and sexual abuse, and neglect. These are outlined below.

## Physical abuse

Physical abuse is the most apparent form of child or young person abuse. It includes any kind of physical harm to a child or young person, which can include hitting, shaking, throwing, poisoning, burning or scalding, drowning and suffocating.

Physical harm may also be caused when a parent fabricates the symptoms of illness in a child, or deliberately induces illness – for example, giving a child so much salt that he or she becomes very ill, so that medical staff think the child has a gastric illness or a brain condition.

## Emotional abuse

Emotional abuse is difficult to define and can be difficult to detect. It involves continual emotional mistreatment which results in significant damage to the child or young person's emotional development. The child or young person may come to feel worthless, unloved, and inadequate or valued only if they meet the expectations or needs of another person. Emotional abuse includes:

- The parent having expectations that are beyond what is suitable for the child or young person's age and development. This includes unreasonable expectations, like continuously trying to force a child to achieve more, and then constantly criticising the child for his or her failures. At the other end of the spectrum, some parents may fail to stimulate their child adequately; for example, keeping a two-year-old child in a playpen with only a few baby toys.
- Preventing a child from participating in normal social interaction with other children, either by keeping the child at home, or by taking the child out but being so overprotective, fearful or controlling that the child cannot join in.
- Failing to protect the child from witnessing the mistreatment of others; for example, cases of domestic violence.

All children and young people will experience some emotional difficulties as part of the ordinary processes of growing up. It becomes abusive if the result is significant damage to the child or young person's emotional development. All cases of child or young person abuse will include some degree of emotional abuse.

## Sexual abuse

Sexual abuse involves forcing or encouraging a child to take part in sexual activities. The child may or may not be aware of what is happening. Activities may involve physical contact (such as rape, including forced anal sex or oral sex) or non-penetrative acts like touching or masturbation.

The abuse may include non-contact activities, such as involving children in looking at or in the production of sexual images online or on mobile phones, watching sexual activities or encouraging children to behave in sexually inappropriate ways.

## Neglect

Neglect means that the parent persistently fails to meet the child's basic physical needs, psychological needs or both. The result is that the child's health or development is significantly impaired.

Neglect can occur during pregnancy if the mother abuses drugs or alcohol, which can have serious effects. Neglect of babies and young children includes the failure to:

- provide adequate food, clothing and shelter
- keep the child safe from physical and emotional harm or danger
- supervise the child adequately, including leaving the child with inadequate carers
- make sure the child is seen promptly by medical staff when ill
- respond to the child's basic emotional needs.

### Research Activity

This section on abuse and neglect draws on guidance from *Every Child Matters*.

- Find out more by reading the guidance in full on this website: www.dcsf.gov.uk/everychildmatters/safeguardingandsocialcare/safeguardingchildren/workingtogether
- Search online for 'Working Together to Safeguard Children'.

## Recognising child abuse

The National Society for the Prevention of Cruelty to Children (NSPCC) states that:

'Children and young people often find it very difficult to talk about the abuse they are experiencing. So adults have a vital role to play in looking out for the possible signs.'

The following section draws on the NSPCC's guide, *Learn how to recognise the signs of child abuse*. It is not always possible to be completely certain that a child is being abused, but there are signs and indicators that all early years practitioners should look out for:

- A baby or toddler who is always crying.
- A child who often has injuries or bruises.
- A child who is often very withdrawn. Withdrawn children are not simply quiet or shy – they shrink from adult attention, lack interest in their surroundings and try to occupy themselves without being noticed.
- A child who is often in very dirty clothes, looks unwashed for a period of time or is very smelly.
- A child who is frequently very hungry.
- A child who is often inappropriately dressed for the weather or time of year. This would include children who often come to the setting in thin T-shirts, shorts or dresses through the winter. It would also include children who come into the setting on a hot day in very warm clothes.
- Any indication that a child is being left home alone, or left unsupervised in unsafe circumstances at home.
- A child who does not receive the medical treatment which he or she needs.
- A child who is mocked, sworn at, constantly joked about and made to feel foolish or useless.
- A child who expresses fear about particular adults, seems reluctant to be picked up by a particular adult, or afraid to be left alone with that person.
- A child with very strong mood swings – anxiety, depression, uncontained anger or severe aggression.
- A child whose sexual knowledge, use of sexual words or sexual behaviour is not appropriate for their age or development.
- A child who is witnessing domestic violence.

- A child who is witnessing significant drug or alcohol abuse.

There may be valid explanations for some of these signs. Equally, there are many other indications of possible abuse, and other circumstances that could be unsafe for a child. The NSPCC advises that:

'The most important thing to remember is that if you have a gut feeling that something is not right, **trust your judgement** and take action.'

## Allegations

Sometimes a child or young person may allege information that leads you to think that he or she is being abused. With young children, this may happen in a number of ways. A child might tell you something directly: 'Mummy and Daddy went out yesterday, and me and Scarlet were scared because we were all alone.' Or a child might use play to communicate – for example, you might observe a child in the home corner shouting at and slapping one of the dolls.

In all cases, your role when a child or young person alleges is to listen very carefully and show concern. Reaffirm that it is good for the child or young person to tell you things that are worrying or upsetting him or her. Say that you believe them. If you are not sure about something a child has said, then ask for clarification: 'I am not sure I quite understood – did you say it was your arm that hurts?'

However, there are also some things that you must *not* do. You must not question or cross-examine a child, or seem to put words into a child's mouth. You would therefore not ask a question such as, 'Does this happen every day?' because the child might just agree with you, or repeat your words. You are there to listen and observe – you are not an investigator.

A child or young person may make an allegation to anyone – their key person, the caretaker, the dinner supervisor, a student on placement. For that reason, it is very important that everyone who comes into contact with children and young people has training on safeguarding and knows what to do if they have any reason to be worried about a particular child or young person.

### Key term

**Allegation** – This is when a child or young person alleges information that causes an adult to be concerned about their safety and wellbeing. This might happen through children talking, acting things out in their play, or drawing and painting. It is essential that early years practitioners listen and watch very carefully, but do not question the child or put words into the child's mouth.

## Procedure for when abuse is suspected

If a child or young person alleges to you, or if you are worried for one or more of the reasons listed by the NSPCC (see page 129):

- Make a note that is as exact as you can make it, recording exactly what the child or young person said, and anything you noticed (signs of an injury, child or young person seeming upset, stressed, angry or ashamed while talking to you). If you have had ongoing concerns, summarise what these are; again, be as accurate as you can.

- Discuss your concerns as a matter of urgency with the named member of staff for safeguarding, however busy that person seems to be.

In most cases, the named member of staff will discuss the concerns with the parent or carer and then make a judgement about what to do next. You should be told what action (if any) is being taken, and why. Responses might include:

- **No action** – for example, in a case where a parent gives a reasonable explanation for their child's injury or behaviour.

- **Advice given** – for example, a parent is advised on what sort of clothes will keep their child warm enough in winter. Staff can then check that the child is appropriately dressed on subsequent days.

- **Support offered** – for example, a parent might agree that she is finding it difficult to manage the child or young person's behaviour, and might welcome the offer of support from a parenting group or an appointment with a clinical psychologist.
- **Referral to family support at the local children's centre** – this will provide structured support and help for the family on a voluntary basis. A similar type of referral might be made to a specialist social work team (Disabled Children's Team, Domestic Violence Project).
- **Referral to Children's Social Care (social services)** – if the named person judges that the child or young person is at risk of significant harm, a written referral will be made to Children's Social Care.

If you have raised a concern and you think that the action being taken is inadequate, meet the named person again. Explain your opinion, referring to what you have observed or heard. Although such conversations are very difficult, they are essential if we are to uphold to the principle that the child or young person's welfare and safety comes first.

If you are a learner, discuss your concerns in confidence with your tutor. Any worried adult is also entitled to contact Children's Social Care or the NSPCC directly. If you have reason to believe your concern is not being acted on, you should do this.

### Research Activity

Read the summary document, *What to do if you're worried a child is being abused*. It is available on this website: www.education.gov.uk/publications/eOrderingDownload/6841-DfES-ChildAbuseSumm.pdf or search online for 'What to do if you are worried a child is being abused'.

## Confidentiality and 'need to know'

In general, you must keep sensitive information confidential. If information circulates too freely, parents can feel very exposed and vulnerable. They may stop sharing information with staff.

## Where appropriate, seek consent before you share information

You might find out on a home visit that a child's mother has a serious mental health difficulty, which is well managed by medication and therapy. However, the medication can make her feel rather tired first thing in the morning, and she tells you that she can struggle to take on information or hold a conversation then. So you might say, 'I will need to tell my manager this, but shall we also let the staff team know, so that they can talk with you at the end of the day and not in the morning?' The parent can then give or withhold consent freely.

### Activity

1 What are the four categories of child abuse?

2 What should you remember to do, if a child or young person alleges to you? What should you avoid doing?

3 Why would early years staff share concerns about a child's welfare or wellbeing with the child's parents, rather than just keeping a record or making a referral?

## Do not disclose information inappropriately

Never disclose any information about a child or young person's welfare in an inappropriate way to people outside the setting or school. For example, you would not tell friends or family about a child protection conference you had attended.

## Put the child or young person's interests first

If sharing information will help to ensure a child or young person's safety, you must do this. In nearly all cases, you would start by explaining to the parent why you wish to share the information and how this would help their child. If a parent refuses, ask for advice and guidance from the named person for safeguarding or the manager/head of the setting. If a parent or carer says something like, 'I did smack her round the head, but you won't tell anyone will you? They'll take her into care,' you will need to explain clearly that you are legally required to pass on information like this.

 **Progress check**

- Working in a team, you should discuss your concerns about children in meetings or with senior staff, as appropriate.
- Understand why you would ask a parent for consent before sharing confidential information with another professional.
- Understand that there are times when you would share information without consent.

# Understand how to respond to evidence or concerns that a child or young person has been bullied

Research suggests that 85 per cent of children aged five to eleven years have experienced bullying in some form, such as name-calling, being hit or kicked. In 2000 a survey of 11- to 16-year-olds found that:

'36 per cent of children said they had been bullied in the last 12 months; 26 per cent had been threatened with violence and 13 per cent had been physically attacked.' (ATL, 2000)

As bullying occurs both inside and outside of schools and settings, the setting should have an anti-bullying policy which clearly sets out the ways in which they try to prevent or reduce bullying, and deal with bullying behaviour when it happens.

## Different types of bullying and the potential effects on children and young people

Bullying can be defined as behaviour that is deliberately hurtful or aggressive, repeated over a period of time and difficult for victims to defend themselves against. There are three main types of bullying:

1 **physical**: hitting, kicking, taking belongings
2 **verbal**: name-calling, insulting, making offensive remarks
3 **indirect**: spreading nasty stories about someone, exclusion from social groups, being made the subject of malicious rumours, sending malicious emails or text messages on mobile phones.

Name-calling is the most common type of bullying. Children and young people can be called nasty names because of their individual characteristics, ethnic origin, nationality, skin colour, sexual orientation or disability. Verbal bullying is common among boys and girls. Boys experience more physical violence and threats when being bullied than do girls. However, physical attacks on girls by other girls are becoming more common. Girls tend to use indirect types of bullying, which can be more difficult to detect and deal with (DfES, 2000).

Any child or young person can experience bullying, but certain factors may make bullying more likely. While there is *never* an acceptable excuse for bullying behaviour, children and young people are more likely to experience bullying if they:

- are shy or have an over-protective family environment
- are from a different racial or ethnic group to the majority of children and young people
- appear different in some obvious respect, such as stammering
- have special needs, such as a disability or learning difficulties
- behave inappropriately or have less developed social and interpersonal skills
- possess expensive accessories, such as mobile phones or computer games.

## Policies and procedures for dealing with bullying

Certain types of bullying may amount to unlawful discrimination, such as bullying on the grounds of age, race, sex, gender, sexual orientation or disability. All settings need to have in place effective systems to deal specifically with the problem of this type of bullying. Anti-bullying policies and procedures are required which include specific reference to bullying in all its forms, including the following:

- bullying on grounds of body image/size/obesity
- homophobic bullying
- racist bullying
- faith-based bullying
- ageist bullying
- disability bullying
- sexist bullying.   (www.nasuwt.org.uk: see the useful resources section at the end of this chapter for their anti-bullying literature)

Children and young people should be provided with information about sources of help and support, such as Barnardo's, Childline, The Samaritans and the National Youth Advocacy Service.

The Early Years Foundation Stage (EYFS) requires that:

'children's behaviour must be managed effectively and in a manner appropriate for their stage of development and particular individual needs'.

Schools are also legally required to have policies and procedures in place to identify and prevent bullying. Every early years setting needs to develop a policy around the support of children's behaviour and the prevention of bullying.

Adults can help to prevent bullying in the following ways:

## Encouraging a culture where children and young people can express how they feel

Sometimes it may feel like a particular child or young person keeps coming to you for help, and this may become wearing. It is, however, important that on every occasion you listen with sympathy and try to help the child or young person.

## Developing effective communication with parents or carers

If a child or young person is being bullied, it may be the parent who first notices that there is something the matter when the child or young person is at home. By working together, you may be able to find out what is happening and take steps to help the child.

## Clearly telling children when their behaviour is not acceptable

Some young children bump into others, grab for equipment first, give others an aggressive look or generally intimidate other children. Sometimes children may deliberately exclude a child from playing within a group. Behaviour like this can quickly escalate to more serious forms of bullying like open aggression, which is either physical (hitting, pushing) or verbal (name-calling). It is important that adults look out for this sort of behaviour and encourage other children to say confidently how it affects them.

## Take firm action when necessary

You may have to remove a child or young person from a situation if necessary, but you can help the child or young person by saying clearly which part of their behaviour is not acceptable, while not being negative towards them personally. This is why you would not say to a child, 'You're being naughty'. It is important that you would follow this up by settling the child back into the play and then spend time in that area, helping all the children to play together.

If bullying is persistent despite your attempts at positive management, you will need to seek advice from the SENCO in your setting or school.

Find out more about bullying by going to www.kidscape.org.uk or searching online for 'Kidscape'.

## Supporting a child, young person and/or their family when bullying is suspected or alleged

Children and young people who are experiencing bullying may be reluctant to attend the setting and may therefore be often absent. They may be more anxious and insecure than others, have fewer friends and often feel unhappy and lonely. They can suffer from low self-esteem and negative self-image; seeing themselves as failures, stupid, ashamed and unattractive. Possible signs that a child or young person is being bullying include:

- suddenly does not want to go to the setting when he usually enjoys it
- unexplained cuts and bruises
- possessions have unexplained damage or are persistently 'lost'
- becoming withdrawn or depressed but refusing to explain.

While the above signs may indicate that a child or young person is being bullied, they may also be symptomatic of other problems such as child abuse (see above).

We have already looked at factors which make bullying more likely. The **behaviour** of some children and young people can also lead to them experiencing bullying, although this does not justify the behaviour of the bullies. For example, some children and young people may:

- find it difficult to play/enjoy leisure with others
- be hyperactive
- behave in ways that irritate others
- bully other children and young people
- be easily roused to anger
- fight back when attacked or even slightly provoked
- be actively disliked by the majority of children and young people using the setting.

Practitioners and the child or young person's parents or carers should work together to identify any such behaviour. The child or young person needs help to improve personal and social skills, including assertiveness techniques and conflict resolution. You may be able to provide support for a child or young person who is being bullied by:

- encouraging the child or young person to talk
- listening to their problems
- believing them if they say that they are being bullied
- providing reassurance that it is not their fault; no one deserves to be bullied
- discussing the matter with a senior colleague
- taking appropriate action, following the setting's policy on anti-bullying.

## Dealing with persistent and violent bullying

Where a child or young person does not respond to the strategies to combat bullying, the setting should take tough action to deal with persistent and violent bullying. The setting should have a range of sanctions to deal with bullying. Everyone within the setting should know what sanctions will be taken. These sanctions should be fair and applied consistently. You can help deal with bullying behaviour by:

- knowing the setting's policy and strategies for dealing with bullying behaviour
- using appropriate sanctions for such behaviour, such as exclusion from certain activities
- providing help for the bully so they can recognise that this behaviour is unacceptable; for example, discussion, mediation, peer counselling
- working with childcarers and parents to establish community awareness of bullying

## Activity

**1** Outline your setting's anti-bullying policy and main strategies for dealing with bullying behaviour.

**2** Give a reflective account of how you have handled concerns about bullying. Remember confidentiality.

**3** Devise an activity to encourage children to speak up about bullying, such as story, discussion, roleplay, drama or poster-making.

- making sure all children and young people know that bullying will *not* be tolerated
- understanding that the setting can permanently **exclude** children and young people who demonstrate persistent bullying behaviour, especially physical violence.

# Understand how to work with children and young people to support their safety and wellbeing

In recent decades, a number of attempts have been made to design programmes for children under five years to help protect themselves against abuse. These have included lessons on 'stranger danger', working with children in groups to explore times when they feel uncomfortable, and teaching children not to keep 'bad secrets'.

There is little or no reliable evidence that such programmes have protected children aged under five years from abuse, and it has been argued that the children merely end up feeling confused, frightened and alarmed. It has also been argued that these approaches can make young children feel some responsibility if they are being abused, because they were unable to do or say what they were taught.

**Figure 7.3** Example of child's anti-bullying poster

It is worth remembering that children in the EYFS do not generally learn effectively through group discussions, or through being shown pictures of dangerous situations. These approaches are most suited to older children in the primary and secondary phases of their education. There are some tried and tested programmes available from the NSPCC, Barnardo's and Kidscape for older children. In the EYFS, a more successful approach is likely to be one which is built into the daily lives of the children in their early years setting or school.

# Supporting self-confidence and self-esteem in young children

The self-confidence and self-esteem of young children can be greatly boosted by a strong key person approach in the setting. Many aspects of this approach support the safeguarding of children.

## Listening and tuning in to a child

This will include the key person noticing changes in a child's behaviour and emotional wellbeing, and developing a trusting relationship so that the child can tell you if things are upsetting him or her. Taking a child's concerns seriously is important. Often, when a child has been bullied or abused in some way, he or she will try to communicate what has happened. The child needs to know that you are there to listen and, most importantly, that you will believe what he or she tells you.

## Allowing a child to express his or her feelings

If a child is allowed to express sadness and anger as well as happiness and enjoyment, she may feel more confident that she can have a range of emotions. The child will therefore be more likely to tell other people how she is feeling.

## Increasing a child's confidence

This involves making a child feel a sense of belonging, and that he is special for many unique qualities. It is important to show a genuine interest in what a child has to say, and to praise him for any achievements. A quick, 'That's lovely, Shivan', is really not enough to show a child that you value him.

## Observing a child and keeping regular records of behaviour

You are in a strong position to note any changes of behaviour or signs of insecurity that could result from child abuse.

**Figure 7.4** This toddler is able to explore the environment confidently because of the security he gains from the presence of his key person

## Working with parents

The emphasis in the key person approach on developing a close relationship with parents is also important. A key person can:

- help a parent to appreciate that a child is finding a particular situation upsetting or difficult
- support a parent with practical advice on general care and clothing
- offer emotional and practical support in cases of family conflict or domestic violence.

# Empowering children and young people to support their own wellbeing and safety

An effective child and young person protection policy will promote a caring and supportive environment in the setting and create an atmosphere in which children and young people feel that they are secure, valued, listened to and taken seriously. The setting's child protection policy should support children and young people's development in ways which foster their security, confidence and independence.

## Protecting themselves

Child protection not only involves the detection of abuse and neglect but also the **prevention** of abuse by helping children and young people to protect themselves. As part of this preventive role you should help children and young people to do the following:

- understand what is and is not acceptable behaviour towards them
- stay safe from harm
- speak up if they have worries and concerns
- develop awareness and **resilience**
- prepare for their future responsibilities as adults, citizens and parents.

Being actively involved in prevention helps children and young people to keep safe both now and in the future. Children and young people need to know how to take responsibility for themselves and to understand the consequences of their actions. Children and young people should know and understand:

- that they all deserve care and respect
- their rights and how to assert them
- how to do things safely and how to minimise risk
- how to deal with abusive or potentially abusive situations
- when and how to ask for help and support.

Critical thinking and decision-making are also essential for helping children to keep themselves safe. You can help them to develop these skills by encouraging them to participate in decision-making within the setting and providing opportunities for cooperation.

You should also encourage children and young people to trust their own feelings and judgement in difficult situations. By learning to trust their inner feelings, they can avoid many potential risky situations. Use roleplay to help them think about what they should do if their friends want them to do something they dislike or feel uncomfortable about, such as going to a party, getting drunk, having sex, shoplifting, taking drugs, etc. Peer pressure can be very strong; encourage them to decide and set limits about what they will or will not do, so that they know how to cope before the situation arises. Make sure that children understand the dangers of situations that may put their personal safety at risk, such as:

- being left at home alone
- playing in deserted or dark places
- being out on their own
- getting lost, for example on outings
- walking home alone, especially in the dark
- talking to strangers
- accepting lifts from strangers, including hitchhiking.

## Risk-taking and developing independence

As children and young people get older, they need opportunities to explore their environment and to develop their independence. To do this safely they will need to know and understand about acceptable risk-taking.

This issue can be explored through stories (such as *Jack and the Beanstalk* for young children) and television programmes. Children can think about and discuss the risks taken by their favourite characters. Encourage them to identify some of the risks they take in their own lives and look at ways in which they can minimise risk. Puppets and roleplay can be used to help them deal with potentially risky situations. Ensure that the children and young people know and understand **The Keepsafe Code** (see www.kidscape.org.uk).

## Seeking help

Children and young people need to know where to go for help and support in difficult situations. They should be encouraged to identify people in the setting and the local community who help them to keep safe. For example, worries about bullying or problems at home may be discussed with a trusted adult; if they get lost they can ask a police officer for assistance.

Encourage children and young people to think of a trusted adult (such as parents or carers, another relative, best friend, teacher, key worker) to whom they could talk about a difficult situation (for example, abuse, bullying, negative peer pressure, etc.). Ensure that they understand that if they go to an adult for help, especially within the setting, they will be believed and supported. Provide them with information about other sources of help and support, such as Childline, The Samaritans.

# Understand the importance of e-safety for children and young people

With the continuing development of new and mobile technologies, the setting has a responsibility to help children and young people to stay safe online. E-safety is a safeguarding issue as part of the wider duty of care for all who work with children and young people. You should have a good understanding of e-safety issues and risks, and how these might relate to the children you work with, including data protection and child protection.

> Discuss ways in which your setting helps children and young people to protect themselves. What sources of help and support are available for children and young people in your setting and the local community?

## Child protection and ICT

The setting has a duty in relation to children and young people to monitor their use of the internet and email in order to protect them from inappropriate, malicious or offensive material, as well as to protect them from paedophiles preying on children via the internet.

## Chat rooms and social networking sites

Children and young people should only be given access to educational chat rooms which should be moderated to ensure that discussions are kept on-topic, and that there is no language or behaviour that is inappropriate.

Guidelines for using **chat rooms** or **social networking** sites in the setting should be included in the setting's policy for using ICT. Children and young people should be taught never to give out personal details that would identify who they are, and never to arrange to meet anyone they have 'met' in a chat room or social networking site. Additionally, children and young people should also be taught not to rely on anyone they have met in a chat room or social networking site for important advice, and if anything makes them feel uncomfortable, not to reply to the message but instead seek advice from a familiar adult such as their key worker, teacher, parent or carer (Becta, 2004).

## Using the internet

The setting should have filtering systems in place to prevent children and young people from accessing inappropriate materials. There should be procedures in place for children and young people to report accidental access to inappropriate material.

The setting should also provide appropriate opportunities within the curriculum to teach internet safety. There should be procedures in place to deal with 'personal alleging' by a child or young person as a result of internet safety education. The setting must have nominated a member of staff who has responsibility for child protection issues. Children and young people's use of the internet, email and/or chat rooms should be regularly monitored to ensure that inappropriate use is not being made. There should be sanctions in place to deal with children and young people who deliberately access inappropriate sites or post bullying or offensive messages (Becta, 2004).

## E-safety for the setting

A setting may have its own website which demonstrates the work of the setting, provides a source of information to parents and develops links with the wider community. The setting website should protect the identity of children; where a child's image appears, the name should not, and vice versa; parental permission should be obtained before using images of children on the website (Becta, 2004).

## Buying online

With a number of internet payment options to choose from (such as debit cards, top-ups and pre-paid cards), children and young people can buy goods and services online even if they do not own a credit card. It is important that they know about e-safety when buying online, especially possible dangers such as being tricked into buying something on a fake website or accidentally giving their personal information to a fraudster. Young people should be made aware of the following important points about buying online:

- Be aware of the potential risks of online shopping such as identity theft and security issues. Criminals could install malicious software (malware) on your computer that might damage your data, cause your PC to run slowly, gather personal information, harm your reputation or be used to steal your money.

- Ensure that your computer has up-to-date anti-virus software and a firewall in place, to provide protection against the potential risks of shopping online.
- Only use online retailers you trust or ones that have been suggested by friends or family.
- Shop around to get the best deals and to check a website's returns and privacy policy before buying anything. When buying things online, always read the small print!
- Ensure that you have strong passwords (a combination of letters, numbers and symbols) on websites you shop online.
- Know what a secure website looks like: look for the padlock symbol in the bottom right of the browser window, and for website addresses which begin with https (the 's' stands for security).
- Print out a copy of any online orders and check your bank statements after you have bought anything online.

## Mobile phones

Internet access is now available on most mobile phones. While this provides opportunities for communication, interaction and entertainment, there are possible risks to children and young people including: accessing potentially harmful content such as pornography; possible dangerous contact with strangers in chat rooms; commercial pressures like spam and intrusive advertising. UK mobile phone operators have taken steps to help protect children and young people from potentially harmful content accessible via their mobile phone, including the following:

- All UK mobile phone operators have to provide an internet filter on their phones to help block accessing material that is potentially harmful to children, such as pornography. However, in most cases parents will need to ask their operator to activate the filter.
- Being registered as a child user will mean that the child cannot access material provided by the mobile operator or its partners that is rated as 18+. All mobile phone users are considered to be children by their mobile operator unless or until they have proved to their mobile operator that they are 18 years old.

- Bluetooth allows a mobile to find and 'talk' to other Bluetooth-enabled mobile phones nearby and vice versa. This means that when activated on a child or young person's mobile phone, they may receive unexpected and unwanted messages from other Bluetooth-enabled phone users nearby, and any personal information stored on their phone (such as their contact list) could be vulnerable. Mobile operators therefore advise that Bluetooth is not enabled on children and young people's phones.
- Chat rooms or games (where you can chat to other users) which are provided by a mobile operator or its partners and which do not have 18+ age-restrictions must be moderated. Different mobile operators may have different moderation policies and systems which may affect the level of safety, so ask the mobile operator about this. Remember that chat rooms accessed on the internet via mobile phone (that is, which are not provided by the mobile operator or its partners) may not be moderated.
- The mobile operator should have systems and procedures in place to help deal with nuisance and malicious phone calls. It is important to let the mobile operator know if their system is failing, both in order to protect children and others using the same service.
- The mobile operator will take action against spam, whether it is text, picture or e-mail. Find out what action the mobile operator is taking and report any spam received on the phone to them.

(Childnet International, 2006)

You can help children and young people to understand the importance of e-safety by giving them the following tips:

- Think about whom you give your mobile phone number to – you do not know where it might end up.
- If you start receiving annoying, nasty or rude texts, remember: do not reply, but do keep a record of it. If any of these things bother you, talk to an adult you trust or report it to your school or mobile phone operator.
- A growing number of viruses are attacking mobile phones, so be careful with what you download onto your mobile.
- If you often receive spam (junk mail) texts from random numbers, report it to your mobile phone operator.
- If you are taking photos or film of your friends and want to upload them to the internet, always check with them first.
- Remember to keep control of your own image too. Once a picture is posted online, it can be copied, changed and distributed without your knowledge. Only upload and exchange photos that you would be happy for everyone to see.

(Childnet International, 2009)

 **In Practice**

Martha is working with a group of five-year-old children when they accidentally access inappropriate material while using the internet. What would you do in this situation?

Weblinks and resources

## Organisations and websites

**National Society for the Prevention of Cruelty to Children (NSPCC)** campaigns against cruelty to children, and runs Childline, the free, confidential helpline for children and young people. The NSPCC also offers services to support children and families, and can investigate cases where child abuse is suspected:
www.nspcc.org.uk

*Working Together to Safeguard Children* is the Government's guide to inter-agency working to safeguard and promote the welfare of children:
www.everychildmatters.gov.uk/workingtogether

**Anna Freud Centre** was established in 1947 by Anna Freud to support the emotional wellbeing of children through direct work with children and their families, research and the development of practice, and training mental health practitioners:
www.annafreud.org

**Kate Greenaway Nursery School and Children's Centre** – this website includes news and policies for a centre based in central London:
www.kategreenaway.ik.org

**Kidscape** is a charity established specifically to prevent bullying and child sexual abuse. The website includes resources for parents, children and professionals, and details of campaigns and training events:
www.kidscape.org.uk

**The National Strategies (Early Years)** is the Government's programme for developing practice in the early years in England, including statutory requirements, advice on best practice, and research findings:
http://nationalstrategies.standards.dcsf.gov.uk/earlyyears

The **NASUWT** publication 'Tackling Prejudiced-Related Bullying' (PDF) is available free:
www.nasuwt.org.uk/InformationandAdvice/Equalities/PrejudiceRelatedBullying/index.htm

**The National Youth Advocacy Service (NYAS)** is a UK charity providing children's rights and socio-legal services. They offer information, advice, advocacy and legal representation to children and young people up to the age of 25, through a network of advocates throughout England and Wales. NYAS is also a community legal service:
www.nyas.net

**Childnet** – their Know IT All website contains resources designed to help educate parents, carers, teachers and young people about safe and positive use of the internet. Available free at:
www.childnet.com/kia/

## Books

Axline, V. (1971) *Dibs, In Search of Self: Personality Development in Play Therapy*. Penguin.

Department of Health (2003) *What To Do If You're Worried A Child Is Being Abused*. DH. (Free copies of this booklet are available via the DH website: www.dh.gov.uk)

Elliott, M. and Kilpatrick, J. (2002) *How to stop bullying: a Kidscape training guide*. Kidscape.

Lindon, J. (2003) *Child Protection*. 2nd Edition. Hodder & Stoughton.

Lindon, J. (2008) *Safeguarding Children and Young People: Child Protection 0-18 Years*. 3rd Edition. Hodder Education.

# 8 Support children and young people's health and safety: Unit CYP Core 3.4

Safety is a basic human need. A safe environment is one in which the child or adult has a low risk of becoming ill or injured. A healthy environment is clean, warm and hygienic. When working with children and young people, you need to know how to provide a safe, healthy environment. This involves knowing how to assess risks to children's safety and to ensure that any such risks are minimised. A fine balance must be achieved which allows children and young people to explore their environment and to learn for themselves, but also ensures that the environment in which children and young people are playing and learning is as safe and healthy as possible.

## Learning outcomes

By the end of this chapter you will:

1. Understand how to plan and provide environments and services that support children and young people's health and safety.

2. Be able to recognise and manage risks to health, safety and security in a work setting or off-site visits.

3. Understand how to support children and young people to assess and manage risk for themselves.

4. Understand appropriate responses to accidents, incidents, emergencies and illness in work settings and off-site visits.

## Supporting children and young people's health and safety

### Planning healthy and safe environments and services

A number of factors must be considered when planning for healthy and safe environments for children and young people. All planning must start with the needs of the individual child or young person. (See also Chapter 4, pages 40–41.)

### The age and developmental capabilities of the children or young people

A room where babies are cared for will need to be warmer than the rest of the rooms, and must have facilities for changing nappies hygienically and the safe provision of bottle-feeds. Outdoor areas for older children and young people need to be planned to allow vigorous physical play with the minimum of risk.

### Specific needs

Children and young people with specific needs, such as a physical disability or a sensory impairment, should have full access to the available activities. Settings should ensure that the environment is planned to suit the individual; sometimes, this will involve adapting the layout or equipment to enable the specific needs to be met.

### The needs of families and carers

Planning should always recognise the needs of families. For example, a setting may have an outbreak of a notifiable infectious disease, such as rubella. This disease can still affect the unborn child in women who are pregnant. It is also important that parents and carers are routinely informed of such occurrences (as well as incidences of head lice in the setting) so that they can help to maintain their own and their family's health.

## The function and purpose of environments and services offered

Not all settings are built for the purpose. Many playgroups and crèches, for example, share their premises with other organisations. Planning should take into account the way in which the setting should function as a safe, healthy environment for children and young people.

## The duty of care

All practitioners who work with children and young people have a duty of care towards them. This means that children and young people's health and safety should be the overriding principle when planning.

## Desired outcomes for the children and young people

All settings must use the statutory desired outcomes relevant to the age group of children provided for. In the EYFS, two of the desired outcomes are *Be healthy* and *Be safe*.

## Lines of responsibility and accountability

Each person working within a setting has a responsibility for the health and safety of children, young people and of staff. There should be a clear 'line of responsibility' so that each worker or practitioner knows to whom they should report and be accountable.

### Key term

**Duty of care** – A requirement to exercise a 'reasonable' degree of attention and caution to avoid negligence which would lead to harm to other people.

## Monitoring and maintaining health and safety

One of the main reasons for maintaining a safe environment is accident prevention. The likelihood of different types of accidents occurring depends on the following factors:

- **The age and developmental capabilities** of the child or young person. For example, bicycle accidents are more likely in older children and young people; accidents involving choking and poisoning are more common in younger children.
- **The environment**: indoor or outdoor, child-aware or not. For example, toddlers visiting a house in which no children live, are more likely to find hazards (such as trailing electrical flexes, loose rugs or unsecured cupboards containing potentially dangerous cleaning products) than in a household with children.
- **The degree of supervision** available. For example, inquisitive toddlers with little appreciation of danger need more supervision in an environment that is not 'child-aware'. At the same time, the adult may be less aware of potential dangers due to distractions; for example, holding an adult conversation with a friend, talking on the phone (especially mobile phones) or in a busy shopping centre where there is much visual stimulation. Staff working in child care and education environments must comply with their home nation's safety requirements regarding safe supervision, including the ratio of staff to children or young people.

## Adult/child ratios

An obvious way of reducing the risk of harm to children and young people is to ensure that there is adequate adult supervision for any activities that are to be undertaken. The number of adults present will depend on:

- the number of children or young people involved
- the age of those involved
- the type of activity.

## Parents, carers and other visitors to the setting

Every setting should have a policy that maintains the safety of the children and young people as well as the

**In Practice**

## Health and safety checks in the setting

It is important that the environment is checked regularly (both before and during activities) to ensure that it is both healthy and safe:

❏ Children should be supervised at all times.

❏ Routine safety checks should be made daily on premises, both indoors and outdoors.

❏ Routine check of security systems – entry phones, locks, visitors' book and name badges etc. to control entry and exit at all times. Children should only be allowed home with a parent or authorised adult.

❏ Make sure that food is stored at the correct temperature and snacks are prepared hygienically.

❏ Prevent accidents by keeping the environment clean, tidy and uncluttered.

❏ All materials and equipment should be in a safe and clean condition – any sharp edges or broken parts should be discarded or repaired before use.

❏ Follow the setting's procedures for dealing with spillages of urine, vomit, blood and faeces.

❏ There must be adequate first aid facilities, and staff should be trained in basic first aid.

❏ Fire drills should be held twice a term in schools and nurseries, and every six weeks in day nurseries.

### Legislation relating to health and safety in child care settings

| | |
|---|---|
| Health and Safety at Work Act 1974 | Management of Health and Safety at Work Regulations 1999 |
| COSSH (Control of Substances Hazardous to Health) 2002 | RIDDOR (Reporting of Injuries, Diseases and Dangerous Occurrences Regulations) 1995 |
| Electricity at Work Regulations 1989 | Manual Handling Operations Regulations 1992 |
| Fire Precautions at Work Regulations 1997 | The Children Act 1989 and 2004 |

**Table 8.1** You should be aware of this legislation

safety of visitors. Policies vary from one setting to another, but most will stipulate the following security measures. Visitors must:

● state the purpose of their visit or whom they are coming to see, and provide identification
● sign into the visitors' book as soon as they arrive and be escorted to the appropriate room by a qualified member of staff
● be supervised at all times by a member of staff.

## Sources of guidance for planning healthy and safe environments and services

Every setting should have a copy of the latest legislation and guidance documents relevant to their service. You could also check on current legislation by accessing the websites listed at the end of this chapter.

## Implementing legislation for health and safety: policies and procedures

Health and safety legislation and policy aims to make sure that all workers, children, young people and families are safe and protected from harm when in work or using services. You do not need to be an expert in this area, but you should be aware of the legal issues and national and local guidance relating to health and safety, and know where to go and whom to ask for advice and support.

The most relevant laws relating to health and safety in childcare settings in the UK are shown in Table 8.1.

## Health and Safety at Work Act 1974

Employers have a duty to:

- make your workplace as safe as possible
- display a health and safety law poster or supply employees with a leaflet with the same information (available from the Health and Safety Executive)
- decide how to manage health and safety; if the business has five or more employees, this must appear on a written health and safety policy.

Employees also have a duty to work safely. If you are given guidance about how to use equipment, you should follow that guidance. You should not work in a way that puts other people in danger.

## COSHH: Control of Substances Hazardous to Health Regulations

Safe workplaces depend on the careful use and storage of cleaning materials and other potentially hazardous substances. Items such as bleach or dishwasher powders, some solvent glues and other materials in your setting can be hazardous. You should have a risk assessment that tells you about these dangers, and what to do in order to minimise the risks involved. Any new person coming to the team must be made aware of what to do.

Every workplace must have a **COSHH** file which lists all the hazardous substances used in the setting. The file should detail:

- where they are kept
- how they are labelled
- their effects

- the maximum amount of time it is safe to be exposed to them
- how to deal with an emergency involving one of them.

Never mix products together as they could produce toxic fumes. Some bleaches and cleaning products, for instance, have this effect.

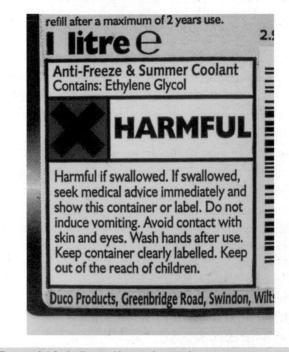

**Figure 8.1** Labelling of hazardous substances

## Food Handling Regulations 1995

If you prepare or handle food (even something as basic as opening biscuits or preparing food for a snack), you need to comply with Food Handling Regulations. These cover many common-sense issues, such as:

- washing your hands before preparing food
- making sure that the surfaces and utensils you use are clean and hygienic
- making sure that food is stored safely, at the correct temperature
- disposing of waste hygienically.

It also includes knowledge of safe practices in the use of chopping boards, having separate sinks for hand washing and preparing foods, how to lay out a kitchen, and so on. There should always be someone at the setting who has completed a Basic Food

Hygiene certificate, to ensure that the guidance is properly followed.

## Fire Precautions (Workplace) Regulations 1997

Fire officers must check all childcare and education premises while they are in the first registration process. They will advise what is needed to make the workplace as safe as possible.

- Evacuation procedures should be in place, known to all the adults, and practised regularly. All available exits should be used at different times, so that everyone can leave the building quickly and safely if an emergency occurs.
- Some exits may be locked to prevent children wandering away or intruders entering, but adults must be able to open them quickly in case of an emergency.
- Designated fire exits must always be unlocked and unobstructed. Fire extinguishers should be in place and checked regularly. A fire blanket is needed in the kitchen.

## Manual Handling Operations Regulations 1992

Lifting and carrying children and moving the equipment used in child care settings could lead to manual handling injuries such as sprains and strains. You should always take measures to protect yourself when lifting children or equipment by following good practice.

Practitioners who work with children and young people with physical disabilities sometimes work in settings which can present significant risks to children, young people and adults. In lifting children and young people with disabilities, often two practitioners need to work together, or there may be a system of hoists to reduce significantly the risk of injury. In this case, instructions on their use would need to be provided by the manufacture of the hoist itself.

If a member of staff is pregnant, she and the manager/teacher have a duty to re-assess any lifting of children and equipment, and to carry out risk assessments accordingly.

If you do have to lift something or somebody from the ground, you should follow these rules:

1 Keep your feet apart.
2 Bend your knees and keep your back upright.
3 Use both hands to get a secure hold.
4 Keep your shoulders level, your back upright and slowly straighten your legs.
5 To put the load down, take the weight on the legs by bending your knees.

## Reporting illness, injury or accident (RIDDOR)

You have a responsibility to report all accidents, incidents and even 'near misses' to your manager. As you may be handling food, you should also report any personal incidences of sickness or diarrhoea. Most settings keep two separate **accident report books** – one for staff and other adults, and one for children or young people (see page 155). These should always be filled in as soon after the incident as possible.

## Policies and procedures

Every childcare and education setting will have policy documents covering such areas as:

- safety
- health and hygiene
- safety at arrival and departure times and on outings
- prevention of illness and first aid
- fire prevention
- staffing ratios and supervision.

 **In Practice**

### Infection control policy

Find out about the infection control policy in your own setting.

❏ When should you wear protective clothing?

❏ When should you wear gloves?

❏ How should you dispose of waste?

❏ Which infectious illnesses should you report to your supervisor and not attend for work?

In group care and education settings, a member of staff is usually nominated as being responsible for health and safety; in a childminder's home or if you are working as a nanny, you can contact the local Childminding Association or nanny agency for information on health and safety.

# Recognising and managing risks to health, safety and security

Practitioners need to be conscious of any risks in the working environment and the potential impact of these risks. They can then plan ahead to avoid hazards and incidents.

## How to identify risks in the setting

### Babies and young children

This group are at particular risk of harm because they:

- lack any appreciation of danger
- are naturally inquisitive
- love to explore and test the boundaries of their world.

You need to help young children to explore within safe boundaries, but to adjust those boundaries according to their capabilities and increasing skill. Useful skills to employ when dealing with inquisitive toddlers include recognising the value of **distraction** – guiding attention away from something dangerous and towards something potentially more interesting, physically removing the child: 'Harry, come with me – I want to show you something . . .'.

Even so, no environment, however carefully planned and designed, can ever be totally without risk to children.

### Older children and young people

This group face different risks. For example, they are more likely to travel to school independently and need to be aware of the principles of road safety. They also need to be aware of the risks involved in using the internet. (See the section on e-safety in Chapter 7, Unit CYP Core 3.3, page 138.)

## Hazards in the work setting and off-site visits

For information on safe practice for off-site visits, please see Chapter 14 ( Unit EYMP 3), page 278.

## Safe working practices: protecting children from common hazards

All areas where children and young people play and learn should be checked for hygiene and safety at the start of every session and again at the end of each session – but do be alert at all times. Look at your setting's written policy for health and hygiene issues. Find out how to clean toys and other equipment from your manager, and remember that many objects (plastic toys and soft toys) end up in children's mouths, which is a good way of passing on and picking up an infection.

Remember that *you* could also be a risk to children and young people's health. For example, if you have a heavy cold or have suffered from diarrhoea or vomiting within the previous 24 hours, you must not attend for work as you could pass on a serious infection to the children or young people.

The home, garden and nursery setting should be made as accident-proof as possible. Remember that playing should be fun and is an important part of growing up. Your role is to make sure that it stays fun and does not lead to a serious accident.

## Health and safety risk assessments

Risk assessment is a method of preventing accidents and ill health by helping people to think about what could go wrong and devising ways to prevent problems. Figure 8.2 illustrates how to carry out a risk assessment.

Look for hazards

Decide who might be harmed and how

Weigh up the risk: a risk is the likelihood that a hazard will cause harm

Decide whether existing precautions are enough

If not, decide what further precautions are needed to reduce risk

Record your findings

**Figure 8.2** How to carry out a risk assessment

## What is the difference between a risk and a hazard?

### Key terms

**Hazard** – A source of potential harm or damage, or a situation with potential for harm or damage.

**Risk** – The possibility of suffering harm or loss; danger.

**Risk assessment** – The assessments that must be carried out in order to identify hazards and find out the safest way to carry out certain tasks and procedures.

In the child care setting **a hazard** may be a substance, a piece of equipment, a work procedure or a child's condition. Examples of hazards in early years settings include:

- toys and play equipment
- chemical hazards, such as cleaning materials and disinfectants
- biological hazards, such as airborne and blood-borne infections
- the handling and moving of equipment and of children
- unsupervised children
- security of entry points and exits

- administration of medicines
- visual or hearing impairment of children.

**Risk** is defined as the chance or likelihood that harm will occur from the hazard. The likelihood is described as 'the expectancy of harm occurring'. It can range from 'never' to 'certain' and depends on a number of factors.

### Example 1: a door

The main entrance to a nursery or primary school may present a **hazard**. The **risks** are:

- that a child might escape and run into the road, or go missing, or
- that a stranger might enter the building.

The likelihood of the **hazard** of the entrance/door posing a **risk** will depend on a number of factors:

- the security of the entrance – for example, can it only be opened by using a key pad or entry phone system, and is the door handle placed high up, out of a child's reach?
- policies and procedures being known to parents and other visitors, such as at collection times.

### Example 2: a damaged or uneven floor surface

This may present a **hazard.** The **risk** is:

- that someone may trip over and become injured.

The likelihood of the **hazard** of the damaged floor posing a **risk** will depend on a number of factors:

- the extent of the unevenness or damage
- the number of people walking over it
- the number of times they walk over it
- whether they are wearing sensible shoes
- the level of lighting.

## Monitoring and reviewing risk assessments

It is important to monitor and review risk assessments as there may have been changes – for example, new equipment introduced or new procedures. After completing an initial risk assessment, a date should be set for the next one. This could be once a term, twice a year or annually, depending on the size of the setting, the number of

## Case Study — A breach of health and safety regulations

A nursery owner was fined £35,000 for breaking health and safety regulations, after a toddler died at the nursery as a result of trapping her neck in the drawstring of a bag. The 16-month-old toddler was described as lively, inquisitive and able to walk. She had been placed in a cot to sleep with a looped drawstring of a bag placed over the side, and became entangled in the loops. She was left unattended for 20 minutes, and when found, she was apparently lifeless. Last year, an inquest jury returned a verdict of unlawful killing after hearing that the toddler was in the care of a 17-year-old student and an unqualified member of staff while senior managers met upstairs. This led to the case against the owner being reopened.

The Crown court judge said staff showed 'gross incompetence' by not acting on warnings from the toddler's parents that she did often wrap things around her neck. The judge said: 'This [*leaving a bag on the cot*] was such an obvious risk that virtually no parent in their own home would have considered this, let alone professionals who should have been responsible.' The prosecuting counsel claimed that although toddlers at the nursery should have been checked every ten minutes, there was a 'conflicting understanding' among staff. He said that a proper risk assessment was not carried out, which meant that bags continued to be left on cots. The nursery owner said: 'There are no words I can say to excuse or lessen the terrible tragedy of [the toddler's] death. As a mother myself, I feel deep sadness and remorse. I accept fully that the ultimate responsibility for her safety lay with me, as the owner.' The judge noted that it was not a case of manslaughter but a breach of health and safety regulations: 'The death of this child is a tragic and heart-breaking incident. It was, however, an accident . . . which should have been foreseen.'

(Adapted from a report in *The Guardian*, 30 October 2008)

1 What factors led to the toddler being unsafe while in nursery care?

2 What sort of risk assessment could have helped to prevent the toddler's death?

3 On a wider subject – do you think that *all* accidents are preventable?

staff changes, changes to the physical environment, additional equipment or resources. When new equipment arrives, a new risk assessment should be completed and the findings added to the original document.

The process of review includes answering the following questions:

- Have there been any changes?
- Are there improvements you still need to make?
- Have you or your colleagues identified a problem?
- Have you learnt anything from accidents or near misses?

# Supporting children and young people to assess and manage risk for themselves

## The importance of a balanced approach to risk management

Children and young people need a safe but challenging environment. Almost every human activity involves a certain degree of risk, and children and young people need to learn how to cope with this. They need to understand that the world can be a dangerous place, and that care needs to be taken when they are negotiating their way round it. For example, when a child first learns to walk, he or she will inevitable fall over or knock into things. This is a valuable part of their learning and a natural part of their development.

Children and young people who are sheltered or overprotected from risk and challenge will not be able to make judgements about their own strengths and skills, and will not be well-equipped to resist peer pressure in their later years. Also, a totally risk-free environment lacks challenges and stimulation; this leads inevitably to children and young people becoming bored and behaving increasingly inappropriately. Simply being *told* about possible dangers is not enough: children and young people need to see or experience the consequences of not taking care.

An important aspect of teaching children and young people about risk is to encourage them to make their own *risk assessments* and think about the possible consequences of their actions. Rather than removing objects and equipment from the environment in case children and young people hurt themselves, adults should teach children and young people how to use them safely. It is important to strike the right balance: protecting children and young people from harm while allowing them the freedom to develop independence and risk awareness.

# The dilemma between the rights of children and health and safety requirements

The challenge for practitioners is balancing the need for safety against the need for children and young people to explore risks. Many adults engage in risky activities such as bungee jumping, skydiving, motor racing, snowboarding, or even drug-taking. All have a potential to cause death, and this is one reason why people enjoy them, for the 'rush'. Similarly, children and young people need to explore their own levels of risk-taking, but in safe environments with qualified first aid personnel at hand should accidents arise. If we do not enable children and young people to take

risks, then they will seek them out when adults are not around.

## The EYFS statutory framework

The EYFS places an obligation on providers to conduct a risk assessment and review it regularly. The guidance on play includes the advice that:

> 'Through play, in a secure but challenging environment with effective adult support, children can take risks and make mistakes.'

The duty to balance keeping children and young people safe with encouraging them to learn actively is further developed in the Principles to Practice cards:

- *A Unique Child – Keeping Safe* says: 'being over-protected can prevent children from learning about possible dangers and about how to protect themselves from harm'.
- *A Unique Child – Health and Well-being* identifies one of the key challenges and dilemmas for practitioners as 'ensuring safety without stopping reasonable risk-taking'.
- *Learning and Development – Play and Exploration* says: 'practitioners always intervene in play if it is racist, sexist or in any way offensive, unsafe, violent or bullying'.
- *Learning and Development – Physical Development* says practitioners should give particular attention to building 'children's confidence to take manageable risks in their play'.

When children and young people undertake a challenging physical activity successfully, they grow in confidence and capability; their skills develop well for their future when they will have to make risk assessments for themselves.

## Supporting children and young people to assess and manage risk

If a child or young person seems at risk of harming herself in some way, the practitioner *must* intervene. Then, using language appropriate to the age and understanding of the child or young person, the adult could ask open-ended questions for the child or

## Case Study    Supporting children to assess and manage risk

Four children are playing in a den they have made in the outdoor play area, using a frame and some cloth. The den looks rather crowded and the children are finding it difficult to carry out their play. Angela, a practitioner, asks them: 'How many children do you think should be in the den? How many of you are in the den? How is it making you feel? What could we do to make it less of a squash?' The children all join in with answers, and after a lively debate, two of the children decide to set up a den for themselves. Angela helps them fetch the equipment and the play resumes.

**Figure 8.3** Children playing in a den

young person to identify why she could come to harm. In this way, the adult and the child/young person work together to reach a solution and children and young people gain a better understanding of why they were stopped how to identify dangers. (They can then carry on, if appropriate.)

As children and young people become older, talk to them about keeping safe and about how to avoid accidents and injury. Children and young people may also be encouraged to assess risks by being given reasons why they may be asked to do something. For example, when asking children to put the cars and trucks back on to the mat, the adult asks why it

should be done and the child learns that if they are not collected, someone may trip over them and could hurt themselves.

# Accidents, incidents, emergencies and illness

## Recognising signs of illness

The responsibility of caring for a child or young person who becomes ill is enormous; it is vital that carers should know the signs and symptoms of illness and when to seek medical aid. When a child or young person is taken ill or is injured, it is vital that the parents or carers are notified as soon as possible. If a child or young person becomes ill while at nursery he or she may have to wait a while to be taken home. In the meantime you should:

- offer support and reassurance to the child or young person, who may feel frightened or anxious
- always notify a senior member of staff if you notice that a child or young person is unwell; that person will then decide if and when to contact the child or young person's parents or carers.

A member of staff (preferably the child or young person's key person) should remain with the child or young person all the time and keep them as comfortable as possible.

You must deal with any incident of vomiting or diarrhoea swiftly and sympathetically to minimise the child or young person's distress and to preserve their dignity. All settings have an Exclusion policy that lets parents know when it is safe for their sick child or young person to return to the group.

# What to do in case of serious illness or injury

1 **Call for help**: Stay calm and do not panic! Your line manager (or designated first aider) will make an assessment and decide whether the injury or illness requires **medical help**, either a GP or an ambulance. He or she will also **contact the parents or carers** to let them know about the nature of the illness or injury.
2 **Stay with the child or young person**; comfort and reassure him or her.
3 **Treat the injury** or **assess the severity of the illness** and treat appropriately. You are not expected to be able to *diagnose* a sudden illness, but should know what signs and symptoms require medical treatment.
4 **Record exactly what happens** and what treatment is carried out.

## What to do when an accident happens

If a child or young person has had an accident, they are likely to be shocked and may not cry

immediately. They will need calm reassurance as first aid is administered, together with an explanation of what is being done to them and why. Parents or carers must be informed and the correct procedures for the setting carried out. If the child or young person needs emergency hospital treatment, parental permission will be needed.

If you work in a setting with others such as a day care facility or school, there is likely to be a designated person who is a qualified in first aid; they should be called to deal with the situation.

**Remember!** It is essential that you do not make the situation worse, and it is better to do the minimum to ensure the child or young person's safety such as putting them into the **recovery position**. The only exception to this is if the child or young person is not breathing or there is no heartbeat.

## Serious conditions

**A child or young person who has sustained a serious injury or illness will need to be seen urgently by a doctor.** For example:

- a head injury or any loss of consciousness
- a wound that continues to bleed after first aid treatment is given
- suspected **meningitis** (see below)
- an asthma attack not relieved by child or young person's inhaler
- fracture or suspected fracture, burns and scalds, foreign bodies
- life-threatening incidents such as seizures, poisoning, choking, **anaphylaxis**, loss of consciousness, respiratory and cardiac arrest.

## Key terms

**Anaphylaxis** – A severe allergic reaction that affects the whole body. It can lead to **anaphylactic shock**.

**Anaphylactic shock** – A potentially fatal immune response when the body system literally shuts down. The most common causes are a severe allergic reaction to insect stings and certain drugs.

| Signs and symptoms of meningitis | |
|---|---|
| **In babies under 12 months:** | **In older children:** |
| Tense or bulging **fontanelles** | Headache |
| A stiffening body with involuntary movements, or a floppy body | Neck stiffness and joint pains; the child may arch the neck backwards because of the rigidity of the neck muscles |
| Blotchy or pale skin | |
| A high-pitched, moaning cry | An inability to tolerate light |
| High temperature | Fever |
| The baby may be difficult to wake | |
| The baby may refuse to feed | |
| Red or purple spots (anywhere on the body) that do not fade under pressure. Do the 'glass test' – see below | |

**Table 8.2** Signs and symptoms of meningitis

## Meningitis

Meningitis is an inflammation of the lining of the brain. It is a very serious illness, but if it is detected and treated early, most children and young people make a full recovery. The early symptoms of meningitis, such as fever, irritability, restlessness, vomiting and refusing feeds, are also common with colds and 'flu. However, a baby with meningitis can become seriously ill *within hours*, so it is important to *act quickly* if meningitis is suspected. Table 8.2 shows the signs and symptoms of meningitis.

### The 'glass test'

Press the side or bottom of a glass firmly against the rash; you will be able to see if the rash fades and loses colour under the pressure. If it *does not* change colour, summon medical aid *immediately*. If spots are appearing on the body, this could be septicaemia – a very serious bacterial infection described as the 'meningitis rash'.

**Figure 8.4** The 'glass test' for meningitis

### Key term

**Fontanelle** – A diamond-shaped soft area at the front of the head, just above the brow. It is covered by a tough membrane and you can often see the baby's pulse beating there under the skin. The fontanelle closes between 12 and 18 months of age.

# Emergency procedures: what to do in the event of a non-medical incident or emergency

There are many different types of emergency (apart from a medical emergency when a person is seriously injured or ill) and it is important to know what procedures to follow, for example:

- if a child or young person goes missing
- in case of fire
- if there is a security incident.

## Missing children

Strict procedures must be followed to prevent a child from going missing from the setting. However, if a child *does* go missing, an established procedure must be followed, for example:

- The person in charge will carry out a thorough search of the building and garden.
- The register is checked to make sure that no other child has also gone astray.
- Doors and gates are checked to see if there has been a breach of security whereby a child could wander out.
- The person in charge talks to staff to establish what happened.

If the child is not found, the parent or carer is contacted and the missing child is reported to the police.

## In case of fire

In the case of fire or other emergency, you need to know what to do to safely evacuate the children and yourselves. Follow the following rules for fire safety:

- No smoking is allowed in any child care setting.
- Handbags containing matches or lighters must be locked securely away out of children's reach.
- The nursery cooker should not be left unattended when turned on.
- Fire exits must be clearly signed.
- Fire procedures should be tested regularly; registers must be kept up to date throughout the day.
- Fire exits and other doors should be free of obstructions on both sides.
- Instructions about what to do in the event of a fire must be clearly displayed.
- You should know where the fire extinguishers are kept and how to use them.
- Electrical equipment should be regularly checked for any faults.

## Evacuation procedures

A plan for an escape route and the attendance register must be up to date so that everyone – children and staff – can safely be accounted for at the meeting point of safety. The attendance record must be taken by the person in charge when the building is evacuated. Clearly written instructions for fire

---

## Case Study — Missing from a nursery

A two-year-old girl walked out of her pre-school nursery one winter morning, leaving her coat behind, and crossed a busy road as she wandered half a mile to her home. The first that the nursery knew of her disappearance was when her furious father turned up demanding to know why he had found his tearful daughter struggling to open their garden gate.

Fortunately, potentially dangerous events like this are very rare, but they should be preventable.

1 How do you think that this could have happened?

2 Consider your own setting and assess whether it could happen there.

3 How could such incidents be prevented?

drills and how to summon the fire brigade must be posted in a conspicuous place in the setting.

## Security issues and violence

Early years settings and schools should be secure environments where children cannot wander off without anyone realising. But they also need to be secure so that strangers cannot enter without a proper reason for being there. Occasionally you might encounter a problem with violence – or threats of violence – from a child's parents or carers. Your setting will have a policy that deals with this issue.

# Recording and reporting accidents, incidents, injuries, signs of illness and other emergencies

## Reporting to parents

All accidents, injuries or illnesses that occur to children and young people in a group setting must be reported to the child or young person's parents or primary carers. If the injury is minor (such as a bruise or a small graze to the knee), the staff will inform parents or carers when the child/young person is collected at the end of the session; or they may send a notification slip home if someone else collects the child. The parents/carers are notified about:

- the nature of the injury or illness
- any treatment or action taken
- the name of the person who carried out the treatment.

In the case of a major accident, illness or injury, the child or young person's parents or primary carers must be notified as soon as possible. Parents/carers need to know that staff members are dealing with the incident in a caring and professional manner, and they will need to be involved in any decisions regarding treatment.

## The Accident Report Book

Every workplace is, by law, required to have an Accident Report Book and to maintain a record of accidents. Information recorded includes:

- name of person injured
- date and time of injury
- where the accident happened (for example, in the garden)
- what exactly happened (Kara fell on the path and grazed her left knee)
- what injuries occurred (a graze)
- what treatment was given (graze was bathed and an adhesive dressing applied)
- name and signature of person dealing with the accident
- signature of witness to the report
- signature of parent or carer.

One copy of the duplicated report form is given to the child's parent or carer; the other copy is kept in the Accident Report Book at the early years setting.

If you are working in the family home as a nanny, you should follow the same reporting procedure, even though you do not have an official Accident Report Book.

## Reporting and recording when a child or young person becomes ill

If a child or young person becomes ill while in a group setting, you should *first* report it to your manager or supervisor and then record the following details in the child or young person's Daily Record:

- when the child or young person first showed signs of illness
- the signs and symptoms: for example, behaviour changes, a high temperature or a rash
- any action taken: for example, taking the temperature or giving paracetamol (with parental permission agreed beforehand)
- progress of the illness since first noticing it: for example, are there any further symptoms?

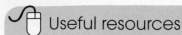 Useful resources

**Organisations and websites**

**British Red Cross** – for information on first aid for children and how to become a qualified first-aider:
**www.redcross.org.uk**

**Child Accident Prevention Trust** is a UK charity, working to reduce the number of children and young people killed, disabled or seriously injured in accidents:
**www.capt.org.uk**

**NHS immunisation information** – for up-to-date information on the current immunisation schedule:
**www.immunisation.nhs.uk**

**Royal Society for the Prevention of Accidents** – for all child safety advice and information:
**www.rospa.com**

# 9 Develop positive relationships with children, young people and others involved in their care: Unit CYP Core 3.5

Children and young people become confident, independent and most resilient where they are secure in the relationships around them. Relationships take time to become established, because they are based on a growing understanding of one another. Effective communication helps children and young people develop confidence, feelings of self-worth and positive relationships with others. It also helps them grow into adults who have positive feelings about themselves and others.

## Learning outcomes

By the end of this chapter you will:

1. Be able to develop positive relationships with children and young people.

2. Be able to build positive relationships with people involved in the care of children and young people.

## Developing positive relationships with children and young people

It is important to establish appropriate and effective relationships with all the people you encounter in your work. This learning outcome requires you to understand the importance of these relationships and to be able to reflect on your own practice.

## Building and maintaining positive relationships

Positive relationships with practitioners provide children and young people with:

- **Emotional security**: when children and young people know that there is someone on their side, who cares and to whom they can turn, they are better able to participate in play and learning activities with confidence. They are also able to manage transitions more easily, such as when separating from their parents in a new setting.
- **Self-esteem**: when practitioners accept children and young people for who they are, it is easier for children and young people to accept themselves and develop good self-esteem.
- **A sense of wellbeing**: children and young people are less likely to exhibit unacceptable behaviour when they feel comfortable in their relationships with others.
- **Ways in which to express their feelings**: having someone they can talk to and share ideas encourages children to develop self-confidence and resilience in all aspects of their lives.

## How to listen to and build relationships with children and young people

### Communicate effectively

The importance of communicating effectively is discussed in Chapter 1 (Unit SHC 31).

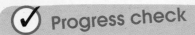 **Progress check**

## How to communicate with children and young people

- **Make eye contact** and show that you are listening: it is very difficult to have a conversation with someone who never looks at you! When talking with very young children, it is usually necessary to stoop down to their level or to sit at a table with them. As noted earlier, it is important to be aware that, in certain cultures, mutual eye contact is considered impolite or disrespectful.
- **Listen carefully** to the child or young person's own spoken language and use it as a basis for conversation. Very young children tend to use one or two words to mean any of a number of things; for example, 'drink' can mean 'this is my drink', 'I want a drink', 'Where is my drink?' or 'You have got a drink'.
- **Repeat** a child's words in a correct form, or a complete sentence. This checks understanding and provides the child with an accurate model for the future. For example, young children often use speech such as 'feeded' instead of 'fed', 'runned' instead of 'ran'. In checking what they mean the adult should use the correct term, for example:

  Child: I feeded carrots to my rabbit.
  Adult: Oh, you fed your rabbit some carrots.
- **Be a positive role model**, speak clearly and use correct grammar and patterns of speech.
- **Use open-ended questions**: encourage children and young people to speak by asking 'open' questions which require an answer in phrases and/or sentences, rather than a simple 'yes' or 'no'; for example, 'Tell me about your party,' instead of 'Did you have a good time at your party?' This opens up opportunities for the child or young person to talk about a range of different things or one single event of his/her own choice. You can always ask more questions as the conversation progresses to check the information, supply additional vocabulary and correct grammar.
- **Use prompts**: these invite the child or young person to say more, to share ideas and feelings. They also tell the child or young person that you are properly listening and interested, that their ideas are important and that you accept them and respect what they are saying. Examples of prompts are: 'Oh, I see,' 'Tell me more,' 'That's interesting.'
- **Listen attentively**: get rid of distractions and pay attention to what the child or young person is saying. It is difficult to pay close attention to what the child or young person is saying if you are busy trying to read at the same time.
- **Respond sensitively**: remember the importance of **non-verbal communication**. Watch out for when a child or young person seems upset or looks sad, and say, 'You seem upset; do you want to tell me about it?'
- **Say 'Please' and 'Thank you' to children and young people**: children and young people deserve the common courtesies that we as adults use with each other. Children and young people will learn by imitating the speech and behaviour of adults.
- **Use appropriate language to help promote self-esteem**: kind words give children and young people more self-confidence and help them to behave better, try harder and achieve more. They communicate love and respect, and also create an atmosphere in which problems can be discussed openly and understandings can be reached.

  For example: a child has spilt her orange juice on the floor. You could say, 'Don't be so clumsy! Just look at the mess you made.' But it would be better to say, 'Here's a cloth. Please wipe the juice up,' and later, 'Thank you for doing such a good job of cleaning the floor.'
- **Do not use inappropriate language that puts children and young people down**: negative words make the child or young person feel bad, and they prevent effective communication. Avoid words which:
  (a) **ridicule**: 'You are acting just like a baby.'
  (b) **shame**: 'I am so ashamed of you.'
  (c) **label**: 'You are a naughty boy.'
  Unkind words, spoken without thinking of their results, make the child or young person feel disliked, and result in low self-esteem. More importantly, unkind words do not help; they only make matters worse.
- **Always be positive**: tell children and young people what **to do** instead of what **not to do**. For example, instead of 'Don't slam the door!' try 'Please shut the door quietly'; instead of 'Don't spill your drink!' say 'Try holding your beaker with both hands.'

## Identify and resolve conflicts and disagreements

Children and young people need to be able to deal with conflict effectively. This is an important life skill and will help children and young people to resolve conflicts in an assertive, but not aggressive, manner. They will be more confident in situations if they feel they can stand up for themselves, without needing others to look out for them. If you see children arguing or fighting, try not to step in straightaway. Most conflicts in early childhood relate to sharing and taking turns. For example, if two children are arguing over whose turn it is to use the computer, stay nearby and observe, and allow the children time to sort the dispute out for themselves. Only step in immediately if a child is being hurt, or is at risk of being hurt.

If you *do* decide to intervene, follow these guidelines:

- Give both children the opportunity to be heard without interruption.
- Invite the children to come up with their own solutions to the problem.
- Acknowledge the feelings and emotions from *both* sides.
- Suggest one or two solutions if necessary.
- Acknowledge the attempts made to resolve conflict: 'That seems like a good idea, Tom. What do you think, Ivan?'

## Be consistent and fair

Children and young people need to feel safe and secure, and they need practitioners to react predictably to situations, showing fairness and consistency. If parents and staff are not consistent in their approaches, children and young people become unsettled and confused, and they do not know what is expected of them. Behaviour then becomes increasingly inappropriate, as they have no real understanding of the acceptable boundaries.

All children and young people need care and attention, support and practical help, but as each child or young person is unique, each will have different needs. It is important that practitioners do the following:

- **Address each child or young person's needs**: for example, a confident, talkative child/young person or a child/young person with behavioural difficulties may take up a lot of your time, but it is important to watch out for the quiet child/young person who seems not to need you when playing quietly alone.
- **Spend time with all the children and young people in your care**: a team approach to planning activities will help to make sure that a balance is achieved for all, and that every child and young person receives individual attention whenever possible.

## Show respect and courtesy

Only when children and young people have learned that other people have feelings of their own, can they start to have empathy and concern for the wellbeing of others. They will then be able to share their feelings with others and to show compassion to friends who are upset. This usually happens at around the age of three to four years.

Children and young people show respect for others when they are treated with respect themselves. Adults should always model respectful and courteous behaviour, both to children and to their colleagues. You can show respect for others by following simple rules of courtesy – by treating other people as you would wish to be treated yourself. From the earliest age, children can learn when to say 'please,' 'thank you' and 'sorry' – all markers of respect for other people's feelings.

### Key term

Empathy – Understanding how other people feel.

## Value and respect individuality

In line with the **CACHE** values, you need to ensure that the child or young person is at the centre of your practice; their needs are **paramount**. This means that each child or young person is valued for his or her individuality. As a practitioner, your role is:

- to listen to children and young people
- not to impose your own agenda on them

- not to single out any one child or young person for special attention
- to ensure that children and young people maintain control over their own play/leisure
- to be friendly, courteous and sensitive to their needs
- to praise and motivate them; display their work
- to speak *to* the child/young person not *at* the child/young person; with young children, this means getting down to their level and maintaining eye contact
- to respect their individuality
- to develop a sense of trust and caring with each child and young person.

## Keep promises and honour commitments

In order to encourage children and young people to trust us, we must keep our promises and honour commitments. If we promise that a child can have a turn on the trampoline tomorrow, then we must remember and keep our promise. Children and young people will then learn that they can trust us and rely on us to honour our commitments.

## Monitor the impact of your own behaviour on others

Every child and young person will react differently to individual adults. You need to be observant in picking up on a child or young person's reaction and body language in response to your own behaviour. For example, you may notice that a child always ignores you when you ask him or her to help with setting out an activity, yet responds positively to another practitioner. Reflect on why this may happen and try to adapt your behaviour appropriately.

## Keep confidentiality as appropriate

Maintaining confidentiality is important for establishing a trusting and respectful relationship. You should only break or breach confidentiality when there is an overriding need to do so. See Chapter 1 (Unit SHC 31), page 2 for more information.

## Recognise and respond appropriately to the power base underpinning relationships

It is important to remember that your relationship with the children and young people in your care is a professional one. You should always be friendly and approachable, but try not to take the place of the child's parents. Similarly, you should communicate with every child and young person at a level which is appropriate to their stage of development and their holistic needs; you should not act as a child would when interacting with one.

Relationships begin before a baby is born, with the care and attention received in the womb. **Bonding** is a term commonly used to describe the strong attachment between a baby and the important people in the baby's life. It used to be thought that babies only bonded with their mothers but research shows that babies can bond to a number of important or significant people. Babies can form an attachment with a variety of others: see Figure 9.1.

Early years practitioners are often concerned, or feel that parents are anxious, about young children becoming 'too attached' to staff. However, babies

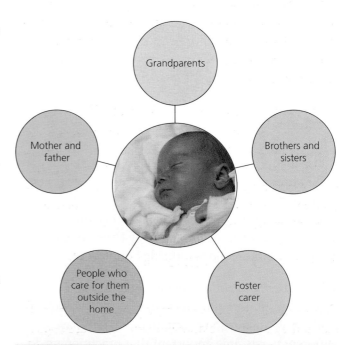

**Figure 9.1** Babies can form attachments with many different people

and young children *need* to form close attachments with significant adults in their lives, and they cannot become too closely attached. Some young children spend many hours in group settings outside the home; they need and ought to develop attachments to their **key person**. Parents who work long hours may experience a conflict of emotions. They want their child to be happy and secure in nursery care, but they do not want to feel forgotten or pushed out. Parents often feel a real anxiety when their child shows affection for their key worker.

## Physical contact with babies, children and young people

Babies and very young children need physical contact; they need to be held and cuddled in order to develop emotionally. Hugging a baby, comforting a child when they are upset, putting a plaster on them, changing their wet pants; these are ways in which adults care for young children every day. However, there is a growing concern among childcare professionals about *touching* children in their care. Researchers say that there is anxiety and uncertainty about what is acceptable and what is not acceptable when it comes to innocent physical contact with children and young people. If teachers and other child care professionals are no longer allowed to offer comforting hugs, or sometimes even to put on a plaster or sun cream, their relationship with the children and young people they look after will certainly suffer.

Your setting should have a **code of conduct** that will give clear guidelines on appropriate physical contact with the children or young people in your care. What is appropriate physical contact with a baby or toddler, such as hugging them when upset or sitting them on your lap to explain something, will not be seen as appropriate in a teenager.

## Building positive relationships with young people

Communication and trust are important if you are to maintain a positive relationship with young people. They need to be able to turn to adults for advice and reassurance. It is easier to help them if

communication channels are kept open and they know that you are there if they want to talk. Relationships with practitioners they see regularly may assume a critical importance when family relationships break down, leaving the young person without the emotional resilience that will be needed in later life. To feel happy and healthy, children and young people want their voices listened to, to be valued as individuals, and their views acted upon.

## Evaluating your own effectiveness

When evaluating your own effectiveness, you need to apply the principles of **reflective practice**. This requires a set of skills that the practitioner must use:

- self-awareness
- the ability to view situations from different perspectives
- the ability to critically analyse and to search for alternative explanations
- the ability to use evidence in supporting or evaluating a decision or position.

Other skills include the ability to integrate new knowledge into existing knowledge, while making a judgement on the incident or situation. **Evaluation** is central to developing any new perspective.

## The reflective cycle

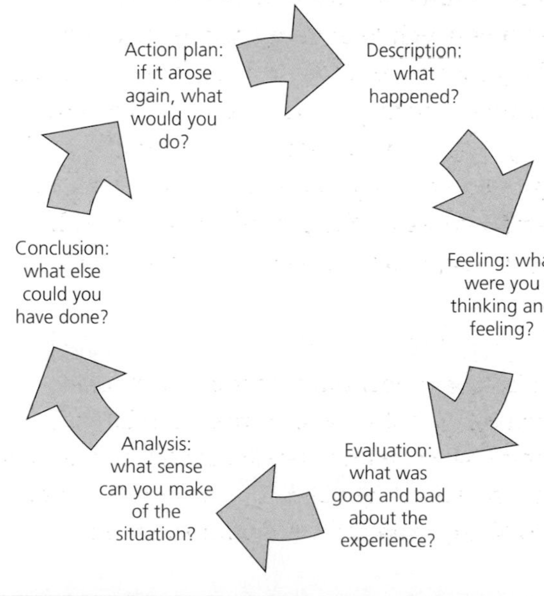

**Figure 9.2** The reflective cycle (G. Gibbs, *Learning by Doing*, FEU, 1988)

## Case Study    Using the reflective cycle

**Description of experience: what happened?**

Claire and I were supervising 12 three-year-old children using the outdoor play equipment, when one of the children, Sasha, climbed to the top of the little slide and pushed Ben very hard so that he fell and bruised his knees. I picked Ben up to examine his knees and to comfort him. Claire rushed towards Sasha and gave her an angry shove, saying 'You naughty girl – now you know what it feels like!' I then told Claire that I was taking Ben indoors to deal with his injury. By the time I came back outside, Sasha was playing happily on the trikes. Ben was no longer crying and he went off to play indoors at the water tray.

**Feelings: how did it make you feel?**

I was quite shaken. I felt that Claire had reacted instinctively and lashed out without thinking first. She has quite a short fuse, but I have never seen her do anything like that before. I was annoyed that I did not say anything to Claire about it.

**Evaluation: what was positive and what was challenging about the experience?**

The positive part about the experience was that ultimately neither child was seriously hurt. The challenging part was that I had not felt able to talk to Claire about it, and felt that the opportunity for telling her how I felt was now lost.

**Analysis: what sense can you make of the situation?**

I lacked assertiveness. I felt ashamed that I had witnessed inappropriate practice and done nothing about it. I think Claire has been under a lot of stress recently as her mother is in hospital. I think I was hesitant to challenge her because she has been working at the setting for a longer time than I have, and because normally I would trust her judgement.

**Conclusion: what else could you have done?**

I could have told Claire that I would like to discuss her behaviour towards Sasha, and could have arranged to see her after work. I could have discussed this with my manager. The incident should have been reported in the incident/accident book.

**Action plan: what would you do if it arose again?**

I would try to remember what I have learned about being assertive without being aggressive. I would definitely speak to Claire about how I felt and hope that it could be discussed rationally.

### Reflective practice: using the reflective cycle

Choose a situation in which you have experienced either success or some difficulty in responding effectively to another's behaviour. Using the reflective cycle, organise your reflections and evaluate your own effectiveness.

# Building positive relationships with people involved in the care of children and young people

## The importance of positive relationships with other carers and parents

The parent or primary carer is a deeply important person to the child or young person, and the relationship between parent/carer and child is always very emotional. Emotional relationships can be a source of great strength, but they can also be very unreasonable at times. It is important to recognise that parents/carers and staff have different kinds of relationships with the children in their care.

Practitioners need to develop consistent, warm and affectionate relationships with children and young people, especially babies, but they do not seek to replace the parents or carers. Babies need to be with the same people every day to develop social relationships, which is why the EYFS requires all early years settings and schools to implement a **key person system**.

Parents, carers and practitioners have one thing in common which is very important: they all want the best for the child or young person. The roles involved are not the same, but they are complementary:

● Practitioners have knowledge of general child and young person development.
● Parents know their own child the best.

For the partnership between parents, practitioners and child/young person to develop well, each needs to be able to trust and respect the other. The self-esteem and wellbeing of the people in the partnership (the parents, the staff members and the child/young person) are important when they are working together. How we feel about ourselves influences how we relate to other people.

Parents or carers may have had bad experiences at school, and when their child joins a group setting, all of those past feelings may come rushing back to the surface. The parent and carer will then be anxious and not feel good about themselves. They might expect your setting to be like the one they went to, and this will make them fear for their child. This is often the case when parents are required to bring their child to the early years setting under a child protection order. Staff will need to be sensitive to the feelings of parents in this sort of situation.

## Understanding the views of parents

It is only by understanding how parents and carers feel that professionals can share effectively what they know and have learned in their own training. This is especially important when working with families from different cultural backgrounds. The assumptions on both sides about what education is and how it should be carried out are often different. Through mutual respect, trust is established. This brings a deep commitment on both sides to working together for the child or young person.

## Respecting differences of opinion

Some parents may hope that their child will learn to read early, and might already have taught the alphabet to their three-year-old child. Do not reject their ideas about how children learn to read, even though your own point of view might be very different as a result of your training. Try asking the parent if they would like to know some of the other 12 or so things children need to know in order to read. Stress that learning each of these things is valuable in itself and that there is no hurry to learn to read. It is more important that children learn at their own pace, as they are more likely to become avid readers as a result.

This does not reject the fact that the parent has taught their child the alphabet, but it does open up all sorts of other possibilities for what the parent can do to help their child to read. The messages to the parent are that the staff also value reading, that they respect the intentions of the parent and that they can be a helpful resource for a family that is teaching a child to read.

See Chapter 1 (Unit SHC 31), page 4 for guidelines on communicating well with parents.

# 10 Working together for the benefit of children and young people: Unit CYP Core 3.6

This chapter will help you to understand the importance of multi-agency and integrated working, and to develop the skills of effective communication for professional purposes. You will also find out how information should be stored and shared with others in your setting.

## Learning outcomes

By the end of this chapter you will:

1. Understand integrated and multi-agency working.

2. Be able to communicate with others for professional purposes.

3. Be able to support organisational processes and procedures for recording, storing and sharing information.

# Understand integrated and multi-agency working

Multi-agency working enables different services and professionals to join forces in order to prevent problems occurring. It is an effective way of supporting children, young people and families with additional needs, and helps to secure improved outcomes. Integrated working involves everyone who works with children and young people, whether part-time or full-time. Any member of the children and young people's workforce (such as an early years practitioner, a nurse, teacher, youth worker, sports coach, social worker) needs to understand the importance of working together in an integrated way and to build it into their everyday practice. Integrated and multi-agency working is also collectively known as **partnership working**.

## Key terms

**Integrated working** – When everyone supporting children and young people works together effectively to put the child at the centre, meet their needs and improve their lives.

**Multi-agency working** – Practitioners from different sectors and professions within the workforce are brought together to provide integrated support to children and their families; for example a 'team around the child' (TAC).

## The importance of multi-agency working and integrated working

Before multi-agency working became the accepted way of working, the parents of a child or young person with special or additional needs would probably face many different appointments with several different people, none of whom would have spoken to each other and all of whom would expect the parents to give a detailed breakdown of their child's disability. Multi-agency working and integrated working is designed to cut across this by bringing together professionals with a range of skills to work across their traditional service boundaries.

### Every Child Matters (ECM)

Multi-agency working is a holistic approach to child care and education and is an important feature of the Government's *Every Child Matters* framework:

The five outcomes for ECM are:

- be healthy
- be safe
- enjoy and achieve
- make a positive contribution
- achieve economic wellbeing.

## The benefits of multi-agency working and integrated working

The key principles of multi-agency and integrated working are openness, trust and honesty, agreed shared goals and values, and regular communication between the different services, agencies and teams of professionals. When performed well, multi-agency working and integrated working enables agencies and professionals to do the following:

- **Maintain a focus on the child or young person** by putting them at the centre of everything they do and by involving them. This ensures that everyone communicates about the 'whole' child or young person.
- **Improve communication and information-sharing**: this involves developing strong partnership links with relevant agencies and within the community.
- Support children, young people and families with additional needs: this helps to secure improved outcomes.
- **Support the early intervention process**: early intervention helps to prevent problems occurring in the first place.
- **Work in an inclusive way**: the needs of every child and young person are valued and supported to ensure active participation in all areas of the setting or curriculum. It also means embedding processes of consultation and engagement with children and families in practice.
- **Reduce inappropriate referrals**: this involves being knowledgeable and well-informed about the roles and functions of other professionals, and understanding when and to whom they can make a referral.
- **Reduce duplication**: this is a key aspect of integrated working: 'Ensuring a child only tells their story once'.

- **Maintain confidentiality**: this means understanding that confidentiality is paramount in helping to build trust and confidence.

## Professionals who may work together to support children and young people

There are many different services and professionals providing integrated support for children and young people: see Figure 10.1.

# Delivering better outcomes through integrated working practices and multi-agency working

Every setting is unique, and the nature of the multi-agency working will vary accordingly. For example, childminders are primarily home-based and will work with a varying number of professionals and agencies according to the needs of the children who are placed with them. In order to meet the needs of families accessing support from a range of professionals, the following systems of multi-agency working have been developed:

## Multi-agency panels, or the Team Around the Child (TAC)

Practitioners remain employed by their home agencies but meet on a regular basis to discuss children and young people with additional needs who would benefit from multi-agency input. An example of this type of working arrangement is a Youth Inclusion and Support Panel (YISP).

## Multi-agency teams

These are made up of practitioners seconded or recruited into the team, making it a more formal arrangement than a multi-agency panel. The team works with universal services (those available to *every* child) to support families and schools, as well as individual children and young people.

## Integrated working practices

Examples of integrated working include Children's Centres and extended schools, which offer access to

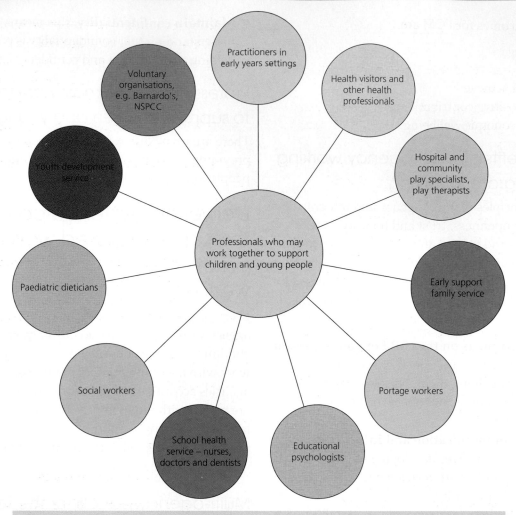

**Figure 10.1** Professionals involved with integrated working

Within the diagram:
- Practitioners in early years settings
- Voluntary organisations, e.g. Barnardo's, NSPCC
- Health visitors and other health professionals
- Youth development service
- Hospital and community play specialists, play therapists
- Professionals who may work together to support children and young people
- Early support family service
- Paediatric dieticians
- Portage workers
- Social workers
- Educational psychologists
- School health service – nurses, doctors and dentists

## Key terms

**Agency** – In this context, this term covers the range of organisations, services and professional groups who provide services to children and their families.

## Key terms

**Extended school** – A school which provides a range of services and activities, often beyond the school day, to help meet the needs of its pupils, their families and the wider community.

a range of integrated, multi-agency services. In children's centres for example, practitioners work in a coordinated way to address the needs of children, young people and families, providing services such as:

- integrated early learning and full daycare
- family support
- health services
- outreach services to children and families not attending the centre
- access to training and employment advice.

# The functions of external agencies

## How multi-agency teams work

Within multi-agency teams, practitioners share a sense of team identity and are generally line-managed by the team leader; they may however maintain links with their home agencies through supervision and training.

Features of multi-agency teams include the following:

- There is a dedicated team leader – also called the **lead professional**.
- There is a good mix of educational, healthcare, social care, youth justice and youth work staff.
- The people who work in the team think of themselves as team members. They are recruited or seconded into the team, either on a full- or part-time basis.
- The team works at a range of levels – not just with individual children and young people, but also small group, family and whole-school work.
- The team is likely to share a base, though some staff may continue to work from their home agencies.
- There are regular team meetings to discuss case working as well as administrative issues.

Examples of multi-agency working include Behaviour and Education Support Teams (BESTs) and Youth Offending Teams (YOTs).

## Key terms

**Lead professional** – The lead professional takes the lead to coordinate provision, and acts as a single point of contact for a child and their family when a TAC (Team around the Child) is required.

## Behaviour and Education Support Teams (BESTs)

These are multi-agency teams bringing together a complementary mix of professionals from the fields of health, social care and education. The aim of a BEST is to promote emotional wellbeing, positive behaviour and school attendance, by identifying and supporting those with, or at risk of developing, emotional and behavioural problems.

- BESTs work with children and young people aged 5 to 18 years, their families and schools. A BEST will aim to intervene early and prevent problems from developing further, and works in targeted primary and secondary schools and in the community, alongside a range of other support structures and services.

- A BEST has a minimum of four to five staff members, who between them have a complementary mix of education, social care and health skills in order to meet the multi-faceted needs of children, young people and their parents.

Schools with BESTs include those with high proportions of pupils with (or at risk of developing) behavioural problems, usually demonstrated in levels of exclusions and attendance.

## Youth Offending Teams

In England and Wales, a Youth Offending Team (YOT) is a multi-agency team coordinated by a local authority, which is overseen by the Youth Justice Board. Scotland and Northern Ireland have very similar systems. YOTs are made up of representatives from:

- the police
- social services
- education
- housing services
- the probation service
- health services
- drug and alcohol misuse services.

Each YOT is managed by a YOT manager who is responsible for coordinating the work of the youth justice services. YOTs aim to identify:

- the needs of each young offender, using a national assessment process
- the specific problems that make the young person offend as well as measuring the risk they pose to others
- suitable programmes to address the needs of the young person, with the intention of preventing further offending.

Occasionally YOT teams organise meetings between young offenders and their victims to encourage apologies and reparation.

## Early Support

Early Support is a Government programme for coordinated, family-focused services for young disabled children and their families in local authorities, hospitals and community-based health

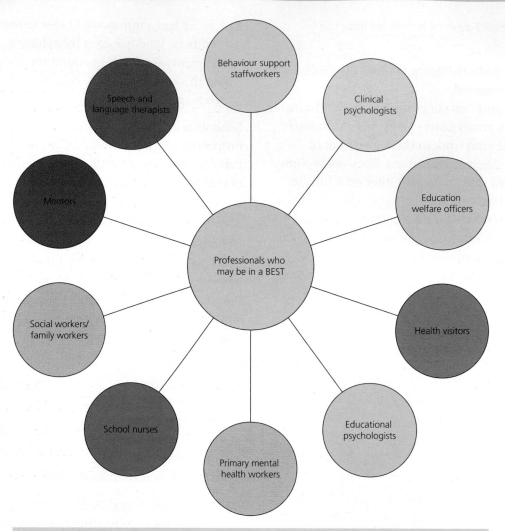

**Figure 10.2** Professionals who may form a BEST

services across England. Families receive coordinated support through key person/worker systems, effective sharing of information between agencies, family support plans and family-held records.

# Common barriers to integrated working and multi-agency working

There are many potential barriers to effective multi-agency working and integrated working.

## Information-sharing

Problems mostly occur around *when* and *how* to share information. Practitioners may be unclear about their individual roles and responsibilities, and worry that they might misjudge the situation and be disciplined for sharing information inappropriately. Team meetings need to be arranged at a convenient time and place for everyone, otherwise non-attendance of various professionals can present a barrier to effective working.

## Case Study    Max

Max is a 3-year-old boy who has learning difficulties and has recently been diagnosed as having autism. Max has a baby sister, Zoe, who is four months old. Six months ago, Max's mother, Carol, was contacted by the local Early Support Team, who helped to find him a place in the nursery at her local children's centre. Max quickly settled in, and although he does not interact with other children he enjoys his time there and has built relationships with two key people. His favourite activity is playing in the sensory room with his mother or a staff member, and he particularly likes the bubble tubes.

Max's key person, Tom, describes Max as a lovely little boy who has difficulties with social and communication skills and who needs supervision at all times to keep him safe as he has very little understanding of danger. As a member of the Early Support Team, Tom coordinates services for Max and his family, and ensures that the appropriate services are in place to support the family. He works closely with Max's parents and immediately made sure that they have access to information about autism in order to understand Max's needs. Tom also helps to coordinate appointments for Max, organises transport to appointments, and makes referrals to other services. For example, he arranged a referral to an occupational therapist to support the family in looking at safety, particularly in the home, and also arranged a referral to the Disability Nursing Team who supports the family in understanding Max's behaviour. Max also has a Portage worker who helps him to interact socially through play. (See Chapter 5, Unit CYP Core 3.1, page 84, for information about Portage home visiting.)

1 List the ways in which Early Support is helping to improve outcomes for Max.

2 Find out how Early Support (or its equivalent programme in Wales, Scotland and Northern Ireland) supports children and families in your own area.

## Key terms

**Information-sharing** – The term used to describe the situation whereby practitioners use their professional judgement and experience on a case-by-case basis to decide whether personal information should be shared with other practitioners in order to meet the needs of a child or young person.

**Organisational culture** – A mixture of the values and beliefs of the people in an organisation.

## Developing a common language

Often there are differences in the organisational cultures of different agencies, and this can lead to difficulties in understanding the specialist terminology and language used by other professionals. Already you will have noticed that there is a whole set of acronyms commonly used in settings with children and young people, such as BEST, CAF, EYFS, ECM, NEET, YSA etc. You do not need to know what they all mean, only the acronyms used in your area of work. You will find a list of acronyms commonly used in settings with children and young people at the end of this book.

## The fear of the 'new'

Some practitioners may feel threatened by new approaches which require them to work differently, across service boundaries. Some may resent being managed by a professional with different skills experiences from their own, and may generally feel out of their 'comfort zone'.

## Lack of understanding of different agency roles

If practitioners do not fully understand the roles and responsibilities of other services and practitioners,

| Children and young people's setting | Services/Professionals |
|---|---|
| **Children's Centre**<br>Integrated local settings set up by Sure Start to provide holistic care to young children and their families | Family information services<br>Play specialists<br>Speech and language therapists<br>Stay and Play Group<br>Toy library<br>Jobcentre<br>Parenting classes, e.g. basic skills, English as an additional language (EAL)<br>Child and family health service<br>Family Support Team (FST)<br>Outreach and family support |
| **Nursery School**<br>Local authority provision for young children | Early education<br>Extended care |
| **School**<br>Local authority provision for children aged 5 to 16 | Education<br>Extended care: breakfast and after-school clubs<br>Education welfare officer<br>Behaviour and Education Support Team (BEST)<br>Counselling services |
| **Youth work**<br>Work with young people aged 13–19<br>Settings vary – school, youth clubs or often outreach work | Education welfare officer<br>Counselling services<br>Drug Action Team<br>Youth offending team worker<br>Primary mental health worker<br>Police and community safety |

**Table 10.1** Multi-agency work with children and young people

they may lack confidence in them and worry that a different agency may not treat the matter confidentially; they may even fear that other practitioners may make things worse for the child, young person or family. Not knowing whom to contact for advice and support with information-sharing can also create barriers to effective multi-agency working. This often leads to anxiety and a lack of confidence.

## Different professional priorities

Team members need to be clear about their goals and their individual roles and responsibilities. Every team member needs to work together to make use of the other professionals' expertise in the best interest of the child, young person and family. It may take time to establish this understanding and to find a way of working together. Making sure that children

and young people are meaningfully involved in planning and decision-making can also cause problems when, for example, a young person does not want his or her parent to be present.

### Assessment practice

**Multi-agency working**

1. How does multi-agency working operate in your area? Find out who would be the relevant 'partners' or agencies in your own work setting.

2. Try to visit one agency such as a children's centre of another department, and find out how referrals are made and how often the multi-agency team meets. Collect as much written information as possible from your visit, to help you when writing up the information required for this unit assessment.

# Referrals between agencies and services

Most children and families who need additional support can obtain it through one of the professionals working in a school or community health setting such as a family worker, health visitor or personal adviser.

Many local authorities have established a **multi-agency referral panel (MARP)** or a similar body. This comprises a team of local professionals from a variety of backgrounds. The panel usually includes the following professionals:

- health visitor
- social worker
- school attendance officer
- school nurse
- psychologist
- youth worker.

The panel meets regularly, working together to produce a holistic solution to an individual child's circumstances. Because every individual has different needs, and possibly a variety of problems, different agencies agree to take the lead on different aspects of a case. No case is closed unless everyone is happy with the outcome.

## Who can make a referral for a multi-agency service?

Children and young people may be able to access support from the multi-agency service by requests initiated by:

- practitioners
- parents and carers
- the child or young person themselves.

## The need to obtain consent

Before making a referral, practitioners are expected to obtain the informed consent either from the parent, carer or the young person to the provision of services. The language they use in these discussions will need to be clear and sensitive to cultural differences and ideas about behavioural and mental health issues.

## The Multi-agency Referral Form

Often the Common Assessment Framework (CAF) form is used as supporting evidence for the referral; it is therefore unnecessary to duplicate the information contained in the CAF assessment on a separate referral form. If not supported by a CAF assessment, then the referrer should use the multi-agency referral form to make detailed notes about the individual child's needs, any other issues they are aware of, and what they have so far done to meet those needs.

## The Common Assessment Framework (CAF)

The Common Assessment Framework (CAF) is a key component of the *Every Child Matters* programme. It is usually used by practitioners to assess the additional needs of a child and his or her family, and to help to identify the services required to meet their needs. The lead professional will usually work with the parents and other agencies to draw up a CAF. It is not always necessary to undertake a CAF for a child – for example if a child is making good progress and the agencies are communicating well together. The CAF begins with information-sharing and assessment of:

- **the child or young person's development**: this is the area in which early years practitioners can usually make the biggest contribution, looking at the child's progress within the framework of the EYFS, including health, and social and emotional development. For young people, the CAF helps to work out what support they might need. This could be a learning mentor for help with the young person's schoolwork, or a drugs worker for help with a drugs problem.
- **parents and carers**: this section looks at the care and support offered to the child or young person, including relationships, stimulation and responding to the child or young person's needs.
- **family and environment**: this takes a wider look at the overall family and environment, and the overall capacity of the parents to support the child or young person's development now and over time.

Drawing on these assessments, the lead professional works with the parents and the TAC to put together an integrated plan to support the child's development.

The CAF recognises that a range of factors may affect children's development and vulnerability. A child with complex needs who has supportive parents and a supportive family environment, with good housing and family income, will be much less vulnerable than a child with a lower level of special need, but who lives in an overcrowded and potentially dangerous flat with a parent suffering from depression. Where a child does not make the expected progress, or where a child is at risk of significant harm, a referral may be made for safeguarding. (This is discussed further in Chapter 7, Unit CYP Core 3.3.)

The CAF has three elements:

1 **A simple pre-assessment checklist**: to help practitioners identify children or young people who would benefit from a common assessment.
2 **A three-step process** (prepare, discuss, deliver) for undertaking a common assessment: this helps practitioners to collect and understand information about the needs and strengths of the child or young person, based on discussions with the child or young person, their family and other practitioners as appropriate.
3 **A standard form**: to help practitioners record and, where appropriate, share with others the findings from the assessment, in terms that are helpful in working with the family to find a response to unmet needs.

# Be able to communicate with others for professional purposes

Sharing information through communicating with others is vital for early intervention to ensure that children and young people receive the services they require. It is also essential for safeguarding and protecting the welfare of individuals, and for providing effective and efficient services which are

---

**Multi-agency working**

A mother comes to the setting to collect her child in the afternoon. She reads the weekly menu and looks angry and upset. You ask if anything is the matter, and she says, 'I've had enough. I've just been at the doctor's with Rhianna and been told to cut out cakes and puddings to help her weight. But I can see here that they have cake, custard and all sorts for pudding in nursery.' You try to explain that the nursery's menus have been checked with the dietician and that each meal is properly balanced, but she storms off.

Think about why early years practitioners should work closely with healthcare professionals in order to help in a situation like this. Discuss your ideas with another learner or in a group. Think together about how a CAF could help this child and her family.

---

coordinated around the needs of an individual or family. The need for every practitioner to have effective communication and teamwork skills is therefore important. See Chapter 1 (Unit SHC 31) for information on developing effective communication skills.

## The importance of clear and effective communication

Effective communication between professionals and agencies is important to make sure that everyone:

- shares information in a clear way that focuses on the individual child or young person
- works towards the same aim: to achieve the best positive outcomes for the child or young person and his or family.

The EYFS Guidance states:
'It is vital to ensure that everyone is working together to meet the emotional, health and educational needs of children in all settings that they attend and across all services provided.'

## Reflective practice: The need for clear and effective communication

Think about the examples below and reflect on why clear and effective communication between different professionals is important in providing for the needs of every child and young person:

- A young person is in foster care and attends more than one setting – school and extended care.

- An 8-year-old child has sickle cell anaemia and attends school but is often in hospital for weeks at a time. Hospital play specialists, hospital teachers and the child's class teacher are all involved in the child's care and education.

- A child with a severe visual impairment attends a mainstream school and has daily support from a dedicated learning support assistant.

- A young child with special educational needs attends a children's centre and is also visited at home by a Portage worker.

# Appropriate communication methods for different circumstances

## Informal communication

Ongoing communication with parents and carers is essential to meet the needs of children and young people. For many parents there can be regular and informal communication when children are brought to, or collected from, the setting. However, it is unusual for both parents to perform this task and, therefore, it is often the same parent who has contact. The methods below can usually work for both parents and practitioners. Finding ways to communicate with parents can sometimes be difficult, especially when staff may not feel confident themselves.

- **Regular contact with the same person**: always meet and greet parents when they arrive. At the

start, it is very important that parents meet the same practitioner – preferably their child's teacher or key person – on a daily basis.

- **A meeting place for parents**: ideally, there should be a room that parents can use to have a drink and a chat together.

Information that applies in the longer term should ideally be given in writing; for example, information concerning food allergies or medical conditions, such as asthma or eczema. As well as informing staff members, notices may also need to be attached to a child's own equipment, lunchbox or displayed in particular areas such as food preparation, nappy-changing. In a school setting the class teacher should ensure that any other adults involved in the child's care receive information as appropriate.

Table 10.2 gives details of appropriate methods of communication.

## Verbal information

Routine information can be exchanged verbally. This usually happens at the start and end of the session, when parents and their child's key person chat informally. (The role of the key person is discussed on page 224.)

### Talking with parents

Always let parents know about their child's positive behaviour and take the opportunity to praise the child in front of their parents. Then if you need to share a concern with them, they will already understand that you are interested in their child's welfare and are not being judgemental.

### Recording information and passing on messages

You will need to record some information the parent has talked to you about, especially if you are likely to forget it! You should always write down a verbal message which affects the child's welfare, so that it can be passed on to other members of staff; for example, someone else is collecting the child, a favourite comfort object has been left at home, the child has experienced a restless night. The person delivering the message also needs confirmation that it will be acted upon. Where there are shift systems

| Method of communication | Role of professional |
|---|---|
| Accident and incident report forms | To record information when a child or young person has been ill or is injured when at the setting.<br><br>These reports are a statutory requirement in all settings. |
| Admission form | All parents fill in an admission form when registering their child.<br><br>This is confidential information and must be kept in a safe place where only staff members have access to it. |
| Email | • To give information about an event<br>• To respond to a request from parent or colleague<br>• To arrange meetings and share documents.<br><br>Ensure confidentiality is maintained by checking recipients and who is to be copied in. |
| Formal letters | • Welcome letter prior to admission to the setting<br>• To give information about parents' evenings or meetings<br>• To alert parents to the presence of an infectious disease within the setting<br>• To advise parents about any change of policy or staff changes.<br><br>Copies of all letters received and sent and a record of all communication be should kept for future reference. |
| Formal reports | These include the CAF and policy documents in the setting.<br><br>(Preparing other formal reports is discussed below.) |
| Home books | To record information from both staff and parents. Home books travel between setting and the home, and record details of the child's progress, any medication given, how well they have eaten and slept, etc. |
| Newsletters | To give information about future events – fundraising fairs, open forums and visiting speakers, etc. |
| Notice boards<br>Display boards | • To give general information about the setting, local events for parents, support group contact numbers, health and safety information, daily menus, etc.<br>• To help parents and visitors feel welcome<br>• To show the names of staff, with their photographs. |
| Personal records | To record your professional development, e.g. attendance at training sessions and certificates gained. |
| Policy and procedure documents | These official documents should be openly available, and parents, carers and young people should be able to discuss them with staff if they have any concerns. |
| Presentations Powerpoint<br><br>Interactive whiteboard | • To present information and data on a range of topics, e.g. food hygiene, safety issues and risk assessment<br>• To clarify new procedures<br>• To explain roles and responsibilities in the setting. |
| Suggestions box | Some settings have a suggestions box where parents, carers and young people can contribute their own ideas for improving the service.<br><br>Any comments received can be addressed in newsletters or on the notice board. |

| Method of communication | Role of professional |
|---|---|
| Telephone | • To share information with parents and professionals<br>• To arrange meetings and visits<br>• To order resources.<br>Make sure that you communicate clearly and that your message has been understood. It is also good practice to make notes to provide a record of calls made and received. |
| Use of an interpreter | Use a language interpreter to support a person for whom English is an additional language.<br>Use British/Irish Sign Language interpreters or visual aids as appropriate to communicate with a parent, child or young person with a hearing impairment. |
| Use of pictorial and design communication aids | Use photographs and visual aids to communicate with a parent who speaks a different language from you.<br>Use Signalong, Makaton and/or PECS (Picture Exchange Communication System) to support children and young people with communication difficulties. |
| Video and DVD | • To share information in training sessions<br>• To record children's development and learning.<br>Remember to follow the rules of confidentiality that apply in your setting when displaying photographs of children. |

**Table 10.2** Appropriate methods of communication

in operation, a strict procedure for passing on messages needs to be established.

## Record-keeping and reports

Keeping good records is an essential part of any work with children, young people and families. Good practice in the area of record-keeping is based on the following principles. Records and reports should:

- **Be legible and grammatically correct**: handwriting must be neat and care should be taken to ensure that records are free from spelling and grammar errors.
- **Help to ensure that children and young people's needs are met**: for example, observation records help to identify children's needs and can inform future practice.
- **Help to safeguard the health and wellbeing of the child or young person**: any concern about the child's health or wellbeing should be recorded and reported to the line manager.

- **Help to provide continuity of service**: so that another member of staff can take over in the event of the practitioner being ill or unavailable.
- **Provide evidence of the practitioner's work**: this will go towards compiling a record of evidence.
- **Contain information that practitioners can use** to monitor and evaluate their work in order to improve their practice.
- **Help managers to monitor and evaluate** the quality and performance of the service to children and young people.

### Reflective practice: Recording information

Think about the last time you wrote a report or record in your work setting. Were you clear about its purpose? Did you have to obtain consent from the child's parents? Evaluate the usefulness of the document.

## Preparing reports

As part of your role, you may need to prepare reports. A report is a formal document which presents facts and findings, and can be used as a basis for recommendations. Certain reports that you may write will be a statutory requirement within the EYFS framework, and must be made available to any Ofsted inspection. These include accident reports, reporting of illnesses or injuries and any report of concerns about a child.

Reports you may be required to write include:

- **An accident or incident report**: this is quite straightforward, and will involve completing a standardised form.
- **A CAF Pre-Assessment checklist or CAF form**: an official form which is focused and easy to complete.
- **A formal report about a project or plan**: for example, a plan to change the use of a room within the setting.

A formal report has a fairly rigid structure, and is usually divided into sections, probably with subheadings performing a very specific task. The language used should be straightforward and to the point, and the report's structure should make it easy to identify the various parts, and to find specific items of information quite quickly. The three general principles of a report are: Why was it done? How was it done? What does it mean?

A formal report usually has the following features:

- **Title page**: include author's name, date and for whom the report is written.
- **Contents list**: list the main sections, sub-sections and any appendices.
- **Introduction**: the background or context to the report and the aims and objectives.
- **Main body or text**: this describes how the study was conducted and gives the facts, findings and results.
- **Conclusions**: this describes what the study has shown, summarising the main points.
- **Any recommendations for the implementation** of a report's findings.

- **Appendices**: include any supporting information here, such as tables, or information that applies only to certain readers.
- **References**: a list of books or articles used or suggestions for further reading.

# Supporting processes and procedures for recording, storing and sharing information

Every setting should have policies and procedures relating to recording, storing and sharing information. All policies should be available to those who have an interest, and may be shared with colleagues, parents and carers and other settings as well as with other agencies and services.

## Information-sharing

The Government produced a 'Guide to information sharing' (2008) for all practitioners working with children and young people. This outlined the important Acts that can be used to develop an information sharing policy in children and young people's services:

- **The Data Protection Act 1998** provides a framework to ensure that information is shared appropriately.
- **The Children Act 2004** on the duty to safeguard and promote the welfare of children.
- ***Working Together to Safeguard Children*** (HMG, 2006): the statutory guidance that sets out how organisations and individuals should work together to safeguard and promote the welfare of children.
- ***What to do if you are worried a child is being abused*** (HMG, 2006).
- **The Education and Inspections Act 2006**, which sets out the duty to promote the wellbeing of pupils to governing bodies of maintained schools.
- The Child Health Promotion Programme (DH, 2008).
- **Local Safeguarding Children Board** (LSCB) policies, procedures, protocols and guidance.

## Guidelines for information sharing: The Seven Golden Rules

1 Remember that the Data Protection Act is not a barrier to sharing information but provides a framework to ensure that personal information about living persons is shared appropriately.

2 Be open and honest with the person (and/or their family where appropriate) from the outset about why, what, how and with whom information will, or could be shared, and seek their agreement, unless it is unsafe or inappropriate to do so.

3 Seek advice if you are in any doubt, without disclosing the identity of the person where possible.

4 Share with consent where appropriate and, where possible, respect the wishes of those who do not consent to share confidential information. You may still share information without consent if, in your judgement, that lack of consent can be overridden in the public interest. You will need to base your judgement on the facts of the case.

5 Consider safety and wellbeing: base your information-sharing decisions on considerations of the safety and wellbeing of the person and others who may be affected by their actions.

6 Necessary, proportionate, relevant, accurate, timely and secure: ensure that the information you share is necessary for the purpose for which you are sharing it, is shared only with those people who need to have it, is accurate and up-to-date, is shared in a timely fashion, and is shared securely.

7 Keep a record of your decision and the reasons for it – whether it is to share information or not. If you decide to share, then record what you have shared, with whom and for what purpose.

The Guidance document also outlined Seven Golden Rules for information sharing (see box).

## Maintain secure storage systems for information

Every setting must provide clear policies and procedures about the recording and storing of information. These are governed by the Data Protection Act 1998. Anyone who keeps records, whether on computers or on paper, should comply with the Data Protection Act. It should be clear to service-users (in this case, young people, parents or carers) for what purpose the data is being kept. Information about a child or young person should also be accessible to his or her parent or carer and shared with them. It is not necessary to do this 'on demand'. A convenient time to be able to discuss the information can be arranged.

## Electronic recording and storing of information

If information is kept on computers or sent by email, steps must be taken to ensure that it could not fall into the hands of unauthorised people (for example, by the use of encryption software).

The National electronic Common Assessment Framework (eCAF) enables authorised, trained practitioners from across the children's workforce to electronically store and share CAF information quickly and securely, and to work together to build a holistic picture of a child or young person's needs. The system reduces the need for children, young people and families to repeat their story for different services.

Information should not be kept for longer than necessary, although accident and incident records will need to be kept in case they are needed for

### Assessment practice

#### Recording and storing information

Find out about the methods used to record and store information about the children and their families in your setting. What information is held? How are such records kept secure? Are computer records password-protected? Who has a right to see the documents held in your setting?

reference at some time in the future. Records must also be stored securely. See also Chapter 1 (Unit SHC 31) for further information on confidentiality and the Data Protection Act.

# Maintaining confidentiality versus the need to disclose information

It is essential to maintain confidentiality when working with children and young people, as it imposes a boundary on the amount of personal information and data that can be disclosed without consent. Confidentiality arises where a person disclosing personal information reasonably expects his or her privacy to be protected, such as in a relationship of trust. It is useful to understand fully the meaning of the terms 'consent', 'disclosure' ('allegation') and 'privacy'.

## Consent

Consent means agreement to an action based on knowledge of what the action involves and its likely consequences. For example, information on a child should only be collected and stored with the consent of the child's parents or carers – and they should have free access to this information on request. The only exceptions to the rule of consent are the very small number of cases where the child might otherwise be at risk of immediate and significant harm if you shared a piece of information with the parent.

## Disclosure

A safeguarding disclosure means the giving out of information that might commonly be kept confidential, to be in compliance with legal regulations or workplace rules. For example, a child tells an adult something that causes him or her to be concerned about the child's safety and wellbeing.

## Privacy

Privacy refers to the right of an individual or group to stop information about themselves from becoming known to people other than those to whom they choose to give the information. For example, when

former Prime Minister Tony Blair's ex-nanny wrote a book about life at Number 10, Downing Street, the Blairs took swift legal action to prevent details being leaked to the press. Tony Blair stated, 'We will do whatever it takes to protect our children's privacy.'

## The right to confidentiality is not absolute

When working within a multi-agency team, private information about the child or young person may often be shared with other professional persons within the team. The obligation to preserve the child's confidentiality then binds *all* professionals equally. Records should only show information which is essential to provide the service, and in many instances should be available to the scrutiny of the child and his or her family (for example, patients have the right to see their medical records).

## Practising confidentiality when working with young people

The need to gain a young person's trust and to build a positive relationship with him or her often leads to misunderstandings. To maintain a trusting relationship, practitioners should:

- **Be explicit with young people** regarding the boundaries within which they work: young people may assume that confidentiality goes further than it actually does. It may be necessary to remind the young person about this if he or she insists on telling the practitioner sensitive information. For example, if a young person tells a practitioner about an illegal practice or abuse by a family member, then the practitioner may need to inform the relevant authorities, so complying with safeguarding procedures.
- **Not lie on behalf of young people** – and it is important that young people are aware of this. For example, if a practitioner witnesses a serious assault or another crime, he or she may be obliged to contact the police or to answer truthfully if questioned later by the police.

## Case Study          Confidential information?

During a coffee break, practitioners are openly chatting about Harry, a child that you know. Apparently, the people he lives with are not his parents, but his grandparents – although they look young enough to be his parents. They are bringing Harry up because their daughter (his mother) was judged to be unable to look after her child. This happened a few years ago when Harry was very young, and he had spent some time in social care before his grandparents gained custody. One practitioner noted that Harry always calls them Mummy and Daddy.

**1** Is this information confidential? If so, why?

**2** Should you inform your line manager of the situation?

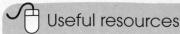 Useful resources

**Organisations and websites**

**Together for Children**: working in partnership with the Department for Education (DfE) to support local authorities (LAs) in their delivery of Sure Start Children's Centres:
**www.childrens-centres.org**

**Connexions**: support, advice and personal development service for 13- to 19-year-olds in England.

**National Parent Partnership Network** and **Parent Partnership Services** (PPS) are statutory services offering information advice and support to parents and carers of children and young people with special educational needs (SEN):
**www.parentpartnership.org.uk**

**National Portage Association**:
**www.portage.org.uk**

**The National Youth Agency** (NYA) works in partnership with a wide range of public, private and voluntary sector organisations to support and improve services for young people. Their particular focus is on youth work and they believe that by investing in young people's personal and social development, young people are better able to live more active and fulfilling lives:
**www.nya.org.uk**

# 11 Understand how to support positive outcomes for children and young people: Unit CYP Core 3.7

The Early Years Foundation Stage (EYFS) states:

'A child's experience in the early years has a major impact on their future life chances. A secure, safe and happy childhood is important in its own right, and it provides the foundation for children to make the most of their abilities and talents as they grow up.'

It is important that you understand how every aspect of a child or young person's environment can have an impact on their lives. A positive environment helps children and young people to become independent, and to have the confidence to learn new skills and gain a sense of belonging.

## Learning outcomes

By the end of this chapter you will:

1. Understand how the social, economic and cultural environment can impact on the outcomes and life chances of children and young people.

2. Understand how practitioners can make a positive difference in outcomes for children and young people.

3. Understand the possible impact of disability, special requirements (additional needs) and attitudes on positive outcomes for children and young people.

4. Understand the importance of equality, diversity and inclusion in promoting positive outcomes for children and young people.

## How the social, economic and cultural environment can impact on the outcomes and life chances of children and young people

Throughout your work with children and young people, you need to keep in mind the uniqueness of every child or young person's situation. This involves understanding the possible impact that the social, economic and cultural environment may have on their personal outcomes and life chances.

### The five outcomes of *Every Child Matters*

The main aim of the EYFS in England is to help children achieve the five outcomes contained in *Every Child Matters*:

- **Stay safe**: protecting children from harm and helping them to stay safe.
- **Be healthy:** helping children to be healthy.
- **Enjoy and achieve:** helping children to enjoy and achieve.
- **Make a positive contribution:** helping children to make a positive contribution to their setting and the wider community.
- **Achieve economic wellbeing**: helping children to achieve economic wellbeing.

# Social, economic and cultural factors

There are a number of factors that have a direct or indirect impact on children and young people's health and wellbeing, and therefore on their outcomes and life chances.

## Personal choice

There are many varieties of family life that differ from the norm, some on which are dictated by lifestyle choices. This personal choice includes nomadic families who may live in a 'mobile' home and travel to different sites, settling in one place for only a short period of time (for example, traveller families). A communal family is one in which two families live together in a house, sharing facilities.

Other families may relate differently to those families with an 'alternative' lifestyle, and sometimes (in the case of traveller families) formal schooling may be disrupted. Some children live in a family where the parents are the same gender; this may also mean that other families relate differently to them.

## Looked-after children

Children who are looked after by local authorities are one of the most vulnerable groups in society. Most looked-after children are in foster care (73 per cent in England, according to Department for Education Statistics for 2010, www.education.gov.uk, Research and Statistics Gateway); approximately 10 per cent are in residential children's homes. Others are cared for in residential schools and placement with parents.

## Poverty

Families living on a low income can cause children's diet, health and wellbeing to suffer. Too often, people experiencing poverty are not treated with respect, either in general or by the people they come into contact with the most. (See page 185 below for further information on the effects of poverty on outcomes for children and young people.)

## Housing and community

Sub-standard housing and urban communities with few shops or amenities mean that children often have little or no space to play safely. Homeless families who are housed in 'hotels' or bed and breakfast accommodation often have poor access to cooking facilities, and have to share bathrooms with several other families. Often children and young people's education is badly disrupted when families are moved from one place to another. Families in rural areas can also feel isolated where transport is limited, although they have more opportunities to play and explore.

## Educational environment

The majority of children and young people attend mainstream educational settings; schools, colleges and all educational settings are inspected and regulated. A minority of children and young people are educated at home or in special schools. A setting that fails to meet the statutory requirements may affect the overall learning potential of children and young people.

## Anti-social behaviour

Children and young people who show anti-social behaviour or break the law run the risk of being excluded from school, and also of becoming looked-after children.

## Health status of self or family member

Children with a chronic physical illness are more likely to suffer from emotional problems or disturbed behaviour as those without illness. This is especially true of physical disorders that involve the brain, such as epilepsy and cerebral palsy. Serious illness or disability can cause a lot of work and stress for everyone in the family, especially the parents. Children who are ill, and those who are frequently in hospital, experience more stressful situations than children without an illness.

## Disability
### Children

Children and young people with disabilities find it difficult to access play and leisure activities which children and young people without disabilities take for granted. See page 190 for more information on the effects of disability on positive outcomes for children.

## Parents or carers

Children and young people who become informal carers (or **young carers**) for their ill or disabled parents or carers are living in a 'role-reversal' where the loss of childhood may have a significant impact on them. They may feel that opportunities which are open to their peers are closed to them, because of their domestic situation and also because they may have missed out on many earlier opportunities. Their behaviour may deteriorate and lead them into truanting and other anti-social behaviours. For some children and young people however, school may be a refuge with opportunities to find supportive adults and participate in 'normal' activities.

### Key terms

**Young carers** – Children and young people under the age of 18 who provide care, assistance or support to another family member.

## Health support

The families who are most in need of health support are often those who are least likely to make use of the services provided. This may be because of lack of information or difficulty in accessing support.

## Addictions in family or self

### Parents or carers

Parents or carers who are addicted to drugs or alcohol are often absent from their children both physically (because they are out looking for drugs) and emotionally (because they are intoxicated by drugs or alcohol). Either way, they are not available to the child. Substance use is often (but not always) associated with poor or inadequate parenting.

### Children and young people

Over time, children may come to see substance use as the norm and start to engage in such behaviour themselves, for example drug or alcohol use. Many children of substance-using parents become young

carers for them and often also for younger siblings. This is a huge responsibility that affects the child emotionally and inhibits their ability to experience a 'normal' childhood by participating in activities outside the home. It can also affect their behaviour at school, for example, through lateness, tiredness and lack of time for homework.

## Bereavement and loss

The physical and emotional wellbeing of parents and/or children suffering significant bereavement (or separation as a result of a recent divorce) can be severely affected. For more informtion on loss, see Chapter 6 (Unit CYP Core 3.2), page 113.

## Family expectations and encouragement

Parents may have unrealistic expectations about their child, or have a poor understanding of their needs. Misunderstanding a child's needs or being inconsistent in their support can lead to the child or young person feeling insecure and having low self-esteem.

## Religious beliefs and customs

Britain is a multi-faith society whose population has become more culturally and religiously diverse in recent years. Religious beliefs and practices have the potential to profoundly influence many aspects of children and young people's lives, including approaches to parenting. Young people need to be able to demonstrate their beliefs without hindrance or harassment; for example, by observing religious dietary rules or wearing religious clothing. When the setting does not fully support their rights they can feel excluded, which will affect their self-esteem.

## Ethnic/cultural beliefs and customs

All children and young people should be able to feel pride in their ethnic origin. This should be on the basis of a feeling of self-affirmation and self-worth, and a positive sense of identity. **Minority ethnic** children and their families often experience racism, which damages their self-esteem, aspirations and expectations. All settings should provide services that are sensitive to and understanding of their needs, and that provide positive affirmation of their racial origins.

## Marginalisation and exclusion

Children whose home life lacks routine and positive discipline or whose basic needs are not met may be marked out as different. Other reasons for children and young people being marginalised include ethnic difference, disability and poverty. Anything that differentiates them from the 'norm' can make them feel isolated or marginalised.

### Key terms

**Minority ethnic** – People belonging to a group whose members share certain characteristics (common history, language, religion, family or social life) that distinguish them from the majority of the population. It covers not just black and Asian groups, but also Irish, Jewish, travellers and other white ethnic groups.

## The impact of poverty on outcomes and life chances

The UK has a very high rate of child poverty: 3.9 million children (one in three) are currently affected according to Barnados (www.barnados.org.uk). This is one of the highest rates in the industrialised world. Children growing up in poverty are significantly more likely to:

- live in poor, overcrowded housing
- have a disability, as parents may not be able to seek employment if they are full-time carers
- be looked-after children (in care)
- live in families where a necessary preoccupation with affording basic provisions can lead to high levels of stress and anxiety, reducing opportunities to enjoy family life
- live with parents from an ethnic minority.

Poorer neighbourhoods are significantly more likely to have:

- comparatively high levels of crime, especially violent crime, according to the Poverty Site (www. poverty.org.uk)

- fewer resources for children and young people; for example, playgrounds, nurseries and playgroups, youth clubs and sporting facilities.

Taken together, the impact of poverty on a child or young person's outcomes and life chances can be considerable. For example, at the time of writing (2011):

- Only three in ten children eligible for free schools meals are judged to be 'developing well' at the end of the EYFS, according to the former Government Department of Children, Schools and Families. 'Developing well' means that the child has a score of 78 or more, and has scored at least six points in every area.
- By the end of primary school education, 65 per cent of children in England eligible for free school meals have achieved the expected Level 4 result in English, compared to 84 per cent of children from families who not eligible for free school meals.
- Out of about 6,000 young people from schools who gained entry to Oxford or Cambridge Universities, 45 were eligible for free school meals (Michael Gove MP, Channel 4 News, 14 February 2010).

### Key terms

**Child poverty** – There is no single agreed definition for 'child poverty' in the UK. However, it is generally understood to describe a child living in a family which lacks the resources that would enable that child to participate in activities and have housing and material goods that are customary in the UK. Child poverty is not only defined by the lack of physical necessities, such as food and clothing.

The Government's *Every Child Matters* strategy aims to reduce the adverse consequences of child poverty. An important part of this strategy is the development of Children's Centres and extended schools, which aim to:

- provide more access to early years education and care for children in poorer neighbourhoods
- provide health services that are easily accessible
- provide places for children to play, and for parents to meet others and make friends
- help parents and carers to access training, adult education and assistance in finding employment

## Activity

### The possible effects of poverty

Consider how poverty affects children and young people. With reference to the children or young people in your care, make notes on the possible effects of poverty on them, using the following pointers:

- **material deprivation**: lack of games, toys and other normal childhood possessions
- **economic deprivation**: family living on a low income
- **social deprivation**: lack of opportunities for socialisation and building relationships
- **educational deprivation**: missing school or off-site visits.

- provide holiday playschemes, sporting and cultural opportunities, and after-school clubs.

## NEET: Poverty and young people

According to *Every Child Matters*, young people aged 16 to 18 who are **NEET** (**N**ot in **E**ducation, **E**mployment or **T**raining) face a future of further unemployment, low income, poor physical health, teenage motherhood and depression. Young people who are **NEET** are more likely to be living unhealthy lifestyles; they are more likely to smoke, drink and have poor diets. They also have more chance of being involved in violent situations and having mental health problems.

## Personal choices and experiences

Children and young people need to be given a voice, so that they can state their choices, contribute their experiences and so take a share in determining their future and outcomes. The United Nations Convention on the Rights of the Child (UNCRC) was introduced in 1989. Articles 12 and 13 relate to the rights of children to participate in decision-making:

'*Article 12:* Every child and young person has the right to express his or her views freely – about everything that affects him or her. The child's or young person's views must be given "due weight" depending on his or her age and maturity. The child or young person has the right to be heard in all decision-making processes, including in court hearings. The child or young person can speak for him or herself, or someone else can speak for him or her.

*Article 13:* Every child and young person has the right to freedom of expression, including the right to all kinds of information and ideas (unless there are legal restrictions).'

## Personal choices in the early years

The EYFS says that every child's individual needs and capabilities should be at the centre of planning and decision-making. Children have an equal right to be listened to and valued, and should be given opportunities to make choices and be involved in decisions that affect their daily lives.

Taking account of the views and feelings of children and young people will also help to safeguard them.

## Hear by Right

Hear by Right is a framework of the National Youth Agency (www.nya.org.uk) which aims to improve practice by involving children and young people in the services provided for them. A set of standards helps practitioners to follow best practice on the safe, sound and sustainable participation of children and young people in the services and activities in which they take part. It is applicable to any organisation working with young people, helping practitioners to provide evidence of the participation that is already happening in their organisation, and then how to plan for improvement where there are gaps.

## In Practice

### Involving children and young people

1. Support children's rights.
2. Encourage children to express their thoughts and feelings.
3. Value their thoughts and feelings when expressed.
4. Offer children the opportunity to make choices.
5. Enable children to be involved in decisions which affect them.
6. Inform parents about what is happening in the setting and about any projects that can involve children in contributing to positive changes in the setting.
7. Encourage a listening ethos in the setting: everyone, including children, parents and members of staff, should feel that their views are valued and that they can contribute positively to the setting.

## The UK Youth Parliament (UKYP)

UKYP is a national charity run by young people for young people. UKYP gives the young people of the UK a platform to be heard by local and national government, providers of services for young people and other agencies who have an interest in the views and needs of young people.

### Research Activity

#### Involving young people

Find out about the way in which young people aged from 11 to 18 years can have a voice through the UK Youth Parliament. What kind of issues do they tend to become involved with?

## How practitioners can make a positive difference in outcomes for children and young people

The *Every Child Matters* agenda focuses on ensuring that all children and young people have the opportunity to achieve five outcomes which are vital to their wellbeing in childhood and later life. The five

*Every Child Matters* outcomes are mapped against the rights set out in the United Nations Convention on the Rights of the Child (UNCRC), an international human rights treaty that grants all children and young people (aged 17 and under) a comprehensive set of rights.

The five outcomes are listed at the beginning of this chapter, and are *universal* ambitions for children and young people, whatever their backgrounds or circumstances. They provide a framework for measuring how circumstances are improving for children and young people. Organisations involved with providing public services to children and young people, including the voluntary and community sector, have to demonstrate how they are working towards ensuring that all children and young people achieve the five *Every Child Matters* outcomes.

## Achieving positive outcomes for children and young people

Every local authority in England has a Children's Trust, which is a partnership of organisations responsible for services for children, young people and their families.

If you are working in England, you will be working within the EYFS framework. Practitioners working elsewhere should consult the frameworks and guidance documents for their home nation, which are:

- **Northern Ireland**: Curricular Guidance for Pre-School Education
- **Wales**: The Learning Country: Foundation Phase (3 to 7 years)
- **Scotland**: Birth to 3: Supporting our youngest children; and The Curriculum for Excellence: 3 to 18 years.

## Safeguarding and protecting children and young people

One of the most important aspects of work with children and young people is safeguarding. Some practitioners will have specific responsibilities, but all practitioners have a role to play in supporting children to achieve the five *Every Child Matters* outcomes – which includes 'Stay Safe'. This outcome includes:

- protecting children and young people from maltreatment
- preventing impairment of children and young people's health or development
- ensuring that children and young people are growing up in circumstances consistent with the provision of safe and effective care.

 **Progress check**

### How to make a positive difference

- Understand how poverty and other factors can affect a child's health, development and learning.
- Ensure that you have a clear understanding of child and young person development (see Chapter 5, Unit CYP Core 3.1).
- Observe children and young people, and use the knowledge gained from observation to plan activities based on their needs and interests.
- Work within your home nation's framework of learning that links to the five outcomes of *Every Child Matters*.
- Follow the EYFS (or other national framework) Practice Guidance documents.
- Keep up to date: read journals, attend courses and workshops to further your professional development.

## Designing services around the needs of children and young people

There is a wide range of services for children and young people and their families. Each service will be designed to ensure that children and young people can achieve positive outcomes, by working towards those in the *Every Child Matters* framework or its equivalent. The facts about the impact of child poverty can make it seem that the problems involved with poorer neighbourhoods can only be resolved by large-scale government intervention. But it is very difficult to plan a programme for a particular community from central government offices in Whitehall. Such programmes are often rather disappointing, costing a great deal but delivering few positive results. An alternative approach is **asset-based community development**.

## Asset-based community development

This approach builds on the strengths of neighbourhoods and communities, rather than just focusing on the problems and what is lacking. When working with parents, asset-based community development highlights the importance of doing the following:

- **Finding out the skills and capabilities of the parent or carer group**: in every neighbourhood, however impoverished, there will be parents with skills in finance who can help run budgets; parents with practical skills in gardening and cooking, and parents who are good with ICT.
- **Building on existing community groups and organisations**: many neighbourhoods have a church, mosque or temple that is well attended, or a thriving community group, club or association. These organisations may offer help and advice to families with young children.
- **Linking with and helping to improve local services**: for example, health centres, schools and hospitals.

## Key terms

**Asset-based community development** – An approach to community development which aims to discover and use the strengths already available in a local community. This is understood as a way of giving choice and power to local communities. It is in contrast to the usual model of trying to establish what is wrong in a community, and sending people (such as more social workers or more police) to fix it.

You can read more about the provision of services for children and young people in Chapter 10 (Unit CYP Core 3.6).

# The importance of active participation

Active participation is about involving children, young people and their families in decision-making at every level. Children and young people have a right to participate in the issues and services that affect them, and their involvement is essential to achieve the best possible outcomes, as set out in the Government's *Every Child Matters* strategy. The United Nation's Convention on the Rights of the Child Article 12 clearly defines children and young people's right to be involved in the decision-making processes that affect them.

The skills you need to promote active participation include:

- **Active listening**: This is discussed in Chapter 1 (Unit SHC 31). It means tuning in to what children, young people and their families say in order to understand their needs and preferences.
- **Responding to feedback**: You need to communicate openly with children and their families, and be willing to adapt your practice to accommodate the views of others.

## Why is active participation important?

Active participation has many benefits for children and young people, and also for services and communities.

## Benefits for children and young people

- Opportunities to build skills in communication, decision-making, resilience, developing positive relationships and confidence.
- Opportunities to learn, to have fun, to achieve accreditation (in certain circumstances).
- Active citizenship: having a voice and being able to influence service provision.
- Updated services which are responsive to children and young people's needs.

## Benefits for services

- Input from a service-user's perspective enables services to plan and deliver more effective services, with better outcomes for children and young people.
- Planning and policy takes place in response to *actual* rather than assumed needs.
- Participation encourages innovative planning and is in line with Government expectations (for example, in the Children's Plan: A Better, brighter future).

## Benefits for communities

- Early involvement of children and young people in decision-making promotes active involvement in communities later in life.
- Opportunities to bring communities together, increasing understanding and respect (for example, meeting the needs of young people for suitable recreational facilities).

# Monitoring and evaluating active participation

**Monitoring** is about collecting information in order to keep track of what is happening in your setting. For example, you can monitor such aspects as who attends (or does not attend) sessions, and feedback received such as reactions or comments from children, young people, parents and colleagues. You can then use this information to think critically about your practice and to help you evaluate.

**Evaluation** is about using monitoring and other collected information, including feedback, interviews

| **Examples of active participation by children and young people** | |
|---|---|
| **Surveys and consultation**: taking part in surveys and consultation events. | **Staff recruitment**: direct involvement in the recruitment and appointment of staff, such as youth workers |
| **Membership of youth forums**: UK Youth Parliament members raising issues of importance to young people. | **Play policies**: children aged five to thirteen years contributing to play policies. |
| **Voluntary groups**: active involvement in participation groups for looked-after young people and those with disabilities. | **Hear by Right**: having a voice in both their school and in their communities outside school (through school councils and other activities). |
| **Developing resources**: websites, leaflets and posters for children and young people: e.g. young people researching and producing an anti-bullying leaflet. | |

**Table 11.1** Examples of active participation

or questionnaires, to make judgements about how successful participation is in your setting. This information can be used to promote and build on a particular area of success and to make changes and improvements where they are needed.

It is important to reflect on your practice and to evaluate it, because evaluation:

- improves practice and promotes change: what you learn can help you to reinforce what is going well and to change what is not.
- helps practitioners to develop, to learn from what they are doing and to take ownership of their practice and its outcomes.

# Supporting children and young people to make positive personal choices and experiences

## Child-centred practice: supporting children and young people

To reflect a genuinely child-centred or young person-centred approach, practitioners need to acknowledge and value the child or young person's voice whenever possible in the planning process. There are advantages to both children and adults in making

your practice child-centred. These include the following points:

- **Services are appropriate for their needs**: insights gained from children can help adults to work more effectively; they can also help to ensure that services are relevant to children's needs.
- **Taking into account the needs of others**: children who learn to express their own needs also learn to consider the needs of others. They may develop skills of cooperation, negotiation and problem-solving.
- **Respect and understanding**: children and parents or carers often work together; this can make relationships stronger and promote greater understanding and respect.
- **Promoting self-esteem and self-worth**: when you involve children and you respect their ideas and their capabilities, they grow in confidence and self-esteem.

There are many factors that affect children and young people; for example, the local environment, their opportunities for play and social interaction, the impact of traffic and noise pollution on their lives, the quality of the streets and housing. On each of these issues, children will have a view and a valid contribution to make.

# TOP TIPS for PARTICIPATION
## what disabled young people want

**Respect us**

"Trust us – we need to trust you"

"If you give us respect – we'll give you respect"

**Be open and honest with us**

"Frustrating when you don't tell us stuff"

"We all make mistakes"

"We ask you questions to help us understand our world and grow as people"

**Prove you're listening to us**

"My voice is my power"

"Tell us what's changed"

"Show us you want to listen"

**Make sure we get something out of it**

"Participation is a great way to help us learn how to make decisions and understand the choices we may face in the future"

"Gives us new skills"

"Empower us"

**Involve us from the start**

"You can find out what's best for us by involving us"

"Don't guess what we want"

**Give us time**

"I know what I want to say – give me time"

"Give me time to get my message ready"

"Help us make decisions by giving us your time – enough time"

**Listen to us**

"If you don't listen to what we want – how can you give us what we want?"

"Listen to me, no one else, listen to me. It's my body. Listen to me, it's my life, listen to me"

**Make it fun!**

"We're teenagers, we're young, we want to learn"

**Involve all of us**

"Don't judge a book by its cover – we can all make choices"

"I may not have speech, but I have a voice – I can give my opinions, I can even argue"

**Support us to make our own decisions**

"I want more choice"

"If you listen to us you can help us get a positive outcome"

making ourselves HEARD!

Council for Disabled Children, NCB
8 Wakley Street, London EC1V 7QE
tel 020 7843 6006
fax 020 7843 6313
email vwright@ncb.org.uk
www.ncb.org.uk/cdc
Charity registration no. 258825

Participation Works

**Produced in partnership with young people from Generate UK and 1Voice**

**Figure 11.1** The *Top Tips for Participation* posters was developed by the Council for Disabled Children and Partnership Works in partnership with young people from Generate UK and 1Voice. The poster highlights in young people's own words what adults can do to better involve them in decisions and issues that affect them. For hard copies please email cdc@ncb.org.uk

## Case Study

### An after-school club for children aged five to six years

Practitioners wanted to find out how children felt about their after-school clubs. Although parents and carers had important views to contribute, they realised that children also had their own perspectives. Through talking with the children, practitioners discovered that:

- they were unhappy about the lighting – it was too gloomy in some clubs

- some children said that they became hungry and wished that food was provided

- some children felt tired and wished that there was somewhere for them to have a quiet time

- they were also concerned about their environment: the paint on the walls, the lighting and their access to the garden and so on.

These were all legitimate and important insights which affected how those children experienced their care, and which could have easily been overlooked by adults who may have a different set of concerns. By placing the child at the centre of their practice, the practitioners developed a greater understanding of the sorts of factors that might affect children's lives.

## Reflective practice: Supporting child-centred practice

Think about how child-centred the practice is in your setting.

- Do you try to involve the child or young person in making decisions about the way in which the setting is organised?
- Are the views of parents and carers taken into account?
- How do you think you could improve your practice and make it more child-centred?

# The possible impact of disability, additional needs and attitudes on positive outcomes

The Equality Act 2010 considers that a person has a disability if he or she has a physical or mental impairment, or a severe disfigurement that:

- is long-term (has lasted for 12 months, is likely to last for at least a further 12 months, or is lifelong)
- has substantial adverse effects on the child's ability to carry out normal day-to-day activities.

## Guidelines for child-centred practice

1 Be aware of children at all times.

2 Think about how your involvement with their families may affect them; be open to engaging with children, listening to them and realising the potential for them to participate and contribute to your work.

3 Recognise (when working with very young children) that they may not be able to contribute in any obvious way, but we still need to be aware of their views.

4 Recognise the value of contributions from any older siblings.

5 Engage with children individually, or as little groups. You can talk with them, they can participate in discussions, community meetings or councils.

6 Encourage children to make scrapbooks, videos, keep diaries, use disposable cameras, make drawings etc.

## Key terms

**Disability** – Under the Equality Act 2010, a person has a disability if they have a physical or mental impairment, and if the impairment has a substantial and long-term adverse effect on their ability to perform normal day-to-day activities.

**Impairment** – Impairment is the loss or limitation of physical, mental or sensory function on a long-term or permanent basis. Often children are described as having a hearing impairment, rather than a hearing disability. A condition, impairment or disfigurement is long-term and has significant, adverse effects on a person's ability to carry out day-to-day activities.

**Special educational need** – A learning difficulty, a behavioural, emotional or social difficulty, or a disability. It can be a short-term or long-term difficulty. A child with a special educational need finds learning or accessing education more difficult than most children of the same age.

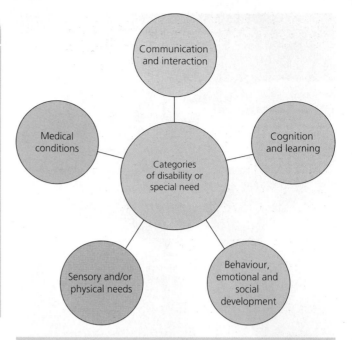

**Figure 11.2** Different categories of disability or special need

## The impact of disability

Children and young people with disabilities and/or special educational needs have needs that are 'in addition' to the general needs of children and young people. Some children have a very obvious and well-researched disability, such as Down's syndrome or cerebral palsy; others may have a specific learning difficulty such as dyslexia. What defines them as children with special needs is the fact that they need **additional support** in some area of development, care or education compared with other children.

There is no absolute way of listing types of disabilities or special educational needs, or of putting a child clearly into a single category. Many children have needs which cross over one or more of the categories in Figure 11.2. Children may also have specific areas of strength in addition to their special needs.

Figure 11.2 gives an overview of the different categories, drawing on the 2001 Special Educational Needs Code of Practice.

## Potential effects of disability on children's life chances and outcomes

Disability can have adverse effects on children's outcomes and life chances, but these potential effects will vary as much as do the children themselves, and will also depend on the nature of the disability and on the amount of support available.

### Communication and interaction

Most children with special educational needs have difficulties in one or more of the areas of communication, interaction and speech. A child might show a delay in his or her speech and language: his or her development might be that which would be expected in a child 6 or 12 months younger. Other children might have a speech difficulty (for example, a stammer or unclear speech), but may understand language perfectly well.

### Cognition and learning

Children with difficulties in this area will find it hard to understand new concepts, solve problems, and learn skills. Children with moderate difficulties in this area will need additional support to develop their learning, possibly including additional time,

**Figure 11.3** James is helped to understand early concepts like full and empty through interesting experiences, like this one outside with water

repetition and practical experiences. Children with severe or complex difficulties in their cognition and learning will need considerable help to develop early concepts like full and empty, over and under. Their play may stay at the level of sensory exploration without moving into pretend or role play. Their communication is likely to be functional (for example, making a need known, like hunger) without the use of language for thinking.

### Behaviour, emotional and social development

Children with these difficulties may present as withdrawn, anxious and isolated; disruptive, aggressive, and behaving in disturbing ways; lacking in concentration and hyperactive; and having difficulties in their social development, such as sharing attention, regulating their emotional state when in a group, or cooperating with others.

### Sensory and/or physical needs

Sensory difficulties can range from the profound and long-term (being deaf or registered blind, for example) to lower levels of visual and hearing impairment, which are sometimes temporary (such as glue ear). Physical impairments can arise from physical causes (for example, lung disease might lead to a child being oxygen-dependent). They can also arise from neurological causes like cerebral palsy, which is usually caused by the failure of part of the brain to develop, leading to a loss of control over certain muscles, posture or balance. Some children may have a combination of profound sensory and physical needs with significant effects on their development.

### Medical conditions

Some medical conditions can affect children's learning. The child's condition may cause him or her to become quickly tired, or may lead to frequent absences for treatment. Examples of this include childhood leukaemia or chronic lung disease. Other medical conditions such as asthma or diabetes may be adequately managed by taking medication and do not need to cause significant interference in the child's development and learning.

## The importance of positive attitudes

It matters a great deal how we 'label' people who are different to us. Generally we are much more aware of individual differences and have a great deal more knowledge about diverse needs and abilities. Yet people with disabilities still experience a great deal of discrimination and prejudice. It is therefore very important to reflect on how we think about people with disabilities, including the terms and labels we use. Settings may exclude children from participation in certain group activities because of their special needs. This exclusion can sometimes be justified on health and safety grounds, but usually could be remedied with some planning and communication with the child's family.

**In Practice**

**Supporting children with special needs**

Practitioners need to:

❏ **understand that all children and young people have different experiences**, interests, skills and knowledge which affect their ability to develop and learn

❏ **focus on the child** and what the child can do, rather than what the child cannot do

❏ **provide a safe and supportive learning environment**, free from harassment, in which the contribution of all children and families is valued

❏ **avoid all stereotypes** and expressions of discrimination or prejudice – for example, assuming that every child with Down's syndrome is always cheerful or assuming that a child with spina bifida will be clumsy.

# The medical and social models of disability

## The medical model

The medical model of disability was used extensively until fairly recently. Disability is seen as a **medical** problem and has the following features:

- Usually the focus is on the disability or impairment, rather than the needs of the person.
- People are identified and labelled according to their impairment.
- If a medical cure is not possible, people are excluded from 'normal' society; they may be shut away in a specialised institution or isolated at home, where only their most basic needs are met.
- The emphasis is on dependence, backed up by the stereotypes of disability that lead to feelings of pity and fear, and patronising attitudes.

The case study below gives an example of the medical model, where the individual is constantly labelled in medical terms.

## The social model

In the social model of disability, people with disabilities are seen as being disabled by society, because of the barriers it creates. These include the following:

- **Attitudinal barriers**: the notion that disabled people are pitiful, incapable, fearful, childlike and

have nothing of value to bring to different situations.
- **Environmental barriers**: limited or no access to schools, shopping and leisure activities; poor lighting, small print, street furniture, poor signage and the use of complex language.
- **Institutional barriers**: the lack of good anti-discriminative legislation; policies, practices and procedures which exclude disabled people; transport, education and housing systems which do not provide for people with impairments.

An example of the social model is a wheelchair user who has a mobility impairment. He or she may be described as being disabled, but is not actually disabled in an environment where he or she can use public transport and gain full access to buildings and their facilities in the same way that someone without his or her impairment would do.

# Different types of support

Many children and young people with learning difficulties will have personal priority needs that are central to their learning and quality of life. Some children and young people may need the provision of a specific therapy or paramedical care, such as supervising medication. Others require existing equipment or activities to be modified or adapted to suit their particular needs. You can often meet the needs of children and young people with disabilities without specialist aids and equipment. Special provision includes the following strategies:

## Case Study — The effects of labelling on Harry, my son

When I first met Harry he was my son. A year later he was epileptic and developmentally delayed. By 18 months he had special needs and he was a 'special' child. I was told not to think about his future.

My husband and I struggled with all this. By the time he was four, Harry had special educational needs and was a 'statemented' child. He was dyspraxic, epileptic, developmentally delayed and had severe and complex communication problems. Two years later (age 6) he was severely epileptic, had cerebral palsy and had communication difficulties. At 8, he had severe epilepsy with associated communication problems; he was showing a marked developmental regression, and he had severe learning difficulties. At 9 he started to attend a mainstream school, with specialist help, and he slowly became my son again. Never again will he be anything but Harry – a son, a brother, a friend, a pupil, a teacher, a person.

*(Adapted from a true account – names have been changed)*

1 How many different labels can you identify in this short account?

2 Why do you think that Harry's mother felt she had 'lost' her son?

---

- Position children and young people so that they learn effectively; for example, by making sure the light falls on the adult's face, so that a child wearing a hearing aid is able to lip-read and a child with a visual impairment can use any residual eyesight to see facial expressions.
- Provide the opportunity to learn sign languages such as Makaton or Signalong.
- Develop the self-esteem of children and young people; for example, by encouraging and praising effort as well as achievement.
- Allow children's behaviour and alternative ways of communicating to be acknowledged and understood.
- Provide appropriate therapies: for example, speech and language, occupational or physiotherapy. (Support from health services is generally set out as non-educational provision in a child's **statement**. However, speech and language therapy may be regarded as either educational or non-educational provision.)
- Plan the use of music, art, drama or movement therapy: these therapies may play a complementary role in the curriculum for individual children and young people, and will need to be planned as part of the whole curriculum.
- Help children and young people to maintain good posture, appropriate muscle tone and ease of movement, and promote skills in independent mobility.
- Promote relaxation and support to help children and young people manage stress and anxiety; some settings use a sensory room, but a quiet, comfortable area will benefit all children.

## Portage

It is useful to find out more about Portage if you are working with very young children. Although the teaching is usually carried out in the child's home, some Portage workers work closely with Children's Centres and other settings.

Portage is a home-based teaching service for the families of pre-school children who show some delay in their development. The service aims to enable parents to teach their own children at home, supported by visits from a Portage Home Visitor supervised by an Educational Psychologist. Central to the Portage philosophy is the emphasis placed on the partnership between parents and professionals in the education and development of their own children.

# The importance of equality, diversity and inclusion in promoting positive outcomes

## Equality, diversity and inclusion

The principles of promoting equality, diversity and inclusion are discussed in Chapter 3 (Unit SHC 33). Children and young people have the following rights:

- **Inclusion**: this means that every child, young person, adult or learner is given **equality of opportunity** to access education and care, by meeting their specific needs.
- **Diversity**: every individual must be respected and acknowledged for their **individuality** – the particular values, attitudes, cultures, beliefs, skills, knowledge and life experience of every individual in a group of people.
- **Equality**: ensuring that everyone has a chance to take part in society on an equal basis and to be treated appropriately, regardless of their gender, race, disability, age, sexual orientation, language, social origin, religious beliefs, marital status and other personal attributes.

Children and young people who experience inequality and discrimination may:

- **be unable to fulfil their potential**, because they are made to feel that their efforts are not valued or recognised by others
- **find it hard to form relationships** with others because of lack of self-worth or self-esteem
- be so affected by the **stereotypes or labels** applied to them that they start to believe in them and so behave in accordance with others' expectations. This then becomes a self-fulfilling prophecy: for example, if a child is repeatedly told that he or she is clumsy, he or she may act in a clumsy way even when quite capable of acting otherwise

- **feel that they are in some way to blame** for their unfair treatment and so withdraw into themselves
- **lack confidence in trying new activities** if their attempts are always ridiculed or put down
- **be aggressive towards others**: distress or anger can prevent children from playing cooperatively with other children.

## Promoting equality, diversity and inclusion

Stereotyped thinking can prevent you from seeing someone as an individual with particular life experiences and interests, and so lead to negative attitudes, prejudice and discrimination. This in turn will have a damaging effect on the individual's outcomes and life chances.

## Examples of stereotyped thinking

1 *Charlie, Ahmed, Rosie and Cara are playing in the role-play area. The practitioner asks Charlie and Ahmed to tidy away the train set and trucks and asks Rosie and Cara to put the dolls and cooking pots away, as it is nearly storytime.*

The assumption here is that dolls and cooking utensils are 'girl' playthings, whereas trains and trucks are 'boy' playthings. The practitioner is reinforcing this stereotype by separating the tasks by gender.

2 *Paul's mother arrives at the school open day. She is in a wheelchair, being pushed by Paul's father. The teacher welcomes the parents and then asks Paul's father if his wife would like a drink and a biscuit.*

The assumption here is that the person in the wheelchair would not be able to understand and reply to what is said to them. This is a common feature of daily life for people who use wheelchairs. They are often ignored and questions are addressed to their companion, often because the other person is embarrassed by the unusual situation and afraid of making a mistake.

3 *Members of staff are having a tea break and discussing a new child who has just started at their school. Julie says, 'I can't stand the way these travellers think they can just turn up at school whenever they feel like it*

*– they don't pay taxes you know and they live practically on top of rubbish dumps . . . poor little scrap, he doesn't know any different.'*

An assumption has been made which is based on prejudice and stereotyped thinking; in this case, travellers are assumed to be 'scroungers' and to live in unhygienic conditions. Such attitudes will be noticed by all the children in the class and may result in the individual child being treated differently, damaging his self-esteem and leading to feelings of rejection.

## Reflective practice: Promoting equality, diversity and inclusion

All children should be represented in the play materials they use within settings. The resources will help children's learning by representing them, being familiar to their home life and assisting in building their self-esteem and self-worth. To help promote equality, diversity and inclusion, consider the following:

### Your displays

- Do these include positive images of children and adults with disabilities? If you are making a display about transport for example, you could include an image of an adult with a disability getting onto an accessible bus.
- Do they include positive images of girls and women as strong and confident, and boys and men as caring and creative? Do you audit the resources, images and books in your setting to ensure that they do not reinforce gender stereotyping and that they include girls and boys stepping outside of traditional gender roles?

### Your layout and organisation

- Is there enough space for a child to negotiate the tables and equipment, if they have a difficulty with their mobility?
- Are displays low-glare, so that they can be seen by people with a visual impairment (laminated sheets can be very hard to read)?

### Your organisational culture

- Do your policies and procedures (and in particular your Equality of Opportunity policy) encourage the development of all children to their full potential?
- Do you use Makaton and visual symbols as a matter of course?
- Do you think carefully about where you position children at group time, taking account of needs such as hearing impairment, visual impairment, and language delay?
- Do leaflets and other forms of information make it clear that you welcome children with special needs and disabilities?

### Your resources

- Do you have dolls and small world play equipment which represent different disabilities, such as people with hearing aids or in wheelchairs?
- Do you represent different ethnicities by having dolls and small world play resources with different skin tones and features?
- Does your role-play area include dressing up clothes from different cultures?

**4** *Eden's mother is a registered heroin addict who has been attending a drug rehabilitation programme for the last few months. Whenever Eden behaves in an aggressive way to other children or to staff, one practitioner always makes a jibe about his home life: 'Eden, you may get away with that sort of thing where you come from, but it won't work here. We know all about you.'*

This is an extreme and very unkind form of stereotyping. It assumes that, because his mother is a drug user, Eden is somehow less worthy of consideration and respect. By drawing attention to his home life, the member of staff is guilty of prejudice and discriminatory behaviour. There is also a breach of the policy of confidentiality.

## Useful websites and resources

**The Centre for Excellence and Outcomes in Children and Young People's Services**
C4EO provides a range of support to drive positive change in the delivery of children's services, and ultimately outcomes for children, young people and their families:
www.c4eo.or.uk

**Child Poverty Action Group**
The CPAG promotes action for the prevention and relief of poverty among children and families with children:
www.cpag.org.uk

**The National Youth Agency**
The NYA works in partnership with young people and with organisations and services to ensure better outcomes for young people:
www.nya.org.uk

**The Council for Disabled Children (CDC)**
This is the umbrella body for the disabled children's sector in England, with links to the other UK nations:
www.ncb.org.uk

**The UK Youth Parliament (UKYP)**
You can read more about this organisation at:
www.ukyouthparliament.org.uk

# SECTION 3

# Early years mandatory pathway units

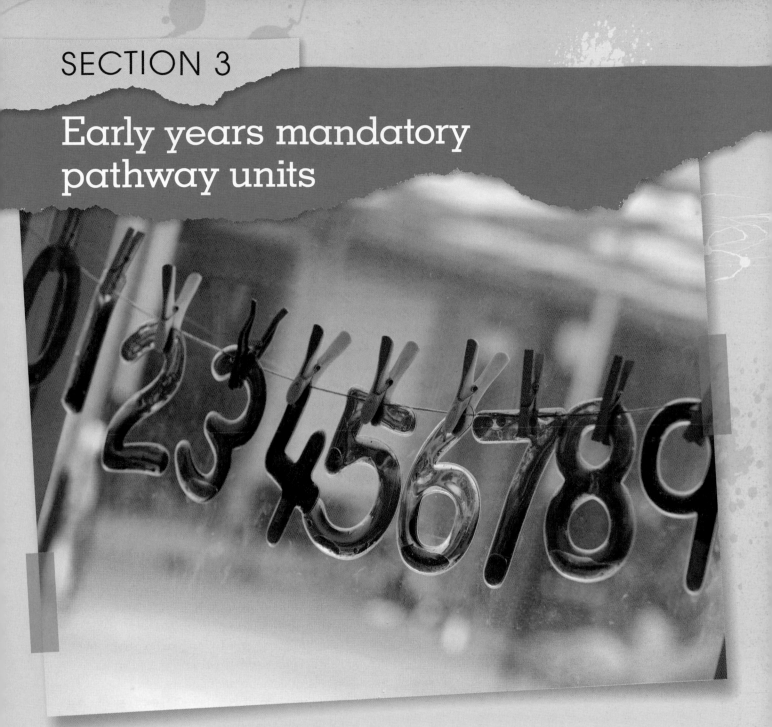

# 12 Context and principles for early years provision: Unit EYMP 1

This unit aims to familiarise learners with the requirements and principles of the early years framework within which they work. The unit also requires skills and knowledge relating to the implementation of the relevant framework. This includes providing environments which deliver the relevant early years framework through planned, purposeful play, with a balance of adult-led and child-initiated activities. It also provides information about working in partnership with children's parents who are the child's first and most enduring educator.

## Learning outcomes

By the end of this Unit you will:

1. Understand the purpose and principles of early years frameworks.
2. Be able to provide environments within the work setting that support and extend children's development and learning in their early years.
3. Understand how to work in partnership with carers.

## Understand the purposes and principles of early years frameworks

As an early years practitioner, you need to understand the purposes and principles of early years frameworks, including:

- The central importance of parents and families for each child's wellbeing and as their first educator

- The importance of a **key person** for each child in each setting, to ensure their wellbeing, so that they develop independence by having someone they can depend upon
- The recognition that babies and young children are competent learners from birth, and the importance to their development of relationships both with other children and with adults
- The need to plan for the individual child using sensitive observations and assessments – schedules, routines and teaching must be guided by the child's needs
- The central role of both indoor and outdoor play in supporting learning – very young children learn by doing, rather than through being told, and also when they are given appropriate responsibility, allowed to make errors, decisions and choices
- The recognition that learning through play and the development of imagination and creativity is a shared endeavour, some of it led by the child and some by an effective practitioner
- The importance of involving key partners, such as health visitors and social workers, in children's successful development and learning
- The value to be placed on diversity; welcoming and genuinely including all children
- What children can already do (rather than what they cannot do) as the starting point of a child's development and learning
- The central importance of competent, committed practitioners to children's outcomes
- Only when high-quality care, development and learning work together will early years provision have the maximum impact on children's development
- Settings should develop effective partnerships not only with parents, but also with other carers, settings and practitioners important to the child;

the experience of the child must be coherent and 'joined-up'

- The importance of 'joined-up' planning and delivery to provide continuity for children who attend more than one setting, e.g. those who are cared for by a childminder and also attend a playgroup or nursery class
- The importance of planning for children who attend for different parts of the day, including the need for rest and relaxation for them and for children attending for long periods
- The need to support effective practice for all children including those following atypical development patterns.

(DfES, 2006a; pp. 3–4)

## Early years frameworks

You should know and understand the frameworks for early years provision used within the relevant UK home nation, e.g. England, Scotland, Wales or Northern Ireland. For example, in England, nursery and pre-school education is provided for within a wide range of settings including pre-school groups, playgroups, nursery centres, day nurseries, nursery schools and reception classes (with pupils aged 4–5 years) in primary schools.

## The Early Years Foundation Stage

Orders and regulations under section 39 of the Childcare Act 2006 brought the **Early Years Foundation Stage** (EYFS) into force in September 2008. All early years providers are required to use the EYFS to ensure a coherent and flexible approach to children's care, learning and development that will enable young children to achieve the five *Every Child Matters* outcomes: staying safe; being healthy; enjoying and achieving; making a positive contribution; and achieving economic wellbeing.

The *Statutory Framework for the Early Years Foundation Stage* sets out the legal requirements relating to learning and development (the early learning goals; the educational programmes; and the assessment arrangements) in Section 2 and the legal requirements relating to welfare (safeguarding and promoting children's welfare; suitable people; suitable premises, environment and equipment;

organisation; and documentation) in Section 3. The learning and development requirements are given legal force by the Early Years Foundation Stage (Learning and Development Requirements) Order 2007 made under Section 39 (1) (a) of the Childcare Act 2006. The welfare requirements are given legal force by Regulations made under Section 39 (1) (b) of the Childcare Act 2006. Together, the Order, the Regulations and the Statutory Framework document make up the legal basis of the EYFS. The requirements in this document have statutory force by virtue of Section 44 (1) of the Childcare Act 2006.

*Practice Guidance for the Early Years Foundation Stage* provides guidance for practitioners on meeting the requirements of the Early Years Foundation Stage (EYFS) framework. It aims to provide useful advice and detailed information on supporting children's learning and development and welfare. The guidance looks in more detail at how to implement the learning and development requirements and the welfare requirements in the *Statutory Framework for the Early Years Foundation Stage* document. There is also guidance on children's development, what to look out for, effective practice and useful hints on planning and resourcing. The sections in 'Development matters' and 'Look, listen and note' also support the continuous assessment that practitioners must undertake.

There are six areas covered by the early learning goals and educational programmes. None of these areas can be delivered in isolation. They are equally important and depend on each other to support a rounded approach to child development. All the areas must be delivered through planned, purposeful play, with a balance of adult-led and child-initiated activities. The six areas of learning and development are:

- Personal, Social and Emotional Development
- Communication, Language and Literacy
- Problem-solving, Reasoning and Numeracy
- Knowledge and Understanding of the World
- Physical Development
- Creative Development.

For detailed information see the *Early Years Foundation Stage (EYFS) Pack* available from the

Department for Education website: www.education. gov.uk/publications/standard/publicationDetail/ Page1/DCSF-00261-2008#downloadableparts

In **Northern Ireland** the early years framework is the *Foundation Stage* which is part of the revised school curriculum introduced in September 2007. Information about the statutory curriculum in Northern Ireland can be accessed from: www. nicurriculum.org.uk

In **Scotland** the national guidance *Pre-Birth to Three: Positive Outcomes for Scotland's Children and Families*, replaces Birth to Three: Supporting our Youngest Children. It includes important information on pre-birth and brain development and it reflects the principles and philosophy which underpin the Early Years Framework and Curriculum for Excellence. For more information visit: www. ltscotland.org.uk/earlyyears/prebirthtothree/index. asp. *Curriculum for Excellence* is Scotland's curriculum for children and young people aged 3 to 18 which replaces A Curriculum Framework for Children 3 to 5 and the 5–14 curriculum. For more information see *Curriculum for Excellence: Supporting the early level* available at: www.ltscotland.org.uk/ earlyyears/curriculum/supportingearlylevel/index. asp

In **Wales** the revised school curriculum for 3- to 19-year-olds has been implemented since September 2008. This includes the **Foundation Phase**, a statutory framework, *Framework for Children's Learning for 3- to 7-year-olds in Wales.* Information about this revised curriculum in Wales is available at: http://wales.gov.uk/topics/educationandskills/ schoolshome/curriculuminwales/arevisedcurriculum forwales/?lang=en

At the moment there is no statutory framework for 0- to 3-year-olds in Wales although in January 2011 the Deputy Minister for Children agreed to work towards taking forward a 'Progress and Development Framework' for 0- to 3-year-olds focusing on the needs of the child before they enter into the Foundation Phase. However, there is an early learning programme, *Flying Start*, which is targeted at 0- to 3-year-olds in the most

disadvantaged communities in Wales. It aims to create positive outcomes in the medium and long term. It is a prescriptive programme, based on international evidence of what works. For more information: http://wales.gov.uk/topics/ childrenyoungpeople/parenting/help/ flyingstart/?lang=en

There is more information on early years frameworks in Chapter 13 (EYMP 2).

## Key terms

**Adult-led activities** – activities in which adults provide specific opportunities to encourage a particular aspect of learning, discuss a particular topic or introduce a particular material, skill or idea.

**Child-initiated activities** – self-chosen activities in which children and young people follow their own ideas, in their own way and for their own reasons.

## Research Activity

Find out about the legal status and principles of the relevant early years framework/s, for your home nation (England, Northern Ireland or Wales). What national and local guidance materials are used in your setting?

# How different approaches to work with children in the early years have influenced current provision in the UK

Throughout history, there have always been people who have been prepared to stand up and fight for what young children need. They are the pioneers who help everyone working with young children, past and present, to move forward. Not all of us have the kind of personality that makes us a pioneer, but we can all do our bit for the children in our care. The pioneers in this chapter are often called educational pioneers, but each one of them cared for children as much as they educated them. They all believed in integrated early years provision. This has a long and respected heritage, and the greatest influence in the UK in the nineteenth century has been that of Friedrich Froebel. Other pioneers include Maria Montessori, Rudolf Steiner, Margaret McMillan and Susan Isaacs.

## Friedrich Froebel (1782–1852)

Froebel, who founded the first kindergarten in 1840, studied for a time with Pestalozzi in his school in Switzerland. Through his observations of children, Froebel learned how important it was for children to have real experiences that involved them in being physically active. Froebel's ideas are now very much part of everyday thinking about the integration of early years services. But most people have never heard of the man himself – only his ideas remain.

Froebel believed that everything links and connects with everything else: he called this the **principle of unity**. But he also believed in what he called the **principle of opposition** – for example, the first 'Gift' is a soft ball, but the second 'Gift' is a hard, wooden ball. He thought that these kinds of contrasts were important in helping children to think. (See below for more details on 'Gifts'.)

A summary of Froebel's ideas:

- Froebel thought that schools should be communities in which the parents are welcome to join their children.
- He believed that parents are the first educators of their child.
- Froebel thought that children should learn outdoors in the garden, as well as indoors. He encouraged movement, games and the study of natural science in the garden.
- He invented finger play, songs and rhymes in the educational context.
- He encouraged the arts and crafts and a love of literature, as well as mathematical understanding.
- He thought that children should have freedom of movement, clothes that are easy to move about in, and sensible food that is not too rich.
- Froebel valued symbolic behaviour deeply, and he encouraged this even in very young children. He realised how important it is for children to

understand that they can make one thing stand for another – for example, a daisy can stand for a fried egg, a twig can stand for a knife, a leaf can stand for a plate, a written word can stand for a name.

- He thought that the best way for children to try out symbolic behaviour is in their play. He thought that, as they pretend and imagine things, children show their highest levels of learning. He thought that children's best thinking is done when they are playing.
- He also designed various items and activities to help symbolic behaviour. He encouraged children to draw, make collages and model with clay.
- He encouraged play with special-shaped wooden blocks, which he called the 'Gifts'.
- He made up songs, movements and dancing, and the crafts that he called his 'Occupations'.
- He allowed children to use the Gifts and Occupations as they wished, without having to do set tasks of the kind that adults usually asked of them. Thus he introduced what is now called free-flow play.

## Research Activity
### Investigating Froebel's work

1. Research a set of wooden hollow blocks and wooden unit blocks (examples of these are made by Community Playthings). Can you find any mathematical relationships between the different blocks? Plan how you could help children to learn about shape, using wooden blocks. Implement your plan, and evaluate your observations with children of 3 to 7 years of age.

2. Try to find 12 examples of finger rhymes. These are songs or rhymes using the fingers for actions. Make a book of them for children to enjoy. Make sure you include a multicultural range of action songs and also think about children with disabilities. Share the book with a child of 2 to 7 years of age. Evaluate your observations.

3. Research what children did in kindergartens in the twentieth century – for example, each child had his or her own little garden.

4. Imagine that you are Friedrich Froebel today. What do you think he might like or dislike about your early years setting?

- He emphasised the expressive arts, mathematics, literature, the natural sciences, creativity and aesthetic (beautiful) things. He believed that each brought important but different kinds of knowledge and understanding.

He also placed great emphasis on ideas, feelings and relationships. Relationships with other children, he believed, were as important as relationships with adults.

## In Practice

❏ Plan how you will organise a garden activity. What equipment will you need? Where will you do this? How will you clear up?

❏ Plant some flowers or vegetables with children, and watch them grow.

❏ Observe a child of 2 to 7 years of age, and evaluate your garden activity in relation to that particular child's cognitive and language development.

## Maria Montessori (1870–1952)

Maria Montessori began her work as a doctor in the poorest areas of Rome, Italy, at the beginning of the 1900s. She worked with children with learning difficulties. She spent many hours **observing** children and this is one of the great strengths of her work. She came to the conclusion, now supported by modern research that children pass through sensitive periods of development when they are particularly receptive to particular areas of learning. Like Piaget (and others), she saw children as active learners.

A summary of Montessori's ideas:

- Montessori devised a structured teaching programme, which she based on her observations of children with learning difficulties; she believed she was making Froebel's work more scientifically rigorous in doing this.
- She also used the work of an educator called Seguin, who had given manual dexterity exercises to children with physical disabilities. He did this

because he believed that if they could learn to use their hands, they would be able to find work later.

- Montessori designed a set of what she called **didactic materials**, which encouraged children to use their hands. Her approach moved children from simple to complex exercises.
- Whereas Froebel stressed the importance of relationships, feelings and being part of a community, Montessori stressed that children should work alone. She thought that this helped children to become **independent learners**.
- For Montessori, the highest moment in a child's learning is what she called the **polarisation of the attention**. This means that the child is completely silent and absorbed in what he or she is doing.
- Unlike Froebel, Montessori did not see the point in play. She did not encourage children to have their own ideas until they had worked through all her graded learning sequence; she did not believe that they were able to do free drawing or creative work of any kind until they had done this. Montessori has had more influence on private schools than on the maintained sector of education.

## Rudolf Steiner (1861–1925)

Steiner believed in three phases of childhood. These involved:

1. The **will**, 0 to 7 years: he believed that the spirit fuses with the body at this stage.
2. The **heart**, 7 to 14 years: he believed that the rhythmic system of the beating heart, the chest and the respiratory system meant that feelings were especially important during this time.
3. The **head,** 14 years onwards: this is the period of thinking.

There are a few schools in the UK that use Steiner's methods. These Waldorf schools are all in the private sector. Like Montessori, Steiner has had less influence on the statutory public sector than on the private sector.

A summary of Steiner's ideas:

- Steiner believed that during the first seven years of life, the child is like a newcomer finding his or her way, and the child's reincarnated soul needs protection.

- The child needs a carefully planned environment in order to develop in a rounded way.
- What the child eats is very important (Steiner was a vegetarian). The child also needs proper rest (rest and activity need to be balanced).
- The child's temperament is also considered to be very important. A child might be calm (**sanguine**), easily angered (**choleric**), sluggish (**phlegmatic**) or peevish (**melancholic**). Often children are a combination of types.
- The golden rule for the adult is never to go against the temperament of the child, but always to go with it.
- Steiner was similar to Froebel in that he believed in the importance of the community. He believed that maintaining relationships with other people is very important, and for this reason children would keep the same teacher for a number of years.
- When children are about to sing and act out a circle game, everyone waits for the last child to join the group. The song is sung many times, so that children who learn quickly learn to help and support children who learn more slowly.
- Steiner's curriculum is very powerful for children with special educational needs who can integrate, because other children are actively helped to care about them.
- Steiner thought the **symbolic behaviour** of the child was important, but in a different way from Froebel. In the first seven years of life, he told special Steinerian fairy tales. He believed that children 'drink' these in and absorb them. He gave them dolls without faces, wooden blocks with irregular shapes, silk scarves as dressing-up clothes and particular colour schemes in rooms (pink at first). Baking, gardening, modelling, painting and singing would all take place in a carefully designed community.

## Margaret McMillan (1860–1931)

Margaret McMillan, like Montessori, began her work using the influence of Seguin. This meant that she emphasised manual dexterity exercises long before Montessori's ideas reached the UK. However, as time went on, she used Froebel's ideas more and more (she became a member of the Froebel Society in 1903).

A summary of McMillan's ideas:

- McMillan believed **first-hand experience** and **active learning** to be important.
- She emphasised relationships, feelings and ideas as much as the physical aspects of moving and learning.
- She believed that children become whole people through play. She thought that play helps them to apply what they know and understand.
- McMillan pioneered nursery schools, which she saw as an extension of, not a substitute for, home.
- She believed in very close partnership with parents; she encouraged parents to develop alongside their children, with adult classes in hobbies and languages made available to them.
- The British nursery school, as envisaged by McMillan, has been admired and emulated across the world. Nursery schools have gardens, and are communities that welcome both parents and children. Such nursery schools stood out as beacons of light in the poverty-stricken areas of inner cities like Deptford and Bradford in the 1920s.
- McMillan said that in a nursery school, families could experience 'fresh air, trees, rock gardens, herbs, vegetables, fruit trees, bushes, opportunities to climb on walls, sandpits, lawns, flowers and flowerbeds and wildernesses'. In her book, *The Nursery School* (published in 1930), she wrote: 'most of the best opportunities for achievement lie in the domain of free play, with access to various materials'.
- Perhaps her most important achievement of all is to have been described as the 'godmother' of school meals and school medical services. She believed that children cannot learn if they are undernourished, poorly clothed, sick or ill, with poor teeth, poor eyesight, ear infections, rickets, and so on. Recent reports emphasise that poor health and poverty are challenges still facing those who work with families in the UK today.
- McMillan placed enormous importance on the training of adults working with children, and on the need for them to be inventive and imaginative in their work.

## Investigating Margaret McMillan's work

Plan an outdoor area for an early years setting. Emphasise the child's need for movement and curiosity about nature, and provide an area for digging and playing in mud. Evaluate your plan.

## Susan Isaacs (1885–1948)

Susan Isaacs, like Margaret McMillan, was influenced by Froebel. She was also influenced by the theories of Melanie Klein, the psychoanalyst (see page 72). Isaacs made detailed observations of children at her Malting House School in Cambridge during the 1930s.

A summary of Isaacs's ideas:

- Isaacs valued play because she believed it gave children freedom to think, feel and relate to others.
- She looked at children's fears, their aggression and their anger. She believed that, through their play, children can move in and out of reality. This enables them to balance their ideas, feelings and relationships.
- She said that young children cannot learn in classrooms where they have to sit at tables and write, because they need to move just as they need to eat and sleep.
- Isaacs valued parents as the most important

educators in a child's life. She spoke to them on the radio, and she wrote for parents in magazines. In her book, *The Nursery Years* (1929), she wrote:

*If the child had ample opportunity for free play and bodily exercise, if this love of making and doing with his hands is met, if his interest in the world around him is encouraged by sympathy and understanding, if he is left free to make believe or think as his impulses take him, then his advances in skill and interest are but the welcome signs of mental health and vigour.*

- Isaacs encouraged people to look at the inner feelings of children. She encouraged children to express their feelings. She thought it would be very damaging to bottle up feelings inside.
- She supported both Froebel's and McMillan's view that nurseries are an extension of the home and not a substitute for it, and she believed that children should remain in nursery-type education until the age of 7 years.
- She kept careful records of children, both for the period they spent in her nursery and after they had left. She found that when they left her nursery and went on to formal infant schools, many of them regressed. Modern researchers have found the same.

## The Reggio Emilia approach

The Reggio Emilia approach to preschool education was started by the schools of the city of Reggio Emilia in Italy after the Second World War. There is much about Reggio Emilia's approach to childcare

## In Practice

### Investigating education and care

1. Research the different ways in which Froebel, Montessori and Steiner would (a) introduce children to a set of wooden blocks and (b) help children to use the blocks.

2. Implement each approach with a group of children in three separate sessions.

3. Evaluate your observations, noting the way your role as an early years worker changed according to which approach you used.

4. Note the differences in the way the children responded, especially in relation to creativity (see Chapter 21), language and communication (see Chapter 16) and play (see below). Which approaches encouraged the child to be a symbol-user? Evaluate your observations.

and education that distinguishes it from other efforts both inside and outside of Italy, and attracts worldwide attention. Of special interest is the emphasis on children's symbolic languages in the context of a project-oriented curriculum. The Reggio Emilia approach is made possible through a carefully articulated and collaborative approach to the care and education of young children.

The key features of the Reggio Emilia approach:

- **Community support and parental involvement** – Reggio Emilia's tradition of community support for families with young children expands on Italy's cultural view of children as the collective responsibility of the state. The parents' role mirrors the community's, at both the school wide and the classroom level. Parents are expected to take part in discussions about school policy, child development concerns, and curriculum planning and evaluation. Because a majority of parents – including mothers – are employed, meetings are held in the evenings so that all who wish to participate can do so.
- **Administrative policies and organisational features** – A head administrator, who reports directly to the town council, works with a group of curriculum team leaders, each of whom coordinates the efforts of teachers from five or six centres. Each centre is staffed with two teachers per classroom (12 children in infant classes, 18 in toddler classes, and 24 in pre-primary classes), one teacher trained in the arts who works with classroom teachers in curriculum development and documentation and several auxiliary staff. There is no principal, nor is there a hierarchical relationship among the teachers. This staffing plan, coupled with the policy of keeping the same group of children and teachers together for a period of three years, facilitates the sense of community that characterises relationships among adults and children.
- **Teachers as learners** – Teachers' long-term commitment to enhancing their understanding of children is at the crux of the Reggio Emilia approach. They compensate for the meagre pre-service training of Italian early childhood teachers by providing extensive staff development

opportunities, with goals determined by the teachers themselves. Teacher autonomy is evident in the absence of teacher manuals, curriculum guides or achievement tests. The lack of externally imposed mandates is joined by the imperative that teachers become skilled observers of children in order to inform their curriculum planning and implementation.
- **The role of the environment** – The organisation of the physical environment is crucial to Reggio Emilia's early childhood programme, and is often referred to as the child's 'third teacher'. The pre-schools are generally filled with indoor plants and vines, and awash with natural light. Classrooms open to a central piazza, kitchens are open to view, and access to the surrounding community is assured through wall-size windows, courtyards, and doors to the outside in each classroom. Entrances capture the attention of both children and adults through the use of mirrors (on the walls, floors and ceilings), photographs, and children's work accompanied by transcriptions of their discussions. These same features characterise classroom interiors, where displays of project work are interspersed with arrays of found objects and classroom materials, with clearly designated spaces for large- and small-group activities.
- **Long-term projects as vehicles for learning** – The curriculum is characterised by many features advocated by contemporary research on young children, including real-life problem-solving among peers, with numerous opportunities for creative thinking and exploration. Teachers often work on projects with small groups of children, while the rest the class engages in a wide variety of self-selected activities typical of pre-school classrooms. The topic of investigation may derive directly from teacher observations of children's spontaneous play and exploration. Project topics are also selected on the basis of an academic curiosity or social concern on the part of teachers or parents, or serendipitous events that direct the attention of the children and teachers. Reggio teachers place a high value on their ability to improvise and respond to children's predisposition to enjoy the unexpected. Regardless of their origins, successful projects are those that

generate a sufficient amount of interest and uncertainty to provoke children's creative thinking and problem-solving and are open to different avenues of exploration. As curriculum decisions are based on developmental and socio-cultural concerns, small groups of children of varying abilities and interests, including those with special needs, work together on projects. Projects begin with teachers observing and questioning children about the topic of interest. Based on children's responses, teachers introduce materials, questions and opportunities that provoke children to further explore the topic. While some of these teacher provocations are anticipated, projects often move in unanticipated directions as a result of problems children identify. Thus, curriculum planning and implementation revolve around open-ended and often long-term projects that are based on the reciprocal nature of teacher-directed and child-initiated activity.

- **The hundred languages of children** – As children proceed in an investigation, generating and testing their hypotheses, they are encouraged to depict their understanding through one of many symbolic languages, including drawing, sculpture, dramatic play and writing. They work together towards the resolution of problems that arise. Teachers facilitate and then observe debates regarding the extent to which a child's drawing or other form of representation lives up to the expressed intent. Revision of drawings (and ideas) is encouraged, and teachers allow children to repeat activities and modify each other's work in the collective aim of better understanding the topic. Teachers foster children's involvement in the processes of exploration and evaluation, acknowledging the importance of their evolving products as vehicles for exchange.

(www.reggioemiliaapproach.net/about.php)

## The HighScope approach

The HighScope approach encourages children to make decisions about their own choice of activities. The HighScope approach encourages active and independent learning by involving children in the planning, doing and reviewing of activities. The children still participate in some adult-directed activities such as story time, PE and other larger group activities as well as work to develop specific skills such as literacy and numeracy in small groups or as individuals. The 'plan-do-review' cycle of planning looks something like this:

1. **Plan:** in a small group with an adult, children discuss which activities they intend to do that session.
2. **Do:** the children participate in the activities of their choice and are encouraged to talk during this time with adults helping to extend the children's language and learning.
3. **Review:** at the end of the session the group come together again to look back on the session's activities.

HighScope is unique in having a 40-year longitudinal study in validation of its work with children. The results of these research studies show how the HighScope approach to early years education produces lasting benefits for children, families and society. The following examples are specific findings from the research studies. Children who had experienced the HighScope approach as adolescents and adults showed: increased social responsibility; increased chance of higher economic status; improved educational performance; increased commitment to long-term relationships. The overall conclusion from research is that children across cultural and socio-economic backgrounds and of varying abilities benefit from the HighScope approach.

HighScope is a quality approach to children's learning that is widely used in the UK. HighScope recognises the uniqueness of each child and develops their self-confidence by building on what they can do.

The key features of the HighScope approach:

- Active Learning – Children learn best by being active – by engaging with people, materials, events and ideas in ways that are direct, immediate and meaningful to them. Every aspect of the HighScope approach supports active learning.
- Personal Initiative – Children have a natural desire to learn. HighScope recognises and supports this.

It encourages children to use their initiative, to plan and to develop their own strengths and interests. The Plan-Do-Review process gives children the opportunity to create and express their intentions, to generate their own learning experiences and to reflect on those experiences.

- Consistency – To become confident, independent learners, children need consistency. The HighScope approach provides this through the daily routine, the organisation of the learning environment and in the ways that adults interact with children.
- Genuine Relationships – Children achieve more when they feel happy and secure. HighScope practitioners bring genuine warmth and trust to their relationships with children. They also respect and value each child's personal and cultural identity.
- Building a Strong Partnership with Parents – HighScope practitioners recognise that parents and practitioners need to form authentic relationships and share their unique knowledge and experience with one another to support children's learning and well-being.
- Appropriate Curriculum – Children need a curriculum that is appropriate to their intellectual, emotional and physical development. The HighScope Curriculum has been developed through extensive observations of young children learning. It is based on key development indicators (formerly Key Experiences) and offers children the foundation of knowledge, skills and ideas that supports the Early Years Foundation Stage while creating confident learners.

(HighScope UK, 2011)

### Research Activity

Investigating different approaches to pre-school education

1. Research the Reggio Emilia approach and the HighScope approach.

2. Note any similarities and differences between these two approaches.

## Common Core of skills and knowledge for the children's workforce

Common Core provides a description of the basic skills and knowledge required by people (including volunteers) whose work brings them into regular contact with children, young people and families. The core skills and knowledge are set out under six headings:

1. Effective communication and engagement with children, young people and families
2. Child and young person development
3. Safeguarding and promoting the welfare of the child
4. Supporting transitions
5. Multi-agency working
6. Sharing information.

The Common Core aims to promote equality, respect diversity and challenge stereotypes, helping to improve the life chances of all children and young people and to provide more effective and integrated services. It also acknowledges the rights of children and young people, and the role of parents, carers and families. The document includes a glossary of terms and a summary of relevant legislation. Another annex provides the *Every Child Matters: Change for Children* outcomes framework, which sets out the desired outcomes for children and young people.

(DfE, 2010)

## Developing a personal and individual approach to learning and development

Valuing children's individuality, ideas and feelings is an important aspect of developing a personal and individual approach to learning and development. This involves being sensitive to children needs. There are *universal needs* that are necessary to *all* children; these needs are physical or **biological needs** such as food, drink and shelter that are essential to *survival*. Then there are **psychological needs** such as love, affection, secure and stable relationships, friendships, intellectual stimulation,

## Activity

List four ways in which you have shown you value children's individuality, ideas and feelings. Include practical examples of working with: boys and girls; children with special needs; children from different social or cultural backgrounds.

independence; these needs are essential to maintaining the individual's *quality of life*.

Remember that children's *individual* needs vary. Meeting the needs of children in childcare settings, especially where children are grouped according to age, can be difficult. Some children will have developmental needs which are in line with the expected **norm** for their chronological age, while others will have needs which are characteristic of much younger or older children. In recognising and attempting to meet children's needs, you should consider each child's age, physical maturity, intellectual abilities, emotional development, social skills, past experiences and relationships. Respecting children and helping them to develop a positive self-image and identity goes a long way towards providing a caring, nurturing and responsive childcare environment.

# Be able to provide environments within the work setting that support and extend children's development and learning in their early years

As an early years practitioner, you should be able to provide environments within the work setting that support and extend children's development and learning in their early years. This includes:

- Providing a stimulating, enjoyable and carefully planned learning environment including the use of indoor and outdoor spaces

- Using everyday routines to enhance learning
- Ensuring a balance between structured and freely chosen play
- Supporting and extending play to encourage learning by using your knowledge of individual children and their preferred learning styles
- Using appropriate materials and support strategies for each child's needs and abilities
- Encouraging children's participation and providing assistance at an appropriate level for each child including supporting children with special needs
- Having high expectations of children and commitment to raising their achievement based on a realistic appraisal of their capabilities and what they might achieve
- Encouraging children to make choices about their own learning
- Changing and adapting plans as required to meet the needs of all the children.

## Providing a stimulating learning environment

It is vital that *all* children have access to a stimulating environment which enables learning, to take place in exciting and challenging ways. To develop into healthy, considerate and intelligent adults, all children require intellectual stimulation as well as physical care and emotional security. Intellectual stimulation through play and other learning opportunities allows children to develop their cognitive abilities and fulfil their potential as individuals.

The children you work with will be constantly thinking and learning, e.g. gathering new information and formulating new ideas about themselves, other people and the world around them. You should provide children with opportunities to:

- Explore their environment and/or investigate new information/ideas
- Discover things for themselves through a wide variety of experiences
- Feel free to make mistakes in a safe and secure environment using 'trial and error'

- Develop autonomy through increased responsibility and working independently
- Encourage and extend their knowledge and skills with appropriate support from adults (and other children)
- Learn to make sense of new information within an appropriate curriculum framework.

It is important to plan and organise an environment for children and families that is welcoming and user-friendly. This involves planning and providing an enabling physical environment for children, including adapting the environment to meet children's needs (according to their ages, abilities and any special needs) and ensuring that any barriers to participation are addressed. It also involves organising space and resources to meet children's needs within an accessible, comfortable and stimulating environment. You should provide a caring, nurturing and responsive environment where children and their families feel valued and respected. You should also facilitate children's personal care by encouraging children to care for themselves as appropriate to their ages, needs and abilities.

The early years setting should be equipped with a basic set of resources and books appropriate to the ages and developmental needs of the children. You should organise resources so that they are equally accessible to all children in the setting and enable choice and independence. You should use ICT to support children's play and learning. You should encourage children to be actively involved in decisions about their environment, e.g. selection of play and learning resources. Children should be taught how to use all resources correctly and safely, with care and respect and with regard for Health and Safety and waste. Remember that resources should reflect the cultural and linguistic diversity of our society. General resources may include:

- *Visual aids:* wall displays including children's work, maps, posters, pictures and posters; interest tables with interesting objects related to topic work; 3D displays of children's work including construction models; videos; computer graphics and books.

- *Indoor and outdoor play equipment* appropriate for the children's ages and levels of development and suitable for children of all abilities, including children with special needs.
- *Groups of tables for group work* including literacy and numeracy activities.
- *Groups of tables for 'messy' practical activities* (e.g. arts and crafts, design technology) including storage for art/design materials and equipment, e.g. paint, paint pots, drying rack; sink for washing paint pots and brushes; basin for washing hands.
- *Computers and printers* with selection of appropriate software.
- *CD players with headphones* with a selection of CDs.
- *Book/story corner* with appropriate range of fiction and non-fiction books, including some dual language books.
- *Quiet area* where children can go for privacy, rest or sleep depending on their individual needs including cushions, mats or cots appropriate to the ages of the children.
- *Whiteboard, over-head projector and teaching base* in settings supporting children's literacy and numeracy skills including marker pens, transparencies, textbooks, teaching manuals and other resources needed by staff on a regular basis.
- *Writing and drawing materials* including a variety of writing tools (crayons, pencils, pens, pastels, chalks); different shapes, sizes and types of paper (e.g. plain, coloured, graph).
- *Specialist resources for specific curriculum areas* stored in the appropriate curriculum resource cupboard/area.
- *Children's work trays* to store individual workbooks, folders for topic work, reading books, reading logs, personal named pencils, crayon tins.
- *Area with individual coat pegs* for children's coats and PE bags.

# Prepare the environment to support and extend children's learning and development

To flourish in their early years, children need opportunities to build their social skills, language and confidence. Children do this best through structured play and talk, interacting with each other and with interested and stimulating adults. The evidence is overwhelming that all children, but particularly those from disadvantaged homes, benefit from high-quality pre-school experiences. (Alexander *et al.* 2009; p. 16)

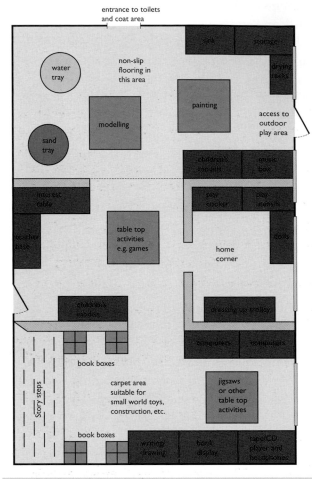

**Figure 12.1** Example of an early years classroom layout

Play is an essential part of development and learning as it contributes to the social, physical, intellectual, communication and emotional wellbeing of children. It is the central way in which children explore and develop an understanding of their environment. Children learn through play. You need to be able to provide opportunities for indoor and outdoor play that support and extend children's development and learning in the early years. When planning play opportunities, you should remember that:

● The play environment should be welcoming and provide maximum opportunities for children and young people to make choices
● Play resources should be varied with sufficient quantities so that children do not have to wait too long to play with materials or equipment
● Children should have lots of opportunities for social interaction with other children and adults.

(Lindon, 2002)

When working with children, you will help to plan how the setting will be organised, both indoors and outdoors, and what play opportunities and resources will be available. However, such planning must take account of children's play needs and be flexible enough to allow them to enjoy play in their own way, and to make their own choices and decisions about play.

## Key terms

**Play needs** – The individual needs of children for play.

## Activity

1. Draw your own plan of an early years setting. Include the following: age range of children; layout of furniture/equipment; areas for play and learning; fire doors/safety equipment; storage areas.

2. Highlight any specific features of the environment that make it suitable for *all* children including those with special needs (e.g. physical disability or sensory impairment) or those from different cultural backgrounds.

3. List ways in which you think the setting maximises sensory experiences and a variety of play and learning opportunities.

When planning opportunities for play, you should remember these important points:

1. Plan play opportunities based on children's play needs and preferences, e.g. find out about children's play and development, observe children's play activities.
2. Involve children in the creation of play environments, e.g. consult them about the play opportunities and play resources they would like in the setting.
3. Create play spaces that children can adapt to their own needs, e.g. flexible play areas to allow children to spread out during their play.
4. Allow children to choose and explore play environments for themselves, e.g. selecting their own play activities and play resources.
5. Allow children to develop through play in their own ways, e.g. freedom to explore and enjoy their chosen play activities in their own way and in their own time.
6. Allow children's play to continue uninterrupted, e.g. participate in their play as and when invited to do so; only intervene in children's play in order to maintain their physical safety or emotional security.
7. Address the possible barriers to accessing play environments that some children may experience, e.g. ensure the setting is inclusive and encourages participation by all the children, including those from ethnic minority backgrounds, and those with disabilities. (See section 'Understand how to support diversity, inclusion and participation in early years settings' in Chapter 15, EYMP 4.)

## In Practice

Describe the planning and provision of play opportunities in your setting.

## Types of play

You should know and understand how to provide opportunities for a wide range of play types. Play types can be grouped into three main areas of play: physical; exploratory; imaginative.

## Activity

List examples of each play type based on your experiences of providing play opportunities for children.

# Providing opportunities for physical play

Children should have plenty of opportunities for physical play, e.g. play apparatus, outdoor play, ball games and swimming. By using their whole bodies, children learn how to control and manage them. The more practice children get to develop gross motor skills, the more agile, coordinated and safe they will be as they grow older. Using lots of energy in physical play is also fun and relaxing. Children also need opportunities to develop their fine motor skills and hand-eye coordination, e.g. playing with stacking toys and jigsaws.

Physical play enables children to:

- Develop body awareness and awareness of spatial relationships, e.g. judging distance between self and other objects
- Understand positional relationships, e.g. going in and out, over and under
- Develop gross motor skills, e.g. participating in individual and group sports
- Develop fine motor skills, e.g. drawing, sewing
- Improve hand-eye coordination and visual perception, e.g. catching a ball, threading a needle.

Activities to encourage children's physical play:

1. **Outdoor play** opportunities should be provided for children everyday, e.g. playing in the outdoor play area, going for walks, going to the park or visiting a playground. As well as the benefits of fresh air, outdoor play offers children more space to develop gross motor skills such as running, hopping, jumping, skipping, throwing and catching a ball, playing football, doing somersaults and cartwheels.
2. **Play apparatus** can be used indoors or outdoors depending on the size of the equipment and the

| Main area of play | Types of play | Example activities |
|---|---|---|
| **PHYSICAL**<br><br>Play activities that provide opportunities for children to develop their physical skills | • **Locomotor play** – play involving movement in all directions for its own sake | • playing chase, tag, hide and seek |
| | • **Mastery play** – play involving control of physical aspects of the environment | • digging holes, building dens |
| | • **Rough and tumble play** – play involving discovering physical flexibility and demonstrating physical skill | • play fighting, chasing |
| **EXPLORATORY**<br><br>Play activities that provide opportunities for children to understand the world around them by exploring their environment and experimenting with materials | • **Exploratory play** – play involving manipulating objects or materials to discover their properties and possibilities | • playing with bricks, sand, water, clay, play-dough |
| | • **Creative play** – play allowing new responses, transformation of information, awareness of connections, with an element of surprise | • enjoying creative activities, arts and crafts, using a variety of materials and tools |
| | • **Object play** – play involving hand-eye coordination to manipulate objects in an infinite variety of ways | • examining novel uses for a paintbrush, brick |
| **IMAGINATIVE**<br><br>Play activities that provide opportunities for children to express feelings and to develop social skills | • **Communication play** – play using words, nuances or gestures | • telling jokes, play acting, singing, storytelling |
| | • **Deep play** – play allowing risky experiences, to develop survival skills and conquer fears | • balancing on a high beam, performing skateboarding stunts |
| | • **Dramatic play** – play dramatising events in which child is indirect participator | • presenting a television show, religious or festive celebrations |
| | • **Fantasy play** – play rearranging the world in a manner unlikely to occur in real life | • playing at being an astronaut or king/queen |
| | • **Imaginative play** – play where conventional rules of the real world not applicable | • pretending to be dog or a superhero |
| | • **Social play** – play involving social interaction that requires following certain rules or protocols | • games with rules, conversations |
| | • **Socio-dramatic play** – play involving enacting intense real life personal or interpersonal experiences | • playing house, shops, hospital, dentist |

| Main area of play | Types of play | Example activities |
| --- | --- | --- |
| | ● **Symbolic play** – play allowing controlled, gradual exploration and increased understanding, without risk | ● using piece of wood to symbolise a person |
| | ● **Role play** – play exploring human activities on basic level | ● doing simple domestic chores, i.e. sweeping with a broom, making telephone calls, driving a car, with or without play equipment |

(NPFA *et al.*, 2000)

**Table 12.1** Play types

space available. Larger play equipment that cannot be easily (or safely) accommodated inside the setting can be used in outdoor play, e.g. climbing apparatus. When using play equipment whether in the setting or at a playground, you must ensure that it is safe for use, as well as appropriate for the children's ages and sizes. Always check play equipment before use.

3. **Jigsaw puzzles** help children with shape recognition as well as developing fine motor skills and hand-eye coordination. Children can tackle standard jigsaws with a few large pieces, increasing the number of pieces as the children grow and improve their physical skills.

4. **Ball games** provide children with opportunities to develop ball skills such as throwing kicking and catching a ball. Younger children need large, lightweight balls to practise their throwing and catching skills. As they get older smaller balls, beanbags and quoits can be used to develop their skills of throwing with more accuracy.

5. **Swimming** is an excellent all-round physical activity. Children are usually ready to learn to swim by the age of 4 or 5 years old. If the setting does not have its own swimming pool, it may be possible to arrange regular outings to a local swimming pool. If not, try to encourage the children in your setting to use their local pool with their families or friends depending on their ages/swimming abilities.

**Figure 12.2** Children using outdoor play equipment

## In Practice

Give examples of physical play activities from your own experiences of working with children.

## Providing opportunities for exploratory play

Exploratory play encourages and extends children's discovery skills. Play is an important way to motivate children and to assist thinking and learning in a wide variety of settings. Children learn from play situations that give them 'hands-on' experience. Exploratory play encourages children to use their senses to discover the properties of different materials in pleasurable and meaningful ways. For example, playing with sand encourages children to consider textures and the functions of sand – getting the right consistency of sand to build sand castles; too wet or too dry and the sand will not stick together.

Exploratory play enables children to:

- Understand concepts such as shape and colour
- Explore the properties of materials, e.g. textures
- Understand volume/capacity and physical forces through sand and water play
- Develop problem-solving skills
- Devise and use own creative ideas.

Activities to encourage children's exploratory play:

1. **Painting** with brushes, sponges, string; finger painting, bubble painting, 'butterfly' or 'blob' painting, marble painting, wax resist painting; printing (e.g. with leaves, potatoes, cotton reels) and pattern-making (e.g. with rollers, stamps).
2. **Drawing** using pencils, crayons, felt tips or chalks on a variety of materials including different kinds paper, card, fabric and wood. Include colouring activities linked to the children's interests by drawing your own colouring sheets, buying ready-made colouring books or using free printable colouring pages from the Internet.
3. **Model making** using commercial construction kits (e.g. *Lego Explore*, *Mega Bloks* and *Stickle Bricks*), wooden blocks or clean and safe 'junk' materials to enable children to create their own designs.
4. **Collage** using glue and interesting materials to create pictures involving different textures, colours and shapes, and provide an enjoyable sensory experience at the same time.

5. **Clay, play-dough and plasticine** can be used creatively; they are also tactile.
6. **Cooking** provides a similar experience to working with play-dough or clay except that the end product is (usually) edible. Remember to include 'no cook' activities such as icing biscuits, making sandwiches or peppermint creams.
7. **Making music** can provide opportunities for children to explore different sounds and to experiment freely with the musical instruments. Provide a range of instruments including: drum, tambourine, castanets, wood blocks, shakers, bell stick, Indian bells, triangle, xylophone and chime bars.
8. **Water play** with plain, bubbly, coloured, warm or cold water helps children learn about the properties of water, e.g. it pours, splashes, runs, soaks. Provide small containers to fill and empty, as well as a sieve and funnel.
9. **Sand play** provides opportunities for exploring the properties of sand, e.g. wet sand sticks together and can be moulded, while dry sand does not stick and can be poured. Use 'washed' or 'silver' sand (not builders' sand which might contain cement). Provide small containers and buckets to fill and empty, as well as sieves and funnels.

### In Practice

Give examples of exploratory play activities from your own experiences of working with children.

## Providing opportunities for imaginative play

Imaginative play provides opportunities for children to release emotional tension and frustration or express feelings such as anger or jealousy in positive ways. Imaginative play also encourages children to look and feel things from another person's viewpoint, as well as developing communication skills to interact more effectively with others. Imaginative play activities such as role play and dressing-up enable children to overcome fears and worries about new experiences or people, to feel more important and powerful, and to feel more

**Figure 12.3** Children engaged in exploratory play

secure by being able to temporarily regress to earlier levels of development.

Imaginative play enables children to:

- Develop language and communication skills
- Practise and rehearse real-life situations
- Improve self-help skills such as getting dressed
- Express feelings in positive ways
- Share ideas and cooperate with other children.

Activities to encourage children's imaginative play:

1. **Role play** includes *domestic play*, e.g. playing/imitating 'mum' or 'dad'; pretending to be a baby while other children act as parents; imitating other role models such as carers, play workers, teachers, characters from television, books; *shop play*, e.g. post office, hairdressers, café where they can explore other job roles. Pretending to visit the dentist, clinic, optician or hospital, setting up a home corner, a health centre or hospital can also provide for this type of play. Imaginative play also includes *drama* activities.

2. **Dressing-up activities** include pretending to be parents, carers, play workers, teachers, film/television super-heroes, characters from games consoles, kings and queens, allow children to experiment with being powerful and in control. Pretending to be someone else can also help children to understand what it is like to be that person and encourages empathy and consideration for others.

3. **Dolls and puppets** can help children to deal with their feelings, e.g. jealousy over a new baby can be expressed by shouting at a teddy or doll. Puppets are a useful way of providing children with a 'voice' and may encourage shy or withdrawn children to express themselves more easily.

4. **Miniature worlds** includes play with small-scale toys such as dolls' houses, toy farms and toy zoos as well as vehicle play, where children can act out previous experiences or situations while sharing ideas and equipment with other children; this can also help them establish friendships.

## In Practice

Give examples of imaginative play activities from your own experiences of working with children.

**Figure 12.4** Child involved in imaginative play

# Planning activities and experiences to support and extend children's learning and development

You will need to plan provision for the children you work with based on your assessment of their developmental progress. You should recognise that children's developmental progress depends on each child's level of maturation and their prior experiences. You should take these into account and have realistic expectations when planning activities and routines to promote children's development.

This includes regularly reviewing and updating plans for individual children and ensuring that plans balance the needs of individual children and the group, as appropriate to your setting. You should know and understand that children develop at widely different rates but in broadly the same sequence. When planning provision to promote children's development, you need to recognise that children's development is holistic even though it is divided into different areas, e.g. **S**ocial; **P**hysical; **I**ntellectual; **C**ommunication and language; **E**motional. You should remember to look at the 'whole' child. You need to look at *all* areas of children's development in relation to the particular aspect of development or learning you are focusing on when planning provision to promote children's development. All the areas must be delivered

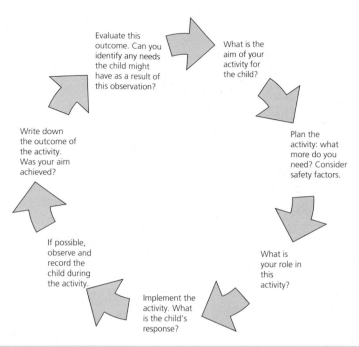

**Figure 12.5** Planning children's activities by Jackie Harding and Liz Meldon-Smith

through planned, purposeful play, with a balance of adult-led and child-initiated activities.

## The planning cycle

Following your observation and assessment of a child's development, learning and/or behaviour, your recommendations can provide the basis for planning appropriate routines and/or activities to encourage and extend the child's skills in specific areas. Effective planning is based on children's individual needs, abilities and interests, hence the importance of accurate and reliable child observations and assessments. Depending on the type of setting, you may also need to plan provision based on the requirements for curriculum frameworks for early education.

When planning activities and experiences for young children, your overall aims should be to:

- Support the care and development of *all* the children you work with
- Ensure every child has full access to the appropriate curriculum
- Meet children's individual developmental and learning needs
- Build on each child's existing knowledge, understanding and skills.

After you have planned and implemented an activity you will need to evaluate it. Some evaluation also occurs during the activity, providing continuous assessment of a child's performance. It is important to evaluate the activity so that you can: assess whether the routine or activity has been successful, e.g. the aims and objectives or outcomes have been met; identify possible ways in which the routine or activity might be modified/adapted to meet the individual needs of the child or children; provide accurate information for the senior practitioner, setting manager or other professionals about the successfulness of a particular routine or activity. The senior practitioner, setting manager or your college tutor/assessor should give you guidelines on how to present your routine and activity plans.

# Monitoring and evaluating

You should draw on everyday observations and assessments and your knowledge of individual children to inform your assessments. After you have planned and implemented activities, you will need to monitor and evaluate the children's progress. Some monitoring and evaluation may occur during the activities, providing continuous assessment of each child's performance (e.g. child observations, checklists, etc.). Some monitoring and evaluation may occur shortly afterwards (e.g. record sheets, formal assessments, etc.). It is important to monitor and evaluate children's progress so that you can: discover if the learning activity has been successful, e.g. the aims and learning objectives or outcomes have been met; consider the ways in which the learning activity might be modified/adapted to meet the needs of the child or children; inform the senior practitioner, teacher, SENCO or other professionals whether or not a particular activity has been successful. You can monitor children's progress by asking yourself questions such as:

1. Did the children achieve the intended learning intentions/objectives? If not, why not?
2. If the children have achieved the learning intentions/objectives, what effect has it had? (e.g. on behaviour, learning, any special needs).
3. Were the learning intentions/objectives too easy or too hard?
4. How did any staff involvement affect the children's achievement?
5. Was the activity and/or overall curriculum plan successful? If not, why not?

You also need to be sensitive to children's individual needs and interests. Remember to observe the children while they are involved in the learning activities, and assess whether you need to change or extend these activities to meet their early learning and developmental needs more fully. The senior practitioner, setting manager or your college tutor/

assessor should give you guidelines on how to record assessments according to curriculum frameworks for early education, as applicable to the setting, local or national requirements.

Despite careful planning, you may find that an activity is not appropriate for all the children you are working with. You need to monitor children's responses to activities and take appropriate action to modify or adapt activities to achieve the intended learning goals/objectives, or provide additional activities to extend their learning. You may need to provide an alternative version of the activity, or you might be able to present the materials in different ways or offer a greater/lesser level of assistance. You may need to modify or adapt activities for the following reasons: the child lacks concentration; the child is bored or uninterested; the child finds the activity too difficult or too easy; the child is upset or unwell (if so, you may need to abandon/postpone the activity).

Children's responses should also be considered when providing support for activities. You should be sensitive to children's needs and preferences. You should take notice of non-verbal responses and preferences demonstrated by the children; these are just as important as what they say. Remember to give the children positive encouragement and feedback to reinforce and sustain their interest and efforts in the learning process. You can use children's positive or negative responses to modify or extend activities to meet each child's needs more effectively. For example, if the learning intentions prove too easy or too difficult, you may have to set new goals. By

## Activity

1. Observe a young child during a play experience.

2. In your evaluation, focus on: the learning intentions/goals achieved by the child, e.g. aspects of development (SPICE), learning new skills or consolidating existing skills; any difficulties the child had in understanding or completing the activity; the strategies used to support the child during the learning activity.

1. Plan and implement a play experience for a young child. You can use the assessment from the previous observation as the starting point for your planning. Include the following: the learning intentions/goals for the child; a list of materials and/or equipment needed for the experience; your intended strategies to support the child during the experience.

2. Review and evaluate the experience afterwards, including any modifications to the experience or any difficulties experienced during the experience.

breaking down activities into smaller tasks, you may help individual children to achieve success more quickly. In modifying plans, you are continuing a cycle of planning and implementing activities.

After the activity, you should use all the available relevant information to evaluate the effectiveness of your planning and implementation of the activity, e.g. responses and/or information from parents, colleagues and other professionals. You must provide feedback about the children's achievements to senior colleagues as appropriate, e.g. the senior practitioner or the class teacher. Any suggested changes to future activity plans should be agreed with the senior practitioner (or class teacher) and other relevant staff.

When planning and implementing activities for children, you should ensure that you make accurate and detailed records of what has been planned and/or implemented in order to: clarify the aims and learning objectives of activity plans; avoid contradictory strategies and unnecessary duplication of work; use the time available more effectively; evaluate the success of plans/activities; provide continuity and progression for future planning.

## Understand how to work in partnership with carers and parents

Early years practitioners need to bear in mind the following facts:

- Every family is different, with different needs and traditions.
- The great majority of parents are concerned to do their best for their child, even if they are not always sure what this might be.
- Each one of us only really knows what it is like to grow up in our own family. Parents almost always like some of the things about their own family and the way they were brought up; but they will be just as likely to wish that other aspects of their upbringing had been different.
- Parents usually welcome help when trying out some alternative ways of doing things. They will not want to change too much, nor will they want rapid changes forced on them by other people. Early childhood practitioners must respect parents' wishes.

## Why do parents choose childcare?

- Many parents need personal space away from their child for part of the day. This may be while the family adjusts to a new baby, or while the parent catches up with chores or simply relaxes.
- It is sometimes thought that all parents want full-time nursery places for their children so that they can work. This is almost certainly not the case. Some parents do want full-time nursery places so that they can work, because they positively want to work. Other parents want full-time nursery places because they have to work, for economic reasons.

## Guidelines for working with parents

- **Support parents** – Begin by seeing yourself as a resource and support that can be used by parents to further their child's best interests.

- **Respect all parents** – The vast majority of parents – including those who abuse their children – love them. It is important not to judge parents, and to respect their good intentions. Almost every parent wants to do the job well, even if on the surface they may not seem to be interested or loving.

- **Recognise the good intentions of parents** – Work positively, with this aim as a central focus. Concentrating on the good intentions of parents helps to give them a positive self-image. Just as children need positive images reflected about themselves, so do parents. The attitude of the staff must therefore be to show parents respect; it is hard bringing up a child.

- **Reinforce the parents' sense of dignity and self-esteem** – Showing parents respect and reinforcing their dignity demonstrates to them that their child also needs respect and a sense of dignity.

- **Using your experience** – If you are not a parent, you will not have experienced some of the things that parents have. If you are a parent, you will only know about being a parent of your own child; you will not know what it is like to be a parent of other people's children.

- Some parents will be required to bring their child to the nursery as a matter of child protection – they will have no choice in the matter.

- Other parents only want part-time nursery places. They may want their child to move in a wider social circle and to have new and interesting experiences.

- Some parents think it is important for their child to have some experiences away from them. Other parents will want to join in with their child – perhaps not every day, but regularly.

# The partnership model of working with carers and parents

The parent is a deeply important person to the child, and the relationship between parent and child is always very emotional. Emotional relationships can be a source of great strength, but they can also be very unreasonable at times. It is important to recognise that parents and practitioners have different kinds of relationships with the children in their care.

Practitioners need to develop consistent, warm and affectionate relationships with children, especially babies, but they should not seek to replace the parents. Babies need to be with the same people each day to develop social relationships. This is why the EYFS requires all early years settings and schools to implement a key person system.

Parents and practitioners have one thing in common that is very important: they all want the best for the child. The roles involved are not the same, but they are complementary:

- Parents know their own child best.
- Practitioners have knowledge of general child development.

If the partnership between parents, practitioners and child is going to develop well, each needs to be able to trust and respect the other. The self-esteem and wellbeing of the people in the partnership are important when they are working together. How we feel about ourselves influences how we relate to other people.

Parents may have had bad experiences at school, and when their child joins a group setting, all those past feelings may come rushing back to the surface. Parents will then be anxious and not feel good about themselves. They might expect your setting to be like the one they went to, and this will make them fear for their child. This is often the case when parents are required to bring their child to the early years

**Figure 12.6** Oliver has come to nursery on World Book Day dressed as a knight; his father, Antonio, helped him with the costume

setting under a child protection order. Staff will need to be sensitive to the feelings of parents in this sort of situation.

## Beginning the partnership – home visits

Home visits enable parents to meet staff on their own territory. The aims and practical arrangements for these visits are discussed in Chapter 14 (EYMP 3).

## Parent handbooks and brochures

Parents appreciate having booklets of their own to keep. An introductory brochure can be given at the first meeting with the key person or teacher. This should contain:

- the address and telephone number of the early years setting or school, plus email and website, if appropriate
- the name of the child's key person and room leader or teacher
- a chart showing the names of all the staff, what they do and their qualifications
- information about the opening and closing times
- details of other services, such as parent-and-toddler groups, drop-ins, toy library, etc., and the contact details for the local children's centre
- information about how the children are admitted, and about fees, if appropriate
- information about what to do if the child is to leave the setting
- information about the age range of the children
- information about what the parent needs to provide – nappies, spare clothes, snacks etc.
- what would happen in the event of late collection, and if a child was lost

## Guidelines for sharing information with parents before the child starts

Parents need to know about:

- settling-in procedures
- how the key person system works, and how their child will be helped if he or she becomes upset, angry, tired or needs a change of clothes
- what type of educational opportunities are offered
- how they can keep up-to-date with their child's development and progress, and share any concerns that may arise
- meals, snacks and how allergies and other dietary requirements – for example, religious ones – are managed
- arrangements for outings and parental permissions
- policy on the use of photographs and video to record children's progress, and for use in displays and publicity.

Some of this information can be shared with parents by going through a photo album or watching a DVD about the setting together. This could show, in a very practical way, the philosophy, activities and timetabling of the day. Seeing the approach 'in action' can help to make sense of questions about how children learn through play, or the approach taken to meals and snacks.

- information about policies on behaviour and bullying, administering medicines, equal opportunities and race equality, inclusion of children with special needs, safeguarding, and making a complaint. Parents also need to be told how to complain directly to Ofsted, should they wish to do so.

Early years settings and schools may develop a range of leaflets and brochures to share important information. Examples might cover the key person approach, learning outdoors, or the curriculum and planning.

### Research Activity

**Planning brochures**

1. Collect some examples of brochures and leaflets from a range of early years settings and schools. You might be able to obtain these by asking friends and family, or downloading them from a range of nurseries' websites. You could start with one of the big chains, e.g., Asquith (go to www.asquithnurseries.co.uk or search online for 'Asquith nurseries').

2. Plan a brochure that will introduce parents to an early years setting. Use photographs or drawings, with brief notes, to make a booklet that shows the philosophy of the setting. The brochure will need to illustrate the range of activities, the daily timetable of events and the rationale behind the organisation.

### Key terms

**Key person approach** – A system within a nursery setting in which care of each child is assigned to a particular adult, known as the key person. The role of the key person is to develop a special relationship with the child, in order to help the child to feel safe and secure in the nursery. The key person will also liaise closely with each key child's parents.

 **Progress check**

- Understand why a parent might choose childcare.
- Work with the team to share information with parents, listening to them as well as talking to them about their child's development and well-being.

## Understanding the views of parents

An advantage of home visits is that practitioners can ask parents about their views on education and care. It is only through understanding how parents feel that practitioners can share effectively what they know and have learned in their own training. This is especially important when working with families from different cultural backgrounds. Assumptions on both sides about what education is and how it should be carried out are often different. Through mutual respect, trust is established. This brings with it a deep commitment on both sides to working together for the child.

Some parents may hope that their child will learn to read early and might already have taught the alphabet to their 3-year-old. Do not reject their ideas about how children learn to read, even though your own point of view might be very different, as a result of your training. Try asking the parents if they would like to know some of the other 12 or so things children need to know in order to read. Stress that learning each of these things is valuable in itself and that there is no hurry to learn to read. It is more important that children learn at their own pace; they are more likely to become avid readers as a result. This does not reject the fact that a parent has taught his or her child the alphabet, but it does open up all sorts of other possibilities for what the parent can do to help the child to read. The messages to the parent are that the staff also value reading, that they respect the intentions of the parent and that they can be a helpful resource for a family that is teaching a child to read.

## Parents keeping records

Practitioners may ask parents to complete a form about their child's current interests and needs, to help with the individual planning for the child. Parents might also be asked to take an observation sheet and complete it at home. Parents can draw or write about interesting things that their child does. Drawing helps parents and practitioners to have a dialogue without the need for words or skilled writing. It can involve, with sensitivity, parents who use a different language or who are not confident about writing. Until recently, many practitioners thought that parents would not want to be involved in record-keeping. However, in the 1980s, as part of the Froebel Early Education Project, the researcher Chris Athey found that parents (several of whom spoke Urdu, but not English) loved to keep observation notes – they drew in order that staff and parents could communicate with each other. Older brothers and sisters often enjoy filling in these observation sheets too. In many settings, parents are encouraged to fill in observation sheets and to meet with practitioners to discuss them.

## Parents coming into the setting for the first time

Some early years settings and schools are unable to organise home visits, and there will be some parents who do not wish to be visited at home. For these parents, the reception they get on their first visit will be especially important, though of course this matters in every setting. Parents may come in to register their child, to visit during an open day or because there is a 'Stay and Play' or other parent-and-child group offered.

## Establishing and maintaining a professional relationship

Hopefully, an atmosphere of trust is initiated during the first meeting with parents. Remember that you are not trying to make *friends* with parents – this is a professional relationship only. Friendships are about choosing each other; they are based on being interested in the same things – for example, the same sort of food, or an activity such as dancing or football. A professional relationship is one in which people do not choose each other. They come together because of the work they do together. Early childhood practitioners and parents come together because they each spend time with and work with the child. You do not have to like someone in order to have a good professional relationship with them.

## Guidelines for welcoming parents and children to an early years setting or school

The following will help parents and children to feel welcome when they first arrive at the setting:

- Parents and visitors are given a friendly welcome by practitioners.
- Clearly sign-posted entrance with arrows to the reception office.
- An attractive display in the entrance area, showing some of the recent activities that children have been involved in.
- Information showing the names of practitioners, with their photographs.
- Photograph albums, slide shows or videos that show children playing, learning and developing.
- The week's menu.
- Positive images and messages about diversity – for example, different languages, ethnicities and genders, with examples of both boys and girls taking part in a full range of activities.
- Including something for children to do in a lobby or entrance area is helpful. One nursery school has a beautiful rocking horse in the entrance hall and this is very popular with the children. One family centre has an aquarium to look at and an interest table with baskets full of shells.

## Guidelines for communicating well with parents

- Maintaining eye contact helps you to give your full attention to a parent.
- Remember that your body language shows how you really feel.
- Try not to interrupt when someone is talking to you. Show positive attention and that you are listening.
- Every so often, summarise the main points of a discussion, so that you are both clear about what has been said.
- If you do not know the answer to a parent's question, say so, and say that you will find out. Do not forget to follow up!
- Remember that different cultures have different traditions. Touching and certain gestures might be seen as insulting by some parents, so be careful.
- If the parent speaks a different language from you, use photographs and visual aids. Talk slowly and clearly.
- If the parent has a hearing impairment, use sign language or visual aids.
- When you are talking together, bear in mind whether or not this is the parent's first child.
- Remember that the parents of a child with a disability may need to see you more often to discuss the child's progress.
- If the parent has a disability, make sure that when you sit together you are at the same level.
- Never gossip.

# Barriers to participation for parents and carers

## Concerns about welfare, development and learning of a child

As an early years practitioner, your first duty is to promote the welfare, development and learning of each child. Sometimes this means raising difficult or sensitive issues with a parent. A key person might need to share a concern with parents that:

- a child has special educational needs
- a child is not getting sufficient support and help at home, or that his or her needs are being neglected
- a child is overweight, or otherwise not in good health.

All of these are sensitive issues. It is important that they are raised in a way that shows concern for a child, not criticism of a parent. However, parents feel highly responsible for their children and their initial reactions may well be defensive ('I do not know why you would think that') or hostile ('It is my business what my child has for breakfast and dinner'). In

## Case Study · · · · · Raising concerns

Ade had been attending nursery for 6 months. Aged 2 years 6 months, she was noticeably overweight. Her clothes never fitted her well – trousers were either far too long and rolled up or very tight around her waist, making her uncomfortable. She avoided outdoor play and indoor physical activities, but on the occasions when she did run, she would quickly become exhausted and would sometimes say her knees were hurting. Ade's mother and father were both very loving towards her. Her father was himself overweight.

After discussion at a staff meeting, Ade's key person – who was very experienced – spoke to Ade's mum. The key person was told that Ade's weight, and her dad's weight, were due to genetic factors and that the family all ate healthily.

Three months later, the nursery's SENCO felt that Ade was noticeably missing out in nursery and reopened discussions. She met with both parents. Ade's key person explained how Ade often felt left out of games with her friends and that her clothes often hampered her. The parents explained that they could not find clothes to fit her properly. The SENCO asked if she could contact the health visitor for further advice, which the parents agreed to.

The health visitor met with the parents and explained that there was a special service locally for overweight children. She said that Ade and the family would be given extra help, and that Ade would not be put on a diet and expected to lose weight. Instead, the emphasis would be on eating healthily, being more active, and keeping her weight stable, so that as she grew, her body mass index (BMI) would reduce. She also explained that the weight on Ade's knees was already causing her discomfort, and that further ill health might follow.

Over the next year, Ade's weight remained about the same. The family changed some of their eating habits, and organised to go swimming together once a week and started walking to nursery. Some clothes for 3-year-olds were found that were a reasonable fit for her, and with encouragement, she started using the nursery bikes. The health visitor and paediatric dietician were very pleased with Ade's progress, and predicted that within a couple of years her weight would be within the usual range. When Ade left for Reception, her parents said that they could not have helped Ade without the help and support of the nursery.

general, if a discussion is sensitively arranged in a confidential space and with a clear focus on the child's best interests, the vast majority of parents will be supportive, even if their first reaction is negative. It is always important to involve senior staff in such discussions – for example, the head teacher, setting manager or SENCO.

## Parents becoming angry or upset

Occasionally, parents might become upset and might shout at you. Many early years settings have a policy on how a member of staff can get help from a senior colleague if there is an emergency of any kind. Make sure that you know about this in advance! Call on the head teacher or manager if you are not sure how to handle a situation. When parents become upset, it is almost always because they are under emotional stress of some kind. The paint spilt on the child's clothing may not seem serious to you, but it might be the last straw for a parent after a stressful day. Try to remain calm and polite; pointing, shouting or moving angrily towards a parent in a situation like this will almost always make things worse. Your line manager will encourage the parent to move away from the public area, and will help by offering a quiet place to talk.

## Parents and carers with other priorities

Sometimes it may appear that a parent prioritises other parts of his or her life at the expense of his or her child's welfare. A parent may work long hours and arrive at the end of the day, at the last minute (or even late), and expect to pick up the child, all ready for home. Meanwhile, the child might be tired out after a long day at nursery and need a few minutes of unrushed care before being ready to go home. A key person can help by offering advice in a friendly and non-critical manner, perhaps pointing out how every evening there is a scene at picking-up time and suggesting some ways of avoiding this. However, it will always be the case that practitioners may not see eye to eye with parents at times but as long as the child is adequately cared for and is developing, practitioners need to accept that in a free society, parents may not always act the way we might like them to.

## Parents and carers having prejudicial attitudes

When working with issues of equality, it is best to put the main emphasis on positive actions, rather than responding to problems. For example, the parent handbook should make it clear that the setting is positive about diversity, celebrates the different languages children speak, and actively opposes discrimination. This should be reinforced through displays and other methods, to establish an atmosphere that is welcoming to all, and opposed to racism and prejudice.

Occasionally, a child in nursery will show discriminatory behaviour that has come from the home environment – for example, a child may make a racist comment, and when this is discussed with the parent, he or she may display the same prejudice.

In these cases, the manager or head teacher will need to be clear about the legal and moral requirement to oppose discrimination, and to help children learn to respect others. The parent needs to be told clearly that such views are not acceptable in an early years setting or school.

## Differences in rules and expectations

Families have a range of approaches to the problems they face. These approaches may contradict what is expected in an early years setting or school – for example, a child might be smacked at home, but expected not to hit in nursery. Children may be made to stay at the table until they have finished their dinner at home, but an early years setting may allow children to choose what they eat, and how much.

The best approach to difficulties like these is to try to build bridges between home and the setting, while accepting that there are differences. Staff and parents can explain to a child that there is a different expectation or rule in nursery, for example. A key person, in response to a parent who does not want the child to play outside on a cold day, might first show sympathy and understanding, then explain the policy on free flow, and finally meet the parent's needs halfway by undertaking to ensure that the child is really well wrapped up, and by arranging a further discussion, if necessary, to explain the nursery's approach.

## Supporting carers in partnership opportunities

There is no *single* way to have a partnership with parents. There needs to be a whole range of ways for parents to access partnership, so that they can find the one that is most suitable for them. Some parents like to have regular home visits and to collect their child quickly at the end of the day, without waiting about for a long chat with the key person. Some parents prefer to use a diary to communicate. In an ideal situation, diaries are updated daily, but more usually they are updated weekly or even monthly. The diary is sent home with the child; parents can add to it and send it back. This is particularly helpful in monitoring the child's progress. Some parents like to come in to the nursery setting to talk to the key worker. Staff may be very tired, however, if they have worked a long shift, and it may be difficult to speak to the parent and to care for the other children who have not yet been picked up. So negotiation and understanding each other's point of view are needed.

Some parents prefer to come to morning or afternoon sessions in the parents' or staff room. Many early years settings now make provision for this. Parents come in to sit with one another and their babies, or to attend a session led by the local health visitor. Subjects covered may include children's feeding routines, sleep patterns and other areas of concern.

Many early years settings and schools store each child's Profile Book in a place where it can be easily picked up and read by the child's parents. This can enable parents to keep up-to-date with the latest observations, assessments and planning for their child. Sometimes parents are encouraged to take the Profile Book home, share it with their child, and add to it themselves. Together with regular reviews when the parent and key person sit down formally together, this type of system can help parents feel that they are up-to-date and are active participants in planning for their child's development and learning.

### Workshops

Parents appreciate workshops run by the setting. These usually take place in the evening; parents come to experience some of the things their children do and staff explain what the children get out of the activities – for example, parents may be surprised to find out about the mathematics that their children are learning when involved in a cooking activity.

### Open days and evenings

These are often popular with parents. They can be purely social or may be a mixture of a social occasion and a workshop or talk. Many early years settings combine these.

 **In Practice**

**Planning a workshop**

1. Plan a workshop for parents that will help them to understand how children learn through activities such as cooking, sand play and painting. Plan the materials you would use for a demonstration, and make instruction cards with diagrams to help parents experiment with the materials.

2. Rehearse what you might say in a presentation to parents about one of the activities.

3. Advertise your workshop to parents and carry out your plan. Do not worry if not many people attend – even one parent taking part will give you valuable experience, and it is common to find that it takes several months of working with parents to encourage high levels of participation.

4. Evaluate how successful your workshop is. Include your own impressions, and information from parental feedback that you have obtained either by talking to the participants or by asking them to fill in an evaluation form.

# Opportunities for parents to feedback on and shape services for children and families

Different early years settings will have a range of management systems, including:

- Maintained nursery schools, and primary schools, will have a legally constituted governing body that includes parent representatives. The governing body will have formal systems for reporting back to all parents and for acting on suggestions and complaints. There will also be systems to survey parents' views on a regular basis.
- Other settings may have a management committee made up of parents and other volunteers. Voluntary and community settings – for example, a pre-school or a community nursery – will often be led by parents of children currently or previously on roll, and be linked to other community and local groups.
- Children's centres will usually have a parents' forum, a gathering of parents who give feedback on the services offered and shape the future direction of the centre.

## Case Study | Mathematics and cooking

Jamal's father said that after a cooking activity he understood the link between doing division sums in mathematics and sharing. He had not wanted to share the biscuits he had made when he cooked. He had been shocked by his own feelings, and it made him understand how Jamal might feel when told that the biscuits must be shared. He had not previously seen this as doing a division sum in mathematics. He thought it was a very good way to learn mathematics.

## Parent volunteers in the early childhood setting

Some parents also enjoy sharing their children's interests. They welcome the opportunity to spend time in the early years setting, working alongside the

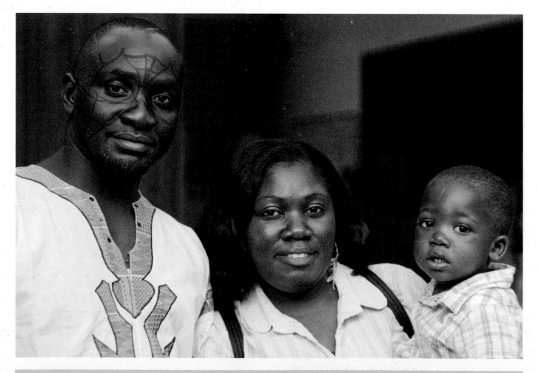

**Figure 12.7** A child and his parents enjoying an open-day event at their local children's centre

staff. This can be very difficult for parents who work, so there should be no pressure to contribute.

Sometimes parents agree to help on a rota system. However, this can be too formal an arrangement for some parents. On the other hand, it does help the staff to know that a particular parent is coming to work with them and they can make sure that the parent is made to feel welcome.

When parents come in to work in the early years setting, although they are giving, they also need to take – this is central to volunteer work. People must receive as much as they give when they volunteer to help; they must find the work rewarding in order to be motivated to volunteer. So, while understanding that the parent has come into the early years setting to help, it is very important not to expect parents to do chores that the staff dislike doing. Most parents have their own washing-up and cleaning at home. They do not necessarily want to come to the early years setting to clean up the paint pots! Parents much prefer doing something that makes them feel relaxed and secure in what might be a new situation for them. They might be a bit nervous about the idea of cooking and tossing pancakes, sewing clothes or taking a group activity at song time. On the other hand, looking at books with individual children in the book area or helping children to sweep the garden leaves might be enjoyable for them. Be sensitive when asking parents to undertake activities.

If a parent is volunteering on a regular basis – for example, a parent who comes in to help every Monday morning – he or she will need:

- an induction (which should be friendly and informal) that explains the organisation, ethos and approach of the setting, including behaviour management, confidentiality and safeguarding
- to be registered with the Independent Safeguarding Authority (from November 2010 for new volunteers).

## Outreach and family support

Considerable research shows that children's development and learning can be greatly enhanced with the support of parents and the availability of play opportunities at home.

This research can lead practitioners in two possible directions:

- **A social control model** of teaching parents to bring up their children. This means the staff show parents examples of what to do, hoping the parents will copy 'good models'. The parents and the home environment they provide are considered to be deficient; there will often be a list of resources and activities that parents are told they should provide.

| **Case Study** | **Parent volunteers** |
| --- | --- |

One father came in to make pancakes. The staff were very grateful because no one could toss a pancake as he could. Everyone had such fun. His commitment was great because he had taken the morning off work to do this on Pancake Day.

A mother, who was a home-based clothes-maker, came into the nursery and made costumes for the home area. She sat in the corner with a sewing machine that belonged to one of the staff. The children loved to watch and to try things on for her. Other parents brought in bits of material that she might be able to use, and they enjoyed chatting to her when they were collecting their children.

Another mother was delighted to have the opportunity to try out her English (she spoke Urdu). She had been learning some songs at her English class, and at group time she enjoyed joining in and singing them. She also sang some songs in Urdu.

A developmental partnership

Pen Green Centre for Children and their Families has led practice in involving parents in understanding and supporting their children's development. This programme includes:

- **action for the parent** – helping parents to reclaim their own education and build up their self-esteem
- **action for the child** – encouraging parents to child-watch, to be involved in and be respectful of their children's learning process and development.

In a system of parents involved in their children's learning (PICL), professionals and staff work closely together, sharing and shaping joint understandings. A parent's unique

knowledge of the child is respected; and professional knowledge about child development is shared with the parent, including:

- understanding children's wellbeing and involvement as they play
- noticing and working with children's schemas.

Video of the child, taken by parents in the family home and by staff in the nursery, provides a way of observing and reflecting on children's play.

Find out more about PICL by going to www.pengreen.org or search online for 'Parents involved in their children's learning'.

- **A developmental partnership** in which professionals do not try to tell parents how to bring up their children. Instead, they seek to identify what the parents think and feel. They respect parents' views and help them to build on what they already know about and want for their children, offering knowledge, information and discussion.

### ✓ Progress check

- Use different ways of sharing information with parents. These might include: keeping a diary about a child which goes home every day, agreeing a convenient regular time to talk, or making a scrapbook that the child can draw in and add photos to, at home and in nursery.
- Understand that complexities can arise with the key person approach; know who in your setting can offer help and support if you need it.

# Effective multi-agency working

Multi-agency working enables different services and professionals to join forces in order to prevent problems occurring in the first place. This means that there is a role for practitioners to work with parents and carers to help them to coordinate the different services and provisions that they may require. For more information about multi-agency working, see Chapter 10 (Unit CYP Core 3.6).

Useful resources

**Websites**

**Child Care** – This is a monthly magazine for all childminders, nannies and child carers.
www.professionalchildcare.co.uk

**Common core of skills and knowledge for the children's workforce** – This document provides a description of the basic skills and knowledge required by people whose work brings them into regular contact with children, young people and families.
http://education.gov.uk/publications/eOrderingDownload/DfES11892005.pdf

**Directgov** – For information on statutory care provision.
www.direct.gov.uk

**Every Child Matters** – This is a framework in England designed to ensure quality provision of children's play and learning.
www.everychildmatters.gov.uk

**HighScope** – HighScope is an American approach to early education and care, with several decades of research into its effectiveness. The website includes books, DVDs and news of training events and conferences in the UK.
www.high-scope.org.uk

**National Children's Bureau** – This charity works to advance the wellbeing of all children and young people across every aspect of their lives.
www.ncb.org.uk

**Nursery World** – The only weekly magazine for early years and childcare practitioners.
www.nurseryworld.co.uk

**Books**

Bilton, H. (2004) *Playing Outside: Activities, Ideas, and Inspiration for the Early Years*. David Fulton Publishers.
Broadhead, P. (2003) *Early Years Play and Learning: Developing Social Skills and Co-operation*. RoutledgeFalmer.
Bruce, T. (2011) *Learning Through Play: Babies, Toddlers and the Foundation Years*. Hodder Education.
Bruce, T. (2011) *Early Childhood Education*. Hodder Education.
Cole, J. *et al.* (2001) *Helping Children Through Activities in the Early Years*. Hodder & Stoughton.
Harding, J. and Meldon-Smith, L. (2000) *Helping Young Children to Develop*. 2nd Edition. Hodder & Stoughton.
Harding, J. and Meldon-Smith, L. (2001) *How to Make Observations and Assessments*. 2nd Edition. Hodder & Stoughton.
Hobart, C. and Frankel, J. (2009) *A Practical Guide to Activities for Young Children*. 4th Edition. Nelson Thornes.
Lindon, J. (2005) *Understanding Child Development: Linking Theory and Practice*. Hodder Arnold.
Palmer, S. and Bayley, R. (2004) *Foundations of Literacy: A Balanced Approach to Language, Listening and Literacy Skills in the Early Years*. Network Educational Press Ltd.
Pound, L. (2005) *How Children Learn: From Montessori to Vygotsky – Educational Theories and Approaches Made Easy*. Step Forward Publishing Ltd.
Siraj-Blatchford, J. and Whitebread, D. (2003) *Supporting ICT in the Early Years*. Open University Press.
Tucker, K. (2005) *Mathematics through Play in the Early Years: Activities and Ideas*. Paul Chapman Publishers.
Whalley, M. (2007) *Involving Parents in their Children's Learning*. 2nd Edition. Paul Chapman.
Wurm, J. (2005) *Working in the Reggio Way: A Beginner's Guide for American Teachers*. St. Paul, MN: Redleaf Press.

# 13 Promote learning and development in the early years: Unit EYMP 2

This chapter aims to prepare the learner to work with children in supporting their learning and development within the relevant early years frameworks within the UK home nations: England, Northern Ireland, Scotland and Wales. The chapter provides detailed information on planning to meet children's needs and providing activities to promote early learning and development.

## Learning outcomes

By the end of this chapter you will:

1. Understand the purpose and requirements of the areas of learning and development in the relevant early years framework.

2. Be able to plan work with children and support children's participation in planning.

3. Be able to promote children's learning and development according to the requirements of the relevant early years framework.

4. Be able to engage with children in activities and experiences that support their learning and development.

5. Be able to review own practice in supporting the learning and development of children in their early years.

## Understand the purpose and requirements of the areas of learning and development in the relevant early years framework

Children are biologically driven to seek out what they need for their development and learning. To do this, they need and depend on other people, and cultural influences are a key part of their development and learning. The curriculum framework has three aspects:

1 **Child** – the child's development and learning, including movement, communication, play, symbolic behaviour, emotional development and relationships (with self and others).

2 **Context** – the access which practitioners create so that every child is helped to develop and learn, and how learning builds on the child's social relationships, family and cultural experiences.

3 **Content** – what the child already knows and understands, together with what the child wants to know more about (the child's interests), and what society and community decide the child needs to know in order to participate and contribute to the community and the wider world. The content of the curriculum is different in every home nation in the UK.

This section explores the areas of learning and development in the early years frameworks of each UK home nation. Information on **documented outcomes** and ways of **assessing and recording** documented outcomes are different for each home nation, and are included below under each home nation heading.

## Principles influencing early childhood curriculum frameworks in the UK

1. The best way to prepare children for their adult life is to give them a childhood that meets their needs and builds on their interests.

2. Children are whole people, who have feelings, ideas, relationships involving a sense of self and others, a sense of awe and wonder, and who need to be emotionally, physically and morally healthy.

3. Children do not learn in neat and tidy compartments. Everything new that they learn links with everything they have already learnt.

4. Children learn best when they are respected and helped to be autonomous, active learners.

5. Self-discipline is emphasised as the only kind of discipline worth having. Children need their efforts to be valued in their own right.

6. There are times when children are especially able to learn particular things.

7. What children can do (rather than what children cannot do) is the starting point for a child's learning.

8. There are many different kinds of symbolic behaviour. These show the inner thoughts, feelings and ideas of the child, through the way they draw, paint, make things, dance, sing, talk/sign, and enjoy making stories, mark-make or pretend-play. The Italian educator Malaguzzi called this the 'hundred languages' of children.

9. Relationships with other people are central to a child's emotional and social wellbeing, and for opening up their possibilities for an intellectual life and a sense of fulfilment.

10. A good education is about the child, the context in which development and learning takes place, and the knowledge and understanding that evolves as part of the child's learning journey.

(Bruce, 1987, 2011; Bruce and Spratt, 2010)

## The early years framework in England

### The Early Years Foundation Stage

The **statutory framework** (which means it is enshrined in law) for the Early Years Foundation Stage (EYFS) aims for quality and consistency in the early years sector through universal standards in relation to both the **welfare requirements** and the **development and learning requirements**.

There are four themes, each linked to a principle. The principles are in tune with the traditional principles outlined in Figure 13.1, which influence early childhood curriculum frameworks in the UK. The themes each have four commitments. This means that practitioners make 16 commitments to the way in which they will work with other people's children.

### Theme 1 – A unique child

**Principle**: Every child is a competent learner from birth, who can be resilient, capable, confident and self-assured.

**Commitments**:

- child development
- inclusive practice
- keeping safe
- health and wellbeing.

### Theme 2 – Positive relationships

**Principle**: Every interaction is based on caring professional relationships and respectful acknowledgement of the feelings of children and their families.

### Key terms

**Statutory framework** – This means that a document is required by law to be followed and carried out in practice. It is not a matter of choice; it is a legal requirement.

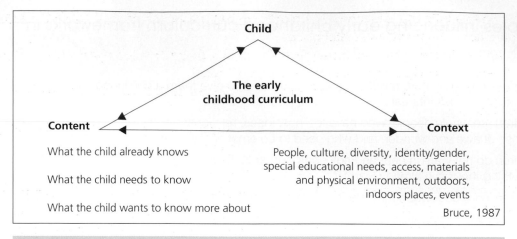

**Figure 13.1** Framework for the early years curriculum (Bruce, 1987)

**Commitments**:

- respecting each other
- parents as partners
- supporting learning
- key person.

## Theme 3 – Enabling environments

**Principle**: The environment plays a key role in supporting and extending children's development and learning.

**Commitments**:

- observation, assessment and planning
- supporting every child
- the learning environment
- the wider context.

## Theme 4 – Learning and development

**Principle**: Children develop and learn in different ways and at different rates, and all areas of development and learning are equally important and interconnected.

**Commitments**:

- play and exploration
- active learning
- creativity and critical thinking
- areas of development and learning.

## The learning and development requirements

There is an aspiration that by the end of the academic year during which a child reaches the age of five, a child will have reached the early learning goals. This is a very contentious area which continues to cause much debate, since few children, especially boys, reach several of the literacy goals. Many early childhood experts have formed the view that these goals are not appropriate for such young children.

The six interconnected areas of development and learning are:

- personal, social and emotional development
- communication, language and literacy
- problem-solving, reasoning and numeracy
- knowledge and understanding of the world
- physical development
- creative development.

Each area depends on the others.

### Planning

Planning needs to balance different areas of development and learning, and play should be central.

### A balance of teaching

Sometimes adults will lead directly (teaching children to cook a recipe, or plant vegetables in the garden). Sometimes adults will lead indirectly, in the way they set up the environment and materials, or engage with children in their play and during their experiences. There needs to be a balance of the adult being involved in direct and indirect teaching, and child-initiated learning.

## Assessment

Throughout the EYFS, ongoing records are kept, called formative assessment records. There is guidance in the *Look, listen and note* sections of the *Practice Guidance*. In the last year of the child's time in the EYFS, the child's level of development and learning must be recorded against the 13 assessment scales derived from the early learning goals. These must be based on the informed observations made of each child, with examples included and clear indication of how the assessment was reached.

In important ways, these summative assessments are marking significant points in the child's learning journey. Some children with complex needs will be assessed using additional tools, but the EYFS aims to be inclusive. Children attending Waldorf-Steiner and Montessori settings will follow the principles of the EYFS in ways that are philosophically appropriate for them.

## The National Curriculum

The National Curriculum sets out the statutory requirements for the knowledge and skills that every child is expected to learn in schools. The National Curriculum framework enables teachers to provide all school-aged children with challenging learning experiences, taught in ways that are both balanced and manageable. It sets out the standards used to measure the progress and performance of pupils in each subject, to help teachers plan and implement learning activities that meet the individual learning needs of pupils.

The National Curriculum applies to children of compulsory school age (5 to 16 years) in schools in England. It sets out what pupils should study, what they should be taught and the standards that they should achieve, and is divided into four key stages:

- **Key Stage 1:** 5- to 7-year-olds (Year groups: 1 and 2)
- **Key Stage 2:** 7- to 11-year-olds (Year groups: 3, 4, 5 and 6)
- **Key Stage 3:** 11- to 14-year-olds (Year groups: 7, 8 and 9)
- **Key Stage 4:** 14- to 16-year-olds (Year groups: 10 and 11).

### Key Stage 1

In Key Stage 1 of the National Curriculum, the compulsory subjects consist of: English, Mathematics, Science, Information and Communication Technology, Design and Technology, History, Geography, Art and Design, Music, Physical Education. In addition there is a non-statutory framework for Personal, Social and Health Education (PSHE) and Citizenship. Primary schools must also provide Religious Education and sex education, although parents may withdraw their children from these lessons if they wish to do so. For more information see: http://nationalstrategies. standards.dcsf.gov.uk/primary

# The early years framework in Scotland

## Birth to 3: supporting our youngest children

This document published in 2005, gives examples and guidance for people working with very young children and for parents. It is not statutory, but its use is encouraged. It gives three features of effective practice: relationships, responsive care, respect.

## Curriculum for Excellence: 3 to 18 years

### The values

The Scottish curriculum framework (3 to 18 years) is underpinned by the values that appear on the ceremonial mace in the Scottish Parliament. These are:

- wisdom
- justice
- compassion
- integrity.

## Defining the curriculum

This new curriculum framework aims to be more flexible, delivering a coherent and enriched curriculum. The curriculum is defined as 'the totality of all that is planned for children and young people throughout their education'.

## The principles on which the curriculum framework is based

The framework is based on the following principles:

- challenge and enjoyment
- breadth
- progression
- depth
- personalisation and choice
- coherence
- relevance.

### The capacities

The purpose of the curriculum framework is captured in four capacities. It aims for every child to be:

- a successful learner
- a confident individual
- a responsible citizen
- an effective contributor.

### Areas of experience and outcomes

These are:

- expressive arts
- health and wellbeing
- languages
- mathematics
- religious and moral education
- sciences
- social studies
- technologies.

Skills for learning, life and work are linked to literacy, numeracy, health and wellbeing.

## Assessment

Assessment is required to support the purposes of learning. This is sometimes described as 'assessment is for learning'.

## The early years and early primary level

The early years and early primary level (3 to 8 years) emphasises active learning, real-life and imaginary situations, and the importance of parents' and children's interests and experiences from home as the starting point from which to extend learning.

## The early years framework in Wales

### The Learning Country: Foundation Phase (3 to 7 years)

The new Foundation Phase will be completed by 1 September 2011, when 6- to 7-years-olds will enter the fourth year of its implementation. By this time, all children from 3 to 7 years will be part of the Foundation Phase in Wales. Practitioners will be required to be trained in the new Foundation Phase.

### Central messages

The basic message of the Foundation Phase in Wales is that it offers children a sound foundation for their future learning through a developmentally appropriate curriculum. It brings more consistency and continuity in a child's learning:

> 'Emphasis has been placed on developing children's knowledge, skills and understanding through experiential learning – learning by doing and by solving real-life problems both inside and outdoors.'

Key elements in the curriculum framework are:

- learning by doing
- the importance of first-hand experience (experiential learning)
- learning through play
- active involvement in learning (not exercises in books)
- time to develop speaking and listening
- time to develop confident readers and writers
- practical mathematical experiences through everyday problem-solving experiences
- emphasis on understanding how things work and finding different ways to solve problems.

In addition, the curriculum places more focus on:

- skills and understanding
- the whole child – personal, social, emotional, physical and intellectual wellbeing
- positive attitudes to learning (enjoying it and wanting to continue the learning)
- giving children high self-esteem and confidence so that they experiment, investigate, learn new things and make new relationships
- encouraging children's development as individuals through creative, expressive and observational skills, and recognising that different children have different ways of responding to experiences
- learning about conservation and sustainability through outdoor, first-hand experiences involving real-life problems.

## The areas of learning

There are seven areas of learning in the Welsh curriculum framework:

- personal and social development, wellbeing and cultural diversity
- knowledge and understanding of the world
- mathematical development
- language, literacy and communication skills
- Welsh language development
- physical development
- creative development.

## Assessment: the Foundation Phase outcomes

At the end of the Foundation Phase when children are 7 years old, there is a statutory teacher assessment of each child. Teachers are required to make rounded judgements of children, based on their knowledge of the way in which a child performs across a range of contexts. Strengths and weaknesses are identified. The child's progress is checked against adjacent outcomes to see which makes the best fit to the child's performance: the best possible match is made. This takes place in the following areas of learning:

- personal and social development, wellbeing and cultural diversity
- language, literacy and communication skills (in English or Welsh)
- mathematical development.

## The early years framework in Northern Ireland

### Curricular Guidance for Pre-School Education

All four countries of the UK have reviewed their early childhood curriculum frameworks recently, and Northern Ireland has developed Curricular Guidance for Pre-School Education. It states that:

'There is no place, at this stage, for the introduction of formal schooling in the sense of an established body of knowledge to be acquired, or a set of skills to be mastered.'

It emphasises that children (3- to 4-year-olds) arrive in early years settings with experiences, and have developed in a number of ways already.

### Guidance

The curricular framework is designed to guide practitioners and settings, but there is an expectation that all will refer to it.

### The areas of learning

There are six areas of learning:

- the arts
- language development
- early mathematical experiences
- personal, social and emotional development
- physical development and movement
- the world around us.

Each area has a section on progress in learning. Throughout, the document is inclusive.

## Primary school education (from 4 years)

The Foundation Stage in primary schools is for children in Year 1 (4- to 5-year-olds) and Year 2 (5- to 6-year-olds). They begin the curriculum which goes through to Stage 4 in the secondary school.

**Cross-curricular** areas (which continue through the education stages) are:

- communication

- using mathematics
- using ICT.

**Thinking skills** are developed to enable the child to:

- think critically and creatively
- develop personal and interpersonal skills and dispositions
- effectively function in a changing world.

**Personal capabilities** aim to encourage:

- lifelong learning
- contributing effectively to society.

## Areas of learning

For Northern Ireland, the areas of learning are:

- language and literacy
- mathematics and numeracy
- the arts
- the world around us
- physical development and movement
- personal development and mutual understanding
- religious education (from which children may be withdrawn as this is defined by the Department of Education and the four main Christian Churches).

There is **assessment for learning**, and reporting to parents through a meeting and an annual report.

> ### The different early years curriculum frameworks in the four UK countries
> 1. Which country has a curriculum framework that includes children from birth? Discuss this with your colleagues. (There are useful websites and resources on page 273.)
> 2. Reflect on the advantages and disadvantages of curriculum frameworks with common themes throughout the different age phases. Discuss.
> 3. If you were a child, what would you find helpful in the different curriculum frameworks? As a practitioner, reflect on what is helpful in the different curriculum frameworks. Discuss with another learner or in a group. Think together about how a CAF could help this child and his or her family.

# Be able to plan work with children and support children's participation in planning

When children feel their efforts are appreciated and celebrated, they learn more effectively. If adults only praise and recognise results (**products of learning**), children are more likely to lose heart and become less motivated to learn.

Planning should therefore focus on process and the efforts which children make (**processes of learning**) as much as the product. An example would be finger-painting rather than hand-prints, so that children can freely make their own patterns in the paint. At the end, the paint is cleared away, with no pressure on children to produce a product. However, staff might photograph the processes involved in finger-painting and display these on the wall, to remind children of what they did. Children love to share process books later with interested adults, other children and their parents or carers.

## Using different sources to plan work for children

Rigid plans hold back learning: they do not meet the learning needs or develop the interests of individual children, and lead to an activity-based curriculum which does not help the group or individual children to develop and learn.

Planning begins with the observation of the child as a unique, valued and respected individual, with their own interests and needs. We could say this is all about getting to know the child, but further general planning is also necessary, because there is only so much that children can learn on their own. They need an environment that has been carefully thought through, plus the right help from adults in using that environment. This aspect of planning ensures that the learning environment indoors and outdoors is balanced in what it offers, so that it helps all children in general, but also caters for individual children.

**Figure 13.2** Children who are just discovering paint also need to experiment with it – painting does not have to have an end product

## Activity

Plan and make a process book, showing the sequence of steps needed for children to do finger-painting. This needs to include making the paint, using it and clearing away, with the children participating at each step. (A process book clearly sets out the step-by-step approach or method of a process or activity using simple text and illustrations such as diagrams, drawings or photographs.)

It is important to have tables at an appropriate height. Children like to stand or work on the floor. They need to be free to move, and often they do not want to sit on chairs (although these should be provided). It is important to offer experiences and activities that allow children to have a choice about this.

It is best to use powder paint as it is more flexible and offers more possibilities than mixed paints, which are also much more expensive. There could be paints with lids on the pots for new painters; and children who are more experienced can mix their own and use pots without lids.

In this way, the curriculum:

- differentiates for individual children
- is inclusive and embraces diversity
- offers experiences and activities which are appropriate for most children of the age range (the group), because it considers the social and cultural context and the biological aspects of children developing in a community of learning
- links with the requirements of legally framed curriculum documents (which include the first three points).

You could use the following sources to plan work for children:

- the children's interests and preferences
- observations and assessments
- the children's mothers, fathers and carers
- your colleagues in the setting
- other professionals such as health visitors.

As appropriate to your particular role, you will need to plan, implement and evaluate curriculum plans according to the requirements of your setting. When planning, implementing and evaluating curriculum plans, your overall aims should be to:

- support *all* the children you work with
- ensure each child has full access to the relevant curriculum
- encourage participation by all children
- meet children's individual learning and development needs
- build on children's existing knowledge and skills
- help all children achieve their full potential.

Your planning should be flexible enough to allow for children's individual interests and unplanned, spontaneous opportunities for promoting children's development and learning. For example, an unexpected snowfall can provide a wonderful opportunity to talk about snow and for children to share their delight and fascination with this type of weather. A child might bring in their collection of postcards, prompting an unplanned discussion about the collections of other children; this could be developed into a 'mini-topic' on collections if the children are really interested. It is important that children have this freedom of choice to help represent their experiences, feelings and ideas.

Planning work also involves working with other people (for example, parents, carers, colleagues and other professionals) to deliver the appropriate curriculum for the children in your setting. You should regularly check and discuss the progress of children with parents, carers and colleagues. Seek additional support especially if children are not progressing as expected, for example by consulting other professionals as appropriate.

Remember to observe the children while they are involved in the learning activities and assess whether you need to change or extend these activities to meet their early learning and developmental needs more fully. Children's responses should also be considered when providing support for learning activities. Be sensitive to children's needs and preferences. You should take notice of non-verbal responses and preferences demonstrated by the children; these are just as important as what they say. Remember to give the children positive encouragement and feedback to reinforce and sustain their interest and efforts in the learning process. You can use children's positive or negative responses to modify or extend activities to meet each child's needs more effectively. For example, if the learning intentions prove too easy or too difficult, you may have to set new goals. By breaking down learning activities into smaller tasks, you may help individual children to achieve success more quickly. In modifying plans, you are continuing a cycle of planning and implementing activities. After the learning activities, you should use all the available relevant information to evaluate the effectiveness of your planning and implementation of the activity; this might include responses from parents, carers, colleagues and other professionals.

## Long-term planning

Long-term planning focuses on the following:

- What is known about the general development and learning needs of most children between birth and 5 years of age.
- General provision arising from this first point, in considering what is planned indoors and outdoors.
- A general sense of direction, making everyone aware of the principles, values and philosophy that support the curriculum.
- A particular emphasis for a period of time (perhaps for several months); for example, the way in which children and adults communicate; how to get the most from the outdoor environment; how to support children settling in to the setting; creativity; play.

## Medium-term planning

This is the way in which the principles and general framework set by the long-term planning are applied. The medium-term plan will need to be **adjusted constantly** because it will be influenced by the observations made of individual children.

For children from birth to 3 years, it needs to include reviews of care routines, key worker relationships and the way in which the day is organised to offer play and experiences, including materials and physical resources.

If short-term planning (see below) is effective, many settings find that medium-term planning becomes unnecessary. If the daily plans are good, they often extend over several weeks and become medium-term plans, which are adjusted slightly each day. This is especially so if the curriculum offers continuous open-ended materials, equipment and resources, indoors and outdoors.

## Short-term planning

This is based on observation sheets of individual children's interests and needs. (If a medium-term plan is used, the observations will inform how to adjust and change the plan so that it is responsive to the individual child's interests and needs.)

One type of plan widely used is called PLOD (possible lines of direction). This was first developed

Example of a medium-term plan
Developed from observations of children into a water theme.
(about 3/4 weeks duration usually, depending on the interest in it from the children).

In a medium-term plan, the focus is on creating a learning enviroment:

- which is well-resourced and well-organised
- where adults are clear about how they will work on specific areas at particular times, and make a bridge between long-term plans for the group as a whole, and short-term immediate action plans for particular children.

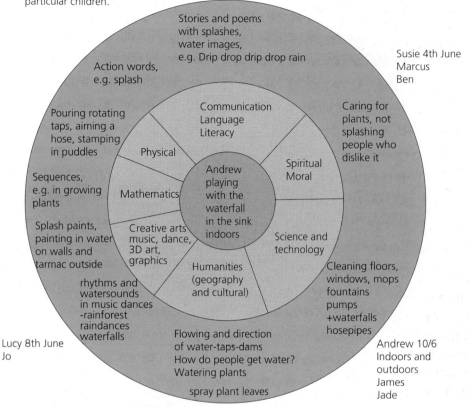

**Figure 13.3** Planning PLOD (possible lines of development)

with staff at Redford House Workplace Nursery at Froebel College in Roehampton, and later developed with staff at Pen Green Children's Centre. These can be used for one child (as in Figure 13.3), or for several children with similar interests.

Many early years settings now focus on particular children on particular days. This means that every child is observed regularly, and the curriculum is planned in a **differentiated** way to cater for the interests and needs of individual children.

## Encouraging children to plan their own learning and activities

Remember, you are planning the play environment. You are not planning the way in which children play

in it. Children need to be able to initiate their own ideas in their play and to be spontaneous. This is only possible if the environment is set up to encourage play.

Quality learning takes place when you are able to match what is offered in the curriculum to the interests and needs of individual children. Effective teaching means helping children to learn, so that they make connections with what they already know, and at times are helped to extend this.

Bear these factors in mind when you plan – quality is more likely to result. If you can help children to enjoy learning, you will have given them a good start, which they will take with them through their lives.

## Case Study — Observation and planning

In one setting, observations of the target child (Andrew) over a week showed that a 'waterfall' consisting of three beakers of graded sizes was greatly used. Andrew lined them up next to the tap so that the water fell exactly as he wanted it to. He had a bowl of corks under the waterfall; he aimed the water at them one by one, to make them bob about.

When the tap was turned on, a waterfall was created, which led to much glee and discussion. The long-term plan identified science as a major area for attention.

The nursery practitioner reported this observation of Andrew to a group of staff. They decided to put the waterfall out again. In addition, they provided a bigger version in the outside area, using buckets and old water trays. They planned who will be in which areas, and aimed for Andrew to learn that water:

- flows
- splashes
- cascades in the outdoor waterfall more than the indoor waterfall
- flows downwards if it can
- makes a trajectory (a moving line)
- has the force to move things that are in its way.

To extend Andrew's interest, the staff planned a visit to the local shopping mall where there is a fountain. They also linked the short-term plans made for Andrew with the medium-term plan (see Figure 13.3) and the long-term plan, which had a focus on knowledge and understanding of the world (science).

Target child observation is explained in Table 6.1 on page 94.

## Case Study — Planning the play environment

Some of the children visited the market and found it fascinating. Back at the setting, the staff set up a market in the garden, with stalls made of upturned cardboard boxes, and play props that were mainly boxes of stones, leaves, conkers, and so on. The children developed their own play, but the important thing was that they had materials such as paper bags to put stones and leaves into, when they pretended to be customers or stallholders.

## Research Activity

Research how play is timetabled in one or all of the following situations:

- an early years setting
- a reception class in a primary school
- the first two years of statutory schooling in primary school.

Both the adult and the child contribute actively when the curriculum is of high quality.

Language helps children to sort and classify things in the world. See Figure 13.4: this little boy is showing through the gesture of holding up the dinosaur that he wants us to look at it. It is his favourite; his eyes coordinate when he looks at it. It is important for children to hold objects and look at them as they play, as this will help later tracking of print on the page of a book. It will also help him if the adult names the dinosaur. Often we use the general word (in this case, dinosaur) instead of giving children the word for the type (Tyrannosaurus rex). This boy is ready to be given this vocabulary and delights in using the correct description of his dinosaur. If he is in a language-rich, enabling environment, he will be able to establish that there are many classes of dinosaurs, and that a Tyrannosaurus rex is different from a brontosaurus. There need to be books of dinosaurs, and people to help him look them up, show them and name them for him.

**Figure 13.4** This little boy is showing through the gesture of holding up the dinosaur that he wants us to look at it.

## Key terms

**Statutory schooling** – The age at which children are legally required to attend full-time education, unless they have the agreement of the local authority that they will be home-educated.

In a small group, discuss how learning is of **poor** quality when:

- an adult directs all the learning
- children lead their own learning all the time
- children colour in outlines given by adults

but is of **good** quality when adults and children take turns to lead and direct.

Research in this textbook to find out more about this and discuss your findings.

 **Progress check**

### Planning for individual children

1. **Observe the child** at different times, in different places, indoors and outdoors, at mealtimes, home time, with different people. What does the child choose to do? What interests the child?

2. **Support the learning**. Are there plenty of opportunities to repeat the experiences which the child has chosen? Is there open and continuous material provision, rather than closed and prescribed activities? Do children have plenty of choice about how they spend their time? What kind of help do the children need? Do adults recognise when help is needed, and do they join children as companions and sensitively engage them in conversations? Do adults know not to interfere when the children are deeply involved?

3. **Extend the learning**. Learning can be extended in two ways:

   - **broadening and deepening the learning** – it is important not to automatically think that children constantly need new experiences. They might need to play with the same dinosaurs for several weeks. If they do, this is an opportunity to help them learn the names of different dinosaurs, what they ate and the habitat they lived in. Dinosaur scenarios could be built with sand and water and plants in seed trays, so that children create their own small worlds about dinosaurs. This is often the best way to extend learning.

   - **onwards and upwards** – it is important not to rush children into new learning when what they really need is to consolidate what they know. A child might have enjoyed cooking roti or bread rolls. Making a carrot cake is a similar experience, but it involves adding eggs and the mixture is stirred and beaten rather than pummelled. These differences could be talked about, but children will need to make the roti and the carrot cakes so that the conversation will be possible. A book of recipes with pictures is helpful – you could make these and laminate them.

## A curriculum that includes all children

When planning activities for children you should remember to include all children (see Chapter 3, Unit SHC 33).

Most children learn in a rather uneven way: they have bursts of learning, and then they have plateaux when their learning does not seem to move forward but they are actually consolidating their learning during this time. This is why careful **observation** and **assessment for learning** of individual children, plus a general knowledge of child development, are very important.

Catching the right time for a particular part of learning during development is a skill, as is recognising the child's pace of learning. Children have their own personalities and moods. They are affected by the weather, the time of day, whether they need food, sleep or the lavatory, the experiences they have, their sense of wellbeing, and their social relationships with children and adults.

Some of the richest learning comes from experiences of everyday living. Examples would be getting dressed, choosing what to do, going shopping, using what you have bought for cooking, using a recipe book, washing up, sharing a story or photographs of shared events (visiting the park), laying the table, eating together, sorting the washing and washing clothes. It is a challenge to find ways of making this manageable for children to take part in with independence, but careful planning makes this both possible and enjoyable, and makes for a deep learning experience.

## Supporting the planning cycle for children's learning and development

Following your observation and assessment of a child's development, learning and/or behaviour, your recommendations can provide the basis for planning appropriate routines and/or activities to encourage and extend the child's skills in specific areas. Effective planning is based on children's individual needs, abilities and interests, hence the importance of accurate and reliable child observations and assessments. Depending on the type of setting, you will also need to plan provision based on the requirements for curriculum frameworks for early learning (see above).

When planning care routines, play opportunities and learning activities, your overall aims should be to:

- support the care and development of *all* the children you work with
- ensure every child has full access to the appropriate curriculum
- meet children's individual developmental and learning needs
- build on each child's existing knowledge, understanding and skills.

### Activity

Describe how *you* plan provision to promote children's learning and development in your setting. Include examples of any planning sheets you use.

## Be able to promote children's learning and development according to the requirements of the relevant early years framework

Although it can seem a daunting task to provide a quality learning environment for children from birth to 7 years, remember that the things that matter most are:

- your relationship and communication with children, their families and the team of staff (that is, people)
- how you support the children in using core experiences and open-ended, continuous material

provision, equipment and resources, both indoors and outdoors.

## Promoting children's learning

Children need:

- people who give them interesting and engaging experiences
- carefully considered and organised materials for indoors and outdoors
- to be greeted and made to feel welcome with their parent/carer as they arrive
- to be connected with their key person when they part from their parent/carer
- to feel physically, socially and emotionally safe, so that their intellectual lives open up as they relax and enjoy learning.

It is very difficult for children when adults do not stay in one place for long enough for children to engage with them in focused ways.

## Layout of indoor and outdoor learning environments

In an inclusive early childhood setting that embraces diversity, the layout and presentation of material provision offers a range of experiences and activities across the birth to 5 years framework.

### Indoor learning environment

Given that children from birth to 6 years learn through the senses, the layout needs to support and extend this kind of learning. The layout from Reggio Emilia and Pistoia in northern Italy has reminded practitioners in the UK of the importance of:

- an attractive and welcoming entrance area, where children and families are greeted, can find and share information, and feel part of a community
- natural light
- the feeling of space without clutter
- making spaces beautiful using natural materials.

The environment also needs to support and actively encourage and extend the symbolic life of the child, making one thing stand for another (such as pretending that a leaf is a plate in the outside playhouse). Understanding cause-and-effect relationships is also very important, and the learning

environment needs to promote this (such as discovering that kicking the ball hard makes it go a long distance, while tapping it with your toes makes it roll only a little way).

 **Progress check**

### Supporting learning

- **The role of the adult** in supporting children's development and learning through developmentally appropriate materials provision, equipment and resources is central. The environment (people and provision) needs to support all children, including those with special educational needs, disabilities, both genders, children from diverse backgrounds and different cultures, or with English as an additional language.

- **Clutter confuses children**. There should be nothing in a learning environment, indoors or outdoors, that has not been carefully thought through and well organised. Children need to know what they are allowed to do, and what they are not allowed to do, and the environment needs to signal to children how it should be used and kept. When children feel insecure, they test boundaries.

- **The space indoors and outdoors should be flexible**, so that it can be set up and transformed for different uses in a variety of ways. Attention should be given to light, because the way that it shines into a building changes the atmosphere. If the sun is shining onto a child's face during story time, it will be difficult for the child to become engaged.

- **The temperature is important**. Being too hot or too cold makes it difficult to learn. Outdoors, children need suitable clothing, for all weathers (and so do the adults!), and indoors, the rooms should have good air circulation to encourage concentration and reduce the spread of infection.

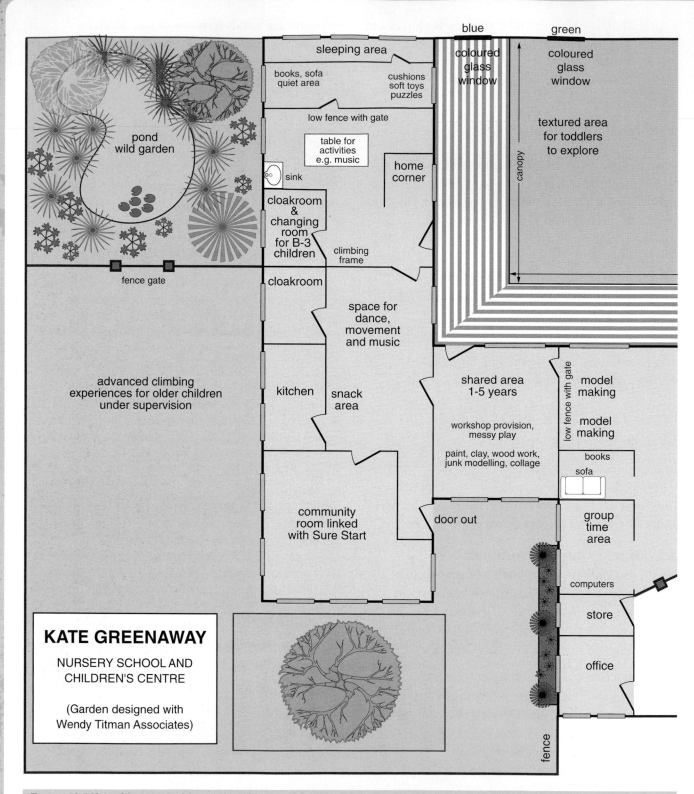

**Figure 13.5** Kate Greenaway Maintained Nursery School and Children's Centre (garden designed with Wendy Titman Associates)

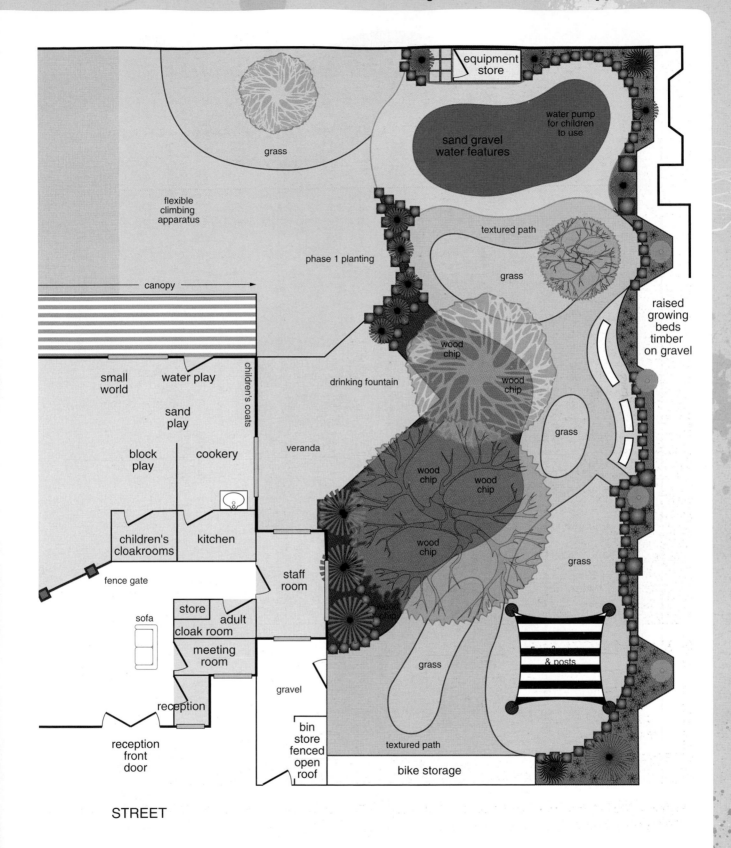

equipment store

sand gravel water features

water pump for children to use

grass

flexible climbing apparatus

phase 1 planting

textured path

grass

canopy

raised growing beds timber on gravel

small world

water play

children's coats

wood chip

drinking fountain

wood chip

sand play

block play

cookery

veranda

grass

wood chip

wood chip

children's cloakrooms

kitchen

wood chip

grass

fence gate

staff room

grass

sofa

store

adult cloak room

meeting room

& posts

reception

gravel

grass

bin store fenced open roof

textured path

reception front door

bike storage

STREET

**GROUND FLOOR**

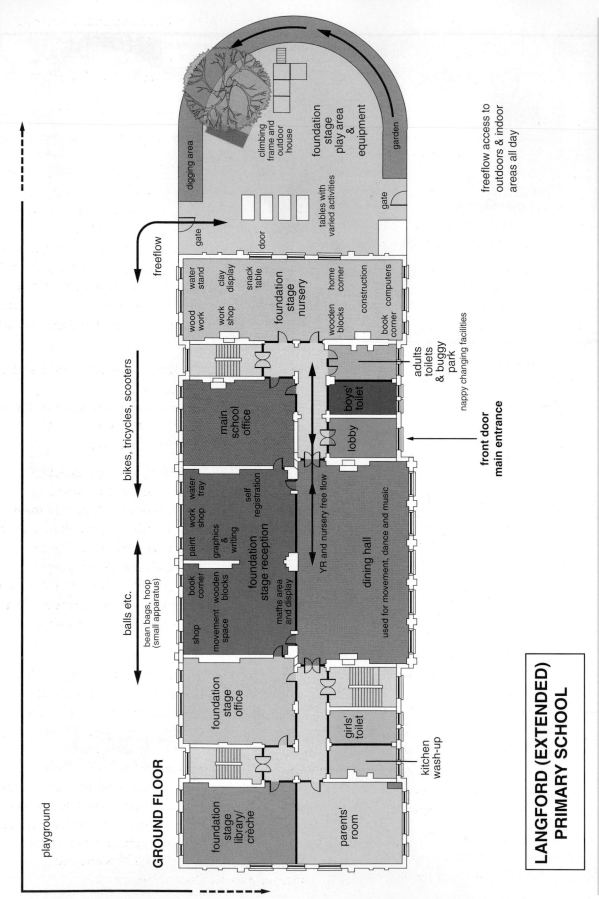

playground

balls etc.

bean bags, hoop (small apparatus)

bikes, tricycles, scooters

digging area

climbing frame and outdoor house

foundation stage play area & equipment

garden

freeflow access to outdoors & indoor areas all day

gate

tables with varied activities

door

freeflow

gate

water stand

clay display

snack table

foundation stage nursery

home corner

construction

computers

book corner

wooden blocks

work shop

wood work

main school office

water tray

paint

work shop

graphics & writing

book corner

wooden blocks

shop

movement space

foundation stage reception

self registration

maths area and display

YR and nursery free flow

dining hall

used for movement, dance and music

lobby

boys' toilet

adults toilets & buggy park

nappy changing facilities

front door main entrance

foundation stage office

foundation stage library/ crèche

parents' room

girls' toilet

kitchen wash-up

**LANGFORD (EXTENDED) PRIMARY SCHOOL**

**Figure 13.6** Langford (extended) Primary School has a Foundation Stage layout, with the nursery class and reception class working together

## Promoting activities and experiences which encourage learning and development in each area of the early years framework

### Personal, social and emotional development

Promoting young children's personal, social and emotional development involves helping them to develop social and emotional skills such as:

- attachments to other people
- positive social interactions
- positive self-image and identity
- socialisation (including behaving in socially appropriate ways)
- sharing and cooperating
- independence and self-reliance (including self-help skills, e.g. feeding, toileting, dressing)
- understanding moral concepts.

### Developing attachments to other people

Babies develop an awareness of others in relation to themselves, for example, people who fulfil their needs for food and drink, warmth and shelter, sleep, physical comfort and entertainment. Babies develop strong attachments to the people they see most often and who satisfy the above needs. One attachment is usually stronger than the others, and this is usually to the baby's mother, but the attachment can be to another family member or to anyone outside the immediate family who spends a significant amount of time with the young child, such as a grandparent or nanny. The security of these early attachments is essential to babies and young children because they provide a firm foundation for promoting:

- emotional wellbeing
- positive relationships with other people
- confidence in exploring the environment.

These early attachments enable children to feel secure about their relationships and to develop trust in others. Security and trust are important elements in the young child's ability to separate from their parents and carers in order to develop their own independence and ideas. (For more information about attachment, see Chapter 5, Unit CYP Core 3.1.)

### Encouraging positive social interactions

Having at least one secure personal relationship with a parent or carer enables children to form other relationships. Consistent, loving care from a parent or carer who is sensitive to the child's particular needs enables the child to feel secure and to develop self-worth. Children observe the behaviour of parents, carers and other significant adults (such as early years practitioners, play workers, teachers and teaching assistants) and their observations affect children's own behaviour, including how they relate to others. A child's ability to relate to others may also be affected by:

- special needs, for example communication and/or social interaction difficulties
- family circumstances such as separation or divorce
- death, abandonment or other permanent separation from parent or main carer.

All children need affection, security, acceptance, encouragement, patience and a stimulating environment. Children deprived of these in the first five to six years of life may find it difficult to relate to other people throughout childhood (and even adulthood). However, children are amazingly resilient and subsequent sustained relationships with caring adults in a supportive environment can help children to overcome early parental separation, rejection or neglect.

Adults who provide inconsistent or inappropriate care may unwittingly encourage inappropriate behaviour in children, which can lead to adults spending less time interacting with the child, resulting in the child having ineffective communication skills as well as difficulties in establishing and maintaining positive relationships with other people. Appropriate social interactions with adults (and other children) in various settings will lead to children being able to demonstrate positive ways of relating to others and using appropriate social skills. (See below.)

## Encouraging children's positive self-esteem

A person's self-esteem is changeable; sometimes we feel more positive about ourselves than at other times. Even if we have had past experiences that resulted in negative or low self-esteem, we can overcome this and learn to feel more positive about ourselves. Self-esteem involves:

- feelings and thoughts about oneself (positive or negative)
- respect or regard for self (or lack of it)
- consideration of self
- self-worth (value of self)
- self-image (perception of self).

How we feel about ourselves depends on a number of factors:

- *who* we are with at the time
- the social context – *where* we are
- current and past relationships
- past experiences (especially in early childhood).

*All* children begin with the *potential* for high self-esteem, but their interactions with others contribute to either encourage or diminish positive self-esteem. Experiences in early childhood have the most significant effect on children's self-esteem; sometimes these effects may not become apparent until adolescence or adulthood, when serious psychological and social problems may result due to very low self-esteem. Children (and adults) are very resilient and can learn to have greater self-esteem even if their earlier experiences were detrimental to their esteem.

## Encouraging children's positive self-image and identity

The development of self-image is strongly linked to self-esteem. Self-image can be defined as the individual's view of their own personality and abilities, including the individual's perception of how other people view them and their abilities. Self-image involves recognising ourselves as separate and unique individuals with characteristics which make us different from others. It also involves a number of factors which influence how we identify with other people, for example, gender, culture, race, nationality, religion, language, social status/occupation, disability/special needs, early experiences and relationships.

As an early years practitioner, you need to be aware of your own self-image and the importance of having positive self-esteem. This may mean that you need to deal with issues regarding your own self-image and raise your own self-esteem before you can encourage children's positive self-image.

Children develop their self-image through interactions with others, starting with family members and gradually including carers, teachers, friends and classmates. Through positive interactions, children learn to value themselves and their abilities, *if* they receive approval, respect and empathy. Early childhood experiences and relationships may have positive or negative influences on children's self-image.

Some children may experience particular difficulties in developing a positive self-image – for example, children with special needs; children from ethnic

## Ten ways to encourage children's positive self-esteem and self-image

1. Treat every child as a valuable individual; every child has unique abilities and needs.
2. Be positive by using praise and encouragement to help children and young people to focus on what they are good at.
3. Help children and young people to maximise their individual potential.
4. Encourage children to measure their achievements by comparing them to their own efforts.
5. Have high but realistic expectations of *all* children and young people.
6. Take an interest in each child's efforts as well as their achievements.
7. Encourage positive participation during play activities, for example, sharing resources, helping others and contributing ideas.
8. Give children and young people opportunities to make decisions and choices.
9. Promote equality of opportunity by providing positive images of children, young people and adults through books, stories and songs.
10. Remember to label the behaviour, not the child, as this is less damaging to their self-esteem. For example, say 'That was an unkind thing to say' rather than 'You are unkind'.

minorities; children who are or have been abused. These children may be experiencing prejudice and/or discrimination on a regular basis, which affects their ability to maintain a positive self-image. By praising all children and encouraging them to feel good about themselves and their achievements, adults can help all children to establish and maintain a positive self-image. Developing and implementing inclusive policies, procedures and strategies will also help.

## Socialisation

Socialisation involves how children relate socially (and emotionally) to other people. Children need to learn how to deal appropriately with a whole range of emotions, including anger and frustration, within a supportive environment. Socialisation occurs through the observation, identification, imitation and assimilation of the behaviour of other people. Children model their attitudes and actions on the behaviour of others. You need to be aware of the significant impact you make on children's social (and emotional) development, and ensure that you provide a positive role model. An essential aspect of socialisation involves getting young children to behave in socially acceptable ways without damaging their self-esteem: that is, rejecting the children's unacceptable behaviour, not the children themselves.

Socialisation begins from birth, as babies interact with the people around them and respond to their environment.

## Developing independence

Children need the freedom to develop their independence in ways that are appropriate to their overall development. Some children may need more encouragement than others to become increasingly independent and less reliant on other people. Children gain independence by:

- developing self-help skills
- making choices and decisions
- taking responsibility for their own actions.

Most children start wanting to do things for themselves from about 18 months to 2 years onwards. While young children want to do things for themselves (for example, getting dressed, making things), they may become frustrated if they cannot do things for themselves. Many conflicts arise between young children and other people as children increase their independence and expand the boundaries of their world.

Adults caring for children should avoid inhibiting the child's need for independence as this can lead to

## Eight ways to encourage children's self-reliance

You can encourage children's self-reliance in the following ways:

1. Provide freedom for children to become more independent.

2. Be patient and provide time for children to do things for themselves. For example, let younger children dress themselves; although it takes longer, it is an essential self-help skill. Children with physical disabilities may need sensitive support in this area.

3. Praise and encourage children's efforts at becoming more independent.

4. Be aware of children's individual needs for independence; every child is different and will require encouragement relevant to their particular level of development. Do not insist that children be more independent in a particular area until they are ready.

5. Be sensitive to children's changing needs for independence. Remember a child who is tired, distressed or unwell may require more adult assistance than usual.

6. Offer choices to make children feel more in control. As they develop and mature, increase the scope of choices. Involve the children in decision-making within the childcare setting.

7. Provide play opportunities that encourage independence; for example, dressing-up is a fun way to help younger children learn to dress independently.

8. Use technology to encourage independence, for example, specialist play equipment, voice-activated word processing, motorised wheelchairs.

either emotional dependence, excessive shyness and an over-cautious nature *or* emotional detachment, anti-social behaviour and a rebellious nature. Adults should also avoid unrestricted independence as the child may be exposed to danger and physical harm (for example, from fire, boiling water, traffic) and/or the child may become selfish and unable to recognise the needs and rights of others. Adults should strike a balance between these two extremes. You should provide a balance between allowing for the individual child's need for independence, and providing supervision with guidelines for socially appropriate behaviour which takes into account the needs of everyone in the early years setting.

## Encouraging children's self-reliance

Encouraging children's self-reliance is an important part of helping them to develop the independence and resilience which will enable them to face life's demands and challenges in preparation for their adult lives. Encouraging self-reliance involves helping children to develop:

- independence (or autonomy) – the ability to think and act for themselves

- dependence on their own capabilities and personal resources
- competence in looking after themselves
- trust in their own judgement and actions
- confidence in their own abilities and actions.

## Developing moral concepts

As part of their social development, children gradually develop moral concepts including:

- knowing the difference between right and wrong, and understanding what is and is not acceptable behaviour
- developing an awareness of fairness and justice, and understanding that goodness is not always rewarded, but that we still need to do what is right
- helping others, including recognising the needs and feelings of others
- sharing, including understanding the importance of turn-taking and cooperation
- developing empathy for others and their beliefs even if we disagree with them, including freedom of speech
- being helped to understand cause and effect relationships.

## Encouraging children to share and cooperate

Encouraging children to take turns is an essential element of helping them to interact appropriately with other children. From about the age of 3, young children begin to cooperate with other children in play activities. By about 5, they should be quite adept at playing cooperatively with other children. Gradually children should be able to participate in more complex cooperative play, including games with rules as their understanding of abstract ideas increases.

We live in a highly competitive society; we all want to be the best, fastest, strongest or cleverest. The media (television, magazines and newspapers) focus our attention on being the best. Most sports and games have only one winner, which means all the other participants are losers. To win is the aim of all contestants. Winning makes the individual feel good, confident and successful; losing makes the individual feel bad, inadequate and unsuccessful. Competitive games can prepare children for the competitiveness of real life. However, competition can also contribute to:

- negative self-image and low self-esteem
- aggressive behaviour
- lack of compassion for others
- overwhelming desire to win at any cost.

Competitive sports and games can be beneficial to children's social development as long as they emphasise:

- cooperation and working as a team
- mutual respect
- agreeing on rules and following them
- participation and the pleasure of taking part are more important than winning
- everyone doing their *personal* best.

As well as being competitive, people can also be sociable and cooperative; we like to be part of a group or groups. Cooperative activities encourage children to:

- be self-confident
- have high self-esteem
- relate positively to others
- work together and help others
- make joint decisions
- participate fully (no one is left out or eliminated)
- have a sense of belonging.

## In Practice

1. Observe a group of children during a play activity or a game. Focus on one child's social and emotional development.

2. In your assessment comment on: the child's level of social interaction; the child's ability to make choices or decisions; the child's use of language to express needs and/or feelings; the child's behaviour during the activity; the role of the adult in promoting the child's social and emotional development; suggestions for further activities to encourage or extend the child's social and emotional development including appropriate resources.

## In Practice

1. Plan, implement and evaluate a play experience which encourages or extends a child's social and emotional development. Use the assessment from your previous observation of the child's social and emotional development as the basis for your planning.

2. Encourage the child to use a variety of social skills and emotional abilities. For example: positive behaviour; independence (such as using self-help skills or making choices); effective communication skills; sharing resources; expressing needs and/or feelings; understanding the needs and feelings of others.

3. Consider how you could meet the needs of children with behavioural difficulties with this experience.

## Ten ways to promote young children's social and emotional development

As an early years practitioner, you need to provide appropriate activities and experiences to promote young children's social and emotional development. You can help to promote children's social and emotional development by:

1. **Using praise and encouragement** to help the children focus on what they are good at. Treat every child in the childcare setting as an individual. Each child has unique abilities and needs. Help the children to maximise their individual potential.

2. **Taking an interest in the children's efforts as well as their achievements**. Remember that the *way* children participate in activities is more important than the end results – for example, sharing resources, helping others and contributing ideas. Encourage the children to measure any achievements by comparing these to their *own* efforts. Foster cooperation, rather than competition, between children.

3. **Giving the children opportunities to make decisions and choices.** Letting children and young people participate in decision-making, even in a small way, helps them to feel positive and important; it also prepares them for making appropriate judgements and sensible decisions later on.

4. **Promoting equal opportunities by providing positive images of children and adults** through: sharing books and stories about real-life situations showing children (and adults) the children can identify with; providing opportunities for imaginative play that encourage the children to explore different roles in positive ways, such as dressing-up clothes, cooking utensils, dolls and puppets.

5. **Being consistent about rules and discipline**. All children need consistency and a clearly structured framework for behaviour so that they know what is expected of them. Remember to label the behaviour, not the children, as this is less damaging to their emotional wellbeing.

6. **Setting goals and boundaries** to encourage socially appropriate behaviour, as suitable to the children's ages and levels of development. Using appropriate praise and rewards can help.

7. **Encouraging the children's self-help skills**. Be patient and provide time for the child to do things independently, for example choosing play activities and selecting their own materials; helping to tidy up; dressing independently during dressing-up.

8. **Providing opportunities for the children to participate in social play**; for example, encourage children to join in team games, sports and other cooperative activities.

9. **Using books, stories, puppets and play people** to help the children understand ideas about fairness, jealousy, growing up and dealing with conflict situations.

10. **Encouraging the children to take turns**, for example, sharing toys and other play equipment. Emphasise cooperation and sharing rather than competition.

## Communication, language and literacy

The aim of the early years practitioner is to support children to develop a love of books, so that they will want to read for pleasure and understanding, information and knowledge, and not just out of duty or under direction.

The areas of the brain that are for movement, gestures, sound and language are close to each other, and form interactive networks.

## Using music to support reading

● Ring games and traditional songs and dances help the brain form connections in a natural way, and this helps children learn to read, and later to write. If you sing, 'Dinner-time, it's dinner-time' to children – especially children with special needs, complex needs or who are learning English as an additional language – you will probably find they understand more easily what you are saying. It helps children to segment the sounds, and to identify and pronounce them.

- The sound of words is important in learning to read, but we have to remember that saying or singing certain words varies in different regions of the same country; for example, 'bath' in the north of England is pronounced differently from in the south. The context is very important too, especially when words are spelt differently; for example, 'When you have *read* this book, you might like to *read* another one.'
- Singing helps children because many of the words rhyme, and this makes the text predictable; it is also more manageable because the poetry is in a verse or small chunk. Clapping the rhythm or dancing to the song while singing also helps the brain to understand the shape of the song.

## Listening to stories

It is important to remember that stories are not always in written form: stories can be told (the Gallic, Celtic and Maori traditions use storytelling powerfully) or told in pictures. Stories have a special way of using language called **book language**, such as, 'Once upon a time. . .'. Children need a wealth of experience of book language before they can read well and become enthusiastic readers. Children need many different forms (genres) of stories.

Think about issues of gender, ethnicity, culture and disability, and be sure that all children see positive images of themselves in the stories you tell and in the books that you offer.

Children need **one-to-one stories**. These are called bedtime-type stories. The child can interact with the reader and become deeply involved. The adult and child can pause, chat, go back and revisit, and read at their own pace.

## In Practice

Select a book for a small-group time, based on your observations of a child. Use the guidelines for selecting appropriate books below to help you.

## Guidelines for selecting appropriate books

- **Everyday events** – these help children to recognise common events and feelings. They help children to heighten their awareness of words that describe everyday situations.

- **Poems** – these help rhyming and rhythm, and the chorus often gives a predictable element; the repetition helps children. This is also true of many stories, but poems are an enjoyable experience for young children, who may not be able to concentrate on a whole story in the early stages.

- **Folk stories** – these introduce children to different cultures. However, avoid stories in which animals behave as if they were humans, or in which animals behave in a way that is out of character (such as a spider saving the life of a fly in an act of bravery). These are called **anthropomorphic stories**. They can confuse young children, who are trying to sort out what is and is not true.

- **True stories** – these lead to an understanding of non-fiction books, which are full of information on different topics and subjects.

- **Make-believe stories** – these lead to an understanding of fiction. Avoid stories of witches and fairies for very young children (under 4 years); children need to be clear about the distinction between reality and imagination, otherwise they may be fearful and have nightmares. Bear in mind that it is one thing for a 4-year-old child to make up their *own* stories about monsters, witches or ghosts (in which the child has control), but if an *adult* introduces these characters, the child may be scared.

- **Action rhymes and finger rhymes** – these help children to predict what is in a text. Predicting is a very large part of learning to read; knowing what comes next is important.

- **Repeating stories** – knowing a story well helps children begin to read. Sometimes adults say, 'Oh, but he is not reading, he just knows it off by heart.' Knowing what comes next is probably one of the most important parts of learning to read.

**Figure 13.7** Sharing a story

**Small-group stories**, with two to four children, are more difficult for children because the adult needs to keep the story going, so cannot allow constant interruptions. Skilled adults are able to welcome many of the children's contributions, but the larger the group, the more important it becomes for children to be able to listen. Large groups, with four to eight children, are less sensitive to the individual needs of children, so these need to be more of a theatre show or performance by the adult, in order to maintain the attention of the children; they cannot be so interactive.

It is better to use **poetry cards** and action songs with very large groups (eight or more children). This gives children the rhythm, intonation and pace, and small, manageable chunks of text in a song. This makes for a good community experience of reading together. Poetry cards can be made out of cardboard boxes, and can be large and rather like theatre props. Children enjoy playing with them afterwards if they are left near the book corner.

Encouraging children to share stories together, whether or not they can read fluently, is very helpful. This encourages emergent readers to **approximate-read**, and to pick out the words they know with confidence. Being able to have a go and to do so with confidence and pleasure is crucial.

## Helping children to read

You can help children to read by enjoying a book or poetry card together, without any pressure. Children can see how a book is used, where to begin, how to turn a page and the direction of print, using pictures as clues, finding familiar words and guessing. Being able to guess and predict what the print says is important. Children are usually fascinated by guesses that go wrong, as they learn to link what they read with meaning, and to work out the words using their increasing ability to segment and blend the graphemes and phonemes. It is important to say, 'What do you think he says next?' Show the child any patterns – for example, a phrase that is repeated – and talk about the letters, words and sentences as you go. Picture cues are very important when learning to read, so talk about these and the clues they give.

Alphabet books and friezes are important as they help children to segment words, while offering a meaningful picture to help the child along. Regularly

### Key terms

**Graphemes** – Letters of the alphabet.

**Phonemes** – Basic sound units capable of conveying meaning, e.g. 's' for 'sat', 'm' for 'mat', 'b' for 'bat'.

singing the alphabet is helpful too. Pointing out children with the same letter at the beginning of their names helps, and there can be fascinating discussions about why George is pronounced with a 'J' sound, while Gary is with a 'G' sound.

Decide as a team which books you will introduce as core texts, to help children become familiar with them. Note which books are favourites of particular children, and use these with the child in the same way. *Above all, remember that learning to read should be fun, and it should hold meaning for the child.*

### In Practice

**Stages of reading**
Observe children aged 3 to 7 years. Identify which children are emergent, beginner and fluent readers. What are the factors that you use to decide this? What can you do to support each child in their enjoyment of books?

### Sounds and how words look
Children need to learn to **segment** (break down) sounds and print. They also need to learn to **blend** (join) sounds and print. They need to begin to see that what they have segmented can be blended back into a word. The ideal age to do this is between 6 and 7 years of age. Using nursery rhymes encourages this; for example, 'Humpty Dumpty':

'Humpty Dumpty sat on a wall,

Humpty Dumpty had a great fall . . .'

Children quickly begin to see that the last chunk is the same (-all), while the beginnings are different ('w' and 'f').

Studies of the brain suggest that the brain loves complexity, and that singing, dancing, moving, doing action songs and seeing print in meaningful patterns are all part of the interconnectedness of different parts of the brain.

### Writing
Writing has two aspects:

- what it says – the construction of meaning
- the look of it – the handwriting and letter shapes (transcription).

When children begin to write, they are constructing a **code**. Most languages have a written code. Writing develops when children begin to use symbols. Often they begin by putting letter-type shapes into their drawings. These gradually get pushed out to the edges of the drawing, to look

**Figure 13.8** Boys writing on whiteboards

more like words and sentences. Practitioners need to observe the shapes, sizes and numbers that children experiment with. Children need to be free to experiment, without criticism or pressure. Left-handed children must never be encouraged to write with the right hand.

Young children find capital letters, which are more linear, easier to write than lower-case letters, which have more curves. It is when children begin to experiment with curves that they are indicating they have more pencil control, so can begin to form letters more easily.

Children need:

- to manipulate and try out different ways of 'writing', using their own personal code. Tracing or copying letters undermines this because their own movement patterns and laying down of neural pathways are an important part of the process
- to explore what writing is
- adults who point out print in books and in the environment – for example, on notices and street signs.

Writing from different cultures is different and should be valued – for example Urdu, Arabic (which is read from right to left) and Chinese (which is read up and down on the page).

It is important not to put children off writing, especially boys. Young children are more likely to enjoy reading and writing if they do not feel under pressure to learn. A child's own name is important to them, and they often write the names of people they love, plus the words 'love from'. Adults can support children's development by talking to them about print, and helping them to pick out their favourite letters (often those in their name).

## In Practice

Select one of the bullet points from the Progress Check on Encouraging creative writing later in life. Carry out the idea and evaluate your findings. How does this work in your work setting?

## Progress check

### Encouraging creative writing later in life

- Learning about different roles, characters and themes is essential if children are going to learn to write stories.
- Having dressing-up clothes to act out stories helps children to create narratives – a skill needed for later writing.
- Ask children to act out a story you have told.
- Encourage children to act out stories that they have made up and which you have written down for them. Vivian Gussin-Paley, in her school in Chicago, did this as a daily part of the curriculum.
- Act out stories in an atmosphere of sharing. This should not involve a performance of the story. The idea is to help children to understand how stories are made. This will help them later when they want to write their own stories.
- It is not helpful to young children to perform stories in school assemblies or in situations with audiences full of strangers (such as for the summer or Christmas show). It is not effective practice to encourage children to perform before they have gone through the sequence: make – share – show. They need to be able to make their own stories and to share these with friends and adults whom they know well, before they perform.
- To perform becomes appropriate only in junior school. Any earlier, and some children begin overacting and playing to the audience rather than becoming involved in the story; other children are put off for ever because of the stress of being made to perform. Waving at people in the audience during a performance may be very sweet for adults to see, but it is a clear sign that the child is not involved in what they are doing and is not ready to perform. The exercise is a failure in terms of involving a child in a story.
- Research suggests that if children are encouraged to play in the early years, they will be better at creative writing at 7 years of age.

## Reasoning, problem-solving and numeracy

Mathematics involves problem-solving and reasoning in particular ways. Problem-solving is part

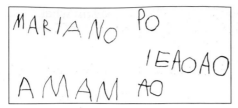

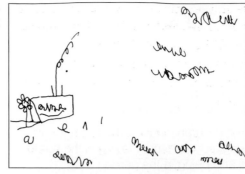

**Figure 13.9** Children's writing

of the whole curriculum, not just mathematics. Children learn about **topological** space (on/off, over/ under, in/out, surrounding, across, near/far) before they learn about **Euclidian** space (circles, squares, and so on).

## Number

Number has several different aspects:

- **matching** – this looks like this (two identical cups in the home corner).
- **sorting** – this looks different from this (the cup and the saucer).
- **one-to-one correspondence** – one biscuit for you, one biscuit for me.
- **cardinal numbers** – the two cups remain two cups, however they are arranged (this means that the child understands the number, such as two).
- **ordinal numbers** – this is first, second, third (for example, the sequence in cooking: first, I wash my hands; second, I put on my apron . . .).

Children learn about number in the following ways:

- reciting – number songs
- nominal understanding – they pick out numbers on house doors, buses, in shops, on shoe sizes, and so on
- subitising – remembering number patterns to recognise how many – for example, four dots, one on each corner of a square, or on a domino (chimpanzees can do this with numbers up to seven)
- counting backwards – 5, 4, 3, 2, 1, lift-off!

There are three counting principles:

1. A number word is needed for every object that is counted. This is the **one-to-one** correspondence principle.
2. The numbers always have the same order, 1, 2, 3 (not 1, 3, 2). This is called the **stable-order** principle.
3. When children count, they have grasped the cardinal number principle if they understand points 1 and 2, because they know that a number is an outcome. This means that when you count, 1, 2, 3, the answer is 3.

## ✓ Progress check

### Number

- Do not do exercises or tasks with young children that are isolated from their experience.

- Remember that children learn mathematics through cooking, tidy-up time, playing in the home area, painting and being in the garden. Mathematics is everywhere.

- Numbers are found on rulers, calibrated cooking jugs, the doors of houses, and so on.

- Counting is only one part of exploring numbers. It is one thing for children to be curious about numbers on calibrated jugs, weights and measures, but they need to be free to experiment and explore. This is very different from formally teaching them numbers through adult-led tasks, unrelated to real life.

## In Practice

Evaluate the learning environment and list the opportunities which children have to see, experience and interact with number situations.

## Understanding time

Time has two aspects:

1. **Personal time**: it feels like a long time before a car journey ends – it might be an hour, but it feels like a day.
2. **Universal time**, including:
   - Succession: Monday, Tuesday, Wednesday . . .
   - Duration: day, night, an hour, a minute . . .

## Shape and size

Children need adults to describe things that are 'bigger than' and 'smaller than' in order to learn that these things are **relative**, not **absolute** sizes. Something is 'big' only in relation to something else. Always use relative terms with children.

Introduce words like 'cylinder' and 'sphere' before 'oblong' and 'circle'. Use everyday things, like tins of food or a football to explain what a cylinder and a sphere look like.

## Length

Use words such as 'longer than' or 'shorter than'. Children need to have rulers and tapes in their environment so that they become aware that things can be measured. Which is the tallest plant? Who has the longest foot? Gradually, they develop an understanding of the exactness of absolute measurements.

## Volume and capacity

'This glass is full.' 'This bucket is nearly empty.' Listen to yourself speak and you will be surprised at how often you use mathematical language in everyday situations.

## Area

You can introduce the concept of area using an example of a blanket that covers the bed mattress. Another example would be a pancake covered with lemon and sugar – the lemon and sugar cover the area of the pancake. Children often explore area in their block play.

## Weight

Introduce the concept of weight using relative ideas: 'This tin of soup is heavier than that apple.' Rather than using a weighing machine, use a balance, so that children see this. Remember that young children need to experience weight physically. They love to carry heavy things. They love to lift each other up, and often carry bags around.

## Case Study    Exploring weight

Kit (aged 3 years) picked up a large piece of ice while out for a walk in the winter. He enjoyed throwing it and watching it skim across an icy stream. He kept saying, 'This is heavy.' His parents helped him to make comparisons: 'Is it heavier than this stone?' 'Is it heavier than this twig?' The natural outdoor environment was an ideal place for Kit to learn about weight.

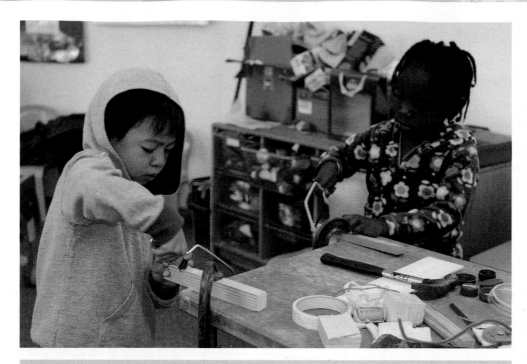

**Figure 13.10** A boy and a girl work side by side, taking care of the tools and of each other's safety

## Computers

The most appropriate computer programs invite children to be interactive. Children benefit from using a word processor and printer, as well as using digital cameras. They enjoy picking out letters and punctuation marks, and through this kind of play they learn about important aspects of reading, writing and numbers, which will be used in a more elaborate way as they get older.

## Creative development

Creative development is important in the following areas:

- arts (dance, music, drama, the visual arts, including sculpture, ceramics and pottery, painting and drawing, collage)
- sciences (biology, chemistry, physics, applied engineering, environmental studies, industry)
- humanities (history, geography, cultural aspects).

 **In Practice**

**Promoting children's creativity in the arts**

Drawing, painting, weaving, collage, sewing, woodwork, sculpture and model-making, and pottery are examples of arts and crafts. Organise art materials for the children to select and use in their own way.

### Creativity in the arts and crafts

Children need experiences such as using clay and paint and woodwork. Representing a dog is quite different when using clay, wood at the woodwork bench, paint, or pretending to be a dog in the home corner. Teach children skills when the need arises. Adults need to be effective observers and tune in to these situations.

Children can make models with clay, wet sand, wax, soap-carving, wood, dough, junk and recycled materials. This will involve them in using sticky tape, scissors, rolling pins, string, wire and other materials. Most of the time, these materials can be

## Guidelines for promoting children's creativity in the arts

Adults often use children's art lessons as a chance to do art for themselves!

**Do not**:

- draw for children
- use templates
- ask children to trace
- ask children to colour in an outline
- ask children to copy your model step by step.

**Do**:

- give children real, first-hand experiences, such as looking at plants or mini beasts in a pond
- give children opportunities to represent things, and to keep hold of their experiences – for example, by making a model of the plant out of clay
- encourage lots of different ideas – it is best when every child in a group has made a different model; this means that children are doing their own thinking and are not dependent on adults for ideas
- remember that children are creative in lots of different ways – arts and crafts is only one area in which children are creative; children can be creative scientists, creative mathematicians, creative writers, and so on.

offered as general areas of provision, available all the time. Clearly, the woodwork can only be used when an adult joins the children, in order to maintain a safe environment.

### Drawing and painting

For **drawing**, it is best to use plain white paper of varied sizes, plus pencils, wax crayons, felt-tip pens, chalks and slates, and charcoal.

For **painting**, there should be powder paints and different thicknesses of brushes. Materials should be stored carefully so that children can take and access what they need when they need it. Children should be offered pots of basic coloured paints, but they should also be able to mix paints, provided they are taught to do so. They simply need the basic colours – red, yellow, blue – and white and black for light and dark shades of colour.

### Book-making

Children love to make books, but need help to do so initially. If they see that you have made recipe books, books of stories and poems, and books for display with information, they will want to do the same.

They need to learn how to fold and cut the paper. An adult may need to be with them so that they do not give up.

## Collage and workshop area

This requires glue, found materials, junk and recycled materials, and scissors. Materials can be set out in attractive baskets or boxes covered in wallpaper. Glue should always be non-toxic.

### Music

Recent studies in neuroscience show that music is important in helping language and memory to develop. Adults naturally sing, 'Up we go', when they lift a baby or toddler out of a pram. Music helps children to remember words, but music is important in its own right. Everyday sounds have rhythm, such as the tick-tock of an alarm clock, tearing paper, shaking a salt cellar, jangling a bunch of keys, fire engines, and so on. Children love to go on listening walks, and to make the sounds they have heard using home-made musical instruments you can help them to make. The importance of singing and listening to a wide range of music from different cultures cannot be overemphasised.

## Case Study
### Creativity in dance, music and drama

You can use what children do naturally – spinning, running, jumping, stamping – to make up a dance. A 'Singing in the Rain' dance was made up by a group of 5-year-old children in Year 1 Key Stage 1, helped by their teacher, Dee De Wet. The children watched a video extract from the film, *Singing in the Rain*, then they experimented with moving about:

- with fancy feet
- by jumping in puddles
- by swishing through puddles
- by dashing about under an umbrella.

They made a dance sequence. Each child had an umbrella and a raincoat, and used the above sequences in line with the traditional music from the film. Every child made up his or her own dance, yet they all danced at the same time, and were sensitive to each other's movement and ideas.

Music is about hearing and making sounds by:

- singing
- making a melody
- clapping rhythms
- making loud and soft sounds (the dynamic)
- making sounds going up and down (the pitch)
- using instruments, to pluck, blow, bow, bang
- singing and dancing action songs and ring games.

The book by Mollie Davies (2003), *Movement and Dance in Early Childhood*, offers more ideas on how to help young children dance, both boys and girls.

## Drama

In their play, children experiment with goodies and baddies, friendship and foes, kindness and unkindness. Penny Holland's work shows how adults can help children to explore these major themes of what it is to be human. Telling children stories and sharing poetry cards with them also helps. Retelling stories with props is beneficial. The adult might help

### Progress check
#### Helping children to make dances

- Use an action phrase – for example, 'shiver and freeze'. Ask the children to move like the words in the phrase.
- Show different objects, perhaps something spiky. Ask the children to move in a spiky way and make a dance.
- Take an idea from nature or everyday life: rush and roar like the wind; be a machine or a clock; dance like shadows moving or fish in an aquarium.
- For inspiration only, use experiences that the children have had very recently.

children to act out the story of Pegasus using a toy horse, with paper wings attached with sticky tape. Children might wear dressing-up clothes to retell the story of *Where The Wild Things Are* by Maurice Sendak, including the rumpus dance.

## Scientific knowledge and understanding

Science is everywhere.

### The physical sciences

- **Electricity**: electrical circuits are easy to make with children and can be used to make a light for the doll's house or the train tracks.
- **Heat**: remember, heat is not just about temperature. Heat is energy; temperature is a measure of how much energy. Cookery is the best way to help children understand about temperature. Making a jelly or ice cream is a good way of looking at coldness. Making something that needs to be cooked in the oven shows children about high temperatures. Look at a central-heating system and the radiators. Think about the sun and how it makes the tarmac on the playground feel warm on a sunny day in the summer. Look at the fridge. Play with ice cubes in the water tray. Again, talk about relative heat. Is this hotter than that? Describe what is happening, think about the cause and effect, why things

**Figure 13.11** This is an example of problem-solving, as well as the satisfaction and engagement which a fulfilled intellectual life brings

## Guidelines for looking at animals

There are reasons why animals, birds and insects have developed as they have done. The following points will give children an introduction to the evolution of the animal world in ways they can understand.

- **Where do animals live?** You can find ants, spiders and birds and look at their habitats. Remember, never kill animals, and always return them to their habitat; make a point of explaining this to the children. You could provide pots containing magnifying glasses, which makes it easier to look at these creatures without squashing them accidentally.
- **What do animals eat?** Study cats, birds and fish, and talk about their diets.
- **How do animals eat?** Talk about claws, type of feet, mouths, beaks, types of teeth, jaws that chew (cows) and jaws that gnash. Study dogs, cats and humans. A bird that eats nuts needs a beak which is a good nutcracker. A bird that catches fish needs a long beak.
- **How do animals protect themselves?** Look at camouflage, claws, tusks, fur for warmth, oil on ducks' feathers to make them waterproof.

**Figure 13.12** The adult is supportive by encouraging the child to water the plants; helping and guiding, but not taking over

happen as they do. Metal feels colder than wood, but why? They are both at room temperature. Does the metal conduct the heat out of your hand?

- **Sound**: listen to the sounds around you. Help children to be aware of them. Children love to record sounds and find ways to imitate sounds they hear. Some sounds are quieter and some are noisier than others. Children are not very concerned about how many decibels a sound is, but they are interested that a shout is louder than a whisper.
- **Light**: use torches and lanterns; make rainbows with prisms; put on puppet shows and have lighting effects; use cellophane® to make different colours of light. Children in Key Stage 1 enthusiastically make light effects for stories they have made up or enjoyed from books. Experiment with shadows and shadow puppets.
- **Gravity**: use parachutes or drop objects from heights.
- **Floating and sinking**: this is a difficult concept. Young children benefit from a waterwheel and different experiments with boats, but true understanding takes time.

### The natural sciences

Use **mixtures** to demonstrate how materials can be changed and recovered (salt and water, sugar and water, earth and water, flour and water, mud pies, and mud and straw to make bricks). All these mixtures have properties that children can explore:

## Guidelines for looking at plants

- Why do plants have leaves? Do all plants have leaves?
- Why is a tree trunk like it is? Do all trees have exactly the same sort of trunk? Make some bark rubbings. Hug trees to see if you can reach all the way round them with your arms.
- Why do flowers have colours? Insects are important for plant life.
- Why do some flowers have scent and nectar? Plants might need to attract insects and birds to visit them.

- Salt and sugar dissolve in water. When the water evaporates, the salt or sugar can be seen again.
- Flour and mud do not dissolve. They become suspended in water.

You can look at transformations using water, ice and steam. You can reverse these, and turn steam into water again.

Study what happens when you cook an egg. You cannot reverse this transformation.

**Low technology** can be explored by looking at activities such as weaving. If you have a frame with string going up and down and from side to side, near the entrance, then children and families will enjoy the in-and-out movement of threading pieces of material, wool, ribbon, and so on. These weavings often become attractive wall hangings in the office or entrance hall of the setting.

It is important to use technology that is easy for children to understand. Examples would be a tin opener, an egg whisk or scissors. Encourage children to use wooden blocks and construction kits.

**High technology** includes digital cameras, tape recorders or CD players for music and stories, computers, word processors and printers, and telephones for conversations. Nowadays, children are able to use these from an early age.

**Figure 13.13** Woodwork is a form of low technology; other forms are egg whisks, waterwheels and bicycles

## Knowledge and understanding of the world

Young children are interested in people, families and homes. They like to learn about what people in the community do. They show this in their role play, and by visiting offices, shops, clinics, the vet, the train station, and so on, they can learn about different communities and develop a sense of geography.

They are also interested in old objects, in what things were like when they were babies or when their parents were babies, and what sort of childhood their

**Figure 13.14** The boy uses fine physical control to place the cylinders and the lion on the top, encouraged by his key person

## Guidelines for floor work

- Give children (aged between 4 and 7 years) a general theme to investigate through floor work – for example, starting low and getting higher.
- Do not make children do just one thing, such as a handstand. There are lots of different ways of changing your balance.
- To help children enjoy creating and solving problems about weight transfer, you can say, 'Can you start on your feet and stop with another bit of you touching the floor?' In this way, you are helping children with reasoning and problem-solving as they think about their own movements.

grandparents had. Collecting artefacts of bygone days and inviting older people to share and talk about their lives, often with the help of photographs, helps children to develop a sense of history. Having a timeline helps too – again, using photos to show the order and sequence of events.

## Physical development

Children need to move as much as they need to eat and sleep. They learn through action and language that gives it meaning. They need to be skilled in a range of movements, using both fine and gross motor skills. They need repetition to consolidate. Movement needs to be appropriate – stroke a dog gently, but throw hard to make a splash with a pebble in a puddle.

### Large apparatus

Large apparatus includes climbing frame, ropes to swing on, planks to walk on with ladders and things

to jump off. Children need to be encouraged to become generally skilled in movement.

### Small apparatus

Small apparatus includes bats, balls, hoops, beanbags, ropes and pushcarts. It is very important to encourage turn-taking and cooperation.

### Floor work

Floor work enables children to explore:

- weight transfer from one part of the body to another
- travel from one spot to another
- flight: the five basic jumps are on two legs, from one leg to the other, on the left leg, on the right leg, from two legs to one leg.

# Be able to engage with children in activities and experiences which support their learning and development

## Working alongside children to support their learning and engaging with them to support sustained shared thinking

It is very difficult for children when adults do not stay in one place for long enough for children to engage with them in focused ways. It does not encourage children to focus either. It is a good idea, as part of planning the curriculum framework in the learning environments indoors and outdoors, to see where there might need to be anchored adults working in depth with children. The following points are important:

- The anchored adult needs to sit at the child's height or on the floor, so as to give full attention to a child or children in one area, while retaining an overview of the rest of the room.
- The practitioner must be free to focus on what the children in a particular area are doing (such as playing with wooden blocks or in the movement corner) and be able to have engaging conversations: listening to what children say and being sensitive to what they do, allowing them plenty of time (such as when cooking together or planting bulbs in the garden).
- Another adult must be free to help children generally – for example, to deal with children's toilet needs, to hang up a painting or comfort a tearful child, or simply to respond to children who ask for help.
- If every adult has a clear understanding of their role in the team, it helps each practitioner to focus on the children and reduces the temptation to chat with other adults instead of engaging with the children.

Sometimes it might appear that children are stuck in their play, because they stay doing something for a long time; it might even appear to be obsessive. However, a child who stays at the workshop area for a long time, dripping glue from a glue stick onto paper and covering the paper until it is soggy, is not necessarily being obsessive. There will be reasons why the child does this, because human behaviour is not random.

The following case studies look at three different children. When the practitioner tunes in to each one,

## Case Study — Developing expertise in the block play area

Some children spend a great deal of time in a particular area, every day. Monty has a favourite – block play. It is important to encourage this, so that he will be able to become a specialist in this area. Help him to develop his skill, making bridges, roofs, walls, and so on. Monty likes to focus on his play for a long time.

Unless practitioners observe and tune in to children, they may be unnecessarily concerned about their actions and behaviour. Perhaps the child needs the right kind of support to get the most out of the learning environment, indoors and outdoors.

In a small group, discuss how you are helping children. What more can you do to support and extend their learning? Children do not know how to use glue, wooden blocks and so on, unless they feel supported and are given the right sort of help, in the right way, at the right time.

## Case Study — Tuning in to children

Nadia (2 years old) is exploring glue and its properties for the first time in her life. She is interested in the way in which the glue falls off the glue stick, and in the soggy mound of glue on the paper. She does not seem to be interested in the function of glue – to join things together. So, does she need to be using this expensive glue? She might gain just as much satisfaction from flour and water glue, which is cheaper. Does she need expensive paper to drip the glue onto? She might learn just as much if the glue is dripped onto newspaper.

It is important to respond sensitively once you have tuned in to a child. Evaluate your practice in relation to this case study. Discuss this in a small group, then take action and try out (implement) the ideas in your practice. In the example explored in the case study, you could consider the following points

1. Always have different kinds of glue available in the workshop. You could offer Nadia flour and water glue in an attractive pot, showing her how she can use it by demonstrating. Chat about the flour glue.

2. When the paper is very soggy, and Nadia wants to continue but it is beginning to flow off the table, replace the paper with newspaper. Chat as you do so, saying you think this might help Nadia to carry out her idea of dripping the glue on the paper.

3. Chatting is important in developing communication – not too much, not too little. Give Nadia key words but in sentences, such as, 'This newspaper will be better, I think, for you to drip your flour glue onto. Let's try it out, shall we?' Nadia might well echo, 'Try it out, shall we'.

4. Chatting is especially important for children with English as an additional language (EAL) and for children with special educational needs (SEN).

we can see that they all have completely different needs. Responding to each child individually is part of creating a rich learning environment indoors and outdoors.

Children usually like to feel that an adult is nearby; it makes them feel safe and secure, especially when they are trying something new and unfamiliar. The first time glue is used or paint is mixed are good examples of this. It is important not to crowd, overwhelm or invade a child's thinking space, but it is vital to support a child's learning by being there for them, smiling and looking interested, and commenting on what they do from time to time; for example, 'You like red best, I think, because I've noticed that you have used it three times in your painting so far.'

We must never underestimate the important of early friendships. Children miss their friends when they are away or ill, and find it more difficult to get involved. A supportive adult is important at these times, offering companionship as the child chooses activities and experiences.

See Chapter 17 (Unit CYPOP 1) for more information on engaging with babies.

### Research Activity

Research the *Core Experiences for the Early Years Foundation Stage* booklet, which shows progression of experiences through the materials provided for children from birth to 5 years. This was developed by staff at Kate Greenaway Nursery School and Children's Centre, building on a Froebelian approach to the curriculum established at Southway Early Childhood Centre and Nursery School (Bedford) and linked to the English EYFS.

## Case Study — Flitting from one thing to the next?

Hayley comes into the garden. She goes to the two-wheeler bikes with no pedals and rides one to the end of the garden. Then she runs to the watering can and picks it up. She walks around with it, drops it on the path and runs to the practitioner who is putting up the sun umbrella. She looks up at its spokes, standing underneath it. Then she goes to the outdoor sandpit, and chooses to play with the wheel, tipping dry sand in and flicking it with her hand as the sand spins round in it. She takes the sand wheel to the water pump and puts it under the spout, pumping water into it and watching it turn.

Hayley seems to be flitting from one thing to the next, yet everything she has chosen to do has the same pattern in it: everything has a core and radials coming out of it – the spokes on the bicycle wheels, the spout on the watering can, the spokes on the umbrella, the sand wheel, which becomes the waterwheel. The researcher Chris Athey would say that she is 'fitting', not 'flitting'.

How should the practitioner respond? Discuss this in a small group, then implement one of your ideas in your practice and evaluate your own practice. What do you need to remember next time?

- Perhaps Hayley would like to be offered similar objects with a core and radials, to broaden her experience.
- The practitioner could have a chat with her as she moves from one thing to another, helping her to build her vocabulary about core and radial objects and what they do (their function).
- The practitioner could take photos of all the objects and make a book of these, calling it 'Hayley's interesting objects'.

# Be able to review own practice in supporting the learning and development of children in their early years

It is important to be a reflective practitioner. You should use official documents; you should not let documents use you! They should be used as something to help you reflect on your practice. They should be a resource to help reflective practice to develop. See Chapter 2 (Unit SHC 32) and Chapter 15 (EYMP 4) for more information about reflective practice and reviewing own practice.

Research shows that children develop and learn through their play and the first-hand experiences they are offered by adults who are interested in what they do, and who support and extend their learning. Children benefit from the relationships and companionship they find with other children. However, none of this can happen if the conditions are not favourable: the role of the adult is crucial in creating, maintaining and planning the general environment.

Useful resources

**Organisations and websites**

**Book Trust Children's Books** encourages children and parents to enjoy reading for pleasure and information; it support adults in reading to young children, recommending a wide range of books, rhymes and stories:
www.booktrustchildrensbooks.org.uk

**Books for Keeps** promotes the use of diverse texts about different cultures, disabilities, gender and age:
www.booksforkeeps.co.uk

**Centre for Literacy in Primary Education** has undertaken pioneering work in supporting and training practitioners to enjoy helping children to love stories and books. It offers excellent training for those working with children in reception and Key Stage 1:
www.clpe.co.uk

**Early Education** – the booklet on *Core Experiences for the Early Years Foundation Stage* from Kate Greenaway Nursery School and Children's Centre can be ordered from this website:
www.early-education.org.uk

**Siren Films** produces high-quality DVDs covering a wide range of topics, such as the first year of life, 2-year-olds, play, attachment and key person, 3- and 4-year-olds, early literacy and schemas in toddlers:
www.sirenfilms.co.uk

**Books**

Brooker, E. (2002) *Starting School: Young Children Learning Cultures*. Open University Press.

Bruce, T. (1987) *Early Childhood Education*. Hodder & Stoughton.

Bruce, T. (2011a) *Cultivating Creativity: Babies, Toddlers and Young Children* Hodder Education.

Bruce, T. (2004) *Developing Learning in Early Childhood*. Paul Chapman Publishing.

Bruce, T. (2011b) *Early Childhood Education*. 4th Edition. Hodder Education.

Bruce, T. (ed.) (2009a) *Early Childhood: A Guide for Students*. 2nd Edition. Sage.

Bruce, T. (2009b) 'Learning through Play: Froebelian Principles and their Practice Today', *Early Childhood Practice: The Journal for Multi-professional Partnerships*, 10(2): 58–73.

Bruce, T. and Spratt, J. (2010) *The Essentials of Communication, Language and Literacy*. 2nd Edition. Sage.

Community Playthings. *Spaces; Creating Places; I Made a Unicorn!* (educational booklets, available at www.communityplaythings.co.uk/resources/request-literature.html).

Davies, M. (2003) *Movement and Dance in Early Childhood*. Paul Chapman Publishing Ltd.

Department for Children, Schools and Families. (2008) *Mark Making Matters: Young Children Making Meaning in All Areas of Learning and Development*. DCSF Publications.

Department for Education and Skills. (2007) *Primary National Strategy: Creating the Picture*. DfES, available at http://publications.teachernet.gov.uk/eOrderingDownload/fs_creating_pic_0028307.pdf

Drury, R. (2007) *Young Bilingual Learners at Home and School: Researching Multilingual Voices*. Trentham Books.

Edgington, M. (2004) *The Foundation Stage Teacher in Action. Teaching 3, 4 and 5 year olds*. 3rd Edition. Sage.

Edwards, C., Gandini, L. and Forman, G. (1998) *The Hundred Languages of Children*. Ablex Publishing.

Greenland, P. (2009) Physical development. In *Early Childhood: A Guide for Students* (ed. T. Bruce). 2nd Edition. Sage.

Gura, P. (ed.) (1990) *Exploring Learning: Young Children and Blockplay*. Paul Chapman Publishing.

Langer, E. (1997) *The Power of Mindful Learning*. Addison-Wesley.

Matthews, J. (2003) *Drawing and Painting: Children and Visual Representation*. 2nd Edition. Paul Chapman Publishing Ltd.

Useful resources (cont.)

Ockelford, A. (1996) *All Join In: A Framework for Making Music with Children and Young People Who are Visually Impaired and Have Learning Difficulties*. RNIB. (This inclusive book, containing music, is also invaluable for all children 0 to 7 years of age.)

Ouvry, M. (2004) *Sounds like Playing: Music in the Early Years Curriculum*. BAECE/Early Education.

Sylva, K., Melhuish, E., Sammons, P., Siraj-Blatchford, I. and Taggart, B. (2004) *The Effective Provision of Pre-School Education (EPPE) Project: Final Report*. DfES/Institute of Education, University of London, available at www.dcsf.gov.uk/research/data/uploadfiles/SSU_FR_2004_01.pdf

Tovey, H. (2007) *Playing Outdoors: Spaces and Places, Risk and Challenge*. Open University Press.

Worthington, M. and Carruthers, E. (2003) *Children's Mathematics: Making Marks, Making Meaning*. Paul Chapman Publishing Ltd.

Ziegler, J. and Goswami, U. (2006), 'Becoming literate in different languages: similar problems, different solutions', *Developmental Science*, 9(5): 429–53.

Community Playthings. *Foundations* (CD-ROM illustrating the value of block play, available at www.communityplaythings.co.uk/resources/request-literature.html).

Department for Education and Skills. (2005) *Celebrating Young Children and Those Who Live and Work with Them* (DVD).

National Assessment Agency. *Early Years Foundation Stage* (DVD, available online by searching for 'early years foundation stage profile exemplification videos').

*Nursery World*, 4 February 2010, pp. 19–22.

# 14 Promote children's welfare and wellbeing in the early years: Unit EYMP 3

This chapter looks at ways of promoting children's physical welfare and wellbeing. To do this, we need to know how to keep children safe and healthy: promoting their safety, preventing infection and ensuring that they receive a balanced, nutritious diet.

## Learning outcomes

By the end of this chapter you will:

1. Understand the welfare requirements of the relevant early years framework.

2. Be able to keep early years children safe in the work setting.

3. Understand the importance of promoting positive health and wellbeing for early years children.

4. Be able to support hygiene and prevention of cross-infection in the early years setting.

5. Understand how to ensure children in their early years receive high quality, balanced nutrition to meet their growth and development needs.

6. Be able to provide physical care for children.

## Understand the welfare requirements of the relevant early years framework

### General welfare requirements: safeguarding and promoting children's welfare

Each of the nations within the UK has a set of welfare requirements or standards that must be met by the provider of early years care. There are three *general* legal requirements and each of these includes *specific* legal requirements. These specific requirements include **statutory** guidance; this guidance informs the provider exactly what is required of them in the early years setting. They are compulsory for all providers of early years care and education.

1 **The provider must take necessary steps to safeguard and promote the welfare of children.** Specific legal requirement areas are:
   a) safeguarding
   b) information and complaints
   c) premises and security
   d) outings
   e) equality of opportunities.

2 **The provider must promote the good health of the children, take necessary steps to prevent the spread of infection and take appropriate action when they are ill.** Specific legal requirement areas are:
   - medicines
   - illness and injuries
   - food and drink
   - smoking.

3 **Children's behaviour must be managed effectively and in a manner appropriate for their stage of development and particular individual needs.** Specific legal requirement area:
- behaviour management.

## Key terms

**General legal requirements** – These are statutory requirements that all early years providers must meet, regardless of type, size or funding of the setting.

**Specific legal requirements** – These expand on the general requirements and must be complied with in the way stated.

**Statutory guidance** – Providers must have regard to and take into account the statutory guidance documentation when seeking to fulfil the general and specific requirements.

## Suitable people

Providers must ensure that adults looking after children, or having unsupervised access to them, are suitable to do so. This includes using safe recruitment and vetting procedures. Adults looking after children must have appropriate qualifications, training and knowledge. Staffing arrangements (such as child:staff ratios) must be carried out to ensure safety and to meet the needs of the children.

## Suitable premises, environment and equipment

Outdoor and indoor spaces, furniture, equipment and toys, must be safe and suitable for their purposes. The provider must conduct a **risk assessment** and review it regularly: at least once a year or more frequently where the need arises. (See Chapter 8, page 150, for more information about risk assessments.)

## Organisation

Providers must plan and organise their systems to ensure that every child receives an enjoyable and challenging learning and development experience which is tailored to meet their individual needs. Every child must be assigned a key person (For more information about the key person role, see page 224. In childminding settings, the childminder is the key person.)

## Documentation

Providers must maintain records, policies and procedures required for the safe and efficient management of the setting and to meet the needs of the children.

## Lines of reporting and responsibility within the work setting

Your setting's health and safety policy will contain the names of staff members responsible for health and safety. All practitioners are responsible for health and safety in any setting. Your responsibilities include:

- taking reasonable care for **your own safety** and that of others
- working with your employer in respect of **health and safety** matters
- knowing about the **policies and procedures** in your particular place of work – these can all be found in the setting's health and safety policy documents
- **not intentionally damaging** any health and safety equipment or materials provided by the employer
- **reporting all accidents**, incidents and even 'near misses' to your manager. As you may be handling food, you should also report any **incidences of sickness** or diarrhoea
- **reporting any hazards** immediately you come across them.

Apart from your legal responsibilities, knowing how to act and being alert and vigilant at all times can prevent accidents, injury, infections and even death; this could be in relation to you, your fellow workers or the children in your care.

# Keeping children safe in the work setting

Children need a safe environment so that they can explore, learn and grow. As they develop, older children need to learn how to tackle everyday dangers so that they can become safe adults.

Children learn some realities of safety the hard way, for example by banging their heads or grazing their knees. You cannot prevent them from hurting themselves altogether, but you can alert them and keep reminding them. You have an important role, not only in keeping children safe and secure but also in teaching them to be aware of safety issues.

## Safe supervision of children while allowing risk and challenge

Safe supervision of children is vital to ensure their safety. Supervising children means far more than just preventing them from doing certain things in case they have an accident. It also involves knowing when to supervise 'at arm's length', to allow children opportunities to tackle more challenging activities. There are certain circumstances when close supervision is essential (for example, when children are playing near or with water) but there should also be times when adults can supervise unobtrusively to give children the chance to try something new. This subject is dealt with in more depth in Chapter 8 (Unit CYP Core 3.4).

## Supporting children's safety when they move in and out of the setting

Every setting should have clear systems in place to ensure the safety of children:

- when being received into the setting
- when departing from the setting, and
- during off-site visits.

During these times, there is often a lot of movement and activity. When children are received into the setting, several children may arrive at once, parents may be in a rush to get to work, and children are keen to rejoin their friends. When leaving the setting, again many children will be leaving at the same time, parents chatting with others and children eager to say goodbye to their friends. During off-site visits, there is usually a great deal of excitement about being in a new place with lots to see and do. Every practitioner should be aware of the policy and procedures that relate to these times in their setting, and should be clear about his or her own role and responsibility.

### Receiving children into the setting

All settings must register children on arrival. A daily register of the names of all the children in the setting at any given time is essential not only in case of an emergency evacuation of the setting, but also so that adequate staff supervision (or staffing ratios) is provided. Many early years settings have door entry phones and a password system for parents and staff to enter the premises. The entrance should be secure so that the door cannot be left open for people to wander in and out. In some settings, one member of staff is stationed at the door, greeting and sharing information with each family as they arrive. Some settings have a designated dropping-off area where a calm atmosphere can be created as parents and carers 'hand over' their child to their key person.

### Ensuring safety on departure

Every setting will have a policy about correct procedure for when parents and carers come to collect their child. Again, a record must be kept so

## Activity

### Receiving children into the setting

Find out about the system for receiving children in your setting:

- Who is responsible for registering the children?
- How does the setting ensure that the entrance door is kept shut between arrivals?
- How smooth is the transition from reception into the setting to each child being with his or her key person?

## Case Study    Problems at home time

Anna is a 3-year-old child who attends a private nursery group four days a week. Her key worker, Jenny, has developed a good professional relationship with Anna's mother and suspects that she and her partner are having problems balancing their home life with their work commitments. Anna's mother, Jane, often arrives late to collect Anna; she is always very flustered and apologetic about it. Anna's father, David, works long hours as a sales rep and is often away from home for weeks at a time. He has only collected Anna on a couple of occasions before, and only when Jane had given prior permission. One Friday afternoon, David arrives at the nursery and explains to Jenny that Jane had rung him to say she was running very late and asked if he could collect Anna on this occasion. When Jenny replies that she must check with the nursery manager before allowing him to take Anna, David becomes very angry and starts to shout about

his rights as a father. As Jenny is trying to reason with him, he suddenly pushes his way past her into the nursery room and scoops Anna up, grabbing her coat from her peg as he rushes out. Five minutes later, Jane arrives and becomes very distressed when she hears what has happened. She tells Jenny that she and David had had an argument that morning and that he had threatened to leave her.

Discuss this case study in class and answer the following questions:

- If you were Jenny (Anna's key worker), what should you do?
- What are the main issues involved in this case study?
- How can the nursery ensure every child's safety at home time?

that it is clear which children are in the setting in case of an emergency. At home time, a member of staff *must* ensure that every child is collected by the appropriate person: the person registered as the child's own parent or carer, or a person who has written authorisation from the parent or carer. If parents know that they will not be able to collect their child on a particular occasion, they should notify the setting, giving permission for another named person to collect their child. The child's key person should, where possible, be responsible for handover at home times. Within the setting's safeguarding children policy, there should be a written statement of the procedures in place for an uncollected child.

## Safety during off-site visits

Any outing away from the children's usual setting (such as trips to farms, parks and theatres) must be planned with safety and security issues as a top

### Reflective practice: Safety at arrival and departure

- Do you know the procedures for arrival and departure in your setting?
- How do you ensure that the person who arrives is authorised to collect the child?
- Do you know what to do if an unknown adult arrives to collect a child?
- Think about the most welcoming and safe way to greet families when they arrive.

priority. Chapter 7 (Unit CYP Core 3.3) also gives information on off-site visits.

Every setting must consider the following points.

### Planning and risk assessment
Visit or find out about the place beforehand and discuss any particular requirements, such as what to

do if it rains, or specific lunch arrangements. A risk assessment should be carried out to include consideration of potential risks in the environment, such as traffic, dogs, ponds or rivers etc.

## Contact numbers

A copy of the children's contact information should be taken on the outing, and the person in charge should regularly check the names of the children against the day's attendance list.

## Parental permission

Parents should be informed of what is involved on the outing, such as what the child needs to bring (such as packed meal, waterproof coat), spending money if necessary (state the advised maximum amount). Parents must sign a consent form that gives the setting permission to take their child off the premises.

## Supervision and staff ratios

There should always be trained staff on any outing, however local and low-key. Usually help is requested from parents so that adequate supervision is ensured. The minimum staff: child ratios are set out in the welfare requirements for every home nation, and must be complied with. The adult to child ratio should never exceed one to four. If the children are under 2 years old or have special needs, then you would expect to have fewer children per adult.

Swimming trips should be attempted only if the ratio is one adult to one child for children under 5 years old. The younger the children, the more adults are required, particularly if the trip involves crossing roads, when an adult must be available to hold the children's hands.

## Head counts

Make sure that you all count the children regularly. Always accompany children to public toilets, telling a colleague how many children you are taking with you.

## Transport

If a coach is being hired, check whether it has seat belts for children. By law, all new minibuses and coaches must have seat belts fitted, and minibus drivers must pass a special driving test.

## First aid kit and medicines

Staff should carry a bag with a simple first aid kit, medication such as inhalers, sun cream, nappies, spare clothes, extra drinks, reins and harnesses.

# Checking the inside and outside environments to ensure safety

All aspects of the indoor and outdoor environments used by children must be checked daily for safety. There should be a system in place for full risk assessments to be carried out at least every year, and this should be updated whenever a new piece of equipment is introduced. The risk assessment should also take into account adaptations that may need to be made in different weather conditions, such as when it is icy underfoot or when it is very hot. Also adaptations may need to be made to allow for children with special needs to play safely. Each practitioner should also know when, how, and to whom they should report any hazard or potential risk in the environment.

# The importance of minimum requirements for space and staff ratios

## Space

When considering the amount of space needed by children to play safely, it is useful to observe the ways in which they play. From observing the movements of children within the setting, practitioners can assess and evaluate the current provision, and work out ways of improving the provision if necessary. For example, you may observe that groups of children always seem to cluster around the bikes, and that allowing free choice may present a hazard. Then, you may decide that it is safer to put in a system where groups of children take it in turns to use the bikes, and you provide running games for the children waiting for their turn. Each home nation sets minimum standards and requirements for use of space in children's settings.

## In Practice

### Checking the environment for safety

- ❏ Worn equipment should be mended or replaced.
- ❏ Equipment should be checked for splinters, sharp edges or peeling paint.
- ❏ Check large apparatus such as climbing frames and trucks for safety catches and safety surfaces.
- ❏ Check that children have enough space to move about safely.

- ❏ Heavy objects should not be on shelves in case they fall on children.
- ❏ All fire exits must be kept free at all times.
- ❏ Doors must not be left half open, especially if there are children with visual impairments, as they bump into them.
- ❏ Objects on shelves should not stick out at a child's head height in case they bump their heads.

## Staffing ratios

The Early Years Foundation Stage (EYFS) in England and the equivalent framework in each of the other home nations give specific minimum requirements for staffing ratios. These ratio requirements set out the minimum numbers of staff that must be present with the children at any time. However, every setting is responsible for considering at all times whether there is adequate supervision of children and ensuring that the needs of the individual children being cared for are met. The ratios relate to staff time available to work *directly* with children. Sufficient suitable staff must be available to cover staff breaks, holidays, sickness and time spent with parents, in order to ensure that the ratio and qualification requirements are always met in relation to the staff working directly with the children. Additional staff may be required to undertake management tasks, prepare meals, maintain premises and equipment, and so on.

The ratios also include any children of staff or volunteers. Under the EYFS welfare requirements,

### Activity

#### Staffing ratios

Find out about the minimum requirements set by the relevant home nation for the age group of children with whom you work.

there must be at least two adults on duty in a setting at any time when children are present.

# Promoting positive health and wellbeing

It is important to view health and wellbeing in a holistic way, just as we view development holistically. There are six aspects of health:

1 **Physical health**: this is concerned with the physical functioning of the body. It is the easiest aspect of health to measure.
2 **Emotional health**: this relates to how we express feelings such as joy, sadness, frustration and fear. It also includes the development of strategies to cope with new, challenging or stressful situations.
3 **Mental health**: this relates to our ability to organise our thoughts coherently, and is closely linked to emotional and social health.
4 **Social health**: this is concerned with how we relate to others and form relationships.
5 **Spiritual health**: this includes religious beliefs and practices, as well as personal codes of conduct and the quest for inner peace.
6 **Environmental health**: an individual's health depends also on the health of the society in which they live. (For example, in areas of famine, health is denied to the inhabitants. Also, unemployed people cannot be described as healthy within a society which only values those who work.)

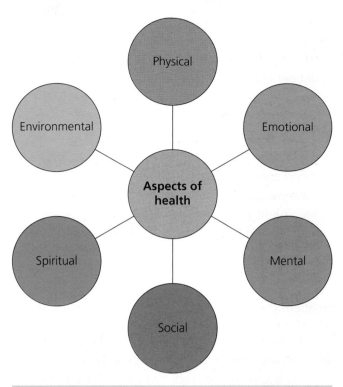

**Figure 14.1** The six aspects of health

It is important to remember that a child with a disability such as cerebral palsy or spina bifida *can* be described as healthy. The important components that determine children's health and wellbeing are feeling happy, being fit and being able to adapt and develop to one's full potential throughout life.

# What do children need to be healthy?

In order to be healthy in its widest sense, children need what children have always needed:

- **nutritious food and drink** – not processed or 'junk' food
- **real play opportunities** – involving physical activity and exercise, not sedentary, screen-based games and entertainment
- **to experience things first-hand** – in a stimulating way, not in a passive way
- **love and support** from (and regular interaction with) the significant adults in their lives
- a **healthy hygienic environment** – with fresh air, sunlight and good hygiene practices

- **to be protected** in safe surroundings where choice and risk-taking are encouraged
- **accommodation and clothing** that is appropriate for the weather and the activities in which they are engaged
- **periods of physical activity, rest and sleep** – where individual sleep and rest patterns are respected.

## Nutritious food and drink

Every child needs to have a balanced, nutritious diet; this is discussed later in this chapter.

## Real play opportunities

Children need play opportunities which stimulate their senses and provide a variety of learning experiences. You can learn more about the importance of play in Chapter 13 (Unit EYMP 2).

## Love and support

Children need love and support if they are to be emotionally and socially healthy. This is discussed in more detail on page 284, in the section on attachment and the key person system.

## A healthy, hygienic environment

Both the environment and children need to be kept clean. Practising good hygiene routines (personal hygiene routines and hygiene routines in the setting) will help to prevent infection and to maintain children's and adult's health. This aspect is also covered later in this chapter.

## Protection

Children need to be safeguarded from hazards in a safe environment, but they also need to be encouraged to make choices and to take risks; this relates to the aspect of emotional health. They also need to be protected from infectious diseases, and this can be supported through child health surveillance, which includes regular health and developmental checks and immunisation against certain serious diseases. See Chapter 7 (Unit CYP Core 3.3) for more information.

## Accommodation and clothing

Children need fresh air and sunlight. Adequate ventilation within the setting is important to help disperse bacteria or viruses transmitted through sneezing or coughing. Make sure that windows are opened to let in fresh air to the setting, but ensure that there are no draughts. The room temperature in the setting should be maintained at between 18 and 21°C.

Babies need to be kept warm but not too hot, especially when sleeping. Rooms for sleeping babies should be kept at a temperature between 16 and 20°C.

Children should be given plenty of opportunities to play outdoors. They should be dressed appropriately for the weather conditions and for their activities.

## Periods of physical activity and rest

Physical activity or exercise is essential for children's growth and development, because it:

- reduces their risk of developing heart disease in later life
- strengthens muscles
- helps to strengthen joints and promotes good posture
- improves balance, coordination and flexibility
- increases bone density, so bones are less likely to fracture.

Apart from these obvious physical benefits, regular exercise develops a child's self-esteem (emotional health aspect) by creating a strong sense of purpose and self-fulfilment. Children learn how to interact and cooperate with other children (social health aspect) by taking part in team sports and other activities. Children also need to have quiet periods of rest and, of course, sleep.

## Sleep and rest

Children vary enormously in their need for rest and sleep. Some children seem able to rush around all day with very little rest, while others need to recharge their batteries by having frequent periods of rest. By the end of the first year, most babies are having two short sleeps during the day – before or after lunch and in the afternoon – and sleeping through the night, although there is much variation between individual children. It is important to have 'quiet periods', even if the baby does not want to sleep.

## Why is sleep important?

Sleep is important to everybody. When we sleep, we rest and gain energy for a new day, and while we dream, we process all the events of our daily life. After a night without enough sleep we often feel exhausted and irritable, but after a good night's sleep we feel rested, refreshed and full of energy. It is important to parents that their child sleeps through the night, as it influences the entire family's life and wellbeing.

Children need more sleep than adults because the brain is developing and maturing, and they are physically growing as well. Sleep is important to child health because:

- it rests and restores their bodies and promotes a feeling of wellbeing
- it enables the brain and the body's metabolic processes to recover (these processes are responsible for producing energy and growth)
- at night, the body produces more growth hormone, which renews body tissues and produces new bone and red blood cells.

## How much sleep do children need?

Children will sleep only if they are actually tired, so it is important that enough exercise and activity is provided throughout the day. Some children prefer to rest quietly in their cots rather than have a sleep during the day; others will continue to have one or two daytime naps even up to the age of 3 or 4 years.

## Bedtime and sleep routines

There are cultural differences in how parents view bedtime and sleep routines. In some cultures it is normal for children to sleep with parents and to have a much later bedtime in consequence. Some families who originate from hot countries where having a sleep in the afternoon is normal, tend to let their children stay up in the evening. Such children are

## Guidelines for sleep and rest routines

When preparing children for a daytime nap or rest, you can help children in the following ways:

- Treat every child as an individual, with individual needs and preferences.
- Find out the child's preferences: some children like to be patted to sleep, while others may need to cuddle their favourite comfort object.
- Make sure that there are no suffocation or choking hazards in the sleeping area.
- Respect the wishes of the child's parents or main carer.
- Keep noise to a minimum and darken the room.
- Each child should have his or her own bedding for hygienic purposes.
- Make sure that children have been to the toilet before trying to fall asleep.
- Ensure that you stay with the children until they fall asleep.
- Reassure them that you (or someone) will be there when they wake up.
- Provide quiet, relaxing activities for those children who do not have a sleep; for example, by reading a book to them or doing jigsaw puzzles.

**Figure 14.2** Sleep is important for health and wellbeing

more likely to need a sleep while in day care; as long as the overall amount of sleep is sufficient for the child, it does not matter.

It is always worth discussing bedtime routines with parents and carers when toddlers are struggling to behave appropriately. Some areas have sleep clinics managed by the health visiting service to help parents whose children have difficulty sleeping. Even after they have established a good sleep routine, children's sleep patterns can become disrupted between the ages of 1 and 3 years. There are thought

to be a number of factors for this, including developmental changes and behavioural issues.

## The effects of insufficient sleep

There is increasing evidence that some children who do not get sufficient sleep experience the following effects. They may:

- exhibit hyperactive behaviour
- be irritable and prone to emotional outbursts such as tantrums
- find it hard to concentrate or settle to any activity
- be more likely to become overweight: both children and adults feel an increased need to eat calorie-rich foods when they are sleep-deprived
- suffer more illness, because lack of sleep affects the ability of their immune system to fight off infections.

All early years practice must take into account any cultural preferences, such as later bedtimes and family circumstances; for example, a family living in bed and breakfast accommodation may have to share bathroom facilities, or bedtime may be delayed to enable a working parent to be involved in the routine.

**In Practice**

**Bedtime routine**

Arrange to visit a family with a young child to talk about the child's bedtime routine. Devise a questionnaire to find out the following:

❑ any problems settling the child to sleep

❑ any problems with the child waking in the night

❑ strategies used to address the problems.

Using the answers from the questionnaire to help you, devise a bedtime routine for a 3-year-old girl who has just started nursery school, and whose mother has 3-month-old twin boys.

Points to include are:

❑ how to arrange one-to-one care for the 3-year-old child

❑ how to avoid jealousy.

## Preventing cot death

Recent research and guidelines have reduced dramatically the incidence of cot deaths in the UK. The principles to follow to help to prevent cot death are detailed in Chapter 18 (Unit CYPOP 2).

# How to promote children's health and wellbeing

As we have seen above, there is more to children's health and wellbeing than simply keeping them safe and physically healthy. Young children also need to be emotionally healthy and to be supported to form attachments within the setting.

## Meeting the attachment needs of children in their early years

For babies and young children to spend any significant amount of time away from their parents and carers, they have to be allowed to form an **attachment relationship** with their key person. There should be clear structures and systems to facilitate this, such as:

- the key person system
- settling-in programmes: to include either home visits or visits to the setting by the parents before their child starts attending
- regular staff time for observation (in order to plan for individual needs) and record-keeping.

## The key person system

The key person system is a welfare requirement in all early years settings in the UK. The role of the key person is as follows:

- Help the baby or child to become familiar with the setting and to feel confident and safe within it.
- Develop a genuine bond with the child (and the child's parents).
- Offer a settled, close relationship.
- Meet the needs of every child in their care.
- Respond sensitively to their feelings, ideas and behaviour.
- Talk to parents to make sure that the child is being cared for appropriately for each family.

The key person needs to spend time with their key child or children during the settling-in period as well as on an ongoing daily basis. You can find out more about the key person role in Chapter 17 (Unit CYPOP 1).

## Key terms

**Key person** – The EYFS defines a key person as the named member of staff assigned to an individual child to support their development and act as the key point of contact with that child's parents.

## The roles of key health professionals and sources of professional advice

Health professionals have an important role in maintaining children's health and in supporting their families. They are able to provide general advice and also specific professional guidance to ensure that children's holistic health needs are met. Parents should always be consulted and asked for their permission before you refer their child to a specialist health professional.

## Sources of professional advice

Specialist health services vary from one local community to another; for example, some local NHS Trusts employ community paediatricians and specialist health visitors. You can find out more about these services by contacting your local NHS Trust, either online or in a reference library. Usually, the first professional to consult will be the GP or family doctor, who can then refer the family to the appropriate specialist.

It is important that you do not overstep the boundaries of your own role. You should always consult parents and gain their consent before referring their child on to other services.

# Supporting hygiene and prevention of cross-infection

In order to keep children healthy, it is important to keep all settings clean and to maintain a standard of hygiene that will minimise the risk of cross-infection.

## Maintaining a clean, hygienic environment

Providing a healthy and hygienic environment for children is vital to their development. A balance also has to be struck where a child is allowed to get dirty when playing, but understands that they will need to wash afterwards. Developing good hygiene routines is important for the following reasons:

1 **It helps to prevent infection and the spread of disease**. Children who play closely together for long periods of time are more likely than others to develop an infection, which can spread very quickly from one child to another.
2 **Being clean increases self-esteem and social acceptance**. Nobody likes to be close to someone who appears dirty or whose clothes smell.
3 **It helps to prepare children for skills of independence and self-caring**. All children benefit from regular routines in daily care. Parents and carers have their own routines and hygiene practices, and these should always be respected (for example, Muslims prefer to wash under running water and Rastafarians wear their hair braided so may not use a comb or brush).

## Providing a hygienic indoor environment

Children need a clean, warm and hygienic environment in order to stay healthy. Although most large early years settings employ a cleaner, there will be many occasions when you have to take responsibility for ensuring that the environment is kept clean and safe; for example if a child has been sick or has had a toileting accident.

All early years settings should have set routines for tidying up and for cleaning the floors, walls, furniture and play equipment; details may be found in the setting's written policy for health and hygiene issues.

## Providing a hygienic outdoor environment

Children benefit from playing in the fresh air, as long as they are dressed appropriately for the weather. All early years settings should be checked regularly to make sure that a safe and hygienic environment is being provided.

## Policies relating to health and hygiene

All early years settings must have a written policy for dealing with health and hygiene issues. The

| Health professional | Role |
| --- | --- |
| Audiologist | An audiologist carries out hearing tests and explains the results of those tests. If a child needs hearing aids, they will identify the best type and arrange for them to be supplied. |
| Clinical psychologist | A clinical psychologist is a health professional who helps children with specific learning problems or with overcoming behaviour difficulties. |
| Dentist | A dentist specialises in the prevention and treatment of dental decay. |
| Dietician | A dietician is a health professional who can advise on diet-related matters. |
| General practitioner (GP) | A GP is a family doctor who works in the community. They are a first point of contact for many families. They deal with children's general health and can refer families to clinics, hospitals and specialists when needed. |
| Health visitor | A health visitor is a qualified nurse or midwife with additional special training and experience in child health. They visit family homes in the early years to check on children's health and development. They give help, advice and practical assistance to families about the care of very young children, normal child development, sleep patterns, feeding, behaviour and safety. |
| Occupational therapist (OT) | An occupational therapist helps children improve their developmental function by therapeutic techniques, environmental adaptations and the use of specialist equipment. OTs are concerned with difficulties that children have in carrying out the activities of everyday life. This could include sitting in a chair, holding a spoon and fork or drinking from a cup. |
| Optometrist/ Ophthalmic optician | An optometrist is a health professional who specialises in measuring children's sight and prescribing glasses. They can identify eye diseases and are usually based at a hospital or optician's clinic, although young children with multi-sensory impairment are more likely to be assessed at a specialist clinic. |
| Orthoptist | An orthoptist is a health professional who specialises in correcting vision by non-surgical means (especially by exercises to strengthen the eye muscles). They often work with ophthalmologists in hospitals, but may also work in a health clinic or visiting a school. They can test children's sight, look at eye movements, assess how well both eyes work together and check for squints (also known as turning eyes). |
| Paediatrician | A paediatrician is a doctor who specialises in working with babies and children. They are often the first point of contact for families who find out their child has an impairment or disability and can offer advice, information and support about any medical condition(s) which a child has. |
| Physiotherapist | A physiotherapist is a health professional specialising in physical and motor development. They can assess a child and develop a tailored treatment plan that might include helping a child to control their head movement, sit, roll over, crawl or walk. Physiotherapists can also teach parents how to handle their child at home for feeding, bathing, dressing and advise on equipment that might help their child's mobility. |
| School nurse | A school nurse may visit a number of mainstream schools in his or her health district to monitor child health and development – by checking weight, height, eyesight and hearing, and by giving advice on common problems such as head lice. They may also be employed in special schools to supervise the routine medical care of children with disabilities. |
| Speech and language therapist | A speech and language therapist is a health professional specialising in communication development and disorders (and associated eating and swallowing difficulties). They offer support and advice to parents of children with any type of communication problem. |

**Table 14.1** Health professionals and their roles

## Guidelines for providing a safe and hygienic indoor environment

- **Adequate ventilation** is important to disperse bacteria or viruses transmitted through sneezing or coughing. Make sure that windows are opened to let in fresh air to the setting, but also ensure that there are no draughts.
- **Cleaning routines**:

  1. All surfaces should be damp-dusted daily. Floors, surfaces and the toilet area must be checked on a regular basis for cleanliness.

  2. All toys and play equipment should be cleaned regularly – *at least* once a week. This includes dressing up clothes and soft toys. Use antiseptic solutions such as Savlon to disinfect toys and play equipment regularly; toys used by babies under 1 year old should be disinfected daily.

  3. Check that sandpits or trays are clean and that toys are removed and cleaned at the end of a play session. If the sandpit is kept outside, make sure that it is kept covered when not in use. Keep sand trays clean by sieving and washing the sand regularly.

  4. Water trays should be emptied daily as germs can multiply quickly in pools of water.

  5. The home area often contains dolls, saucepans and plastic food; these need to be included in the checking and in the regular wash.

  6. Apart from routine cleaning, you should always clean up any spills straightaway; both young children and adults often slip on wet surfaces.

- Use paper towels and tissues, and dispose of them in covered bins.
- Remove from the nursery any toy which has been in contact with a child who has an infectious illness.
- Throw out any plastic toys that have cracks or splits in them, as germs can multiply in these places. Particular care should be taken to keep hats, head coverings and hairbrushes clean in order to help prevent the spread of head lice.
- Animals visiting the nursery or nursery pets must be free from disease, safe to be with children and must not pose a health risk. Children should *always* be supervised when handling animals, and you must make sure that they always wash their hands after touching any pet.
- A no smoking policy must be observed by staff and visitors.

## Guidelines for ensuring a hygienic outdoor environment

- Check the outdoor play area daily for litter, dog excrement and hazards such as broken glass, syringes or rusty cans.
- Follow the sun safety code; provide floppy hats and use sun cream (SPF15) to prevent sunburn (if parents or carers give their permission).
- Check all play equipment for splinters, jagged edges, protruding nails and other hazards.
- Supervise children at all times.
- Keep sand covered and check regularly for insects, litter and other contamination.
- Keep gates locked and check that hinges are secure.

## Guidelines for addressing health and hygiene issues

- Always wear disposable gloves when dealing with blood, urine, faeces or vomit.
- Always wash your hands after dealing with spillages, even if gloves have been worn.
- Use a dilute bleach (hypochlorite) solution to mop up any spillages (or product specified by your setting's policy).
- Make sure paper tissues are available for children to use.
- Always cover cuts and open sores with adhesive plasters.
- Food must be stored and prepared hygienically.
- Ask parents to keep their children at home if they are feeling unwell or if they have an infection.
- Children who are sent home with vomiting or diarrhoea must remain at home until at least 24 hours have elapsed since the last attack.

guidelines above include points that are often part of the policy document.

## Preventing cross-infection

Cross infection is the spread of infection from one person to another. Infections are very common in childhood and are responsible for the majority of illnesses that occur in babies and children under the age of 5 years. A particular concern for early years settings is that young children often lack basic hygiene skills and must rely on others for their care. Shared toilets and washing facilities, toys, equipment and utensils further increase cross-infection risks. Repeated close physical contact with other children, adults and at-risk areas of the environment (such as toilet facilities) increases the risk of acquiring infections.

### What is cross-infection?

Infections are caused by bacteria, fungi and viruses. These pathogenic (disease-causing) organisms or germs can spread in various ways, the main methods being:

- **airborne**: the germs are carried by the air, such as the chicken pox virus
- **droplet spread**: infectious droplets of moisture are coughed or breathed out during infection. They settle on surfaces and may be transferred to another person's eyes or mouth, usually by their hands

- **direct contact**: the germs are spread by touching someone who has the infection, such as scabies or impetigo
- **indirect contact**: the germs are spread by coming into contact with dirty equipment or other materials.

## The importance of hand-washing

Effective hand-washing is an essential way of preventing cross-infection in early years settings. Some simple facts illustrate the importance of regular hand-washing in preventing the spread of infection:

- The number of bacteria on fingertips doubles after using the toilet.
- Bacteria can stay alive on our hands for up to three hours.
- 1,000 times as many bacteria spread from damp hands than from dry hands.
- Even after thorough washing, certain bugs can remain under long fingernails.
- Right-handed people tend to wash their left hand more thoroughly than their right hand, and vice versa.
- Millions of bacteria can hide under rings, watches and bracelets.

### How you should wash your hands

We all think we know how to wash our hands, but many of us do not do it properly. Figure 14.3 shows how we often miss certain parts of our hands when washing them.

## A step-by-step guide to effective hand-washing

**1**  Wet your hands thoroughly under warm running water and squirt liquid soap onto the palm of one hand.

**2**  Rub your hands together to make a lather.

**3**  Rub the palm of one hand along the back of the other and along the fingers. Then do the same with the other hand.

**4**  Rub in between each of your fingers on both hands and around your thumbs.

**5**  Rinse off the soap with clean running water.

**6**  Dry hands thoroughly on a clean dry towel, paper towel or air dryer.

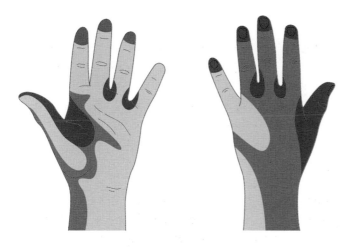

**Figure 14.3** Parts commonly missed when washing hands

### When you should wash your hands

You should wash your hands **before**:

- starting work – this is particularly important when working in any caring environment
- preparing food
- eating
- putting a plaster on a child or giving medicines, etc.
- looking after babies and young children,

**between** handling raw foods (meat, fish, poultry and eggs) and touching any other food or kitchen utensils, and **after**:

- handling raw foods, particularly meat, fish and poultry and raw eggs in their shells
- going to the toilet

- coughing or sneezing (into your hands or a tissue)
- touching your hair or face
- playing outside
- touching rubbish/waste bins; cleaning cat litter boxes or using chemical cleansers
- changing nappies
- caring for someone who is ill, especially with tummy upsets
- handling and stroking pets or farm animals; gardening, even if you wear gloves
- smoking.

## Waste disposal

All types of waste (nappies, used tissues and food scraps) can contain germs and must be disposed of promptly and correctly. Children should not be able to gain access to any waste bins.

## Children who become ill in the setting

It is often in an early years setting that a child first shows signs and symptoms of an infectious illness. The setting's policy will outline the time period that children need to stay away in the event of a common infectious disease, such as chicken pox or measles. If the child becomes ill in the setting, he or she should be kept away from other children while waiting to be taken home. This will help to prevent cross-infection.

## Safe preparation and storage of food and milk

Young children are particularly vulnerable to the bacteria that can cause food poisoning or

## Guidelines for disposing of waste

- **Always** wear disposable gloves when handling any bodily waste, such as blood, urine, vomit and faeces. Always dispose of the gloves and wash your hands after dealing with such waste, even though gloves have been worn.
- A dilute bleach (hypochlorite) solution should be used to mop up any spillages.
- Different types of waste should be kept in separate covered bins in designated areas; food waste should be kept well away from toilet waste.
- Soiled nappies, dressings, disposable towels and gloves should be placed in a sealed bag before being put in a plastic-lined, covered bin for incineration.
- Always cover any cuts and open sores with waterproof adhesive plasters.

## Guidelines for the safe storage of food

- Keep food cold. The fridge should be kept as cold as possible without actually freezing the food (1–5°C or 34–41°F).
- Cover or wrap food with food wrap or microwave cling film.
- Never refreeze food which has begun to thaw.
- Do not use foods that are past their sell-by or best-before date.
- Always read instructions on the label when storing food.
- Once a tin is opened, store the contents in a covered dish in the fridge.
- Store raw foods at the bottom of the fridge so that juices cannot drip onto cooked food.
- Thaw frozen meat completely before cooking.

gastroenteritis. Bacteria multiply rapidly in warm, moist foods and can enter food without causing the food to look, smell or even taste bad. So it is very important to store, prepare and cook food safely, and to keep the kitchen clean.

Hands are the most obvious way in which a person can contaminate food because they touch utensils, work surfaces and the food itself when being prepared, served or eaten. Nails can also harbour dirt and bacteria and should be kept short and clean

at all times. Even healthy people carry food poisoning bacteria on their bodies. These can be spread to the hands through touching parts of the body that contain them, such as the nose, mouth or bottom and then from the hands to the food.

## At risk: babies and young children

Babies and very young children are at particular risk from food poisoning. They have immature immune systems, and infection can spread very quickly if there is a lack of supervised thorough hand-washing after using the toilet and before eating, and from touching contaminated toilet seats and tap handles. Many young children also put their hands, fingers and thumbs in their mouths frequently, so their hands should be kept clean.

### Key terms

**Gastroenteritis** – Inflammation of the stomach and intestines, often causing sudden and violent upsets. Diarrhoea, cramps, nausea and vomiting are common symptoms.

## Guidelines for the safe preparation and cooking of food

- Always wash hands in warm water and soap and dry on a clean towel, before handling food and after handling raw foods, especially meat.
- Wear clean protective clothing which is solely for use in the kitchen.
- Keep food covered at all times.
- Wash all fruits and vegetables before eating. Peel and top carrots, and peel fruits such as apples.
- Never cough or sneeze over food.
- Always cover any septic cuts or boils with a waterproof dressing.
- Never smoke in any room which is used for food.
- Keep work surfaces and chopping boards clean and disinfected; use separate boards for raw meat, fish, vegetables etc. to avoid cross-contamination.
- Make sure that meat dishes are thoroughly cooked.
- Avoid raw eggs. They sometimes contain *salmonella* bacteria, which may cause food poisoning. (Also avoid giving children *uncooked* cake mixture, home-made ice creams, mayonnaise, or desserts that contain uncooked raw egg.) When cooking eggs, the egg yolk and white should be firm.
- When re-heating food, make sure that it is piping hot all the way through, and allow to cool slightly before giving it to children. When using a microwave, always stir and check the temperature of the food before feeding children, to avoid burning from hot spots.
- Avoid having leftovers – they are a common cause of food poisoning.

## Storing formula milk

The Department of Health guidelines state that storing formula milk for any length of time increases the risk of infection. They recommend that every feed be made up fresh, only as the baby needs it. If this is not possible (for example, because of an outing), then ready-to-use liquid formula should be used.

## Storing breast milk

Mothers who are breastfeeding their baby may bring in their expressed breast milk, either fresh or frozen, in sterilised bottles. The Department of Health recommends that breast milk can then be stored:

- in the fridge for up to five days at 4°C or lower
- for two weeks in the ice compartment of a fridge
- for up to six months in a freezer.

Frozen breast milk should be defrosted in the fridge and given to the baby straight away. It must never be re-frozen once it is thawed.

# The importance of high quality, balanced nutrition

A healthy diet consists of a wide variety of foods to help the body to grow and to provide energy. It must include enough of these nutrients (proteins, fats, carbohydrates, vitamins, minerals and fibre) as well as water to fuel and maintain the body's vital functions.

### Key terms

**Nutrients** – Nutrients are the essential components of food which provide the individual with the necessary requirements for bodily functions.

## In Practice

**Basic food hygiene**

When serving food and clearing away after meals and snacks, you should observe the rules of food hygiene:

❑ Wash your hands using soap and warm water and dry them on a clean towel.

❑ Wear clean protective clothing.

❑ Ensure that any washing-up by hand is done thoroughly in hot water, with detergent (and use rubber gloves).

❑ Cover cups/beakers with a clean cloth and air-dry where possible.

❑ Drying-up cloths should be replaced every day with clean ones.

❑ Never cough or sneeze over food.

# Types of food

Types of food can be arranged into five groups, based on the **nutrients** they provide. To ensure a balanced, healthy diet, some foods from each group should be included in a child's diet every day.

## Group one: Carbohydrates (bread, other cereals and potatoes)

Foods in this group are needed to provide energy. They also contain vitamins and minerals. Foods in this group include rice, all types of bread, breakfast cereals, pasta, potato and couscous. Wholemeal bread, wholegrain cereals and potatoes in their skins all increase the fibre content of the diet. Bran should *not* be given to children as an extra source of fibre as it can interfere with the absorption of calcium and iron, and may also cause stomach cramps.

All meals throughout the day should include foods from this group.

### For children aged between 1 and 4 years

A mixture of some white and some wholegrain varieties of bread should be offered; this is because the fibre content from *only* wholegrain cereals would be too high for toddlers. Excess fibre can fill up the stomach and reduce their food intake, leading to a restriction of their energy and nutrient intake.

## Group two: Fruit and vegetables

Fruit and vegetables are full of vitamins, minerals and fibre, all of which are needed to maintain good health. They are also very low in fat. Many children will eat slices of raw vegetables or salad in place of cooked vegetables, such as carrots, cucumber, tomato or peppers. Children who are reluctant to eat vegetables should be given fruit or fruit juice instead. Fruit and vegetables are best eaten raw, because their vitamin content is easily destroyed by cooking and processing.

A fruit or vegetable that is high in vitamin C should be included in children's diets every day; for example, tomatoes, citrus fruits such as oranges and grapefruit, kiwi fruit and sweet peppers.

## Group three: Milk and dairy foods

Foods in this group are needed to provide energy, and also to store energy in the body and insulate it against the cold. Whole milk and full-fat dairy products are a good source of vitamin A, which helps the body to resist infections and is needed for healthy skin and eyes. Children require about one pint (500 ml) of milk each day to ensure an adequate intake of calcium which is needed to develop strong bones and teeth. Goats' milk or calcium-enriched soya milk and their products can be directly substituted for cows' milk. If a child cannot achieve this milk intake, equivalent amounts of calcium can be taken from yoghurt, cheese, fromage frais etc.

Reduced-fat milks should not generally be given to children under 5 years because of their lower energy and fat-soluble-vitamin content. However, semi-skimmed milk may be introduced from 2 years of age, provided that the child's overall diet is adequate.

## Group four: Meat, fish and alternatives

Young children need protein and iron to grow and develop. Meat, fish, eggs, nuts, pulses (such as beans, lentils and peas) and foods made from pulses (such as tofu, hummus and soya mince) are very good sources of protein and iron. When eggs, pulses and nuts are served, a food or drink high in vitamin C should also be included in the meal to ensure good absorption of iron.

Children should be given one or two portions from this group each day. Meat and fish also contain zinc, which is important for healing wounds and making many of the body's processes function properly.

### Nuts

Children under 5 should not be offered whole nuts as they may cause choking. Peanut butter and ground or chopped nuts in recipes are fine, but always be aware of the risk of nut allergy (see page 298 later in this chapter).

## Group five: Fatty and sugary foods

Fats and oils are found in the foods from the four groups; for instance, meat and cheese contain fat and some vegetables contain oil. They provide toddlers with energy and vitamins A, E and D. Olive, walnut, rapeseed and soya oils give a good balance of omega fats.

Sweets, cakes, chocolate and crisps are all **high-energy** foods, but they have little other nutritional value. If children eat a lot of these foods, they run the risk of putting on weight and suffering tooth decay. However, children may be offered *limited* amounts of foods with extra fat or sugar – biscuits, cakes, chocolate, crisps and sweet drinks – as long as these items are not *replacing* food from the other four food groups.

Sweetened drinks should be well diluted and offered with food at a meal or snack to lessen their tendency to cause dental decay. Salty snacks such as crisps should be offered only rarely.

## Minerals and vitamins: Iron, calcium and vitamin D in children's diets

### Iron

Iron is an important dietary mineral involved in different bodily functions, including the transport of oxygen in the blood. This is essential in providing energy for daily life. Lack of iron often leads to anaemia, which can hold back both physical and mental development. Children most at risk are those who are poor eaters or on restricted diets.

Iron comes in two forms, either:

- in foods from **animal sources** (especially meat) which is easily absorbed by the body, or
- in **plant foods**, which is not quite so easy for the body to absorb.

If possible, children should be given a portion of meat or fish every day, and kidney or liver once a week. Even a small portion of meat or fish is useful because it also helps the body to absorb iron from other food sources.

If children do not eat meat or fish, they must be offered plenty of iron-rich alternatives, such as egg yolks, dried fruit, beans and lentils, and green leafy vegetables. It is also a good idea to give foods or drinks that are high in vitamin C at mealtimes, as this helps the absorption of iron from non-meat sources.

### Calcium and vitamin D

Children need calcium for maintaining and repairing growing bones and teeth, and for the correct functioning of muscles and blood clotting. Calcium is:

- found in milk, cheese, yoghurt and other dairy products
- only absorbed by the body if it is taken with vitamin D.

The skin can make all the vitamin D that a body needs, when it is exposed to gentle sunlight. People with darker skin are at greater risk of vitamin D deficiencies (such as rickets) because increased pigmentation reduces the capacity of the skin to manufacture the vitamin from sunlight. Sources of vitamin D include milk, fortified breakfast cereals, oily fish, meat, fortified margarine and tofu.

The UK health departments recommend that children under the age of 5 be given vitamin drops that contain vitamins A, C and D.

## The dangers of too much salt

Salt (sodium chloride) should be avoided as far as possible in the diets of young children, as their kidneys are not mature enough to cope with large amounts. It is important to be aware that many common foods, such as cheese, manufactured soup, packet meals and bread, are already quite high in added salt. Children will receive sufficient salt for their dietary needs from a normal balanced diet without adding any to food as it is cooked or at the table.

On average, children today are eating twice the recommended amount of salt. The recommended nutrient intake (RNI) for infants aged between 1 and 3 years is not more than 1.25g of salt every day; children aged between 4 and 6 years should consume no more than 1.75g. Many manufactured foods are marketed at children, and some of these can top their daily salt requirement in just one serving: a bag of crisps, for example. A small can (200g) of pasta shapes in tomato sauce contains *twice* the daily RNI of salt for a child aged between 1 and 3 years, and a third more than the daily RNI for child aged between 4 and 6 years.

## Dietary fibre

Dietary fibre (or roughage) is found in cereals, fruits and vegetables. Fibre is made up of the indigestible parts or compounds of plants, which pass relatively unchanged through our stomach and intestines. Fibre is needed to provide roughage to help to keep the food moving through the gut. A small amount of fibre is important for health in children under the age of 5 years, but too much fibre can cause problems as their digestive system is still immature. It could

also reduce energy intakes by 'bulking up' the diet. Providing a mixture of white bread and refined cereals, white rice and pasta as well as a few wholegrain varieties occasionally helps to maintain a healthy balance between fibre and nutrient intakes.

## Providing drinks for children

An adequate fluid intake will prevent dehydration and reduce the risk of constipation. Milk and water are the best drinks to give between meals and snacks as they do not harm teeth when taken from a cup or beaker. You should offer children something to drink several times during the day.

- Water is a much under-rated drink for the whole family. It quenches thirst without spoiling the appetite; if bottled water is preferred it should be still, not carbonated (fizzy) as this is acidic. More water should be given in hot weather in order to prevent dehydration.
- Research into how the brain develops has found that water is beneficial; many early years settings now make water available for children to help themselves.
- Milk is an excellent nourishing drink which provides valuable nutrients.

### Other drinks

All drinks that contain sugar can be harmful to teeth and can also take the edge off children's appetites. Examples are flavoured milks, fruit squashes, flavoured fizzy drinks, and fruit juices (containing natural sugar).

Unsweetened *diluted* fruit juice is a reasonable option for children (but not as good as water or milk), but ideally should only be offered at mealtimes. Low-sugar and diet fruit drinks contain artificial sweeteners and are best avoided.

Tea and coffee should *not* be given to children aged under 5 years, as they prevent the absorption of iron from foods. They also tend to fill children up without providing any nourishment.

For children aged 1 to 5 years:

- Offer around six to eight drinks per day from a beaker or cup (although more may be needed in very hot weather or when they are very active). One drink for this age group will be about 100–150 ml.

- Sweetened drinks, including diluted fruit juice, should only be consumed *with* (rather than between) meals, to reduce the risk of dental decay. Consumption of sugar-free fizzy or fruit-based drinks, although not recommended, should also be confined to mealtimes because the high acidity level of these drinks can cause dental decay.

## Planning balanced meals, snacks and drinks

Our eating habits, tastes and preferences are shaped very early on – in part by the example set to us by our parents and other carers, and by the food offered in childhood. These early influences often shape our ideas about food and eating throughout school and adult life. Some children can be choosy about the food they eat. This can be a source of anxiety for parents and for those who work with the children. However, as long as children eat some food from each of the **five food groups** – even if they are the same old favourites – there is no cause for worry.

### Meals and snacks

Most children really do need to eat between meals. Their stomachs are relatively small and so they fill up and empty faster than adult stomachs. Sugary foods should *not* be given as a snack, because sugar is an appetite depressant and may spoil the child's appetite for the main meal to follow.

The following foods have a high concentration of nutrients in a relatively small portion:

- breakfast cereal and milk
- toasted crumpet or teacake
- yoghurt or fromage frais
- glass of milk
- cheese and crackers or oatcakes
- crunchy muesli and yoghurt
- fresh fruit
- nuts, seeds or dried fruit
- fruit smoothies
- slice of fruit loaf or malt loaf.

**Figure 14.4** Enjoying a healthy snack

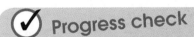

### Progress check

**A balanced diet**

1. List the five main food groups which provide nutrients in the diet.
2. Which food group provides children with energy? Give four examples of foods in this group.
3. Why is it important for children to have calcium in their daily diet?

## Respecting the individual

Every child is unique, and gradually develops a whole catalogue of likes, strong dislikes and mild preferences regarding food and mealtimes. For example:

- Some children like their food covered in sauces while others prefer it dry.

- Some like every food kept separate from the others on the plate.
- Many do not like 'tough' meat or foods that are difficult to chew.

It is important to respect a child's likes and dislikes and offer alternative foods from the same food group where necessary. With time, tastes often change, so it is important to keep offering young children different foods.

## Food allergies

A food allergy is an abnormal response (an allergic reaction) of the immune system to otherwise harmless foods. Up to 5 per cent of children have food allergies. Most children outgrow their allergy, although an allergy to peanuts and some other tree nuts is considered life-long. There are eight foods that cause 90 per cent of all food allergic reactions. These are:

- peanuts
- soy
- tree nuts (such as almonds, walnuts, pecans etc.)
- wheat
- milk
- shellfish
- eggs
- fish.

Milk is the most common cause of food allergies in children, but peanuts, nuts, fish and shellfish commonly cause the most severe reactions.

## What are the symptoms of an allergic reaction?

Symptoms of an allergic response can include:

- vomiting
- hives (or urticaria) – an itchy raised rash usually found on the trunk or limbs
- itching or tightness in the throat
- diarrhoea
- eczema
- difficulty in breathing
- cramps
- itching or swelling of the lips, tongue or mouth
- wheezing.

Allergic symptoms can begin within minutes and up to one hour after ingesting the food.

## Anaphylaxis

In rare cases of food allergy, just *one bite* of food can bring on **anaphylaxis**. This is a severe reaction that involves various areas of the body simultaneously. In extreme cases, it can cause death.

Anaphylaxis is a sudden and severe potentially life-threatening allergic reaction. It can be caused by insect stings or medications, as well as by a food allergy. Although potentially any food can cause anaphylaxis, peanuts, nuts, shellfish, fish and eggs are foods that most commonly cause this reaction.

Symptoms of anaphylaxis may include all those listed above for food allergies. In addition, the child's breathing is seriously impaired and the pulse rate becomes rapid.

Anaphylaxis is fortunately very rare, but is also very dangerous:

- Symptoms can occur in as little as 5 to 15 minutes.
- As little as half a peanut can cause a fatal reaction in severely allergic individuals.
- Some severely allergic children can have a reaction if milk is splashed on their skin.
- Being kissed by somebody who has eaten peanuts for example, can cause a reaction in severely allergic individuals.

## Emergency treatment of anaphylaxis

1 **Summon medical help immediately**. The child will need oxygen and a life-saving injection of adrenaline.
2 **Place the child in a sitting position** to help relieve any breathing difficulty.
3 Be prepared to resuscitate if necessary.

In some settings attended by a child or children known to be at risk from anaphylaxis, the staff may be trained to give the adrenaline injection by Epipen.

## How can food allergies be managed?

The only way to manage food allergies is strictly to avoid the foods to which the child is allergic. It is important to learn how to interpret ingredients on food labels and how to spot high-risk foods. Many children outgrow earlier food-allergic symptoms as they get older, but parents will need professional support and advice to ensure that their child is receiving a safe, balanced diet.

### Key terms

**Allergy** – Abnormal sensitivity reaction of the body to substances that are usually harmless.

**Anaphylaxis** – An immediate and severe allergic response; a shock reaction to a substance.

## Food intolerances

Food intolerance is an adverse reaction to some sort of food or ingredient that occurs **every time** the food is eaten, but particularly if larger quantities are consumed. Food intolerance is not the same as:

- a food allergy, because the immune system is not activated
- food poisoning, which is caused by toxic substances that would cause symptoms in anyone who ate the food.

Food intolerance does not include **psychological** reactions to food; it is much more common than food allergy.

Some babies develop an intolerance to cows' milk protein; the most common symptoms are vomiting, diarrhoea and failure to thrive. After weaning, foods most likely to cause an adverse reaction in babies are hen's eggs, fish, wheat and other cereals, citrus fruits and pork.

Sometimes an adverse reaction will be temporary (perhaps following an illness), but the offending food should always be removed from the child's diet. Dietetic advice should be sought before any changes to a balanced diet are made.

## Coeliac disease

Coeliac disease is a condition in which the lining of the small intestine is damaged by **gluten**, a protein found in wheat and rye. In babies, it is usually diagnosed about three months after weaning onto solids containing gluten, but some children do not show any symptoms until they are older. Treatment for coeliac disease is by gluten-free diet which needs to be maintained for the rest of the person's life. All formula milks available in the UK are gluten-free, and many manufactured baby foods are also gluten-free. Any cakes, bread and biscuits should be made from gluten-free flour, and labels on processed foods should be read carefully to ensure that there is no 'hidden' wheat product in the ingredients list.

**Note** that commercially available 'Play-doh' is made from 40 per cent ordinary flour, as is the homemade variety used in nurseries and playgroups. Extra vigilance is needed by staff to stop children with coeliac disease from putting it in their mouth; even safer, dough can always be made using gluten-free flour.

## Diabetes

*Diabetes mellitus* occurs in one out of every 500 children under the age of about 16 years, and results in difficulty in converting carbohydrate into energy due to the underproduction of insulin. Insulin is usually given by daily injection, and a diet sheet will be devised by the hospital dietician. It is important that mealtimes be *regular* and that some carbohydrate (group one food) be included at every meal. Children with diabetes should be advised to carry glucose sweets whenever they are away from home in case of **hypoglycaemia** (low blood sugar).

# Dietary requirements of different cultural or religious groups

The UK is home to a multicultural and multi-ethnic society. The Asian community represents the largest ethnic minority in the UK, about 1.25 million people. Asian dietary customs are mainly related to the beliefs of the three main religious groups: Muslims (or Moslems), Hindus and Sikhs. It is important to find out from parents about any specific dietary requirements concerning the foods that can be prepared and served for their children.

## Food and festivals from different cultures

Particular foods are associated with certain religious festivals; for example, mince pies at Christmas and pancakes on Shrove Tuesday in the Christian tradition, and in the Hindu tradition poori are eaten at Diwali. Providing foods from different cultures within an early years setting is a very good way of celebrating these festivals. Parents of children from ethnic minority groups are usually very pleased to be asked for advice on how to celebrate festivals with food, and may even be prepared to contribute some samples.

## Research Activity

### Different traditions

Find out about the dietary requirements and restrictions in *one* cultural or religious group, different from your own. Choose from:

- Jewish
- Muslim (Islamic)
- Hindu
- Rastafarian.

## Cultural needs

The nursery school where you are working has 22 white British children and one child from Turkey. The nursery teacher says, 'We only offer English food here because we do not have any children from ethnic minorities.' Discuss this statement and decide what your approach would be if you were in charge of the nursery.

## Vegetarians

Children who are on a vegetarian diet do not eat meat or fish, so they need an alternative to meat, fish and chicken as the main sources of protein. These could include cheese and eggs, milk and pulses (lentils and beans).

They also need enough iron; it is more difficult to absorb from vegetable sources than from meat, so a young child needs to obtain iron from sources such as:

- leafy green vegetables – such as spinach and watercress
- pulses (beans, lentils and chick peas)
- dried fruit (such as apricots, raisins and sultanas)
- some breakfast cereals.

It is easier to absorb iron from our food if it is eaten *with* foods containing vitamin C foods such as fruit and vegetables or diluted fruit juices at mealtimes.

## Vegans

A vegan diet completely excludes *all* foods of animal origin; that is, animal flesh, milk and milk products, eggs, honey and all additives that may be of animal origin. A vegan diet is based on cereals and cereal products, pulses, fruits, vegetables, nuts and seeds. Human breast milk is acceptable for vegan babies.

## Ethical and environmentally-aware diets

Some parents will only buy and use food that has been ethically produced, such as organic foods, foods approved by the Soil Association and/or Fairtrade products.

| Muslims | Hindus | Sikhs |
|---|---|---|
| Muslims practise the Islamic religion, and their holy book, The Koran, provides them with their food laws.<br><br>Unlawful foods (called haram) are: pork, all meat which has not been rendered lawful (halal), alcohol and fish without scales.<br><br>Wheat, in the form of chapattis, and rice are the staple foods.<br><br>The Koran dictates that children should be breastfed up to the age of 2 years.<br><br>Fasting: during the lunar month of Ramadan Muslims fast between sunrise and sunset; fasting involves abstinence from all food and drink, so many Muslims rise early to eat before dawn in order to maintain their energy levels. Children under 12 years and the elderly are exempt from fasting. | Wheat is the main staple food eaten by Hindus in the UK; it is used to make types of bread called chapattis, puris and parathas. Orthodox Hindus are strict vegetarians as they believe in Ahimsa – non-violence towards all living beings – and a minority practise veganism. Some will eat dairy products and eggs, while others will refuse eggs on the grounds that they are a potential source of life.<br><br>Even non-vegetarians do not eat beef as the cow is considered a sacred animal, and it is unusual for pork to be eaten as the pig is considered unclean. Ghee (clarified butter) and vegetable oil are used in cooking.<br><br>Fasting: common for certain festivals, such as Mahshivrati (the birthday of Lord Shiva). | Most Sikhs will not eat pork or beef or any meat that is killed by the halal method. Some Sikhs are vegetarian, but many eat chicken, lamb and fish. Wheat and rice are staple foods.<br><br>Fasting: Devout Sikhs will fast once or twice a week, and most will fast on the first day of the Punjabi month or when there is a full moon. |

| Afro-Caribbean diets | Jewish diets | Rastafarians |
|---|---|---|
| The Afro-Caribbean community is the second largest ethnic minority group in the UK. Dietary practices within the community vary widely. Many people include a wide variety of European foods in their diet alongside the traditional foods of cornmeal, coconut, green banana, plantain, okra and yam. Although Afro-Caribbean people are generally Christian, a minority are Rastafarians. | Jewish people observe dietary laws which state that animals and birds must be slaughtered by the Jewish method to render them kosher (acceptable). Milk and meat must never be cooked or eaten together, and pork in any form is forbidden.<br><br>Shellfish are not allowed as they are thought to harbour disease. Only fish with fins and scales may be eaten.<br><br>Fasting: The most holy day of the Jewish calendar is Yom Kippur (the Day of Atonement), when Jewish people fast for 25 hours. | Dietary practices are based on laws laid down by Moses in the Book of Genesis in the Bible. These laws state that certain types of meat should be avoided. The majority of followers will only eat Ital foods, which are foods considered to be in a whole or natural state. Most Rastafarians are vegetarians and will not consume processed or preserved foods. No added salt; no coffee. |

**Table 14.2** Multicultural provision and dietary implications

# Educating children and adults in effective food management

In recent years there has been increasing public concern about the quality of children's diets, rapidly increasing rates of child obesity, diet-related disorders, and low consumption of fruit and vegetables by children. Different conditions may occur in childhood which are often directly related to a poor or unbalanced diet; these are a result of either malnutrition or under-nutrition, and include:

- **failure to thrive** (or faltering growth): poor growth and physical development
- **dental caries** or tooth decay: associated with a high consumption of sugar in snacks and fizzy drinks
- **obesity**: children who are overweight are more likely to become obese adults
- **nutritional anaemia**: due to an insufficient intake of iron, folic acid and vitamin B12
- **increased susceptibility to infections**: particularly upper respiratory infections, such as colds and bronchitis.

## Children who are overweight or underweight

It is much more difficult to interpret weight in children than it is in adults. This is because children are still growing, so you need to take into account their age, height and gender. Experts use a special 'weight for height calculator' to work out whether a child is in the healthy weight, overweight or very overweight range.

Sometimes parents are unaware that their child is overweight or obese, or that he or she regularly consumes much more high-calorie foods and drinks than others of the same age. Obesity can lead to emotional problems as well as to the physical problem of being more prone to infections: an overweight child may be taunted by others, and will be unable to participate in the same vigorous play as their peers. A child who is diagnosed as being overweight will usually be prescribed a diet low in fat and sugar, and high-fibre carbohydrates are encouraged, such as wholemeal bread and other cereals. The child who is suddenly not permitted crisps, chips and snacks between meals will need much support and encouragement from parents and other adults. If you observe that a child seems either overweight or underweight for their height, then it is important that parents are consulted and that professional help is sought.

## Food refusal

Many children go through phases of refusing to eat certain foods or not wanting to eat anything much at all. This is particularly common in children up to the age of 5, and is a normal part of growing up and asserting their independence. Eating can quickly become a focus for conflict and tension at home, with parents feeling anxious and out of control. Food refusal often starts because it is one of the few ways in which children can exert influence over their parents. Reasons for food refusal in young children include the following:

### Slower growth and small appetites

Growth slows down in a child's second year. This means that toddlers often have small appetites and need less food. Children eat according to their appetite, and this can vary from day to day. Some children eat in spurts; they may eat much one day and very little the next. It also depends on how active they have been during the day.

### Distraction

Young children have no concept of time. Their world has become an exciting place to explore and food can seem less important when there are so many other things to do.

### Grazing and snacking

Toddlers rarely follow a traditional meal pattern. They tend to need small and regular snacks. Parents may offer sweets or crisps throughout the day so that children 'won't go hungry'. Children then become even less inclined to eat their meals when they know that they can fill up on their favourite snacks. Large quantities of milk or other drinks throughout the day also take the edge off a child's appetite.

### Fussy eating and food fads

Showing independence is part of normal child development, and this often includes refusing to eat foods 'to see what will happen'. It is quite normal for children to have certain times when their food choices become very limited. For example, they will only eat food prepared and presented in a certain way. Some decide they do not like mixed-up food or different foods touching each other on the plate, and they develop strong likes and dislikes that frequently change.

### New textures and tastes

Children are experimenting with, or being asked to try, new textures and tastes. Rejecting a food does not always mean the child does not like it; they may eat it the very next day. Many adults reject certain foods that are eaten widely in other cultures, such as sheep's eyeballs or dog.

### Seeking attention

Children are testing their parents' reactions and learning the effects of their uncooperative behaviour. They have learnt to say 'no' and may welcome all the attention they are getting by refusing to eat (or taking ages to eat) a lovingly prepared meal.

## How to cope with food refusal

Research shows that one-third of all parents worry that their child is not eating enough, but unless they are ill, young children will never voluntarily starve themselves. If a child seems to be healthy and energetic, they are almost certainly eating enough. There is plenty of advice for parents and carers from health experts and child dieticians on how to cope with their child's refusal of food, including the following tips:

- Never force-feed a child, either by pushing food into his mouth or by threatening punishment or withdrawal of a treat.
- Keep calm and try not to make a fuss of whether their child is eating or not. Instead, try to make mealtimes pleasant, social occasions, because if children associate mealtimes with an enjoyable event, they will want to repeat it.
- Encourage self-feeding and exploration of food from an early age, without worrying about the mess.
- Offer alternative foods from every food group: if a child dislikes cheese, they may eat yoghurt.
- Provide healthy, nutritious snacks between meals as these play an important part in the energy intake of young children. Ideas include fresh and dried fruits, crackers with cheese or peanut butter, yoghurt, plain biscuits, scones or buns.

- Avoid giving sweets and crisps between meals to children who refuse food at mealtimes.

# Providing physical care for children

It is important to provide physical care for children which is appropriate to their individual needs and their stage of development. The routine care of children's skin, hair and teeth is discussed in Chapter 18 (Unit CYPOP 2). For this learning outcome, you will need to read through the section from pages 381 to 391 to understand how to provide physical care, and also the section below which focuses on children from 3 years and older.

## Encourage learning and development during routines

As they grow and develop, young children should be encouraged to develop self-care skills in their personal care routines. These skills include being able to:

- wash their hands
- use the toilet independently
- dress themselves
- brush their hair
- pour drinks and to feed themselves.

Many of these skills are learned through children copying adult behaviour.

## Supporting independence and self-care

Children like to feel independent, but sometimes they need an adult's encouragement to feel that they are capable and that adults believe that they can do it. Teaching independence with self-care skills such as hand-washing, brushing teeth, and dressing and undressing is an important step in development that can be achieved when children are supported in a positive and encouraging way.

### Hand-washing

Hand-washing is an important skill that children need to learn. It can be made into a fun activity by singing 'This is the way we wash/dry our hands . . .

on a cold/hot and frosty/sunny morning'. Children soon learn that hand-washing is a routine task that must always be done after going to the toilet, before meals and after playing outdoors.

## Dressing and undressing

Children need plenty of time and support to learn how to dress and undress themselves. You can help by breaking the process down into steps and encouraging them when they have mastered the first step by offering descriptive praise (see below).

## Toileting

It is important to encourage self-care skills when children are using the toilet independently. They should be encouraged to pull their own pants down and shown how to wipe their bottoms – for example, showing girls how to wipe from the front to the back. You also need children to learn that going to the toilet is a private activity and to withdraw by partially closing the door while remaining nearby in case help is needed.

## Brushing teeth

It is essential to establish a tooth-brushing routine. Children should brush after meals, after snacks, and before bedtime, so that it becomes a lifelong habit. Offering children a choice during routines increases the likelihood that they will do the activity and gives them a sense of control. So for example, when brushing teeth, you could say, 'Do you want to use the minty toothpaste or the strawberry toothpaste?'

## Engaging with children during care routines to support their learning and development

### Encourage

It is very important that you encourage *all* attempts when the child is first learning how to do a routine. If you discourage children because it was not done *quite* right, their attempts at trying might stop.

### Practice makes perfect

Remember that young children need a lot of practice (and support) before they are able to carry out new

tasks independently. As children gain the skills required for the task, we need to slow down the routine and expect that it might take extra time to complete.

### Step by step

Break down activities and tasks and activities into easy, manageable steps; for example:

- Cut food up into bite-size pieces.
- Have well-defined places to pack away toys.
- Use a non-slip mat under a baby's bowl when feeding.
- Use child-size cutlery and a drinking cup with a lid to avoid spills.
- Use a footstool to reach the bathroom basin.
- Use small steps and a toilet seat to make the child feel more secure when going to the 'big' toilet.
- Choose clothing with bigger buttons and shoes with velcro fastenings.

### Support

It is important to let children know that you understand their feelings when they are becoming frustrated, and that you will support them so that they feel successful. For example: 'I know it's hard to get your hands really dry; let me help'.

### Praise

Praise every little attempt to do any step. Attention to a child's use of a new skill will strengthen that skill. Effective praise is **descriptive praise**; for example, 'Thank you for putting your cup on the side there – it stopped it from being knocked over', or 'Putting your shoes on all by yourself so quickly was great as now we have more time to play outside'. Children will learn that when you offer descriptive praise (rather than just saying 'Clever boy'), you are teaching them what you like and why you liked it. They are more likely to do it again.

### Modelling

First, model how to do the first step and then say, 'Now you show me'. Show one step at a time, allowing time for the child to process the information and imitate what you did before moving to the next step.

# Regulations concerning management of medicines

Some children have illnesses or chronic medical conditions which are controlled by medication. Children with asthma or allergies will require the medication to be kept in the setting in case it is needed. Procedures to follow for the storage and administration of any medicines must comply with the regulations of your home country.

In England, the EYFS issued a guidance document: *Managing Medicines in Schools and Early Years Setting*. This requires settings to do the following:

1 **Policy**: Have a policy about the management and administration of medicines.
2 **Written record**: every medicine given to children must be written down, and this record is shared with the child's parents or carers.
3 **Parent consent forms**: ensure that parent consent forms have been completed, giving permission for each and every medicine prior to it being administered. The consent form must be very precise and contain the following information:

  • full name of child and date of birth
  • name of medication and strength
  • who prescribed it
  • dosage to be given in the setting
  • how the medication should be stored (such as in the fridge) and the expiry date
  • any possible side effects that may be expected
  • signature, printed name of parent and date.

If the administration of the medicine requires any technical or medical knowledge, individual training should be provided for the staff team from a suitably qualified health professional. The manager will decide who administers the medication in your setting. It might be on a voluntary basis; often the child's key person takes the responsibility, or the task could form part of an employee's contract.

It is good practice for two members of staff to be present when administering medication, and for each of them to sign the record sheet, which should include date, time, dosage, and space for the parent's or carer's signature when he or she collects the child.

The Control of Substances Hazardous to Health Regulations 1994 (COSHH) states that medicines should be kept in a safe place, preferably in a locked cupboard, clearly labelled with the child's name. The exception to this rule is the use of inhalers for children with asthma. The inhaler should be kept nearby for the child, in a place easily reached by an adult yet out of reach of other children (for example, a high shelf).

# Lifting and handling children and equipment in the work setting

Lifting and carrying children and moving the equipment used in early years settings could lead to manual handling injuries such as sprains, strains and back injuries. The setting's policy will give guidance on how to manage lifting and handling tasks. The setting should also have carried out a risk assessment to cover situations where practitioners might be expected to lift or carry children or pieces of equipment.

Firstly, think about the task and make your *own* risk assessment before lifting or moving children or equipment. If you think that it is too heavy to lift: do not do it! Seek assistance and advice from your line manager instead.

Secondly, if you *do* have to lift something or somebody from the ground, you must protect your back from injury by following these rules:

1 Keep your feet apart.
2 Bend your knees and keep your back upright.
3 Use both hands to get a secure hold.
4 Keep your shoulders level, your back upright and slowly straighten your legs.
5 To put the load down, take the weight on the legs by bending your knees.

Settings for practitioners who work with children with physical disabilities can present risks to both children and adults. In lifting children with disabilities, often two practitioners need to work together, or there may be a hoist or lifting pad to help reduce the risk of injury. In this case, instructions on their use would need to be provided by the manufacturer. If a member of staff is pregnant, it is important for the setting to re-assess any lifting of children and equipment and to carry out risk assessments accordingly.

 Websites and resources

**Websites**
**The Food Standards Agency**
The Food Standards Agency carries out a range of work to make sure that food is safe to eat, including funding research on chemical, microbiological and radiological safety, as well as food hygiene and allergy:
**www.food.gov.uk**

**Weight Concern**
Weight Concern is a registered charity set up in 1997 to tackle the rising problem of obesity in the United Kingdom:
**www.weightconcern.org.uk**

**Books**
Meggitt, C. (2003) *Food Hygiene and Safety*. Heinemann Educational Publishers.

# 15 Professional practice in early years settings: Unit EYMP 4

The early years sector is a dynamic and vitally important sector which requires high standards of professional practice. Those who work in the early years sector play a crucial role in shaping the lives of future generations. This chapter covers the range of early years settings and the current policies and influences on the early years sector. It includes how to support diversity, inclusion and participation in early years settings, and covers the application of principles and values in day-to-day practice. The chapter revisits the issues of professional practice, reflection and review, and requires a focused approach to the development of strategies to address professional development in areas identified as challenging.

## Learning outcomes

*By the end of this chapter you will:*

1. *Understand the scope and purposes of the early years sector.*
2. *Understand current policies and influences on the early years sector.*
3. *Understand how to support diversity, inclusion and participation in early years settings.*
4. *Be able to review own practice in promoting diversity, inclusion and participation in early years settings.*

## Understand the scope and purposes of the early years sector

Young children need both education and care. Children are not made up of separate parts: a child is a whole person. It is inappropriate to talk about either education of or caring for young children. Instead, the term 'integrated early years settings' is used to describe places that provide education and care for young children. Children need good physical and health care as much as they need new, interesting and stimulating experiences.

## The range of early years settings reflects the scope and purpose of the sector

A statutory service is one that is provided by the state. Some statutory services are provided by central government and funded from central taxation, such as the National Health Service (NHS). Others are provided by local government and funded by a combination of local and central taxation, such as education and social service departments.

### Children's services

From 2006, education and social care services for children have been brought together under a **Director of Children's Services** in every local authority in England. In Scotland, Wales and Northern Ireland, local authorities nominate a senior officer and elected member/non-executive director to take the lead responsibility for children.

Social services provide a range of care and support for children and families, including:

**Figure 15.1** A private day nursery

- families where children are assessed as **being in need** (including disabled children)
- children who may be suffering '**significant harm**' – for example, from violence in the home or from some form of child abuse (this aspect of social work is known as **child protection**)
- children who require **looking after** by the local authority (through fostering or residential care)
- children who are placed for **adoption**.

## Education services for children

The **Department for Education** (DfE) is headed by the Secretary of State for Education, and is responsible for deciding on policies and funding to the local education authorities.

Currently, all 3- and 4-year-old children are entitled to free early education for 12.5 hours per week for 38 weeks of the year. Children under the age of 5 years may attend any of the following:

- maintained (or state) nursery schools
- nursery classes attached to primary schools
- playgroups or preschools in the voluntary sector
- privately run nurseries
- children's centres
- home learning environment (HLE): many young children are cared for by childminders (in the childminder's home), nannies or grandparents.

## Maintained nursery schools

Maintained nursery schools are part of the provision made by some local education authorities.

Maintained nursery schools offer either full-time or part-time places for children of 3 years to the equivalent of the end of Reception. Exceptionally, children may start at 2 years and 6 months, but only if there is a recommendation and joint decision by the education, health and social services departments. There is a head teacher who has specialist training in the age group, and graduate-trained teachers working with qualified nursery nurses. Adult:child ratios are 1:10 in England and Wales, and 1:13 in Scotland and Northern Ireland.

## Nursery classes and nursery units

**Nursery classes** are attached to primary schools. The head teacher of the primary school may or may not be an expert in early years education. The class teacher will be a trained nursery teacher, who will work alongside a fully qualified nursery nurse. **Nursery units** are usually in a separate building, with a separate coordinator. They are larger than a nursery class, but will have the same adult:child ratio as the nursery class, which is 1:15. Like the nursery class, these units come under the management of the head teacher, who may or may not be trained to work with this age group.

## Local authority day nurseries

Local authority day nurseries are funded by social services and offer full-time provision for children under school age. They cater mainly for families who may be facing many challenges and who need support. They provide care from 8 a.m., often until 7 p.m., and are registered and inspected every year. Staffing levels are high, the usual ratio being one staff member for every four children. Some local authority day nurseries also operate as family centres, providing advice, guidance and counselling to families with difficulties.

## Extended services

In June 2005, the Government launched the prospectus, *Extended schools: Access to opportunities and services for all*, outlining the vision of extended schools. This vision is for all children to be able to access the following, through schools, by 2010:

- high-quality 'wraparound' child care, provided by the school site or other local providers, available 8 a.m. to 6 p.m. all year round
- a varied menu of activities, such as homework

clubs and study support, sport, music tuition, special interest clubs and volunteering
- parenting support, including information sessions for parents at key transition points, parenting programmes and family learning sessions
- swift and easy referral to a wide range of specialist support services, such as speech and language therapy, family support services and behaviour support
- providing wider community access to ICT, sports and arts facilities, including adult learning.

### Research Activity

#### Investigating education and care

Research the age at which children start compulsory schooling in six countries, including one country in each of the following regions: Africa, Asia, Europe and Australia/New Zealand. You can use the internet to help you to find this information.

## Integrated care and education for children

Recent legislation has led to a number of reforms in the delivery of care and education to children. While the school system remains largely unchanged, the statutory services for children from birth to 5 years are becoming increasingly integrated. This involves a new structure for the delivery of an integrated service, to include:

- Children's Trusts
- Early Years Foundation Stage (see Chapter 13, Unit EYMP 2 for more information on the EYFS)
- children's centres
- local authority day nurseries (see above).

## Children's Trusts

Children's Trusts are organisations in England which bring together health, education and social services for children, young people and families. Some take on responsibility for *all* children's services, from child protection to speech therapy, while others will focus on particularly vulnerable children, such as those with disabilities. The trusts employ a range of professionals, such as:

- social workers
- family support workers
- health visitors
- school nurses
- educational psychologists
- speech and language therapists
- child and adolescent mental health professionals.

Children's Trusts are currently underpinned by the Children Act 2004 duty to cooperate and to focus on improving outcomes for all children and young people. Trusts can also include Sure Start local programmes. Other local partners may include: housing, leisure services, the police, youth justice, independent sector organisations such as voluntary organisations, and community sector organisations such as churches. They will be led by local 'children's champions', whose role is to advocate the interests of children across different services.

Integrated early childhood services must include:

- early years provision (integrated child care and early education)
- social services
- relevant health services – for example, health visitors, antenatal, postnatal care
- services provided by Jobcentre Plus to assist parents to obtain work
- information services.

## Research Activity

### What kind of provision?

Research the early years provision made by your local authority.

1. What proportion of 4-year-old children are in reception classes?

2. What kind of provision is offered to most 3-year-old children and their families?

## Sure Start

Sure Start was an extensive government programme launched in the late 1990s as a cornerstone of the Government's drive to eradicate child poverty in 20 years, and to halve it within a decade. The first Sure Start local programmes were established in 1999, with the aim of improving the health and wellbeing of families and children from before birth to 4 years, so that they can flourish at home and when they begin school. The first centres were established in the most disadvantaged areas in the UK.

Sure Start local programmes were delivered by local partnerships and work with parents-to-be, parents, carers and children, to promote the physical, intellectual and social development of babies and young children. All Sure Start local programmes are now called Sure Start Children's Centres.

The coalition government states that it is committed to Sure Start children's centres as these play a crucial role in early intervention, ensuring that vulnerable families can get the help they need when they need it, as well as tackling issues early and helping to prevent costly problems from emerging later on. The government wants the network of children's centres to be retained but for them to focus much more effectively on those families who need them the most.

According to the Department for Education, there is enough money in the system, through the new Early Intervention Grant, to keep the existing network of children's centres open. Some children's centres have already closed and a further 250 are likely to close during 2011.

However, local authorities still have statutory duties under the Childcare Act 2006 in relation to the provision of children's centres – in particular to carry out consultation before opening, closing or significantly changing children's centres, and to secure sufficient provision to meet local need so far as is reasonably practicable. See the Department for Education website for statutory guidance about Sure Start children's centres –

http://www.education.gov.uk/
childrenandyoungpeople/earlylearningandchildcare/
surestart/a0074514/sure-start-childrens-centres-
statutory-guidance?cid=LAemail&pla=17Feb2011&t
ype=email

## Children's centres

The majority of children's centres will be developed
from Sure Start local programmes, neighbourhood
nurseries and Early Excellence Centres. Sure Start
children's centres are places where children under 5
years old and their families can receive holistic,
integrated services and information, and where they
can access help from multi-disciplinary teams of
professionals. Children's centres serve children and
their families from the antenatal period until
children start in Reception or Year 1 at primary
school. They also offer a base within the
community, linking to other providers of day care,
such as childminder networks and out-of-school
clubs.

Each centre offers the following services to families
with babies and preschool children:

- high quality early learning integrated with full day
  care provision (a minimum of ten hours a day, five
  days a week, 48 weeks a year)
- family support services
- a base for a childminder network
- child and family health services, including
  antenatal services
- support for children and parents with special
  needs
- links with Jobcentre Plus, local training providers
  and further and higher education institutions.

Children's centres may also offer other services,
including:

- training for parents – for example, parenting
  classes, basic skills, English as an additional
  language
- benefits advice and information
- toy libraries.

 **Progress check**

- Integrated early years settings are places that
  provide both education and care for young
  children.
- The EYFS enables children to learn through a
  range of activities and emphasises the importance
  of learning through play.
- All 3- and 4-year-old children are entitled to free
  early education for 12.5 hours per week for 38
  weeks of the year.
- Sure Start children's centres provide early
  education integrated with health and family
  support services, and child care from 8 a.m. to
  6 p.m.

## Voluntary services and self-help agencies for children and families

These are health, education and social care services
that are set up by **charities** to provide services which
local authorities can buy in, benefiting from their
expertise. Voluntary organisations are:

- non-profit-making
- non-statutory
- dependent on donations, fund-raising and
  government grants.

For example, **Children England** is an organisation
whose members are all registered charities that work
with children, young people and their families. They
range from very large national organisations, such as
**Barnardo's**, to small, locally based charities, such as
Mudiad Ysgolion Meithrin, which supports Welsh-
medium playgroups in Wales.

Voluntary organisations often arise because:

- there is a gap in services (for example, the
  Salvation Army provides hostels for homeless
  people)
- there is a need for a campaign, both to alert the
  public to an issue and to push for action to be
  taken (for example, Shelter, a pressure group for
  the homeless).

Within any local authority in the UK, there are child
care and education settings which come into the

category of voluntary or self-help provision. Two examples are community nurseries and the Pre-school Learning Alliance community preschools.

## Community nurseries

Community nurseries exist to provide a service to local children and their families. They are run by local community organisations (often with financial assistance from the local authority) or by charities such as Barnardo's and Save the Children. Most of these nurseries are open long enough to suit working parents or those at college. Many centres also provide or act as a venue for other services, including:

- parent and toddler groups
- drop-in crèches
- toy libraries
- after-school clubs.

## Pre-school Learning Alliance community preschools

Pre-school Learning Alliance community preschools (playgroups) offer children aged between 3 and 5 years an opportunity to learn through play.

- They usually operate on a part-time sessional basis. Sessions are normally two and a half hours each, morning or afternoon.
- The staff plan a varied curriculum which takes into account children's previous experiences and developing needs.
- The EYFS is adapted by each group to meet the needs of their own children and to allow them to make the most of a variety of learning opportunities that arise spontaneously through play.
- At many pre-school playgroups, parents and carers are encouraged to be involved, and there are often parent and toddler groups meeting at the same sites.

## Families Information Services

This service was set up by the government to provide information for parents about the range and costs of child care in their area. Their website has links to all local authorities: www.childcarelink.gov.uk. Parents without internet access could write directly to their local authority for printed information.

### Research Activity

**Voluntary organisations**

1. Write down the names of ten voluntary organisations (charities) that come into your mind. Research what these organisations do.
2. Now find ten voluntary organisations that you had not previously heard of. Find out what these organisations do.
3. Write down reasons why some voluntary organisations are better known to the public than others.

### Key terms

**Statutory service** – Any service provided and managed by the state or government, such as the NHS or a local authority day nursery.

**Voluntary organisation** – An association or society which has been created by its members rather than having been created by the state, such as a charity.

## The UK private sector

This sector comprises businesses that make profits. In education, this includes private nurseries. Private nurseries, hospitals and schools are legally required to be registered and inspected, and to follow guidelines laid down in law and by local authorities.

## Day nurseries, nursery schools, preparatory schools and kindergartens

- Private nursery schools and private day nurseries are available for those parents who can afford them, and some financial support is available to parents through government schemes. In addition, there are workplace nurseries which subsidise places so that staff and students in institutions can take up this form of care.
- These are required to appoint qualified staff, and to meet the National Standards for Day Care.

## Childminders, nannies and grandparents: home learning environment

- Children are looked after in their own homes by grandparents or nannies, or in the childminder's home.
- Childminders are offered training through the National Childminding Association.
- Nannies sometimes live with a family, but not always. Sometimes, they look after children from several different families.

# Understand current policies and influences on the early years sector

You should know and understand the current policies, frameworks and influences that are appropriate to your relevant UK Home Nation, either England, Scotland, Wales or Northern Ireland. For example, in England early years education is provided for in a wide range of settings including pre-school groups, playgroups, nursery centres, day nurseries, nursery schools and reception classes (with pupils aged between 4 and 5 years) in primary schools.

## Early Years Foundation Stage

Orders and regulations under section 39 of the Childcare Act 2006 brought the **Early Years Foundation Stage** (EYFS) into force in September 2008. All early years providers are required to use the EYFS to ensure a coherent and flexible approach to children's care, learning and development that will enable young children to achieve the five *Every Child Matters* outcomes: staying safe; being healthy; enjoying and achieving; making a positive contribution; and achieving economic wellbeing.

The EYFS applies to all schools and registered early years providers in the maintained, private, voluntary and independent sectors attended by children from birth to 5 years. This includes reception and nursery classes in maintained and independent schools; day nurseries; childminders; playgroups; after-school and breakfast clubs; holiday play schemes; children's centres. The following groups do not have to use the EYFS: mother and toddler groups; nannies; short-term, occasional care such as crèches. Chapter 13 (Unit EYMP 2) gives detailed information on the early years frameworks for England, Wales, Scotland and Northern Ireland.

## Children's needs and rights

In the past decade there has been a major shift in attitude towards children's rights. In the past children's rights were mainly concerned with children's basic welfare needs. Now as well as their basic rights to life, health and education, children are viewed as having a much wider range of rights including the right to engage in play activities, to express their views and to participate in making decisions that affect them directly. Children's rights, as stated in the UN Convention on the Rights of the Child, are clear and universal: they apply to all children. Also, while children's individual needs may differ, they all have the same rights. Children's rights are based on their needs, but emphasising rights rather than needs demonstrates a commitment to viewing and respecting children as valued citizens. (See also The Children's Rights Alliance for England: www.crae.org.uk)

## The United Nations Convention on the Rights of the Child

As an early years practitioner you must know and understand the basic requirements of the United Nations Convention on the Rights of the Child. These rights are for children and young people (up to the age of 18 years). The United Nations (UN) approved the Convention on the Rights of the Child on 20 November 1989; the UK government ratified (agreed to uphold) it on 16 December 1991. Countries that have ratified the Convention are legally bound to do what it states and to make all laws, policy and practice compatible with the Convention. The only two countries in the world that have not signed the Convention are the USA and Somalia.

There are 54 articles in the UN Convention on the Rights of the Child. The articles cover four different groupings of rights: survival, protection, development and participation. Each article outlines a different right. A summary of the articles most relevant to the early years sector are listed below:

**Article 1**: Everyone under 18 years of age has all the rights in this Convention.

**Article 2**: The Convention applies to everyone whatever their race, religion, abilities, whatever they think or say, whatever type of family they come from.

**Article 3**: All organisations concerned with children should work towards what is best for each child.

**Article 4**: Governments should make these rights available to children.

**Article 12**: Children have the right to say what they think should happen, when adults are making decisions that affect them, and to have their opinions taken into account.

**Article 13**: Children have the right to get and to share information as long as the information is not damaging to them or to others.

**Article 14**: Children have the right to think and believe what they want and to practise their

religion, as long as they are not stopping other people from enjoying their rights. Parents should guide their children on these matters.

**Article 15**: Children have the right to meet together and to enjoy groups and organisations, as long as this does not stop other people from enjoying their rights.

**Article 19**: Governments should ensure that children are properly cared for, and protect them from violence, abuse and neglect by their parents or anyone else who looks after them.

**Article 23**: Children who have any kind of disability should have special care and support so that they can lead full and independent lives.

**Article 28**: Children have a right to an education. Discipline in schools should respect children's human dignity. Primary education should be free.

**Article 29**: Education should develop each child's personality and talents to the full. It should encourage children to respect their parents, and their own and other cultures.

**Article 30**: Children have a right to learn the language and customs of their families, whether these are shared by the majority of people in the country or not.

**Article 31**: All children have a right to relax and play, and to join in a wide range of activities.

**Article 39**: Children who have been neglected or abused should receive special help to restore their self-respect.

(From 'What Rights?' Leaflet by UNICEF: www.unicef.org.uk)

## National legislation relating to children's rights

As an early years practitioner you must know and understand the basic requirements of national legislation relating to children's rights. You also need to know and understand how to carry out research

**Figure 15.2** Example of child's poster about children's rights

## Activity

1. Find out more about the UN Convention on the Rights of the Child.

2. Check whether copies of the Convention and related materials are available in your setting and/or the college library.

3. Design a poster and/or leaflet outlining the Articles most relevant to early years settings, such as Articles 1–4, 12–15, 19, 23, 28–31 and 39. You could encourage the children in your setting to design their own posters/leaflets about these rights.

on children's rights and identify the implications for your setting.

## The Children Act 1989

This Act provided a step in the right direction towards implementing the articles of the UN Convention on the Rights of the Child within the UK. The Act came into force on 14 October 1991 and is concerned with families and the care of children, local authority support for children and their families, fostering, childminding and day care provision. The Children Act 1989 is particularly important because it emphasises the importance of putting the child first. In summary, the Act states that:

- What is best for the child must always be the first consideration.
- Whenever possible, children should be brought up in their own family.
- Unless the child is at risk of harm, a child should not be taken away from their family without the family's agreement.
- Local authorities must help families with children in need.
- Local authorities must work with parents and children.
- Courts must put children first when making decisions.
- Children being looked after by local authorities have rights, as do their parents.

The **Children Act 2004** provides the legislative framework for whole-system reform to support the Government's long-term plans to improve the lives of children and their families. The first Children's Commissioner for England was appointed in March 2005. Children's Commissioners in the other home countries of the UK are each required by law to promote and safeguard the rights of children. In England, the Children's Commissioner's general function is limited to 'promoting awareness of the views and interests of children in England' (section 2.1).

The Children Act 2004 together with *Every Child Matters: Change for Children* published in December 2004 by the Department for Education and Skills (DfES) set out the Government's direction for 150 local programmes of change which bring together local authority, health, criminal justice services, voluntary and community organisations and other local partners to deliver improved services for children.

This national framework enables organisations providing services to children (including hospitals, schools, the police and voluntary groups) to access the same information and work together to protect children from harm and help them achieve what they want and need. Children have a greater say about the issues that affect them both as individuals and collectively. Table 15.1 outlines the outcomes which the Children Act 2004 promotes.

**The Childcare Act 2006** provides a legal entitlement to accessible high quality childcare and services for children under 5 years old and their families. The Act places a duty on local authorities to ensure that childcare services meet the needs of working parents, especially those with low incomes or children with special needs, and to ensure that parents have access to the full range of information they may need as parents.

The Act simplified the childcare and early years framework by introducing the new Early Years Foundation Stage which supports the delivery of integrated care and education of children aged birth to 5 years. For more information about the Act see: www.education.gov.uk/childrenandyoungpeople/earlylearningandchildcare/a0071032/childcare-act-2006

## Research Activity

1. Investigate children's rights in your local community.
2. Find out what local provision is being made to meet these rights, such as statutory services and voluntary organisations.

## Key terms

**Children's needs** – these include basic welfare needs such as food, shelter and physical care as well as communication and interaction with others; in addition, educational needs are also important, such as opportunities for play and learning which are appropriate for each child's age/level of development.

**Children's rights** – the universal entitlements to life, health, education, play and consultation which applies to *all* children aged birth to 18 years.

## The Equality Act 2010

This Act provides a single legal framework with clearer legislation to effectively tackle disadvantage and discrimination. The main provisions of the

## What the outcomes mean

### 1. Be healthy:

- physically healthy
- mentally and emotionally healthy
- sexually healthy
- healthy lifestyles
- choose not to take illegal drugs.

### 2. Stay safe from:

- maltreatment, neglect, violence and sexual exploitation
- accidental injury and death
- bullying and discrimination
- crime and anti-social behaviour in and out of school
- insecurity and instability.

### 3. Enjoy and achieve:

- ready for school
- attend and enjoy school
- achieve stretching national educational standards at primary school
- achieve personal and social development and enjoy recreation
- achieve stretching national educational standards at secondary school.

### 4. Make a positive contribution:

- engage in decision-making and support the community and environment
- engage in law-abiding and positive behaviour in and out of school
- develop positive relationships and choose not to bully or discriminate
- develop self-confidence and successfully deal with significant life changes and challenges
- develop enterprising behaviour.

### 5. Achieve economic wellbeing:

- engage in further education, employment or training on leaving school
- ready for employment
- live in decent homes and sustainable communities
- access to transport and material goods
- live in households free from low incomes.

(DfES, 2004b)

**Table 15.1** Outcomes promoted by the Children Act 2004

Equality Act were introduced from October 2010 while the rest will be phased in until 2013. The Act came into force for employment and education in October 2010. A draft code of practice for schools should be available in May 2011.

The fundamental difference from previous equality legislation is that new groups are now provided the same levels of protection from discrimination across all the protected characteristics and all sectors. See Chapter 2 (Unit SHC 32).

Here is a summary of the key changes:

- Protecting people from discrimination in the recruitment process. It is now unlawful for employers to ask job applicants questions about disability or health before making a job offer, except in specified circumstances.

- Protecting people discriminated against because they are perceived to have, or are associated with someone who has, a protected characteristic (such as protecting carers from discrimination).
- Protecting pregnant women and mothers from discrimination: mothers can breastfeed their children in places like cafes and shops and not be asked to leave. The Act also prohibits schools from discriminating against pupils who are pregnant or new mothers.
- The new Equality Duty will require public authorities to consider the needs of all the protected groups in, for example, employment and when designing and delivering services (this is not yet in place).
- Changing the definition of gender reassignment, by removing the requirement for medical supervision.
- Harmonising the thresholds for the duty to make reasonable adjustments for disabled people.
- Extending protection in private clubs to sex, religion or belief, pregnancy and maternity, and gender reassignment.

(EHRC, 2010)

## Social and economic influences

The **National Service Framework for Children, Young People and Maternity Services** was set up by the Department of Health in 2004, and one of its main aims is to help parents find and stay in learning or work, including having high-quality, affordable child care (for both pre-school and school-aged children) and child-friendly working practices.

At the moment every parent is entitled to receive **child benefit**, a *universal*, tax-free payment that can be claimed for each child under the age of 16 years. However, from 2013 households that contain at least one higher-rate or top-rate taxpayer will no longer be entitled to child benefit; these households will have to either stop claiming child benefit completely or have the money reclaimed in taxes.

There are also *targeted* benefits for families to help with the extra costs of child care. The family's

income is assessed (by means testing) to find out if they are in need of financial support:

- **Sure Start Maternity Grant** – a one-off payment to help pay for provisions for a first baby if the parent(s) are on a low income.
- **Working Tax Credit** – a specific element supports the cost of registered or approved child care for working parents. The child care element can help with up to 70 per cent of child care costs.
- **Time off ('parental leave')** – a working parent can take up to 13 weeks' parental leave for each child until his or her fifth birthday (the entitlement is greater if the parent has a disabled child). The parent's employer does not *have* to pay the parent when he or she takes this leave, but they might do so as part of the employment package.
- **Flexible working** – parents, foster parents and guardians have a right to request a flexible working pattern if they have a child aged under 6 years or a disabled child under 18 years. Various conditions apply but the employer has to consider any request for flexible working seriously.
- **Child maintenance** – the Child Support Agency (CSA) is part of the Department for Work and Pensions (DWP). The CSA's role is to make sure that a parent who lives apart from his or her child contributes financially to the child's upkeep by paying child maintenance. Child maintenance is money paid to help cover the child's everyday living costs. The parent with whom the child does not normally live (the non-resident parent) is responsible for paying child maintenance to the parent or other person, such as a grandparent or a guardian, with whom the child normally lives (the parent with care).
- **New Deal for Lone Parents** – a voluntary government programme which gives people on benefits the help and support they need to look for work, including training and preparing for work.

## Evidence-based practice and the early years

Everyday practice in early years settings is influenced by many factors such as: staff training in work with young children; staff experiences of working with different children and families; on-the-job learning and training with colleagues; watching television programmes relating to the early years; research into current early years practice in magazines, journals and on the internet. Professional practice involves keeping up-to-date with the reported findings of research studies, and considering how these can be applied in the setting.

However, you should choose your sources of information carefully and exercise caution when interpreting research findings. For example, some research studies may be superficial, as they are based on a small number of children; some pieces of research may contradict each other; some research is often poorly reported by the general media.

In recent years, an example of a useful research project relating to the early years is Effective Provision of Pre-school Education (EPPE) – an influential, soundly-based academic research project on a significant scale, which has confirmed the value of early learning through guided play, especially for children from low income families (Tassoni *et al.*, 2010; p. 280).

### Research Activity

Research information about the EPPE project at: http://eppe.ioe.ac.uk

Find out about other current research relevant to the early years sector.

# Understand how to support diversity, inclusion and participation in early years settings

As an early years practitioner you must know and follow the setting's strategies, policies, procedures and practice for supporting diversity, inclusion and participation. You also need to know and understand how to develop and implement these as consistent with your role and responsibilities in the setting. Remember that to develop effective policies, procedures and practice, everyone should be involved at some level including staff, children and their parents or carers.

You need to know how to judge whether the early years setting is inclusive and supportive of diversity, and be able to demonstrate that you support inclusion and diversity through your words, actions and behaviours in the setting. You must know and understand the importance of promoting the setting to children who may experience barriers to participation, such as children with disabilities or those from other minority groups.

For more information on equality, diversity, inclusion and participation, see Chapter 3 (Unit SHC 33).

## What is diversity?

Diversity refers to the differences between individuals and groups in society arising from gender, ethnic origins, social, cultural or religious background, family structure, disabilities, sexuality and appearance (Griffin, 2008).

**Cultural diversity** can be defined as ethnic, gender, racial and social differences within a situation, institution or group. In education, cultural diversity means the coexistence of different ethnic, gender, racial and social groups within one social unit – the school. By valuing and promoting cultural diversity, the school can encourage positive attitudes to other social units such as the local community or wider society.

## What is inclusion?

Inclusion may be defined in a variety of ways. There is a common assumption that inclusion is mainly about integrating disabled children or those identified as having special educational needs into mainstream settings. Inclusion should increase the participation not just of children with 'special needs' but of any child whose participation may be impeded or enhanced.

Inclusion means reducing discrimination on the basis of gender, class, disability, sexual orientation, ethnicity, faith and family background. Inclusion involves the recognition and conviction that all children and young people have rights to a broad education, appropriate support and to attendance at their local early years settings or school (Ainscow *et al.*, 2006).

**Inclusive practice** in the setting can be defined as words and actions which encourage the participation of *all* children (including those with disabilities or from other minority groups) within a mainstream setting. See Chapter 3 (Unit SHC 33) for guidelines on inclusive practice in early years settings.

## What is participation?

As an early years practitioner you must protect and promote young children's rights by supporting equality of access to your setting. This includes providing information for children, families and communities which promotes participation and equality of access. You should be able to implement transparent procedures and information about access to provision that meet the needs of all children.

Children from all backgrounds must be welcomed, and practitioners should ensure that barriers to participation are identified and removed. The views and preferences of children should be sought and respected, and your practice should be adapted to the children's ages, needs and abilities. You could involve relevant local community groups in the setting and provide information on community resources, such as childcare services, play provision, sport and leisure activities, local libraries, support groups, multicultural resources, specialist equipment for people with disabilities.

Children should know their rights and responsibilities in the context of your setting, and you should also provide information about equality of access to children and families, including representative groups and individuals; for example, current and potential new users of the early years setting, children and their families who found services hard to access such as those with disabilities or from different ethnic groups.

Information can be provided in a variety of ways including: leaflets, newsletters, newspapers, magazines; public notice boards; open days; exhibitions; the internet. Select the most effective way to reach your target audience; for example, provide leaflets in community languages, ensure that posters show positive images of people with disabilities and from different ethnic groups (Sure Start, 2003c)

### Activity

Describe ways in which your setting has provided information that promotes participation and equality of access to all relevant community groups, including those who have found services hard to access such as people with disabilities or from different ethnic groups.

## The importance of anti-discriminatory/anti bias practice

Anti-discriminatory or anti bias practice in the setting can be defined as words and actions which prevent discrimination and prejudice towards any individual or group of people, and actively promote equal opportunities. This means ensuring that all children, parents, colleagues and other professionals are treated in an unbiased, fair and non-prejudiced way. All policies, procedures and strategies in the setting should demonstrate a positive and inclusive attitude towards all individuals, regardless of age, gender, race, culture or disability.

Anti-discriminatory practice must underpin all work with children, young people and their families. Early years settings have an important role to play in promoting anti-discriminatory practice by offering equality of opportunity and being inclusive of all children.

Anti-discriminatory practice is about the implementation of the setting's equal opportunities policy in all aspects of the setting including curriculum planning, delivery and evaluation. It is

- Find out about your setting's policies and practices for inclusion, including equal opportunities and special educational needs.
- Briefly outline the setting's procedures for inclusion and anti-discriminatory practice, including your role in implementing these procedures.
- Describe how you apply anti-discriminatory practice in your work with children.

the responsibility of the adults in the setting to ensure that all children have an opportunity to participate in activities and achieve their maximum learning potential. When working with young children, adults must model good practice in what they say, how they say it and their actions.

## Challenging discrimination and prejudice

All early years settings have an equal opportunities policy, with procedures in place to ensure that it is implemented. You must follow your setting's policy and procedures together with any relevant legal requirements when dealing with these issues. As an early years practitioner you should:

- Challenge discrimination or prejudice when necessary. (For example, if a colleague makes a derisory comment about a person's race, culture or disability, you should tell them why it is unacceptable to express their views in this way.)
- State that you will not condone views that discriminate against another person.
- Provide support for children and adults who experience discrimination or prejudice by encouraging them to respond with positive action.

See Chapter 3 (Unit SHC 33) for more detailed information about discrimination and combating prejudice in early years settings.

## Key terms

**Anti-discriminatory practice** – taking positive action to counter discrimination and prejudice.

## Case Study

Mae is working as a nursery nurse in a reception class. While talking to Mae in the staff room, a colleague makes a negative comment about the background of one of the pupils. What would you do in this situation?

## Applying anti-discriminatory/anti bias practice

Children are influenced by images, ideas and attitudes that create prejudice and lead to discrimination or disadvantage. Children are not born with these attitudes; they *learn* them. You have an important role to play in promoting children's positive attitudes towards themselves and other people. In addition, you must not have stereotyped views about children's potential, nor have low expectations of children based on culture, gender or disability.

As an early years practitioner you should do the following:

- Recognise and eliminate racial discrimination.
- Have high but realistic expectations for *all* children.
- Maximise every child's motivation and potential.
- Encourage each child to feel a positive sense of identity.
- Ensure that the childcare environment reflects positive images.
- Challenge stereotypes in the media, literature and everyday life.

**Figure 15.3** Supporting diversity, inclusion and participation

- Give all children the opportunities to play with a wide variety of toys, games and play equipment.
- Support the children to develop ideas of equality among their peers.
- Expect the same standards of behaviour from all children regardless of culture, gender or disability.
- Recognise children with disabilities as individuals, not by their condition or impairment (for example,

refer to 'a child *with* autistic tendencies' not 'an autistic child').
- Encourage the 'able' world to adapt to those with disabilities, not the other way round.

See Chapter 3 (Unit SHC 33), page 34 for guidelines to help individuals promote diversity, equality of opportunity and inclusion.

## Activity

1. Compile a resource pack that supports diversity, inclusion and participation in the early years. You might include the following information and resources: posters, wall charts, photographs and pictures; booklets and leaflets; suggested activities to support diversity, inclusion and participation; book list of relevant children's books and stories; list of useful organisations and addresses.

2. Plan, implement and evaluate at least one activity suggested in your resource pack.

## Involving children in decision-making

As an early years practitioner, you must know and understand the importance of encouraging young children to make choices and involving children in decision-making. This includes encouraging children to take responsibility for everyday tasks within the setting. Young children are quite capable of making their own decisions and this helps to develop their independence and extends their own communication skills even further. Chapter 11 (Unit CYP Core 3.7) gives more information on supporting children to make decisions.

Children have the right to be consulted and involved in decision-making about matters that affect them (UN Convention on the Rights of the Child, Article 12 – see page 312 above). Involving children in decision-making within your setting will help you to provide better childcare provision based on the children's real needs rather than adult assumptions about children's needs. It will also help you to promote social inclusion by encouraging the children to participate as active citizens in their local community.

# Be able to review own practice in promoting diversity, inclusion and participation in early years settings

Effective practice requires committed, enthusiastic and reflective practitioners with a breadth and depth of knowledge, skills and understanding. To be an effective, reflective practitioner, you should use your own learning to improve your work with children and their families in ways which are sensitive, positive and non-judgemental. Through initial and ongoing training and development, you can develop, demonstrate and continuously improve your:

- relationships with both children and adults
- understanding of the individual and diverse ways in which children develop and learn
- knowledge and understanding in order to actively

### Activity

How does your setting involve children in decision-making?

support and extend children's learning in and across all areas and aspects of learning
- practice in meeting all children's needs, learning styles and interests
- work with parents, carers and the wider community
- work with other professionals.

(DfES, 2005a)

The **Key Elements of Effective Practice (KEEP)** provides a framework for early years practitioners to: reflect on their work; understand what effective practice looks like; record their qualifications; formulate their self-development plan; allow managers to understand staff experience/ qualifications and training needs to support the development of the setting. KEEP supports self-appraisal, appraisal, quality assurance, self-evaluation and performance management as it links the needs of children, parents, the setting *and* practitioners (DfES, 2005a). You can find this document on the following website page: http://education.gov.uk/publications/eOrderingDownload/DfES%201201%202005.pdf

KEEP has been developed alongside and is consistent with **The Common Core of Skills and Knowledge for the Children's Workforce** which sets out the six areas of expertise that everyone working with children, young people and families should be able to demonstrate. For further details, see this website: http://education.gov.uk/publications/eOrderingDownload/DfES11892005.pdf

Voice, the union for education professionals (including teaching, childcare and support staff as well as students), has an **Early Years and Childcare Code of Practice**. The code provides guidance for all practising professional early years practitioners in carrying out their duties and responsibilities. You will find it useful to bear these guidelines in mind when working with young children and their families. You can download the full text at this website page: www.voicetheunion.org.uk/index.cfm/page/_sections.contentdetail.cfm/navid/28/parentid/366/id/1172/_sa/17

**Activity**

Outline the standards of professional early years practice expected from you and your colleagues. (This information may be included in a code of practice for staff which may be in the staff handbook and/or set out in best practice benchmarks such as KEEP.)

## The importance of reviewing your own practice as part of being an effective practitioner

You need to know and understand clearly the exact role and responsibilities of your work as an early years practitioner. Review your professional practice by making regular and realistic assessments of how well your working practices match your role and responsibilities. Share your self-assessments with those responsible for managing and reviewing your work performance, for example during your regular discussions/meetings with your colleagues or with your line manager.

You should also ask other people for feedback about how well you fulfil the requirements and expectations of your role. You can also reflect on your own professional practice by making comparisons with appropriate models of good practice, such as the work of more experienced practitioners within the early years setting.

## Reflective analysis of own practice

As an early years practitioner you need to know and understand the techniques of reflective analysis:

- questioning what, why and how
- seeking alternatives
- keeping an open mind
- viewing from different perspectives
- thinking about consequences
- testing ideas through comparing and contrasting
- asking 'what if?'
- synthesising ideas
- seeking, identifying and resolving problems.

(NDNA, 2004)

### Self-evaluation

Self-evaluation is needed to improve your own professional practice, and to develop your ability to reflect upon routines/activities and modify plans to meet the individual needs of the children you work with. When evaluating your own practice you should consider the following questions:

- Was your own particular contribution appropriate?
- Did you choose the right time, place and resources?
- Did you intervene enough or too much?
- Did you achieve your goals (such as objectives/outcomes for the child or children and yourself)? If not, why not? Were the goals too ambitious or unrealistic?
- What other strategies/methods could have been used? Suggest possible modifications.

**Activity**

1. How do you monitor the processes, practices and outcomes from your work?

2. Give examples of how you evaluate your own professional practice including: self-evaluation; reflections on your interactions with others; sharing your reflections with others; using feedback from others to improve your own evaluation.

3. Describe how you have used reflection to solve problems and improve practice.

- Who to ask for further advice (such as senior practitioner, setting manager, other professional)?

# Dealing with difficulties and challenges encountered in professional practice in promoting diversity, inclusion and participation in early years settings

Your own attitudes, values and behaviour impact on your work with young children and their parents. Your attitudes, values and behaviour should demonstrate your commitment to diversity, inclusion and participation. You need to be able to think clearly and fairly about issues related to diversity, inclusion and participation. This will enable you to care for young children with due attention to their individual needs as well as promoting their development and early learning in ways which open up opportunities for their future. The words you use to express yourself affect the development of your own attitudes, values and behaviour. The language you use moulds the way you think and may lead you to distorted or limited opinions. Language reflects and influences how you think about yourself and others. Language can reinforce the development of stereotyped and prejudiced ideas or it can help you to think more constructively and treat others respectfully (Griffin, 2008).

Prejudice and discrimination can have negative impact on young children, including damaging their self-esteem and limiting their future potential. Discrimination goes against the principles and values of practice in working with children and young people and denies them their rights (see above), so it is essential to base your professional practice on anti-discriminatory practice (see above). This involves taking positive action to help children and young people to learn positive attitudes, behaviour and language which are not discriminatory against others.

Adults working with children, young people and their parents must not behave in ways that reinforce stereotypes. For example, when presenting learning activities you should ensure that the examples used reflect positive yet realistic images of the people in the local community, rather than stereotypes.

It can be very tempting to pigeon-hole people into certain categories and make large assumptions about their life experience. Establish ground rules – ensure that all pupils are aware of their obligations to work and play in an anti-discriminatory way. This means that if a situation should arise, everyone, including the person who has created the problem, knows what to expect.

All resources used in the learning environment need to be checked to ensure that they are not creating barriers to access or learning. It is your responsibility to check that any learning materials used (such as videos or handouts) encourage positive attitudes and promote anti-discriminatory practice. The learning environment has to be accessible. OHP acetates should be clear enough to allow people with different levels of eyesight to see them without discomfort. Always back up OHPs with handouts. Avoid using pale colours when writing on acetates or flipcharts. Be aware that some colours cause problems for people with colour blindness.

It is never pleasant to have caused unintentional offence. The best thing to do is to acknowledge that the person is offended. Apologise and ask what you could say in the future to avoid giving offence. It may be good to emphasise that you are learning about these things all the time and want to promote anti-discriminatory practice (Morrison, 2010).

## Challenging prejudice and discrimination

As an early years practitioner, you should:

- Challenge discrimination or prejudice when necessary
- State that you will not condone views that discriminate against another person
- Provide support for children and adults who experience discrimination or prejudice by encouraging them to respond with positive action.

You cannot ignore prejudice or discriminatory behaviour among young children. It is not helpful to overreact to a child's discriminatory behaviour or to resort to labelling a child as racist or sexist. Children are influenced by the adults at home, in their local community and in the media. Children may learn to behave in aggressively discriminatory ways because they observe members of their family and local community behaving like that, using prejudiced language and showing little respect for others. Young children may have heard and observed adults or older children speaking and behaving in discriminatory ways, so they may not understand that the language and behaviour they are repeating is wrong. Point out to children that you know that some people do speak and behave in prejudiced and discriminatory ways, but that this is not acceptable in your setting because it is rude and unfair (Griffin, 2008).

Ensure that you know and understand the correct procedures to follow if a child demonstrates discriminatory language or behaviour. These procedures are likely to be the same as when dealing with bullying behaviour – see the section on bullying in Chapter 7 (Unit CYP Core 3.3). You also need to know and follow the procedures for challenging an adult's discriminatory language or behaviour – always follow the relevant procedures in your setting.

You have a responsibility to intervene when discrimination occurs and try to create a positive learning experience. Effective practice in response to a child's abusive remarks relating to another person's skin colour, gender, disability, social background or appearance includes the following:

- Never ignore or excuse one child's discriminatory behaviour towards another child, as this is as unacceptable as allowing them to inflict physical pain on that child
- Do not feel that you will make things worse by drawing attention to what has been said or done

– if you do not respond, you give the impression that you condone the discriminatory behaviour

- Intervene immediately, pointing out to the child who has behaved in a discriminatory way that what was said or done is hurtful and that unfair or cruel behaviour will not be accepted, but do not suggest that the child will be punished
- If necessary, point out anything that is untrue and give the correct information and new vocabulary
- Help the child to learn from the situation, to see the consequences of their actions and to understand why their behaviour is regarded as unacceptable or inappropriate, using phrases such as 'How would you feel?'
- Do not leave the child with the feeling that you dislike them personally for what they have said or done – make it clear that what you will not tolerate is what they have said or how they have behaved in this particular instance
- Help the child to find ways of expressing their own strength through things they are good at and can achieve, and support them in building their self-esteem in positive ways, showing that you value them for who they are (Griffin, 2008; p. 208).

Challenging children's discriminatory language or behaviour takes a consistent and patient approach. However, challenging the discriminatory comments or behaviour of adults can be difficult and requires strength and courage. When challenging adults about their discriminatory ways, use a similar approach as with children, for example:

- Challenge the remark or behaviour, politely but firmly
- Choose your time and place – you may not want to speak strongly in front of children or young people, but you should act as soon as you can
- Remain as calm as possible but make it clear that you find the remark or behaviour offensive or inappropriate

## Research Activity

1. Find out about your setting's procedures for dealing with a child who demonstrates discriminatory language or behaviour.

2. Find out about your setting's procedures for challenging the discriminatory language or behaviour of other adults.

- Remember that if you let the incident pass, you are contributing to the person feeling that it is acceptable to speak or behave in that way
- Offer support to the person who has been the object of the remark or excluding behaviour
- Offer accurate information if the person's comments or actions seem to arise from ignorance of the implications of what they are saying or doing (Griffin, 2008; p.215).

 ## Useful resources

### Organisations and websites
*Child Care* is a monthly magazine for all childminders, nannies and child carers:
www.professionalchildcare.co.uk

**Council for Awards in Care, Health and Education** (CACHE) is the specialist awarding organisation for qualifications in health, care and education:
www.cache.org.uk

**Daycare Trust** is a national child care charity which provides information for parents, child care providers, employers, trade unions, local authorities and policymakers:
www.daycaretrust.org.uk

**Directgov** gives information on statutory care provision:
www.direct.gov.uk

**Every Child Matters** is a framework in England designed to ensure quality provision of children's play and learning:
www.everychildmatters.gov.uk

**National Children's Bureau** is a charity which works to advance the wellbeing of all children and young people across every aspect of their lives:
www.ncb.org.uk

*Nursery World* is the leading magazine for everyone working in early years education and care. It includes job adverts, news and in-depth articles on good practice:
www.nursery-world.co.uk

### Books
Alderson, P. (2000) *Young Children's Rights: Exploring Beliefs, Principles and Practice.* Jessica Kingsley Publishers.
Bruce, T. (2011) *Early Childhood Education.* Hodder Education.
Bruce, T. (ed.) (2010) *Early Childhood: A Guide for Students.* Sage.
Department of Health. (1989) *An Introduction to The Children Act 1989.* HMSO.
Dryden, L. (2005) *Essential Early Years.* Hodder Arnold.
Griffin, S. (2008) *Inclusion, Equality and Diversity in Working with Children.* Heinemann.
Hartley, M. (2005) *The Assertiveness Handbook.* Sheldon Press.
Knowles, G. (2009) *Ensuring Every Child Matters.* Sage Publications.
Lindenfield, G. (2000) *Self Esteem: Simple Steps to Developing Self-reliance and Perseverance.* HarperCollins.
Lindon, J. (2006) *Equality in Early Childhood: Linking Theory and Practice.* Hodder Arnold.
Miller, L. *et al.* (2005) *Developing Early Years Practice.* David Fulton Publishers.
Mitchell, A. (2001) *Study Skills for Early Years Students.* Hodder & Stoughton.
Page-Smith, A. and Craft, A. (2008) *Developing Reflective Practice in the Early Years.* Open University Press.
Smidt, S. (2002) *A Guide to Early Years Practice.* 2nd Edition. Routledge.
Stacey, M. (2009) *Teamwork and Collaboration in Early Years Settings.* Learning Matters.
UK Committee for UNICEF. (2000) *The Convention on the Rights of the Child.* UNICEF.

# 16 Support children's speech, language and communication: Unit EYMP 5

This chapter aims to provide a basis for understanding the importance of speech, language and communication for a child's overall development. It explores the ways in which those working with children can support the development of speech, language and communication skills. Communication is a complex, two-way process, reliant on a wide range of skills including listening, understanding and means of expression as well as interaction. Consideration of the complexity of this process, and the many factors which can affect it, will help you to communicate effffectively and to support children's communication.

## Learning outcomes

By the end of this chapter you will:

1. Understand the importance of speech, language and communication for children's overall development.

2. Understand the importance and the benefits of adults supporting the speech, language and communication development of the children in the setting.

3. Be able to provide support for the speech, language and communication development of the children in the setting.

4. Be able to contribute to maintaining a positive environment that supports speech, language and communication.

## Understand the importance of speech, language and communication for children's overall development

We use speech, language and communication to interact with each other. Humans are social animals and desire the company of others. We use language as the most effective means of communicating with other people. Communication is a key factor in the social interaction which is essential for our daily lives. This applies to babies and young children as well as older children and adults. Babies and young children use their communication skills (however limited these may be) to express their needs and desires in an egocentric way; they use language as a means of self-preservation.

Speech, language and communication are important for children's overall development because they are used to:

- interact with others
- explore the environment
- make sense of everyday experiences
- access information and understand concepts
- organise thoughts and formulate ideas
- express own feelings and understanding the feelings of others.

(See the section on the interrelated areas of development in this chapter, pages 332–4.)

# Understanding the terms speech, language, communication, and speech, language and communication needs

The word **language** is often used to describe the process of speaking and listening, but it is much more than just **communication**. Language is what makes humans different from all other animals. All animals, including humans, communicate through the use of signals. For example, a cat hisses and its tail bristles when it feels threatened, and a dog may bark to indicate that there is an intruder. Humans also communicate using signals such as body language and gesture; what makes us different is the use of symbols (such as words) to indicate more complex needs and feelings. While animals are only able to deal with the here and now, humans can use language to store and later recall ideas, feelings and past experiences, and to look forward to the future.

Humans have the ability to utilise language by use of a recognised system of symbols which includes a common understanding of what those symbols mean. Anyone could make up their own language system, but they would not be able to communicate with others unless they shared this system or code with them. For example, in Britain the majority of people use the language system 'English', so that they can communicate effectively in an English-speaking society. There are many other language systems as indicated by the many languages and alphabet systems used around the world.

At first, babies and young children are not able to use a complex language system; it takes time for them to learn the code of their particular home or community language. While they are learning this code, babies and young children use other ways to communicate their needs and feelings to other people, using for example body language, gestures and facial expressions. However, these symbols can only be interpreted by others; adults do not always know exactly what the young child is trying to communicate, which can be very frustrating for both adult and child! A baby's cry may indicate a need for food, sleep, cuddle, play or nappy change. The adult's interpretation of a baby's cry will depend on how well they know this particular baby and their understanding of this baby's needs.

Many people think that language equals **speech**, but there are many ways to communicate besides talking. Humans are able to use language from birth using non-verbal communication. For example, a baby may communicate in the following ways: crying in negative response or to gain attention; moving whole body/limbs in response to sound; turning head towards human voice; using eye contact; smiling in positive response; experimenting with sounds (for example, babbling).

Communication involves:

- sending information (verbally or non-verbally)
- receiving information
- interpreting information
- understanding information.

## Key terms

**Speech** – verbal communication; the act of speaking; the articulation of words to express thoughts, feelings or ideas.

**Language** – a recognised, structured system of gestures, signs and symbols used to communicate.

**Communication** – the transmission of thoughts, feelings or information via body language, signals, speech or writing.

## What is communication with and without words?

Communication is probably one of the most important ways in which we develop and learn throughout life. Babies, children and adults communicate all the time. However, 80 per cent of communication is without words. Even when we use the spoken word (verbal communication), we continue to communicate non-verbally.

We communicate in order to understand ourselves and develop a strong, confident sense of our identity, and to understand and relate to other people, their

**Figure 16.1** These babies are communicating with each other in non-verbal ways. The object is used as an invitation to open up communication between them

feelings, ideas and thoughts. See Figure 16.2, which demonstrates that communication does not always require words. The adult holds the child in a way that makes the child feel secure. They share an experience: the adult smiles, looking at the child, which gives an atmosphere of warm affection, without overwhelming. The child is sitting in a relaxed way, with one foot under the other, and feels confident about looking at what is happening around them. They are not feeling rushed or under pressure.

## In Practice

### Communicating

Sit with a child, either between 1 and 3 years, 3 and 5 years, or 5 and 7 years. Note the communications you have between you that do not depend on words. Make a list of examples.

Not all human beings communicate through a spoken language, for one reason or another, but the vast majority of people in the world do. What is

more, they often speak two or three languages fluently from an early age.

## Key terms

**Receptive language** – Learning to listen and understand language: the child listens, watches people talking, and begins to understand what is being said.

**Expressive language** – Learning to speak and to use language. This involves using the face expressively, making gestures and speaking (or signing).

## Gestures, pointing, props, signals and links

The educational psychologist Jean Piaget (1896–1980) stressed the importance of personal and individual ways of communicating through expressing thoughts, ideas, feelings and relationships, as well as the shared and agreed forms of language. His work has been particularly important in supporting the development of communication in children with disabilities such as profound deafness, and for children with complex needs. His work is also useful in looking at babies

# Developing communication skills and addressing speech, language and communication needs

Children (and adults) use many different ways to communicate. These **modes of language** are essential to being able to communicate effectively with others and to being fully involved in a wide range of social interactions. The different modes of language can be described as:

- non-verbal communication
- thinking
- listening
- speaking
- reading
- writing.

Every mode of language involves a variety of communication skills which are inter-related. Some of the skills are required in more than one mode; for example, reading and writing both involve the processing of oral language in a written form.

You should provide opportunities for children to develop the necessary communication skills so that they can become competent at using these different modes of language. Opportunities for talk are especially helpful in promoting language development and the use of communication skills. Some children may be limited in their ability to use some modes of language due to sensory impairment or other special needs.

**Figure 16.2** There are several kinds of communication here that do not involve words

and toddlers, who use personal language more than conventional spoken or signed language.

Personal communication can include:

- gestures
- pointing
- props – the handbag represents mother when she goes for coffee, and the child knows she is coming back because her handbag is there
- signals that give evidence – the footprint in the sand tells us someone was there
- links – the child has a teddy bear while the parent or carer is away that links the child to them; the communication is personal between this child and this parent or carer.

## Key terms

**Modes of language** – The different ways to communicate, including non-verbal communication, listening, speaking, thinking, reading and writing.

All children have individual **speech, language and communication needs**, but some may have *additional* speech, language and communication needs that affect their ability to communicate and interact effectively with others. For example:

- Communication and interaction needs affecting the ability to communicate or socially interact with others, such as autistic spectrum disorders

- Behavioural and/or emotional needs affecting the ability to communicate or socially interact with others, such as attention deficit disorders

- Cognition difficulties affecting the ability to process language, such as dyslexia
- Sensory impairment affecting the ability to use some aspects of language, such as hearing impairment (which may limit use of spoken language) and visual impairment (which may limit use of written language)
- Physical disabilities affecting articulation of sounds, such as cleft palate.

*'Children and young people with speech, language and communication needs (SLCN) have difficulties in communicating with others; it may be that they cannot express themselves effectively or they may have difficulties in understanding what is being said to them. Alternatively those who support them may not understand their way of communicating.*

*Children and young people may have difficulties across one or many of the different elements of speech, language and communication resulting in a communication breakdown. This may be minor and temporary, or it may be complex and long-term. Under this umbrella term, there will be many different labels used. The term 'needs' refers both to the needs of the individual and to what society can do to support their inclusion. It implicitly looks both at the individual and the environment in which children play, learn, communicate and live.'*

(From a leaflet 'Explaining Speech, language and Communication Needs (SLCN)' produced by the Communications Consortium)

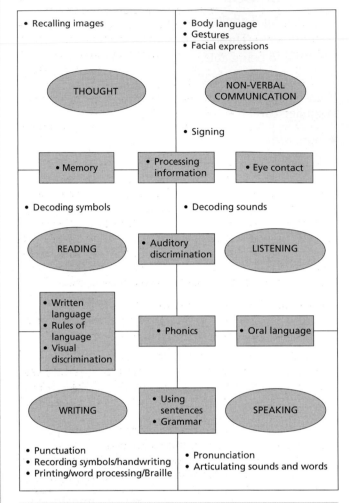

**Figure 16.3** The inter-related modes of language

## Activity

Look at Figure 16.3. Use the headings from the diagram and list examples of activities/experiences which could encourage each skill. Your list might look something like this:

| Modes of language | Skills | Example activities |
|---|---|---|
| Thought | Recalling images | Drawing/painting of event |
| Speaking | Oral language | Discussion or news time |
| Listening | Processing information | Listening to instructions |
| Reading | Phonics | Songs/stories |
| Writing | Written language | Recording news |
| Non-verbal communication | Body language | Drama or role play |

## Key terms

**Aphasia** – Partial or total loss of the ability to express and/or comprehend spoken or written language, resulting from damage to the brain caused by injury or disease.

**Articulation** – The ability to produce speech sounds.

**Asperger's syndrome** – An autistic spectrum disorder (see below), characterised by severe impairment of social interactions and by restricted interests and behaviours; however, unlike autism, there is usually no delay in the development of language, cognitive function and self-help skills.

**Attention deficient disorders** – A syndrome, usually diagnosed in childhood, characterised by a persistent pattern of impulsiveness, a short attention span, and often hyperactivity, and interfering especially with academic, occupational and social performance.

**Autistic spectrum disorders** – A group of difficulties characterised by impairment of development in multiple areas including social interaction, verbal and non-verbal communication skills and imaginative activity, as well as by restricted interests and behaviours; includes autism and Asperger's syndrome.

**Cleft palate** – A child with a cleft lip and/or palate has structural damage to their top lip, palate or both, due to the failed development of these areas of the mouth during the early weeks in the womb. A series of operations is essential to correct this impairment; this may result in significant language delay as correct speech cannot be articulated until the gaps in lips and/or palate have been successfully mended. Speech and language therapy may be necessary later.

**Cognition difficulties** – These can be divided into general learning difficulties and specific learning difficulties. Children with **general learning difficulties** have below-average cognitive abilities across all areas of learning and often have delayed development in other areas; they may be socially and emotionally immature and/or have problems with gross/fine motor skills. General learning difficulties are divided into **mild, moderate** and **severe or profound** learning difficulties. Children with **specific learning difficulties** show problems in learning in one particular area of development. For example: a child with **dyslexia** has difficulties in acquiring literacy skills; a child with **dyscalculia** has difficulties in acquiring numeracy skills; a child with **dyspraxia** has difficulties with the way the brain processes information which affects the co-ordination of movement.

## Key terms

**Hearing impairment** – This may range from a slight impairment to profound deafness. The loss may affect one or both ears at different levels. There are two types of hearing impairment. **Conductive hearing loss** involves the interference of the transmission of sound from the outer to the inner ear. This may be due to congestion or damage to the inner ear. The loss may be temporary or permanent; it makes sounds seem like the volume has been turned down. **Sensori-neural loss** is a rare condition that is more likely to result in permanent hearing impairment. The damage to the inner ear results in distorted sounds where some sounds are heard but not others.

**Physical disabilities** – Some children may be severely disabled by physical difficulties due to damage to the neurological system which controls motor functions, e.g. cerebral palsy and spina bifida; some children have relatively minor difficulties, such as dyspraxia. Some children have multiple disabilities, affecting several physical functions, such as hearing or visual impairment combined with motor disorders. Some physical and medical problems are congenital; others emerge later on.

**Speech, language and communication needs** – are additional or special needs that affect a person's ability to communicate and interact effectively with others.

**Visual impairment** – Vision can be considered to be impaired if, even with the use of contact lenses or glasses, a person's sight cannot be fully corrected. Children who wear glasses to correct short or long sight are not considered to be visually impaired. Children with normal vision in only one eye (monocular vision) are not considered to be visually impaired, because one eye enables them to see quite well for most activities; however, they will have difficulties with 3D perception and judging distances.

## Research Activity

Find out more about the definitions for speech, language, communication, and speech, language and communication needs.

Explain in your own words what each of these terms means:

- speech
- language
- communication
- speech, language and communication needs.

## The sequence of communication and language development

### From birth to 1 year

The first year of a baby's life is sometimes called 'prelinguistic'. This is a rather misleading term. It is more positive and helpful to think of a baby as someone who communicates without words, and who is developing everything needed for conversations in spoken/signed language. This is sometimes called the period of emerging language.

### From 1 to 4 years

From the second year of the baby's life until about the age of 4 years, there is the period of language explosion. Every aspect of language seems to move forward rapidly at this time. It is the best time to learn other languages, or to become bilingual or multilingual.

### From 4 to 8 years

At this age, children are consolidating their communication and language learning. They build on what they know about communication with themselves, with other people, developing better articulation, and using more conventional grammar patterns. They think about who they are talking to, with greater sensitivity and awareness. They are also more attentive to the context in which they are talking, and the situation. They can put their ideas and feelings into words more easily than when they were toddlers.

## Interrelated areas of development

### How language supports emotional development

Children experience difficulties when they are not able to put their feelings into words or to express them in any way. This has a damaging impact on their sense of self and identity, and on their self-

**Figure 16.4** These two have a trusting relationship, knowing that they have a boundary around hurting each other

## Activity

Observe one of the following either in the home setting or the early childhood setting:

- baby aged 6 to 12 months
- child aged 1 to 3 years
- child aged 3 to 5 years
- child aged 5 to 7 years.

Note sounds: vowels (ah, eh, ee, aye, oh, yu) and consonants such as p, g, b. Look at Table 16.1 and the charts of normative development on language development in Chapter 5, (Unit CYP Core 3.1) and analyse your observations.

Does the baby/child use single words or holophrases (single-word utterances that express several thoughts, ideas or feelings)? Does the child speak in sentences? Evaluate the language development of the child.

| Age range | Speech, communication and language development |
|---|---|
| **0 to 3 months** | • Recognises familiar voices<br>• Stops crying when hears familiar voices<br>• Aware of other sounds<br>• Turns head towards sounds<br>• Responds to smiles<br>• Moves whole body in response to sound/to attract attention<br>• Pauses to listen to others<br>• Makes noises as well as crying, e.g. burbling. |
| **3 to 9 months** | • Responds with smiles<br>• Recognises family names, but cannot say them<br>• Enjoys looking at pictures and books<br>• Even more responsive to voices and music<br>• Participates in simple games, e.g. 'peep-po'<br>• Tries to imitate sounds, e.g. during rhymes<br>• Starts babbling, uses single syllable sounds, e.g. 'daa', 'baa' and 'maa'<br>• From about 7 months uses two syllable sounds, e.g. 'daada', 'baaba', 'maama'<br>• Shouts to attract attention. |
| **18 months to 2 years** | • Uses language to gain information, e.g. starts asking 'What dat?'<br>• Repeats words said by adults<br>• Acquires 1–3 words per month; by 2 years has vocabulary of about 200 words<br>• Participates in action songs and nursery rhymes<br>• Continues to enjoy books and stories<br>• Uses telegraphic speech e.g. speaks in 2–3 word sentences such as 'Daddy go' or 'Milk all gone'. |
| **2 to 3 years** | • Has vocabulary of about 300 words<br>• Uses more adult forms of speech, e.g. sentences now include words like that, this, here, there, then, but, and<br>• Can name main body parts<br>• Uses adjectives, e.g. big, small, tall<br>• Uses words referring to relationships, e.g. I, my, you, yours<br>• Asks questions to gain more information<br>• Sings songs and rhymes<br>• Continues to participate in action songs<br>• Continues to enjoy books/stories<br>• Can deliver simple messages. |
| **3 to 4 years** | • Has vocabulary of between 900 and 1000 words<br>• Asks lots of questions |

| Age range | Speech, communication and language development |
|---|---|
| | • May use vocabulary of about 1500 to 2000 words |
| | • Uses more complex sentence structures |
| | • Asks even more questions using what, when, who, where, how and especially why! |
| | • Shows interest in more complex books and stories |
| | • May develop early reading and writing skills such letter and sound recognition |
| | • Gives more detailed accounts of past events |
| | • Vocalises ideas and feelings |
| | • Can listen to and follow more detailed instructions |
| | • Can deliver more complex verbal messages |
| | • Continues to enjoy songs and rhymes |
| | • Shows interest in simple poetry. |
| 5 to 8 years | • Has extensive vocabulary; by 7 years may use as many as 4000 words |
| | • Uses more complex sentence structures |
| | • Develops reading skills and improves comprehension skills |
| | • Develops writing skills (but possibly at slower rate than reading skills) including more accurate spelling, punctuation and joined-up writing |
| | • Continues to enjoy books, stories and poetry; by age 7 can recall the story so far if book read a chapter at a time |
| | • Gives very detailed accounts of past events and can anticipate future events |
| | • Vocalises ideas and feelings in more depth |
| | • Listens to and follows more complex instructions |
| | • Appreciates simple jokes due to more sophisticated language knowledge |
| | • Uses literacy skills to communicate and to access information e.g. story and letter writing, use of dictionaries, encyclopaedia, computers, Internet, e-mail. |

**Table 16.1** The sequence of speech, communication and language development

confidence. If children are full of anger, anxiety, frustration or fear, they need to express this. Talking about feelings is just as important as talking about ideas. Children who cannot explain or put into words/signs how they feel often have temper tantrums or show other kinds of challenging behaviour.

Unless children develop the language of **emotion**, they will not be able to express their feelings in ways that others find acceptable. This will cause difficulties with relationships and will have a damaging influence on their **social** development. See Figure 16.4: children need to learn to express

themselves for their own social development and to protect themselves. This child is learning the language of 'Please be gentle', 'That hurts', 'Please could you stop doing that because I don't like it', 'I'm a bit worried that if you squeeze my ears it might hurt me', and so on.

## Language and thinking

Language and thinking are often considered to be particularly closely linked. Can we think without words? Some researchers have suggested that we cannot have concepts without having language (spoken or signed languages such as BSL). Certainly, language is important for abstract thinking. It would be difficult to have an idea of what is fair or honest without any language. But some ideas can be expressed without words or sign language, and feelings and relationships often do not need language at an abstract level.

## How language supports behaviour

We use language to set limits and firm boundaries for children's behaviour. To do this, adults need to effectively communicate and exchange information with children according to their ages, needs and abilities. Language plays an important part in encouraging children to behave in acceptable ways as it enables them to:

- Understand verbal explanations of what is and is not acceptable behaviour
- Understand verbal explanations of why certain behaviour is not acceptable
- Express their own needs and feelings more clearly
- Avoid conflicts when handled by sensitive adults
- Reach compromises more easily
- Have a positive outlet for feelings through discussion and imaginative play.

Language and communication support behaviour by enabling young children to demonstrate these aspects of acceptable and positive behaviour:

- Being fairly independent
- Being realistically self-controlled
- Having some understanding of the needs and rights of others
- Participating in group activities
- Making friends with other children
- Meeting the challenge of new experiences without too much anxiety.

Children model their attitudes and actions on the behaviour of others. They imitate the actions and speech of those who are closest to them, for example acting at being 'mum', 'dad', 'key worker' or 'teacher'; copying the actions and mannerisms of adults around the home, childcare setting or school. All adults working with children need to be aware of the significant impact they make on children's development, including their behaviour, by

providing positive role models. Observing the communication and interactions of parents and other significant adults (such as early years practitioners) affects children's own behaviour, how children deal with their own feelings and how children relate to others. This is why it is so important for adults to provide positive role models for children's behaviour.

## How language supports social development

Children often talk out loud to themselves when they:

- feel frustrated and they are trying to understand something
- need to talk to themselves about how they feel
- are trying to organise an idea they are developing
- are trying out an idea and want to talk it through with themselves
- want to tell themselves what to do (give themselves an instruction).

Talking out loud to yourself is often described by researchers as 'egocentric speech'. It is helpful for children, as the bullet points above show. Gradually children begin to be able to put themselves in someone else's shoes, providing that person's experience links with their own. They move from being self-centred to being self-relating to being other-people-centred. This does not mean that the child is initially selfish; it just means they are becoming increasingly able to see something from someone else's point of view as well as their own.

It takes years for children to understand the difference between informal and formal situations. Going into school assembly or sitting at the table for a meal in a group are formal occasions, and children who have not experienced formal situations may need sensitive help. Too much time spent in formal situations is not good for a child's development and learning. Assembly time is difficult for young children because they have to sit, often in an uncomfortable position, for a long time, and be passive (not make an active response). Fortunately, it is becoming unusual for children below the age of 5 years to attend assemblies.

Even very young children readily learn about eating together in a group. They soon enjoy asking those next to them if they would like some vegetables passed to them, or saying 'thank you' for their second helping, or talking about what they like to eat. Mealtimes can be a very appropriate way of introducing children to formal gatherings in ways that allow them to enjoy participating. It is important that children are encouraged to be active, helping each other and themselves, enjoying chatting to people on their table and helping with the clearing away.

## How language supports learning

Effective communication is not just about conversations with young children. It also involves children being able to understand and use *the language of learning*. That is, the language needed to: understand concepts; participate in problem-solving; develop ideas and opinions.

Language helps children (and adults) to:

- talk to ourselves (see above) – children and adults often talk out loud to themselves; as we develop our language skills, what we say out loud becomes 'internal speech', so that we are increasingly able to think of the words rather than saying them out loud
- move from the here and now into thoughts about the past or the future, and back again
- use and make different symbols, from spoken/ signed language to the languages of dance, music, mathematical symbols, drawings, sculptures and models
- develop ideas, some of which become concepts, and put them into words
- express creative and imaginative thoughts and ideas
- express and communicate personal ideas
- think in abstract ways
- plan
- express feelings, think about emotional responses and manage them, becoming increasingly self-disciplined.

See Figure 16.5: although there is a conversation going on here, there are quite long pauses while the practitioner does the next bit of face painting. She holds the little girl's chin gently and the child trusts her. The child chose to have her face painted with a butterfly, and they have talked about the colour and the antennae on her forehead. Both are taking this seriously, so there are no jerky movements or loud talking. This needs to be a quiet time, with words said calmly.

# The potential impact of speech, language and communication difficulties on development

Some children may have speech, language and communication difficulties that affect their development, including their ability to communicate and interact effectively with others. For example: autistic spectrum disorders; behavioural and/or emotional difficulties; cognition difficulties affecting the ability to process language; hearing impairment; physical disabilities affecting articulation of sounds.

The potential impact of the wide range of communication difficulties varies greatly – from severe mental impairment to slight problems with social interaction (see Table 16. 2). The potential effects on each child's development depend on the severity of their speech, language and communication difficulties. Give children plenty of opportunities to join in, to express opinions and to interact with other children. Remember to focus on each child as a unique person with individual strengths, rather than focusing on the child's particular difficulties – that is, focus on what they *can* do rather than what they cannot.

**Figure 16.5** Communication can help to build trust

| Potential short-term impact | Potential long-term impact |
|---|---|
| Difficulty in communicating and interacting effectively with others, e.g. making friends | Difficulty in relating to other people, e.g. establishing and maintaining relationships |
| Difficulty with the articulation of sounds | Inability to understand the thoughts, feelings and needs of others |
| Cannot articulate thoughts into words quickly enough | Unable to express their own thoughts, feelings and needs effectively to others |
| Poor social skills | Social isolation |
| Difficulties in using verbal and/or non-verbal communication | Aggression, loss of control or mood swings |
| Difficulties with structuring language | A track record of inappropriate behaviour |
| Difficulties understanding language (receptive difficulties) | Lack of confidence in group situations |
| Difficulties using language (expressive difficulties) | Anxiety and/or depression |
| Difficulties learning to read and write | Very low self-esteem |
| Difficulties in acquiring communication skills | Reclusive and reluctant to talk |
| Easily distracted and inattentive | Unfulfilled potential and/or dependence on others |

**Table 16.2** The potential short- and long-term impacts of speech, language and communication difficulties on children's development

# Understand the importance and the benefits of adults supporting the speech, language and communication development of the children in own setting

It is important that children spend time with people who speak fluently, so that they hear the patterns of the language they are trying to learn. A stimulating environment which encourages children to talk is crucial. Hearing other people speak fluently means hearing something the child is able to understand: if the adult says, 'Oh dear, you've bumped your knee. Shall I rub it better?' and points at the child's knee and makes a rubbing mime, then the child has enough clues to understand what is being said. This is very important for young children, children with language delay and children who are learning English as an additional language.

Children learn by doing, so language is best learned when children are active in their learning. The practitioners might say to a 3-year-old child, 'You've got to the top of the slide, haven't you? Are you going to come down now?'

## Supporting communication in the early years

From the moment a baby is born, communicating begins. Babies have a different kind of cry for different situations: they cry for food, to say they are tired or with distress or pain. Babies listen to people's voices; they like the human voice more than other sounds. Babies 'call out' for company, as they become lonely if they spend too much time alone.

When we talk to babies, we speak in a high-pitched tone, in short phrases, placing emphasis on the key words and using a great deal of repetition. This is called parentese. However, in some cultures adults do not speak to babies in parentese. Instead, the babies watch their mothers working and talking with other adults.

When we converse with babies, we look at the baby and the baby looks at us. Eye contact is part of communication. Visually impaired babies respond by becoming still and listening intently, whereas sighted babies 'dance' in response to speech. Adults will pause and be still when they have said something to the baby, and the baby will usually 'reply' in babble, moving as he or she does so. We move when we talk to babies (body language).

Communication between babies, children and adults involves:

- facial expressions – smile, frown, raised eyebrow, eye contact
- gesture and body language – hugs, beckoning, clapping hands, shrugs, jumping with surprise, being stiff and ill at ease, feet and arms moving in response to someone talking to you
- moving together (in synchrony) in a proto-conversation – this can be either mirroring each other or imitating the other's movements and sounds
- movements of the hands and face are especially important for communication and language development
- pauses – these are very important; often we do not give babies and young children enough time to make their response
- rhythms, tone and melody of a language (musical aspects) – these are important in developing communication and spoken language
- intonation – the voice may be used to express fear, anger, pleasure, wanting to play, cooing, relaxing, and so on
- researchers have found that babies will finish a phrase in a musical way, adding a note that seems to complete it when they respond to people talking to them; this seems to be cross-cultural
- spoken language and sign languages (such as BSL) – these are agreed codes that develop according to the cultures in which they arise
- verbal or sign language – a child might say 'oggie' for dogs and all animals, so that only close family

understand what the baby is saying; this is a personal language, not yet a shared language beyond a close circle of people

- Makaton – a communication system that uses agreed and shared signs but is not a full language
- objects of reference – these build a personal communication system with an individual child, and are only shared between the child, the family and practitioners working with the child and the family.

## The positive effects of adult support for children and their carers

Positive effects may include improvements in: speech, language and communication skills; social interaction; behaviour; emotional development/self-confidence.

Praise and encouragement are essential components when supporting young children's speech, language and communication development. Young children need immediate and positive affirmations or rewards to show that their language and learning are progressing in accordance with the adult's (and child's) expectations. Adults should emphasise the **positive** aspects of young children's attempts at developing their speech, language and communication skills. Children gain confidence and increased positive self-esteem when they receive praise/rewards for their efforts and achievements, including encouragement to try new activities and experiences.

There are four main methods used to praise and encourage children:

1. **Verbal,** for example: 'praise' assemblies; positive comments about the child's behaviour or activities, such as 'Well done, Tom! This is a lovely story! Tell me what happened next.'
2. **Non-verbal,** for example: body language, leaning forward or turning towards a child to show interest in what the child is communicating; facial expressions: smiling; sign language – 'good boy/girl!'

3. **Symbolic,** for example: 'smiley faces' for carefully done work or positive behaviour; stickers for being a good listener or for reading well; stars or merit points for attempting and/or completing tasks.
4. **Written,** for example: merit certificates; written comments in head teacher's book; newsletter recording achievements; comments written (or stamped) on child's work such as 'Well done!' or 'Good work!'

### Activity

What methods do you use to provide positive praise and encouragement for the efforts and achievements of children in your setting?

Children's social and emotional development is closely linked with their language development, as communication involves social interaction with at least one other person. Confidence, self-esteem and self-image affect the way we all interact with other people, so this will necessarily affect the development of communication skills. (See sections on self-esteem and self-image in Chapter 14, Unit EYMP 3.)

## Varying levels of language among children entering early years provision

To participate fully in all aspects of education (and society), children need to successfully develop a wide range of language and communication skills. Adults working with young children need to be aware of the wide variety of language experiences which young children bring to the early years setting, and the environmental/social factors or special needs which may affect language development. Depending on their individual language experiences, some young children may not have reached the same level of language development as their peers or they may lack effective communication skills, while some children may be ahead of what is usually expected for children their age (for example, they may already have some reading skills).

Language development is affected by many factors, not just a child's chronological age. Some children may have special needs which affect their ability to communicate effectively with others (see above).

Other factors which affect children's speech, language and communication include poverty, race/culture, parental expectations and language experiences at home and in education settings (see below). Another important factor to remember is that physical maturity also plays a part in children's language development. Babies need to have physical control over their vocal chords, tongue, lips and jaw muscles to be able to articulate the sounds necessary to form their first words.

In addition, children (and adults) have two important areas of vocabulary usage: **passive vocabulary** – the language used by others which they can *understand* – and **active vocabulary** – the words which they actually *use* themselves. Children (and adults) can recognise and understand a larger number of words than they can speak (or write) themselves, whatever their level of development. The size of an individual's vocabulary (like all aspects of language development) depends on their language experiences, especially access to books and reading.

# Be able to provide support for the speech, language and communication development of the children in your own setting

You need to be able to demonstrate methods of providing support for speech, language and communication development, taking into account the age, specific needs, abilities and interests, and

## In Practice

Observe a small group of children involved in a language activity.

In your assessment, comment on each child's language and communication skills:

❏ Use of verbal language (e.g. vocabulary, sentence structure, babbling, imitating sounds)

❏ Use of non-verbal communication (e.g. body language, gestures, facial expressions, signing)

❏ Level of participation in the group situation (e.g. frequency of language, need for prompts from other children/adults)

❏ Level of social interaction (e.g. ability to take turns in speaking and listening, following instructions for the activity or rules of a game).

Suggest practical ideas to assist the children's language and communication skills in future activities.

## In Practice

❏ Plan, implement and evaluate a language activity for a small group of children, such as news time, circle time, discussion, story time or phonics session.

❏ You could use your suggestions from the previous observation as the starting point for planning this activity.

❏ The activity should encourage the children's active participation, including attentive listening and communicating with others during the activity, as well as supervising and maintaining the children's interest throughout the activity.

home language (where this is different to that of the setting) of the children in your setting. These methods may include: adapting your own language; scaffolding the child's language; giving children the time and opportunity to communicate; facilitating communication between children; learning through play; working with carers.

## Adapting your own language

It is important to communicate with children in a manner that is clear and concise and appropriate to their ages, needs and abilities. This involves: using words and phrases that children will understand; actively listening to children; responding positively to children's views and feelings; clarifying and confirming points to reinforce children's knowledge and understanding. When communicating with children: ask and answer questions to prompt appropriate responses from them and to check their understanding; encourage them to ask questions and contribute their own ideas; adapt communication methods to suit their individual language needs if they have special needs such as a hearing impairment or they are bilingual.

## Scaffolding the child's language

As well as enabling children to use language, early years practitioners can also help young children to understand the *rules of language*. Once children start to combine words to make sentences, they progress through various stages as the structure and organisation of language becomes gradually more systematic. This systematic structuring of language is called **grammar**. For example:

- **Stage 1:** Very young children use simple two- or three-word phrases or sentences. Grammatical indicators are not present at this stage: no plurals, e.g. 'Many car'; no possessive 's', e.g. 'Tom teddy'; no tense markers such as 'ed' or 'ing', e.g. 'It rain'; no auxiliary verbs such as 'is' or 'do', e.g. 'No like cake'. Young children only use nouns, verbs, adjectives and adverbs such as 'now' or 'soon'.
- **Stage 2:** Young children begin to use grammatical indicators that were previously missing. Note the irregular use of past tense forms, e.g. 'camed'

(came) and 'goed' (went), and plurals, e.g. 'sheeps' (sheep). Gradually, children begin to use grammar in increasingly adult forms.

Children do not learn grammar through imitation alone; they need opportunities to discover the rules of language for themselves by experimenting and being creative with words in a variety of situations.

Early years practitioners can help children with grammar by repeating back the correct form of language when the child makes a grammatical error. Some examples are:

- **Possessive pronouns** – the child says, 'This Tom hat and that Teena hat', so the adult replies, 'Yes, that is *your* hat and this is *my* hat'.
- **Possessive 's'** – the child says, 'Here Marley boots and teacher boots', so the adult replies, 'Yes, these are Marley's boots and those are Ms Kamen's boots'.
- **Plurals** – the child says, 'We saw sheeps', so the adult replies, 'Yes, we saw *some sheep* at the farm'.
- **Tense markers** – the child says, 'The cat goed out', so the adult replies, 'Yes, the cat *went* outside', or the child says, 'Mummy come!', so the adult replies, 'Yes, your mummy is com*ing* into the nursery now'.
- **Auxiliary verbs** – the child says, 'We done play dough', so the adult replies, 'Yes we *did* make play dough this morning', or the child says, 'We is walking to the park', so the adult replies, 'Yes, we *are* walking to the park'.
- **Negatives** – the child says, 'I not eat 'nana', so the adult replies, 'I see you *haven't* eaten your banana'.
- **Questions** – the child asks, 'More?', so the adult asks, 'Would you like some more milk?'

You should give positive feedback, praise and encouragement to all children by commenting positively on their efforts to communicate in different ways. Remember to be positive towards each child's attempts at language and communication by considering children's individual interest and abilities, valuing children's home or community language(s), and being aware of children's special language needs. (See relevant sections below.)

# Giving children the time and opportunity to communicate

Early years practitioners need to provide appropriate opportunities for language and to ask the right type of questions to stimulate communication. You can do this by providing a wide range of materials and by encouraging young children to talk about their interests, what they are doing and what is happening around them. You need to provide appropriate activities and experiences to enable young children to develop their speech, language and communication skills in meaningful situations, for example, providing opportunities for children's self-expression and self-evaluation through discussion, news time, circle time, painting, drawing, writing, music making, drama and dance.

# Facilitating communication between children

The early years practitioner needs to act as a **facilitator** by providing opportunities for communication between children. For example:

- Talking about their day, experiences and interests with other children and adults
- Talking about special events such as birthdays, a new baby, religious festivals
- Talking during imaginative play activities: playing with pretend/role play equipment such as dressing-up clothes, home play area, play shop, puppets; playing with dolls, teddies and other cuddly toys; playing with small-scale toys such as toy cars, garages and road systems, train set, dolls' houses
- Playing games and puzzles
- Problem-solving during activities such as mathematics, science and technology
- Follow-up discussion after an activity or event, such as watching a DVD/television or a live performance, listening to a story or recorded music
- Co-operative group work
- Talking while doing activities – not necessarily related to the task!

# Learning through play

Early years practitioners need to provide opportunities for play which are appropriate to the children's ages/levels of development, especially activities and materials which encourage language and communication, such as:

- Toys and other interesting objects to look at and play with, such as household objects (remember safety)
- Sounds to listen to, including voices, music, songs and rhymes, and noise-makers such as commercial and home-made musical instruments
- Construction materials including wooden bricks, plastic bricks and 'junk' modelling
- Natural materials, such as water, sand, clay, dough and cooking ingredients
- Creative materials, such as paint, paper and glue
- Imaginative play materials (see above)
- Outdoor activities and outings including playgrounds, gardening, visits to parks and museums, swimming.

# Working with parents and carers

Early years practitioners also need to work with parents and carers to encourage their support and participation in activities which help to develop children's speech, language and communication both at home and in the setting. For example, encourage parents and carers to:

- Share books and stories (appropriate to the age/level of development of their children) at home, including cloth books, board books, activity books, pop-up books, picture books, audio books, simple textbooks and encyclopaedias
- Visit their local library, including special story sessions for the under-fives
- Share books and stories with children in the setting, for example bilingual story time
- Participate in activities within the setting, for example cooking, sewing and gardening activities
- Participate in special events in the setting, such as festivals
- Participate in special events outside the setting, such as visits to parks, museums, farms and wildlife centres.

## Key terms

**Facilitator** – Person who makes things easier by providing the appropriate environment and resources for learning.

 **In Practice**

Based on your own experiences of working with children, describe an example for *each* of these methods:

❏ adapting own language

❏ scaffolding the child's language

❏ giving children the time and opportunity to communicate

❏ facilitating communication between children

❏ learning through play

❏ working with parents/carers.

 **In Practice**

Observe a small group of three or four children with an adult. Note examples of turn-taking and any of the things you would expect to find in a conversation that have been identified in this chapter. Was there a difference in the number of times individual children spoke in the group? In what way? Evaluate the pros and cons of small groups and large groups.

*Every Child a Talker* (ECaT) is a developmentally appropriate approach that emphasises the importance of a supportive and stimulating environment in which children are encouraged to develop communication and language. It supports the work of the Early Years Foundation Stage in England, in home learning environments (childminders) and in group settings of all kinds.

It helps practitioners to:

● identify what helps communication and language to develop

● audit their language provision and plan appropriately

● work with children with English as an additional language (EAL)

● make the most of everyday activities and experiences that promote communication and language

● make a good partnership with parents.

See the way in which the adult is talking to the child in Figure 16.6: she is at the child's level, and shows that she finds it interesting through her body language (putting her head on one side and looking directly at the child to establish contact). The child

**Figure 16.6** Using non-verbal communication is essential when working with young children

shows that she welcomes this by her relaxed facial expression and her arms. Note that her arms are bending onto her shoulders, which is what we do when we feel relaxed, and her hands are opened out too (clenched hands would indicate that the child felt tense). All of this is non-verbal communication, but it tells us a great deal about the warmth, sensitivity and respect in the social interaction and relationship of the child and adult.

## Promoting language diversity

We live in a multicultural society where a huge variety of languages are used to communicate. We are surrounded by different accents, dialects and other ways of communicating, such as sign language. All children should have an awareness and understanding of other people's languages, while still feeling proud of their own **community language** and being able to share this with others. Settings where only English (or Welsh) is spoken still need an awareness of other languages to appreciate fully the multicultural society they live in.

While promoting language diversity, we need to remember that we live in a society where English is the dominant language; developing language and literacy skills in English is essential to all children if they are to become effective communicators both in and outside the setting. Most children starting nursery or school will speak English even if they have a different cultural background. However, there are some children who do start nursery or school with little or no English because they are new to this country or English is not used much at home.

A shared language is essential to provide children with opportunities to communicate and share cultural experiences. You should ensure that children's community language(s) are equally valued and that you support the language development of children with bilingual home backgrounds, for example including community languages in displays, notices, books, magazines, etc.

Bilingual means 'speaking two languages', which applies to some children (and practitioners) in settings in the United Kingdom. 'Multilingual' is used to describe someone who uses more than two languages. The term 'bilingual' is widely used for all children who speak two or more languages.

The Early Years Foundation Stage (EYFS) recommends that practitioners 'encourage children

to recognise their own unique qualities and the characteristics they share with other children. Discussions which take place in a positive way result in children having good feelings about themselves, feeling neither inferior nor superior to others.' (Griffin, 2008; pp.102–3)

To value and promote language diversity, the early years setting should provide and use resources which reflect the diverse cultures of our society as a whole. For example:

- Puzzles, books, dolls, puppets and small world figures from a variety of ethnic and cultural backgrounds and family groupings – use these regularly and talk to the children about them
- Pretend play materials representing everyday items (such as cooking utensils and clothing) used in a range of cultures – ensure they are treated with respect and show children how to use unfamiliar items, e.g. draping a sari, using a wok
- Books with dual language or script – show children that English is not the only language spoken and written
- Paints and crayons offering a full range of skin tones so that children can portray people from a variety of ethnic backgrounds accurately – ensure that they are always available, not just as part of a special project.

(Griffin, 2008; p.106)

You can support the language needs of bilingual children by:

- Encouraging the children to use their community languages some of the time; this promotes security and social acceptance, which will make learning English easier
- Inviting parents/grandparents to read or tell stories in community languages or to be involved with small groups for cooking, sewing or art and design activities
- Using songs and rhymes to help introduce new vocabulary
- Using play activities and/or games to encourage and extend language.

Bilingual children do not see their use of different languages as a difficulty. Early years practitioners need to maintain this attitude and to encourage all bilingual children to see their linguistic ability as the asset it really is in our multicultural society.

## Key terms

**Community language** – main language spoken in a child's home.

 **In Practice**

❑ Give examples of how your setting promotes language diversity and encourages children to use their community languages.

❑ How do (or could) you provide support for the communication skills of bilingual children?

## Supporting special language needs

*All* children have individual language needs, but some children may have *additional* or *special language needs* that affect their ability to communicate effectively with others. Being able to structure and use language is an enormous task for everyone; it takes the first seven to eight years of life to learn how to form all the different sounds correctly. Some sounds are more difficult to pronounce than others, for example: s, sh, scr, br, cr, gr and th. Most young children have problems with these sounds at first, but eventually are able to pronounce them properly.

Some children may have difficulties with structuring language, such as problems with:

- The articulation of sounds, syllables and words (as mentioned above)
- Grammar or syntax – words, phrases or sentence structure
- *Understanding* language (**receptive** difficulties) and/or *using* language (**expressive** difficulties).

Children with delayed language development go through the same sequence of language development as other children, but at a much slower rate.

Disordered language development is more likely to be caused by:

- Minimal brain damage affecting areas relating to language
- Physical disabilities affecting the articulation of sounds
- Sensory impairment affecting hearing or visual abilities
- Cognitive difficulties affecting the ability to process language.

Many of the activities already suggested in this chapter will be suitable for *all* children, including those with special language needs. Some pupils, especially those with severely delayed or disordered language development, may need specialist help from a speech and language therapist.

## Language delay or difficulty

There are a variety of reasons why language may be delayed:

- The child may be growing up and spending time in environments that are not supporting the development of communication and language.
- The child may have a learning difficulty that makes it a challenge to process language – for example, aphasia, Asperger's syndrome, autism or Down's syndrome.
- The child may have a hearing or visual impairment.

For children with language delay, it may be necessary to support their language development with the help of a speech and language therapist, a specialist language teacher and other professionals, such as health visitors who work in the home context with families and young children.

Not being able to talk or listen with ease can cause frustration, loneliness and a feeling of powerlessness. It can be very difficult for some children to listen and talk – for example, those who have a hearing impairment, severe learning difficulties, moderate learning difficulties or physical challenges such as cerebral palsy. It is very important that every child is encouraged to find ways of communicating with other people. A considerable minority of children are now helped to learn sign language or sign systems

(Makaton), or to use personal references which help them to communicate. It is important to remember that gestures and touch are effective forms of communication, as well as shared signs, finger spelling and computers and keyboards.

- **British Sign Language** (BSL) is now an official language, using signs rather than words. Children with profound hearing loss are often taught BSL.
- Some children with disabilities and special educational needs are taught **Makaton**, which is a simpler communication system than BSL. It uses shared signs, but it is not a full language.
- Some children use **PECS** – pictures/symbols that help them to think ahead or think back about what they will do and what they have done. This is an example of a non-verbal augmentative communication system.
- A small number of children with disabilities and complex needs will not use a communication system that is understood by others. They will continue to use personal communication signs, which only those close to them will understand. They are helped to find ways to communicate that are right for them and their families and close friends through **objects of reference**, a system devised by Professor Adam Ockelford.

## In Practice

Describe how you have provided (or could provide) support for children with special language needs in your setting. Include examples for children with additional communication and/or interaction needs.

## Using day-to-day activities to encourage young children's speech, language and communication development

Adults working with children need to spend time listening carefully to individual children and to what children have to communicate in small or large group situations such as news time or story sessions.

Informal 'conversations' are an important part of communicating with children. When adults are not actively involved in the children's activities, perhaps because they are putting up displays or preparing materials for later activities, they should always be willing to listen to the children, who will undoubtedly approach them to start up a conversation. Children can learn a great deal about language and the world around them from the spontaneous, unplanned communications that occur during everyday activities such as break/playtime, milk/juice time, meal times, setting up/clearing away play and learning activities.

Many of the following day-to-day activities allow children the opportunity to talk and listen in relaxed, informal situations. They allow children and adults to share their experiences in a natural way through situations which may be similar to their home experiences such as meal times. Activities which can encourage young children's speech, language and communication development include:

- **Natural materials:** sand, water, play dough, clay
- **Domestic activities:** milk/juice times, meal times, tidy up times, cooking and washing up, washing clothes. (Remember children's safety.)
- **Books:** sharing books and stories with an individual or small group
- **Displays:** interest tables, wall displays, posters
- **Animals:** pets in the setting and/or in the home
- **Toys/hobbies:** special days/times for 'show and tell' when children can talk about their special interests or favourite objects
- **Special occasions:** birthdays, festivals, preparing for visits or visitors.

## Encouraging conversations and group discussions

Conversations need to:

- be two-way
- involve sharing feelings and ideas
- involve thinking of each other
- be a real exchange of feelings and ideas between children and other children, and between children and adults
- include turn-taking as the conversation flows

- involve thinking about what will be of interest to each other, as well as things that are of interest to oneself.

## One-to-one conversations with young children

Young children are beginning to establish a strong sense of self, realising that they are a separate person; this is why their favourite words are often 'no' and 'mine'.

Researchers have noticed that although toddlers often turn their backs on their mother (or other adults they are familiar with and have a close relationship with, such as their key person) and say 'No!' to a suggestion, they do in fact take up and imitate the idea offered to them. Adults need to be aware of this, and to realise that when a toddler says 'No!' they really mean they want to do something for themselves, and to make the decision for themselves, rather than feeling controlled. It is all part of developing a strong sense of self.

Remember:

- Children need to be spoken to as individuals.
- They need to spend time with adults who are patient with them and who listen to them. It is hard for young children to put their feelings and thoughts into words, and it takes time, so adults need to be aware of this. It is very tempting to prompt children and say things for them. Instead, try nodding or saying, 'Hmm'. This gives children time to say what they want to.
- Do not correct what children say. Instead, elaborate on what they have said, giving them the correct pattern. For example, Shanaz, at 2 years, says, 'I falled down.' The adult replies, 'Yes, you did, didn't you? You fell down. Never mind, I will help you up.'
- It is important that all children experience unrushed, one-to-one conversations with adults and with other children – for example, when sharing a drink together at the snack table, chatting while using the clay or sharing a book together.
- Value and respect the child's language and culture.

- Have genuine conversations with children, using gestures, eye contact and props.
- Encourage children to listen to and enjoy stories, including those of their own culture.
- Introduce 'book language', such as 'Once upon a time . . .'

## Small group discussions

Children need help when taking part in group discussions. Groups should be no more than four to eight children, and wherever possible should be with the key person whom the children know well. Having to wait for a turn frustrates young children, as does having to wait until everyone is sitting quietly. It is best to start a song or a dance with plenty of actions, so that everyone can join in from the beginning of the group time. Children are then much more likely to be willing to sit quietly for a story.

In a small group, children can take part in the discussion more easily. Group times should be no longer than ten to fifteen minutes in length.

## Children who do not speak

It is important that children who do not speak when they attend a group setting are not put under pressure to speak. But it is also important to create an environment that encourages children to communicate and talk/sign. This can be achieved by:

- observing to see how the child spends the day in the setting – share your observations with your line manager and the team
- checking that a silent child can see and hear – this is very important
- bearing in mind that a child under emotional stress may become withdrawn and will need sensitive encouragement to talk/sign
- inviting a child to talk about something during small group time, or perhaps in a one-to-one story, but respecting their decision if they turn down the invitation to speak, so that they do not feel bad about it
- using stories and rhymes with props and pictures to make them easy to understand

- making sure that the child has understood what you have said – it may be necessary to try different ways of explaining something
- remembering that other children can often explain something to another child in a way that helps them to understand.

**In Practice**

Nathan (aged 6 years) is a quiet and shy child who needs lots of encouragement to participate in group discussions. He enjoys books and ICT activities. Suggest ways in which you can encourage his communication skills.

# Evaluate the effectiveness of speech, language and communication support for children in your own setting.

You need to evaluate the effectiveness of speech, language and communication support for children in your setting as this will enable you to:

- Understand the wide range of speech, language and communication development demonstrated by young children
- Know and understand the sequence of children's development
- Use this knowledge to link theory and practice in your own setting
- Assess children's language and development and communication skills
- Plan activities appropriate to children's individual language needs.

## Observing children's speech, language and communication

Adults working with young children need to be able to look and to listen attentively to how children communicate. By observing carefully, you can discover the range and variety of language used by the children in your setting and improve your own skills in providing appropriate opportunities for encouraging and extending children's speech, language and communication development.

Regular observations are also helpful in identifying any potential problems children may have with their speech, language and communication skills. The observing adult can identify the ways in which each child communicates, how the child interacts with others, the child's social skills, and any difficulties the child has in communicating.

A continuous record of a child's language difficulties (for example, in a diary format) can help the adult to identify specific problems. Working with parents, colleagues and specialist advisers (if necessary), the early years practitioner can then plan a suitable programme to enable the child to overcome these difficulties. Observations can provide a check that children's language is progressing in the expected ways.

You can observe children's language in a variety of situations. Remember we all use language in some form in *everything* we do. For example, you could observe the following situations:

- A child talking with another child or an adult
- An adult talking with a small group of children
- A small group of children engaged in a role play activity
- A child playing alone
- Small or large group discussions such as news time or circle time
- An adult reading or telling a story to a child or group of children
- A child or group of children participating in a creative activity such as painting or drawing
- A child or children playing outside
- A child involved in a literacy activity such as writing news, a story or a poem.

**Research Activity**

Find out about the policies in your setting with regard to child observations, language assessments, record keeping and confidentiality. Remember to keep this information in mind when doing your own observations of children within the setting.

## Evaluating children's speech, language and communication

Once you have recorded your observation of the child's language and communication skills, you need to assess this information in relation to:

- The aims of the observation
- What you observed about this child's language and communication skills in *this* situation
- How this compares to the expected language development for a child of this age
- Any factors which may have affected the child's language ability such as the immediate environment, significant events, illness, the child's cultural or linguistic background, and any special needs
- How the adult supported the child's speech, language and communication.

Your college tutor or assessor should give you guidelines on how to present your observations.

## Planning to support a child's speech, language and communication

Following your observation and assessment of a child's speech, language and communication, your recommendations can provide the basis for planning appropriate activities and experiences to encourage or extend the child's abilities in these areas.

Effective planning is based on children's individual needs, abilities and interests, hence the need for accurate child observations and assessments. These needs have to be integrated into the curriculum requirements of your particular setting; for example, themes and activities may be related to the Early Years Foundation Stage.

When you have decided on the appropriate activities and experiences (in consultation with colleagues and/or parents as relevant to your setting), you can then implement them. Remember to evaluate the plan afterwards. Further observations and assessments will be necessary to maintain up-to-date information on each child's developmental needs.

## In Practice

Observe a young child communicating with another child or adult. Focus on the child's speech, language and communication skills. In your assessment, comment on:

- ❏ any vocabulary used by the child
- ❏ the complexity of the child-centred structure
- ❏ any non-verbal communication used, such as body language, gestures, facial expressions

- ❏ the child's level of social interaction. For example, did the child appear confident when speaking? Did the child have a friendly and relaxed manner? Did the child need coaxing to communicate?
- ❏ the role of the adult in supporting the child's speech, language and communication.

## In Practice

Plan, implement and evaluate a language activity such as:

- ❏ Circle time, news time or discussion
- ❏ Story time
- ❏ Nursery and/or finger rhymes
- ❏ Early reading activities such as phonics.

Use the information gained from your previous observation (including your recommendations for encouraging or extending one child's language and communication skills) as a starting point for this activity.

Remember to review and evaluate the activity afterwards.

# Be able to contribute to maintaining a positive environment that supports speech, language and communication

## The importance of the environment in supporting children's speech, language and communication

While there are often differences between children's language experiences, it is very important for the early years setting not to exacerbate those differences.

Remember that while you may sometimes have limited control over the environmental/social factors outside the setting, you can and should help to maximise opportunities within your setting for enabling language development and encouraging communication skills by providing a stimulating, language-rich environment.

A well-planned and stimulating environment is essential to children's language development. Play and conversation are important elements in this development because it is through these that young children learn about themselves, other people and the world around them.

## Review evidence about the key factors that provide a supportive speech, language and communication environment

It is important to plan and organise an environment for children and families that is welcoming and user-friendly. This involves planning and providing an enabling physical environment for children, including adapting the environment to meet

**Figure 16.7** A language-rich environment

children's needs (according to their ages, abilities and any special needs) and ensuring that any barriers to participation are addressed. It also involves organising space and resources to meet children's needs within an accessible, comfortable and stimulating environment. You should provide a caring, nurturing and responsive environment where children and their families feel valued and respected.

Key factors that provide a supportive speech, language and communication environment may include: the physical environment; staff roles and responsibilities; training needs and opportunities; views of the child; appropriate involvement of carers.

## The physical environment

When planning and providing an enabling physical environment for children you must ensure that the setting meets regulatory health and safety requirements. You must maintain procedures for risk assessment and health and safety including maintaining children's safety during play and learning activities. (For detailed information see Chapter 2, Unit SHC 32.)

The precise way the environment is organised to support children's speech, language and communication depends on:

- The type of setting and the age range of the children
- Any specific curriculum requirements, such as the Early Years Foundation Stage
- The resources for particular activities
- The developmental needs of the children

- The play and/or learning objectives for the children
- Behaviour management strategies
- The inclusion of children with special needs.

## Staff roles and responsibilities

Quality early years provision for young children can only be delivered through caring, personal relationships between young children and early years practitioners. In group settings such as a crèche or day nursery, a key person (or key worker) system is essential to provide links between individual practitioners and individual children. The key features of an effective key person system are:

- The same practitioner is responsible for the physical needs of a small number of individual young children who need to be able to recognise the face of the person who changes them, feeds them or to whom they wake from a nap
- The key person responds sensitively to individual young children, knows their preferences and develops personal rituals of songs, smiles and enjoyable 'jokes'
- The key person develops a friendly relationship with each child's parent(s), sharing ideas about the child and communicating important information about the day or the child's state of health
- The key person observes, assesses and records the learning and development of their key children.

(Lindon, 2002a)

To become skilful communicators, babies and children need to be with people who have meaning

## Guidelines for organising the physical environment

- Fire exits must not be obstructed, locked or hidden from view.
- Chairs, tables and play equipment must be the correct size and height for the ages/levels of development of the children.
- Books, jigsaws, computers and art and design materials need to be used in areas with a good source of light, near a natural source of light if possible.
- Water, sand, art and design activities need to be provided in areas with appropriate floor surfaces and with washing facilities nearby.
- Any large or heavy equipment that has to be moved for use should be close to where it is stored.

for them and with whom they have warm and loving relationships, such as their family or carers and, in a group situation, a key person whom they know and trust. To give all children the best opportunities for effective development and learning in communication, language and literacy, early years practitioners should give particular attention to the following areas:

- Helping children to communicate thoughts, ideas and feelings and build up relationships with adults and each other
- Giving daily opportunities to share and enjoy a wide range of fiction and non-fiction books, rhymes, music, songs, poetry and stories
- Allowing children to see adults reading and writing, and encouraging children to experiment with writing for themselves through making marks, personal writing symbols and conventional script
- Identifying and responding to any particular difficulties in children's language development at an early stage.

(DCFS, 2008; pp.41/42)

## Activity

Describe the role of a key person (or key worker) in your setting.

Early help is very important and effective early assistance with communication difficulties can prevent more complex problems later on. Early intervention is important because:

- Language and communication skills are essential to the learning process
- Language has a vital role in the understanding of concepts
- The main foundations of language are constructed between the ages of 18 months and 4½ years, during which time the majority of children fully integrate language as part of the thinking and learning process
- It is easier to assist with language development and communication skills during this critical

three-year period than to sort out problems once children have reached school age
- Effective communication skills are essential to positive social interaction and emotional well-being.

## Training needs and opportunities

To provide effective support for a child's speech, language and communication, practitioners may need to access additional training opportunities.

The role of the early years practitioner is crucial in planning and resourcing a challenging environment which extends and develops children's speech, language and communication. To do this effectively, the early years setting should provide time and space for knowledge-sharing and support for continuous professional development for all staff. This includes reflective practice, self-evaluation and informed discussion to identify the setting's strengths and priorities for development that will improve the quality of provision for all children.

A continuously improving early years setting will have well-qualified and experienced staff who:

- Are appropriately trained, with up-to-date skills and qualifications
- Are motivated and supported to raise their skills and qualification level to level 3 and beyond
- Engage in regular cycles of planning and review, informed by accurate record-keeping, including information on children's learning progress (and the relevant early years framework)
- Understand and engage in informed reflective practice – both individually and in groups
- Work collaboratively within the setting to share knowledge, question practice and test new ideas – with high aspirations for every child
- Support quality improvement processes in the setting, recognising how these processes can extend effective practice and help improve outcomes for every child
- Are keen to share best practice with other practitioners through local, regional and national networking
- Work together with other practitioners and parents to support transitions, both between settings and between the setting and school

- Are committed to the development of sustained shared thinking by offering encouragement, clarifying ideas and asking open questions which support and extend children's thinking and help them make connections in learning – while ensuring a balance between adult-led and child-initiated activities
- Work in partnership with parents – sharing information and involving them in their child's continuous learning and development.

(DCFS, 2008; p.9)

There are a number of agencies which offer advice, support and/or training for children's speech, language and communication development. For example: health visitors; speech and language therapists; educational psychologists; portage workers; advisory teachers; charities such as Afasic, National Autism Society, RNIB and RNID.

## Research Activity

Find out about training relating to supporting children's speech, language and communication which is available in your setting and/or the local community.

## The views of the child

You should provide a caring and responsive environment by:

- providing flexible routines to support children's wellbeing
- explaining any foreseeable changes to the child's environment clearly and honestly
- providing reassurance, explanations and comfort for any unforeseen changes
- being flexible and responsive to children's changing needs and circumstances.

You should allow children to take responsibility for themselves and others by providing opportunities which encourage them to become more independent according to their age, needs and abilities. This includes taking the child's views into account and providing opportunities for children to make choices

or be involved in decision-making, for example, choosing play activities and/or resources.

Early years practitioners should also take account of the views of the child by:

- Showing sensitivity to the many different ways in which children express themselves non-verbally
- Encouraging children to communicate their thoughts, ideas and feelings through a range of expressive forms, such as body movement, art, dance and songs
- Talking about things which interest young children, and listening and responding to their ideas and questions
- Listening to children and taking account of what they say in response to them
- Showing interest in the words children use to communicate and describe their experiences
- Valuing children's contributions and using them to inform and shape the direction of discussions
- Talking to children about what they have been doing and helping them to reflect upon and explain events – for example, 'You told me this model was going to be a tractor. What's this lever for?'
- Making books with children of activities they have been doing, using photographs of them as illustrations.

(DCFS, 2008)

## Appropriate involvement of parents/carers

Positive working relationships with parents/carers are essential to provide continuity of care for young children. Partnership between parents and practitioners depends on regular and open communication where contributions from both parties are acknowledged and valued. Friendly communication on a regular basis ensures continuity and consistency in providing shared routines and timing any necessary changes. Parents and practitioners can keep up-to-date with what a young child has learned or is nearly ready to do through regular conversation when they can exchange information and share delight about the young child's discoveries and interests (Lindon, 2002a).

Early years practitioners have a key role to play in working with parents to support their young children's speech, communication and language development. Regular information should be provided for parents about activities undertaken by the children, for example, through wall displays, photographs and examples of children's work. Early years practitioners should also talk to parents to ensure that the needs of the child are being met appropriately, and that records of development and progress are shared with parents and other professionals as necessary.

Early years practitioners can work in partnership with parents to support young children's speech, communication and language development by:

- Creating positive relationships with parents by listening to them and offering information and support
- Finding out from parents how they like to communicate with their baby, noting especially the chosen language
- Finding out from parents how children make themselves understood at home; confirm which is their preferred language
- Recognising and valuing the importance of all languages spoken and written by parents and children
- Communicating with parents to exchange and update information about babies' personal words
- Encouraging parents whose children are learning English as an additional language to continue to encourage use of the first language at home; explain that strong foundations in a home language support the development of English
- Using rhymes from a variety of cultures and asking parents to share their favourites from their home languages
- Explaining to parents the importance of reading to children, asking about favourite books and offering book loans
- Sharing and reflecting with parents on children's progress and development, ensuring that appropriate support is available where parents do not speak or understand English

- Discussing with colleagues and parents how each child responds to activities, adults and their peers; build on this to plan future activities and experiences for each child.

(DCFS, 2008)

Take the time each day to chat briefly with the parents when you hand the child back into their care. Keep it short so that the child can interact with the parents as soon as possible. Sort out how you will share more detailed information about the child with the parents, for example keeping a diary or daily log of the child's day including food/drink intake, hours slept, play and early learning activities done, any developmental progress made. You could also make a brief note of any specific plans for the next day, for example reminders about outings such as going swimming or to the library. The parents can also use the diary/daily log to share information with you, for example if the child did not sleep well the night before, and reminders about immunisations, dental check-ups or returning library books.

## In Practice

Describe how you have contributed to maintaining a positive environment that supports children's speech, language and communication. Include information on: the physical environment; staff roles and responsibilities; training needs and opportunities; views of the child; appropriate involvement of parents or carers.

# Demonstrate how settings use the environment to provide effective support for speech, language and communication for all children

The early years setting needs to provide the space and opportunities for effective communication to take place and to enable children (and adults) to use the different modes of language. Suitable areas need to be created to facilitate the development of children's language and communication skills. For example:

- **Writing tables** enabling children to 'make their mark' using a variety of writing tools (crayons, pencils, pens, pastels, chalks) on different shapes, sizes, textures and types of paper (plain, coloured, tissue, graph)
- **Displays,** including interest tables, displays of children's work in construction models, wall displays and posters to provide a stimulus for talk
- **Simple science and mathematics equipment,** including sand and/or water trays to encourage exploration and conversation
- **Pretend play areas** – home play area, shop, cafe, post office or space station to encourage language and communication skills through imaginative play
- **Book displays and story corner** to promote children's interest in books and to develop their early literacy skills
- **ICT equipment,** including audio-visual aids and computers to extend the children's range of language and literacy skills, for example games and activities to encourage letter and sound recognition.

## The importance of labelling

Very young children respond to labels even before they can read them; they will ask adults what labels say. Using pictures or objects as well as written words helps children to make sense of labels and to develop their own literacy skills.

Labelling introduces young children to one of the important purposes of written language: providing information or directions. Labels encourage children's independence in reading and writing. A special place for children to keep their belongings (whether on a hook, in a drawer, tray or basket) clearly labelled with each child's name, is an essential part of the effective language-rich environment. With very young children, a picture on the left-hand side of the label helps them to remember to work from left to right in reading and writing activities. See Figure 16.8 for an example.

**Figure 16.8** A label with a picture and name

Labels on important everyday objects in the setting assist children's early literacy skills and help to extend their vocabulary within a meaningful context. Where possible use sentences rather than single words: see Figure 16.9.

**Please put the crayons back here.**

Please close the **door.**

**Figure 16.9** Using sentences in labels

Clearly labelled areas and storage can help extend children's language as well as aiding the development of their social skills and independence: see Figure 16.10.

**4 Four** children can play with the **sand.**

**Figure 16.10** Labels can extend children's language as well as their social skills

## Promoting language by taking responsibility

Effective communication is also promoted by encouraging children to take responsibility for everyday tasks within the setting. Young children are quite capable of making their own decisions, and this helps to develop their independence and extends their communication skills even further. For example, children as young as 4 years old can be responsible for: tidying up their own activities, getting equipment out (under adult supervision for safety reasons, of course); choosing their own activities; following written and/or pictorial instructions for tasks/activities to be done that day; recording weather and other data.

To give all children the best opportunities for effective speech, communication and language development, early years practitioners should provide an enabling environment by:

- Planning an environment that is rich in signs, symbols, notices, numbers, words, rhymes, books, pictures, music and songs that take into account children's different interests, understanding, home backgrounds and cultures
- Allowing plenty of time for children to browse and share these resources with adults and other children
- Providing opportunities for children who may need to use alternative communication systems to discover ways of recording their ideas and to gain access to texts in an alternative way, for example through ICT
- Providing time and relaxed opportunities for children to develop spoken language through sustained conversations between children and adults, both one-to-one, in small groups and between the children themselves
- Allowing children time to initiate conversations, respecting their thinking time and silences and helping them to develop the interaction
- Showing particular awareness of, and sensitivity to, the needs of children learning English as an additional language, using their home language when appropriate and ensuring close teamwork between practitioners, parents and bilingual workers so that the children's developing use of English and other languages support each other.

(EYFS, p. 42)

### Activity

Describe how your setting provides a language-rich environment which encourages opportunities for appropriate activities and experiences to enable children to develop their speech, language and communication.

Useful resources

**Organisations and websites**
**Talk to Your Baby**
This organisation is part of the National Literacy Trust, and has campaigned for front-facing pushchairs which encourage adults to talk to children and show them exciting experiences. Many adults use the mobile phone and ignore children as they push them along, so that babies and toddlers do not have the opportunity for interesting and shared conversations with their parents/carers:
**www.talktoyourbaby.org.uk**

**Siren Films**
Siren Films produces high-quality DVDs covering a wide range of topics including early literacy and schemas in toddlers:
**www.sirenfilms.co.uk**

**Books**
Alcott, M. (2002) *An Introduction to Children with Special Needs.* Hodder & Stoughton.

Browne, A. (2009) *Developing Language and Literacy 3–8.* 3rd Edition. Sage.

Bruce, T. and Spratt, J. (2008) *Essentials of Literacy from 0–7.* Sage.

Cole, J. *et al.* (2001) *Helping Children Through Activities in the Early Years.* Hodder & Stoughton.

Conteh, J. (ed.) (2006) *Promoting Learning for Bilingual Pupils 3–11: Opening Doors to Success.* Sage.

Godwin, D. and Perkins, M. (2002) *Teaching Language and Literacy in the Early Years.* David Fulton Publishers.

Griffin, S. (2008) *Inclusion, Equality & Diversity in Working with Children.* Heinemann.

Harding, J. and Meldon-Smith, L. (2000) *Helping Young Children to Develop.* 2nd Edition. Hodder & Stoughton.

Hobart, C. and Frankel, J. (2009) *A Practical Guide to Activities for Young Children.* 4th Edition. Nelson Thornes.

Miller, L. *et al.* (2005) *Developing Early Years Practice.* David Fulton Publishers.

Nyland, B., Ferris, J. and Dunn, L. (2008) 'Mindful hands, gestures as language: Listening to children'. *Early Years,* 28(1): 73–80.

Palmer, S. and Bayley, R. (2004) *Foundations of Literacy: A Balanced Approach to Language, Listening and Literacy Skills in the Early Years.* Network Educational Press.

Ramsey, R. D. (2002) *How to Say the Right Thing Every Time: Communicating Well with Students, Staff, Parents and the Public.* Corwin Press.

Siraj-Blatchford, J. and Clarke, P. (2000) *Supporting Identity, Diversity and Language in the Early Years.* Open University Press.

Trevarthen, C. (2004) *Learning about Ourselves from Children: Why a Growing Human Brain Needs Interesting Companions.* Perception-in-Action Laboratories, University of Edinburgh.

Wall, K. (2006) *Special Needs and Early Years: A Practitioner's Guide.* Paul Chapman Publications.

Whitehead, M. (2010) *Language and Literacy in the Early Years 0–7.* 4th Edition. Sage.

# SECTION 4

# Optional units

**17** Work with babies and young children to promote their development and learning (CYPOP 1)

**18** Care for the physical and nutritional needs of babies and young children (CYPOP 2)

**19** Lead and manage a community-based early years setting (CYPOP 3)

**20** Promote young children's physical activity and movement skills (CYPOP 4)

**21** Supporting disabled children and young people and those with specific requirements (CYPOP 6)

# 17 Work with babies and young children to promote their development and learning: Unit CYPOP 1

The first three years of a child's life are a time of rapid growth and development, and early years practitioners are in the privileged position of being able to both watch and support babies and young children as development unfolds. Sharing the pride and delight of a baby or toddler in their newly discovered skills is one of the pleasures of working with this age group. This chapter looks at ways in which you can promote their development and learning.

## Learning outcomes

By the end of this chapter you will:

1. Understand the development and learning of babies and young children.

2. Be able to promote the development and learning of babies and young children.

3. Understand the attachment needs of babies and young children.

4. Be able to engage with babies and young children and be sensitive to their needs.

5. Be able to work in partnership with carers in order to promote the learning and development of babies and young children.

## The development and learning of babies and young children

It is very important that you understand the ways in which children develop and learn new skills. In Chapter 5 (Unit CYP Core 3.1), the main patterns of holistic development are discussed. You will need to look again at these tables to gain a good understanding of the developmental norms.

## The pattern of development in the first three years of life

As children become more mobile (usually after their first birthday), they need to have access to a wider variety of toys and activities. It is important to know and understand the usual stages of development as well as being able to recognise differences between individual babies and children. See Chapter 5 (Unit CYP Core 3.1) for full details on the developmental stages of babies and young children.

## How development and learning are interconnected

Development and learning are different concepts, but they are very closely connected.

- **Development** is about the general way in which a child *functions*. For example, Noah (aged 2 years) can run and jump, but he cannot hop or skip yet. He runs across spaces and jumps to music. Noah's development is spontaneous, and depends on his physical progress, his ability to think about a concept of 'hop' or 'skip', his mood, and whether he has seen someone else hop or skip.

- Learning is sometimes described as cognitive development, because it involves thought, memory, perception and concentration – all activities carried out by the brain. However, learning is closely connected to other aspects of development:
  - Sensory learning: babies learn through their senses about the sounds, smells and objects they see and feel around them
  - Emotional learning (or emotional intelligence): babies and young children learn how adults respond to their needs and how it feels to be smiled at – and to smile back
  - Motor skills learning (or muscle memory): young children learn gross and fine motor skills using the part of the memory that is used in repetitive muscle movement, for example in remembering how to ride a bike or play a musical instrument.

Learning occurs in a specific situation, at a specific moment, or when a specific problem needs to be tackled. People help young children to learn by creating environments and atmospheres which promote learning. For example, Noah is taken to a fair, where he learns to jump in a new way, on an inflatable castle.

# Variations in the rate and sequence of development and learning

## Level of stimulation

Babies and young children are naturally curious and fast learners, but they need plenty of play, stimulation and exercise to allow their brains to grow and develop. Babies need a wide variety of sensory experiences and for babies and toddlers stimulation can also be provided through talking with them, reading with them and creating opportunities for indoor and outdoor play and exercise.

Children are held back in their learning if they are not allowed to develop. There have been tragic instances of this in the orphanages of Romania, where children who had been left sitting in a cot all day were held back intellectually (even if only temporarily) because their general development was not allowed to move forward.

## Disabilities and learning difficulties

It is important to take care that children with disabilities are not held back in their learning just because their general development is constrained in some way. For example, the child with a hearing impairment needs to communicate, otherwise learning about relating to other people will be held back. Use of facial expression, gestures and baby signing will all help the young child's general development. The child can then, in particular situations, communicate, learn to think and socialise.

## Giftedness

People who are gifted and talented in music, dance and mathematics tend to show promise early in their lives. The most important thing is that adults provide a rich and stimulating learning environment, indoors and outdoors, which encourages children to develop and extend their thinking, understand and talk about their feelings, and understand themselves and others.

It is frustrating for gifted children when they are constrained and held back in their learning. It is also important to remember that however gifted a child may be in a particular aspect, he or she is still a child, and needs all the things that any child needs. A gifted child should not be put under pressure to behave and learn in advance of his or her general development.

## The importance of people: learning before sitting

Being a baby can be very boring. Babies depend on adults to bring interesting experiences to them, as they cannot move about enough to reach for things when sitting, or crawl or walk to get them. Bored, unhappy babies cannot learn much, and the important period of babyhood, when so much learning is possible, will then be lost. Studies of child development suggest that the first years of life are of great importance for development and learning, and also that this is the time when the child's willingness and ability for future learning are set. Imagine what it would be like if you spent long periods on your back with only a ceiling to look at; or you were in a pram in the garden with a plastic cover hiding your view of the sky and trees; or you could hear voices, but could not see who was talking because they were standing behind you.

## Learning in different ways

Some researchers think that different children (and adults) have different learning styles. The idea is that they learn better through some channels than others. This is sometimes expressed as VAK:

- **Visual** – emphasis on learning by looking
- **Auditory** – emphasis on learning by listening
- **Kinaesthetic** – emphasis on learning by feedback from body movement and tactile experience.

Other researchers prefer the idea that children learn through all the senses. This is sometimes called **multi-sensory learning**: even if one sense works best for an individual child, his or her learning will be better supported if adults offer experiences that involve all the senses. Pummelling clay, splashing with paint, jumping in puddles, swinging, riding a bike, doing a drawing and making marks with chalk on stones are all multi-sensory experiences.

**Figure 17.1** Jumping in puddles is a multi-sensory experience

## The importance of play

Research into the brain and human development demonstrates that there are some overarching mechanisms in the brain that influence a child's development and learning. Communication and movement are examples of these, and so is play. Play helps children to become imaginative and to develop symbols (making one thing stand for another). These are important aspects of human development. Play involving symbolic and imaginative aspects of development is a very powerful mechanism in the brain which allows children to begin to transform experiences and to make sense of them.

Play helps children to apply their learning. It is not so much about the new things that children learn, but how they begin to try things out, make sense of what they have been learning and put it to use. Play is important because it helps children to:

- reflect on life
- bring together and organise what they have been learning
- have opportunities to apply what they have been learning and to experiment safely, away from the dangers of the real world
- think flexibly
- transform what they know from the literal and real to the imagined and created.

## The potential effects on development of pre-conceptual, pre-birth and birth experiences

### Pre-conceptual care

Pre-conceptual care means that both partners work to reduce known risks (such as smoking, alcohol consumption and recreational drugs) before trying to conceive, in order to create the best conditions for an embryo to grow and develop into a healthy baby; in other words, actively planning for a healthy baby. Caring for the woman's health is particularly important because in the very early weeks of pregnancy she may not even know she is pregnant.

## Pregnancy

Different factors may affect the growth and development of the foetus while in the womb:

### Diet during pregnancy

Every pregnant woman hears about 'eating for two', but the best information available today suggests that this is not good advice. Research shows that it is the quality (not quantity) of a baby's nutrition before birth that lays the foundation for good health in later life. Therefore, during pregnancy, women should eat a well-balanced diet, and also should do the following:

- **Avoid pre-packed foods** and any foods which carry the risk of salmonella or listeria (such as soft or blue-veined cheeses, pate, liver and raw meat). Listeria can cause miscarriage, premature labour or severe illness in a newborn baby.
- **Take folic acid tablets and have a diet rich in folic acid**: when taken both pre-conceptually and in pregnancy, folic acid helps the development of the brain and spinal cord, and also helps to prevent defects such as **spina bifida**. Sources of folic acid include broccoli, nuts and whole grain cereals.

### The mother's age and number of pregnancies

Complications of pregnancy and labour are slightly more likely above and below these ages:

- **Younger mothers**: below the age of 16 years, there is a higher risk of having a small or premature baby, of becoming anaemic and suffering from high blood pressure. In addition, emotionally and socially, very young teenagers are likely to find pregnancy and motherhood hard to cope with, and they will need a great deal of support.
- **Older first-time mothers**: first-time mothers over the age of 35 run an increased risk of having a baby with a chromosomal abnormality. The most common abnormality associated with age is Down's syndrome. A woman in her twenties has a chance of only one in several thousand of having an affected baby, but by 40 years the risk is about one in every 110 births, and at 45 the risk is about one in every 30.
- **Number of pregnancies**: some problems occur more frequently in the first pregnancy than in later

ones, such as breech presentation, pre-eclampsia (see below), low birth weight and neural tube defects. First babies represent a slightly higher risk than second and third babies. The risks begin to rise again with fourth and successive pregnancies; this is partly because the uterine muscles are less efficient, but it also depends to a certain extent on age and on the social factors associated with larger families.

### Key terms

**Chromosomal abnormality** – An abnormality in the number or structure of chromosomes. Chromosomes are the structures that hold our **genes**.

**Genes** – The individual instructions that tell our bodies how to develop and function. They govern our physical and medical characteristics, such as hair colour, blood type and susceptibility to disease.

### Maternal health

The majority of pregnancies proceed without any major problems. Women often experience minor physical problems, but these do not affect their own health or their baby's development. Every pregnant woman will be closely monitored during pregnancy in case she develops a condition called **pre-eclampsia.** This is a complication of later pregnancy that can have serious implications for the wellbeing of both mother and baby. The oxygen supply to the baby may be reduced and early delivery may be necessary. It is characterised by:

- a rise in blood pressure
- oedema (swelling) of hands, feet, body or face due to fluid accumulating in the tissues
- protein in the urine.

In severe cases, pre-eclampsia may lead to **eclampsia**, in which convulsions (seizures) can occur. This can occasionally threaten the life of both mother and baby. If pre-eclampsia is diagnosed, the woman is admitted to hospital for rest and further tests.

### Multiple birth pregnancies

Multiple birth pregnancies (where there is more than one baby) always need special care and supervision. The main risk when there is more than one baby is that they will be born too early (be premature), and this risk rises with the number of babies. Usually, women expecting twins or more babies are admitted to hospital for the birth; twins may be delivered vaginally provided both babies are in the head-down position, but triplets and quadruplets are usually born by Caesarean section.

## Smoking

Smoking during pregnancy cuts the amount of oxygen supplied to the baby through the placenta. Babies born to mothers who smoke are more likely to be born prematurely or to have a low birth weight. (It is also important to continue not to smoke after the baby is born, as babies born into a household where there is a smoker are more at risk of cot death, chest infections and asthma.)

## Alcohol

Alcohol can harm the foetus if taken in excess. Babies born to mothers who drank large amounts of alcohol throughout the pregnancy may be born with foetal alcohol syndrome. These babies may have characteristic facial deformities, stunted growth and mental retardation. Even moderate drinking may increase the risk of miscarriage.

## Key terms

**Caesarean section** – A Caesarean section (sometimes referred to as a C-section) is when the baby is delivered through an incision in the mother's abdomen and uterus. It is used when a woman cannot give birth vaginally or if the baby is in distress or danger.

**Neural tube defects** – This term includes anencephaly, encephalocoele and spina bifida. These conditions occur if the brain and/or spinal cord, together with its protecting skull and spinal column, fail to develop properly during the first month of embryonic life.

**Pre-eclampsia** – A condition that a mother may develop late in pregnancy, marked by sudden oedema, high blood pressure and protein in the urine. It can lead to eclampsia where the mother has convulsions; antenatal care staff monitor women carefully for the warning signs.

**Premature (or preterm) baby** – A premature baby is one who is born before 37 weeks of gestation.

**Spina bifida** – This condition occurs when the spinal canal in the vertebral columns is not closed (although it may be covered with skin). Individuals with spina bifida can have a wide range of physical disabilities. In the more severe forms the spinal cord bulges out of the back, the legs and bladder may be paralysed, and obstruction to the fluid surrounding the brain causes hydrocephalus.

## Substance misuse

Most drugs taken by the mother during pregnancy will cross the placenta and enter the foetal circulation. Some of these may cause harm, particularly during the first three months after conception:

- **Prescription drugs**: drugs are sometimes prescribed by the woman's doctor to safeguard her health during pregnancy, such as antibiotics or anti-epilepsy treatment. This has to be very carefully monitored to minimise any possible effects on the unborn child.
- **Non-prescription drugs**: drugs such as aspirin and other painkillers should be checked for safety during pregnancy.
- **Illegal drugs**: recreational drugs such as cocaine, crack and heroin may cause the foetus to grow more slowly. Babies born to heroin addicts are also addicted, and suffer painful withdrawal symptoms. They are likely to be underweight and may even die.

## Infection

Viruses and small bacteria can cross the placenta from the mother to the foetus, and may interfere with normal growth and development. During the first three months of a pregnancy, the foetus is particularly vulnerable. The most common problematic infections are:

- **Rubella (German measles)** – a viral infection which is especially harmful to the developing foetus as it can cause congenital defects such as blindness, deafness and mental retardation. All girls in the UK are offered immunisation against rubella before they reach childbearing age, and this measure has drastically reduced the incidence of rubella-damaged babies.
- **Cytomegalovirus (CMV)** – this virus causes vague aches and pains, and sometimes a fever. It poses similar risks to the rubella virus such as blindness, deafness and mental retardation, but – as yet – there is no preventative vaccine. It is thought to infect as many as 1 per cent of unborn babies, of whom about 10 per cent may suffer permanent damage.
- **Toxoplasmosis** – an infection caused by a tiny parasite. It may be caught from eating anything infected with the parasite, including:
  - raw or undercooked meat, including raw cured meat such as Parma ham or salami

- unwashed, uncooked fruit and vegetables
- cat faeces and soil contaminated with cat faeces
- unpasteurised goat's milk and dairy products made from it.

In about one-third of cases, toxoplasmosis is transmitted to the foetus and may cause blindness, hydrocephalus or mental retardation. Infection in late pregnancy usually has no ill effects.

- **Syphilis**: a bacterial sexually transmitted disease (STD). It can only be transmitted across the placenta after the 20th week of pregnancy, and causes the baby to develop congenital syphilis or even lead to the death of the foetus. If the woman is diagnosed as having the disease at the beginning of pregnancy, it can be treated satisfactorily before the 20th week.

## Birth

The majority of babies are born safely, usually in hospital, but sometimes in a special midwife-led unit or at home.

Most women give birth vaginally, but sometimes the delivery is **assisted** medically, using forceps, vacuum delivery or a Caesarean section.

### Forceps delivery

Forceps are like tongs that fit around the baby's head to form a protective 'cage'. They are used during the second stage of labour to help deliver the head under the following circumstances:

- to protect the head during a breech delivery (when the baby presents bottom first)
- if the mother has a condition, such as heart disease or high blood pressure, and must not over-exert herself
- if the labour is very prolonged and there are signs of foetal distress
- if the baby is very small or pre-term (premature).

### Vacuum delivery (ventouse)

This is an alternative to forceps, but can be used before the cervix is fully dilated; gentle suction is applied via a rubber cup placed on the baby's head.

### Caesarean section

A Caesarean section is a surgical operation performed under either a general or an epidural anaesthetic; the baby is delivered through a cut in the abdominal wall. The need for a Caesarean section may be identified during pregnancy and is called an **elective** (planned) operation; for example, when the woman is expecting twins or triplets. A Caesarean section may be performed as an emergency in the following circumstances:

- when induction of labour has failed
- when there is severe bleeding
- when the baby is too large or in a position (such as breech) which makes vaginal delivery difficult
- in placenta *praevia* – when the placenta is covering the cervix
- in cases of severe foetal distress
- if the mother is too ill to withstand labour.

### Birth trauma

Occasionally, a baby may suffer from foetal distress during the birth process. This is usually caused by a lack of oxygen to the baby's brain (anoxia). During labour, midwives and doctors look out for signs of foetal distress and will often accelerate the delivery by using forceps.

### Premature birth

Babies who are born before the 37th week of pregnancy are premature babies. Around 10 per cent of babies are born before 38 weeks of pregnancy, and most of them weigh less than 2,500 g. The main problems for premature babies are as follows:

- **Temperature control** – heat production is low and heat loss is high, because the surface area is large in proportion to the baby's weight, and there is little insulation from subcutaneous fat.
- **Breathing** – the respiratory system is immature and the baby may have difficulty breathing by him or herself; this condition is called respiratory distress syndrome (RDS). This is caused by a deficiency in surfactant, a fatty substance that coats the baby's lungs and is only produced from about 22 weeks of pregnancy.
- **Infection** – resistance to infection is poor because the baby has not had enough time in the uterus to acquire antibodies from the mother to protect against infection.
- **Jaundice** – caused by immaturity of the liver function.

## Premature and multiple births: potential effects on development

The extent to which prematurity and multiple births affect the healthy development of the foetus and baby varies a great deal and is linked to how *early* a baby or babies are born. Babies born earlier than 34 weeks may need extra help breathing, feeding and keeping warm. The earlier they are born, the more help they are likely to need in these areas.

**Post-term babies** (those born after the expected date of delivery, after 40 weeks of pregnancy) may also experience problems with breathing, feeding and keeping warm. This is because the placenta stops functioning after about 42 weeks, and so fails to provide the larger baby with enough oxygenated blood.

Advances in the medical and nursing care of babies born prematurely have meant that many babies born after 35 weeks are able to breathe and feed independently, and their healthy development is not usually affected. However, babies who are born very early – such as around 25 weeks – require intensive neonatal care, which means being nursed in incubators (to maintain their body temperature) and receiving medical assistance with breathing and feeding. These vulnerable babies have a higher risk of developing hearing and sight problems and learning difficulties, than those who are born at full term.

## Current research: studies in brain development and learning

Current research into the development and learning of babies and young children focuses on neuroscience. In the past, some scientists thought the brain's development was determined genetically, and that brain growth followed a biologically predetermined path. Now neuroscientists believe that most of the brain's cells are formed *before* birth, but most of the connections among cells are made during infancy and early childhood. They refer to the 'plasticity' of the brain and believe that:

- early experiences are vital to healthy brain development
- the outside world shapes the development of a baby's brain through experiences that a child's

senses – vision, hearing, smell, touch and taste – take in.

It is estimated that at birth, a baby's brain contains thousands of millions of neurons, or nerve cells, and that almost all the neurons that the brain will ever have are present. Babies start to learn in the womb, particularly in the last three months. When they are born, babies are able to recognise familiar sounds and they have already developed some taste preferences. The brain continues to grow for a few years after birth, and by the age of 2 years, the brain is about 80 per cent of the adult size.

The neurons are connected together to form even more billions of different neural pathways. Whenever we have a new experience, a new neural pathway in the brain is used. Each new experience changes our behaviour – this is called **learning**. If the experience is repeated, or the stimulus is very strong, more nerve impulses are sent along the new pathway. This reinforces the learning process and explains why repetition helps us to learn new things. Repetition strengthens the connections between neurons and makes it easier for impulses to travel along the pathway. This process is commonly known as **hard-wiring**, and 90 per cent of the hard-wired connections will be complete by the age of 3. It is very important to our understanding of brain development in early childhood, and explains and illustrates the long-lasting impact of early experiences.

### Key terms

**Neuroscience** – Studies of the brain which provide evidence to help early years specialists working with young children.

# Promoting the development and learning of babies and young children

In the Early Years Foundation Stage (EYFS), observation, assessment and planning make up one of the commitments under the heading of '*Enabling*

## Case Study    'Leaving baby to cry could damage brain development'

'It is not an opinion but a fact that it's potentially damaging to leave babies to cry,' says parenting guru Penelope Leach. Using saliva swab tests, scientists have been able to measure high levels of the stress hormone cortisol in distraught babies whose cries elicit no response from parent or carer. Neurobiologists say that high cortisol levels are 'toxic' to the developing brain. Leach is not saying it is bad for babies to cry, but that crying, in the first year or so, is the only way a baby can gain a response. Denying a response, she argues, can have long-term emotional consequences.

By contrast, Gina Ford, author of best-selling parenting manual, *The Contented Little Baby Book*, advises that parents can leave a baby to cry for a while if he is clean and fed and burped. When they put a baby down to sleep at night, they can return if he cries but must not make eye contact.

Penelope Leach has co-directed the UK's largest research project into different forms of child care for children aged under 5 years. Her own research work, she says, has shown that having a mother, father or carer who responds to the baby is a crucial factor in their development, outweighing the effects of poverty and disadvantage. Acknowledging that it is contentious, Leach says: 'If you really, really don't want a baby to make any difference, you could try not having one.' She is not talking about the mother who cannot reach the cot for five minutes after the baby has started to cry, 'But you can tell by sound and, quite frankly, by sight whether a baby is working herself into a lather,' she says.

Adapted from an article in *The Guardian*, April 2010

1. Discuss the issues raised in the case study.
2. How important do you think it is to be able to refer to scientific research in your practice?

 **In Practice**

### Keeping up to date with research
In order to improve and promote evidence-based practice, practitioners could:

❏ engage regularly in continuing professional development activities – workshops, courses etc.

❏ explore issues around improving the quality of provision for children and families

❏ share findings on good practice by contributing to websites such as Learning and Teaching Scotland, Research into Practice and others relevant to your area

❏ subscribe to new e-bulletins, publications or websites, such as the Foundation Stage Forum

❏ reflect regularly on different aspects of practice with colleagues, children and parents, and focus on what is done and why

❏ encourage children to adopt a 'finding-out' culture so that research is regarded as a natural tool.

*Environments'*. The frameworks for early years education in Scotland, Wales and Northern Ireland also emphasise the importance of practitioners closely observing children in order to assess their progress. Adults working with children in their early years need to be motivated and enthusiastic as they play alongside children, and support their learning. It is through these everyday interactions and relationships that practitioners help children to develop positive attitudes and a strong desire to learn.

# Assessments of development and learning needs

In Chapter 6 (Unit CYP Core 3.2), you learned about the different observation methods that can be used to build up a picture of individual children and groups of children, that will support practitioners in making assessments of their development and learning needs. You will need to re-visit this chapter in order to decide the best ways of observing babies and young children to ensure that their needs are provided for in a positive and inclusive environment. In particular, look at the KEEP (Key Elements of Effective Practice) framework on page 95 to help you plan learning opportunities after observing and assessing children.

## Getting it right

*Getting it right for every child* (Scottish Parliament, 2008) is a national approach (often referred to as *Getting it right*) which supports staff working with children in Scotland to improve their wellbeing and life chances. It is founded on ten core components, which can be used by all those working with babies and children as they play their part in making sure that Scotland's children are healthy, achieving, nurtured, active, respected, responsible, included and, above all, safe. These are the eight *Wellbeing Indicators* which are used during the assessment and planning process, and are illustrated in the wellbeing wheel in Figure 17.2. The *Wellbeing Indicators* are the basic requirements for all children and young people to grow, develop and reach their full potential.

The needs of babies and toddlers differ from those of older children. For example, babies spend much of their time sitting and so may need adults to bring experiences to them; toddlers are active explorers who will need more careful supervision and support than older children when trying out a new activity. Both the indoor and outdoor environment need to be planned with their specific learning needs in mind.

Goldschmied and Jackson maintain that:

'Creating a satisfactory visual environment is not a once-for-all job but something that needs to happen continuously. Just as at home we are

**Figure 17.2** Wellbeing indicators (Scottish Government, *Pre-birth to Three: Positive Outcomes for Scotland's Children and Families*)

constantly making small adjustments and improvements, changing pictures from one place to another, moving a lamp or a plant, a nursery will only look inviting and cared for if the same kind of process is going on.'

# Indoor and outdoor environments

Babies and toddlers need a rich, stimulating environment that will promote their holistic development. Provision will be much the same as for older children in early years settings, with activities appropriate to their stage of development. See also Chapter 13 (Unit EYMP 2) for further information.

## Key terms

**Environment** – the provision that is made for children in which they can learn, play and relax. It encompasses both the physical environment (such as the layout, equipment and furniture) and the 'emotional' environment (the atmosphere or ambience that is created).

| Activities and toys to provide | Area of learning and skills development |
|---|---|
| **In the first year** | |
| Mobile | Sensory: especially vision – awareness of colour, shape and movement |
| Rattle | Physical: gross and fine manipulative skills |
| Songs and rhymes | Emotional, intellectual and language: emotional reassurance; repetition helps babies to predict and recognise words |
| Bath time and water toys (in washing-up bowl) | Emotional: express feelings; intellectual and sensory: learn about cause and effect, shape, texture, colour; language: descriptive words |
| | Physical: hand–eye coordination, fine motor skills |
| Activity centre | Sensory: awareness of texture, shape, colour |
| | Physical: hand–eye coordination and motor skills |
| **When the baby can sit unsupported** | |
| Treasure basket | Physical: gross and fine motor skills; sensory (all) |
| | Intellectual: helps concentration and exploratory play; |
| | Emotional: release of tension by banging objects, promotes independent playing |
| Saucepans and wooden spoons; plastic or foam bricks | Emotional: release of tension by banging objects |
| | Intellectual: helps concentration and exploratory play |
| Reading a book | Emotional: close contact |
| | Intellectual: exposure to 'book' language |
| Ball – for rolling to and from baby | Physical: hand–eye coordination, motor skills |
| | Sensory development: vision, touch |
| | Social: encourage turn-taking |
| | Intellectual: cause and effect |
| **From 1 to 3 years** | |
| Trucks and trolleys for pushing and pulling | Physical: walking skills, balance and coordination |
| | Emotional: confidence, independence |
| Wheeled toys to sit on and move with the feet | Physical: balance, large muscle development, steering skills and coordination |
| | Intellectual: learn about speed, distance, space, cause and effect |
| Cardboard boxes | Physical: motor skills – getting in and out of boxes, balance and coordination |
| | Emotional and social: using box as den or cooker or table |
| Duplo; large threading toys | Physical: fine manipulative skills – grasping, passing, picking up objects with finger and thumb |
| | Intellectual: creativity, learn about cause and effect |
| Play dough; 'gloop'; paints and crayons | Physical: fine manipulative skills |
| | Emotional: creativity and aesthetic appreciation |

| Activities and toys to provide | Area of learning and skills development |
|---|---|
| **From 1 to 3 years** | |
| Balls (large, soft), balloons etc. according to child's ability | Physical: motor skills – gross and fine, hand–eye coordination |
| | Social skills: taking turns |
| Bricks for building towers; stacking cups and beakers; jigsaws; posting boxes | Physical: fine manipulative skills, hand–eye coordination |
| | Intellectual: learn about cause and effect |
| | Emotional: self-reliance |
| Comfort objects; soft toys; cuddles and hugs | Emotional: security and reassurance |
| Messy play – finger painting, wet sand, water play, mud, 'gloop', play dough and clay | Creative: imagination |
| | Emotional: expression of feelings |
| Picture books; action rhymes and songs; interest tables at which children can handle various objects | Intellectual, language and social development |
| Heuristic play | Physical: gross and fine motor skills |
| | Sensory: all |
| | Intellectual: helps concentration and exploratory play |
| | Emotional: release of tension by banging objects, promotes independent playing |
| Bath toys and water play | Intellectual: early concepts of sinking, floating, volume and capacity |
| Mealtimes | Skills of independence as children learn to feed themselves; social and emotional development |

**Table 17.1** Age-appropriate toys and activities for children from birth to 3 years

## Providing an appropriate level of challenge

Children need a safe and predictable environment. When children feel safe, they explore and enjoy stimulating provision that has been planned for them. Opportunities to experience planned risk and challenge through play encourage young children to gain confidence in their abilities and in making decisions. Children are biologically driven to assess the risk, but only if they are constantly encouraged to use these processes – for example, toddlers can be encouraged to come down the stairs (under supervision) sliding on their tummies, feet first. They will pause and check where they are every few steps,

### Reflective practice: Managing risk and challenge

- What do you think is meant by risk and challenge in the context of play?
- Consider an activity you have recently carries out with a child or group of children. Reflect upon how they experienced risk and challenge during the activity.
- How could you introduce new challenges and improve children's understanding and management of risk through play?

**Figure 17.3** Playing with a posting toy

making their own risk assessment. Children who are not supported to make their own risk assessments by an adult sensitive and helpful to their needs are more likely to have accidents.

## Sensory stimulation

Everything a baby tastes, hears, sees, feels and smells, and all of a baby's own movements will influence the way the brain makes its connections, so the more varied and appropriate the play experiences we offer, the better these neural pathways are formed. It is important to give babies interesting sensory experiences, as well as the love and care that are essential. Babies will appreciate this, and will cry less when they are engaged with their senses and are perceptually aware. This kind of awareness leads to early concepts (an important aspect of intellectual development), which researchers are beginning to discover are formed earlier than was previously thought. Our feelings, thoughts and physical selves all work together as we learn.

## Quiet, calming spaces

Sometimes babies need to be quiet, but they still need to feel that people are near. Of course, it is important that the sun is not in their eyes, and that they are comfortable in temperature and with a clean nappy. Babies need times to:

- look at a mobile
- listen to gentle music playing
- hear the birds singing as they lie in a pram under a tree, looking through the branches at the patterns of the leaves against the sky
- sit propped up in a specially designed chair and watch what is going on
- watch other children
- follow voices they know because they spend time with them and love them
- receive warmth and affection.

Toddlers also need spaces and time in which to be calm and quiet. Many settings provide comfortable sofas in a cosy, enclosed space, which help young children to feel 'at home' and where they can share books or enjoy time with other young children or adults.

## Environments planned and organised around individual needs

Every setting needs to have routines so that they can plan and organise staff resources and equipment effectively. However, these routines should include a degree of flexibility. This means that practitioners should be able to respond to a child's individual learning needs as they are observed and identified. Many early years settings now focus on particular children on particular days. This means that each child is observed regularly, and activities are planned in a differentiated way to provide for the interests and needs of individual babies and children.

## Planning play-based activities based on assessments

In Chapter 12 (Unit EYMP 1), we looked at play patterns that may be observed in toddlers (see page 214), and these provide a useful framework for planning activities. Activities that most babies and toddlers will enjoy are:

● treasure basket play
● heuristic play
● water play
● play with gloop.

## Treasure basket play

Elinor Goldschmied pioneered treasure baskets for sitting babies, which are now widely used in most settings. It is very important that they are presented to babies in the correct way, or the baby will not gain the full benefit of the learning offered by the treasure basket. Make sure that the basket is the correct shape, height and size. It is distressing for the baby if it tips as they lean on it, or if they are unable to reach the objects on the other side; it is also uncomfortable to sit at a basket which is too high (like an adult sitting at a table when the chair is too low for the table height). The baby needs the companionship of an adult who sits near them (usually on a chair that is near to the ground in height) but does not join in – simply being there as an anchor, smiling when shown objects, but saying nothing. When adults are concentrating (perhaps writing and thinking hard), it would interrupt the flow of thought and the deep focusing to have someone make suggestions or ask questions and try to make conversation with them.

Ideally, the treasure basket experience will take place away from the hurly-burly of the main area, perhaps screened off, to signal to other, older, more mobile children that this is a quiet area, set aside for sitting babies to concentrate and learn.

The objects should not be made of plastic, but of natural materials or metals that can be washed and kept clean. This is because plastic does not offer much to the range of senses through which babies learn. As objects become shabby they should be removed, and there should be new objects to keep the interest of the baby who has regular use of the basket. As your observations of a baby build, you will be able to select objects with that baby's interests in mind. The baby who loves to bang and bash objects will choose different ones from the baby who loves to dangle and shake objects. It is very satisfying to try to work out what a baby will particularly enjoy exploring, especially when you have built on your observations successfully.

Babies need sufficient objects to be able to select from, so the basket should be full enough to encourage this. Examples would be: a small wooden brush, a small cardboard box, a loofah, a wooden spoon, a small metal egg whisk, a bath plug and chain, a small bag of lavender, a large feather.

Of course, you will need to make a risk assessment based on your observations of what a baby needs. Never put an object in the treasure basket that makes you anxious about its safety for a baby, and remember that some babies have allergies. Remember also that some babies are less adventurous than others and will need more support and encouragement to enjoy the treasure basket.

 **In Practice**

### A natural treasure basket
Babies learn about their environment using all their senses – touch, smell, taste, sight, hearing and movement. A treasure basket is a collection of everyday objects chosen to stimulate the different senses. Babies have the chance to decide for themselves what they want to play with, choosing in turn whichever object they want to explore.

1. Choose a sturdy basket or box – one that does not tip over easily.

2. Fill the basket with lots of natural objects or objects made from natural materials so that the baby has plenty to choose from. For example:

❑ fir cones

❑ large seashells

❑ large walnuts

❑ pumice stone.

## Heuristic play

Mobile babies and toddlers (crawling or bottom-shuffling) can be offered heuristic play experiences, which, like the treasure basket, were first developed by Elinor Goldschmied. The term 'heuristic' comes from the Greek word for 'to find' or 'to discover'.

Children need to be comfortable. Rather than a cold, draughty floor, they need a warm, inviting floor space, without lots of clutter, to capture their attention. The space needs to be prepared in advance so that children come upon the carefully spaced piles of objects when they enter the area. All the objects are collected from everyday use, rather than toys.

One pile might include spheres, circular objects and cylinders, such as a cotton reel, a bobble from a hat, a bracelet. Another might be of metal objects, such as tins with smoothed edges, or a metal tea caddy. The adult sits quietly and provides a calm and concentrating atmosphere that supports the child's explorations without intervening, except to say something like, 'Yes, you have a lovely tin,' but only if the child brings it to them. Otherwise, a warm smile is sufficient and the child then returns to his or her explorations.

The session varies in length, but careful observation will signal to the adult when to draw things to a close. Often children stay concentrating for half an hour. A further ten minutes or so should be taken to clear up with the children, who are encouraged to put the collections into the right type of bag. This is then hung on the wall, with the children watching. As long as children's efforts are valued, they enjoy helping. They do not respond well when nagged or criticised for putting an object in the wrong bag: they need encouragement and positive, sensitive support.

## Water play

Children enjoy playing with water – at bath time for babies and later on, filling up water containers, using a washing-up bowl or water tray. They will be learning mathematical concepts – when containers are empty or full, or heavy or light. Young children enjoy splashing through puddles on outdoor walks and seeing how objects float in puddles or streams. It is of course essential that adults supervise all children playing with water, and that they remove the water when it is no longer being used.

## Play with gloop

Gloop is simply cornflour mixed with water until it is a runny milkshake consistency. Food colouring can be added and children of all ages love to play with it as it can appear 'solid' but as soon as it is handled, it runs like water through the fingers. It can be played with indoors or outside if you put it on a tray.

## Tailoring activities to children's needs

For this assessment criterion you need to be able to show that you can provide activities that are tailored to meet the needs of babies and young children. The best way to show this is to observe the children during an activity and then evaluate it in terms of their enjoyment and learning development. It is also useful to obtain feedback from a colleague who has observed the activity and noted how effectively you engaged with the child or children. See Chapter 6 (Unit CYP Core 3.2) for observation and evaluation techniques.

# The attachment needs of babies and young children

When children receive warm, responsive care, they feel safe and secure. Secure attachments are the basis of *all* the child's future relationships. Because babies experience relationships through their senses, it is the expression of love that affects how a young child develops and helps to shape later learning and behaviour. They will grow to be more curious, get along better with other children, and perform better in school than children who are less securely attached. All parents find separation difficult, whether or not they have formed a strong attachment with their child.

The EYFS (in England and Wales), *The National Guidance: Pre-Birth to Three* (in Scotland), and the

*Early Years (0–6) Strategy* (in Northern Ireland) place the focus on the importance of relationships in the development of children aged under 2 years, and the emphasis on having persons who spend time observing the infant in order to plan for their individual needs.

This learning outcome links to Chapter 14 (Unit EYMP 3); see page 284 on attachment.

This learning outcome links to Chapter 14 (Unit EYMP 3); see page 284 on attachment.

### Key terms

**Attachment** – A warm, affectionate and supportive bond between child and carer that enables the child to develop secure relationships.

## The benefits of the key person system in early years settings

Practitioners need to develop consistent, warm and affectionate relationships with children, especially babies, although they should not seek to replace the parents. Babies need to be with the same people everyday to develop social relationships. This is why the EYFS requires all early years settings to implement a key person system.

### What is a key person?

A key person is:

- a named member of staff who has more contact with the child than other members of staff
- someone to build relationships with the child and parents
- someone who helps the child become familiar with the provision
- someone who meets children's individual needs and care needs (such as dressing, toileting etc.)
- someone who responds sensitively to children's feelings, ideas and behaviour
- the person who acts as a point of contact with parents.

## The importance of loving, secure relationships

Babies learn and begin to make sense of the world through responsive care and loving, secure relationships. These relationships are equally important with their primary carer(s) and with their key person in the setting.

Babies and children who do not have loving, secure relationships with the important people in their lives are likely to find it difficult to settle and to enjoy being in the setting. This in turn may lead to difficulties with concentration, with engaging with others and with their general ability to learn.

## The possible effects of poor quality attachments

When babies learn that they can rely completely on at least one person for their physical and emotional needs, they form what is known as a **secure attachment**. A baby or child who has internalised a strong attachment figure is then able to separate from that attachment figure and make relationships

### In Practice

#### The key person system

In early years settings, every child should be allocated to a key person, who ideally is responsible for:

- ❏ the routine daily hands-on care, such as feeding, washing, changing etc.
- ❏ observing the child's development
- ❏ encouraging a wide range of play activities tailored to the child's individual needs
- ❏ recording and reporting any areas of concern
- ❏ liaising with the child's primary carers or parents and establishing a relationship which promotes mutual understanding.

Any setting that uses the key person system should also have a strategy for dealing with staff absence or holidays.

with other important adults in their lives. Recent research has shown that settings that do not provide for a strong attachment figure can cause harm to babies and children.

## Emotional security

Babies and children need to be able to trust others in order to feel emotionally secure. When there has been insecure or poor attachment – whether it is with their primary carer or parent, with adults in a setting, or both – they begin to show anti-social behaviour and aggression towards others. Poor quality attachments may also lead to youth offending or anti-social behaviour.

## Effects on mental health

Babies and young children with poor quality attachments may show less interest in exploring their environment than those with secure attachments. They may also display anxiety and even depression later on in life, although it is difficult to predict the cause and effect relationship as there are many other factors at work.

## Effects on relationships with parents and professional carers

A baby's primary attachment is at its most intense between the ages of 6 months and 1 year, and it is then that the baby is likely to be acutely distressed when being left with a new carer. Babies who have experienced poor attachments at home may not feel able to trust the new carer enough to be able to form an attachment relationship. This is an unconscious self-defence mechanism – the baby does not want to experience emotional distress again.

# Engaging with babies and young children and being sensitive to their needs

Adults need to demonstrate a sensitive and caring approach through words and facial expressions. Providing companionship, time and physical

---

## Case Study — Attachments

Maya is 11 months old and has recently started attending a local children's centre. Jennie, her key person, has observed that she appears uninterested in the adults in the centre, and also does not seem to notice a difference between regular staff and strangers who visit. Maya shows no anxiety or distress when her mother leaves her every day, and Jennie is worried that there does not seem to be a close relationship between Maya and her mother. She has also observed that Maya does not seem to engage properly with play activities – she appears listless and apathetic, but rarely cries.

What should Jennie do in this situation to ensure that Maya's needs are being met?

---

affection is essential if babies and toddlers are to feel safe, secure, respected and valued.

## Allowing time for babies and young children to respond

Babies and young children look for reactions and responses from people around them, and they often mirror what they see. They respond to facial expressions, tone of voice, body language, eye contact and the kind of care they receive. Babies and toddlers need time to be allowed to process the information they receive from your tone of voice and facial expression, so it is important to be patient and wait for their response.

## Showing affection

Babies and young children need to be shown physical signs of affection – holding and cuddling. For babies, this will increase their feelings of emotional security. Adults should take the cue from toddlers and let them decide if they want to be held or cuddled.

## Talking and singing

When we have a conversation with babies, we look at the baby and the baby looks at us. When the baby has had enough of a chat, he or she will turn his or her head away and drop the eye contact, as if to tell us that they are tired and need a break from the conversation. We tend to talk to babies in a high-pitched tone, in short phrases, placing emphasis on the key words and using a great deal of repetition. This is known as 'motherese' or 'fatherese'. Using plenty of language when caring for babies and toddlers – for example, describing what you are doing when feeding them or during mealtimes – will help to promote communication and language development.

Singing and saying nursery rhymes are an important way of providing emotional security as well as promoting language development. Babies and toddlers should enjoy regular times when their key person holds them and sings to them.

## Playful activity with babies and young children

Playing alongside babies and toddlers helps them to learn in many ways – including the social skills they need to play with other children. It is useful to use a range of games and activities, so that you can follow the interests and preferences of individual children. Many babies and toddlers develop favourite play activities, which they want to repeat many times. The following examples are popular with babies and toddlers:

- **Peek-a-boo**: sit close in front of the baby and cover your face with your hands, then open them and gently say: 'Boo!' You can vary the game by peeping round the side of your hands or moving to different parts of the room.
- **Hand and finger puppets**: have one puppet for yourself and one for the baby. Create your own stories, using funny voices and allow time for a response.
- **Water play**: fill a low, wide container with a few centimetres of water and place it on the ground. Float small objects such as flowers or corks in the water and let the baby reach and splash. Always supervise children when playing with water.
- **Hide and seek**: show the baby a toy, then hide it under a towel or small blanket and help the baby to find it.
- **Stacking beakers and blocks**: with the baby watching, build a tower and then show how to knock it down. After a few demonstrations, the baby will probably want to knock it down him- or herself.
- **Action rhymes**: make a language game for toddlers from the song, 'Here we go round the mulberry bush'. Touch various body parts and sing, 'This is the way we touch our nose . . . head . . . hand . . .' and so on.

## How babies express their emotions, needs and preferences

It is important to learn how babies communicate so that you can identify their needs and respond to them sensitively. This involves becoming a **responsive caregiver**. Responsive care means knowing and accepting children, and respecting that they are *unique* individuals. As we have seen, babies make sense of the world through adults, and the

 In Practice

**Playing with babies and children under 3 years**
- ❏ Observe the child's current interests and plan an appropriate activity.
- ❏ Do not rush the child: let the child play for as long as he or she likes in his or her chosen way.
- ❏ Encourage the child with friendly gestures, smiles and words.
- ❏ Allow the child to repeat actions and games.
- ❏ Encourage conversations, talking and then waiting for a response.

responses that they receive let them know that the significant adults in their lives are consistent, reliable and trustworthy, and responsive to their needs.

There are various factors which, when taken together, result in responsive care giving:

- attachment (see page 374)
- communicating with babies
- trust
- emotional security
- reflection and tuning in.

## Communicating with babies

Babies send many cues or signals to the adults who care for them without saying a word. They communicate their needs and preferences through various methods, including:

- the sounds which they make
- the way in which they move
- their facial expressions
- the way in which they make or avoid eye contact.

Adults need to respond affectionately to these signals, and show that they have understood and that they care.

## Trust

Children become securely attached and begin to trust when someone:

- smiles back at them
- comforts and reassures them when they are upset
- feeds them when they are hungry.

Research shows that babies who receive quick and affectionate responses to their expressed needs, typically learn to cry much less and sleep more at night. At the same time, when babies are calmed by being comforted or fed, the brain's stress-response systems are turned off. Babies' brains begin to create the network of cells (neural pathway) that help them learn to soothe themselves.

**Remember**: You cannot spoil a young baby by responding to his or her needs.

## Emotional security

When unhappy, babies will often frown or switch their focus from the carer to objects in the room. This is their way of expressing their feelings. As babies gain more experience with their carers' soothing responses to their signals of unhappiness, babies begin to develop their own pattern of soothing self-regulation; for example, by babbling to themselves before going to sleep or on waking. A key component of self-regulation is the baby's emotional security.

## Reflection and tuning in

Responsive adults need to be reflective and in tune with what babies are telling them. This enables adults to make sensitive and informed decisions about how to respond appropriately. Effective practitioners pay close attention, for example, to how individual babies like to be fed, what they like to eat, and the way that they prefer to be comforted.

## In Practice

### Being a responsive caregiver

To be a responsive caregiver, you need to understand the holistic development of babies and children. You also need to:

- ❏ be interested, affectionate, loving and responsive
- ❏ hold, touch, rock, sing and smile at babies and children
- ❏ build an understanding of the needs and temperaments of each child

- ❏ continually observe each baby or toddler to discover what skills he is ready to explore and eventually master
- ❏ have an overall plan for each day – one which includes materials and activities that are appropriate for the development stage of each child
- ❏ always work to enhance sensitivity and respect.

# Managing transitions for babies and young children

## Guidelines for managing transitions for babies and young children

- **Routines**: build in routines that are welcoming and familiar.
- **Settling in**: invite parents or carers to stay with the child as they adjust to their new environment.
- **Comfort object**: encourage children to bring a familiar object from home, such as a teddy or blanket.
- **Planning**: plan for the transition (if expected) and involve colleagues who also know the child to ensure a smooth transition.
- **Emotional support**: provide opportunities for discussion, stories and play, helping children to express their feelings.
- **Tuning in**: observe gestures and body language and tune in to what is being communicated.
- **Siblings**: provide opportunities for siblings who attend the setting to see one another regularly throughout the day.

### Reflective practice: Managing transitions

- How does your setting ensure that transition from home to setting is as smooth as possible?
- Thinks of ways in which you could improve transition experiences for children and families.

## The importance of rest and sleep

Chapter 14 (Unit EYMP 3) discusses the importance of rest and sleep for children's health. Although it is important to provide opportunities for rest for babies

### Case Study — Active communication

Charlie (aged 10 months) plays with the xylophone that his key person, Sarah, has given him. He then lies down and begins whining. Sarah sits him up and plays the xylophone as she talks to him softly. 'Now, it's your turn, Charlie!' she says enthusiastically. Charlie stops whining and plays with the xylophone again as Sarah strokes his hair and says, 'Charlie is making a lovely sound'. Sarah is quick to respond to Charlie's 'cue' that he is unhappy as she helps him to control his feelings. Once he is calm and begins playing with the xylophone again, Sarah reassures him further by talking to him softly as she strokes his hair. In her daily interactions, Sarah often 'contains' a baby; that is, she helps the baby to remain involved in an activity.

1. Why are musical instruments particularly useful in this situation?
2. How could Sarah best engage Charlie's attention?

and toddlers, it should not be thought that rest is a substitute for sleep.

Sleep is important for learning. It helps the memory to embed rich learning experiences with people, objects, events and places. Getting the right amount of rest is crucial for the learning of babies and young children. Not all babies will need to sleep at the same time, and it is inappropriate practice for a setting to expect all babies to have their nappies changed at the same time and to sleep at the same time. These are very individual things.

It is important for babies to feel that they are near someone when they sleep. Some babies sleep best on a mat on the floor of a quiet area that is gated, with a cover to keep them warm; others sleep better in a darkened room, in a cot kept for them. This area should not be too full of stimulation; it is important to relax and let go when falling asleep. Neutral colouring is best, and the room should not be cluttered.

It is also important to keep to the sleep-time rituals and patterns that are familiar to the baby at home.

Some babies need to have a cuddle, being lowered into their cot as they fall asleep. Others might not sleep on an adult's lap, but need to be in a cot in a quiet room with their teddy, in order to fall asleep.

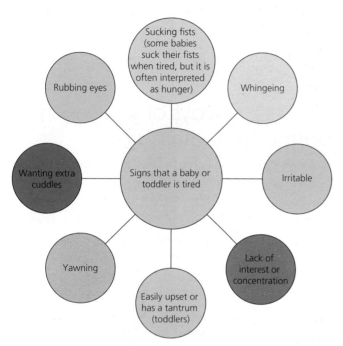

**Figure 17.4** You need to be able to read a baby's signs

# Working in partnership with parents and carers

Working with parents and carers involves understanding and respecting differences, individual circumstances and the changing needs of children and their families. It is essential that all staff working with families respect and value parents and their role. This learning outcome has links with Chapter 1 (Unit SHC 31), so it is important to read the information on page 4 of that chapter.

## The primary importance of mothers, fathers and carers

In all family set-ups, parents and carers will have a central role in their children's lives. They:

- are the first and most enduring carers and educators of their child
- know and understand their own child best
- have specific legal responsibilities towards their child
- give their child a strong sense of identity and belonging
- have skills and experience that can be of value to the early years setting
- are partners with early years practitioners in the care and education of their child.

## Exchanging information with parents and carers

Staff in early years settings will need a certain amount of information from the child's parents or carers. They record information about the baby or child's routines, interests and preferences; also they need to know about any medical conditions, allergies or special needs.

Parents need to know about:

- settling-in procedures
- how the key person system works, and how their child will be helped if he or she becomes upset, angry, tired or needs a change of clothes
- what type of educational opportunities are offered
- how they can be updated with their child's development and progress, and share any concerns that may arise
- meals, snacks and how allergies and other dietary requirements are managed (such as religious requirements)
- arrangements for outings and parental permissions
- policy on the use of photographs and video to record children's progress, and for use in displays and publicity.

Some of this information can be displayed on a Parent's noticeboard or in a brochure. Information about the individual child's progress will be

## In Practice

### Planning a workshop

1. Plan a workshop for parents that will help them to understand how children learn through activities such as cooking, sand play and painting. Plan the materials you would use for a demonstration, and make instruction cards with diagrams to help parents experiment with the materials.

2. Rehearse what you might say in a presentation to parents about one of the activities.

3. Advertise your workshop to parents and carry out your plan. Do not worry if not many people attend – even one parent taking part will give you valuable experience, and it is common to find that it takes several months of working with parents to encourage high levels of participation.

4. Evaluate the success of your workshop.

5. Include your own impressions and information from parental feedback that you have obtained either by talking to the participants or by asking them to fill in an evaluation form.

communicated to the parents or carers in the form of a daily or weekly diary, or a similar system.

## Progress check

### Sharing information with parents and carers

- Use different ways of sharing information with parents. These might include: keeping a diary about a child which goes home everyday, agreeing a convenient regular time to talk, or making a scrapbook that the child can draw in and add photos to, at home and in nursery.
- Understand that complexities can arise with the key person approach; know who in your setting can offer help and support if you need it.

## Evaluating ways of working in partnership with carers

Not every parent or carer is able (or indeed wants to) become closely involved with the setting. Some however are happy to offer their time and expertise to come to the setting to help with a cooking, sewing or other activity, or to help when children go on an outing. Others might be involved in planning or recruitment, or with administrative tasks, such as producing a newsletter. It is important to be able to communicate effectively with parents and to obtain feedback from them about their involvement.

## Useful resources

### Books

Goldschmied, E. and Jackson, S. (2004) *People Under Three: Young children in day care*. 2nd Edition. Routledge.

Department of Health. *Birth to Five*. Given free to all parents in England. Chapter 5 covers learning and playing. **www.nhs.uk/Planners/birthtofive**

# 18 Care for the physical and nutritional needs of babies and young children: Unit CYPOP 2

Babies and young children are totally dependent on others to meet their physical and nutritional needs. This chapter looks at ways in which we can provide for these fundamental needs.

## Learning outcomes

By the end of this chapter you will:

1. Be able to provide respectful physical care for babies and young children.

2. Be able to provide routines for babies and young children which support their health and development.

3. Be able to provide opportunities for exercise and physical activity.

4. Be able to provide safe and protective environments for babies and young children.

5. Be able to provide for the nutritional needs of babies under 18 months.

6. Understand how to provide for the nutritional needs of young children from 18 to 36 months.

# Providing respectful physical care for babies and young children

## Culturally and ethnically appropriate care

Parents develop their own way of caring for their child which reflects their culture and personal preferences. It is important to consult parents and carers about these ideas and preferences. This involves respecting their decisions and acknowledging them as being the people who know their child best. We can then use this knowledge to plan individualised and culturally sensitive care.

## Caring for a baby's skin

A baby's skin is soft and delicate, yet is also tough and pliant. Young babies do not have to be bathed every day because only their bottom, face and neck, and skin creases become dirty, and because the skin may tend to dryness. If a bath is not given daily, the baby should have the important body parts cleansed thoroughly – a process known as 'topping and tailing', which limits the amount of undressing and helps to maintain good skin condition. Whatever routine is followed, the baby needs to be handled gently but firmly, and with confidence. Most babies learn to enjoy the sensation of water and are greatly affected by your attitude. The more relaxed and unhurried you are, the more enjoyable the whole experience will be.

## Topping and tailing

Collect all the equipment you will need before you start:

- changing mat
- cotton-wool swabs
- bowl of warm water
- clean clothes and a nappy
- water that has been boiled and allowed to cool
- lidded buckets for soiled nappies and used swabs, and clothes
- protective cream, such as Vaseline.

## Bathing

You may be responsible for bathing a baby, particularly if you are working in the home environment. You need to check with parents about their preferred methods of bathing. Some parents prefer to wash their baby using running water – for example, using a shower or a shower attachment in the bath. Cultural preferences in skin care should be observed; for example, cocoa butter or special moisturisers are sometimes applied to babies with black skin, and their bodies may be massaged with oil after bathing.

*Before you start*, ensure that the room is warm and draught-free, and collect all necessary equipment:

- small bowl of boiled water and cotton swabs (as for 'topping and tailing' procedure)
- changing mat
- two warmed towels
- brush and comb
- baby bath filled with warm water – test temperature with your elbow, not with hands as these are insensitive to high temperatures; the water should feel warm but not hot
- lidded buckets
- clean nappy and clothes
- toiletries and nail scissors.

## Hand and face washing

Babies and toddlers need to have their hands washed frequently. This is because they are constantly picking things up and putting their hands in their mouths, and they may also pick up an infection. It is

## Guidelines for topping and tailing

- Babies do not like having their skin exposed to the air, so should be undressed for the shortest possible time. Always ensure the room is warm – no less than 20°C (68°F) – and that there are no draughts.
- Have a soft towel ready to wrap the baby in afterwards.
- Wash your hands. Remove the baby's outer clothes, leaving on his or her vest and nappy. Wrap the baby in the towel, keeping the arms inside if a young baby.
- Using two separate pieces of cotton wool (one for each eye, which will prevent any infection passing from one eye to the other) squeezed in the water which has boiled and been allowed to cool, gently wipe the baby's eyes in one movement from the inner corner outwards.
- Gently wipe all around the face and behind the ears. Lift the chin and wipe gently under the folds of skin. Dry each area thoroughly by patting with a soft towel or dry cotton wool.
- Unwrap the towel and take the baby's vest off, raise each arm separately and wipe the armpit carefully. The folds of skin rub together here and can become sore. Again, dry thoroughly.
- Wipe and dry the baby's hands.
- Take the nappy off, place in a disposable bag and place in a lidded bucket.
- Clean the baby's bottom with moist swabs, then wash with soap and water; rinse well with flannel or sponge, pat dry and apply protective cream if necessary and with parental consent.
- Put on clean nappy and clothes.

## Guidelines for a bathing routine

- Undress the baby except for the nappy and wrap the baby in a towel while you clean the face, as for 'topping and tailing'.
- Wash the baby's hair before putting him or her in the bath: support the head and neck with one hand, hold the baby over the bath and wash the head with baby shampoo or soap; rinse the head thoroughly and dry with second towel.
- Unwrap the towel around the baby's body, remove the nappy and place it in bucket.
- Remove any soiling from the baby's bottom with cotton wool; remember to clean baby girls from front to back to avoid germs from faeces entering the urethra or vagina.
- Lay the baby in the crook of one arm and gently soap the body front and back with baby soap. (If preferred, use baby bath liquid added to the bath beforehand.)
- Lift the baby off the towel and gently lower him or her into the water, holding him or her with one arm around the back of the neck and shoulders, reaching to the far arm to stop him or her from slipping.
- Talk to the baby and gently swish the water to rinse off the soap, paying particular attention to all skin creases – under arms, between legs and behind knees. Allow time for the baby to splash and kick, but avoid chilling.
- Lift the baby out and wrap in a warm towel; dry the baby thoroughly by patting, not rubbing.
- Baby oil or moisturiser may now be applied to the skin; do not use talcum powder with oils as it will form lumps and cause irritation.
- Check if fingernails and toenails need cutting. Always use blunt-ended nail scissors and avoid cutting nails too short.
- Dress the baby in clean nappy and clothes.

important to build regular hand washing into routine care – washing their hands before and after eating. Most young children dislike having their faces washed as they feel they are being suffocated. Always use a clean cloth and wipe each part of the face separately and gently. Dry thoroughly with a soft towel.

## Protection from sun

Babies benefit from being outside in the fresh air for a while each day. When air is trapped in a building it becomes stale, the level of humidity rises and there is an increased risk of infections spreading. When working in nurseries, practitioners should ensure that rooms are well ventilated and that there are opportunities for babies to go outside. Sunlight is beneficial too, but care should be taken with babies and young children:

- Keep all children out of the sun when it is at its most dangerous, between 11 am and 3 pm; those caring for young children should plan outdoor activities to avoid this time unless children are well protected by hats and sun protection cream. Permission must be obtained from the child's parent or guardian before applying sunscreen creams.
- Specialists advise keeping babies up to 9 months of age out of direct sunlight altogether to prevent the risk of developing skin cancer in later life.
- Use sun hats with a wide brim that will protect face, neck and shoulders on older babies.
- Use sun protection cream on all sun-exposed areas.
- Use sunshades or canopies on buggies and prams.

## Hair

Most parents will style their own children's hair. If we need to care for their hair while they are in the setting, it is important to follow the parents' preferences; for example, using a wide-toothed comb, or using hair oil rather than shampoo.

## Features of head lice

| | |
|---|---|
| • They are tiny grey-brown insects with six legs. | • Head lice only live in human scalp hair: they cannot be caught from animals. |
| • They have mouths like small needles which they stick into the scalp and use to drink the blood. | • They are unable to fly, hop or jump. They cling to hair shafts and climb swiftly between them. |
| • Head lice are not the same as nits, which are the cases or shells of eggs laid by female lice, 'glued' on to the hair shafts. Nits remain glued in place after the lice hatch; they are pinhead sized and pearly white. | |
| • Head lice are between 1 and 3 mm in size – from pin head to match head length (see Figure 18.1). | • Head lice generally remain close to the scalp, for warmth, food and cover, and do not wander down the hair shafts. They move away in response to disturbance. |
| • Head lice do not discriminate between clean and dirty hair, but cease to move around in really wet hair. | • They are caught just by head-to-head contact with someone who is infested. When heads touch, the lice simply get across by climbing through the dry hair. |

**Table 18.1** Features of head lice

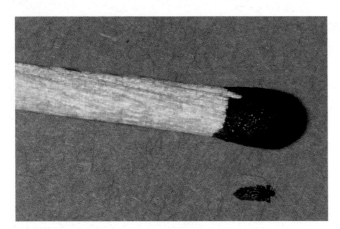

**Figure 18.1** Head louse

## Head lice

Head lice are a common affliction. Anybody can catch head lice, but they are particularly prevalent among young children, 3 to 11 years old, probably because they tend to put their heads together when playing.

See Table 18.1 for detailed information on head lice.

Many people only realise that they have head lice when the itching starts, usually after two to three months. The itching is due to an allergic reaction to the louse bites which takes time to develop. Sometimes a rash may be seen on the back of the neck where lice droppings (a black powder, like fine pepper) irritate the skin.

## Treatment

The Community Hygiene Concern charity (www.chc.org) has developed the '**bug buster**' kit; this contains specially designed combs, which are used in wet hair to detect and cure lice methodically, without having to subject children to chemical treatments. This method has been approved by the UK Department of Health. (See Figure 18.2.)

## Prevention

The best way to prevent lice is for families to learn how to check their own heads reliably. National Bug Busting Days are educational days that many schools in the UK take part in. The aim is to inform children and their parents about the behaviour of head lice and how to detect and remove them. Co-ordinating Bug Busting Days across the country can help to prevent head lice circulating. See www.chc.org for more information about Bug Busting for schools.

## Teeth

Although not yet visible, the teeth of a newborn baby are already developing inside the gums. A baby's first teeth are called milk teeth and these begin to appear at around 6 months. Dental care should begin as soon as the first tooth appears, with visits to the dentist starting in the child's second year. Teeth need cleaning *as soon as they appear*, because plaque sticks to the teeth and will cause decay if not removed.

**Figure 18.2** The bug buster kit

## In Practice

### Caring for teeth

❑ Use a small amount (a smear) of baby toothpaste on a soft baby toothbrush or on a piece of fine cloth (such as muslin) to clean the plaque from the teeth. Gently smooth the paste onto the baby's teeth and rub lightly. Rinse the brush in clear water and clean his or her mouth.

❑ Brush twice a day – after breakfast and before bed.

❑ After the first birthday, children can be taught to brush their own teeth – but will need careful supervision.

❑ They should be shown when and how to brush, that is, up and down away from the gum. They may need help to clean the back molars.

❑ Avoid sugary drinks, sweets and snacks between feeds or mealtimes.

Caring for the first teeth, even though they are temporary, is important for the following reasons:

1 This develops a good hygiene habit which will continue throughout life.
2 Babies need their first teeth so that they can chew food properly.
3 First teeth guide the permanent teeth into position. If first teeth are missing, the permanent teeth may become crooked.
4 Painful teeth may prevent chewing and cause eating problems.
5 Clean, white shining teeth look good.

## Nappy area

Young babies will need several changes of nappy each day, whenever the nappy is wet or soiled. As with any regular routine, have everything ready before you begin:

● a plastic-covered padded changing mat
● baby lotion

## Research Activity

### Caring for a baby's teeth

Prepare a leaflet for parents showing how teeth develop in a young baby and how to ensure their healthy development. Include tips for making caring for the teeth an enjoyable routine activity.

● nappy sacks for dirty nappies
● baby bath liquid
● a bowl of warm water (or baby wipes)
● barrier cream, such as zinc and castor oil cream, when required
● cotton wool
● new, clean nappy.

It is important to pay attention to the differences between boys and girls when cleaning the nappy area – see the guidelines below. If you are using a

## Guidelines for cleaning the nappy area

1. Wash your hands and put the baby on the changing mat.

2. Undo the clothing and open out the nappy. It is quite common for baby boys to urinate just as you remove the nappy, so pause for a few seconds with nappy held over the penis.

3. Clean off as much faeces as possible with the soiled nappy.

4. **Boys**: moisten cotton wool with water or lotion and begin by wiping his tummy across, starting at his navel. Using fresh cotton wool or baby wipes, clean the creases at the top of his legs, working down towards his anus and back. Wipe all over the testicles, holding his penis out of the way. Clean under the penis. Never try to pull back the foreskin. Lift his legs using one hand (finger between his ankles) and wipe away from his anus, to buttocks and to back of thighs.

5. **Girls**: use wet cotton wool or baby wipes to clean inside all the skin creases at the top of her legs. Wipe down towards her bottom. Lift her legs using one hand (finger between her ankles) and clean her buttocks and thighs with fresh cotton wool, working inwards towards the anus. Keep clear of her vagina and never clean inside the lips of the vulva.

6. Dry the skin creases and the rest of the nappy area thoroughly. Let the baby kick freely and then apply barrier cream if required and with parental consent.

special changing table or bed, make sure the baby cannot fall off.

**Never** leave the baby unattended on a high surface. As long as there are no draughts and the room is warm, the changing mat can be placed on the floor.

## Taking into account the preferences of parents and carers

Every setting will have its own policies and procedures concerning the physical care of babies and young children. However, it is also important to work in partnership with parents and this involves taking into account the preferences of parents and carers, whether these are tied to cultural customs or to personal preferences. For example, parents may express a preference for:

● only using organic, environmentally-friendly products, including skin care products and foods
● practising baby-led weaning (see page 396)
● using a dummy when their baby is put down for a sleep and at certain other times.

Provided that the parent's preference does not conflict with professional practice in the setting, their preferences should be noted and complied with.

## Providing respectful and personalised physical care

Babies and young children need to form relationships with adults who are warm, responsive and respectful. When providing physical care, we should always be aware of the child's individual needs and preferences, and help them to enjoy care routines.

## Procedures which protect babies, young children and practitioners

Early years settings generally keep babies and children safe by having good procedures for issues such as safer recruitment and general management. Intimate, personal care such as nappy changing, toileting, dressing and undressing should be coordinated by a key person. When developmentally appropriate, young children should be asked to *consent* to offers of intimate care. You might say, for example, to a toddler in the toilet: 'Would you like me to help pull your pants down?' rather than just going ahead and doing it. All settings are required to have a policy to deal with allegations made against staff.

## In Practice

### Procedure for changing nappies in a group setting

Nappy changing is an important time and you should ensure that the baby feels secure and happy. Singing and simple playful games should be incorporated into the procedure to make it an enjoyable experience. Every setting will have its own procedure for changing nappies. The following is an example:

❏ Nappies should be checked and changed at regular periods throughout the day.

❏ A baby should never knowingly be left in a soiled nappy.

1 Collect the nappy and the cream if needed. Put on apron and gloves. Ensure that you have warm water and wipes.

2 Carefully put the baby on the changing mat, talking to them and reassuring them.

3 Afterwards dispose of the nappy and discard the gloves.

4 Thoroughly clean the nappy mat and the apron with an anti-bacterial spray.

5 Wash your hands to avoid cross-contamination.

6 Record the nappy change on the baby's **Nappy Chart**, noting the time, whether it was wet or dry or if there has been a bowel movement. Also note any change you have observed – such as in colour or consistency of the stools, or if the baby had difficulty in passing the stool. Also, note if there is any skin irritation or rash present.

❏ Check nappy mats for any tears or breaks in the fabric and replace if necessary.

**Never leave a baby or toddler unsupervised on the changing mat**

For information on disposing of waste in the early years setting, see Chapter 14 (Unit EYMP 3).

## In Practice

### Respectful care

❏ Let a baby or child know in advance what you intend to do.

❏ Use positive facial expressions and reassuring words.

❏ Remember that physical touch reassures babies and toddlers.

❏ Let them 'go' at their own pace. Do not hurry a baby or child when feeding or dressing them.

❏ Give the baby or child your whole attention when carrying out a personal care activity.

❏ Where possible, involve the baby or child in the care routine. A baby can hold the clean nappy for you; a toddler can be supervised washing his or her own face.

However, no system alone can protect children; in 2009, a nursery worker, Vanessa George, was jailed for a minimum of seven years after admitting abusing toddlers at the nursery and photographing the abuse. A review into the case concluded that the environment had enabled a culture to develop in which staff did not feel able to challenge some inappropriate behaviour by George. The review also found that an 'informal' recruitment process was partly to blame. See Chapter 7 (Unit CYP Core 3.3) for more information on making complaints about staff.

# Routines for babies and young children that support their health and development

Good routines can provide valuable opportunities for promoting health and development, whether in a home or group setting. Everyday care routines for babies and children under 3 years provide opportunities for the promotion of:

- **intellectual and language skills**: talking to babies and children when carrying out routine care promotes communication skills and understanding.
- **emotional development**: babies and children feel secure when handled and treated in an affectionate and competent manner.
- **social skills**: young children see and understand that they are treated equally when routines are carried out, and will learn the concepts of sharing and taking turns. They will also experience a feeling of belonging, which is very important.
- **development of independence**: good routines allow time and space for toddlers to try to do things for themselves, rather than being rushed by the adult.

## Daily and weekly routines

Routines should be planned and organised around the needs of individual babies and children. The routines should ensure that each baby or child has all his or her personal care needs met in a positive environment. Factors to take into consideration when planning and implementing routines include:

- sleep, rest and stimulation
- feeding
- nappy changes
- stage of development
- play preferences.

## Sleep, rest and stimulation

Physical care routines should promote physical and sensory development, and provide babies and young children with stimulation. Outings and visits need to be planned in advance and will become part of the weekly routine. Babies and toddlers need periods of quiet and rest as well as regular opportunities for naps.

## Feeding

Feeding routines also need to be planned; babies should not have to wait for their feeds. Recent research has suggested that babies should be weaned before 6 months to avoid developing allergies. This may lead to a change in the Department of Health guidelines, which currently recommends waiting until a baby is 6 months old before weaning. You need to keep up to date with the latest Government guidelines.

Routines for meal and snack times for toddlers should include allowing time for them to feed themselves and planning to make the experience as enjoyable as possible. Special dietary needs and parental preferences must always be taken into account.

## Nappy changes

Nappies must be changed regularly to avoid nappy rash, and should always be changed immediately after they have been soiled. Whenever possible, the baby's key person should change the baby's nappy as this helps to develop a close, trusting relationship and enables the key person to report any concerns to the parents.

## Play preferences

It would be very boring if babies and children were all routinely offered the same activities every day – even when they appear to enjoy them. Planning routines for play should take account of their play preferences but it is important to introduce new activities in order to promote their learning and development.

## Stage of development

Understanding about the sequence of development as well as the stage which each baby or child is going through will help you to plan for the future. For example, a 7-month-old baby who enjoys sitting can be helped to become more mobile if you place a few toys just out of his reach. Observations of the way in which a child is developing will help the planning process.

## Showing respect and sensitivity during everyday care routines

The importance of showing respect when working with babies is discussed earlier in this chapter. The key person system is fundamental to children's wellbeing; he or she gets to know the child and their family well, and is the best person to be able to plan for their needs in a sensitive way.

## The principles of effective toilet training

Newborn babies pass the waste products of digestion automatically – in other words, although they may appear to be exerting a physical effort when passing a stool or motion, they have no conscious control over the action. Parents used to boast with pride that all their children were potty-trained at 9 months, but the reality is that they were lucky in their timing! Up to the age of 18 months, emptying the bladder and bowel is still a totally automatic reaction – the child's central nervous system (CNS) is still not sufficiently mature to make the connection between the action and its results.

## Recognising that a child is ready to move out of nappies

There is no point in attempting to start toilet training until the toddler shows that he or she is ready, and this rarely occurs before the age of 18 months. The usual signs are:

- increased interest when passing urine or a motion: the child may pretend-play on the potty with their toys
- they may tell the carer when they have passed urine or a bowel motion, or look very uncomfortable when they have done so
- they may start to be more regular with bowel motions, or wet nappies may become rarer; this is a sign that the bladder is developing
- they can stand on their feet and sit on a potty seat or a toilet. Some experts assess a child's readiness

by their ability to climb stairs using alternate feet, that is, one foot per step.

## When to start toilet training

Toilet training should be approached in a relaxed, unhurried manner. If the potty is introduced too early or if a child is forced to sit on it for long periods of time, he or she may rebel and the whole issue of toilet training will become a battleground.

Toilet training can be over in a few days or may take some months. Becoming dry at night takes longer, but most children manage this before the age of 5 years. Before attempting to toilet train a child, make sure that he or she has shown that he or she is ready to be trained. Remember that, as with all developmental milestones, there is a wide variation in the age range at which children achieve bowel and bladder control.

## Dealing with accidents

Even once a child has become used to using the potty or toilet, there will be occasions when they have an 'accident' – that is, they wet or soil themselves. This happens more often during the early stages of toilet training, as the child may lack the awareness and control needed to allow enough time to get to the potty. Older children may become so absorbed in their play that they simply forget to go to the toilet.

You can help children when they have an accident by:

- not appearing bothered; let the child know that it is not a big problem, just something that happens from time to time
- reassuring the child in a friendly tone of voice and offering a cuddle if he or she seems distressed
- being discreet – deal with the matter swiftly; wash and change the child out of view of others and with the minimum of fuss
- encouraging an older child to manage the incident themselves, if they wish to do so; but always check tactfully afterwards that they have managed this
- following safety procedures in the setting – for example, wear disposable gloves and deal appropriately with soiled clothing and waste.

## Guidelines for toilet training

- **Be positive and supportive to the child's efforts**: be relaxed about toilet training and be prepared for accidents.

- **Structuring the physical environment to facilitate training**: have the potty close at hand so that the child becomes familiar with it and can include it in his or her play. It helps if the child sees other children using the toilet or potty. It is also helpful if children are dressed in clothes that are easy for them to manage by themselves, such as pull-up trousers rather than dungarees.

- **Working in partnership with carers**: it is important to work closely with parents so that we take a similar approach to toilet training, otherwise the child may become anxious. If a parent starts training their toddler when there is a new baby due, be prepared for some accidents. Many children react to a new arrival by regressing to baby behaviour.

- **Encouraging and praising**: always praise the child when he or she succeeds and do not show anger or disapproval if the opposite occurs; the child may be upset by an accident. It is important not to over-encourage children as this can make them anxious about letting you down.

- **Treating child with respect and avoiding guilt**: do not show any disgust for the child's faeces. He or she will regard using the potty as an achievement and will be proud of them. Children have no natural shame about their bodily functions (unless adults make them ashamed).

- **Establishing a routine**: offer the potty regularly so that the child becomes used to the idea of a routine, and learn to read the signs that a child needs to use it. Cover the potty and flush the contents down the toilet. Always wear disposable gloves. Encourage good hygiene right from the start, by washing the child's hands after every use of the potty.

- **Flexible personalised approach**: some children feel insecure when sitting on a potty with no nappy on – try it first still wearing a nappy or pants if the child shows reluctance. The child may prefer to try the 'big' toilet seat straightaway; a toddler seat fixed onto the normal seat makes this easier. Boys need to learn to stand in front of the toilet and aim at the bowl before passing any urine; you could put a piece of toilet paper in the bowl for him to aim at. Some children are frightened when the toilet is flushed; be tactful and sympathetic. You could wait until the child has left the room before you flush.

- **Providing plenty of fluids and fibre to prevent hard stools**: children need to drink plenty of water or other drinks in order for them to learn what having a full bladder feels like. They also need to be given foods that contain fibre (such as fruit and vegetables) to prevent constipation.

## Activity

### Toilet training

1. Arrange to interview a parent or carer who has recently toilet trained a child.

2. Try to find out the methods they used and any problems they encountered.

3. Write a report of the methods used.

In small groups, make a colourful, eye-catching wall display that provides tips for parents and carers on toilet training.

## Toilet training

In class, discuss the problems that can arise with toilet training and compare the strategies used by different families.

# Providing opportunities for exercise and physical activity

## The importance of exercise and physical activity

In Chapter 14 (Unit EYMP 3), we looked at the importance of physical activity and exercise for children. Apart from their importance for children's health and wellbeing, physical play and exercise also have a positive impact on developing social skills. Babies and toddlers need:

- daily play routines to encourage their enjoyment of physical activity

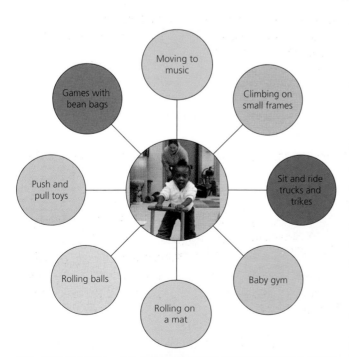

**Figure 18.3** Activities to support physical play

- safe floor surfaces and sufficient space for crawling or bottom-shuffling
- periods of rest after physical play and exercise – to build up their stamina.

## Supporting babies' or young children's exercise and physical activity

There are many different ways in which we can support babies' or young children's physical play. It is important to supervise them closely when playing and to offer encouragement and praise. Figure 18.3 shows appropriate activities to support physical play.

# Providing safe and protective environments for babies and young children

Babies and young children have no awareness of possible risks and dangers in their environment. It is up to the adults to ensure that the environment is safe and protective.

## Policies and procedures

Every setting should have a health and safety policy, along with procedures that outline how the policy can be followed. It is fundamental to your practice that you understand the policies, and that you are always alert to the possibilities of an accident occurring. The main dangers for babies and toddlers in the setting are:

- cot death (see page 395)
- falls
- choking and suffocation
- poisoning
- drowning
- electrocution.

## Preventing falls

The safest place for babies is on the floor or in a playpen if they have to be left unattended for a short period (for example, if you need to attend to another child). They must never be left alone on any surface

– falling from a surface is one of the most common causes of accidents and injury to young babies, sometimes causing head injury or fractures.

Before, during and after play sessions you will need to check for and remove any items that may prove an obstruction. Always be aware of children with special needs – for example, those with mobility problems or a visual impairment. Whenever children are playing with or near water – even indoors at the water play area – they must be constantly supervised. Running and playing in the garden or outdoor play area is good for children's health and fitness, but active play always increases the risk of accidents happening. All children will trip and fall at some time, but children should not be put at risk of serious injury.

## Preventing choking

Babies are most at risk from choking when left unsupervised either eating or playing. Young children are most at risk of choking when they are tired, crying or running around.

## Preventing poisoning

The peak age for accidents with poisons is 1 to 3 years, when children are highly mobile and inquisitive. When young children explore the world, they use all their senses, including taste. They typically put everything in their mouth to find out what it is.

## Preventing drowning

Babies and young children can drown in only 5 cm of water. This puts them at risk of drowning in paddling pools, baths and buckets. They should never be left in the bath even for a moment, and even if an older brother or sister is in the bath with them. Water trays and paddling pools should be emptied immediately after supervised use.

## Guidelines for preventing choking

- Never leave small items within a baby or toddler's reach – be extra vigilant when working in a setting where older children leave their toys around.
- Follow the age-appropriate symbols on toys and equipment.
- Never leave a child propped up with a bottle or feeding beaker.
- Keep plastic bags and wrap away from babies and toddlers.
- Always supervise babies and toddlers when they are eating and drinking.
- Never give peanuts to children under 4 years as they can easily choke or inhale them into their lungs, causing infection and lung damage.
- Make sure you know what to do if a child is choking.

## Guidelines for preventing poisoning

- Make sure that all household chemicals are out of children's reach.
- Never pour chemicals or detergents into empty soft drink or water bottles.
- Keep all medicines and tablets in a locked cupboard.
- Use childproof containers.
- Teach children not to eat berries or fungi in the garden or park.

## Guidelines for preventing burns, scalds and electrocution

- Never carry a hot drink through a play area or place a hot drink within reach of babies or young children.
- Check the temperature of feeds and meals.
- Make sure the kitchen is safe for children – kettle flexes coiled neatly, cooker guards used and saucepan handles turned inwards.
- Make sure the kitchen is inaccessible to children when no one is in it: use safety gates or adult locks.
- Never smoke in early years settings; keep matches and lighters out of children's reach.
- Check that the electric sockets are covered with socket covers when they are not in use, and that there are no trailing wires on the floor or where children could grab them.

## Preventing burns, scalds and electrocution

As children learn to crawl, climb and walk, the risk of scalds or burns increases. Nearly half of all severe burns and scalds occur in children under 5 years old.

## Safety features within the environment

The most important way of ensuring that babies and children are kept safe and protected is for the adults in the setting to take responsibility for supervision. In addition, most settings use a variety of safety devices to help prevent accidents. These include the following:

- Baby evacuation trolley – can transport up to six babies in the event of emergency evacuation; useful in a large nursery setting.
- Cushioned corner covers – for tables and shelves with sharp corners.
- Drawer, cupboard and window locks – to prevent children trapping their fingers and also gaining access to cupboard contents, or falling from windows.
- Harnesses – to prevent falls, babies must be secured in highchairs and pushchairs with a three-point harness.
- Reins – to keep children safe when walking near roads and ponds.
- Finger protector – attaches between the door and the door frame and prevents children's fingers getting trapped.
- Safety gates – to prevent children from entering areas of potential danger, such as a kitchen, garden or stairs.
- Plug safety covers – plastic cover preventing anything being pushed into an electrical socket.

## Supervision and risk management

Babies and young children need a stimulating environment in which they feel safe but not overprotected. You need to strike a balance between the needs of children to explore independently, and concerns about safety. They should never be left unsupervised unless they are asleep.

Read more about managing risk in Chapter 8 (Unit CYP Core 3.4).

## Sudden infant death syndrome

Sudden infant death syndrome (SIDS) is often called 'cot death'. It is the term applied to the sudden unexplained and unexpected death of an infant. The reasons for cot deaths are complicated and the cause is still unknown. Although cot death is the commonest cause of death in babies up to 1 year old, it is still *very rare*, occurring in approximately two out of every 1,000 babies. Recent research has identified various **risk factors**, such as adults smoking near the baby, babies becoming overheated, and the baby's sleep position.

## Guidelines for reducing the risk of cot death

- **Temperature**: do not let the baby become too hot. Keep baby's head uncovered; babies over 1 month of age should never wear hats indoors, as small babies gain and lose heat very quickly through their heads. The room where an infant sleeps should be at a temperature that is comfortable for lightly clothed adults: 16–20°C.

- **Sleep position**: place the baby on his or her back to sleep, tucked in with head and shoulders above the sheet and blanket. If the baby is a natural tummy-sleeper, keep turning him over and tuck in securely with blankets (as long as the weather is not too hot); a musical mobile may help to keep him happy while lying on his back.

- **Feet-to-foot**: place the baby with their feet to the foot of the cot, to prevent wriggling down under the covers. A pillow should never be used for sleeping.

- **Smoking**: do not let anyone smoke in the same room as a baby, or near to them. Adults should not handle babies immediately after they have been smoking, as it takes 20 minutes for an adult's breath to return to normal and eliminate the chemical-filled smoke.

- **Dummies**: it is possible that using a dummy at the start of any sleep period reduces the risk of cot death. Guidance from the NHS however says that evidence is not robust, and that not all experts agree they should be promoted.

- **Illness**: learn to recognise the signs and symptoms of illness and know how to respond.

- **Know how to resuscitate a baby**: learn and practise on a special baby resuscitation mannequin how to perform artificial ventilation and cardiac massage. This should always be practised under the supervision of a qualified first-aider.

 **In Practice**

### First aid

In pairs, rehearse the procedure to follow if a young baby is found 'apparently lifeless' in his cot. Use a baby resuscitation mannequin to test each other's skills.

Note: Professional supervision will be required.

### Research Activity

#### Sudden infant death syndrome

The Foundation for the Study of Infant Deaths (FSID) publishes the latest research on sudden infant death syndrome on its website: www.fsid.org.uk. Find out about its recent campaigns. Using the information, prepare a poster that includes up-to-date advice for parents.

# The nutritional needs of babies under 18 months

A nutritious and balanced diet will help to ensure the health, growth and development of children under 18 months, and will be the basis of good eating habits that can last a lifetime. It helps to prevent childhood nutritional disorders such as iron deficiency and anaemia, vitamin D deficiency and rickets, growth problems, tooth decay, constipation and eating difficulties. Also it may help prevent both child and adult obesity and their consequences. It is important to follow current guidelines from the Government, as they provide the best advice on nutrition for everyone, based on the latest available research. You can find guidance on all the following nutrition topics on the Department of Health website and the Food Standards Agency website.

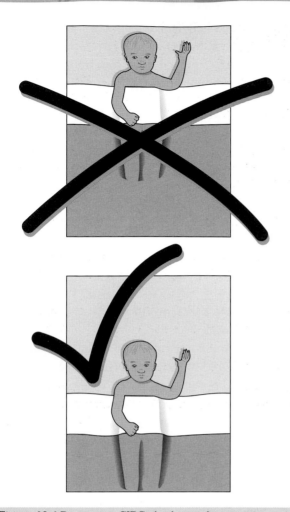

**Figure 18.4** Preventing SIDS: the feet-to-foot position

# The nutritional needs of babies

The way in which babies are fed involves more than simply providing enough food to meet nutritional requirements. For the newborn baby, sucking milk is a great source of pleasure and is also rewarding and enjoyable for the mother. The *ideal* food for babies to start life with is breast milk, and **breastfeeding** should always be encouraged as the first choice in infant feeding; however, mothers should not be made to feel guilty or inadequate if they choose not to breastfeed their babies.

## Breast milk

Breast milk provides all the nutrients the baby needs in the correct balance for human growth. There are proven advantages in breastfeeding, which include the following benefits for the baby:

- **Hygienic**: the milk is sterile and at the correct temperature; there is no need for bottles or sterilising equipment.
- **Can help prevent infection**: breast milk initially provides the infant with maternal antibodies and helps protect the child from infection: for example, against illnesses such as diarrhoea, vomiting, chest, ear and urine infections, eczema and nappy rash.
- **Prevents babies being overweight**: the child is less likely to become overweight, as overfeeding is not possible and the infant has more freedom of choice as to how much milk he or she will suckle.
- **Bonding**: sometimes it is easier to promote the mother–infant bonding by breastfeeding, although this is certainly not always the case.
- **Prevents constipation**.

## Formula milk

Although the ideal will always be breast milk, parents may choose to use formula milk for their babies for a variety of reasons:

- Breastfeeding is harder for some mothers than others; for example, if a new mother does not receive the support she needs to establish breastfeeding, the 'let-down' reflex (when milk flows from the ducts towards the nipple) is more difficult to be stimulated.
- Some babies can have medical conditions that make breastfeeding difficult; for example, they may have tongue-tie or have been born prematurely.
- The mother may have to return to work and find that bottle-feeding is more convenient when leaving her baby in the care of others.
- Many new mothers feel that there is a bottle-feeding culture in the UK. Breastfeeding is often seen as an embarrassing activity when carried out in front of others.

The important thing is that a mother makes her own choice and is happy that her baby is feeding properly.

## Weaning

Weaning is the gradual introduction of solid food to the baby's diet. The reasons for weaning are to:

- meet the baby's nutritional needs – from about 6 months of age, milk alone will not satisfy the baby's increased nutritional requirements, especially for iron
- satisfy increasing appetite
- develop new skills – using feeding beaker, cup and cutlery
- develop the chewing mechanism; the muscular movement of the mouth and jaw also aids the development of speech
- introduce new tastes and textures; this enables the baby to join in family meals, thus promoting cognitive and social development.

## When to start weaning

Current guidelines from the Department of Health and Food Standards Agency state that babies should be given solid food for the first time when they are 6 months old. Before then, parents are urged to give their infants just milk – and preferably breast milk. Giving solids too early (often in the mistaken belief that the baby might sleep through the night) places a strain on the baby's immature digestive system; it may also make him or her fat and increases the likelihood of allergy. If parents do choose to introduce solid foods before 6 months, they should consult their health visitor or GP first. Babies who are born prematurely should not be introduced to solid foods just because they have reached a certain age or weight. They will need individual assessment before weaning.

When the following three key signs are present together, it means that the baby is ready for solid food:

- They can stay in a sitting position while holding their head steady.
- They can coordinate their eyes, hands and mouth (they can look at food, grab it and put it in their mouths themselves).
- They can swallow their food (if they are not ready, most of it will be pushed back out).

### Preparing a weaning plan

Before preparing a weaning plan, you need to find out from parents about any dietary requirements or preferences they may have linked to their religious,

cultural or other beliefs. For example, some parents may want their baby to follow a vegetarian diet; some may want to bring foods from home or try baby-led weaning (see below).

## Stages of weaning

Every baby is different. Some enjoy trying new tastes and textures, moving through weaning quickly and easily, while others need a little more time to get used to new foods.

- **Stage 1** (around 6 months): give puréed vegetables, puréed fruit, baby rice, finely puréed dhal or lentils. Some soft finger foods can also be given: soft fruit pieces, cooked vegetable pieces or sticks, cooked pasta pieces, crusts of bread or toast, cheese cubes. Milk continues to be the most important food.
- **Stage 2** (about 6 to 8 months): widen the variety of foods offered to include all fruits, vegetables, meats, fish, eggs, pulses, bread, rice, pasta and other cereals. Liver should be limited to one serving per week because of the very high vitamin A content. Provide mashed food with soft lumps, and soft finger foods. Meat may still need to be puréed but can be mashed if it is very soft. Peanut butter (but not whole or chopped nuts) can be introduced unless the child or family has a history of allergy-related illness, such as eczema or hay fever. Milk feeds decrease as more solids rich in protein are offered.
- **Stage 3** (about 9 to 12 months): move on to 'lumpier' foods – minced and chopped family foods such as pasta, pieces of cooked meat, soft cooked beans, pieces of cheese; finger foods such as raw fruit and vegetable sticks, as well as a variety of family foods such as sandwiches, toast or any of the food previously described above; additional fluids such as diluted unsweetened fruit juice or water. Three regular meals should be taken as well as drinks. Cows' milk (only full-fat) can safely be used at about 12 months.

### Baby-led weaning

Some parents use a technique for weaning their babies called baby-led weaning (BLW). This involves letting the baby select those items of food that can be held or grasped by them and taken to their mouth.

Starter foods may include pieces of broccoli, carrot or fruit cut into 'chip' shapes and offered to the baby on a tray. The use of bowls and weaning spoons is discouraged. The principles behind this way of feeding babies are as follows:

- Baby-led weaning offers babies the opportunity to discover what other foods have to offer, as part of finding out about the world around them.
- It utilises their desire to explore and experiment, and to mimic the activities of others.
- It enables the transition to solid foods to take place as naturally as possible, by allowing the baby to set the pace of each meal, and maintaining an emphasis on play and exploration rather than on eating.

For more information, visit this website: www.babyledweaning.com

## Foods to avoid for babies under 12 months

Table 18.2 states which foods to avoid and why, during a child's first year.

## Preparing formula feeds

A young baby's immune system is not as strong or as well developed as an adult's system. This means that babies are much more susceptible to illness and infection. Good hygiene is therefore very important when making up a feed. All equipment used to feed a baby must be sterilised. Bottles, teats and any other feeding equipment need to be cleaned and sterilised before each feed. If they are not, it may cause sickness and diarrhoea.

All formula feeds must be made up in accordance with the manufacturer's instructions and following strict hygiene guidelines.

## Types of formula milk

There are three different types of formula milk:

- cows' milk-based formula
- hydrolysed protein formula
- soya-based formula.

Most babies can have cows' milk-based formula, unless there is a health or dietary reason why they cannot.

## Cows' milk-based formula

Most baby formula milks are based on cows' milk, which is modified to resemble breast milk as closely as possible. Carbohydrate, protein and fat levels are adjusted, and vitamins and minerals are added. There are also special types of formula manufactured for premature babies. The protein in milk can be

## In Practice

### Preparing formula feeds

❑ **Prepare each feed freshly** and correctly, using boiled water at a temperature of at least 70°C.

❑ Before making up a feed, **clean and disinfect** the surface which you are going to use.

❑ **Wash your hands thoroughly** before washing bottles prior to sterilising them and before preparing feeds every time.

❑ Always use a **sterilised bottle and teat**.

❑ **Stand the bottle on a clean surface.** Keep the teat and cap on the upturned lid of the steriliser. Do not put them on the work surface.

❑ **Boil the water**. After it is boiled, let the water cool for *no more* than 30 minutes.

❑ **Follow manufacturer's instructions** on how to make up the feed (sizes of scoops vary with different makes).

❑ **Cool the formula** to a safe temperature before feeding. To cool, hold the bottom half of the bottle under cold running water, with the cap covering the teat. Test the temperature of the feed by dropping a little onto the inside of your wrist. It should feel *warm* to the touch, not hot.

❑ **Throw away** any feed not used within two hours.

| Food | Reasons for avoiding this food |
|------|-------------------------------|
| Salt | Do not add salt to any foods you give to babies, because their kidneys cannot cope with it. The baby foods on sale are not allowed to contain salt. Limit the child's intake of foods that are high in salt (such as cheese, bacon and sausages). Avoid giving any processed foods that are not made specifically for babies such as pasta sauces and breakfast cereals, because these can also be high in salt. |
| Sugar | Do not add sugar to the food or drinks you give to babies. Sugar could encourage a sweet tooth and lead to tooth decay when the first teeth start to come through. If you give the baby stewed sour fruit, such as rhubarb, you could sweeten it with mashed banana, breast or formula milk. |
| Honey | Do not give honey until the baby is 1 year old. Very occasionally, honey can contain a type of bacteria that can produce toxins in a baby's intestines. This can cause serious illness (infant botulism). After a baby is a year old, the intestine matures and the bacteria cannot grow. |
| Cows' milk | Cows' milk must not be given as a drink for babies under 1 year old because their digestive system cannot cope with the proteins. |
| Shark, marlin and shellfish | Avoid giving any shark, swordfish or marlin to a baby because the levels of mercury in these fish can affect a baby's growing nervous system. Avoid giving raw shellfish to babies to reduce their risk of developing food poisoning. |
| Low-fat, low-calorie and high-fibre foods | These are not suitable for babies. Babies have small stomachs and are growing quickly, so they need small portions of foods that contain lots of nutrients and calories. |
| Nuts | Whole nuts, including peanuts, should not be given to children under 5 years old as they can choke on them. As long as there is no history of food or other allergies in the child's family, peanuts can be given if crushed or in the form of peanut butter, but not before the baby is 6 months old. |
| Raw and lightly cooked eggs | Make sure eggs are cooked until the yolk and white are solid: uncooked or partially cooked eggs may contain bacteria that can result in food poisoning. |

**Table 18.2** Foods which babies should avoid

broken down into curds (casein) and whey. There are two main types:

- **First-stage formula**. These milks consist mostly of whey, with a casein-to-whey ratio of 40:60, which is about the same as breast milk. They are suitable for a baby from birth up to about a year, and are thought to be easy to digest.
- **Second-stage formula**. These milks consist of mostly casein, with a casein-to-whey ratio of 80:20. They take longer to digest and are often promoted as being for hungrier babies.

## Hydrolysed-protein formula milk

This is a formula milk which is specially designed for babies with an allergy or intolerance to cows' milk. If a baby has a cows' milk allergy, the protein in the milk will cause an allergic reaction. If the baby has

an intolerance to cows' milk, the baby will have difficulty in digesting the lactose (sugar) in the milk.

Hydrolysed-protein formula milks are based on cows' milk and have the same nutritional value as standard formula milk. However, the protein in the milk is hydrolysed, which means it is broken down so that babies are less likely to react to it. These milks are also generally lactose-free, so babies who have an intolerance to cows' milk can digest them easily.

## Soya-based formula

Soya-based formula is made from soya beans. It is modified with vitamins, minerals and nutrients to make it suitable for formula milk. It should only be given on the advice of a doctor, health visitor or paediatrician. Even though manufacturers market their soya formulas as suitable for babies from birth, health professionals do not recommend them for babies under 6 months.

## Follow-on milks

These are milks with higher protein and mineral content than ordinary infant formula, and are sold as suitable for babies from 6 months old. Follow-on milks are advertised as more nutritious than cows' milk, because they contain added iron, vitamins and minerals. Health professionals say that the main benefit is for babies over 12 months (when they can be having cows' milk), and are not necessary if the baby is having a good diet.

# The nutritional needs of young children from 18 to 36 months

Young children, especially those under the age of 3, need a wide variety of nutrients to ensure that the body grows, develops normally and continues to function well. Because toddlers are growing rapidly and are extremely active, they need a diet that is higher in fat and lower in fibre than that recommended for adults and children over 5 years. A toddler's daily energy requirement is around three times greater than an adult's.

## Planning meals for young children

A healthy diet for young children combines foods from each and all of the **five food groups**:

1. **Bread, cereals and potatoes**: serve at each meal and offer some as snacks. Offer a mixture of white and wholegrain varieties of bread and cereals.
2. **Fruit and vegetables**: serve at each meal and aim for about five servings per day. Offering foods from this group at each meal will teach toddlers that a meal should always have fruit and vegetables. Set a good example by eating fruit and vegetables yourself.
3. **Milk, cheese and yoghurt**: serve three times a day. Toddlers need less milk than babies under 12 months. There are also some vitamins that are only found in fats, which is why foods such as

whole milk, yoghurt and cheese are so important. All toddlers should drink whole (full-fat milk) until they are 2 years old. Children above this age who are eating well can change to semi-skimmed milk.

4. **Meat, fish and vegetarian alternatives such as eggs, pulses and lentils**: one or two servings a day for non-vegetarians; two or three servings a day with a high vitamin C content for vegetarians. Oily fish such as mackerel, sardines and salmon are a good source of omega 3 fats, and should be served regularly.
5. **Foods high in fat and sugar**: include these every day in addition to, but not instead of, the other food groups. Once the child is 2 years old, you can gradually lower the amount of fat in their diet. Some foods will increase the levels of saturated or 'bad' fat in the diet. Cheap burgers, crisps, chips, biscuits, cakes and fried foods are all high in saturated fat. It can help to think of these sorts of foods as 'extras' once the child has eaten well from the four other main groups.

## Drinks

Young children should have six to eight drinks a day to ensure adequate hydration and to prevent constipation. Milk and water are the best drinks to give between meals and snacks as they will not harm teeth.

Young children do not need as much milk as in their first year of life. Fruit juices should be diluted one-part juice to ten-parts water, and given with meals and snacks. They are acidic and dissolve tooth enamel when given on their own. Fruit squashes with sugar or sweeteners are also acidic and should be well-diluted. Bottles and reservoir cups should not be used because they bathe the gums and sensitive milk teeth in acid for longer, which increases the risk of dental decay and enamel.

## Government guidance

It is important to review the setting's food policy to ensure that it is in line with current government recommendations. Information is available on the Food Standards website and on the NHS Birth to Five website.

## Guidelines for providing for the nutritional needs of young children

- A healthy balance of nutrients will be supplied by combining foods from each and all of the five food groups.
- Young children should eat according to their appetites rather than to set serving sizes.
- Young children may eat better some days than others. A balanced combination should therefore be averaged out over the week rather than judged on a day-to-day basis.
- This combination involves mixing high calorie foods (the foods that provide more energy) and low calorie foods so that not too many calories are consumed.
- Adults should eat with young children and praise them when they eat well, as this will encourage them to enjoy their meals.
- Fussy eaters, or others who may not be having enough vitamins in their diet, may need to have a daily vitamin A and D supplement. A health visitor or dietician would advise on this.

## Working with parents and carers

Parents and carers should be involved in the planning of meals for their children. This will enable young children to try new foods at a group setting as well as including foods from their home environment.

## Food allergies and intolerances

Foods to be avoided for this age group are those listed in Table 18.2. When planning meals and snacks for young children, it is important that we know which foods to avoid and also that we find out about food allergies and intolerances that a child may develop. For further information on food allergies and intolerances, see pages 296–7 in Chapter 14 (Unit EYMP 3).

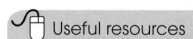

### Assessment practice

Using the information above:

1. Plan a week's meals for a group of children aged between 18 months and 36 months. You can find examples of foods in the five food groups on the NHS Birth to Five website and also in Chapter 14 (Unit EYMP 3).

2. Explain how the weekly plan meets the nutritional needs of young children.

3. Describe how you have based your plan on current government guidance and from information from children's parents and carers.

4. Describe the difference between a food allergy and a food intolerance. Why is it important that you know about these? Why is it important to work closely with parents and carers when planning meals for young children?

### Useful resources

**Organisations and websites**
The **Food Standards Agency** is responsible for food safety and food hygiene across the UK: www.food.gov.uk

**Birth to five** is a guide to parenting in the early years and has 150 pages of NHS-accredited information, videos and interactive tools:
www.nhs.uk/Planners/birthtofive

# 19 Lead and manage a community-based early years setting: Unit CYPOP 3

This unit is about providing leadership and management in a community-based setting that promotes the engagement, involvement and participation of parents. Your role as an early years practitioner may involve working in an organisation or group that is run by a management committee, for example, parent and toddler groups, playgroups and pre-schools. This usually involves working within community-based provision whose main purpose is to support children's care, learning and development in partnership with their families.

## Learning outcomes

By the end of this Unit you will:

1. Understand the purposes, benefits and key features of community based early years provision.

2. Be able to lead the team in a community-based early years setting.

3. Be able to engage parents as partners in the community-based early years setting.

4. Be able to engage parents in the management/decision-making processes of early years setting.

5. Be able to provide learning opportunities to support parents' participation in a community-based early years setting.

6. Be able to manage the resource, regulatory and financial requirements for a community-based early years setting.

## Understand the purposes, benefits and key features of community-based early years provision

Community-based early years provision includes pre-schools, playgroups, parent and toddler groups, crèches, community nurseries, children's centres and out of school clubs.

## The purpose and features of a community-based setting

All early years providers have to follow a structure of learning, development and care for children. In England this is called the Early Years Foundation Stage (EYFS) and it enables children to learn through a range of activities. The main principles of the EYFS are as follows:

- children learn through play
- providers work closely with parents
- the child's learning at home is taken into account
- parents and guardians are kept up to date on the child's progress
- it is inclusive – it ensures the welfare, learning and all-round development of children with different backgrounds and levels of ability, including those with special educational needs and disabilities.

The EYFS applies to all schools and registered early years providers in the maintained, private, voluntary and independent sectors attended by children from birth to 5 years. This includes:

- reception and nursery classes in maintained and independent schools
- day nurseries
- childminders
- playgroups
- after-school and breakfast clubs
- holiday play schemes
- children's centres.

The following groups do not have to use the EYFS:

- mother and toddler groups
- nannies
- short-term, occasional care – for example, crèches.

(Detailed information about the EYFS is in Chapter 13, EYMP 2.)

## Pre-schools and playgroups

Community pre-schools and playgroups offer children aged between 3 and 5 years an opportunity to learn through play:

- They usually operate on a part-time sessional basis. Sessions are normally 2.5 hours each, morning or afternoon.
- Staff plan a varied curriculum that takes into account children's previous experiences and developing needs.
- The Early Years Foundation Stage is adapted by each group to meet the needs of their own children and to allow them to make the most of a variety of learning opportunities that arise spontaneously through play.
- At many pre-school playgroups, parents and carers are encouraged to be involved, and there are often parent and toddler groups meeting at the same sites.

## Community nurseries

Community nurseries exist to provide a service to local children and their families. They are run by local community organisations – often with financial assistance from the local authority – or by charities such as Barnardos and Save the Children. Most of these nurseries are open long enough to suit working parents or those at college. Many centres also provide, or act as a venue for, other services, including:

- parent and toddler groups
- drop-in crèches
- toy libraries
- after-school clubs.

## Children's centres

The majority of children's centres were developed from Sure Start local programmes, neighbourhood nurseries and Early Excellence Centres. Sure Start Children's Centres are places where children under 5 years old and their families can receive seamless, holistic, integrated services and information, and where they can access help from multidisciplinary teams of professionals. Children's centres serve children and their families from the antenatal period until children start in Reception or Year 1 at primary school. They also offer a base within the community, linking to other providers of day care, such as childminder networks and out-of-school clubs.

Each centre offers the following services to families with babies and pre-school children:

- good-quality early learning integrated with full day care provision (a minimum of 10 hours a day, 5 days a week, 48 weeks a year)
- family support services
- a base for a childminder network
- child and family health services, including antenatal services
- support for children and parents with special needs
- links with Jobcentre Plus, local training providers and further and higher education institutions.

Children's centres may also offer other services, including:

- training for parents – for example, parenting classes, basic skills, English as an additional language
- benefits advice and information
- toy libraries.

## Out-of-school clubs

Out-of-school clubs and extended schools offer:

- high-quality 'wraparound' child care, provided by the school site or other local providers, available 8 a.m. to 6 p.m. all year round
- a varied menu of activities – for example, homework clubs and study support, sport, music tuition, special interest clubs and volunteering
- parenting support, including information sessions for parents at key transition points, parenting programmes and family learning sessions
- swift and easy referral to a wide range of specialist support services – for example, speech and language therapy, family support services and behaviour support providing wider community access to ICT, sports and arts facilities, including adult learning.

## Research Activity

### What kind of provision?

Research the early years provision made by your local authority.

1. What community-based early years provision is available for 0 to 3 year olds?
2. What community-based early years provision is available for 3 to 5 year olds?

## How a community-based early years setting can be an agent of community development

A community-based early years setting can play a positive role in building a stronger community. For example, by increasing opportunities for all children to play, through developing new facilities and maximising the use of existing ones. A community-based early years setting also encourages community development by recognising and valuing the crucial role parents and carers play in their child's learning and development and engages them as partners in service development.

The early years setting influences the developing attitudes of the children within it and can be a powerful vehicle for the promotion of understanding and practice of equal opportunities. Every member (or potential member) of the setting should be regarded as of equal worth and importance, irrespective of his/her creed, culture, class, race, gender, sexuality and/or disability.

An important aspect of community development is to find out what children, parents, carers and others in the local community think about the setting and the services provided. You should know how to gain and use feedback from people in the local community about early years provision, including representative groups and individuals, e.g. current and potential new users of the early years setting, individuals who may experience barriers to access such as those with disabilities, relevant colleagues within the setting. Feedback can be gained *informally* through discussions with individuals or small groups or *formally* using meetings or questionnaires. Ensure that you listen and respond to the views and experiences of people in the local community, especially those of children and their parents or carers. Try to include their suggestions when planning to make changes or improvements to the childcare setting. (See section on involving children in decision-making in Chapter 1, Unit SHC 31.)

## The benefits arising from community-based early years provision for children, parents/carers, the early years setting, and the local community

There are many benefits arising from community-based early years provision for young children, their parents/carers, the early years setting and the local community.

Benefits for children include:

- The early years are a period of formative learning and development and can have a significant influence on the rest of a child's life
- Early years services offer the care and education children need to give them the best start in life
- Children may receive a better start in life so that they are ready to succeed, live longer and lead healthier lives

- Early years settings enrich the lives of children to become confident and successful individuals learning through play.

Benefits for parents include:

- Parents and carers and the wider family have the greatest influence on children, particularly in the early years
- Early years settings develop partnerships with parents/carers in ways which help them to provide nurturing and stimulating family environments that give children the best start in life
- Early years settings support parents and carers to improve parenting skills that secure better outcomes for their families.

Benefits for the early years setting include:

- Collaborative working and partnership in the early years setting helps to deliver the relevant early years framework
- Encouragement of integration and sharing of services and a more cost-effective use of scarce resources between local and national childcare agencies
- Supports the development of appropriate approaches which enable children and their parents/carers to be active participants in the services they use.

Benefits for the local community include:

- Early years settings support on service developments that engage and empower families as well as strengthen communities
- Enables parents to choose early years and childcare services with the child's welfare driving the decision, rather than economics
- Collaboration and support across the early years sector and increased emphasis on the value of voluntary sector community-based services which offer flexible, engaging, innovative and holistic approaches
- Providing early interventions and services that help children experience the best start to life that prevents later, often more costly, interventions.

# Be able to lead the team in a community-based early years setting

As an early years practitioner, you may be responsible for the management of a community-based early years setting either as the setting manager or senior practitioner in one of these types of setting – children's centre, community project, crèche, day nursery, holiday play scheme, out-of-school club, play bus, play centre, playgroup, pre-school or Sure Start programme.

## Leadership skills in own practice

The early years setting should have a clear management structure with management duties carried out by different members of the management team. The people in the management team usually share the management of the early years setting with one person having overall responsibility. Members should know what their key responsibilities are within the management team.

To lead the team in a community-based early years setting effectively you need to know and demonstrate leadership skills in your own practice. For example:

- **Effective communication:** remember confidentiality in discussions with colleagues concerning any problem associated with their work; respect parental rights to enquiry, consultation and information with regard to the development and learning of their children; respect the confidentiality of information relating to children, unless the disclosure of such information is either required by law or is in the best interests of that particular child.
- **Negotiation and empathy:** demonstrate an awareness of the work-related needs of others; express any criticism of colleagues or parents in a sensitive manner and avoid hurtful comments of a personal nature; never denigrate a colleague or parent in the presence of others; respect the joint responsibility that exists between the setting and the parents of the children who attend the setting.

- **Consistency and fairness:** act with compassion and impartiality; never distort or misrepresent the facts concerning any aspect of the development and learning of children.
- **Leading change and modelling good practice:** remember that the social, intellectual and physical welfare and emotional wellbeing of the children is the prime purpose and first concern; always have proper regard for the health, safety and well-being of children, parents, colleagues and yourself; seek to establish a friendly and co-operative relationship with the parents, your colleagues and the management committee; be aware of the involvement of the local community in the life of the setting and understand its social, economic and ethnic needs and problems; recognise the need of the local community to use the setting facilities, subject to the requirements of the setting, especially within shared buildings such as community centres and church halls.
- **Effective conflict management:** recognise and respond to issues that affect your team's ability to work effectively in the setting, including dealing appropriately with difficulties and conflict situations that affect your working relationships with colleagues or parents; many difficulties and conflicts within the setting can be resolved through open and honest discussion; you can act as a mediator to help those involved in a disagreement or conflict to reach a satisfactory agreement or compromise; where serious difficulties or conflict situations cannot be resolved, use the setting's grievance procedure to deal with them – the management committee, the local authority and relevant trade unions may be involved.
- **Coaching and facilitation skills:** respect the status of colleagues and parents, particularly when making any assessment or observations on colleagues' work; staff members should actively seek to develop their personal skills and professional expertise, this includes parent helpers (see sections below on staff development and mentoring).

# Implement activities with the setting's staff team to share and promote their understanding of good practice

Developing productive working relationships with colleagues involves a knowledge and understanding of the following: providing effective support for colleagues; staff induction; supervision in the setting; staff appraisals; motivating colleagues; staff development; resolving conflicts; grievance and disciplinary procedures; mentoring and coaching in the setting (see below).

## Providing effective support for colleagues

Developing productive working relationships with colleagues is important because this helps to maintain a positive childcare environment that benefits children, parents and staff. As a member of a team, you need to develop productive working relationships with your colleagues by: being supportive towards them; helping to reduce sources of stress; challenging discrimination and prejudice; improving your own performance. (See Chapter 15, Unit EYMP 4.)

You can provide effective support for colleagues by being an attentive listener. Listening carefully to colleagues will enable you to recognise possible signs of stress. You can then respond in the following ways: be sympathetic and understanding; offer to help directly if you can; give information on sources of help and advice, for example, help available within the setting, national and local advice lines, the Citizens' Advice Bureau and counselling services such as Relate. If you have concerns about a colleague with a serious problem, you could consult the management committee or your professional body about what to do next but always remember to maintain confidentiality, especially if the colleague concerned has told you something in confidence. (See information on confidentiality in Chapter 1, Unit SHC 31.)

## Staff induction

Induction provides new members of staff with the opportunity to learn about the early years setting and what is expected of them. It can be helpful to compile a **staff induction pack** including: welcome letter; statement of principles and values; copies of essential policies and procedures, e.g. equal opportunities, health and safety, child protection, fire and emergency procedures; information about the setting's administration, e.g. registration and consent forms, monitoring forms, risk assessment, timesheets; names of staff and their main roles and responsibilities; the management structure of the setting; details of who to contact if they have any problems; general information and publicity about the setting; floor plan of the building.

Sometimes it might be appropriate to ask the practitioner who is leaving to stay on during the new practitioner's first week. The departing practitioner can share the workload and help the new member of staff to familiarise themselves with their new working environment. They can also help the new member of staff to gain a greater understanding of the exact duties and responsibilities they are expected to undertake in the early years setting.

## Staff appraisals

Staff appraisals or reviews are a formal way for you to keep up-to-date with the work performance of your colleagues and to identify their ongoing training needs. Staff appraisals usually take place once a year. Staff appraisals should have an agreed format, e.g. a form to be completed by the

practitioner prior to the appraisal meeting that will form the basis of discussion at the actual appraisal meeting.

## Staff development

Good quality and appropriate staff development and training can have a huge, positive impact on workplace performance which, in turn, can greatly enhance the play and learning experiences of the children using the early years setting. To be effective, staff development should take into account the needs of individual staff members and the needs of the setting as a whole.

When providing learning opportunities for your colleagues, you should start by identifying their learning needs, e.g. what additional knowledge and skills do they need to work more effectively? Staff appraisals can help you to identify these learning needs. Once their learning needs have been identified, you need to agree with your colleague(s) on an appropriate training course or qualification that will help to meet their learning needs.

When considering staff development you will have a choice of training options including: sending staff on existing training courses (as a group or individually); inviting trainers in to the setting to run sessions for you; running in-house training. Another aspect of staff development is to look at ways that your colleagues can pass on their knowledge, skills and experience to other practitioners, e.g. training as early years trainers or assessors. Training opportunities should be also be offered to parents and carers, as well as staff members, including meetings with speakers, discussion groups, reading materials, e.g. books, factsheets and information packs.

Each member of staff should have a Personal Development Plan or Continuing Professional Development Plan that includes training and personal development goals and how these relate to the aims of the childcare setting. (See section on agreeing a personal development plan in Chapter 2, Unit SHC 32.)

## In Practice

Describe how you identify the learning needs of your colleagues and provide training opportunities to meet these needs.

## Mentoring in the early years setting

Mentoring is a structured approach to supporting a colleague by pairing an experienced member of the team with a less experienced member of the team, e.g. trainee on modern apprenticeship. Mentoring is a very effective way for colleagues to share knowledge, skills and experience.

Mentoring involves: 'shadowing' (e.g. watching the work of a more experienced colleague); learning 'on the job' (e.g. developing new skills; asking and answering every day questions); introducing other people in the early years setting; providing guidance and constructive criticism; agreeing and setting daily objectives; reviewing progress; providing feedback to manager on progress; identifying further training needs; providing friendly and reassuring support.

The stages involved in planning the mentoring process:

1. Identify development needs and expectations of trainees.
2. Recruit mentors and provide them with training and guidance on mentoring activities.
3. Match mentors with trainees to form mentoring pairs.
4. Mentoring pair negotiates a mentoring agreement based on development needs.
5. Devise an individual development plan based on development objectives.
6. Implement individual development plans.
7. Mentoring agreement concluded.

8. Evaluate the individual development plan and the mentoring process.

### Research Activity

Find out about the support for trainees in your setting:

- Which training programmes are available in your setting, e.g. modern apprenticeships, etc.
- What resources, facilities, information and support are available to help trainees?
- Which documents and activities are available to help trainees in the early stages of mentoring?

### Give mentoring support

To be an effective mentor you need the following important skills and personal qualities: good interpersonal skills including being a good listener; good coaching/counselling skills (see below); appropriate workplace experience; honesty and integrity; you must be well informed about the work of the setting and other relevant agencies; demonstrate enthusiasm; patience; reliability; be a reflective practitioner; be committed to supporting trainees.

Giving effective mentoring support involves: setting aside enough time for each mentoring session; helping trainees to express and discuss ideas and any concerns affecting their experience in the workplace; giving trainees information and advice that will help them to be effective in the workplace; giving trainees opportunities that help them understand and adapt to the working environment; identifying ways of developing trainees' confidence in performing activities in the workplace; helping trainees take increasing responsibility for developing their skills in the workplace; giving trainees the opportunities to gain experience in the workplace to increase their confidence and self-development; helping trainees look at issues from an unbiased and objective point of view that helps them make informed choices; giving trainees honest and constructive feedback; identifying when the mentoring relationship needs to change to still be effective and agree any changes with the trainee; identifying when the mentoring relationship has reached a natural end and review the process with the trainee; agreeing what extra support and help the trainee needs or can access; planning how to provide extra support and help (NDNA, 2004).

## In Practice

Give a reflective account of how you have supported learners by mentoring in the workplace. Include detailed information on how you: plan the mentoring process; set up and maintain the mentoring relationship; provide mentoring support.

# Implement strategies to create and maintain a team culture among all of the staff and parents in a community-based early years setting

Much of adult life involves working with other people usually in a group or team. Individuals within a team affect each other in various ways. Within the team there will be complex interactions involving different personalities, roles and expectations, as well as hidden agendas that may influence the behaviour of individual members of the team. Teamwork is essential when working closely and regularly with other people over a period of time.

**Effective teamwork** is important because it helps all members of the team to:

- **T**ake effective action when planning and/or assigning agreed work tasks
- **E**fficiently implement the agreed work tasks
- **A**gree aims and values which set standards of good practice
- **M**otivate and support each other
- **W**elcome feedback about their work
- **O**ffer additional support in times of stress
- **R**eflect on and evaluate their own working practices
- **K**now and use each person's strengths and skills.

As a manager or team leader in an early years setting, you must know and understand: your exact role and responsibilities; the exact roles and responsibilities of each member of your team; how to contribute to effective team practice; how to participate in team meetings.

## Effective communication with colleagues

You should know how to communicate effectively with members of your team. Effective communication is essential for developing effective team practice. Effective lines of communication are also important to ensure that all members of the team receive the necessary up-to-date information to enable them to make a full contribution to the life of the early years setting. Make sure you use any notice boards, newsletters and/or staff bulletins to advise team members of important information. You can also use informal opportunities such as breaks or lunch times to share information, experiences and ideas with colleagues. You might find a communications book or file may be useful as well as regular meetings with members of your team. As an experienced early years practitioner you can make a valuable contribution to the induction or on-going training of new practitioners possibly acting as a mentor (see section above).

## Activity

List the methods you use to share information with colleagues in your setting.

## Team objectives

You must also know and understand the purpose, objectives and plans of your team including: how to set and achieve team objectives which are SMART (Specific, Measurable, Achievable, Realistic and Time-bound) in consultation with team members; demonstrate to team members how their personal work objectives contribute to team objectives (see section on developing your personal development objectives in Chapter 2 and section on staff development in this chapter). You should also be aware of the types of support and advice that team members may require (see section on providing support for colleagues).

## Activity

Describe how you set and achieve team objectives in consultation with your team members.

## Resolving conflicts

Conflicts can arise in even the best-run early years settings. The resolution of conflict situations within the setting requires the senior practitioner to work with colleagues. Whenever possible, it is better for colleagues to find their own solutions with the senior practitioner or manager acting as a **facilitator** or **mediator.** Sometimes a colleague may not make allowances for parent/carer's particular problems or does not show respect for the needs and rights of parents/carers. Conflicts must be handled sensitively and resolved as quickly as possible to avoid creating a negative, unpleasant atmosphere for all those in the setting which can have a detrimental effect on the wellbeing of the children. Personal problems may also affect a colleague's working relationships with others in the setting. The senior practitioner or manager should have a one-to-one discussion and suggest where sources of help might be found. (See above for information on providing effective support for colleagues.)

## Key terms

**Conflict situation** – verbal or physical disagreement, e.g. arguments, fighting, disputing rules.

**Facilitator** – person who makes things easier by providing the appropriate environment and resources for learning.

**Mediator** – a person who acts as an intermediary between parties in a dispute.

## Activity

Describe how you have responded or would respond to a conflict situation as senior practitioner or manager in a childcare setting. (Be tactful and remember confidentiality.)

## Grievance and disciplinary procedures

The Employment Rights Act 1996 requires that all employees who work for more than 16 hours a week have a contract, a formal written agreement stating their terms and conditions of employment. This statement should also include information about the setting's grievance and disciplinary procedures. The Employment Act 2002, sections 35–38, deals with changes to the rules concerning written particulars of employment, including ensuring the statement complies with the Act's requirements for minimum statutory internal grievance and disciplinary procedures.

If an employee has a grievance relating to their employment, they are entitled to invoke the setting's grievance procedure (which may be part of a local authority agreement) and should be included in the staff handbook. The grievance should be raised initially with their line manager (e.g. the senior practitioner). The grievance should be raised orally in the first instance, although the employee may be requested to put it in writing. If the grievance relates to the employee's line manager, then the grievance should be referred to their line manager's line manager (e.g. the setting's manager).

The early years setting will expect reasonable standards of performance and conduct from all staff members. Details of the disciplinary procedure (which may be part of a local authority agreement) should be included in the staff handbook. If an employee is dissatisfied with a disciplinary decision they should in the first instance contact the setting manager usually within five working days of the date of the decision.

## Activity

Outline the grievance and disciplinary procedures for practitioners in your setting.

# The effectiveness of own practice in implementing the principles of community-based early years provision

When administering provision within the early years setting, you must be committed to promoting understanding of the values and principles of children's care, learning and development (see page 17 in Chapter 2, Unit SHC 32).

## Basic management skills

To manage a community-based early years setting effectively, you also need to know and understand basic management skills. Basic management skills can be divided into four main categories:

1. **Managing people:** recruiting and retaining colleagues; motivating staff; providing training opportunities; managing difficult team members and dealing with personality clashes; dealing with disciplinary issues; working with parents and carers; managing children's behaviour.
2. **Managing activities:** effective planning and organisation, e.g. activity plans, work rota, holidays, etc; monitoring children's care, learning and development.
3. **Managing resources:** securing funding; organising finances; managing a budget; obtaining appropriate resources.
4. **Managing information:** registration including following legal requirements; day-to-day administration, e.g. daily attendance registers; establishing, developing and evaluating quality assurance systems.

# Be able to engage parents as partners in the community-based early years setting

As an early years practitioner, you should have a strong commitment to children and their parents. You should behave towards parents at all times in a manner that shows personal courtesy and integrity.

## Activity

1. Make a list of your management skills.

2. Are there any particular skills that you need to work on and improve?

This includes: helping parents to feel welcome and valued in the setting; seeking to establish a friendly and cooperative relationship with parents; never distorting or misrepresenting the facts concerning any aspect of their children's care, learning and development; respecting the joint responsibility that exists between the setting and parents for the development and wellbeing of their children; respecting parental rights to enquiry, consultation and information with regard to the development of their children.

The setting should recognise that working in partnership with parents is an important part of developing positive relationships between the setting and the local community. As appropriate to the type of setting, you should encourage parents to become actively involved in the life of the setting (see below).

# Establish and maintain a relationship of partners with the parents/carers of children in an early years setting

As an early years practitioner you should establish and maintain a relationship of partners with the parents/carers of children in an early years setting including:

- Understanding that parents and carers are partners who have the lead role and responsibility for their children
- Understanding the value of the role of parents and carers, and know how and when to refer them to further sources of information, advice or support
- Understanding the importance of building good

relationships with children and their parents or carers

- Establishing a rapport and building respectful, trusting, honest and supportive relationships with children and their families or carers, which make them feel valued as partners
- Building a rapport and developing relationships using the most appropriate forms of communication (for example, spoken language, visual communication, play, body and sign language, information and communication technologies) to meet the needs of the individual child as well as their parents or carers
- Holding conversations at the appropriate time and place, understanding the value of regular, reliable contact and recognising that it takes time to build a relationship.

(CWDC, 2010; pp. 6–9)

## Exchange information with parents about the progress of their child's learning and development

You will need to exchange information with parents about the progress of their child's learning and development. You may need to give parents positive reassurance about what their children are doing in the setting, for example, explaining the benefits of play to their child's development and learning.

Good communication is central to working with children and their parents or carers. It helps build trust, and encourages parents to seek advice and use services. It is key to establishing and maintaining relationships, and is an active process that involves listening, questioning, understanding and responding.

When exchanging information with parents remember the following points:

- Know that communication is a two-way process
- Communicate appropriately to match the personal circumstances and needs of the person you are talking to
- Know how to listen to people, make them feel valued and involved

- Use clear language to communicate with all parents and carers, including people who find communication difficult, or are at risk of exclusion or under-achievement
- Actively listen in a calm, open, non-judgemental, non-threatening way and use open questions
- Acknowledge what has been said, and check you have heard correctly
- Ensure that parents and carers know they can communicate their needs and ask for help.

(CWDC, 2010; pp. 6–8)

### In Practice

Give examples of how your setting exchanges information with children and families. Examples may include: copy of the setting's brochure or information pack; posters, leaflets and newsletters; sample registration form; letters about outings; home/setting diary; daily log; review sheets; meeting agendas.

## Involve parents in decisions about plans and activities to progress their child's learning and development

Effective communication extends to involving children and their parents or carers in the design and delivery of services and decisions that affect them. It is important to consult the people affected and consider opinions and perspectives from the outset. Involving parents in decisions affecting their child can have a positive effect on supporting their children to achieve positive outcomes.

Remember the following points:

- Decide together how to involve parents or carers in the choices to be made
- Consult the child or young person, and their parents or carers from the beginning of the process
- Make informed judgements about how to involve children, young people, parents and carers in decisions as far as is possible and appropriate

**Figure 19.1** Working with parents in a community-based early years setting

- Take account of their views and what they want to see happen
- Be honest about the weight of their opinions and wishes.

(CWDC, 2010; pp. 6–9)

## Involve parents in the activities of the early years setting

You should provide information to individual families who could benefit from participating in groups and ensure that activities provided are inclusive, stimulating and of interest to all participants. You should help family members settle into the group and agree ground rules for group sessions with participants. You should also manage and minimise dissent within the group. Encouraging families to become involved in the setting is an important part of developing links with the local community. You can encourage families to be involved in the setting by ensuring that families feel welcome in a setting that is friendly and accessible.

You should encourage parents to become actively involved in the life of the setting, for example, as parent helpers or volunteers in the setting or as participants in committees, special events, outings

and other activities. Remember you should encourage parental involvement without putting pressure on parents who may have other commitments such as work, caring for younger children or elderly relatives.

You could actively encourage parents to:

- Help in the setting, e.g. help with play and learning opportunities, help with the provision of food and drinks, help with administration, help with preparation for trips and outings
- Share their expertise, e.g. arts and crafts, bilingual storytelling, etc.
- Join in with outings, e.g. visits to parks, playgrounds and sports facilities
- Participate in special events, e.g. puppet shows, theatre groups
- Fund-raising for the setting, the local community, local and national charities
- Help to promote the service to other families in the local community.

You can involve parents in the activities of the early years setting by:

- **Providing the parent with an overview of the planning for activities,** e.g. a brochure or information pack outlining the work of the setting; a booklet with a brief introduction to the relevant early years curriculum such as the Early Years Foundation Stage (EYFS); a leaflet promoting the service to other families in the local community

- **Giving guidance to the parent on which activity/activities in which to participate,** e.g. posters and leaflets inviting parents to join in with sessions as parent helpers, help with fundraising or join the committee; regular newsletters including suggestions on how parents can participate – helping with play and learning opportunities, the provision of food and drinks, administration, or preparation for trips and outings; verbal and written requests for parents to join in with activities such as outings (visits to parks, playgrounds and sports facilities) or special events (festival celebrations, puppet shows, theatre groups), as well as fund-raising for the setting, the local community, or local and national charities; sign-up sheets for helping during sessions or with specific activities; a suggestion box for ideas for future activities

- **Explaining the purposes of the activity in which the parent participates,** e.g. a booklet about the benefits of play to children's development and learning; an activity guide sheet outlining the purpose of the activity (such as to encourage and extend children's language and communication), how the activity will help different aspects of children's learning and development, the resources needed and the parent's involvement in the activity

- **Working with a parent to enable her or him to share a specific interest/skill with the setting's children,** e.g. encouraging parents to share their expertise such as: painting, drawing, pottery and other art techniques; bilingual storytelling; music, dance and drama; gardening, knitting, sewing, weaving, computer skills. Provide parents with tips on how they can share their particular expertise with young children, such as keeping it simple, using a step-by-step approach and giving instructions appropriate to the age/level of development of the children

- **Creating opportunities for parents to contribute to the play materials provided for the children by the setting,** e.g. making or mending materials for imaginative play, such as dressing-up clothes, dolls' clothes, puppets; collecting clean household 'junk', such as empty cereal boxes, for construction models

- **Supporting parents to participate in the setting's curriculum provision for its children,** e.g. a booklet with a brief introduction to the relevant early years curriculum, such as EYFS; a booklet linking the early years curriculum to children's development and learning, with suggestions for possible activities and how the parents may be involved.

## In Practice

1. Describe how you encourage families to attend and participate in your setting. Give examples from your own experiences of working with families.

2. Describe how you have involved parents in the running of group sessions. You could include information on how you: ensure parents understand and support the values of the setting; provide information on ground rules and play setting procedures; find opportunities appropriate to their needs and skills; monitor their involvement and providing guidance and support.

3. Describe how you have managed and minimised dissent within the group. Remember confidentiality.

# Be able to engage parents in the management/decision-making processes of early years setting

Your role may involve working in an organisation or group that is run by a management committee, e.g. parent and toddler groups, playgroups and pre-schools. This usually involves working within community-based provision whose main purpose is to support children's care, learning and development in partnership with their families.

## Explain the role of the parent management committee/ support group in a community-based early years setting

The management committee is responsible for the management of the pre-school, playgroup or parent and toddler group. The majority of management committee members are parents of the children who attend the setting. The management committee is responsible for anything from organising a fundraising event to negotiating with the landlord over terms of the lease for the setting's accommodation. All decisions regarding the operation of the setting are the responsibility of the committee. The committee can delegate the implementation of decisions to staff, but the committee retains the responsibility for those decisions. A committee is the employer of all staff in the pre-school setting. It has overall responsibility for recruitment, wages, salaries, tax and national insurance, appraisals, contracts of employment and terms and conditions. The committee also has responsibility for things like developing a business plan, accounts, budgeting, funding, insurance, membership fees (e.g. Pre-school Learning Alliance membership), accommodation costs, staff wages and volunteer expenses, admission costs, and publicity costs. The committee, together with staff, is also responsible for health and safety, risk assessment, insurance and first aid, as well as policy making (PSLA, 2004).

You may be employed by a management committee to work as a playgroup or pre-school leader/ supervisor in a pre-school or playgroup setting which works with children aged between 2 and 5 years. The sessions may be full-day or part-day, e.g. 2½ hour sessions. The emphasis in the setting is on children learning through play and parental involvement in all aspects of the pre-school or playgroup should be encouraged.

As a pre-school or play group supervisor, you will be responsible for the preparation of long-, medium- and short-term plans using the appropriate curriculum framework, e.g. Early Years Foundation Stage. (See Chapter 13, Unit EYMP 2.) You will be responsible for organising and planning appropriate play and learning activities for the children (according to the appropriate curriculum framework); supervising staff on a day-to-day basis; reporting to the management committee on a regular basis.

Your responsibilities may also include managing the setting's petty cash system; liaising with the management committee, local authority and other agencies as necessary, to ensure that all regulatory requirements are met; providing the management committee with operational plans and reports as required.

As a pre-school or playgroup supervisor, you should send weekly updates of key information to the committee so that any problems can be identified quickly and action taken immediately. Regular full committee meetings should be held at which the supervisor should be present. A formal agenda should be used, based on key information and important issues for the setting. At the conclusion of the meeting, clear actions should be delegated (Sure Start, 2003b).

### Activity

Outline how you prepare and present operational plans and reports to a management committee.

## Demonstrate support to parents' involvement in the parent management committee/support group of a community-based early years setting

As a pre-school or play group supervisor, you will plan and supervise the daily programme of activities. This includes ensuring that staff and volunteers provide appropriate stimulation and support to the children, organising the key person or key worker system and supervising staff and volunteers on a daily basis. You will also implement observation and record keeping systems to regularly assess children's progress and monitoring the effectiveness of assessment procedures.

You may also be responsible for helping to monitor the quality of teaching, participating in staff appraisals and identifying in-service training needs, as well as attending in-service training and meetings as required. You should also liaise with parents including exchanging information about their children's progress and encouraging parents' involvement.

You should ensure that the setting is a safe environment for children, staff and others by ensuring hygiene standards and safety procedures are implemented at all times and fire drills are regularly practised; this also includes ensuring records are properly maintained, e.g. daily register, accident/incident book (see Chapter 8, Unit CYP Core 3.4). You should help to maintain the setting's policies and procedures including those on confidentiality, equal opportunities, inclusion, special needs and child protection.

## Activity

Give examples of how you implement management committee policies and procedures.

# Be able to provide learning opportunities to support parents' participation in a community-based early years setting

Part of your role within the setting involves providing learning opportunities to support parents'

participation in a community-based early years setting. You may be involved in activities such as: identifying individual needs; providing appropriate learning opportunities; checking on the progress of parents; giving feedback to parents; reviewing the potential for e-learning support for parents; helping parents to apply their learning; giving ongoing support to parents.

You should know how to identify and use different learning opportunities, e.g. observation, presentations, workshops, simulation, role play and practical experience. You should also know how to structure learning opportunities and how to choose and prepare appropriate materials including technology-based materials (see below).

You should put information in order and use language which is appropriate for parents. You should be able to put parents at their ease, for example, be approachable and communicate with parents in a sensitive way. You should provide parents with positive feedback and encourage them to recognise their own achievements. You should check parents' understanding and progress by asking questions and by observing and assessing the skills they demonstrate during learning opportunities.

You should know how to recognise the things that are likely to prevent learning, e.g. parents who may have difficulties accessing some learning activities such as people with disabilities or from different ethnic groups. You should know how to overcome these difficulties by providing appropriate support and resources.

# Utilise the informal learning opportunities arising from parents' participation in activities to promote the learning and development of their own child and the setting's children

You should help parents recognise the value and importance of play to children's development, emphasising the exploratory nature of play and its contribution to development. You should help parents and children to identify opportunities for sharing play and learning activities together, including identifying resources and opportunities for play in everyday activities. You should support parents in play activities with their own children and the setting's children. You should encourage parents to include non-stereotypical opportunities and experiences, e.g. boys as well as girls should have opportunities to play with dolls, dressing up clothes and join in cooking activities; girls as well as boys should have opportunities to play with toy cars, construction kits and join in ball games. You should encourage parents' involvement in their children's play activities in ways that enhance their development and reinforce positive relationships with their children.

You should assist parents to apply their learning by: giving parents the opportunities to practise skills, apply their knowledge and obtain experience in a structured way; consider using technology-based support for parents, including e-support; identifying opportunities for parents to achieve agreed learning objectives and give them positive feedback on their progress; identifying opportunities to use different learning opportunities and agree action with parents; giving parents clear and accurate

information on the resources available to help them apply their learning; giving parents positive feedback on the learning experience and the outcomes achieved; identifying anything that prevents learning and review this with parents; explaining to parents about any ongoing support available to them.

You should know and understand how to identify the opportunities available for parents to apply their learning. You should provide information on the resources and ongoing support that is available to them. You need to know how to analyse and use developments in learning and new ways of delivery such as technology-based learning; you need to know how to choose and prepare technology-based materials. You should ensure that everyone acts in line with health, safety and environmental protection legislation and best practice (see Chapter 8, Unit CYP Core 3.4).

## Provide parents with information about resources to enable them to develop the knowledge and skills

Part of your role may involve providing parents with information about resources to enable them to develop the knowledge and skills to participate effectively in the parent management committee or support group of the setting. This could include helping parents to:

- Identify possible sources of information, e.g. access advice and support networks
- Identify personal and study goals, e.g. complete a written assignment or practical task
- Develop their own ideas and how to present these
- Work out how to do management committee or support group tasks, e.g. participating in meetings, understanding budgets, fundraising
- Develop time management, e.g. prioritise tasks, plan for study time and social life
- Develop study skills including where to find information, e.g. developing word-processing skills, using the Internet.

(See useful resources at the end of this chapter.)

### Research Activity

Compile a booklet for parents about children's play. Include information on:

- The value and importance of play to a child's development

- How physical, exploratory and imaginative play contribute to children's development

- The sequence of social play

- A chart of developmentally appropriate play opportunities and resources suitable for the children in your setting

- How parents can be involved in children's play activities in ways that promote the learning and development of their own child and the setting's children.

# Be able to manage the resource, regulatory and financial requirements for a community-based early years setting

Every early years setting keeps a variety of records, including essential personal information for each child using the facility. The setting will also have contact details of the person responsible for the setting, staff and volunteers. Early years settings also have records relating to administrative duties, e.g. permission slips for educational visits/outings and requisition forms for equipment and materials. Records may also include: observations and assessments of children's developmental progress and activity plans with evaluations of the effectiveness of the activities provided; individual education plans and reviews for children with special educational needs. There will also be staff records relating to job applications and appointments.

## The regulatory requirements of the work setting and the lines of responsibility and reporting

When leading and managing a community-based early years setting, you will be involved in meeting regulatory requirements, e.g. statutory requirements for registration and inspection. This includes: identifying regulatory requirements relevant to your setting; planning for inspection in consultation with your colleagues; collecting required evidence; taking appropriate action to meet requirements.

## Identify regulatory requirements

You should identify regulatory requirements relevant to your setting, for example, the early years framework for your home country – England, Northern Ireland, Scotland and Wales. You must know and understand the criteria for early years provision in your setting with regard to:

- Premises and equipment
- The provision of food and drink, including guidelines for healthy eating
- Health and safety, including first aid and fire safety
- Staff numbers/ratios, suitability and qualifications
- Management of information systems and records, including confidentiality
- Curriculum requirements for the under-5s, e.g. Early Years Foundation Stage.

For example, in England, the Statutory Framework for the Early Years Foundation Stage (EYFS) includes the welfare requirements that all early years providers must meet. It is an offence to fail to comply with certain welfare requirements.

The general welfare requirements are:

1. **Safeguarding and promoting children's welfare**
   - *The provider must take necessary steps to safeguard and promote the welfare of children.*
   - *The provider must promote the good health of the children, take necessary steps to prevent the spread of infection, and take appropriate action when they are ill.*
   - *Children's behaviour must be managed effectively and in a manner appropriate for their stage of development and particular individual needs.*

2. **Suitable people to look after children**
   - *Providers must ensure that adults looking after children, or having unsupervised access to them, are suitable to do so.*
   - *Adults looking after children must have appropriate qualifications, training, skills and knowledge.*
   - *Staffing arrangements must be organised to ensure safety and to meet the needs of the children.*

3. **Suitable premises, environment and equipment**
   - *Outdoor and indoor spaces, furniture, equipment and toys must be safe and suitable for their purpose.*

4. **Organisation**
   - *Providers must plan and organise their systems to ensure that every child receives an enjoyable and challenging learning and development experience that is tailored to meet the children's needs.*
   - *Providers must maintain records, policies and procedures required for the safe and efficient management of the settings and to meet the needs of the children.*

(DCSF, 2008; pp.19–20)

### Research Activity

What are the regulatory requirements for your early years setting?

## Plan for inspection in consultation with colleagues

The Childcare Act 2006 introduced two new registers for people caring for children – the Childcare Register and the Early Years Register. The Childcare Register is a register of providers who are registered by Ofsted to care for children from birth to 17 years. The register has two parts: the voluntary part which providers who are not eligible for compulsory registration may choose to join (mainly people looking after children aged 8 and over, or providing care in the child's home); the compulsory part which providers must join if they care for one child or more from the 1 September following their fifth birthday until they reach their eighth birthday (Ofsted, 2010; p. 6). Unless exempt, the following must be registered by Ofsted on the Early Years Register: maintained and independent schools directly responsible for provision for children from birth to the age of 3; childcarers, such as childminders, day nurseries, pre-schools and private nursery schools, providing for children from birth to the 31 August following their fifth birthday (Ofsted, 2010; p. 8). For more information about registration on the Childcare Register and the Early Years Register see: www.ofsted.gov.uk.

You and your colleagues can prepare for inspection in the following ways:

- **Know, understand and implement the principles and statutory guidance of the Early Years Foundation Stage, including the learning and development and welfare requirements** so that children receive a high standard of care and early education.
- **Put right any weaknesses identified in your last Ofsted inspection report** – If your provision has been inspected before, check your last report and think carefully about the changes and improvements you have made since then.
- **Complete the Ofsted self-evaluation form** – Completing the self-evaluation form is an indication that you are continually seeking to improve your provision for children's learning, development and welfare. If you complete other self-evaluation documents and/or are part of a

quality assurance scheme, please be ready to point this out when the inspector comes to visit.

- **Keep any information about how parents view your service and any improvements you have made as a result** – This information will give a fuller picture of your provision and help the inspector to see how well you work with parents to ensure the best outcomes for their children.

- **Demonstrate that you work with other providers who provide the Early Years Foundation Stage for the children in your care** – Close working between early years providers and professionals from other agencies, such as local and community health services, is vital for the identification of children's learning needs. Shared knowledge and advice will provide children with the best possible learning opportunities and environment. If the children who attend also receive the Early Years Foundation Stage in other settings, you should be able to show how you work with them to complement activities they provide and provide a good programme overall for the children.

(Ofsted, 2010; pp. 26–27)

### In Practice

1. How do you plan for inspection? Give examples from your own experience of working with colleagues to prepare for inspection.

2. Complete the Ofsted self-evaluation form. This is available at:

   www.ofsted.gov.uk/Ofsted-home/Forms-and-guidance/Browse-all-by/Other/General/Early-years-online-self-evaluation-form-SEF-and-guidance-For-settings-delivering-the-Early-Years-Foundation-Stage

## Collect required evidence

All early years providers must keep certain written records. Your setting must have the following documents ready to show the inspector:

- A record of complaints received from parents and their outcomes. From time to time, parents may

complain to you about your provision. You are likely to resolve these complaints without involving Ofsted. However, you must show the inspector a record of any written complaint parents have made that relates to one or more of the requirements of the Early Years Foundation Stage. This will help the inspector to check with you that the information on complaints that will go in the report is accurate

- A record of all medicines administered to children
- A record of accidents and first aid treatment
- A record to demonstrate that the required Criminal Records Bureau checks have been carried out, including the number and date of issue of the enhanced Criminal Records Bureau disclosure, in respect of all people who work directly with children or who are likely to have unsupervised access to them
- A record of the following information for each child in your care: full name; date of birth; the name and address of every parent and carer who is known to the provider; which of these parents or carers the child normally lives with; emergency contact details of the parents and carers
- A record of the name, home address and telephone number of the provider and any other person living or employed on the premises
- A record of the name, home address and telephone number of anyone who will regularly be in unsupervised contact with the children attending the early years provision
- A daily record of the names of the children looked after on the premises, their hours of attendance and the names of the children's key workers
- A record of risk assessment, clearly stating when it was carried out, by whom, the date of review and any action taken following a review or incident. A risk assessment must be carried out for each specific outing with the children.

(Ofsted, 2010; p. 28)

All early years providers are expected to implement the following policies and procedures. All early years providers (except childminders) are expected to have written copies of these policies and procedures:

- A safeguarding children policy and procedure

- A policy for ensuring equality of opportunities and for supporting children with special educational needs and/or disabilities
- A policy for administering medicines, including effective management systems to support individual children with medical needs
- A behaviour management policy
- A procedure for dealing with concerns and complaints from parents
- A procedure to be followed in the event of a parent failing to collect a child at the appointed time
- A procedure to be followed in the event of a child going missing
- A procedure for the emergency evacuation of the premises.

(Ofsted, 2010; p. 28)

- Ensuring colleagues' personal details are correct and up-to-date
- Ensuring children's developmental records are up-to-date and based on observations
- Reviewing materials and equipment to ensure they meet health and safety requirements
- Reviewing curriculum plans and amending where necessary so they meet objectives
- Ensuring records of children's attendance, contact details and other essential information are up-to-date
- Keeping accurate and legible records of meetings and discussions
- Working with colleagues to develop confidence in the inspection process to provide positive benefit for children and their families.

(NDNA, 2004)

## Activity

Check that you have collected the required evidence. Use the above list to help you.

## Take appropriate action to meet requirements

As part of your role in meeting the regulatory requirements in the early years setting, you must be able to take appropriate action to meet regulatory requirements. This includes:

- Reviewing and updating policies and procedures
- Examining premises and making any necessary changes prior to inspection

## How human resources are managed within the setting

Adults are one of the most important resources in the setting. Ensure that your setting is making the best use of human resources (e.g. practitioners, parent helpers and volunteers) in order to: respond to children's play needs and preferences; stimulate children's play and development; encourage children's ideas, opinions and active participation; provide appropriate support for children's self-directed play; safeguard children's health and wellbeing.

When managing human resources within the setting, you must have a clear knowledge and understanding of the following: effective planning and organisation within the childcare setting; allocating work in your team including job rotation

## Activity

1. Outline the regulatory requirements for your setting.

2. Describe how you plan for inspection in consultation with colleagues.

3. List the different sources of evidence and records required for inspection.

4. Outline how you have taken appropriate action to meet regulatory requirements.

and effective delegation; monitoring work in your team; monitoring children's care, learning and development; making the best use of the available resources.

## Effective planning and organisation within the setting

Staff meetings are essential for effective planning and organisation within the setting. Such meetings also provide regular opportunities to share day-to-day information and to solve any problems. Staff meetings should be held regularly – about once every four to six weeks. Ensure that there is an agenda for the meeting and that the minutes of the meeting are recorded and can be easily accessed by staff. Encourage colleagues to share best practice, knowledge and ideas on developing appropriate play and learning activities in the setting. As well as general staff meetings, you should also have regular team meetings for the more detailed planning of routines, play and learning activities as well as the allocation of work within your area of responsibility.

## Allocating work in your team

You can allocate work and responsibilities in a variety of ways. For example:

- *Responsibility for an area:* Each practitioner (or group of practitioners) is responsible for a specific area of the setting and promoting children's care, learning and development within that area, e.g. baby room, toddler room, pre-schoolers. The practitioner(s) will provide support for the individual needs of the children in that area, including appropriate adult supervision or intervention as and when necessary. This includes working with any parent helpers.
- *Responsibility for an activity:* Each practitioner and/or parent helper is responsible for a specific activity, e.g. arts and crafts. The adult stays with the same activity throughout the day/week and is responsible for: selecting and setting out materials or helping the children to access these for themselves; encouraging the children's interest and participation in the activity; providing appropriate adult supervision or intervention as

required; helping children to clear away afterwards.
- *Responsibility for a group of children:* Each practitioner is responsible for a small group of children as their key person or key worker. The practitioner helps them to settle into the childcare setting. The practitioner is responsible for: greeting their group of children on arrival; encouraging the children's care, learning and development in the setting; establishing and maintaining a special relationship with each child and their family. (See the role of the key person on page 224).
- *Responsibility for an individual child:* A practitioner may have special responsibility for a child with a disability. The practitioner will be responsible for: ensuring that child's particular needs are met in an inclusive way within the setting; ensuring they have the necessary materials to participate in routines and activities including any specialist equipment; establishing and maintaining a special relationship with the child and their family. (See the role of the key worker on page 463.)

## Job rotation

Job rotation involves giving colleagues (including parent helpers) the opportunity to experience other roles within the setting. It can be an interesting and positive way for colleagues to gain varied work experience and to develop new skills. It can also be extremely useful when covering staff absences. A staff rota can be a useful way to ensure the fair allocation of work within the setting. Use the rota to share out some of the more routine jobs within the setting, e.g. washing paint pots. If you use a rota, make sure you give adequate notice of changes to the rota so that your colleagues know what areas and activities they are responsible for that particular week.

## Effective delegation

Effective delegation is another important factor in managing a setting. Delegation involves motivating your colleagues to carry out specific tasks to enable you to focus on the jobs that you need to do. Delegation also enables you to make use of the particular strengths and skills of your colleagues.

Remember, developing effective delegation takes time and practice.

## Eight steps to effective delegation

You can demonstrate effective delegation by:

1. **Finding the right person:** consider existing and potential abilities, attitude and personality.
2. **Consulting first:** allow your colleagues to be involved in deciding what is to be delegated.
3. **Thinking ahead:** do not wait for a crisis to occur and then delegate; try to delegate in advance.
4. **Delegating whole tasks:** where possible, delegate a complete task to a colleague, rather than just a small section of a task.
5. **Specifying expected outcomes:** make it clear what outcomes are expected from your colleagues.
6. **Taking your time:** especially if you have been under-delegating or are dealing with less experienced staff. A gradual transfer of responsibility will allow both you and your colleagues to learn what is involved.
7. **Delegating the good and the bad:** if you delegate the tasks that are pleasant to do and also those that are not so pleasant, your colleagues will have the opportunity to gain valuable, realistic experience of many types of jobs.
8. **Delegating, then trusting:** when you delegate a task to a colleague, together with the responsibility for getting it done, you then need to trust that person to complete the job to your specified and mutually agreed requirements.

(Wandsworth EYDCP)

## Monitoring the work of your team

When monitoring the progress and quality of work of individuals or teams within your area of responsibility, you should encourage your colleagues to take responsibility for their own work tasks and to use existing feedback systems to keep you informed of work progress. When establishing procedures for monitoring work in the setting include the following:

- Formal procedures (e.g. reports, formal meetings, mentoring, staff appraisals, supervision)
- Informal procedures (e.g. observations, informal meetings, conversations)

- The type of information required (e.g. checklists, evaluation sheets, progress reports)
- When the information will be delivered to you or others in the team (e.g. daily, weekly, monthly, half-termly, termly, annually)
- The form of the information (e.g. verbal, written, email, audio-visual)
- Where and how the information will be delivered (e.g. meeting, face-to-face, presentation, electronic)
- The amount of detail required.

(Wandsworth EYDCP)

## How systems of resource management operate in the work setting

Every setting should be equipped with appropriate play resources appropriate to the age range of the children. You should know how to obtain and/or create the resources needed for a range of play spaces. You may need to work within the budget available for resources and, if necessary, find alternative ways to obtain or create resources. Children benefit from a wide range of play resources, not just those that are commercially produced. Depending on the setting, you should be able to provide a wide selection of play resources. For example:

- Recycled materials to provide opportunities for children to construct models, etc.
- The outdoor environment to provide opportunities for exploring the natural world, e.g. gardening, visiting local parks and playgrounds
- Natural materials to provide opportunities for exploring different materials and their properties, e.g. sand, water, cooking ingredients
- Homemade materials for creative activities, e.g. homemade play dough (encouraging children to make the play dough themselves enriches their play and learning experience)
- Clean unwanted clothing for dressing up activities (recycling again!) not just commercially produced outfits
- Space for children's imaginary games that require little or no props
- Commercially produced resources which are well-made, durable and safe for children's use, as

1. Give examples of effective planning and fair allocation of work within your area of responsibility. You could include copies of planning sheets, minutes from a staff or team meeting and a work rota.

2. Describe how you use effective delegation to motivate your colleagues to carry out specific tasks.

3. Outline the ways in which you monitor work in your team.

well as being good value for money, e.g. construction kits and tools, climbing equipment, child-size domestic play equipment. Remember, quality is more important than quantity.

Remember to make use of any community resource facilities such as book loans from local libraries (usually free to non-profit organisations) and borrowing play equipment from toy libraries. Contact the local authority or disability charities for information on schemes they may operate for hiring or purchasing specialist play equipment for children with disabilities.

Resources for the setting should include:

1. *Consumables* (resources that are used up) such as paint, glue, paper; ingredients for cooking activities; food and drinks for meals/snacks; cleaning materials. Keep track of these resources to ensure that they do not run out, by doing regular stock takes and reporting to the person responsible for reordering.
2. *Equipment* (resources that are not used up) such as furniture, books, computers and play equipment, e.g. climbing frames, construction kits, board games. Check these resources for wear and tear to ensure they are safe for continued use and report any problems or damage to the person responsible for resources.
3. *Finance* for the play setting, e.g. money needed to buy consumables and new equipment, pay staff

wages, pay for the rent and/or maintenance of the building.
4. *Adults*, e.g. the people who run and organise the setting. They may be paid staff, parent helpers or volunteers.

You may be responsible for replenishing consumables (e.g. pencils, paper and card, paint, cooking ingredients, exercise and textbooks) and replacing old or damaged equipment (e.g. furniture, books, computer software and play equipment) as necessary. You should ensure that stock levels are monitored on a regular basis.

**In Practice**

Outline the methods you use to obtain appropriate resources for your setting.

# How financial systems in the setting are operated and accountability maintained according to appropriate standards

Part of your responsibilities when leading and managing a community-based early years setting (e.g. pre-school or playgroup) will be to work with the management committee to identify funding streams for the group. Groups should be clear about their funding requirements. A business plan will help clarify specific needs and should include realistic budgets. A business plan is usually part of the application for funding as it provides information about why the funding is required (PSLA, 2006).

When identifying possible funding streams, the best place to start is the early years unit at your local authority. Staff there will be able to provide advice about local funding. Local authorities may have revenue and capital funding available to help sessional groups move into full day care and some sustainability funding may also be available in your area. This may all come under the umbrella of Sure Start funding. Local authorities also coordinate the **Early Years Education funding** provided by the DfE. This is also known as **Nursery Education Grant** (NEG) and it funds free early years education places for 3 and 4 year olds. Other sources of funding include: Lloyds TSB Foundation; Futurebuilders England; Big Lottery Fund; Local Network Fund for

Children and Young People (England); European Social Fund (ESF); European Regional Development Fund (ERDF); Neighbourhood Renewal Fund (PSLA, 2006). (For more information about Early Years Education funding and other sources of funding download the Pre-school Learning Alliance's *Funding Factsheet* available free at: www.pre-school.org.uk/resources/fundingfactsheet.pdf. For additional information see: *Getting Funding from Charitable Trusts* – www.pre-school.org.uk/resources/trusts.pdf and *Developing Effective Funding Applications* – www.pre-school.org.uk/resources/fundingapplications.pdf

# Administer budgets and financial arrangements according to the procedures of the setting

As a setting manager or senior practitioner, you may be responsible for administering budgets and financial arrangements according to the procedures of your setting. To manage a budget, you will need to know how to prepare, submit and agree a budget for a set period, e.g. for each month. You can do this with a monthly budget report setting out the setting's expected income and expenditure. The monthly budget report also provides details of the setting's actual income and expenditure using information from the cashbook. The monthly budget reports provide the information for the setting's profit and loss statement at the end of the year. Monthly budget reports provide accurate figures for the setting's cash flow forecast and they also form the basis for the next year's business forecast. Using a computer, you may be able to set up the setting's budget on a spreadsheet to enable income and expenditure to be updated easily on a daily basis. By law, all businesses have to keep records of their income and expenditure. Keeping such records will also help you to manage the finances of the setting more efficiently and help to prevent/detect fraud or theft. (Sure Start, 2003).

You should keep records of all the setting's **income** which may come from a variety of sources, e.g.

## Activity

Give examples of how you: identify and suggest potential sources of funding to support the provision; investigate funding streams in partnership with others; check that your provision is eligible for funding.

grants, funding, donations and, where applicable, payments from parents whose children use the early years provision. You should also keep records of all the setting's **expenditure** such as: receipts of anything purchased by the setting for the setting; details and receipts of costs, e.g. rent, rates and utility bills; details of wages paid to employees; invoices for equipment repairs or replacements; invoices for travel expenses; invoices for training expenses (Sure Start, 2003).

You should monitor the setting's *actual* financial performance against the agreed budget. The most common way to do this is to update and review the budget on a monthly basis. Record all transactions in a cashbook so that you can see at a glance all the income and expenditure for the childcare setting. Use the cashbook on a daily basis to record transactions as they occur so that your records are up-to-date. You should also have a petty cash book for staff to record the purchase of small items such as

| Item | Actual amount this month | Budgeted amount for the month | Variance |
|---|---|---|---|
| *Income* | | | |
| Fees | £1,970 | £1,888 | +£82 |
| Grant | £1,333 | £1,385 | -£42 |
| Total income | £3,303 | £3,273 | +£30 |
| *Outgoings* | | | |
| Staff costs | £2,395 | £2,339 | -£56 |
| Play and craft materials | £308 | £247 | -£61 |
| Catering supplies | £342 | £321 | -£21 |
| In-service training | £190 | £175 | -£15 |
| Rent and rates | £95 | £95 | 0 |
| Office running costs | £66 | £71 | +£5 |
| Total outgoings | £3,396 | £3,248 | -£148 |
| **Net surplus/deficit** | -£93 | £25 | -£118 |

**Figure 19.2** Monthly budget sheet

### Activity

Outline the methods you use to manage a budget in your setting.

books, crayons, ingredients for cooking activities, etc. You, or a designated member of staff, should be responsible for managing the petty cash system including keeping all receipts and keeping a locked box with the petty cash 'float'. The petty cash box should be kept in one place and locked at all times (Sure Start, 2003).

Useful resources

**Organisations and websites**
**Early Years Foundation Stage** – the statutory requirements and practical guidance for the EYFS:
**www.nationalstrategies.standards.dcsf.gov.uk/earlyyears**

The Pre-School Learning Alliance **website has a designated area for parents** – see:
**www.pre-school.org.uk/parents**

**The BBC Parenting website** which has information for parents of children from birth to teenage including support and information on a range of topics such as family matters, play, learning as well as links to relevant television programmes and useful websites – see
**www.bbc.co.uk/parenting**

**The National Family and Parenting Institute** which provides information and advice for parents including a Parent Services Directory – see:
**www.nfpi.org/templates/psd/**

**The Parents Centre** website –
**www.parentscentre.gov.uk**

**Books**
Ashman, C. and Green, S. (2004) *Self-Development for Early Years Managers*. David Fulton Publishers.
Brockbank, A. and McGill, I. (2006) *Facilitating Reflective Learning Through Mentoring and Coaching*. Kogan Page Ltd.
Daly, M. *et al.* (2004) *Early Years Management in Practice: A Handbook for Early Years Managers*. Heinemann Educational Secondary Division.
Dryden, L. (2005) *Essential Early Years*. Hodder Arnold.
Hobart, C. and Frankel, J. (2003) *A Practical Guide to Working with Parents*. Nelson Thornes.
Lyus, V. (1998) *Management in the Early Years*. Hodder & Stoughton.
PSLA (2004) *Planning a Pre-school Curriculum: Making it Work for You*. Available to order from the Pre-school Learning Alliance: www.pre-school.org.uk
Ramsey, R. D. (2002) *How to Say the Right Thing Every Time: Communicating Well with Students, Staff, Parents and the Public*. Corwin Press.
Smith, A. and Langston, A. (1999) *Managing Staff in Early Years Settings*. Routledge Falmer.

# 20 Promote young children's physical activity and movement skills: Unit CYPOP 4

This chapter looks at the importance of physical activity to children's holistic development and health. It focuses on gross motor and movement skills, and on ways in which these can be planned and evaluated.

## Learning outcomes

By the end of this chapter you will:

1. Understand the importance of physical activity and the development of movement skills for young children's development, health and wellbeing.

2. Be able to prepare and support a safe and challenging environment for young children which encourages physical activity and the development of movement skills.

3. Be able to plan and implement physical activities for young children.

4. Be able to build opportunities for physical activity into everyday routines for young children.

5. Be able to evaluate the effectiveness of provision in supporting young children's physical activity and movement skills.

## The importance of physical activity and the development of movement skills

Physical activity is essential for children's growth and development, because it:

- reduces their risk of developing heart disease in later life
- strengthens muscles
- helps strengthen joints and promotes good posture
- improves balance, coordination and flexibility
- increases bone density, so that bones are less likely to fracture.

Apart from these obvious physical benefits, regular exercise develops a child's self-esteem by creating a strong sense of purpose and self-fulfilment; children learn how to interact and cooperate with other children by taking part in team sports and other activities.

## The importance of physical activity for young children's holistic development

Physical activity and the development of movement skills help children to develop holistically in the following areas:

- **Expressing ideas and feelings**: children become aware that they can use their bodies to express themselves by moving in different ways as they respond to their moods and feelings, to music or to imaginative ideas.

- **Developing skills requiring coordination** of different parts of the body: for example, hands and eyes for throwing and catching, legs and arms for skipping with a rope.
- **Exploring what their bodies can do** and become aware of their increasing abilities, agility and skill. Children's awareness of the space around them and what their bodies are capable of can be extended by climbing and balancing on large-scale apparatus, such as a climbing frame, wooden logs and a balancing bar, and by using small tricycles, bicycles and carts.
- **Cooperating with others** in physical play and games. Children become aware of physical play both as individuals and as a social activity: in playing alone or alongside others, in playing throwing and catching with a partner, in using a seesaw or push cart, or in joining a game with a larger group.
- **Developing increasing control of fine movements** of their fingers and hands (fine motor skills). For example, playing musical instruments and making sounds with the body, such as clapping or tapping, helps develop fine motor skills in the hands and fingers, while also reinforcing the link between sound and physical movement. Helping with household tasks – washing up, pouring drinks, carrying bags – also develops fine motor skills.
- **Developing balance and coordination**, as well as an appreciation of distance and speed; energetic play that involves running, jumping and skipping helps children to develop these skills.
- **Developing spatial awareness**: for example, dancing and moving around to music develops a spatial awareness while also practising coordination and muscle control.

# Effects on short- and long-term health and wellbeing

Physical activity and exercise are no longer a regular feature in many children's lives. Some children never walk or cycle to school, or play sport. Instead, many of them spend hours in front of a television or computer. Children need to be physically active in order to prevent harmful effects on their health, in both the long and short term. Current guidelines from the Chief Medical Officer state that children and young people should be spending a minimum of one hour of moderate intensity physical activity per day. At least twice a week this should include activities to improve bone health, muscle strength and flexibility. The hour can be made up from various shorter sessions and a mixture of different activities. For example, it could include a mixture of physical play, games, dance, cycling, a brisk walk to school, sports, various outdoors activities, and so on.

## Short-term health

Physical activity boosts energy, and helps to alleviate stress and anxiety. Children who are physically active are more likely to fall sleep easily and to sleep for longer. They are also less likely to develop infections, such as colds and flu, because their immune system is made stronger by having regular exercise and sufficient sleep.

## Long-term health

Physical activity in young children also helps in the long term, with:

- **controlling weight** – and so preventing **obesity**. A recent study found that teenagers who carry a gene for obesity are less likely to become overweight or obese if they are physically active for an hour a day. If an overweight child becomes an overweight or obese adult, they are more likely to suffer from health problems, including diabetes, stroke, heart disease and cancer.
- **increasing bone density** in children and helping to maintain strong bones in adolescents. It also slows down bone degeneration later in life. This can help to prevent osteoporosis, a condition when bones become brittle and more prone to break.
- **reducing blood pressure**: if you have high blood pressure, you are more likely to have a stroke or heart attack.
- **reducing the risk of diabetes**: keeping active can help lower the risk of developing type 2 diabetes later on in life.
- **reducing the risks of some kinds of cancer**.

## Wellbeing

Children who are physically active have improved psychological wellbeing. They gain more self-confidence and have higher self-esteem. Children benefit from playing outdoors in the fresh air and having lots of space in which to move freely. They also benefit socially from playing alongside other children and making friends.

## The development of movement skills

This chapter focuses mostly on movement skills: motor skills, locomotion and balance. Development follows a sequence:

- **From simple to complex**: for example, a child will walk before he or she can skip or hop.
- **From head to toe**: for example, head control is acquired before coordination of the spinal muscles. Head control is important from birth, in order for the baby to feed.
- **From inner to outer**: for example, a child can coordinate his or her arms to reach for an object before he or she has learned the fine manipulative skills necessary to pick it up.
- **From general to specific**: for example, a young baby shows pleasure by a massive general response (eyes widen, legs and arms move vigorously, etc.). An older child shows pleasure by smiling or using appropriate words and gestures.

## The development of motor skills

The sequence of development of movement skills involves firstly gross motor skills, which involve control of large muscles in the body. This is followed by development of fine manipulative skills, which depend on small muscle coordination.

- **Gross motor skills** use the large muscles in the body (the arms and legs) and include walking, running, climbing, etc.
- **Fine motor skills** use the smaller muscles and include:
  - gross manipulative skills which involve single limb movements, usually the arm; for example throwing, catching and sweeping arm movements
  - fine manipulative skills which involve precise use of the hands and fingers for drawing, using a knife and fork, writing, doing up shoelaces and buttons.

## The skills of locomotion and balance

**Locomotion** uses large movements and is the ability to move around on one's own. It is central to the pattern of development changes that occur at the end of the baby's first year, and begins with crawling or bottom shuffling.

**Balance** is the first of all the senses to develop. It is crucial to posture, movement and **proprioception.** The 8-month-old child who rolls backwards and forwards across the floor with no particular goal in sight, is preparing his or her balance for sitting, standing, and walking.

**Figure 20.1** This child is using balance skills (bending and squatting) and fine motor skills (picking up) to pick up the block

### Key term

**Proprioception** – The sense that tells the baby the location of the mobile parts of his or her body (for example, his or her legs) in relation to the rest of him or her – in other words, where his or her own body begins and ends.

| Travel<br>*Travelling movements where the child moves from one point to another* | Object control<br>*Objects being sent, received or travelled with* | Balance and coordination |
|---|---|---|
| • walking<br>• running<br>• skipping<br>• jumping<br>• hopping<br>• chasing<br>• dodging<br>• climbing<br>• crawling | • throwing<br>• catching<br>• picking up<br>• kicking<br>• rolling<br>• volleying<br>• striking<br>• squeezing<br>• kneading | • bending<br>• stretching<br>• twisting<br>• turning<br>• balancing<br>• squatting<br>• transferring<br>• landing<br>• hanging |

**Table 20.1** Movement skills

## Eye–hand coordination

The ability to reach and grasp objects in a coordinated way requires months of practice and close attention. In the first months after birth, eye–hand coordination takes effort, but by around 9 months of age, babies can usually manage to guide their movements with a single glance to check for accuracy; for example, when feeding themselves with a spoon.

## Foot–eye coordination

The ability to execute actions with the feet, guided by the eyes is necessary for many movement activities: for example, climbing stairs, and kicking or dribbling a ball.

There are several aspects of movement skills, which are outlined in Table 20.1.

## Links to other aspects of development

Physical development is linked to other areas of development, such as emotional, social, cognitive and language development. Each affects and is affected by the other areas. For example:

- **Emotional development**: once babies have mastered crawling, they are free to explore the world on their own. They become more independent and confident when away from their familiar adults.
- **Cognitive development**: the ability to reach and grasp objects (usually achieved at around 6 months) develops their understanding of the nature of objects. This often results in a surprise, for example, when they try to pick up a soap bubble or a shaft of sunlight. Babies are interested in *edges*, for example, of a book on a floor. Where does one object end, and the next object begin?
- **Language development**: when children are taking part in movement activities, there are plenty of opportunities to talk, using new vocabulary related to physical activity – such as faster, higher, etc.
- **Social development**: playing with other children is very important for learning social skills such as fairness and turn-taking. Children also learn to appreciate the abilities of others and gain confidence in interacting socially with their peers through structured physical play.

# Preparing and supporting a safe and challenging environment

The early years environment here means both the indoor and the outdoor environment. Each area should be carefully planned and prepared to provide opportunities for physical activity and the development of movement skills.

## Preparing the environment

The following factors are important in planning for physical activity that is inclusive (includes all children and uses both indoor and outdoor environments).

### Time

You will need to allow sufficient time for babies and children to become familiar with newly introduced equipment and activities, and also to practise both new and existing skills.

### Space

You need to plan for sufficient space, both indoors and outdoors, to set up appropriate activities for physical play. Movement is important but it does require a lot of room. Additional space may be necessary for children who have physical disabilities or motor impairments, to take into account specialised equipment and also extra professional support such as physiotherapy or occupational therapy.

### Indoor and outdoor environments

Opportunities for physical activity should be provided both inside and out. Regular sessions of indoor physical play are particularly important when the weather limits opportunities for outdoor play. The outdoors can provide a scale and freedom for a type of play that is difficult to replicate indoors. For example, outdoors there are opportunities for children to:

- dig a garden
- explore woodland and climb trees
- run on the grass and roll down a grassy slope
- pedal a car across a hard surface.

Visits to swimming pools can help children to enjoy and gain confidence in the water at an early stage.

## Providing variety, risk and challenge in play

**Play England** states that:

> 'All children both need and want to take risks in order to explore limits, venture into new experiences and develop their capacities, from a very young age and from their earliest play experiences.'

Physically challenging activities that involve safe risk-taking help children to build and extend their strength and fitness levels. You need to plan activities that are interesting to children, and that offer physical challenges and plenty of opportunities for physical activity. When assessing risk and challenge in physical play, you need to decide whether the activity is developmentally appropriate. Children quickly become frustrated if activities are *too* challenging or difficult; but they also lose interest in activities that are lacking in challenge or that they find too easy.

## Problem-solving in physical play

Children need to develop the skills of making assessments and solving problems. Any conscious movement involves making judgements or assessments. Assessment of the situation and of your ability (speed, power, etc.) will help you to make the appropriate movement. For example, a child might make an assessment of:

- how hard to throw
- how fast to run
- how much effort to use to jump so high
- when to begin to stop.

## Meeting the needs of all children
### Girls and boys

Boys are routinely offered more opportunities for energetic play – for example, rough and tumble games with parents and early introduction to football games. You need to offer the same opportunities for physical play to boys *and* girls.

## Disabled children

Some children may need special equipment for physical play or they may need to have existing equipment adapted; for example, a child with cerebral palsy may have limited control over his or her body movements and need to use a tricycle with differently positioned handles or pedals.

## Children with special needs

A child with a hearing impairment can be encouraged to dance to music as they can usually feel the vibrations through the floor. Many children with learning difficulties will have personal priority needs that are central to their learning and quality of life. Some children may need the provision of a specific therapy or paramedical care, for example, supervising medication. Others need to have existing equipment or activities modified or adapted to suit their particular needs.

## Children of different ages

Babies need physical play just as much as do older children. From just a few weeks old, babies can be placed on the floor and encouraged to kick their legs freely. Activities need to be planned that are developmentally appropriate for every child or group of children.

## Keeping children safe

Children who play in a physically safe environment are more likely to develop confidence, self-esteem and self-reliance. In modern society it is often dangerous for children to play outside in the street. Safety considerations have had a huge impact on what parents and carers allow their children to do, and the freedom to play outdoors out of a carer's sight is now extremely rare.

It is therefore very important that when children attend group settings they can be physically safe. Safety issues should always be in mind when working with young children so that accidents are prevented. This is called **assessing the risk** because adults are thinking ahead about possible physical danger to children. Children need to be supervised carefully; it is important for adults never to sit with their back to the group, either indoors or outdoors. Without supervision, children might become involved in unacceptable or inappropriate behaviour, such as throwing stones at a window or snatching a tricycle from another child.

## Case Study — A child-centred outdoor environment

The design of Cowgate Under 5s Centre reflects the centre's philosophy inspired by the educationalist Friedrich Froebel, who believed that children learn best through spontaneous child-centred play, and that they should be surrounded by kindness, understanding and beauty.

Good design has enabled a wide range of experiences to be offered within a small space. Nearly all of the resources are made from natural materials, have been chosen to enhance the children's curiosity, and provide both challenge and risk. There are two timber houses at either end of the site (one of which is two storeys high); a pergola with climbing plants; bird boxes, feeders and insect homes; a sand pit; a rabbit run with a rabbit; planted beds with sensory plants such as rosemary and lavender; an adventure playground with a rope climb, wobbly bridge and tyre swing; a greenhouse for growing; large-scale musical instruments; a raised wet area and a seating area with a storytelling seat.

The children are allowed to use all the equipment at all times as a member of staff is always present. First thing in the morning, the doors are opened wide and the children are free to move between the indoors and outdoors.

How does the Cowgate Under 5s Centre provide for children's physical activity?

Why is it important for children to play outdoors?

## The importance of natural outdoor environments

We have seen how important movement is and how it requires a lot of room. The natural outdoor environment – such as woodland, fields and beaches – provides young children with a wonderful and constantly varying 'playground'. An exciting outdoor space provides an opportunity for children to explore the environment at their own individual levels of development.

# Planning and implementing physical activities

## Opportunities for physical activity

When planning physical activities, you need to consider the following factors:

- **Observation**: before planning how to provide physical activity, take some time to observe children's natural and spontaneous movements. You should observe:
  1 how they move
  2 their object control skills
  3 their coordination and balance skills
  4 which activities individuals prefer.
  You can observe their movement and object control skills, and plan their physical play by extending an activity: for example, a baby who is sitting but not yet moving (crawling or bottom shuffling) could be supported in trying to move if you provide some exciting objects that are just out of reach.
- **Balance of child-initiated and adult-led activities**: the EYFS in England requires that a balance between those activities initiated by the child and those that are adult-led.
- **Range of skills and movements**: you need to consider the wide range of motor skills, movement skills and balance and coordination when planning activities.
- **Time**: children need to be allowed to play at their own pace. Some children are slow to begin and may need support to attempt a new skill.

**Figure 20.2** Playing hopscotch involves many movement skills such as jumping, skipping, hopping, turning and balancing

### Reflective practice: Managing risks and challenges

Think about the way in which risk and challenge is managed in your setting.

- Have you encouraged a child to assess the risks involved in a particular activity, and to work out for themselves how to manage the risk? Did you have to intervene to support the child?
- Have you encouraged a child to try a more challenging activity?
- Have you helped a child to talk through potential problems during a play activity?
- How could you improve the way in which you support children to understand and assess risks?

- **Interests**: children need to have their interests valued and taken into account when planning. This is where your observations of children playing will be useful.

## Developmentally appropriate activities

Table 20.2 suggests a range of developmentally appropriate activities. For children with disabilities or special needs, you may need to seek advice from other professionals and their parents when planning play for them.

# Meeting the individual movement skills needs of children

Table 20.2 provides ideas for developmentally appropriate activities for babies and children.

## Planning for physical activities

Children need to feel motivated to be physically active. You can support them to develop movement skills through:

### Key terms

**Child-initiated activity** – Child-initiated activity is wholly decided upon by the child, based on the child's own motivation, and remains under the child's control. It may involve play of many types, or it may be seen by the child as an activity with a serious purpose to explore a project or express an idea which the child may not see as pure play.

**Adult-led activities** – Adult-led activities are those which adults initiate. The activities are not play, and children are likely not to see them as play, but they should be **playful** – with activities presented to children which are as open-ended as possible, with elements of imagination and active exploration that will increase the interest and motivation for children. As well as focused activities with groups of children, adult-led activities can include greeting times, story times, songs and even tidying up.

## Case Study — Taking your cue from children

Rebecca, Shana and Chris work in pre-school with children aged 3 to 5 years. On quieter days, they like to take the children to the local park. One day, they plan an outing with ten children. Rebecca, the room leader, ensures that they have drinks, first aid kit and mobile phone with them. She has checked that all the parents and carers have signed up-to-date outing permission slips. As they walk through the park, 4-year-old twins Chloe and Oscar run ahead to a fallen tree. The other children are delighted by their find and rush to join them. Rebecca decides that they will stop here to let the children play. The staff help the children to climb and balance, and encourage them to jump off the lower end of the tree trunk onto the soft grass. The children love the activity and it promotes much discussion when they return to the setting.

The next time they plan to go to the park, Rebecca includes Shana and Chris in thinking of ways to promote the children's movement skills as they play. They decide to take quoits,

markers and a canvas tunnel, and they set about making an obstacle course that incorporates the fallen tree as a central obstacle. The children are shown the course, and how to complete it and are supported to have a go, one at a time. The children waiting for their turn join in with the staff, shouting encouragement. Chris decides to vary the course after every child has had a turn, and he involves the children in helping him. The children are encouraged to offer their ideas, and are supported in working as a team to put the objects in the right places.

1. List the areas of development being promoted.

2. How are the children being empowered during this activity?

3. This activity can be extended in many ways to promote children's movement and balance skills. Think of other activities that could be used with the children, incorporating the children's interests, such as the fallen tree.

| Age and motor skills development | Activities for movement skills | Activities for fine manipulative skills |
| --- | --- | --- |
| **By 6 months:** | | |
| • grasps adult finger<br>• arm and leg movements jerky and uncontrolled<br>• holds a rattle briefly | • gentle bouncing games on the carer's knee to songs<br>• encourage baby to kick, lying on back and front, to build muscles in neck and back<br>• swinging in a baby swing to promote balance | • rattles and soft, squashy toys<br>• books<br>• waterproof books in bath |
| **By 9 months:** | | |
| • rolls from front to back<br>• sits up unsupported<br>• may crawl or bottom shuffle<br>• grasp object and passes it from one hand to other | • encourage balance by placing toys around seated baby<br>• encourage mobility by placing objects just out of reach<br>• play 'rolling over' games with them | • picture books<br>• toys to transfer safely to the mouth<br>• simple musical instruments, e.g. xylophone |
| **By 12 months:** | | |
| • sitting for longer periods<br>• mobile – crawling or rolling<br>• may be walking, usually with hand/s held<br>• stands, holding on to furniture | • push and pull brick trolleys<br>• roll balls to and from baby<br>• low climbing frames<br>• swimming sessions | • stacking and nesting toys<br>• messy play<br>• painting and drawing |
| **By 18 months:** | | |
| • walking independently<br>• bends and squats to pick up objects<br>• climbs up and down stairs with help<br>• uses pincer grasp to pick up small objects | • walker trucks, pull-along animals etc.<br>• low, stable furniture to climb on<br>• space to run and play<br>• trips to parks and woodland<br>• low climbing frames<br>• swimming sessions | • posting toys and shape sorters<br>• threading toys<br>• jigsaw puzzles<br>• hammer and peg and pop-up toys<br>• messy play, sand and water play<br>• play dough |
| **By 2 years:** | | |
| • runs and jumps<br>• rides a tricycle propelling with feet<br>• walks up and down stairs | • toys to ride and climb on<br>• space to run and play<br>• ball play: throwing and catching<br>• trips to parks and woodland<br>• swimming sessions | • threading toys<br>• jigsaw puzzles<br>• messy play, sand and water play<br>• play dough<br>• models to build (e.g. Duplo®) |
| **By 3 years:** | | |
| • rides a tricycle using pedals<br>• walks and runs<br>• jumps from a low step<br>• stands on one foot and walks on tiptoe | • climbing frames<br>• scooters and tricycles<br>• trips to parks and woodland<br>• swimming sessions<br>• dancing to music | • creative activities: painting, drawing, modelling<br>• jigsaw puzzles<br>• messy play, sand and water play<br>• play dough |

| Age and motor skills development | Activities for movement skills | Activities for fine manipulative skills |
|---|---|---|
| **By 3 to 4 years:** | | |
| • walks with arms swinging<br>• climbs upstairs with one foot on each step and downwards with two feet on each step<br>• catches, throws, kicks and bounces a ball<br>• can stand, walk and run on tiptoe | • balls and bean bags for throwing and catching<br>• simple running games<br>• rope swings, climbing frames, slides, suitable trees<br>• party games such as musical statues<br>• running to music: fast or slow, loudly or quietly according to the music<br>• trips to parks and woodland<br>• swimming sessions<br>• party games such as musical statues<br>• running to music: fast or slow, loudly or quietly according to the music<br>• bikes with stabilisers | • creative activities: painting, drawing, modelling<br>• jigsaw puzzles<br>• messy play, sand and water play<br>• small world play |
| **By 4 to 5 years and beyond:** | | |
| • good sense of balance<br>• catches, throws and kicks a ball<br>• runs up and down stairs, one foot per step<br>• can run and dodge lightly on the toes<br>• climbs, skips and hops forwards on each foot separately<br>• shows good coordination and fine motor skills | • climbing frames, rope swings<br>• skipping ropes and hoops<br>• hopping and jumping<br>• action songs and games<br>• riding tricycles, bikes, with or without stabilisers<br>• trampoline<br>• simple running games<br>• team sports<br>• trips to parks and woodland<br>• obstacle courses for bike riders | • dressing and undressing practice<br>• creative activities: painting, drawing, modelling<br>• small world play<br>• construction toys |

**Table 20.2** Activities which are developmentally appropriate for babies and young children

• valuing and following their interests (letting them initiate an activity)
• praise
• encouragement
• appropriate guidance.

Your plan should:

1 Meet the individual movement skills needs of babies and children.
2 Promote the development of movement skills.
3 Encourage physical play.

Whenever possible, you should involve children in your planning – by finding out what they would like to do and what equipment they would like to use.

**Figure 20.3** This boy enjoys playing on the climbing apparatus

# Building opportunities for physical activity into everyday routines

Children need to have opportunities for physical activity every day. They need opportunities to walk, run, jump, climb and swing. Most of these activities will take place outdoors, but there are other ways in which you can build in opportunities for physical activity in the setting. Everyday routines are those that are usually built in to a setting's provision and include:

- dressing and undressing
- hanging up their own coats
- tidying up and putting away equipment
- wiping and setting tables for meals and snacks
- pouring their own drinks
- washing and drying up.

## The importance of physical activity in everyday routines

Helping children to develop physical skills in everyday routines will promote their confidence and self-esteem, as well as providing a positive pattern for later in life. Children also need to have opportunities to go for a walk every day, so that being outside and walking in the fresh air becomes a regular, enjoyable experience.

## How to provide opportunities in practice

It is important to stand back and consider how physical activity is built into your own practice. It is often quicker and easier to do things ourselves, but children can be encouraged to develop self-help and social skills if we build opportunities into our practice. Toddlers can be asked to fetch their own coat or shoes for example, or you could make a game out of tidy-up time, involving children in sweeping up and putting away the toys they have been playing with.

## How planned physical activities are implemented

Again, careful observation is vital to the successful implementation of a plan. You will need to observe the way in which children are playing, and be ready to adapt the activity if it does not seem to be meeting the children's needs and stimulating their interest. Sometimes your plan might be 'taken over' by the children. They may find a different way of playing with a piece of equipment, or they may introduce other play props into their play. You need to be flexible and prepared to adapt or even abandon the activity to include their intervention.

Think about the way in which risk and challenge is managed in your setting.

Think about a session in your setting:

- How many opportunities are there for children to be engaged in everyday routines that could involve physical activity?
- How much time do children spend outdoors? Are these opportunities limited by rainy or cold weather?
- How could you improve the provision of physical activity opportunities?

# Evaluating the effectiveness of provision in supporting young children's physical activity and movement skills

When evaluating the effectiveness of our provision and practice, we need to be able to identify and record ways of continually improving our practice.

## Assessing the effectiveness of planned provision

The main way of evaluating our practice is by observing children's participation and assessing whether their needs have been met. The following points should be considered:

## Observing and assessing children

Select one child (or a group of children) and carry out a structured observation over a number of sessions or a few weeks. Your aims are to find out:

- how their physical activity has been supported – in particular their progression in movement skills, and
- how their confidence has improved.

## Obtaining feedback

*From the child or children*

You can obtain direct feedback from the child or children by listening to them and noting their comments or by asking them questions. It is usually easy to see whether children have enjoyed a physical activity, as they will often be clamouring to do it again.

*From colleagues and parents*

Parents know their own child best and they are often able to provide valuable insight into the effectiveness of activities. Colleagues are often well placed to give feedback as they may be able to observe children during an activity. Feedback can also be obtained by filming the children during the activity and observing the children's reactions and comments.

## Identifying and recording areas for improvement

Having obtained feedback, you now need to identify areas for future development. This can be recorded as an action plan. You should draw up a plan that identifies:

- areas for improvement
- reason for action
- detail of action to be taken
- equipment and resources needed
- date for implementation.

## Reflecting on your own practice

Reflect on your daily practice and think about how well you provide appropriate physical play experiences for the children you work with. For example:

- How do you consider the balance between child-initiated activity and adult-led activity?
- Do you join in with physical activity?
- How do you enable children and their parents to express opinions and be listened to?
- How confident are you in planning for children's individual needs and in observing and assessing their progress?
- How do you ensure that there is sufficient challenge in the activities you provide?
- How can you improve your practice?

Useful resources

**Websites**
**JABADAO** is a national charity which works in partnership with the education, health, arts and social care sectors to bring about a change in the way people work with the body and movement:
**www.jabadao.org**

**Play England** promotes free play opportunities for all children and young people, and works to ensure that the importance of play for children's development is recognised:
**www.playengland.org.uk**

**Books**
Bruce, T. (2010) *Early Childhood: A Student Guide*. 2nd Edition.
Meggitt, C. (2006) *An Illustrated Guide to Child Development*. 2nd Edition.

# 21 Supporting disabled children and young people and those with specific requirements: Unit CYPOP 6

Supporting children and young people with disabilities and/or specific requirements involves establishing the strengths and needs of children and young people in partnership not only with their families but also in collaboration with other agencies. In addition, it involves the identification and provision of appropriate resources to enable inclusion and participation. The unit is designed to assess competence in the support of disabled children or young people and those with specific requirements in partnership with their carers. It also includes partnership working with other agencies and professionals.

## Understand the principles of working inclusively with disabled children and young people and those with specific requirements

The principles and values of equality, diversity and inclusion should underpin all work with children and young people. The Common Core of Skills and Knowledge for the children and young people's workforce sets out common values for those working with children, young people and families that promote equality, respect diversity and challenge stereotypes (Griffin, 2008).

As a practitioner, you must know and understand the articles of the United Nations Convention on the Rights of the Child (see Chapter 3, Unit SHC 33). The articles cover rights for **all** children (up to the age of 18 years). However, Article 23 refers to disabled children specifically:

> Children who have any kind of disability should have special care and support so that they can lead full and independent lives.

### Learning outcomes

By the end of this Unit you will:

1. Understand the principles of working inclusively with disabled children and young people and those with specific requirements.

2. Be able to work in partnership with families with disabled children or young people and those with specific requirements.

3. Be able to support age and developmentally appropriate learning, play or leisure opportunities for disabled children or young people and those with specific requirements.

4. Be able to evaluate, support and develop existing practice with disabled children and young people and those with specific requirements.

5. Understand how to work in partnership with other agencies and professionals to support provision for disabled children and young people and those with specific requirements.

As a practitioner, you should contribute to the inclusion of disabled children and young people and those with specific requirements by:

- Seeking information about children and young people from families and external support agencies
- Assessing and responding to the child or young person's individual needs
- Identifying barriers to participation
- Taking steps to remove barriers to participation
- Supporting children and young people's participation and equality of access
- Involving and consulting children, young people and families to support equality of access
- Developing individual plans to meet each child or young person's needs
- Requesting additional resources or a statutory assessment where appropriate.

## The legal entitlements of disabled children and young people for equality of treatment

You must know, understand and follow the relevant legislation regarding disabled children and young people for equality of treatment; this includes supporting the setting in carrying out its legal duties.

### Legislation relating to equality

**The Equality Act 2010** received Royal assent on 8 April 2010. This Act provides a single legal framework with clearer legislation to effectively tackle disadvantage and discrimination. The main provisions of the Equality Act were introduced from October 2010 while the rest will be phased in over 2010–13. The Act came into force for employment and education in October 2010. The fundamental difference from current anti-discriminatory legislation is that new groups are now provided the same levels of protection from discrimination across all the protected characteristics and all sectors.

Key changes relating to the legal entitlements of disabled children and young people include:

- Protecting people discriminated against because they are perceived to have, or are associated with

someone who has, a protected characteristic, for example, protecting carers from discrimination. The Equality Act will protect people who are, for example, caring for a disabled child or relative. They will be protected by virtue of their association to that person.
- Extending the equality duty to require the public sector to take into account the needs of all protected groups (except marital and civil partnership status). The new Equality Duty will require public authorities to consider the needs of all the protected groups in, for example, employment and when designing and delivering services. Although timescales for this Duty are to be confirmed with the government.
- Harmonising the thresholds for the duty to make reasonable adjustments for disabled people.

(EHRC, 2010)

### Legislation and guidance relating to children and young people in need

Families have the right to expect practical support from services such as health and education. Part III of the **Children Act 1989** provides the legal basis for the provision of local services for children in need below the age of 18 years. The Children Act 1989 places a specific duty on agencies to cooperate in the interest of children in need. The Children Act 1989 uses the following criteria to define children in need:

*'A child shall be taken to be in need if –*
*a. he is unlikely to achieve or maintain or to have the opportunity of achieving or maintaining, a reasonable standard of health or development without the provision for him of services by a local authority . . .*
*b. his health or development is likely to be significantly impaired, or further impaired, without the provision for him of such services; or*
*c. he is disabled.'*

(Children Act 1989, section 17:10)

The ***Framework for the Assessment of Children in Need and their Families (2000)*** provides a systemic framework to help practitioners identify children in need and assess the best approach to help children in need and their families (see Figure 21.1).

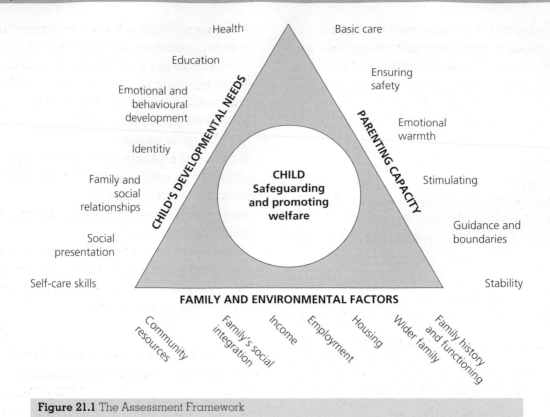

Figure 21.1 The Assessment Framework

## Legislation relating to children with special educational needs (SEN)

**The Education Act 1996** defines children with special educational needs as:

*(a) Having a significantly greater difficulty in learning than the majority of children of the same age*

*(b) Having a disability which either prevents or hinders the child from making use of educational facilities of a kind provided for children of the same age in schools within the area of the local education authority*

*(c) An under 5 who falls within the definition at (a) or (b) above or would do if special educational provision was not made for the child.*

(HMSO, 1996, The Education Act 1996; Part IV, Chapter 1, Section 312)

**The Special Educational Needs and Disability Act 2001** amends Part 4 of the **Education Act 1996** to make further provision against discrimination, on the grounds of disability, in schools and other educational establishments. This Act strengthens the right of children with SEN to be educated in mainstream schools where parents want this and the interests of other children can be protected. The Act also requires local education authorities (LEAs) to make arrangements for services to provide parents of children with SEN with advice and information. It also requires schools to inform parents where they are making special educational provision for their child and allows schools to request a statutory assessment of a pupil's SEN (www.drc-gb.org).

*The Special Educational Needs Code of Practice 2001* gives practical advice to Local Education Authorities, maintained schools and others concerning their statutory duties to identify, assess and provide for children's SEN. This code came into effect on 1 January 2002 and re-enforces the right for children with SEN to receive education within a mainstream setting and advocates that schools and LEAs implement a graduated method for the organisation of SEN. The code provides a school-based model of intervention (Early Years Action or School Action, Early Years Action Plus or School Action and Statutory Assessment) for children with

SEN to enable *all* children to have the opportunities available through inclusive education. Accompanying the code is the *Special Educational Needs Toolkit* which expands on the guidance contained in the code. This Toolkit is not law but does provide examples of good practice that LEAs and schools can follow.

## SEN and Disability Green Paper

The coalition government has published its proposals for changing the system through which families of children and young people with SEN and disabilities receive their support. The Green Paper entitled *Support and Aspiration: A New Approach to Special Educational Needs and Disability* provides details of how the government intends to:

- Reduce bureaucracy
- Improve transparency in how resources are allocated
- Abolish the categories of early years/school action and early years/school action plus and replace them with one SEN category that will cover both early years settings and schools
- Simplify the assessment process by replacing

statements of SEN with one assessment that will cover support from education, health and social care. The government intends to introduce these Education, Health and Care Plans by 2014
- Make assessments more independent by exploring whether voluntary and community organisations could coordinate them
- Give parents and families a greater degree of control of their services by introducing more personal budgets
- Improve the support for young people as they move into adulthood
- Improve the way agencies work together to support children and families with consideration being given to what role the voluntary and community sector can play.

(DfE, 2011)

For more information about the SEN and Disability Green Paper see: www.education.gov.uk/childrenandyoungpeople/sen/b0075291/sen-and-disability-green-paper-executive-summary/

## In Practice

Outline your setting's procedures for ensuring that individual education plans (IEP) for children are in place and regularly reviewed. Provide examples of the relevant forms, e.g. an individual education plan; review sheets for child's comments, parents' comments and staff comments; record of review. Remember confidentiality.

## Key terms

**Special educational needs** – all children have *individual* needs, but some children may have *additional* needs due to physical disability, sensory impairment, learning difficulty or emotional/behavioural difficulty.

# The principles of working inclusively placing the child in the centre

As an early years practitioner you must know and follow the setting's inclusion strategies, policies, procedures and practice. You also need to know and understand how to develop and implement these as consistent with your role and responsibilities in the early years setting. Remember that to develop effective inclusion policies, procedures and practice, everyone should be involved at some level including staff, children and their parents or carers.

## Inclusive and anti-discriminatory practice

**Anti-discriminatory practice** in the setting can be defined as words and actions which prevent discrimination and prejudice towards any individual or group of people and actively promote equal opportunities. This means ensuring that all children, parents, colleagues and other professionals are treated in an unbiased, fair and non-prejudiced way. This includes ensuring that all the setting's policies, procedures and strategies demonstrate a positive and inclusive attitude towards all individuals regardless of age, gender, race, culture or disability.

**Inclusive practice** in the setting can be defined as words and actions which encourage the participation of *all* children (including those with disabilities or from other minority groups) within a mainstream setting. This means ensuring that all children are valued as individuals and are given appropriate support to enable them to participate fully in the play and learning activities provided by the setting.

As an early years practitioner, you should know how to judge whether the setting is inclusive and supportive of diversity. You should be able to demonstrate that you support inclusion and diversity through your words, actions and behaviours in the setting. You must know and understand the importance of promoting the setting to children who may experience barriers to participation, e.g. children with disabilities or those from other minority groups. Inclusion is about the child's right to: attend the local mainstream setting; be valued as an individual; be provided with all the support needed to thrive in a mainstream setting. Inclusive provision should be seen as an extension of the childcare setting's equal opportunities policy and practice. It requires a commitment from the entire staff, parents and children, to include the full diversity of children in the local community. This may require planned restructuring of the whole childcare environment to ensure equality of access.

## Facilitate access and participation for children with disabilities and specific requirements

As an early years practitioner, you must know and understand how to identify good inclusive provision and practice in the setting. Kidsactive define inclusive provision as:

*'provision that is open and accessible to all, and takes positive steps in removing disabling barriers, so that disabled and non-disabled people can participate'*

(Douch, 2004)

The following inclusion indicators may help you to identify whether inclusion is being put into practice in your setting.

## Inclusion indicators

1. **Visitors can see:**
   - Nobody makes a fuss about the presence of disabled children.
   - Activities are designed around the interests and enthusiasms of all children who attend and with regard to any dislikes or impairments they may have.
   - Each person, adult or child, is welcomed on arrival.
   - All children, including disabled children, have choices and are able to exercise those choices.
2. **The leader/manager:**
   - Has sought out families, schools and services for disabled children and built links to promote the involvement of disabled children.
   - Runs regular staff meetings designed to enable staff to reflect on their practice together and develop good future practice.

**Figure 21.2** An inclusive setting

- Can identify action taken and progress made towards inclusion, and also the things he or she still needs and plans to do to make the setting more inclusive.

3. **The staff:**
   - Have received disability equality training and/or attitudinal training and continue to undertake other training relating to inclusion.
   - Feel that they are consulted and informed by the leader/manager.

4. **Disabled and non-disabled children**
   - Report being involved in making rules/policies or 'having a say in what goes on'.
   - Say they are generally happy with the setting.

5. **Parents of disabled and non-disabled children:**
   - Feel welcome and valued.
   - Say they are consulted about how best to meet their children's needs.

6. **Policies and paperwork indicate that:**
   - A commitment to inclusion is explicit in public and internal documentation.
   - Staff that have particular support roles with individual disabled children are full members of the team and have job descriptions which stress the inclusion of the child, rather than just one-to-one support.

(Douch, 2004)

## Supporting children with specific requirements

As an early years practitioner, you should be actively involved in contributing to the inclusion of children with specific requirements, including those with hearing or visual impairment, physical disabilities, communication difficulties, learning difficulties, emotional difficulties or behavioural difficulties (see below).

## Ten ways to support children with specific requirements

You can help children with specific requirements to participate in the full range of activities by:

1. Providing a stimulating, language-rich childcare environment which is visually attractive, tactile and interactive.
2. Maximising the use of space in the setting to allow freedom of movement for *all* children (including those who are physically disabled or visually impaired).
3. Ensuring accessibility of resources including any specialist equipment.
4. Providing opportunities for all children to explore different materials and activities.

5. Encouraging children to use the abilities they do have to their fullest extent.

6. Providing sufficient time for children to explore their environment and materials; some children may need extra time to complete tasks.

7. Encouraging independence, e.g. use computers, word processing, tape recorders.

8. Praising all children's *efforts* as well as achievements.

9. Supporting families to respond to their children's specific requirements.

10. Accessing specialist advice and support for children with specific requirements.

## Key terms

**Anti-discriminatory practice** – taking positive action to counter discrimination and prejudice.

**Inclusive practice** – identifying barriers to participation and taking positive action to eliminate those barriers and encouraging participation in the full range of activities provided by the setting.

## In Practice

1. Find out about your setting's inclusion strategies, policies, procedures and practice.

2. Explain your role and responsibilities in developing, implementing and reviewing strategies, policies, procedures and practice for inclusion.

## Service-led and child- and young person-led models of provision for disabled children and young people

Service-led models of provision for disabled children and young people are often more concerned with the needs of the service and professionals than with needs of the service-users, i.e., the children, young people and their parents or carers. The traditional service-led model of service delivery and the traditional roles which have supported that model are changing. Personalisation means that rather than professionals telling people what services they should

have, they will listen to service-users concerns and understand what they want to do, to live their lives more independently. Professionals will design and deliver services to meet those needs. There will need to be much greater flexibility in the workforce and an ability to deliver far wider services, as well as those being currently delivered. Being child- or young person-led requires a service to offer children and young people a range of ways to participate and make informed choices that will result in making services 'child-centred'. For example, children choose which local setting or activity they would like to attend and the lead professional or key worker follows the child's choice and supports the people who work there to welcome that child. This is a child-led and not a service-led model.

## The difference between the social model and medical model of disability

The **medical model of disability** sees disabled people with disabilities as having the problem. Disabled people have to adapt to fit into the world as it is. If this is not possible, then they are excluded in specialised institutions or isolated in their homes. The medical model of disability emphasises the person's impairment and provides support for stereotypical views of disability that evoke pity, fear and patronising attitudes towards disabled people. The medical model creates a cycle of dependency and exclusion. In addition, the design of the physical environment (e.g. play, leisure, school and work facilities) present disabled people with many barriers, making it very difficult or sometimes impossible for their needs to be met and limiting their day-to-day activities (Disability Equality in Education: www.diseed.org.uk).

The **social model of disability** views the barriers that prevent disabled people from participating in any situation as what disables them. The social model suggests that disabled people are individually and collectively disadvantaged by a complex form of institutional discrimination as fundamental to our society as sexism and racism. Disabled people are often made to feel that it is their fault that they are

| Medical Model Thinking | Social Model Thinking |
| --- | --- |
| Child or young person is faulty | Child or young person is valued |
| Diagnosis | Strengths and needs defined by self and others |
| Labelling | Identify barriers and develop solutions |
| Impairment becomes focus of attention | Outcome-based programme design |
| Assessment, monitoring, programmes of therapy imposed | Resources are made available to ordinary services |
| Segregation and alternative services | Training for parents and professionals |
| Ordinary needs are put on hold | Relationships nurtured |
| Re-entry if normal enough *or* permanent exclusion | Diversity welcomed: child is included |
| Society remains unchanged | Society evolves |

**Table 21.1** The differences between the medical and social models of disability (From the Disability Equality in Education website)

different. The only difference is that they have an impairment that limits their physical, mental or sensory functions. Restructuring physical environments and accepting people with disabilities for who they are without fear, ignorance and prejudice benefits everyone (Disability Equality in Education: www.diseed.org.uk).

## In Practice

Describe your role and responsibilities in contributing to the inclusion of children or young people with disabilities or specific requirements in your setting.

## The importance of advocacy

Advocacy can be defined as helping and supporting someone else to speak up for what they want. This can involve expressing their views or acting on their behalf, to secure services that they require or rights to which they are entitled. Key concepts in advocacy are: equality, inclusion, empowerment and rights (www.advocacy.force9.co.uk).

An advocate provides relevant information and helps parents and children or young people to understand their rights and entitlements. An advocate will help to ensure that these rights and entitlements are upheld. An advocate will also offer practical help such as helping to prepare for, and representing the parent/child at, meetings (for example at reviews or an assessment), writing letters on their behalf and making phone calls, where necessary, to other agencies. An advocate will also talk to social and health professionals on their behalf, if necessary. An advocate will provide information regarding services in the local area and, if necessary, help to get in touch with them. Advocacy is important as it aims to make a fairer balance of power between individuals, groups and professionals. If necessary, advocates will challenge the decisions that professionals make on behalf of parents/carers and their children. An advocate can also offer emotional support to carers, for example, sitting down and spending time listening to the difficulties and concerns the parent/carer or child may have.

www.claspthecarerscentre.org.uk/
page?page=Advocacy

## The importance of facilitated advocacy for children or young people who require it

Parents usually act as their children's advocates, recognising that certain choices and decisions (e.g. those relating to health, education and any specific requirements) affect how their children's particular needs are met, as well as their children's life chances. Some parents may not be able to act as advocates (for various reasons, for example, limited communication skills or mental health problems) so facilitated advocacy may be required. For children and young people in public care, the local authority as **corporate parent** is expected to fulfil the role of advocate. Foster carers, residential care workers, designated teachers and social workers (and in some cases parents) have a clear role in day-to-day advocacy, e.g. accessing appropriate services to ensure that individual children and young people in care receive the support they need when they need it. Local authorities should ensure that primary carers, social workers and teachers have the necessary training to enable them to act as effective advocates. Local authorities may also have independent advocacy arrangements which children and young people or their carers/parents may use in order to access services to meet special needs or to challenge placement choices (DfEE, 2000a). For more information see *Your Voice Your Choice: A guide for children and young people about the National Advocacy Standards* by Voice for the Child in Care, available from the website: www.dfes.gov.uk/qualityprotects/ then click on 'Your Voice Your Choice'.

## The importance of the personal assistant role

Some children and young people may require personal assistance in the form of individualised support for living in the community, by a paid assistant other than a healthcare professional, for at least 20 hours per week. Some disabled children and young people living in the community may require assistance to perform tasks of daily living (e.g. bathing and eating) and participate in normal activities due to permanent disabilities. Disabled children and young people may have difficulty performing particular activities as a result of disabilities and their participation in education, social life, and other areas may be limited as a result of interactions among impairments, activities and environment (WHO 2003).

Personal assistance is paid support provided for disabled children and young people in various settings to enable them to participate in mainstream activities. Personal assistants might help with bathing, dressing, moving around during the day, shopping, and so on. Personal assistance is designed for people with permanent disabilities so it is indefinite and ongoing; this differs from rehabilitative services and services provided for fixed periods of time. Personal assistance aims to improve mental and physical health by increasing participation, including social activities, the ability to participate in spontaneous activities, time outside the home, and mobility (Mayo-Wilson, 2008).

Increased participation and inclusion in activities of daily life may have positive effects on the social functioning, development, mental and physical health of children and young people. There are lots of ways to increase participation by disabled children and young people, such as designing school timetables to enable pupils with disabilities to engage in age-appropriate activities with their peers. Disabled children and young people may require interventions tailored to their specific requirements, lifestyles and living arrangements. Assistive devices, skills training, physiotherapy, education and human support help disabled children and young people control their lives appropriately and engage in normal activities (Mayo-Wilson, 2008).

## The importance of encouraging the participation of disabled children

As an early years practitioner, you must protect and promote children or young people's rights by supporting equality of access to your setting. This includes providing information for children, families and communities that promotes participation and equality of access. You should be able to implement transparent procedures and information about access to provision that meet the needs of all children and young people. You must welcome children or young people from all backgrounds and ensure that barriers to participation are identified and removed. You should seek and respect the views and preferences of children, adapting your practice to the children or young people's ages, needs and abilities. You should involve all relevant local community groups in the setting and provide information on community resources, e.g. childcare services, play provision, sport and leisure activities, local libraries, support groups, multicultural resources or specialist equipment for people with disabilities. You should provide information to children about their rights and responsibilities in the context of your setting.

## Providing information that promotes participation and equality of access

As an early years practitioner, you will be responsible for providing information about equality of access to children, young people and families including representative groups and individuals, e.g. current and potential new users of the setting, children, young people and their families who have found services hard to access, such as those with disabilities or from different ethnic groups. You can provide information in a variety of ways including: leaflets, newsletters, newspapers, magazines; public notice boards; open days; exhibitions; the Internet. Select the most effective way to reach your target audience, e.g. provide leaflets in community languages, ensure posters show positive images of people with disabilities and from different ethnic groups. Try different styles to appeal to different target groups, e.g. information aimed at children and/or young people will be different to that aimed at their parents/carers (Sure Start, 2003).

### In Practice

Describe appropriate ways that your setting has provided information to promote participation and equality of access to all relevant community groups, including those who have found services hard to access such as people with disabilities or from different ethnic groups.

As a practitioner, you should help disabled children and young people and those with specific requirements to participate in the full range of activities and experiences by identifying and taking steps to overcome barriers to communication, as well as identifying and taking steps to overcome barriers to participation in the full range of activities and experiences.

## Ten ways to help children with specific requirements to participate in activities

You can help disabled children and those with specific requirements to participate in the full range of activities and experiences by:

1.  Providing a stimulating language-rich learning environment which is visually attractive, tactile and interactive.
2.  Adapting the environment (e.g. the layout of furniture) and maximising the use of space in the setting to allow freedom of movement for *all* children (including those who with physical disabilities or visual impairment).
3.  Ensuring accessibility of materials and equipment.
4.  Providing opportunities for all children to explore different materials and activities, as well as offering alternative activities, if appropriate.
5.  Encouraging children to use the senses they have to their fullest extent.
6.  Providing sufficient time for children to explore their environment and materials; some children may need extra time to complete tasks.
7.  Implementing adaptations that can be made without the use of special aids and equipment and/or identifying and deploying specialist aids and equipment as necessary.
8.  Encouraging independence, e.g. use computers, word processing, tape recorders.
9.  Praising *all* children's *efforts* as well as achievements.
10. Ensuring adults involved are knowledgeable about children's disabilities and specific requirements and confident in their roles and responsibilities.

## Be able to work in partnership with families with disabled children and young people and those with specific requirements

As a practitioner, you should support families to respond to their children's needs by working in partnership with parents. Establishing partnerships with parents is very important as parents are the child's primary carers and may have detailed specialist knowledge about their child. Working in partnership with families is crucial for both parents and practitioners as it:

- Increases parents' understanding of the learning process
- Enables parents to reinforce tasks being undertaken by their child in the setting by engaging in similar activities with their child at home
- Allows two-way communication between practitioners and parents
- Enables shared knowledge about the individual child
- Enhances the overall understanding of the child's needs in the setting and home.

(Gatiss, 1991)

Most parents are usually keen to be actively involved in their children's learning. You should inform parents about the activities their child is involved in within the setting and suggest ways in which the parents can complement the work of the setting such as:

- Encouraging family members to participate in observing and identifying the needs of children
- Working through an agreed programme with an understanding of its steps towards progress, e.g. home-school literacy and numeracy programmes and Portage schemes
- Helping with individual and group activities in both indoors and outdoor settings
- Supporting other professionals working with their child either in the setting or at home, e.g. physiotherapist, speech and language therapist
- Assisting with activities outside the setting, e.g. outings to the local library, park, playground or swimming.

## The concepts and principles of partnership with carers of disabled children and young people and those with specific requirements

Parents usually know more about their children and their children's specific requirements, so it is important to listen to what parents have to say. You should, therefore, actively encourage positive relationships between parents (or designated carers) and the setting. You should only give information to parents consistent with your role and responsibilities within the setting, e.g. do not give recommendations concerning the child's future learning needs directly to parents, if this is the responsibility of another professional. Any information shared with parents must be agreed with the relevant colleagues such as the child's key worker. When sharing information about a child with their parents, ensure it is relevant, accurate and up-to-date. Always follow the confidentiality requirements of the setting.

When liaising with parents about the specific requirements of their children, you should consider the family's home background and the expressed wishes of the parents. You must also follow the setting's policies and procedures with regard to specific requirements, e.g. inclusion strategies, policies, procedures and practices. You may need to give parents positive reassurance about their children's care, learning and development. Any concerns or worries expressed by a child's parents should be passed immediately to the appropriate person in the setting. If a parent makes a request to see a colleague or other professional, then you should follow the relevant setting policy and procedures.

## Activity

Suggest practical ways to support families to respond to their children's needs.

## In Practice

Outline the methods you use to negotiate and assess needs, in consultation with children and their parents.

## In Practice

Give examples of how your setting exchanges information with parents with regard to their children who have specific requirements, e.g. information packs, regular reviews, individual education plans, home-school diaries.

You should ensure that families are active participants in early intervention. You are working *with* families, not doing things *for* them; hence the importance of involving families in goal-setting. There should be clear roles between parents and professionals. You must recognise and acknowledge families' feelings about intervention and specialist help. You should be able to show empathy and understanding for parents' views about contact with social services and other statutory agencies. For example, parents may have worries about: being vulnerable to child protection enquiries and losing their children; being perceived as failed or 'bad' parents; losing control once other agencies are involved, i.e. forfeiting parenting responsibility. Parents value family support services which include: open, honest, timely and informative communication; social work time with someone who listens, gives feedback, information, reassurance and advice, and who is reliable; services which are practical and tailored to particular needs and accessible; an approach which reinforces and does not undermine their parenting capacity (DH, 2000).

Knowledge and understanding of the Assessment Framework (see above) will enable you to contribute to the assessments of children in need. It is essential that you are clear about:

❑ The purpose and anticipated outputs from the assessment

❑ The legislative basis for the assessment

❑ The protocols and procedures to be followed

❑ Which agency, team or professional has lead responsibility

❑ How the child and family members will be involved in the assessment process

❑ Which professional has lead responsibility for analysing the assessment findings and constructing a plan

❑ The respective roles of each professional involved in the assessment

❑ The way in which information will be shared across professional boundaries and within agencies, and be recorded

❑ Which professional will have responsibility for taking forward the plan when it is agreed.

(DH *et al.*, 2000; p. 7)

You should discuss and agree an assessment plan with the child and family to ensure that they understand who is doing what, when and how the various assessments will be used to assess the child's needs and to plan intervention. To do this, you must know and understand the principles underpinning the Assessment Framework. Assessments:

❑ Are child-centred

❑ Are rooted in child development

❑ Are ecological in their approach

❑ Ensure equality of opportunity

❑ Involve working with children and families

❑ Build on strengths, as well as identify difficulties

❑ Are inter-agency in their approach to assessment and the provision of services

❑ Are a continuing process, not a single event

❑ Are carried out in parallel with other action and providing services

❑ Are grounded in evidence-based knowledge.

(DH *et al.*, 2000; p. 10)

## The types of support and information carers may require

Being a parent is hard work and many families are under stress. All families may experience difficulties at some time which may affect their children. For example: family bereavement, physical or mental health problems, marital breakdown, sudden unemployment, multiple births or having a child with special needs. Some parents are not well prepared for the ups and downs of parenthood and may find particular times in their children's lives more stressful than others, e.g. when their children are toddlers or teenagers. Most parents can cope with one problem at a time but not with a combination of problems all at once or in close succession. Many families under stress have adequate support from family, friends or community services and do not need or seek additional support. Some families do not have such a network of support and so require additional support through paid childcare (e.g. childminder or private day nursery) or from statutory or voluntary agencies such as befriending by a volunteer (e.g. Home-Start) or targeted services from health, education and social services (e.g. Portage, Sure Start) (DH *et al.*, 2000).

However, some very young children may continue to experience difficulties even with input from skilled early years practitioners; these children and their parents may require additional or specialist support to maximise their development. It is important, if early years practitioners are concerned about a child's behaviour, learning or development, to contact the relevant support service. Such action may be part of Early Years Action Plus or statutory assessment (DfES, 2001).

Children and young people may be defined as in need in many different circumstances including: disadvantaged children and young people who would benefit from extra help from public agencies; children and young people looked after in statutory care; children and young people on the Child Protection Register; children and young people with disabilities. Families referred to or seeking help will have differing levels of need ranging from advice, practical support and short-term intervention to detailed assessment and long-term intervention (DH *et al.*, 2000). Examples of early interventions include: cognitive behaviour therapy; counselling; crisis intervention; family therapy; Home-Start; Portage; National Autistic Society Early Bird Programme; the Nippers Project (Nursery Intervention for Parents and Education Related Services); special nursery provision; Sure Start.

## Family support

A single point of contact for the family (such as a key worker, link worker or care coordinator), with a holistic view of the child and family, can help the family to find out about what services are available and the roles of different agencies, and to get professionals to understand their needs. Families with a single point of contact report better relationships with services, fewer unmet needs, better morale, fewer feelings of isolation and burden, more information about services, greater satisfaction, and more parental involvement than families without this service. Care coordination should ensure that the family's needs for information, advice and help are identified and addressed (DH, 2001).

Types of support and information include:

- Communication aids such as learning to use sign language, Makaton, speech board
- Social and emotional support such as coming to terms with the impact of disability on own family
- Financial support such as claiming benefits
- Information about services and availability such as housing adaptations
- Information about children's and families' rights
- Information for parents about their child's condition and how they can support their child's development
- Information for children and young people about their condition and treatment, about how to live with the condition and how to overcome disabling barriers
- Support that enables families to do activities together, as a whole family
- Short-term breaks and domiciliary services
- Accessible and appropriate play and leisure services.

### Research Activity

Find out about the services available to provide support and information for families with disabled children and young people in your local area. Examples may include counselling services, domiciliary services, special nursery provision, play and leisure services, Portage, Home-Start and Sure Start.

## Demonstrate in own practice partnership working with families

Your work with children and families should be underpinned by effective adult–child and adult–adult communication. You are responsible for effective communication with families to establish positive relationships based on trust and openness. You should encourage families to discuss any concerns and share information likely to impact on their children's health, wellbeing or developmental progress. Remember these important points:

- Express yourself simply and clearly and use concepts which are familiar to both children and their parents
- Match your explanations of new ideas to the children's ages and levels of understanding
- Be aware of the possible impact of emotional distress on families' understanding
- Find out about the families' fears and offer them reassurances
- Give families plenty of opportunities for asking questions
- Repeat, simplify, expand and build on explanations, if appropriate
- Use communication tools such as games, prompt cards, books and videos.

(DH, 2000)

# Be able to support age and developmentally appropriate learning, play or leisure opportunities for disabled children or young people and those with specific requirements

Your role includes enabling disabled children and young people and those with specific requirements to gain access to age and developmentally

appropriate learning, play or leisure opportunities. Your role may also involve information sharing, networking, training, supporting and advising – working both with the child/family, as well as with the relevant professionals and agencies involved.

## Demonstrate in own practice engagement with disabled children and young people

Time, commitment and good communication skills are essential to engaging with disabled children. You need to spend time with both the child and family to gain their trust and build their relationship within the setting. You can demonstrate your engagement with disabled children and young people in the following ways:

- Liaising with the child/family to understand the child or young person's particular requirements for accessing the setting, e.g. home visits, talking with the child/family about their needs
- Work with colleagues and the child/family to identify how best to meet those requirements from the beginning, e.g. establishing links with key worker, induction programme
- Ensure the setting recognises and develops its existing good practice as the basis for welcoming any child or young person, e.g. all staff have disability awareness and/or inclusion training
- Show the child and family how the setting is able to meet the needs of children and young people, e.g. disabled access, specialist equipment, individual programmes
- Identify any additional resources required to meet the child or young person's needs and work with the family to obtain these resources, e.g. medical interventions, recruitment of additional staff, loan or purchase of equipment, sign language or inclusion training.

## Encourage children and young people to express their preferences and aspirations

Children and young people have the right to be consulted and involved in decision-making about matters that affect them; they have the right to have their opinions taken into account when adults are making decisions that affect them according to Article 12 of the UN Convention on the Rights of the Child. Children should have opportunities to be involved in the planning, implementation and evaluation of policies that affect them or the services they use (CYPU, 2001).

Involving children in decision-making within your setting will help you to provide better provision, based on the children's real needs rather than adult assumptions about children and young people's needs. It will also help you to promote social inclusion by encouraging the children and young people to participate as active citizens in their local community. You should encourage children and young people to express their preferences and aspirations in their chosen way of communication. To do this, you may need to communicate with them in their home language or preferred method of communication such as Makaton or British Sign Language.

A person's sense of self-efficacy (or self-direction) is about qualities of optimism, persistence and believing that one's own efforts can make a difference. There are two important ways that you can help children to develop a sense of self-efficacy, by encouraging them to define their own outcomes and involving them in the development of services. Involving children and young people in planning their care is a crucial way of promoting a sense of self-efficacy, as it provides them with a sense of stability and control. Encouraging them to develop goals or outcomes can help promote a more positive sense of what the future might hold and how to reach it (Bostock, 2004).

## Five ways to promote children and young people's self-efficacy

You can encourage children and young people to make their views known, define their own outcomes and participate in service development by:

1. Involving children and young people in discussions about their needs and their future.
2. Helping children and young people to contribute to care plans and reviews; ensuring that their

wishes are always considered and, where possible, addressed.
3. Giving clear information and making sure children and young people know about: why special provision is being made for them; their rights; future plans and how they can influence these.
4. Trying to regard children and young people as resources (not as problems) in the process of seeking solutions in their lives.
5. Encouraging children and young people to make choices, declare preferences and define outcomes for themselves; respecting these preferences.

(Bostock, 2004)

### Activity

Give examples of how you encourage children and young people to make their views known, define their own outcomes and participate in service development.

## Demonstrate in own practice how to work with children or young people and their families to assess a child or young person's learning, play or leisure needs, identifying solutions to any barriers according to the principles of inclusion

You can assess a child or young person's learning, play or leisure needs through: observations; information from others; preferences of the child or young person; findings solutions to obstacles; looking at how to overcome barriers.

Compared to non-disabled children, disabled children do not participate in sport and leisure activities as much – disabled children and young people spend more time at home and more time watching television than non-disabled children and young people. Young people in particular report difficulties accessing social and leisure facilities – they want access to opportunities which promote friendships, and offer opportunities to go out into the community, join in with leisure activities, and develop skills in an entertaining setting.

Disabled children and young people and their parents have identified several barriers to participation in inclusive activities, including unsuitability or lack of local facilities, lack of accessible transport, high cost and lack of money, the attitudes of staff and members of the public, and the lack of personal support.

Achieving participation in inclusive play and leisure services requires a multi-agency approach, involving leisure, education, social services, transport and housing. Inclusion is something that has to be actively supported. It does not simply mean that they will join in activities together.

Possible solutions to any barriers include:

- Involving disabled children and their parents in service planning
- Ensuring that disabled children and young people are able to attend the same facilities as non-disabled children and young people
- Providing accessible transport to and from the facilities
- Providing staff with knowledge and training on disabilities and inclusion issues
- Providing adequate resources and staffing to assist children and young people during activities
- Providing suitable environments, such as soft-play facilities, which are barrier-free and minimise the effects of differences in children's abilities
- Actively encouraging children and young people to join in activities together.

(DH, 2001)

## Twenty ways to work with children and young people and families to promote inclusion

In order to work with children and young people and their families to assess a child's learning, play or leisure needs and to identify solutions to any barriers, according to the principles of inclusion, you need to:

1. Empower parents and their children in a child or young person-centred and play-centred way.
2. Be an effective communicator, facilitator and coordinator.
3. Be creative in obtaining resources, developing links and networks.
4. Interact diplomatically, liaise strategically and be approachable at all levels, e.g. with parents, providers, children, both individually and in groups.
5. Be a patient, persistent mediator and advocate.
6. Have a determined, persistent and positive 'can do' attitude – not taking 'No' for an answer!
7. Know what services are available for disabled and non-disabled children and young people in your local area.
8. Maintain a current and accurate 'directory' for effective signposting (include statutory, voluntary, segregated, separate, inclusive and mainstream support services, play and leisure opportunities).
9. Get to know the service quality and the key contacts of those in your directory.
10. Take time to really get to know the children and young people, parents/carers, providers, agencies and organisations. Remember, it takes time to build trust and respectful relationships.
11. Develop a principled statement of how your setting plans to do things inclusively – e.g. a policy for inclusive play.
12. Identify, agree and work within inclusive underpinning values and principles.
13. Look at the language you use and ensure that it reflects the social model of disability. The terms 'disabled children' and 'non-disabled children' are currently recommended.

14. Be clear what the service and workers stand for (mission/vision, purpose and what you all aim to achieve).

15. Monitor what is happening at present in a variety of ways and from different perspectives.

16. Assess whether or not there is a requirement to change policy or practice if monitoring shows a mismatch between provision and expectations.

17. Identify what could be improved upon and why.

18. Work with service users and providers to agree how improvements could be made.

19. Make the necessary changes to ensure your service is effective.

20. Record and monitor action to be taken to improve practice and/or policy, with specific timescales.

(KIDS Playwork Inclusion Project, 2006)

### Research Activity

1. Find out about available services for disabled and non-disabled children and young people in your local area.

2. Compile a current and accurate 'directory' of local statutory, voluntary, segregated, separate, inclusive and mainstream support services, play and leisure opportunities.

3. Look at how your setting can develop (or improve) a policy for inclusive play. You might find the briefing 'Planning for Inclusion' a useful starting point. This can be downloaded from the Kids website: www.kids.org.uk/Shared_ASP_Files/UploadedFiles/kids/95B56F89-207C-4FB9-B791-05CCD0C79204_PlanningforInclusion-Makingyourplaystrategyinclusive.pdf

## Supporting children and young people with disabilities and those with specific requirements

You need to know and understand the details about particular disabilities as they affect the children and young people in your setting and your ability to provide a high quality service. Children and young people with disabilities and those with specific requirements in your setting may include children with hearing impairment, visual impairment, physical disabilities, behavioural difficulties, emotional difficulties, communication difficulties and learning difficulties. Some children and young people may require additional support in the setting due to specific requirements such as additional sensory and/or physical needs as a result of hearing, visual and/or physical impairment. As children and young people with sensory or physical impairments may be dependent on others for some of their needs, it is essential to provide opportunities for them to be as independent as possible. Give them every chance to join in, to express opinions and to interact with their peer group. Remember to focus on each child as a unique person with individual strengths rather than focusing on the child or young person's particular disabilities, e.g. what they *can* do rather than what they cannot.

The Association of Teachers and Lecturers (ATL) website has a useful guide to supporting disabled children and those with specific requirements: *Achievement for all: working with children with special educational needs in mainstream schools and colleges.* Revised in 2010 and available free from: www.atl.org.uk/publications-and-resources/classroom-practice-publications/special-education-needs.asp

 **In Practice**

Provide examples of how you have supported disabled children and young people and those with specific requirements to enable them to participate in the full range of activities and experiences in your setting, e.g. encouraging the child to participate in activities, or modifying activities to meet the child's individual learning, play or leisure needs.

## Develop a plan with an individual child or young person to support learning, play or leisure needs

When working with children and young people, you should maintain a balance between flexibility and consistency in your approach to time allocation to ensure that the needs of individual children are met.

**Figure 21.3** Adult supporting a child with additional communication needs

An individual support plan will ensure that this time allocation takes into account:

- The individual child or young person's learning, play or leisure needs in terms of staffing, resources and equipment, e.g. mobility and communication aids
- The management of medical issues and personal care routines, e.g. epilepsy or difficulties with eating and drinking
- Approaches to minimising the impact of sensory and physical impairments, e.g. the use of specialised lighting or appropriate positioning of equipment
- Individual counselling and the management of difficult emotions and behaviour, e.g. helping the child recognise what triggers outbursts and how to respond
- The use of therapeutic treatments, e.g. speech and language therapy, physiotherapy, hydrotherapy, etc.

An effective individual support plan builds on the child's understanding of their own support needs, as well as the views and contributions of parents, carers, families and others. An individual support plan uses the expertise and involvement of a range of professionals from different agencies that may

include therapists, nursing staff, social workers and representatives from the voluntary sector. An individual support plan can make a significant contribution to an effective and inclusive environment for a disabled child or young person, by ensuring that parts of therapeutic programmes are successfully integrated in the activities of the setting (QCA, 2001).

Your contribution to the planning of an individual support plan will depend on your exact role and responsibilities within the setting. You may be involved in developing a plan with an individual child to support learning, play or leisure needs. You may be involved in a variety of planning sessions and meetings, or simply be required to implement the plans of others such as teachers and/or specialists. An individual support plan may be either short-term (e.g. a week, a month or half term) or long-term (e.g. a term, several months or a whole year) and can cover a range of developmental and learning needs, including social, physical, intellectual communication or emotional. A plan for several months or the whole year will, of course, require more work than a plan for a week or two. An individual support plan should be based on detailed observations and assessments of the child or young person's learning and

## In Practice

Observe a child with specific requirements over a period of time (e.g. a week, a month or half a term) which is appropriate to your role in the setting. Using your observations, assess the child's development and make suggestions for the child's future learning needs.

As part of your role in the planning process, you may be involved in making suggestions for the specific content of an individual support plan. You will work in conjunction with colleagues, the special educational needs coordinator (SENCO) and possibly a specialist such as an educational psychologist, speech and language therapist, physiotherapist or occupational therapist.

The individual support plan should include:

❏ The child or young person's age and level of development

❏ The specific area of impairment or special need

❏ The intended length of the plan

❏ Where and when the plan is to be implemented, e.g. at home, in the setting or both

❏ Details of the activities to be provided to support learning, play or leisure needs

❏ Who will provide the activities and any necessary support

❏ The resources required, including any specialist equipment.

---

development. These assessments will include information from parents and appropriate professionals, as well as the observations and assessments made by you and your colleagues.

## Implement the learning, play or leisure plan according to own role and responsibility

As appropriate to your own role and responsibilities, you will implement the individual support plan, including providing activities to support the child's learning, play or leisure needs. It is essential that you understand your own role (and that of colleagues) in the planning and implementation of the programme.

In addition to following the general information on promoting learning and development (see Chapter 13), you also need to consider implementing activities in ways that maximise benefit to the child or young person. For example:

● Implement at a time when the child is receptive
● Avoid unnecessary distractions for the child
● Keep disruptions to the usual routines of the setting to a minimum
● Use appropriate resources, including any specialised learning materials and/or equipment.

## Explaining and evaluating its effectiveness and suggesting changes for the future

Throughout the implementation of the individual support plan, you will need to keep accurate and detailed records of the child or young person's progress and responses to the activities, in order to feed back information to colleagues, parents and other relevant people such as specialists. You can record significant aspects of the child or young person's participation levels and progress during the activity, as soon as possible or shortly afterwards, so that you can remember important points.

## Be able to evaluate, support and develop existing practice with disabled children and young people and those with specific requirements

You should be able to evaluate, support and develop existing practice with disabled children and those

## In Practice

Develop a possible individual support plan for a child or young person with specific requirements, based on your observations and assessments from the previous activity.

You could do an outline plan to include the following:

❏ Spidergram of activities and/or skills to be developed using headings appropriate to your setting and the child's learning, play or leisure needs, e.g. the Early Years Foundation Stage

❏ List of the planning and preparation for the activities, including resources and organisation

❏ Inclusion of the child or young person's activities into the usual routines of the setting, including any necessary modifications

❏ Your role in supporting the child during the activities

❏ Any health and safety issues

❏ Timetable of the first week's activities from the plan

❏ Detailed description of the implementation of at least one activity from the plan (remember to review and evaluate this activity afterwards)

❏ Review and evaluate the whole plan.

If you have never done an outline plan before, ask your tutor for guidance or advice on a format which might be more appropriate to your role within the setting.

---

with specific requirements. For example, looking at the characteristics of quality inclusion:

- Through their attitudes and behaviour, children, practitioners and parents demonstrate how unremarkable it is that disabled children are part of a wide cross-section of the local community using the setting
- Children's interests, interactions or enthusiasms lead their play, and activities take into account individual likes, dislikes as well as access or support requirements
- Everyone is welcomed on arrival and wished well on departure in a way that suits them
- Each child is respected and valued as an individual with equal rights and choices, and is given equality of opportunity to exercise those rights and choices
- Each child is supported when he or she chooses to play with others, to play alongside others, to play alone or not to take part in the activity
- Risks are assessed and managed to enable each child to experience and enjoy risky play, while managing their preferences and their own and others' safety
- Children and adults each initiate communication with one another in a variety of ways
- Each child has opportunities to actively participate in formal and informal consultation, using their

chosen communication methods, so that they can express their views and opinions on the play sessions and the setting as a whole

- All children report that practitioners seek their views, and listen and act on their requests
- Each child indicates they are happy in the play/childcare environment, and have opportunities to experience a range of emotions
- Each child is encouraged to show their parent(s) what they have been doing, in their own way.

(PIP, 2008)

## Demonstrate in your own practice how barriers which restrict children and young people's access are overcome

You should be able to demonstrate, in your own practice, how barriers that restrict children's access are overcome. For example, you should be able to:

- Sensitively address the cause and effects if any child is consistently being excluded from other children's play, but wishes to participate in that play or activity
- Show awareness of potential barriers to accessing activities fully, and understand that attitudes, environments, structures and policies may

disadvantage particular children, and challenge these barriers as appropriate

- Ensure reasonable adjustments for access have been made, and continue to be made, to the activities and social environments in and around the setting.

(PIP, 2008)

(See previous information in this chapter about identifying solutions to any barriers.)

# Explain the importance of evaluating and challenging existing practice and becoming an agent of change

You should be able to explain the importance of evaluating and challenging existing practice and becoming an agent of change, as this will enable you to improve inclusive practice, both in the setting and the wider community. To do this you (and your colleagues) should:

- Be highly responsive, thinking and adapting practice to be a resource to individual or groups of children, intervening, offering support or working as a team, as appropriate
- Have had rights-based training relating to disability and other equality, diversity and inclusion matters
- Reflect on how own attitudes may impact on the children and their families
- Keep informed or feel you are kept informed by managers/leaders/advisers and consulted on practice and organisational developments
- Use positive language consistently and be able to explain why certain terminology is preferred
- Describe the systems in place that enable appropriate response(s) to support the specific requirements of individual children
- Use pictures, equipment and resources to reflect disabled people's lives, as part of a wider representation of the diverse backgrounds and experiences of children and the community
- Develop links with disabled people who can contribute effectively as part of a wide cross-section of adults involved in the work of the setting

- Provide a variety of opportunities and methods for all parents to be involved in formal and informal consultations, to influence what happens in the setting, and to feel comfortable in approaching practitioners without feeling they are imposing
- Develop links with families, schools and services for disabled children, as part of a commitment to give all local children and their families genuine opportunities to participate in the setting.

(PIP, 2008)

# Explain how and when to use policies and procedures to challenge discriminatory, abusive or oppressive behaviour

All settings have policies and procedures to ensure equality and inclusion. You must follow your setting's policy and procedures together with any relevant legal requirements when challenging discriminatory, abusive or oppressive behaviour. See the section 'Challenging discrimination and prejudice' in Chapter 15.

# Describe the impact of disability within different cultures and the importance of culturally sensitive practice

The positive role of parents or carers leads to *optimal* child or young person development from birth to adulthood. All children and young people have biological and psychological needs (see page 76) but there are a variety of ways of meeting these needs. You must respect and accept the differences of family life which vary according to culture, class and community. There is no perfect way to raise children, so you must avoid value judgements and stereotypes. Assessing children and young people's developmental needs is a complex process which requires all relevant aspects of a child's life experience to be addressed. For children of Asian, African or Caribbean origin, including children of mixed heritage, assessments should address the impact that racism has on a particular child and family and ensure that the assessment process itself does not reinforce racism through racial or cultural stereotyping (DH, 2000).

Children and young people's opportunities for achieving optimal outcomes, depend on their parents' abilities to respond appropriately to their children's needs, at different stages of their lives. Most parents want to do the best for their children and have their best interests at heart. However, good parenting requires certain permitting circumstances, such as necessary life opportunities and facilities (e.g. adequate housing, satisfactory education and/or training, regular employment, reasonable income, access to affordable childcare and leisure facilities). There are many factors that may inhibit the way parents respond to their children and prevent parenting at a level necessary to promote optimal outcomes in children. These factors include: alcohol problems; drug use; mental illness; domestic violence; ignorance about child development; lack of a supportive partner; the parents' negative childhood experiences such as rejection, abandonment, neglect and feeling unloved; parents' low self-esteem; lack of resilience factors in parents' own childhood (DH, 2000).

There may be problems in interpreting needs, e.g. differences in the rate of development of children with similar background, disabilities, etc. Remember all children and young people are unique individuals and develop at their own rate (see Chapter 5, Unit CYP Core 3.1). Some children and young people may be 'behind' in some areas of development but may 'catch up' with support from their parents/carers and the usual early years experiences (e.g. parent and toddler group,
playgroup, nursery class) *without* the need for intervention.

# Explain the importance of systems of monitoring, reviewing and evaluating services for disabled children and young people

You should collect relevant background information from available sources including children (according to their ages, needs and abilities), their families, health and social services. You should record information according to your setting's agreed formats and procedures. You should ensure that records are regularly updated and kept according to the procedures of the setting including, adherence to confidentiality and data protection requirements.

## In Practice

Describe how you collect, record and update background information about children and young people with specific requirements. Include examples of relevant formats and procedures, e.g. child observation and assessments, individual education plans.

Monitoring and evaluating services for children and families helps to ensure the needs of children and their families are met by:

❏ Ensuring mechanisms are in place to enable joint planning between health, education and social services

❏ Helping parents and carers understand what is likely to happen next and how they can best encourage children's developmental progress

❏ Marking progress and celebrating achievement in children and young people who are facing significant challenges

❏ Informing discussion between families and professionals who work with them

❏ Highlighting development that is not following an expected pattern, where additional or different intervention may be required

❏ Evaluating the impact of any early intervention and support that has been provided

❏ Including measures of consumer satisfaction/ client feedback.

(DfES, 2004a)

## In Practice

Outline the procedures you use to monitor and evaluate services to ensure the needs of children and families are met. Include information on how you:

❏ Regularly review children and young people's individual needs

❏ Discuss services and provision with individual families

❏ Regularly liaise with colleagues and other professionals

❏ Agree and implement any changes to ensure children's needs are met

❏ Keep accurate records of meetings and discussions.

# Understand how to work in partnership with other agencies and professionals to support provision for disabled children and young people and those with specific requirements

In addition to liaising with parents, you will also need to liaise with other professionals regarding disabled children and those with specific requirements, as well as providing effective support for colleagues in the setting (see below). You may be involved in coordinating a network of relationships between staff at the setting and other professionals from external agencies such as:

- **Local education authority,** e.g. educational psychologist, special needs support teachers, special needs advisers, specialist teachers, education welfare officers
- **Health services,** e.g. paediatricians, health visitors, physiotherapists, occupational therapists, speech and language therapists, play therapists, school nurses, clinical psychologists
- **Social services department,** e.g. social workers; specialist social workers: sensory disabilities, physical disabilities, mental health or children and families

- **Charities and voluntary organisations**, e.g. AFASIC, British Dyslexia Association, Council for Disabled Children, National Autistic Society, RNIB, RNID, SCOPE.

## Research Activity

Find out which external agencies and other professionals are connected with the care and support of disabled children and those with specific requirements at your setting.

# The roles and responsibilities of partners that are typically involved with disabled children and young people and those with specific requirements

Statutory services include health, education and social services. A number of different services or agencies may work together to support children and their families. Support services provided by different statutory agencies should be carefully coordinated to meet the needs of children and families more effectively. Some areas already provide a single multi-agency service for young children and families which bring together health, education and social services, e.g. children's centres (see page 402).

The **Right from the Start Template** is a working document designed to help professionals develop the policies, procedures and practice required to ensure that more families with disabled children receive a better service. The principles and good practice

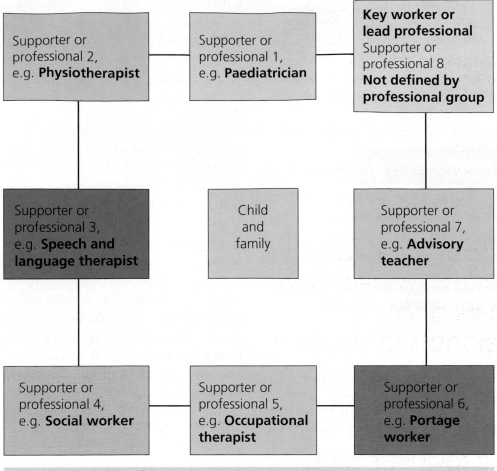

**Figure 21.4** Team Around the Child approaches

framework included in the *Right from the Start Template* are applicable to professionals working with **all** children in need, not just children with disabilities – see www.rightfromthestart.org.uk

## The role of the key worker or lead professional

The key worker is a named professional who assists families in accessing information and support from specialist services. Sometimes the key worker is known as the lead professional. In *Team Around the Child* approaches (see Figure 21.4), a professional with regular contact with the family takes on the role of key worker or lead professional, as well as their existing responsibilities for supporting the family. The core responsibilities of the key worker are:

● Making sure the family have all the information they need and, where necessary, help families to understand and use the information received

● Ensuring everyone (e.g. other agencies) has up-to-date information about the child and family
● Coordinating assessment support and intervention
● Ensuring a joint plan is formulated which keeps the family at the centre of decision-making and involves all the professionals and agencies in contact with the child
● Facilitating the regular review and updating of support plans
● Maintaining regular contact with the family and, where appropriate, provide emotional support.

(DfES, 2004a)

The *Framework for the Assessment of Children in Need and their Families* provides a systemic framework to help professionals identify children and young people in need and assess the best approach to help children in need and their families (see above).

You must know and follow your setting's procedures and protocols for sharing information – see the relevant sections in this book on confidentiality, the basic provisions of the Data Protection Act relevant to early years settings, the setting's requirements regarding confidentiality and the confidentiality of information relating to abuse.

## In Practice

Describe how you work with other agencies to help families access specialist support.

Include information on how you exchange information with families and other agencies, such as keeping records of contacts and information in line with agreed policies and procedures, e.g. confidentiality and data protection procedures.

## Analyse examples of multi-agency and partnership working from practice

Disabled children and young people and those with specific requirements may often have support from other professionals from external agencies. To provide the most effective care and support for disabled children and young people, it is essential that the working relationships between the setting staff and other professionals run smoothly and that there are no contradictions or missed opportunities, due to lack of communication. Liaising with other professionals will enable you to involve colleagues with the work of the specialists in a number of ways, for example: planning appropriate support for the child within the setting; assisting children to perform tasks set by a specialist; reporting the child's progress on such tasks, e.g. to the child's parents.

Any interactions with other professionals should be conducted in such a way as to promote trust and confidence in your working relationships. Your contributions towards the planning and implementation of joint actions must be consistent with your role and responsibilities in your setting. You should supply other professionals with the relevant information, advice and support as appropriate to your own role and expertise. If requested, you should be willing to share information, knowledge or skills with other professionals. You should use any opportunities to contact or observe the practice of other professionals from external agencies to increase your knowledge and understanding of their skills/expertise in order to improve your own work (and that of your colleagues) in planning and supporting children's learning and development.

## Key terms

**Specialist** – person with specific training/additional qualifications in a particular area of development, e.g. physiotherapist, speech and language therapist, educational psychologist.

## Activity

Compile an information booklet which includes the following:

- Links with other professionals from external agencies established by your setting
- A diagram which illustrates how you and your colleagues work with other professionals to provide effective support for disabled children and young people in your setting
- Your role and responsibilities in liaising with other professionals to support disabled children and their parents
- Where to obtain information about the roles of other professionals in the local area.

Useful resources

## Websites

**Advisory Centre for Education (ACE):** an independent, registered charity, which offers information about state education in England and Wales for parents of school age children.
www.ace-ed.org.uk

**Contact a Family:** this website is for families who have a disabled child and those who work with disabled children or are interested to find out more about their needs.
www.cafamily.org.uk

**Centre for Studies in Inclusive Education (CSIE)** is an independent centre working in the UK and overseas to promote inclusion and end segregation. It is funded by donations from trusts, foundations and grants.
www.csie.org.uk

**Department for Education:** this government website contains information on disabilities, special education needs, schools, curriculum and many other education related topics.
www.education.gov.uk

**Equality and Human Rights Commission:** have a statutory remit to promote and monitor human rights; and to protect, enforce and promote equality across the seven 'protected' grounds – age, disability, gender, race, religion and belief, sexual orientation and gender reassignment.
www.equalityhumanrights.com

**PACT (Participation, Advocacy, Consultancy and Training):** this project aims to support and empower disabled children and young people by working creatively and collaboratively to deliver a wide-ranging programme of direct services and accredited training.
www.childrenssociety.org.uk/what-we-do/helping-children/our-programmes/disabled-children/pact

## Books

Alcott, M. (2002) *An Introduction to Children with Special Needs*. Hodder & Stoughton.
ATL (2010) *Achievement for All: Working with Children with Special Educational Needs in Mainstream Schools and Colleges*. Association of Teachers and Lecturers. (Available free from: www.atl.org.uk)
Contact a Family (2004) *Caring for Disabled Children: A Guide for Students and Professionals*. (Available from: www.cafamily.org.uk/students.pdf)
Dare, A. and O'Donovan, M. (2005) *Good Practice in Caring for Young Children with Special Needs*. 2nd Edition. Nelson Thornes.
DfES. (2001) *The Special Educational Needs Code of Practice 2001*. DfES. (Available free at: www.teachernet.gov.uk/_doc/3724/SENCodeOfPractice.pdf)
Dickins, M. and Denziloe, J. (2004) *All Together: How to Create Inclusive Services for Children and Their Families*. National Children's Bureau.
Harding, J. and Meldon-Smith, L. (2000) *How to Make Observations and Assessments*. 2nd Edition. Hodder and Stoughton.
Horwath, J. (2001) *The Child's World: Assessing Children in Need*. Jessica Kingsley Publishers.
Limbrick-Spencer, G. (2001) *The Key Worker: A Practical Guide*. Handsel Trust Publications.
Lindon, J. (2005) *Understanding Child Development: Linking Theory and Practice*. Hodder Arnold.
Mortimer, H. (2001) *Special Needs and Early Years Provision*. Continuum International Publishing Group.
Wall, K. (2006) *Special Needs and Early Years: A Practitioner's Guide*. Paul Chapman Publications.
Wilson, R. (2003) *Special Educational Needs in the Early Years*. Routledge Falmer

# Appendix: Useful acronyms

| | |
|---|---|
| ADD | Attention Deficit Disorder |
| ADHD | Attention Deficit Hyperactivity Disorder |
| ASBO | Anti-Social Behaviour Order |
| ASD | Autistic Spectrum Disorder |
| BASW | British Association of Social Workers |
| BEST | Behaviour and Education Support Team |
| BME | Black and Minority Ethnic |
| BTEC | Business and Technology Education Council |
| C&G | City and Guilds |
| CAB | Citizens Advice Bureau |
| CACHE | Council for Awards in Care, Health and Education |
| CAF | Common Assessment Framework |
| CAFCASS | Children and Family Court Advisory and Support Service |
| CAMHS | Child and Adolescent Mental Health Services |
| CCLD | Children's Care, Learning and Development |
| CCW | Care Council for Wales |
| CRE | Commission for Racial Equality |
| CWDC | Children's Workforce Development Council |
| CWN | Children's Workforce Network |
| CYP | Children and Young People |
| DCS | Director of Children's Services |
| DH | Department of Health |
| DTI | Department for Trade and Industry |
| EBSD | Emotional, Behavioural and Social Difficulties |
| ECaT | Every Child a Talker |
| ECM | Every Child Matters |
| ELPP | Early Learning Partnership Project |
| EPPE | Effective Provision of Pre-School Education Project |
| EWO | Education Welfare Officer |
| EYFS | Early Years Foundation Stage |
| EYP | Early Years Professional |
| EYPS | Early Years Professional Status |
| FPI | Family and Parenting Institute |
| FST | Family Support Team |
| FSW | Family Support Worker |
| FYJ | Forum for Youth Justice |
| GP | General Practitioner |
| IQF | Integrated Qualifications Framework |
| LLUK | Lifelong Learning UK |
| LP | Lead Professional |

| | |
|---|---|
| LRN | Learning Resource Network |
| LSC | Learning and Skills Council |
| LWS | Local Workforce Strategy |
| MAT | Multi-agency Team |
| NASWE | National Association of Social Workers in Education |
| NCB | National Children's Bureau |
| NCERCC | National Centre for Excellence in Residential Child Care |
| NCH | National Children's Home (The Children's Charity) |
| NCMA | National Childminding Association |
| NCVCCO | National Council of Voluntary Child Care Organisations |
| NDNA | National Day Nurseries Association |
| NEET | Not in Education, Employment or Training |
| NGfL | National Grid for Learning |
| NISCC | Northern Ireland Social Care Council |
| NOS | National Occupational Standards |
| NVQ | National Vocational Qualification |
| OCW | One Children's Workforce |
| Ofsted | Office for Standards in Education |
| PHCT | Primary Health Care Team |
| PLA | Pre-school Learning Alliance |
| PRU | Pupil Referral Unit |
| QCA | Qualification and Curriculum Authority |
| QTS | Qualified Teacher Status |
| RNIB | Royal National Institute for the Blind |
| RNID | Royal National Institute for the Deaf |
| SEAL | Social and Emotional Aspects of Learning |
| SEN | Special Educational Needs |
| SENCO | Special Educational Needs Co-ordinator |
| SSDA | Sector Skills Development Agency |
| SSSC | Scottish Social Care Council |
| TAC | Team Around the Child |
| UCAS | University and Colleges Admission Service |
| VRQ | Vocationally Related Qualification |
| YCPS | Youth Crime Prevention Strategy |
| YCS | Youth and Community Service |
| YISP | Youth Inclusion and Support Panel |
| YJB | Youth Justice Board |
| YOS | Youth Offending Service |

# Index

Note: page numbers in **bold** refer to key terms.